A PLUME BOOK

COSMOS AND PSYCHE

RICHARD TARNAS is a professor of philosophy and cultural history at the California Institute of Integral Studies in San Francisco, where he founded the graduate program in Philosophy, Cosmology, and Consciousness. He also teaches psychology and cultural history at Pacifica Graduate Institute in Santa Barbara. A graduate of Harvard University and Saybrook Institute, he is the author of *The Passion of the Western Mind*, a history of the Western world views from the ancient Greek to the postmodern that became both a bestseller and a required text in many universities.

Supplementary material for *Cosmos and Psyche*, including the author's schedule of public lectures and seminars, interviews, reviews, and reader comments, a comprehensive index, additional essays, and related links, can be found at Cosmosandpsyche.com.

"It is hard to think of many books written in the past century that will still be read two hundred years from now. *Cosmos and Psyche* will top that short list. It is majestic, sweeping, and profound. This will be a book for the ages. It will stand over time with the seminal expressions of the human spirit."
—William Van Dusen Wishard, author of *Between Two Ages: The 21st Century and the Crisis of Meaning*

"Breathtaking in the scope and scale of its vision, this extraordinary book shatters our cosmological assumptions as it awakens us to a living universe and its creative intelligence. Tarnas succeeds masterfully in bringing his encyclopedic knowledge forged in writing the critically acclaimed *Passion of the Western Mind* to the task of discerning the archetypal pulse of history. Spellbinding, eloquent, compelling, *Cosmos and Psyche* will be a marker for an entire generation."
—Christopher Bache, professor of philosophy and religious studies, Youngstown State University, and author of *Dark Night, Early Dawn*

"Some rare books, presenting very challenging evidence after decades of research, have the power to transform a whole culture. It happened with the groundbreaking works by Copernicus, Darwin, and Freud. It may happen now with *Cosmos and Psyche*. Searching beneath the depths of the psyche Tarnas has found the heights of the cosmos. This book will radically transform the way we see cultural and political history, individual life journeys, and our sense of participation in the universe."
—Jordi Pigem, author of *La odisea de Occidente* (The Odyssey of the West)

Cosmos *and* Psyche

Intimations of a New World View

RICHARD TARNAS

A PLUME BOOK

PLUME
Published by Penguin Group
Penguin Group (USA) Inc., 375 Hudson Street, New York, New York 10014, U.S.A.
Penguin Group (Canada), 90 Eglinton Avenue East, Suite 700, Toronto, Ontario, Canada M4P 2Y3
(a division of Pearson Penguin Canada Inc.)
Penguin Books Ltd., 80 Strand, London WC2R 0RL, England
Penguin Ireland, 25 St. Stephen's Green, Dublin 2, Ireland (a division of Penguin Books Ltd.)
Penguin Group (Australia), 250 Camberwell Road, Camberwell, Victoria 3124, Australia
(a division of Pearson Australia Group Pty. Ltd.)
Penguin Books India Pvt. Ltd., 11 Community Centre, Panchsheel Park, New Delhi – 110 017, India
Penguin Group (NZ), 67 Apollo Drive, Mairangi Bay, Auckland 1311, New Zealand
(a division of Pearson New Zealand Ltd.)
Penguin Books (South Africa) (Pty.) Ltd., 24 Sturdee Avenue, Rosebank,
Johannesburg 2196, South Africa

Penguin Books Ltd., Registered Offices: 80 Strand, London WC2R 0RL, England

Published by Plume, a member of Penguin Group (USA) Inc. Previously published in a Viking
edition.

First Plume Printing, May 2007
10 9 8 7 6 5 4 3 2 1

 REGISTERED TRADEMARK — MARCA REGISTRADA

CIP data is available.
ISBN 0-670-03292-1 (hc.)
ISBN 978-0-452-28859-1 (pbk.)

Printed in the United States of America
Original hardcover design by Daniel Lagin

To my family and friends,
who waited patiently so long

Evening star, you bring all things
which the bright dawn has scattered . . .

Sappho

Contents

Preface

Skepticism is the chastity of the intellect, Santayana declared, and the metaphor is apt. The mind that seeks the deepest intellectual fulfillment does not give itself up to every passing idea. Yet what is sometimes forgotten is the larger purpose of such a virtue. For in the end, chastity is something one preserves not for its own sake, which would be barren, but rather so that one may be fully ready for the moment of surrender to the beloved, the suitor whose aim is true. Whether in knowledge or in love, the capacity to recognize and embrace that moment when it finally arrives, perhaps in quite unexpected circumstances, is essential to the virtue. Only with that discernment and inward opening can the full participatory engagement unfold that brings forth new realities and new knowledge. Without this capacity, at once active and receptive, the long discipline would be fruitless. The carefully cultivated skeptical posture would become finally an empty prison, an armored state of unfulfillment, a permanently confining end in itself rather than the rigorous means to a sublime result.

It is just this tension and interplay—between critical rigor and the potential discovery of larger truths—that has always informed and advanced the drama of our intellectual history. Yet in our own time, at the start of a new millennium, that drama seems to have reached a moment of climactic urgency. We find ourselves at an extraordinary threshold. One need not be graced with prophetic insight to recognize that we are living in one of those rare ages, like the end of classical antiquity or the beginning of the modern era, that bring forth, through great stress and struggle, a genuinely fundamental transformation in the underlying assumptions and principles of the cultural world view. Amidst the multitude of debates and controversies that fill the intellectual arena, our basic understanding of reality is in contention: the role of the human being in nature and the cosmos, the status of human knowledge, the basis of moral values, the dilemmas of pluralism, relativism, objectivity, the spiritual dimension of life, the direction and meaning—if any—of history and evolution. The outcome of this tremendous moment in our civilization's history is deeply uncertain. Something is dying, and something is being born. The stakes are high, for the future of humanity and the future of the Earth.

No recital is necessary here of the many formidable and pressing problems—global and local, social, political, economic, ecological—facing the world today. They are visible in every headline in our daily news, monthly journals, and annual state of the world reports. The great enigma of our situation is that we have unprecedented resources for dealing with those problems, yet it is as if some larger or deeper context, some invisible constraint, were negating our capacity and resolve. What is that larger context? Something essential seems to be missing in our understanding, some potent but intangible factor or set of factors. Can we discern the more fundamental conditions in which our many concrete problems might ultimately be rooted? What are the most important *underlying* issues that confront the human mind and spirit in our era? Focusing particularly on the "Western" situation, centered in Europe and North America though now variously and acutely affecting the entire human community, we can observe three especially fundamental factors:

First, the profound metaphysical disorientation and groundlessness that pervades contemporary human experience: the widely felt absence of an adequate, publicly accessible larger order of purpose and significance, a guiding metanarrative that transcends separate cultures and subcultures, an encompassing pattern of meaning that could give to collective human existence a nourishing coherence and intelligibility.

Second, the deep sense of alienation that affects the modern self: here I refer to not only the personal isolation of the individual in modern mass society but also the spiritual estrangement of the modern psyche in a disenchanted universe, as well as, at the species level, the subjective schism separating the modern human being from the rest of nature and the cosmos.

And third, the critical need, on the part of both individuals and societies, for a deeper insight into those unconscious forces and tendencies, creative and destructive, that play such a powerful role in shaping human lives, history, and the life of the planet.

These conditions, all intricately interconnected and interpenetrating, surround and permeate our contemporary consciousness like the atmosphere in which we live and breathe. From a longer historical perspective, they represent the distillate of many centuries of extraordinary intellectual and psychological development. The compelling paradox of this long development is that these problematic conditions seem to have emerged from, and be subtly interwoven with, the very qualities and achievements of our civilization that have been most progressive, liberating, and admired.

It was this complex historical drama that I explored in my first book, *The Passion of the Western Mind*, a narrative history of Western thought that followed the major shifts of our civilization's world view from the time of the ancient Greeks and Hebrews to the postmodern era. In that book, published in 1991, I examined and attempted to understand the great philosophical, religious, and scientific ideas and movements that, over the centuries, gradually brought forth the world and world view we inhabit and strive within today. As with many such works that seem to take hold of their authors until they are completed, I was moved to write that book for more reasons than I fully grasped when I began the ten-year task. But my principal motive from the start was to provide, for both my readers and myself, a preparatory foundation for the present work. For while *The Passion of the Western Mind* examined the history that led to our current situation, *Cosmos and Psyche* addresses more precisely the crisis of the modern self and modern world view, and then introduces a body of evidence, a method of inquiry, and an emerging cosmological perspective that I believe could help us creatively engage that crisis, and our history itself, within a new horizon of possibility. I hope this book will point towards an enlarged understanding of our evolving universe, and of our own still-unfolding role within it.

R.T.

Cosmos *and* Psyche

I

The Transformation of the Cosmos

In each age of the world distinguished by high activity, there will be found at its culmination, and among the agencies leading to that culmination, some profound cosmological outlook, implicitly accepted, impressing its own type on the current springs of action.

—Alfred North Whitehead
Adventures of Ideas

Our psyche is set up in accord with the structure of the universe, and what happens in the macrocosm likewise happens in the infinitesimal and most subjective reaches of the psyche.

—C. G. Jung
Memories, Dreams, Reflections

The Birth of the Modern Self

The modern self began to emerge, with astonishing force and speed, just over five hundred years ago. There is scarcely a major figure or idea in the preceding cultural and intellectual history of the West that did not contribute to the formation of the modern self, nor has there been any aspect of our existence subsequently untouched by its unique character and potency. One can date the period of its emergence in many ways, but it is illuminating to see that historical epoch as framed by two definitive, symbolically resonant events, Pico della Mirandola's *Oration on the Dignity of Man* in 1486 and Descartes's *Discourse on Method* in 1637—that is, the extraordinary century and a half that extends from Leonardo, Columbus, Luther, and Copernicus to Shakespeare, Montaigne, Bacon, and Galileo—climaxing, in a sense, in the Cartesian *cogito ergo sum*, "I think, therefore I am." We could extend this crucial window, this threshold of transformation, by precisely another fifty years to encompass the 1687 publication of Newton's *Principia*, by which time the full foundation had been laid for the modern world and the sovereign confidence of the modern mind. Not just a revolution had occurred but a new Genesis. Thus Alexander Pope's telling epigram for the Enlightenment:

> Nature and Nature's laws lay hid in night:
> God said, Let Newton be! and all was Light.

But the dawn had already begun to break in Pico della Mirandola's *Oration*, the Renaissance manifesto for the new human self. Composed for the opening of a great gathering of philosophers invited to Rome by Pico himself, the *Oration* described the Creation in a characteristically Renaissance synthesis of ancient Greek and Judaeo-Christian sources, combining the biblical Genesis and Plato's *Timaeus* for its mythic narrative. But Pico then went further, in prophetic anticipation of the new form of the human self about to be born: When God had completed the creation of the world as a sacred temple of his glory and wisdom, he conceived a desire for one last being whose relation to the whole and to the divine Author would be different from that of every other creature. At this ultimate moment God considered the creation of the human being, who he hoped would come to know and love the beauty, intelligence, and grandeur of the divine work. But as the

Creator had no archetype remaining with which to make this last creation, no assigned status for it within the already completed work, he said to this final being:

> Neither a fixed abode nor a form that is thine alone nor any function peculiar to thyself have We given thee, Adam, to the end that according to thy longing and according to thy judgment thou mayest have and possess what abode, what form, what functions thou thyself shalt desire. The nature of all other beings is limited and constrained within the bounds of laws prescribed by Us. Thou, constrained by no limits, in accordance with thine own free will, in whose hand We have placed thee, shalt ordain for thyself the limits of thy nature. We have set thee at the world's center that thou mayest from thence more easily observe whatever is in the world. We have made thee neither of heaven nor of earth, neither mortal nor immortal, so that with freedom of choice and with honor, as though the maker and molder of thyself, thou mayest fashion thyself in whatever shape thou shalt prefer.

Thus the brilliant Pico, twenty-three years old, gave the prophecy. A new form of human being announces itself: dynamic, creative, multidimensional, protean, unfinished, self-defining and self-creating, infinitely aspiring, set apart from the whole, overseeing the rest of the world with unique sovereignty, centrally poised in the last moments of the old cosmology to bring forth and enter into the new. In the decades that followed, the prodigious generation that emerged immediately after this prophetic declaration brought forth the decisive moment that in childbirth is called "crowning"—that dramatic stage when the head of the new child begins to appear. Within the time span of a single generation surrounding the year 1500, Leonardo, Michelangelo, and Raphael created their many masterworks of the High Renaissance, revealing the birth of the new human as much in da Vinci's multiform genius and the godlike incarnations of the *David* and the Sistine *Creation of Adam* as in the new perspectival objectivity and poietic empowerment of the Renaissance artist; Columbus sailed west and reached America, Vasco da Gama sailed east and reached India, and the Magellan expedition circumnavigated the globe, opening the world forever to itself; Luther posted his theses on the door of the Wittenberg castle church and began the enormous convulsion of Europe and the Western psyche called the Reformation; *and* Copernicus conceived the heliocentric theory and began the even more momentous Scientific Revolution. From this instant, the human self, the known world, the cosmos, heaven and earth were all radically and irrevocably transformed. All this happened within a period of time briefer than that which has passed since Woodstock and the Moon landing.

It was of course no accident that the birth of the modern self and the birth of the modern cosmos took place at the same historical moment. The Sun, trailing clouds of glory, rose for both, in one great encompassing dawn.

The Dawn of a New Universe

It must have been a breathtaking experience to have been among those earliest scientific revolutionaries of the modern era, Copernicus and his immediate successors—Rheticus, Giese, Digges, Bruno, Maestlin, Kepler, Galileo—as they first began to grasp the stupendous truth of the heliocentric theory. The sense of cosmic upheaval and wonder would have been nearly inexpressible. A view of the Earth and its place in the universe that had governed the human mind virtually without question for untold thousands of years was now suddenly recognized to be a vast illusion. We in the twenty-first century, long accustomed to living in the new universe those Renaissance visionaries first revealed, must call upon a profound act of the intellectual imagination to enter again into that dramatic moment of transition between worlds. To have it suddenly dawn upon one that the great Earth itself, the most obviously stationary and immovable entity in the cosmos, upon which one had lived in changeless solidity all one's life, was in fact at that moment moving freely through space, through the heavens, spinning and circling around the Sun in an immensely expanded universe—no longer the absolute fixed center of that universe, as had been assumed since the beginning of human consciousness, but rather a planet, a wanderer, an exalted celestial body in a new cosmos whose dimensions and structure and meaning were now utterly transfigured: such a revelation must have filled the mind and spirit with an awe seldom known in human history.

Yet it is not just the sheer magnitude of the Copernican revelation that so easily escapes us today. We also tend to forget, and conventional histories of the Scientific Revolution tend to overlook entirely, the degree to which the original discovery was charged with intense spiritual significance. The early scientific revolutionaries perceived their breakthroughs as divine illuminations, spiritual awakenings to the true structural grandeur and intellectual beauty of the cosmic order. These were not merely abstract conceptual innovations or empirical findings of purely theoretical interest. They were not, as had been true of astronomy since classical antiquity, merely instrumentalist mathematical constructs, epicyclic elaborations ingeniously devised for the purpose of marginally increasing predictive accuracy. The new discoveries were triumphant fulfillments of a sacred quest. For thousands of years, the celestial and terrestrial realms had been regarded as unalterably separate realities, as incommensurable as the divine was to the human. Because of their extreme complexity, the true nature of the planetary motions had come to be seen as fundamentally beyond the capacity of the human intellect to understand. Concerning heavenly and divine matters, it seemed, only the Bible could reveal the truth; human astronomy could produce nothing but artificial constructions, as through a glass darkly. But now the true reality of the divinely ordered cosmos had finally been revealed. The deep mysteries of the universe were suddenly unfolding within the awestruck minds of the new scientists through the grace of a sovereign Deity whose glory was now dramatically unveiled. The stunning mathematical harmonies and aesthetic perfection of the new cosmos disclosed the workings of a transcendent intelligence of unimaginable power and splendor. In that very epiphany, the human intelligence that could grasp such workings was itself profoundly elevated and empowered.

The heliocentric discovery thus became the source and impetus for a tremendously magnified confidence in human reason. It revealed the human being's divinely graced capacity for direct, accurate knowledge of the world at the most encompassing macrocosmic level, something never before known in the entire history of Western astronomy. It was specifically this unprecedented claim to cosmological truth, the claim to represent the objective reality of the great universe, not just a useful instrumentalist fiction, that made the Copernican revolution so revolutionary, so emancipatory, as the very paradigm of modern humanity's new power of self-definition and cosmic illumination through reason.

Moreover, contrary to the human-decentering consequences later drawn from the Copernican shift, all of the great Copernicans from Copernicus through Newton were deeply convinced that the cosmic order was expressly created to be known and admired by the human intelligence. Here and now, after millennia of dark ignorance in an exile that had been as much spiritual as intellectual, the human mind had finally achieved direct contact with the true cosmic order as the divine mind had long intended. Only thus can we understand the full exaltation of Kepler, the pivotal figure of the Copernican revolution, as he announced his discovery of the third law of planetary motion, which completed the early mathematical foundation of the heliocentric theory:

Now, since the dawn eighteen months ago, since the broad daylight three months ago, and since a few days ago, when the full Sun illuminated my wonderful speculations, nothing holds me back. I yield freely to the sacred frenzy; I dare frankly to confess that I have stolen the golden vessels of the Egyptians to build a tabernacle for my God far from the bounds of Egypt. If you pardon me, I shall rejoice; if you reproach me, I shall endure. The die is cast, and I am writing the book— to be read either now or by posterity, it matters not. It can wait a century for a reader, as God himself has waited six thousand years for a witness.

A new universe had dawned, and the Sun, whose luminous centrality Copernicus and Kepler perceived as the very image of the Godhead, seemed to shine on the world a new light of divine intelligibility. Yet as Kepler's words remind us, these first discoverers were altogether alone in their new cosmos, alone in a way we today can hardly comprehend. Now that Copernicus and Kepler and the rest are seen as but the first of millions to recognize the new universe, it is easy to forget how supremely isolated they were. During their lifetimes, there were no millions but rather just one or two, later a handful, who wrote letters to each other from one country to another secretly encouraging each other in their scarcely believable conviction. To put ourselves in their position, we would have to imagine that we had made an epochal discovery that would be rejected out of hand not only by the untutored masses but by virtually all the major intellectual and cultural authorities of the time—all the most distinguished university professors, the most respected scientists, the Nobel Prize winners, the pope and other religious leaders, the most prominent philosophers, the scholarly contributors to the *New York Review of Books* and the *Times Literary Supplement*—all the conscientious and learned guardians of the cultural world view. For decade after decade our new conception of the cosmos would be, when noticed at all, forthrightly condemned by just about everyone who counted—dismissed and ignored as absurd nonsense or, if necessary, attacked and suppressed as a dangerous heresy.

Copernicus himself had anticipated such a reaction. In his preface to the *De Revolutionibus,* he predicted that as soon as certain people heard of his thesis they would "cry out that, holding such views, I should at once be hissed off the stage." Recalling the Pythagoreans' habit of imparting their "noble and arduously won discoveries" only to an inner circle of friends and intimates, Copernicus stated that he had long hesitated to publish his work lest it be despised by those too unintelligent or prejudiced to comprehend it. And despised it was, by even the most advanced and innovative thinkers of the time. History textbooks have long made us aware that the major religious authorities of the time, first Protestant and later Catholic, vehemently opposed the Copernican theory. Even before the *De Revolutionibus* was published Luther is reported to have said, "People gave ear to an upstart astrologer who strove to show that the Earth revolves, not the heavens or the firmament, the Sun and the Moon. . . . This fool wishes to reverse the entire science of astronomy; but sacred Scripture tells us that Joshua commanded the Sun to stand still, and not the Earth." And in his *Commentary on Genesis*, Calvin wrote: "Who will venture to place the authority of Copernicus above that of the Holy Spirit?" Yet secular intellectuals were equally dismissive: "No one in his senses," said the influential liberal philosopher Jean Bodin, "or imbued with the slightest knowledge of physics, will ever think that the Earth, heavy and unwieldy from its own weight and mass, staggers up and down around its own center and that of the Sun; for at the slightest jar of the Earth, we would see cities and fortresses, towns and mountains thrown down."

The new theory conflicted not only with common sense, and not only with literal interpretations of certain passages of the Bible, but with the most cogent and long-established principles of physics and cosmology. Most of the leading academic scientists of the day thought the idea so implausible as not to require serious examination. Impressive scientific arguments (for example, concerning falling objects on the Earth) and rigorous astronomical observations (such as the absence of annual stellar parallax) strongly contradicted the heliocentric hypothesis. In the light of scientific assumptions then current, the new idea seemed altogether unreasonable. Arguments we find compelling today were not compelling then. Without an entirely new cosmological framework and new principles of interpretation through which to view the data, all the arguments and evidence for a moving Earth lacked force. Both physically and philosophically, the new theory was "impossible." Though it depended in part on hard-won conceptual advances made by the Scholastics of the medieval universities, its implications radically challenged the entire medieval world view. Today we can easily lose sight of what a bold, almost reckless act of faith supported the revolutionaries' belief in their new world. It certainly was not empirically "proven." Little wonder that to bolster their fledgling hypothesis and give themselves encouragement, the early Copernicans repeatedly brought up the names of every ancient authority they could—Aristarchus, the Pythagoreans, Heraclides—as precursors of their own view.

It was not primarily empirical considerations nor, in the narrow modern sense, "rational" factors that were decisive in persuading the early Copernican revolutionaries to pursue and elaborate the heliocentric hypothesis. These were necessary but not sufficient conditions for such a radical change. It was, above all, powerful spiritual and even aesthetic intellectual predispositions that made the crucial difference. And it was these predispositions—influenced by Renaissance Humanism and Neoplatonism, Hermetic esotericism, and Christian mysticism, all supporting a vastly expanded mystical-mathematical cosmology—that effectively transformed the significance of the rational and empirical factors. To conceive and propose the new vision of the cosmos required a new Humanist confidence in the world-completing, self-realizing power and role of the human being, capable of grasping and articulating the true forms of the divinely created universe. To be attracted to the heliocentric conception required as well a Platonic-Pythagorean conviction that the Creator of the universe expressed the divine intelligence through mathematical forms and geometric harmonies of an eternal, transcendent nature, and that the problem of the apparent planetary motions, bewilderingly complex, veiled a simpler, elegant truth. It further demanded a Neoplatonic apprehension of the Sun as a visible reflection of the central Godhead, a living metaphor of the divine creative principle, whose luminous radiance and glory made it the most appropriate body in the heavens to be the cosmic center. To adopt the Copernican idea in those first decades took above all an overriding passion for a certain kind of intellectual beauty and precision, a sensibility that so valued elegance, harmony, simplicity, and coherence as intrinsic qualities of the divine heavens that one would be willing to ignore both the evidence of the senses and the arguments from contemporary physics against the movement of the Earth, confident that in time adequate explanations could be found.

The first Copernicans had experienced a kind of inner conversion. Their epiphany was at once intellectual and spiritual, psychological and cosmological, and all their research and thinking served the new vision by which they were happily possessed. Their intuition ran ahead far in advance of all the theoretical and empirical work that had to be done before the new theory could be fully justified and grounded. Even a century after Copernicus, in the *Dialogue Concerning the Two Chief World Systems*, Galileo underscored this point:

> You wonder that there are so few followers of the Pythagorean opinion [that the Earth moves] while I am astonished that there have been any up to this day who have embraced and followed it. Nor can I ever sufficiently admire the outstanding acumen of those who have taken hold of this opinion and accepted it as true: they have, through sheer force of intellect done such violence to their own senses as to prefer what reason told them over that which sensible experience showed them to be the contrary. For the arguments against [the Earth's rotation] we have examined are very plausible, as we have seen; and the fact that the Ptolemaics and the Aristotelians and all their disciples took them to be conclusive is indeed a strong argument of their effectiveness. But the experiences which overtly contradict the annual movement [of the Earth around the Sun] are indeed so much greater in their apparent force that, I repeat, there is no limit to my astonishment when I reflect that Aristarchus and Copernicus were able to make reason so conquer sense that, in defiance of the latter, the former became mistress of their belief.

For the Copernican hypothesis to be made reasonable, an entirely new conception of "reason" itself had to be forged: new ways of deciding what counts as truth, new ways of recognizing patterns, new forms of evidence, new categories of interpretation, a new understanding of causality. Long-established rules of scientific methodology had to be overturned. An entirely new epistemology and ontology had to be formulated. The nature of the Copernican revolution was so fundamental that what had to be rethought was not only all the conventional scientific theories but the entire established hierarchy of humanity's place in the universal scheme of things: its relation to the rest of nature and to the cosmos, its relation to the divine, the basis for its morality, its capacity for certain knowledge, its historical self-understanding.

Such a radical transformation could not happen overnight. For the cultural mind and psyche to support that transformation, the passage of entire generations was required, including the deaths of the many intellectual authorities who were incapable of escaping the hold of the reigning paradigm. The required change was not just physical but metaphysical: The entire world needed to be revisioned. In the end, the implications of the great shift—cosmological, religious, moral, epistemological, psychological, existential—were so far-reaching that it would take centuries to work them out, even to become conscious of them.

Gradually, the passage of time, and heroic efforts against powerful opponents and entrenched assumptions, brought about the complete triumph of the Copernican shift. Yet as the modern age progressed, the passage of yet more time brought forth, with what now seems a fateful inevitability, a succession of new consequences and elaborations out of the deep matrix of the Copernican revolution that could scarcely have been more paradoxical, revealing implications often sharply antithetical to the cosmological vision of its originators. Its larger meaning has been transformed with each succeeding age, and is, today, still unfolding.

Two Paradigms of History

A paradox concerning the character and fate of the West confronts every sensitive observer: On the one hand, we recognize a certain dynamism, a luminous, heroic impulse, even a nobility, at work in Western civilization and Western thought. We see this in the great achievements of Greek philosophy and culture, and in the profound moral and spiritual strivings of the Judaeo-Christian tradition. We see it embodied in the Sistine Chapel and other Renaissance masterpieces, in the plays of Shakespeare, in the music of Beethoven. We recognize it in the brilliance of the Copernican revolution and the long sequence of dazzling scientific advances in many disciplines that have unfolded in its wake. We see it in the titanic space flights of a generation ago that landed men on the Moon, or, more recently, in the spectacular images of the vast cosmos coming from the Hubble Space Telescope that have opened up unprecedented perspectives reaching back in time and outward into space billions of years and light-years to the primal origins of the universe itself. No less vividly, we find it in the great democratic revolutions of modernity and the powerful emancipatory movements of our own era, all with deep sources in the Western intellectual and spiritual tradition.

Yet at the same time, if we attempt to perceive a larger reality beyond the conventional heroic narrative, we cannot fail to recognize the shadow of this great luminosity. The same cultural tradition and historical trajectory that brought forth such noble achievements has also caused immense suffering and loss, for many other cultures and peoples, for many people within Western culture itself, and for many other forms of life on the Earth. Moreover, the West has played the central role in bringing about a subtly growing and seemingly inexorable crisis—one of multidimensional complexity, affecting all aspects of life from the ecological and economic to the psychological and spiritual. To say that our global civilization is becoming dysfunctional scarcely conveys the gravity of the situation. For many forms of life on the Earth, catastrophe has already begun, as our planet undergoes the most massive extinction of species since the demise of the dinosaurs. How can we make sense of this tremendous paradox in the character and meaning of the West?

If we examine many of the major debates in the post-traditional intellectual culture of our time, it is possible to see looming behind them two fundamental paradigms, two great myths, diametrically opposite in character, concerning human history and the evolution of human consciousness. As genuine myths, these underlying paradigms represent not mere illusory beliefs or arbitrary collective fantasies, naïve delusions contrary to fact, but rather those enduring archetypal structures of meaning that so profoundly inform our cultural psyche and shape our beliefs that they constitute the very means through which we construe something *as* fact. They invisibly constellate our vision. They filter and reveal our data, structure our imagination, permeate our ways of knowing and acting.

The first paradigm, familiar to all of us from our education, describes human history and the evolution of human consciousness as an epic narrative of human progress, a long heroic journey from a primitive world of dark ignorance, suffering, and limitation to a brighter modern world of ever-increasing knowledge, freedom, and well-being. This great trajectory of progress is seen as having been made possible by the sustained development of human reason and, above all, by the emergence of the modern mind. This view informs much, perhaps most, of what we see and hear on the subject and is easily recognized whenever we encounter a book or program with a title such as *The Ascent of Man, The Discoverers, Man's Conquest of Space*, or the like. The direction of history is seen as onward and upward. Humanity is typically personified as "man" (*anthropos, homo, l'uomo, l'homme, el hombre, chelovek, der Mensch*) and imaged, at least implicitly, as a masculine hero, rising above the constraints of nature and tradition, exploring the great cosmos, mastering his environment, determining his own destiny: restless, bold, brilliantly innovative, ceaselessly pressing forward with his intelligence and will, breaking out of the structures and limits of the past, ascending to ever-higher levels of development, forever seeking greater freedom and new horizons, discovering ever-wider arenas for self-realization. In this perspective, the apex of human achievement commenced with the rise of modern science and democratic individualism in the centuries following the Renaissance. The view of history is one of progressive emancipation and empowerment. It is a vision that emerged fully in the course of the European Enlightenment of the seventeenth and eighteenth centuries, though its roots are as old as Western civilization itself.

As with all powerful myths, we have been, and many perhaps remain, largely unconscious of this historical paradigm's hold on our collective imagination. It animates the vast majority of contemporary books and essays, editorial columns, book reviews, science articles, research papers, and television documentaries, as well as political, social, and economic policies. It is so familiar to us, so close to our perception, that in many respects it has become our common sense, the form and foundation of our self-image as modern humans. We have been so long identified with this progressive understanding of the human project, and particularly of the modern Western project, that it is only in recent decades that we have begun to be able to see it as a paradigm—that is, to be able to see, at least partly, from outside its sphere of influence.

The other great historical vision tells a very different story. In this understanding, human history and the evolution of human consciousness are seen as a predominantly problematic, even tragic narrative of humanity's gradual but radical fall and separation from an original state of oneness with nature and an encompassing spiritual dimension of being. In its primordial condition, humankind had possessed an instinctive knowledge of the profound sacred unity and interconnectedness of the world, but under the influence of the Western mind, especially its modern expression, the course of history brought about a deep schism between humankind and nature, and a desacralization of the world. This development coincided with an increasingly destructive exploitation of nature, the devastation of traditional indigenous cultures, a loss of faith in spiritual realities, and an increasingly unhappy state of the human soul, which experienced itself as ever more isolated, shallow, and unfulfilled. In this perspective, both humanity and nature are seen as having suffered grievously under a long exploitative, dualistic vision of the world, with the worst consequences being produced by the oppressive hegemony of modern industrial societies empowered by Western science and technology. The nadir of this fall is the present time of planetary turmoil, ecological crisis, and spiritual distress, which are seen as the direct consequence of human hubris, embodied above all in the spirit and structure of the modern Western mind and ego. This second historical perspective reveals a progressive impoverishment of human life and the human spirit, a fragmentation of original unities, a ruinous destruction of the sacred community of being.

Something like these two interpretations of history, here described in starkly contrasting terms for the sake of easy recognition, can be seen to inform many of the more specific issues of our age. They represent two basic antithetical myths of historical self-understanding: the myth of Progress and what in its earlier incarnations was called the myth of the Fall. These two historical paradigms appear today in many variations, combinations, and compromise formations. They underlie and influence discussions of the environmental crisis, globalization, multiculturalism, fundamentalism, feminism and patriarchy, evolution and history. One might say that these opposing myths constitute the underlying argument of our time: Whither humanity? Upward or downward? How are we to view Western civilization, the Western intellectual tradition, its canon of great works? How are we to view modern science, modern rationality, modernity itself? How are we to view "man"? Is history ultimately a narrative of progress or of tragedy?

John Stuart Mill made a shrewd, and wise, observation about the nature of most philosophical debates. In his splendid essay on Coleridge, he pointed out that both sides in intellectual controversies tended to be "in the right in what they affirmed, though in the wrong in what they denied." Mill's insight into the nature of intellectual discourse shines light on many disagreements: Whether it is conservatives debating liberals, parents arguing with their children, or a lovers' quarrel, almost invariably something is being repressed in the service of making one's point. But his insight seems to apply with particular aptness to the conflict of historical paradigms just described. I believe that both parties to this dispute have grasped an essential aspect of our history, that both views are in a sense correct, each with compelling arguments within its own frame of reference, but also that they are both intensely *partial* views, as a result of which they both misread a larger story.

It is not simply that each perspective possesses a significant grain of truth. Rather, both historical paradigms are at once fully valid and yet also partial aspects of a larger frame of reference, a metanarrative, in which the two opposite interpretations are precisely intertwined to form a complex, integrated whole. The two historical dramas actually constitute each other. Not only are they simultaneously true; they are embedded in each other's truth. They underlie and inform each other, implicate each other, make each other possible. One might compare the way the two perspectives coalesce while appearing to exclude each other to those gestalt-experiment illustrations that can be perceived in two different, equally cogent ways, such as the precisely ambiguous figure that can be seen either as a white vase or as two black profiles in silhouette. By means of a gestalt shift in perception, the observer can move back and forth between the two images, though the figure itself, the original body of data, remains unchanged.

One is reminded here of Niels Bohr's axiom in quantum physics, "The opposite of a profound truth may well be another profound truth," or Oscar Wilde's "A Truth in art is that whose contradictory is also true." What is difficult, of course, is to see both images, both truths, simultaneously: to suppress nothing, to remain open to the paradox, to maintain the tension of opposites. Wisdom, like compassion, often seems to require of us that we hold multiple realities in our consciousness at once. This may be the task we must begin to engage if we wish to gain a deeper understanding of the evolution of human consciousness, and the history of the Western mind in particular: to see that long intellectual and spiritual journey, moving through stages of increasing differentiation and complexity, as having brought about both a progressive ascent to autonomy and a tragic fall from unity—and, perhaps, as having prepared the way for a synthesis on a new level. From this perspective, the two paradigms reflect opposite but equally essential aspects of an immense dialectical process, an evolutionary drama that has been unfolding for thousands of years and that now appears to be reaching a critical, perhaps climactic moment of transformation.

Yet there is another important party to this debate, another view of human history, one that instead of integrating the two opposing historical perspectives into a larger, more complex one appears to refute them both altogether. This third view, articulated with increasing frequency and sophistication in our own time, holds that *no* coherent pattern actually exists in human history or evolution, at least none that is independent of human interpretation. If an overarching pattern in history is visible, that pattern has been projected onto history by the human mind under the influence of various non-empirical factors: cultural, political, economic, social, sociobiological, psychological. In this view, the pattern—the myth or story—ultimately resides in the human subject, not the historical object. The object can never be perceived without being selectively shaped by an interpretive framework, which itself is shaped and constructed by forces beyond itself and beyond the awareness of the interpreting subject. Knowledge of history, as of anything else, is ever-shifting, free-floating, ungrounded in an objective reality. Patterns are not so much recognized in phenomena as read into them. History is, finally, only a construct.

On the one hand, this robust skepticism that pervades much of our postmodern thought is not far from that necessary critical perspective that allows us to discuss paradigms at all, to make comparisons and judgments about underlying conceptual structures such as those made above. Its recognition of the radically interpretive factor in all human experience and knowledge—its understanding that we are always seeing by means of myths and theories, that our experience and knowledge are always patterned and even constituted by various changing a priori and usually unconscious structures of meaning—is essential to the entire exercise we have been pursuing.

On the other hand, this seemingly paradigm-free relativism, whereby *no* pattern or meaning exists in history except as constructed and projected onto history by the human mind, is itself clearly another paradigm. It recognizes that we always see by means of myths and interpretive categories, but fails to apply that recognition consistently to itself. It excels at "seeing through," but perhaps has not seen through enough. In one sense, this form of the postmodern vision may be best understood as a direct outgrowth, possibly an inevitable one, of the progressive modern mind in its ever-deepening critical reflexivity—questioning, suspecting, striving for emancipation through critical awareness—reaching here in its most extreme development what is essentially a stage of advanced self-deconstruction. Yet this perspective may also be understood as the natural consequence of the Enlightenment vision beginning to encounter its own shadow—the darkly problematic narrative articulated by its opposing historical paradigm—and being challenged and reshaped by that encounter. For just this reason, the deconstructive postmodern perspective may represent a crucial element in the unfolding of a new and more comprehensive understanding. There is a deep truth in this view, though it too may also be a deeply partial truth, an essential aspect of a much larger, more embracing, and still more richly complex vision. The postmodern mind may eventually be seen as having constituted a necessary transitional stage between epochs, a period of dissolving and opening between larger sustained cultural paradigms.

To begin to explore how all this might be so, and to understand better the historical and philosophical context for the perspective introduced in this book, let us take a more precise look at the basic nature of the modern world view.

Forging the Self,
Disenchanting the World

Our world view is not simply the way we look at the world. It reaches inward to constitute our innermost being, and outward to constitute the world. It mirrors but also reinforces and even forges the structures, armorings, and possibilities of our interior life. It deeply configures our psychic and somatic experience, the patterns of our sensing, knowing, and interacting with the world. No less potently, our world view—our beliefs and theories, our maps, our metaphors, our myths, our interpretive assumptions—constellates our outer reality, shaping and working the world's malleable potentials in a thousand ways of subtly reciprocal interaction. World views create worlds.

Perhaps the most concise way of defining the modern world view is to focus on that which distinguishes it from virtually all other world views. Speaking very generally, what sets the modern mind apart is its fundamental tendency to assert and experience a radical separation between subject and object, a distinct division between the human self and the encompassing world. This perspective can be contrasted with what has come to be called the primal world view, characteristic of traditional indigenous cultures. The primal mind does not maintain this decisive division, does not recognize it, whereas the modern mind not only maintains it but is essentially constituted on it.

The primal human being perceives the surrounding natural world as permeated with meaning, meaning whose significance is at once human and cosmic. Spirits are seen in the forest, presences are felt in the wind and the ocean, the river, the mountain. Meaning is recognized in the flight of two eagles across the horizon, in the conjunction of two planets in the heavens, in the unfolding cycles of the Moon and Sun. The primal world is ensouled. It communicates and has purposes. It is pregnant with signs and symbols, implications and intentions. The world is animated by the same psychologically resonant realities that human beings experience within themselves. A continuity extends from the interior world of the human to the world outside. In the primal experience, what we would call the "outer" world possesses an interior aspect that is continuous with human subjectivity. Creative and responsive intelligence, spirit and soul, meaning and purpose are everywhere. The human being is a microcosm within the macrocosm of the world, participating in its interior reality and united with the whole in ways that are both tangible and invisible.

Primal experience takes place, as it were, within a world soul, an *anima mundi,* a living matrix of embodied meaning. The human psyche is embedded within a world psyche in which it complexly participates and by which it is continuously defined. The workings of that *anima mundi,* in all its flux and diversity, are articulated through a language that is mythic and numinous. Because the world is understood as speaking a symbolic language, direct communication of meaning and purpose from world to human can occur. The many particulars of the empirical world are all endowed with symbolic, archetypal significance, and that significance flows between inner and outer, between self and world. In this relatively undifferentiated state of consciousness, human beings perceive themselves as directly—emotionally, mystically, consequentially—participating in and communicating with the interior life of the natural world and cosmos. To be more precise, this *participation mystique* involves a complex sense of direct inner participation not only of human beings in the world but also of human beings in the divine powers, through ritual, and of divine powers in the world, by virtue of their immanent and transformative presence. The participation is multidirectional and multidimensional, pervasive and encompassing.

By contrast, the modern mind experiences a fundamental division between a subjective human self and an objective external world. Apart from the human being, the cosmos is seen as entirely impersonal and unconscious. Whatever beauty and value that human beings may perceive in the universe, that universe is in itself mere matter in motion, mechanistic and purposeless, ruled by chance and necessity. It is altogether indifferent to human consciousness and values. The world outside the human being lacks conscious intelligence, it lacks interiority, and it lacks intrinsic meaning and purpose. For these are human realities, and the modern mind believes that to project what is human onto the nonhuman is a basic epistemological fallacy. The world is devoid of any meaning that does not derive ultimately from human consciousness. From the modern perspective, the primal person conflates and confuses inner and outer and thus lives in a state of continuous magical delusion, in an anthropomorphically distorted world, a world speciously filled with the human psyche's own subjective meaning. For the modern mind, the only source of meaning in the universe is human consciousness.

Another way we might describe this situation would be to say that the modern mind engages the world within an implicit experiential structure of being a subject set apart from, and in some sense over against, an object. The modern world is full of objects, which the human subject confronts and acts upon from its unique position of conscious autonomy. By contrast, the primal mind engages the world more as a subject embedded in a world of subjects, with no absolute boundaries between or among them. In the primal perspective, the world is full of subjects. The primal world is saturated with subjectivity, interiority, intrinsic meanings and purposes.

From the modern perspective, if I see the world as if it were communicating humanly relevant meaning to me in some purposeful, intelligent way, as if it were laden with meaning-rich symbols—a sacred text, as it were, to be interpreted—then I am projecting human realities onto the nonhuman world. Such an attitude toward the world is regarded by the modern mind as reflecting an epistemologically naïve state of awareness: intellectually undeveloped, undifferentiated, childish, wishfully self-indulgent, something to be outgrown and corrected through the development of a mature critical reason. Or worse, it is a sign of mental illness, of primitive magical thinking with delusions of self-reference, a condition to be suppressed and treated with appropriate medication.

We can illustrate the basic difference between primal and modern experience with a simple diagram (Figure 1), in which the inner circle representing the primal self has a porous boundary, suggesting its radical permeability and embeddedness with respect to the world, while the inner circle representing the modern self is formed by a solid line, suggesting the modern experience of a sharp distinction and dichotomy between subject and object, inner and outer. In the primal mind, the shaded area, representing the presence of conscious intelligence and interiority, the source of meaning and purpose, passes without dis-

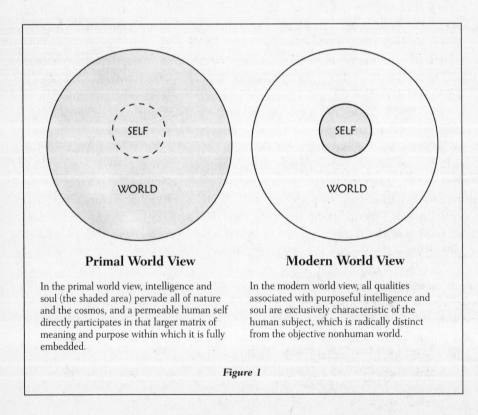

Primal World View

In the primal world view, intelligence and soul (the shaded area) pervade all of nature and the cosmos, and a permeable human self directly participates in that larger matrix of meaning and purpose within which it is fully embedded.

Modern World View

In the modern world view, all qualities associated with purposeful intelligence and soul are exclusively characteristic of the human subject, which is radically distinct from the objective nonhuman world.

Figure 1

tinction through the entire self/world complex. In the modern mind, the shaded area is located exclusively within the boundary of the self.

The systematic recognition that the exclusive source of meaning and purpose in the world is the human mind, and that it is a fundamental fallacy to project what is human onto the nonhuman, is one of the most basic presuppositions—perhaps *the* basic presupposition—of modern scientific method. Modern science seeks with obsessive rigor to "de-anthropomorphize" cognition. *Facts* are out there, *meanings* come from in here. The factual is regarded as plain, stark, objective, unembellished by the human and subjective, undistorted by values and aspirations. We see this impulse clearly evident in the emergence of the modern mind from the time of Bacon and Descartes onward. If the object is to be properly understood, the subject must observe and analyze that object with the utmost care taken to inhibit the naïve human tendency to invest the object with characteristics that are properly attributable only to the human subject. For genuine and valid cognition to occur, the objective world—nature, the cosmos—must be viewed as something fundamentally lacking in all those qualities that are subjectively, inwardly most present to the human mind as constituting its own being: consciousness and intelligence, sense of purpose and intention, capacity for meaning and communication, moral and spiritual imagination. To perceive these qualities as existing intrinsically in the world is to "contaminate" the act of knowing with what are in fact human projections.

It is easy for us today, still under the influence of the modern vision that reifies modern experience and assumptions as absolute, to believe we truly understand the primal vision when we see it as simply the naïve consequence of primitive fears, wishes, and projections. But to discern more impartially the difference between these two world views, we must grasp the stubborn fact that the primal cosmos was universally *experienced,* for countless millennia, as tangibly and self-evidently alive and awake—pervasively intentional and responsive, informed by ubiquitous spiritual presences, animated throughout by archetypal forces and intelligible meanings—in a manner that the modern perception does not and perhaps cannot recognize.

Of course this fundamental difference between the primal and the modern did not arise instantly in the seventeenth century, but evolved over thousands of years, in many forms and through many cultural developments. Not just modernity but the entire human project can be seen as impelling the gradual differentiation between self and world. An emergent distinction between subject and object seems to have been present already at the very birth of Homo sapiens, with its novel capacity and impulse to consciously plan rather than act automatically on instinct, to rely on one's own wits and will to make one's way in the world, to manipulate and control nature rather than be so embedded in it as to be its passive subject. As soon as our species first developed linguistic symbolization, we began to differentiate ourselves further from the world, objectifying our experience in ways that could articulate the world's acting on us and our acting on the world. As soon as we first used a tool, we began to act as a subject vis-à-vis an object. All the epochal advances in human evolution—bipedalism and an upright posture, the larger and more complex brain, the making of tools, the control of fire, the development of hunting-and-gathering societies, the division of labor, the domestication of plants and animals, the formation of settled communities and then large urban centers, the increasingly complex and hierarchical social organization, the evolving capacities for linguistic, religious, and artistic symbolization, the emergence of the earliest forms of science and philosophy— all these both reflected and impelled new stages in the progressive differentiation of the human self from the encompassing world.

A memorable image at the beginning of Kubrick's film *2001: A Space Odyssey* captures one aspect of this larger coherence in the vector of the human epic. In the opening sequence, entitled "The Dawn of Man," a protohuman primate has just made the primordial discovery of using a tool for the first time, successfully employing a large bone as a weapon in a life-and-death struggle. In the ecstasy of that discovery, he hits the bone over and over again on a rock, on which it eventually shatters and, soaring high into the air, metamorphoses in slow motion into an orbiting space satellite at the turn of the twenty-first century. In that single montage we see the entire Promethean trajectory, the alpha and the omega of the Promethean quest to liberate the human being from the bonds of nature through human intelligence and will, to ascend and transcend, to gain control over the larger matrix from which the human being was attempting to emerge. This quest climaxes in modernity, especially in modern science, where the dominant goal of knowledge is ever-increasing prediction and control over an external natural world seen as radically "other": mechanistic, impersonal, unconscious, the object of our powerful knowledge.

From the time of Bacon and Descartes, Hobbes and Locke, and more pervasively in the aftermath of the Enlightenment, the modern understanding is gradually so transformed that the world is no longer seen as a locus of pregiven meanings and purposes, as had been true not only in the immemorial primal vision but also for the ancient Greeks, medieval Scholastics, and Renaissance Humanists. With the full ascension of the modern mind, the world is no longer informed by numinous powers, gods and goddesses, archetypal Ideas, or sacred ends. It no longer embodies a cosmic order of meanings and purposes with which the human self seeks to be aligned. Rather, the world is viewed as a neutral domain of contingent facts and potential means to our secular purposes. In Max Weber's famous term at the beginning of the twentieth century, which developed Schiller's insight of a century earlier, the modern world is "disenchanted" *(entzaubert):* It has been voided of any spiritual, symbolic, or expressive dimension that provides a cosmic order in which human existence finds its ground of meaning and purpose. Instead, the world is viewed entirely in terms of neutral facts, the detached rational understanding of which will give the human being an unprecedented capacity to calculate, control, and manipulate that world.

Yet such a great shift in understanding also accomplishes something else of scarcely less importance for the modern self. Disenchantment, the denial of intrinsic meaning and purpose, essentially *objectifies* the world and thereby denies *subjectivity* to the world. Objectification denies to the world a subject's capacity to intend, to signify intelligently, to express its meaning, to embody and communicate humanly relevant purposes and values. To objectify the world is to remove from it all subjective categories, such as meaning and purpose, by perceiving these as projections of what are now regarded as the only true subjects, human beings. This in turn tremendously magnifies and empowers human subjectivity: the felt interior capacity of the human being to be self-defining, self-revising, self-determining—to be both outwardly world-shaping and inwardly consequential and autonomous. It makes possible a new freedom from externally imposed meanings and orderings that had previously been seen as embedded in the cosmos, and that had typically been upheld and enforced by traditional structures of cultural authority, whether religious, social, or political. Charles Taylor has well described the consequences of this deep shift for the modern self:

> One of the powerful attractions of this austere vision, long before it "paid off" in technology, lies in the fact that a disenchanted world is correlative to a self-defining subject, and that the winning through to a self-defining identity was accompanied by a sense of exhilaration and power, that the subject need no longer define his perfection or vice, his equilibrium or disharmony, in relation to an external order. With the forging of this modern subjectivity there comes a new notion of freedom, and a newly central role attributed to freedom, which seems to have proved itself definitive and irreversible.

Depriving the world of subjectivity, of its capacity for intentional significance, by objectification and disenchantment radically enhances the human self's sense of freedom and autonomous subjectivity, its underlying conviction that it can shape and determine its own existence. Simultaneously, disenchantment enhances the human being's capacity to view the natural world as primarily a context to be shaped and a resource to be exploited for human benefit. As the world loses its traditional structures of pregiven meaning, as these are successively "seen through" and deconstructed, the conditions of human existence—both outer and inner—become increasingly open to change and development, ever more subject to human influence, innovation, and control. It was through just this extraordinary shift of vision that there developed an effective psychological and philosophical foundation for the rapid ascent of modern science, secular society, democratic individualism, and industrial civilization.

The history of the human mind's movement from a state of *participation mystique* to a more fully differentiated mode of awareness is in many respects the history of the human mind itself. Impelled by the powerful human drive to achieve ever-greater autonomy relative to the conditions of existence, virtually the entire evolution of human consciousness has served this psychological and epistemological impulse to distinguish the human self from the world, subject from object, part from whole. The Promethean project seems to be intrinsic to the human condition. Yet this project has been carried out most vigorously and brilliantly by the Western mind, above all by the modern mind, that avatar and apex of Promethean progress.

If we look again at the comparison (Figure 2) between the primal experience of *participation mystique* and the modern experience of a subject-object dichotomy, we can readily see what has happened in the process of moving from the world view depicted on the left to that depicted on the right. In the long evolution from primal to modern consciousness, there has taken place a complexly intertwined and interpenetrating two-sided process: on the one hand, a gradual *differentiation* of the self from the world, of the human being from nature, of the individual from the encompassing matrix of being; on the other hand, a gradual *disenchantment* of the world, producing a radical *relocation* of the ground of meaning and conscious intelligence from the world as a whole to the human self alone. What once pervaded the world as the *anima mundi* is now seen as the exclusive property of human consciousness. The modern human self has essentially absorbed all meaning and purpose into its own interior being, emptying the primal cosmos of what once constituted its essential nature.

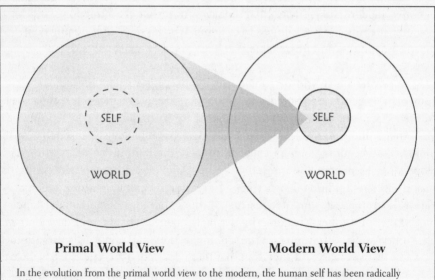

Primal World View   **Modern World View**

In the evolution from the primal world view to the modern, the human self has been radically differentiated from the world, and the ground of meaning and purposeful intelligence has been relocated from a now-disenchanted cosmos to an empowered autonomous human self.

Figure 2

But we misunderstand this evolutionary process if we consider it only in the generally secular terms so far discussed. The modern differentiation of the autonomous human self and the disenchantment of the empirical cosmos were also profoundly influenced and even impelled by the historical evolution of religion, again particularly in the Western context—ancient, medieval, and early modern. From its beginnings, the Western self was informed by the momentous disclosure of humanity's special relationship to a transcendent divine reality, a monotheistic supreme being who was both the creator of the world and the ultimate locus of meaning and value: "Man was made in the image of God." Thus God's absolute uniqueness, separation, and superiority with respect to the mundane world of mortal finitude and unredeemed nature deeply strengthened the human being's sense of uniqueness, separation, and superiority with respect to the rest of nature and the created universe.

Modifying our diagram accordingly, we can recognize the crucial intervening stage in the evolution from the primal world view to the modern one provided by this immense religious development. With the revelation of a transcendent divine being as the ultimate ground of meaning and value, supraordinate to and separate from the empirical world of nature, combined with the human being's unique association with that transcendent divinity, an enormous intellectual and psychological step is taken in the separative elevation of the human from a universe gradually voided of intrinsic meaning. In the monotheistic revelation, a self-subsistent divine Subject created the world as Object, within which the special human subject and its divinely ordained history unfolds. As the diagram in Figure 3 suggests (and as Descartes's careful arguments for the existence of God at the birth of modern philosophy affirm), what eventually becomes the modern self receives its unique ontological status from its privileged association with the transcendent divine reality that stands above an empirical cosmos that has been increasingly emptied of all inherent significance and value apart from the human.

This epochal transformation of the triadic relationship between divinity, humanity, and the world was already set in motion with the emergence of the great world religions and philosophies of transcendence during that period of the first millennium BCE named by Karl Jaspers the Axial Age. The differentiation between self, world, and God was given special force and new definition with the unfolding of the biblical tradition from the later Hebrew prophets through early Christianity to Saint Augustine and the medieval era. It was decisively forwarded, and in a sense absolutized, by the Reformation's militant desacralizing of the world in service of the human being's exclusive allegiance to the sovereign majesty of the Creator. Finally, in the wake of the Scientific Revolution and Enlightenment, this privileged position of the human vis-à-vis rest of creation was assumed and expanded in entirely secular terms—here too, partly as a result of forces set in motion by the Western religious legacy—as the modern self progressed in its unprecedented development of autonomy and self-definition.

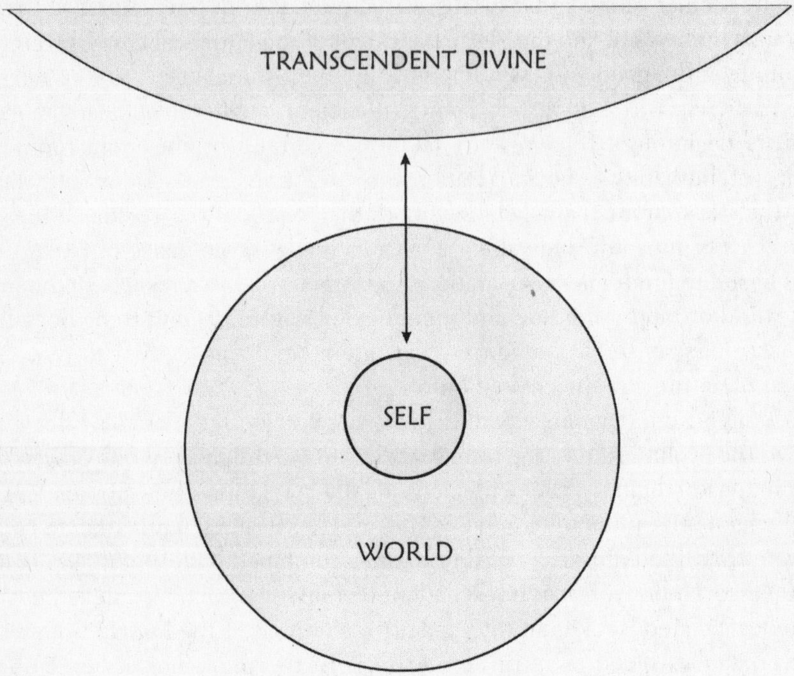

Western Religious World View

In the Western religious world view that emerged between the primal and modern, forming a link between them, the human self bears a unique relationship to a transcendent divinity that is separate from and sovereign over the created world, a world that is increasingly perceived as devoid of meaning and purpose other than that associated with the human self.

Figure 3

A host of significant complications and exceptions, ambiguities and nuances could be usefully discussed concerning this long and complex historical development.[1] But speaking very broadly, we may say here that as the human self, guided by its evolving cultural, religious, philosophical, and scientific symbolizations, has gained increasing substantiality and distinction with respect to the world, that self has increasingly appropriated all the intelligence and soul, meaning and purpose it previously perceived in the world, so that it eventually locates these realities exclusively within itself. Conversely, as the human being has appropriated all the intelligence and soul, meaning and purpose it previously perceived in the world, it has gained more and more substantiality and distinction with respect to the world, accompanied by ever-greater autonomy as those meanings and purposes are seen as ever more malleable to human will and intelligence. The two processes—constellating the self and appropriating the *anima mundi*—

have been mutually supportive and reinforcing. But their joint consequence has been to gradually empty the external world of all intrinsic meaning and purpose. By the late modern period, the cosmos has metamorphosed into a mindless, soulless vacuum, within which the human being is incongruently self-aware. The *anima mundi* has dissolved and disappeared, and all psychological and spiritual qualities are now located exclusively in the human mind and psyche.

It appears that this evolutionary trade-off has fostered the emergence of a centered autonomous self, one decisively set off from yet dynamically engaged with the encompassing world, a world that in turn has been voided of all those qualities with which the human being is uniquely identified. The forging of the self and the disenchantment of the world, the differentiation of the human and the appropriation of meaning, are all aspects of the same development. In effect, to sum up a very complex process, *the achievement of human autonomy has been paid for by the experience of human alienation*. How precious the former, how painful the latter. What may be viewed as the fundamental epistemological strategy of the evolving human mind—the systematic separation of subject from object—one carried forth to its fullest extent by the modern mind, has proved to be powerfully effective and indeed liberating. Yet many of that strategy's long-term consequences have also proved to be highly problematic.

The Cosmological Situation Today

In the course of the past century, the modern world view has seen both its greatest ascendancy and its unexpected breakdown. Every field and discipline, from philosophy, anthropology, and linguistics to physics, ecology, and medicine, has brought forth new data and new perspectives that have challenged long-established assumptions and strategies of the modern mind. This challenge has been considerably magnified and made more urgent by the multitude of concrete consequences produced by those assumptions and strategies, many of them problematic. As of the first decade of the new millennium, almost every defining attitude of the modern world view has been critically reassessed and deconstructed, though often not relinquished, even when failure to do so is costly. The result in our own, postmodern time has been a state of extraordinary intellectual ferment and fragmentation, fluidity and uncertainty. Ours is an age between world views, creative yet disoriented, a transitional era when the old cultural vision no longer holds and the new has not yet constellated. Yet we are not without signs of what the new might look like.

Recently there have been emerging from the deconstructive flux of the postmodern mind the tentative outlines of a new understanding of reality, one very different from the conventional modern view. Impelled by developments in many fields, this shift in intellectual vision has encompassed a wide range of ideas and principles, among which can be identified a few common themes. Perhaps the most conspicuous and pervasive of these can be summed up as a deeper appreciation of both the multidimensional complexity of reality and the plurality of perspectives necessary to approach it. Closely related to this new appreciation, as both cause and effect, is a critical reappraisal of the epistemological limits and pragmatic consequences of the conventional scientific approach to knowledge. This reappraisal includes a more acute sensitivity to the ways in which subject and object are mutually implicated in the act of knowing, a revised understanding of the relationship of whole and part in all phenomena, a new grasp of complex interdependence and subtle order in living systems, and an acknowledgment of the inadequacy of reductionist, mechanistic, and objectivized concepts of nature.

Other major characteristics of this emerging intellectual vision include a deeper understanding of the pivotal role of the imagination in mediating all human experience and knowledge; an increased awareness of the depth, power, and complexity of the unconscious; and a more sophisticated analysis of the nature of symbolic, metaphoric, and archetypal meaning in human life. Behind many of these themes can be seen a rejection of all literalistic and univocal interpretations of reality—of the tendency, as Robert Bellah has put it, to identify "one conception of reality with reality itself." Equally fundamental to this shift is a growing recognition of the need for and desirability of a radical opening of the mainstream Western intellectual and cultural tradition to the rich multiplicity of other traditions and perspectives that have evolved both within the West and in other cultures.

Yet this emphatic embrace of pluralism has been balanced by—and to a great extent been in the service of—a profound impulse for reintegration, a widely felt desire to overcome the fragmentation and alienation of the late modern mind. Underlying the variety of its expressions, the most distinctive trait of this new vision has been its concern with the philosophical and psychological reconciliation of numerous long-standing schisms: between human being and nature, self and world, spirit and matter, mind and body, conscious and unconscious, personal and transpersonal, secular and sacred, intellect and soul, science and the humanities, science and religion.

For some time this emerging consensus of convictions and aspirations has seemed to me, as to many others, the most interesting and hopeful intellectual development of our age and perhaps the one most likely to produce a viable successor to the rapidly deteriorating modern world view. Yet from its beginning this new vision or paradigm has confronted a seemingly insurmountable problem. The present world situation could hardly be more ripe for a major paradigm shift, and many thoughtful observers have concluded that such a shift, when it comes, should and very probably will be based on principles resembling those just cited. But to succeed in becoming a broad-based cultural vision, or even to achieve its own implicit program of psychological and intellectual integration, this new outlook has been lacking one essential element, the sine qua non of any genuinely comprehensive, internally consistent world view: a coherent cosmology.

In retrospect it is evident that the fundamental intellectual turning point of Western civilization was the Copernican revolution, understood in its largest sense. Nothing so effectively bestowed confidence in the supreme power of human reason. Nothing so emphatically and comprehensively affirmed the superiority of the modern Western mind over all others—all other world views, all other eras, all other cultures, all other modes of cognition. Nothing emancipated the modern self from a cosmos of established pregiven meanings more profoundly or more dramatically. It is impossible to think of the modern mind without the Copernican revolution.

Yet the luminosity of that great revolution has cast an extraordinary shadow. The radical displacement of the Earth and humanity from an absolute cosmic center, the stunning transference of the apparent cosmic order from the observed to the observer, and the eventual pervasive disenchantment of the material universe were all paradigmatic for the modern mind, and these have now come to epitomize humankind's underlying sense of disorientation and alienation. With the heavens no longer a separate divine realm and with the Earth no longer embedded in a circumscribed celestial order of planetary spheres and powers, humanity was simultaneously liberated from and thrust out of the ancient–medieval cosmic womb. The essential nature of reality underwent an immense shift for the Western mind, which now engaged a world possessed of entirely new dimensions, structure, and existential implications.

For all the exalted numinosity of the Copernican birth, the new universe that eventually emerged into the light of common day was a spiritually empty vastness, impersonal, neutral, indifferent to human concerns, governed by random processes devoid of purpose or meaning. At a deep level human consciousness was thereby radically estranged and decentered. It no longer experienced itself as an essential expression and focus of an intrinsically meaningful universe. "Before the Copernican revolution," wrote Bertrand Russell, "it was natural to suppose that God's purposes were specially concerned with the earth, but now this has become an unplausible hypothesis": mankind must instead be regarded as a "curious accident." The Copernican revolution was the modern mind's prototypical act of deconstruction, bringing both a birth and a death. It was the primordial cataclysm of the modern age, a stupendous event which destroyed an entire world and constituted a new one.

Not only the subsequent evolution of modern cosmology, from Newton and Laplace to Einstein and Hubble, but virtually the entire modern intellectual trajectory has sustained and magnified the primary Copernican insight: Descartes, Locke, Hume, Kant, Schopenhauer, Darwin, Marx, Nietzsche, Weber, Freud, Wittgenstein, Russell, Heidegger, Sartre, Camus. From seventeenth-century rationalism and empiricism to twentieth-century existentialism and astrophysics, human consciousness has found itself progressively emancipated yet also progressively relativized, unrooted, inwardly isolated from the spiritually opaque world it seeks to comprehend. The soul knows no home in the modern cosmos. The status of the human being in its cosmic setting is fundamentally problematic—solitary, accidental, ephemeral, inexplicable. The proud uniqueness and autonomy of "Man" have come at a high price. He is an insignificant speck cast adrift in a vast purposeless cosmos, a stranger in a strange land. Self-reflective human consciousness finds no foundation for itself in the empirical world. Inner and outer, psyche and cosmos, are radically discontinuous, mutually incoherent. As Steven Weinberg famously summarized modern cosmology, "The more the universe seems comprehensible, the more it also seems pointless." With the encompassing cosmos indifferent to human meaning, with all significance deriving ultimately from the decentered and accidental human subject, a meaningful world can never be more than a courageous human projection. Thus did the Copernican revolution establish the essential matrix for the modern world view in all its disenchanting ramifications. The most celebrated of human intellectual achievements, it remains the watershed of human alienation, the epochal symbol of humanity's cosmic estrangement.

Here we face the crux of our present predicament. For it is this post-Copernican cosmological context that continues to frame the current effort to forge a new paradigm of reality, yet that context, utterly at variance with the deep transformations now being urged, thereby confounds them. Although many of the post-Copernican ramifications (Cartesian, Kantian, Darwinian, Freudian) have been grappled with, criticized, and reconceived to one extent or another, the great starting point for the whole trajectory of modern consciousness remains untouched. The cosmological metastructure that implicitly contained and precipitated all the rest is still so solidly established as to be beyond discussion. The physical sciences of the past hundred years have flung open wide the nature of reality, dissolving all the old absolutes, but the Earth still moves—along with, now, everything else, in a postmodern explosion of centerless, free-floating flux. Newton has been transcended but not Copernicus, who has rather been extended in every dimension.

For all the notable strides made in deconstructing the modern mind and moving towards a new vision, whether in science, philosophy, or religion, nothing has come close to questioning the larger Copernican revolution itself, the modern mind's first principle and foundation. The very idea is as inconceivable now as was the idea of a moving Earth before 1500. That most fundamental modern revolution, along with its deepest existential consequences, still prevails, subtly yet globally determining the character of the contemporary mind. The continuing implacable reality of a purposeless cosmos places an effective glass ceiling on all attempts to reconstruct or soften the various alienating post-Copernican ramifications, from Descartes's subject-object dualism to Darwin's blind evolution. A straight line of disenchantment extends from astronomy and biology to philosophy and religion, as in Jacques Monod's well-known synopsis of the human condition in the later twentieth century: "The ancient covenant is in pieces: Man knows at last that he is alone in the universe's unfeeling immensity, out of which he emerged only by chance."

From the cosmological perspective, the various movements now pressing for the creation of a more humanly meaningful and spiritually resonant world have been taking place in an atomistic void. In the absence of some unprecedented development beyond the existential framework defined by the larger Copernican revolution, these less primordial intellectual changes can never be more than brave interpretive exercises in an alien cosmic environment. No amount of revisioning philosophy or psychology, science or religion, can forge a new world view without a radical shift at the cosmological level. As it now stands, our cosmic context does not support the attempted transformation of human vision. No genuine synthesis seems possible. This enormous contradiction that invisibly encompasses the emerging paradigm is precisely what is preventing that paradigm from constituting a coherent and effective world view.

As a long line of thinkers from Pascal to Nietzsche have recognized, the cosmic spaces of meaningless vastness that surround the human world silently oppose and subvert the meaning of the human world itself. In such a context, all human imagination, all religious experience, all moral and spiritual values, can only too readily be seen as idiosyncratic human constructs. Despite the many profound and indispensable changes that have taken place in the contemporary Western mind, the larger cosmological situation continues to sustain and enforce the basic double bind of modern consciousness: Our deepest spiritual and psychological aspirations are fundamentally incoherent with the very nature of the cosmos as revealed by the modern mind. "Not only are we not at the center of the cosmos," wrote Primo Levi, "but we are alien to it: we are a singularity. The universe is strange to us, we are strange in the universe."

The distinctive pathos and paradox of our cosmological situation reflects a deep historical schism within modern culture and the modern sensibility. For the modern experience of a radical division between inner and outer—of a subjective, personal, and purposeful consciousness that is incongruously embedded in and evolved from an objective universe that is unconscious, impersonal, and purposeless—is precisely represented in the cultural polarity and tension in our history between Romanticism and the Enlightenment. On the one side of this divide, our interior selves hold precious our spiritual intuitions, our moral and aesthetic sensibilities, our devotion to love and beauty, the power of the creative imagination, our music and poetry, our metaphysical reflections and religious experiences, our visionary journeys, our glimpses of an ensouled nature, our inward conviction that the deepest truth can be found within. This interior impulse has been carried in modern culture by Romanticism, understood in its broadest sense—from Rousseau and Goethe, Wordsworth and Emerson all the way through to its spirited renascence, democratized and globalized, in the post-Sixties counterculture. In the Romantic impulse and tradition, the modern soul found profound psychological and spiritual expression.

On the other side of the schism, that soul has dwelled within a universe whose essential nature was fully determined and defined by the Scientific Revolution and Enlightenment. In effect, the objective world has been ruled by the Enlightenment, the subjective world by Romanticism. Together these have constituted the modern world view and the complex modern sensibility. One could say that the modern soul's sustaining allegiance has been to Romanticism, whereas the modern mind's deeper loyalty has been to the Enlightenment. Both live within us, fully yet antithetically. An impossible tension of opposites thereby resides deep in the modern sensibility. Hence the underlying pathos of the modern situation.

The biography of the modern soul has taken place completely within a disenchanted Enlightenment cosmos, thereby contextualizing and rendering the entire life and striving of the modern soul as "merely subjective." Our spiritual being, our psychology, is contradicted by our cosmology. Our Romanticism is contradicted by our Enlightenment, our inner by our outer.

Behind the Enlightenment/Romanticism division in high culture (mirrored in the academic world by the "two cultures" of science and the humanities) looms the deeper and more ancient cultural schism between science and religion. In the wake of the Scientific Revolution, many spiritually sensitive individuals have found resources to help them cope with the human condition in the modern cosmological context in ways that, to one extent or another, answer their religious longings and existential needs. Paradoxically, it seems to be this very context, with its absolute erasure of all inherited orders of pregiven cosmic meaning, that has helped make possible in our time an unprecedented freedom, diversity, and authenticity of religious responses to the human condition. These have taken a multitude of forms: the pursuit of the individual spiritual journey drawing on many sources, the personal leap of faith, the life of ethical service and humanitarian compassion, the inward turn (meditation, prayer, monastic withdrawal), involvement with the great mystical traditions and practices from Asia (Hindu, Buddhist, Taoist, Sufi) and from diverse indigenous and shamanic cultures (Native North American, Central and South American, African, Australian, Polynesian, Old European), recovery of various gnostic and esoteric perspectives and practices, the pursuit of psychedelic or entheogenic exploration, devotion to creative artistic expression as a spiritual path, or renewed engagement with revitalized forms of Jewish and Christian traditions, beliefs, and practices.

Yet all these engagements have taken place in a cosmos whose basic parameters have been defined by the determinedly nonspiritual epistemology and ontology of modern science. Because of science's sovereignty over the external aspect of the modern world view, these noble spiritual journeys are pursued in a universe whose essential nature is recognized—whether consciously or subconsciously—to be supremely indifferent to those very quests. These many spiritual paths can and do provide profound meaning, solace, and support, but they have not resolved the fundamental schism of the modern world view. They cannot heal the deep division latent in every modern psyche. The very nature of the *objective* universe turns any spiritual faith and ideals into courageous acts of *subjectivity,* constantly vulnerable to intellectual negation.

Only by strenuously avoiding the reality of this contradiction, and thus engaging in what is in essence a form of psychological compartmentalization and denial, can the modern self find any semblance of wholeness. In such circumstances, an integrated world view, the natural aspiration of every psyche, is unattainable. An inchoate awareness of this underlies the reaction of religious fundamentalists to modernity, their rigid refusal to join the seemingly impossible spiritual adventure of the modern age. But for the more fully embracing and reflective contemporary sensibility, with its multiple commitments and alertness to the larger dialectic of realities in our time, the conflict cannot be dismissed so readily.

The problem with this dissociative condition is not merely cognitive dissonance or internal distress. Nor is it only the "privatization of spirituality" that has become so characteristic of our time. Since the encompassing cosmological context in which all human activity takes place has eliminated any enduring ground of transcendent values—spiritual, moral, aesthetic—the resulting vacuum has empowered the reductive values of the market and the mass media to colonize the collective human imagination and drain it of all depth. If the cosmology is disenchanted, the world is logically seen in predominantly utilitarian ways, and the utilitarian mind-set begins to shape all human motivation at the collective level. What might be considered means to larger ends ineluctably become ends in themselves. The drive to achieve ever-greater financial profit, political power, and technological prowess becomes the dominant impulse moving individuals and societies, until these values, despite ritual claims to the contrary, supersede all other aspirations.

The disenchanted cosmos impoverishes the collective psyche in the most global way, vitiating its spiritual and moral imagination—"vitiate" not only in the sense of *diminish* and *impair* but also in the sense of *deform* and *debase*. In such a context, everything can be appropriated. Nothing is immune. Majestic vistas of nature, great works of art, revered music, eloquent language, the beauty of the human body, distant lands and cultures, extraordinary moments of history, the arousal of deep human emotion: all become advertising tools to manipulate consumer response. For quite literally, in a disenchanted cosmos, nothing is sacred. The soul of the world has been extinguished: Ancient trees and forests can then be seen as nothing but potential lumber; mountains nothing but mineral deposits; seashores and deserts are oil reserves; lakes and rivers, engineering tools. Animals are perceived as harvestable commodities, indigenous tribes as obstructing relics of an outmoded past, children's minds as marketing targets. At the all-important cosmological level, the spiritual dimension of the empirical universe has been entirely negated, and with it, any publicly affirmable encompassing ground for moral wisdom and restraint. The short term and the bottom line rule all. Whether in politics, business, or the media, the lowest common denominator of the culture increasingly governs discourse and prescribes the values of the whole. Myopically obsessed with narrow goals and narrow identities, the powerful blind themselves to the larger suffering and crisis of the global community.

In a world where the subject is experienced as living in—and above and against—a world of objects, other peoples and cultures are more readily perceived as simply other objects, inferior in value to oneself, to ignore or exploit for one's own purposes, as are other forms of life, biosystems, the planetary whole. Moreover, the underlying anxiety and disorientation that pervade modern societies in the face of a meaningless cosmos create both a collective psychic numbness and a desperate spiritual hunger, leading to an addictive, insatiable craving for ever more material goods to fill the inner emptiness and producing a manic techno-consumerism that cannibalizes the planet. Highly practical consequences ensue from the disenchanted modern world view.

The ambition to emancipate ourselves as autonomous subjects by objectifying the world has in a sense come full circle, returned to haunt us, by turning the human self into an object as well—an ephemeral side effect of a random universe, an isolated atom in mass society, a statistic, a commodity, passive prey to the demands of the market, prisoner of the self-constructed modern "iron cage." Thus Weber's famous prophecy:

> No one knows who will live in this cage in the future, or whether at the end of this tremendous development entirely new prophets will arise, or there will be a great rebirth of old ideas and ideals, or if neither, mechanized petrification, embellished with a sort of convulsive self-importance. For of the last stage of this cultural development, it might well be truly said: "Specialists without spirit, sensualists without heart; this nullity imagines that it has attained a level of civilization never before achieved."

Defined in the end by its disenchanted context, the human self too is inevitably disenchanted. Ultimately it becomes, like everything else, a mere object of material forces and efficient causes: a sociobiological pawn, a selfish gene, a meme machine, a biotechnological artifact, an unwitting tool of its own tools. For the cosmology of a civilization both reflects and influences all human activity, motivation, and self-understanding that take place within its parameters. It is the container for everything else.

This, therefore, has become the looming question of our time: What is the ultimate impact of cosmological disenchantment on a civilization? What does it do to the human self, year after year, century after century, to experience existence as a conscious purposeful being in an unconscious purposeless universe? What is the price of a collective belief in absolute cosmic indifference? What are the consequences of this unprecedented cosmological context for the human experiment, indeed, for the entire planet?

It was Friedrich Nietzsche who seems to have recognized most intensely the full implications of the modern development, and experienced in his own being the inescapable plight of the modern sensibility: the Romantic soul at once liberated, displaced, and entrapped within the vast cosmic void of the scientific universe. Using hyper-Copernican imagery to depict the dizzying annihilation of the metaphysical world and death of God wrought by the modern mind, and reflecting that peculiarly tragic combination of self-determining will and inexorable fate, Nietzsche captured the pathos of the late modern existential and spiritual crisis:

What were we doing when we unchained this earth from its sun? Whither is it moving now? Whither are we moving? Away from all suns? Are we not plunging continually? Backward, sideward, forward, in all directions? Is there still any up or down? Are we not straying as through an infinite nothing? Do we not feel the breath of empty space? Has it not become colder? Is not night continually closing in on us?

If we again look at the diagram illustrating the difference between the primal and the modern experience of the world, taking into account the full effect of the post-Copernican, post-Nietzschean situation, we see the extremity of the late-modern human's differentiation and alienation in the cosmos (Figure 4). The source of all meaning and purpose in the universe has become at once infinitesimally small and utterly peripheral. The lonely island of human meaning is now so incongruent, so accidental, so ephemeral, so fundamentally estranged from its vast surrounding matrix, as to have become, in many senses, insupportable.

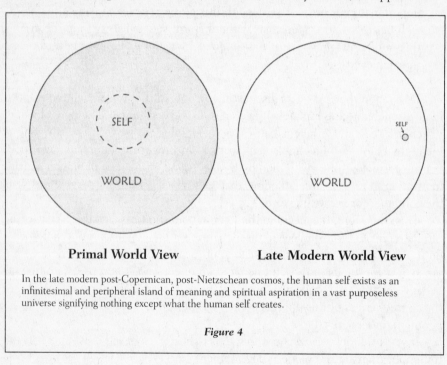

Primal World View   **Late Modern World View**

In the late modern post-Copernican, post-Nietzschean cosmos, the human self exists as an infinitesimal and peripheral island of meaning and spiritual aspiration in a vast purposeless universe signifying nothing except what the human self creates.

Figure 4

Yet it is perhaps the very starkness and self-contradictory absurdity of this situation that suggests the possibility of another perspective. The modern mind has long prided itself on its repeated success in overcoming anthropomorphic distortions in its understanding of reality. It has constantly sought to purify its world view from any naïve anthropocentrism and self-fulfilling projections. Each revolution in modern thought from Copernicus onward, each great insight associ-

THE COSMOLOGICAL SITUATION TODAY 35

ated with a canonical name in the grand procession—from Bacon and Descartes, Hume and Kant to Darwin, Marx, Nietzsche, Weber, Freud, Wittgenstein, Heidegger, Kuhn, and the entire postmodern turn—has brought forth in its own manner another essential revelation of an unconscious bias that had until then blinded the human mind in its attempts to understand the world. The gist and consequence of this long, incomparably intricate modern and postmodern epistemological development has been to compel us with ever-increasing acuity to recognize how our most fundamental assumptions and principles, so long taken for granted as to fully escape our notice, imperceptibly bring into being the very world we consider unarguably objective. As the post-Kuhnian philosopher of science Paul Feyerabend recognized:

> A change of universal principles brings about a change of the entire world. Speaking in this manner we no longer assume an objective world that remains unaffected by our epistemic activities, except when moving within the confines of a particular point of view. We concede that our epistemic activities may have a decisive influence even upon the most solid piece of cosmological furniture—they may make gods disappear and replace them by heaps of atoms in empty space.

Let us, then, take our strategy of critical self-reflection one crucial and perhaps inevitable step further. Let us apply it to the fundamental governing assumption and starting point of the modern world view—a pervasive assumption that subtly continues to influence the postmodern turn as well—that any meaning and purpose the human mind perceives in the universe does not exist intrinsically in the universe but is constructed and projected onto it by the human mind. Might not this be the final, most global anthropocentric delusion of all? For is it not an extraordinary act of human hubris—literally, a hubris of cosmic proportions—to assume that the exclusive source of *all meaning and purpose in the universe* is ultimately centered in the human mind, which is therefore absolutely unique and special and in this sense superior to the entire cosmos? To presume that the universe utterly lacks what we human beings, the offspring and expression of that universe, conspicuously possess? To assume that the part somehow radically differs from and transcends the whole? To base our entire world view on the a priori principle that whenever human beings perceive any patterns of psychological or spiritual significance in the nonhuman world, any signs of interiority and mind, any suggestion of purposefully coherent order and intelligible meaning, these *must* be understood as no more than human constructions and projections, as ultimately rooted in the human mind and *never* in the world?

Perhaps this complete voiding of the cosmos, this absolute privileging of the human, is the ultimate act of anthropocentric projection, the most subtle yet prodigious form of human self-aggrandizement. Perhaps the modern mind has been projecting soullessness and mindlessness on a cosmic scale, systematically filtering and eliciting all data according to its self-elevating assumptions at the very moment we believed we were "cleansing" our minds of "distortions." Have we been living in a self-produced bubble of cosmic isolation? Perhaps the very attempt to de-anthropomorphize reality in such an absolute and simplistic manner is itself a supremely anthropocentric act.

I believe that this criticism of the hidden anthropocentrism permeating the modern world view cannot be successfully countered. Only the blinders of our paradigm, as is always the case, have prevented us from recognizing the profound implausibility of its most basic underlying assumption. For as we gaze out now at the immense starry heavens surrounding our precious planet, and as we contemplate the long and richly diverse history of human thinking about the world, must we not consider that in our strangely unique modern commitment to restrict all meaning and purposive intelligence to ourselves, and refusing these to the great cosmos within which we have emerged, we might in fact be drastically underestimating and misperceiving that cosmos—and thus misperceiving, at once overestimating and underestimating, ourselves as well? Perhaps the greater Copernican revolution is in a sense still incomplete, still unfolding. Perhaps a long-hidden form of anthropocentric bias, increasingly destructive in its consequences, can now at last be recognized, thus opening up the possibility of a richer, more complex, more authentic relationship between the human being and the cosmos.

Questions and issues like these compel us to direct our attention with new eyes both outward and inward. Not *only* inward, as we habitually do in our search for meaning, but also outward, as we seldom do because our cosmos has long been regarded as empty of spiritual significance and unable to respond to that search. Yet our gaze outward must be different from before. It must be transformed by a new awareness of the interior: The questions and issues we have confronted here require us to explore yet more deeply the nature of the self that seeks to comprehend the world. They press us to discern yet more clearly how our subjectivity, that tiny peripheral island of meaning in the cosmic vastness, subtly participates in configuring and constellating the entire universe we perceive and know. They compel us to examine that mysterious place where subject and object so intricately and consequentially intersect: the crucial meeting point of cosmology, epistemology, and psychology.

II

In Search of a Deeper Order

There are more things in heaven and earth, Horatio,
Than are dreamt of in our philosophy.

—William Shakespeare
Hamlet (First Folio)

Two Suitors: A Parable

Imagine, for a moment, that you are the universe. But for the purposes of this thought experiment, let us imagine that you are not the disenchanted mechanistic universe of conventional modern cosmology, but rather a deep-souled, subtly mysterious cosmos of great spiritual beauty and creative intelligence. And imagine that you are being approached by two different epistemologies—two suitors, as it were, who seek to know you. To whom would you open your deepest secrets? To which approach would you be most likely to reveal your authentic nature? Would you open most deeply to the suitor—the epistemology, the way of knowing—who approached you as though you were essentially lacking in intelligence or purpose, as though you had no interior dimension to speak of, no spiritual capacity or value; who thus saw you as fundamentally inferior to himself (let us give the two suitors, not entirely arbitrarily, the traditional masculine gender); who related to you as though your existence were valuable primarily to the extent that he could develop and exploit your resources to satisfy his various needs; and whose motivation for knowing you was ultimately driven by a desire for increased intellectual mastery, predictive certainty, and efficient control over you for his own self-enhancement?

Or would you, the cosmos, open yourself most deeply to that suitor who viewed you as being *at least* as intelligent and noble, as worthy a being, as permeated with mind and soul, as imbued with moral aspiration and purpose, as endowed with spiritual depths and mystery, as he? This suitor seeks to know you not that he might better exploit you but rather to unite with you and thereby bring forth something new, a creative synthesis emerging from both of your depths. He desires to liberate that which has been hidden by the separation between knower and known. His ultimate goal of knowledge is not increased mastery, prediction, and control but rather a more richly responsive and empowered participation in a co-creative unfolding of new realities. He seeks an intellectual fulfillment that is intimately linked with imaginative vision, moral transformation, empathic understanding, aesthetic delight. His act of knowledge is essentially an act of love and intelligence combined, of wonder as well as discernment, of opening to a process of mutual discovery. To whom would you be more likely to reveal your deepest truths?

This is not to say that you, the universe, would reveal nothing to the first suitor, under the duress of his objectifying, disenchanting approach. That suitor would undoubtedly elicit, filter, and constellate a certain "reality" that he would naturally regard as authentic knowledge of the actual universe: *objective* knowledge, "the facts," as compared with the subjective delusions of everyone else's approach. But we might allow ourselves to doubt just how profound a truth, how genuinely reflective of the universe's deeper reality, this approach might be capable of providing. Such knowledge might prove to be deeply misleading. And if this disenchanted vision were elevated to the status of being the *only* legitimate vision of the nature of the cosmos upheld by an entire civilization, what an incalculable loss, an impoverishment, a tragic deformation, a grief, would ultimately be suffered by both knower and known.

I believe that the disenchantment of the modern universe is the direct result of a simplistic epistemology and moral posture spectacularly inadequate to the depths, complexity, and grandeur of the cosmos. To assume a priori that the entire universe is ultimately a soulless void within which our multidimensional consciousness is an anomalous accident, and that purpose, meaning, conscious intelligence, moral aspiration, and spiritual depth are solely attributes of the human being, reflects a long-invisible inflation on the part of the modern self. And heroic hubris is still indissolubly linked, as it was in ancient Greek tragedy, to heroic fall.

The postmodern mind has come to recognize, with a critical acuity that has been at once disturbing and liberating, the multiplicity of ways in which our often hidden presuppositions and the structures of our subjectivity shape and elicit the reality we seek to understand. If we have learned anything from the many disciplines that have contributed to postmodern thought, it is that what we believe to be our *objective* knowledge of the world is radically affected and even constituted by a complex multitude of *subjective* factors, most of which are altogether unconscious. Even this is not quite accurate, for we must now recognize subject and object, inner and outer, to be so deeply *mutually* constituted as to render problematic the very structure of a "subject" knowing an "object." Such a recognition—hard-won and, for most of us, still being slowly integrated—can initially produce a sense of intellectual disorientation, irresolution, or even despair. Each of these responses has its time and place. But ultimately this recognition can call forth in us a fortifying sense of joyful co-responsibility for the world we elicit and enact through the creative power of the interpretive strategies and world views we choose to engage, to explore, and to evolve with.

What is the cure for hubristic vision? It is, perhaps, to *listen*—to listen more subtly, more perceptively, more deeply. Our future may well depend upon the precise extent of our willingness to expand our ways of knowing. We need a larger, truer empiricism and rationalism. The long-established epistemological strategies of the modern mind have been both relentlessly limiting and unconsciously "constructing" a world it then concludes is objective. The objectifying ascetic rationalism and empiricism that emerged during the Enlightenment served as liberating disciplines for the nascent modern reason, but they still dominate mainstream science and modern thought today in a rigidly undeveloped form. In their simplistic myopia and one-sidedness, they seriously constrain our full range of perception and understanding.

The disenchanting strategy can be said to have served well the purposes of its time—to differentiate the self, to empower the human subject, to liberate human experience of the world from unquestioned pregiven structures of meaning and purpose inherited from tradition and enforced by external authority. It provided a powerful new basis for criticism and defiance of established belief systems that often inhibited human autonomy. It also at least partly succeeded in disciplining the human tendency to project onto the world subjective needs and wishes. But this differentiation and empowerment of the human being has been striven for so single-mindedly as to now be hypertrophic, pathologically exaggerated. In its austere universal reductionism, the objectifying stance of the modern mind has become a kind of tyrant. The knowledge it renders is literally narrow-minded. Such knowledge is at once extremely potent and deeply deficient. A little knowledge may be a dangerous thing, but a massive amount of knowledge based on a limited and self-isolating set of assumptions may be very dangerous indeed.

The remarkable modern capacity for differentiation and discernment that has been so painstakingly forged must be preserved, but our challenge now is to develop and subsume that discipline in a more encompassing, more magnanimous intellectual and spiritual engagement with the mystery of the universe. Such an engagement can happen only if we open ourselves to a range of epistemologies that together provide a more multidimensionally perceptive scope of knowledge. To encounter the depths and rich complexity of the cosmos, we require ways of knowing that fully integrate the imagination, the aesthetic sensibility, moral and spiritual intuition, revelatory experience, symbolic perception, somatic and sensuous modes of understanding, empathic knowing. Above all, we must awaken to and overcome the great hidden anthropocentric projection that has virtually defined the modern mind: *the pervasive projection of soullessness onto the cosmos by the modern self's own will to power.*

Objectifying the world has given immense pragmatic power and dynamism to the modern self but at the expense of its capacity to register and respond to the world's potential depths of meaning and purpose. Contrary to the coolly detached self-image of modern reason, subjective needs and wishes have unconsciously pervaded the disenchanted vision and reinforced its assumptions. A world of purposeless objects and random processes has served as a highly effective basis and justification for human self-aggrandizement and exploitation of a world seen as undeserving of moral concern. The disenchanted cosmos is the shadow of the modern mind in all its brilliance, power, and inflation.

As we assimilate the deepening insights of our time into the nature of human knowledge, and as we discern more lucidly the intricate mutual implication of subject and object, self and world, we must ask ourselves whether this radically disenchanted cosmology is, in the end, all that plausible. Perhaps it was not as truly neutral and objective as we supposed, but was in fact a reflection of historically situated evolutionary imperatives and unconscious needs—like every other cosmology in the history of humanity. Perhaps disenchantment is itself another form of enchantment, another highly convincing mode of experience that has cast its spell over the human mind and played its evolutionary role but is now not only limiting for our cosmological understanding but unsustainable for our existence. Perhaps it is time to adopt, as a potentially more fruitful hypothesis and heuristic starting point, the second suitor's approach to the nature of the cosmos.

Of the many disciplines that have begun to challenge the dominance of the disenchanted universe, there is one field in particular whose development over the past century has brought forth a series of insights, concepts, and data of unexpected relevance to the cosmological crisis I have outlined here. It is that discipline and its historical evolution, which is closely intertwined with the larger history of the modern self, to which we now turn our attention.

The Interior Quest

The history of a culture, the inner history of a civilization, can sometimes bear suggestive resemblances to the unfolding of an individual human life. In Joseph Campbell's classic description of the archetypal journey of the hero—the liberator, the shaman, the mystic, the creator, the discoverer of new worlds—a dramatic progression takes place that involves certain characteristic stages: a decisive separation from the community, detaching the self from the larger whole in which it has until then been embedded; an experience of the physical and spiritual life of the world as undergoing a great danger, an encroaching shadow, a fall into ruin; and a radical shift of emphasis from external realities to the interior realm, moving "from the world scene of secondary effects to those causal zones of the psyche where the difficulties really reside." There follows a dark night of the soul, an interior descent, bringing a crisis of meaning, a transformative encounter with human suffering and mortality, and a disorienting dissolution of the self's basic structures of identity and being. Only through such a descent does the hero penetrate to a source of greater knowledge and power opened by a direct experience of the archetypal dimension of life. Along the way of this perilous journey certain humble clues and anomalies unexpectedly appear that challenge and destabilize the confident knowledge of the old self, yet ultimately point the way to the threshold of another world.

In the dramatic evolution of the Western psyche, which has proved so consequential for the planet, the enduring archetypal patterns visible in the myths of the hero also seem to function with extraordinary potency at the level of history and the collective cultural psyche. But if so, the shift in context from myth to history, and from the individual person to a civilization, has involved a surprising change in the terms of the narrative. For in the history of Western thought and culture, the community and larger whole from which the heroic self was separated was not simply the local tribal or familial matrix, but rather the entire community of being, the Earth, the cosmos itself. Different stages of such a separation, descent, and transformation have taken place in each great epoch of Western cultural history, in what in retrospect appears not unlike a vast evolutionary rite of passage played out on the stage of history and the cosmos, and now reaching an especially precarious moment of truth.

We see such a pattern in late antiquity, against the backdrop of classical civilization's ruinous decline, as the ancient cosmological vision eventually reached an opaque boundary within the overarching fixed structure of the geocentric Ptolemaic-Aristotelian universe. The complexity of the celestial movements was seen as increasingly inscrutable, the power of the planetary spheres over human life increasingly all-determining. The cultural psyche could not penetrate farther under that established set of assumptions and was thereby forced to go within, to move deeply into the interior world of the human soul and spirit, and bring forth a new form of being. So it was at this moment, after the intense struggles and epiphanies of late biblical Judaism and early Christianity, Gnosticism, and the mystery religions, amidst the skeptical and religious crisis of the late classical age, that there took place the great interior journey of Saint Augustine, and then of the entire medieval West he so profoundly influenced and anticipated.

So too in the modern world, but on a new scale and with a more radical separation: As the larger implications of the Copernican revolution gradually emerged in the course of the modern era, the impenetrable boundaries of the disenchanted cosmic vision began again to force the cultural psyche to the interior. Pascal was among the first to confront the dark entailments of the new cosmic reality: "The eternal silence of these infinite spaces fills me with dread." Kant, though filled with wonder by those same spaces, struggled mightily to overcome the stark disjunction between "the starry heaven above me and the moral law within me," the realm of science and the realm of religion. Finally Nietzsche, fully recognizing the plight of the modern self in the scientifically revealed cosmos, "straying as through an infinite nothing," began his paradigmatic descent into the interior depths. Thus he foreshadowed the depth psychology that was conceived and developed in the immediate aftermath of that descent, by Freud and Jung in Europe and, in a different but closely related mode, by William James in America. Against the historical background of the great crises, both inner and outer, that overtook modern civilization, the twentieth century became, as Peter Homans has observed, "the psychological century."

It was Freud who first recognized the deep affinity and continuity linking the Copernican revolution with the depth psychology revolution. As the former event had irrevocably transformed the outer cosmos, so the latter irrevocably transformed the inner cosmos, in each case radically overturning humankind's naïve conviction of its centrality as the price for radically enlarging the compass of its vision. Just as the Copernicans had displaced the Earth from the center of the universe to reveal a much larger unknown cosmos of which the Earth was now but a tiny peripheral fragment, the Freudians displaced the conscious self from the center of the inner universe to reveal the much larger unknown realm of the unconscious. The modern self had to acknowledge that it was not master of its own house, as the confident Cartesian *cogito* had implied, but was rather a peripheral epiphenomenon of far more powerful processes working unfathomed beyond the boundaries of its awareness.

Both revolutions, cosmological and psychological, were simultaneously decentering and emancipatory. But where Copernicus's came as the modern self began its great *ascent*, with Leonardo and Columbus, Luther and Montaigne, Bacon and Galileo, Descartes and Newton, by contrast Freud's emerged at the other end of the trajectory as the modern self began its great *descent*, with Nietzsche and Weber, Kafka and Picasso, Heidegger and Wittgenstein, Woolf and Beauvoir, Camus and Beckett. The two revolutions heralded, as it were, the dawn and sunset of the modern self's solar journey: While the Copernican revolution impelled and symbolized the outward-moving ascent and construction of the modern self that began in the Renaissance and brought forth the Enlightenment, the depth psychology revolution reflected the inward-turning descent and deconstruction of the self that commenced at the end of the nineteenth century and brought forth the postmodern era.

This arc-like symmetry revealed itself in yet another important way. For each revolution was also both disenchanting and spiritually renewing in its effects. But whereas the Copernican awakening of outward ascent began within an ambiance of spiritual exaltation and then moved gradually but inexorably towards the random mechanistic universe of the later modern world view, the unfolding of the depth psychology revolution of inward descent enacted rather the reverse sequence. Freud, by temperament and intellectual commitment, emphasized from the start the disenchanting implications of the psychological awakening: all psychic motivation rooted in unconscious biological instinct; all human experience and aspiration, no matter how elevated or sublime, reduced finally to mechanistic impulse. Yet even Freud, in the poetic and mythic cast of his vision and his enduring emotional investment in archaic numinosity (classical mythology, dream interpretation, ancient religious icons, cultic secrecy), betrayed signs of an underlying ambivalence. James and Jung, however, with different sensibilities from Freud's, pointed decisively to more spiritually expansive potentials of the new discoveries, and ultimately to a vaster and more mysterious inner universe than Freud had been able to acknowledge. Like the Copernican revolution, depth psychology resulted from the extraordinary convergence of a multiplicity of intellectual and cultural streams, and proved to be just as generative and paradoxical in its developing vision.

Of all the fields and disciplines of the modern intellectual world, it was uniquely depth psychology, by the very nature of its historical moment, its cultural sources, and its therapeutic aims, that located itself at the precise intersection of the two great polarities of the modern sensibility, the Enlightenment and Romanticism. With roots nourished by both streams, depth psychology was a tradition inspired not only by the scientific principles of Newton and Darwin but also by the imaginative aspirations of Goethe and Emerson—hence the promise it held for so many as a *via regia* for healing the schisms of the modern self. Depth psychology took up the enduring passions and concerns of the Romantic project, exploring the depths of consciousness and the unconscious, emotion and instinct, memory and imagination, visions, dreams, myth, art, creativity. It pursued introspection to new heights and abysses, examined the psyche's shadows and pathologies, discerned hidden motivations, ambivalence, and ambiguity. It studied the mysteries of religious experience, ancient rituals and shamanic initiations, mystical revelations and gnostic doctrines, esoteric traditions and divinatory practices, the wisdom and visions of many other cultures and other ages.

All this it did with an Enlightenment commitment to lucid rational analysis and systematic investigation as it sought therapeutically effective knowledge in a context of collective empirical research. Throughout their lives James, Freud, and Jung pressed the scientific mind beyond its conventional limits to engage realities known by visionaries and poets, mystics and initiates. Striving to combine the intellectual rigor of scientific observation with the intuitive insight of the poetic and spiritual imagination, depth psychology attempted to bring the light of reason to the deep mysteries of human interiority, yet often witnessed the converse: the light of reason reevaluated, transformed, and deepened by the very mysteries it sought to illuminate.

Moreover, as especially Jung understood, depth psychology engaged the Enlightenment's epistemological challenge set by Kant as it attempted to discern the deep structural principles that inform human subjectivity, those enduring patterns and forms that unconsciously permeate and configure human knowledge and experience (hence Jung's understanding of depth psychology as the direct successor and heir of critical philosophy). Yet contrary to Kant's narrow list of a priori categories, those underlying forms were repeatedly discovered, beginning with Nietzsche and Freud and above all by Jung and his successors, to be mythic, symbolic, even numinous in nature, pervading and impelling human consciousness from the unconscious depths. Such a discovery fundamentally undermined the Enlightenment project to extend rational mastery over the inner world in the same manner it had done, or appeared to have done, so successfully over the outer world. With depth psychology, reason revealed ever-expanding and deepening interior realities that challenged reason's compass. The very nature of those disclosures ultimately subverted Freud's reductionist Enlightenment assumptions and moved the modern mind, from James and Jung onward, to engage and assimilate dimensions of consciousness and principles of the subjective universe that could no longer be easily accommodated by what James saw as the prematurely "closed universe" of conventional scientific belief.

Just as depth psychology subverted the naïve orthodoxies of the scientific mind while extending the range of scientific inquiry, so it subverted the naïve orthodoxies of traditional religion while extending the range of spiritual inquiry. The relationship of depth psychology to religion was complex. The directions opened by both James and Jung pointed towards the human universality of spiritual aspiration, contrary to the secularist assumptions of much modern thought, and provided new grounds for affirming the religious dimension of life as essential to psychological health and wholeness. Insights into transcultural archetypal structures underlying the world's religions brought new understanding to the human quest for spiritual meaning. That understanding proved to be both enriching and relativizing. On the one hand, it undermined absolutist claims by various religious traditions to unique spiritual authority, thus freeing many individuals from their dogmatic chains while honoring their spiritual quests. On the other hand, the new insights also made possible for many an unexpected spiritual renewal and deepening of relationship to the central symbols of those same traditions, now seen and understood in a larger, less literal, more directly meaningful and experientially vivid light.

Especially affected were those many spiritual seekers whose experience of the sacred no longer readily fit within the structures of their inherited religious tradition, a phenomenon increasingly widespread in the late modern and postmodern era. For these, depth psychology provided new ways of articulating their encounter with the numinous, and affirmed the many fruitful sources of spiritual disclosure from which the human psyche could draw beyond those sanctioned by a particular tradition—nonordinary states of consciousness, creativity, dreams, intimate relationships, sexuality and the body, nature, sacred traditions and transformative practices from other eras and cultures. Like science, religion possessed its own tendencies towards reifying a prematurely closed interpretation of the universe. Depth psychology offered an evolving frame of reference that opened the horizon of authentic religious experience to engage the mysteries of human existence beyond the constraints and mutual antagonisms widely characteristic of the world's religious traditions.

Given the modern mind's radical divisions between self and world and between conscious and unconscious, the continuing centrality in twentieth-century thought of depth psychology can be recognized as in some sense inevitable. For the radiant emergence of the modern rational self—the highly focused, centered, empowered, detached, objectifying, self-reflective and self-identifying Cartesian consciousness—effectively constellated an "unconscious," as light creates shadow, which then needed to be theorized, explored, and painstakingly integrated. The discovery of the unconscious was thus significant on many fronts, with multiple implications needing to be addressed—not only psychological and therapeutic but cultural and historical, philosophical and political, existential and spiritual. Jung described that significance in the strongest possible terms: "We have not understood yet that the discovery of the unconscious means an enormous spiritual task, which must be accomplished if we wish to preserve our civilization."

The fate of depth psychology was nevertheless problematic throughout the twentieth century. It provided the modern mind with a host of irreplaceable insights and concepts, from the discovery of the unconscious itself, both personal and collective, to the understanding of the ego's various mechanisms of defense, the psyche's symbolic modes of expression, and the dynamics of psychospiritual transformation. But because the larger cultural world view within which depth psychology was embedded continued to sustain the basic schism between human self and disenchanted world, the reintegration and healing of the modern psyche could go only so far. The problem was indirectly reflected in criticism from scientific disciplines indifferent or antagonistic to the Romantic project that charged depth psychology with an alleged lack of objectivity and empirically measurable results. These scientistic critiques were effectively refuted by psychologists, as well as by philosophers such as Jürgen Habermas, who affirmed depth psychology's emancipatory potential through deepened self-understanding. In contrast with the physical sciences, its essential focus was on meanings that can never be quantified. Yet the discipline continued to be constrained by a more encompassing problem: Its insights were apparently relevant only to the psyche, to the subjective aspect of things, not to the world in itself. Those insights could not change the larger cosmic context within which the human being sought psychological integrity and spiritual fulfillment. That primal rupture remained untouched, and unhealed.

Within the established structure of the modern world view, no matter how subjectively convincing might be the psychological evidence for a transcendent spiritual dimension, an archetypal realm, an *anima mundi,* a universal religious impulse, or the existence of God, the discoveries of psychology could reveal nothing with certainty about the actual constitution of reality. The experiences and inner knowledge explored by depth psychology could be regarded only as an expression of the human psyche and its intrinsic structures. Human spirituality and religion were still, in effect, confined to the subjective universe. What existed beyond this could not be said. Depth psychology had perhaps rendered a deeper and richer inner world for the modern soul, but the objective universe known by natural science was still materialistically opaque and purposeless. With the chasm in the modern world view between religious, Romantic, and depth psychological interiority on the one hand and the mechanistic world picture of the physical sciences on the other, there appeared to be no possibility for an authentic bridge or mediation between self and world, subject and object, psyche and cosmos. At its core and essence, modernity had constellated a seemingly irresolvable tension of opposites, a fundamental antithesis between an objectivist cosmology and a subjectivist psychology.

The great descent of the modern self had reached an apparently intractable impasse. Extending into and permeating every aspect of human experience, this metaphysical and epistemological predicament in one form or another engaged virtually every major thinker of the twentieth century. Many courageous responses to this encompassing dilemma emerged in the course of that century, some resigned to its inevitability, others anticipating its transformation. Among the latter, from within the field of depth psychology itself, the study of one provocative category of phenomena in particular has suggested with special directness that the chasmic division between interior self and objective world might not be absolute.

Synchronicity and Its Implications

Most of us in the course of life have observed coincidences in which two or more independent events having no apparent causal connection nevertheless seem to form a meaningful pattern. On occasion, this patterning can strike one as so extraordinary that it is difficult to believe the coincidence has been produced by chance alone. The events give the distinct impression of having been precisely arranged, invisibly orchestrated.

Jung first described the remarkable phenomenon he named synchronicity in a seminar as early as 1928. He continued his investigations for more than twenty years before at last attempting a full formulation in the early 1950s. He presented his influential, still-evolving analysis of synchronicity in the final paper he gave at the Eranos conferences, and immediately followed this with a long monograph. Developed in part through discussions with physicists, particularly Einstein and Wolfgang Pauli, the principle of synchronicity bore parallels to certain discoveries in relativity theory and quantum mechanics. Yet because of its psychological dimension, Jung's concept possessed a special relevance for the schism in the modern world view between the meaning-seeking human subject and the meaning-voided objective world. From the beginning, it has held a unique position in contemporary discussions, having been simultaneously described by physicists as posing a major challenge to the philosophical foundations of modern science and by religious scholars as holding deep implications for the modern psychology of religion. With each decade, increasing numbers of books and heightened attention, both scholarly and popular, have been devoted to the concept and the phenomenon.[1]

Jung took particular interest in meaningful coincidences, in the beginning no doubt because their frequent occurrence had exerted a considerable influence on his own life experience. He also observed that in the therapeutic process of his patients such events repeatedly played a role, sometimes a powerful one, especially in periods of crisis and transformation. The dramatic coincidence of meaning between an inner state and a simultaneous external event seemed to bring forth in the individual a healing movement toward psychological wholeness, mediated by the unexpected integration of inner and outer realities. Such events often engendered a new sense of personal orientation in a world now seen as capable of embodying purposes and meanings beyond the mere projections of human subjectivity. The random chaos of life suddenly appeared to veil a deeper order. A subtle sign, as it were, had been given, an unexpected color in the pale void of meaning—an intimation, in William James's phrase, of "something more."

Accompanying the more profound occurrences of synchronicity was a dawning intuition, sometimes described as having the character of a spiritual awakening, that the individual was herself or himself not only embedded in a larger ground of meaning and purpose but also in some sense a focus of it. This discovery, often emerging after a sustained period of personal darkness or spiritual crisis, tended to bring with it an opening to new existential potentialities and responsibilities. Both because of this felt personal import and because of its startling metaphysical implications, such a synchronicity carried a certain numinosity, a dynamic spiritual charge with transformative consequences for the person experiencing it. In this respect, the phenomenon seemed to function, in religious terms, as something like an intervention of grace. Jung noted that such synchronicities were often kept secret or carefully guarded, to avoid the possibility of ridicule concerning an event possessing such significant personal meaning.

The classic example of a pivotal synchronistic experience is Jung's well-known description of the "golden scarab" case:

My example concerns a young woman patient who, in spite of efforts made on both sides, proved to be psychologically inaccessible. The difficulty lay in the fact that she always knew better about everything. Her excellent education had provided her with a weapon ideally suited to this purpose, namely a highly polished Cartesian rationalism with an impeccably "geometrical" idea of reality [as in Descartes's characteristic mode of logical demonstration]. After several fruitless attempts to sweeten her rationalism with a somewhat more human understanding, I had to confine myself to the hope that something unexpected and irrational would turn up, something that would burst the intellectual retort into which she had sealed herself. Well, I was sitting opposite her one day, with my back to the window, listening to her flow of rhetoric. She had had an impressive dream the night before, in which someone had given her a golden scarab—a costly piece of jewelry. While she was still telling me this dream, I heard something behind me gently tapping on the window. I turned round and saw that it was a fairly large flying insect that was knocking against the window-pane from outside in the obvious effort to get into the dark room. This seemed to me very strange. I opened the window immediately and caught the insect in the air as it flew in. It was a scarabaeid beetle, or common rose-chafer (*Cetonia aurata*), whose gold-green colour most nearly resembles that of a golden scarab. I handed the beetle to my patient with the words, "Here is your scarab." This experience punctured the desired hole in her rationalism and broke the ice of her intellectual resistance. The treatment could now be continued with satisfactory results.

The acute coincidence between the symbolically resonant image that the woman had experienced in her dream the night before and was just then recounting and the spontaneous appearance at the window of an insect that was "the nearest analogy to a golden scarab that one finds in our latitudes" effectively broke through the intellectual armoring that had been blocking her psychological development. Now "her natural being could burst through . . . and the process of transformation could at last begin to move."

In another such instance, recounted in Esther Harding's notebooks, a patient whose dreams were filled with sexual imagery kept attempting to interpret the dreams in nonsexual symbolic terms, despite Jung's efforts to persuade her of their more plausible straightforward meaning. On the day of her next appointment, two sparrows fluttered to the ground at the woman's feet and "performed the act."

On rare occasions a synchronicity proves to have an extraordinary power through its impact on an historically significant individual, so that it ultimately plays a pivotal role in the collective life of the larger culture. The famous coincidence that formed a turning point in the life of Petrarch took place at the climax of his ascent of Mont Ventoux in April 1336, an event that has long been regarded by scholars as representing the symbolic beginning of the Renaissance. For many years Petrarch had sensed a growing impulse to ascend the mountain, to see the vast panorama from its peak, though doing such a thing was virtually unheard of in his time. Finally choosing the day, with his brother for a companion, he made the long ascent, marked by intense physical exertion and inward reflection. When he at last attained the summit, with clouds below his feet and winds in his face, Petrarch found himself overwhelmed by the great sweep of the world that now opened out to him—snowcapped mountains and the sea in the distance, rivers and valleys below, the wide expanse of skies in every direction. James Hillman recounts the event:

At the top of the mountain, with the exhilarating view of French Provence, the Alps, and the Mediterranean spread before him, he had opened his tiny pocket copy of Augustine's *Confessions*. Turning at random to book X, 8, he read: "And men go abroad to admire the heights of mountains, the mighty billows of the sea, the broad tide of rivers, the compass of the ocean, and the circuits of the stars, and pass themselves by. . . ."

Petrarch was stunned at the coincidence between Augustine's words and the time and place they were read. His emotion both announced the revelation of his personal vocation and heralded the new attitude of the Renaissance. . . . Petrarch draws this crucial conclusion from the Mont Ventoux event: "Nothing is admirable but the soul" (*nihil praeter animum esse mirabile*).[2]

Petrarch was so moved by the coincidental force of Augustine's words that he remained silent for the entire descent down the mountain. He at once recognized the coincidence as part of a larger pattern of such transformative moments that had happened to others in the history of spiritual conversions: "I could not believe that it was by a mere accident that I happened upon them. What I had there read I believed to be addressed to me and to no other, remembering that Saint Augustine had once suspected the same thing in his own case." For indeed Augustine had undergone a nearly identical experience at his own momentous spiritual turning point: In the garden of Milan in 386, in a frenzy of spiritual crisis, he heard a child's voice from a nearby house mysteriously repeating the words "Tolle, lege" ("Pick up and read"). Uncertain of their significance, he finally opened at random a copy of Saint Paul's epistles and there read words that spoke with uncanny precision to the nature of his lifelong conflict and its resolution, immediately after reading which "the light of certainty flooded my heart and all dark shadows of doubt fled away" (*Confessions*, VIII, 29).

Here too Augustine's emotion in the garden of Milan both announced the revelation of his personal vocation and heralded the new attitude of the Christian epoch being born. A thousand years later, Augustine's own words randomly encountered provided a strikingly similar catalyzing force for Petrarch on Mont Ventoux. This time the synchronistic epiphany unfolded in a new direction and with different consequences—one revelation in the garden, pointing to Christianity and the Middle Ages, the other on the mountain, pointing to the Renaissance and modernity.[3]

Jung believed that synchronicities generally seemed to serve the same role as dreams, psychological symptoms, and other manifestations of the unconscious, namely, to compensate the conscious attitude and move the psyche from a problematic one-sidedness toward greater wholeness and individuation. Not only did the unexpectedly externalized pattern of meaning seem to represent more than mere chance coincidence; it also appeared to serve a definite purpose, impelling the psyche toward a more complete psychological and spiritual realization of the individual personality. This self-realization was achieved through a deeper integration of conscious and unconscious, which ultimately required of the individual a discerning surrender of the usual conscious attitude of knowing superiority. In this view, the perceptive interpretation of synchronistic phenomena, as with all expressions of the unconscious, rather than inflating the egocentric importance of the individual in a narcissistic manner, could correct precisely these tendencies and open the psyche to a larger vision.

An instructive example of this self-critical, compensatory approach toward synchronicity in Jung's own life was recounted by Henry Fierz when he described a meeting with Jung in the 1950s. Fierz had come to discuss whether Jung thought a manuscript by a scientist who had recently died should be published. At the appointed hour of five o'clock, Fierz arrived for the meeting and the discussion began:

> Jung had read the book and he thought that it should not be published, but I disagreed and was for publication. Our discussion finally got rather sharp, and Jung looked at his wristwatch, obviously thinking that he had spent enough time on the matter and that he could send me home. Looking at his watch he said: "When did you come?" I: "At five, as agreed." Jung: "But that's queer. My watch came back from the watchmaker this morning after a complete revision, and now I have 5:05. But you must have been here much longer. What time do you have?" I: "It's 5:35." Whereon Jung said: "So you have the right time, and I the wrong one. Let us discuss the thing again." This time I could convince Jung that the book should be published.

Here the synchronistic event is of interest not because of its intrinsic coincidental force but because of the meaning Jung drew from it, essentially using it as a basis for challenging and redirecting his own conscious attitude. The unexpected stopping and resulting error of the watch was immediately recognized by Jung as paralleling—and as thereby bringing to his attention—what he then suspected might be a comparable stoppage and error in his own thinking about the matter at hand. He was alert to the fact that the two events, one inner and the other outer, would have taken place at virtually the same moment. Rather than automatically assuming that there could be no significant connection between the state of his watch and the state of his thinking, which would certainly be the usual assumption, his immediate intuition was of a larger field of meaning underlying and patterning all that happened in the room at the time. In that field, events having no apparent causal connection in the conventional sense could be recognized as participating in a more subtly ordered whole, a larger pattern of meaning that was discernible to the prepared mind—even if that meaning challenged his conscious attitude.

For Jung, the symbolic connection between the two events was as transparently intelligible as if he were reading a newspaper, and he acted accordingly. What made the correlation between the inner and outer events intelligible was the presence of two factors: first, a developed capacity for thinking and perceiving symbolically, a cultivated sensitivity to metaphoric and analogical patterns that connect and thereby illuminate diverse phenomena; and second, an episte-mological openness to the possibility that such meaning can be carried by the outer world as well as the inner, by all of nature and one's surrounding environment, not just by the human psyche.

Yet the recognition of synchronicities requires subtle judgments made in circumstances usually pervaded by ambiguity and open to multiple interpretations. The suggestive patterning and often delicate precision of detail in such coincidences notoriously escape the net of objectivistic assessments and experimental tests. Synchronicities seem to constitute a lived reality the experience of which depends deeply on the sensitive perception of context and nuance. For synchronicities have a shadow side, as in the exaggeration of the trivial to discover a self-inflating meaning. Another form this shadow can take is the paranoid's morbidly narrow interpretation of coincidences in terms of other people's malign plots cunningly directed at the self, or psychotic delusions of self-reference. Such interpretations are, as Jung once suggested, pre-Copernican, egocentric. They center the world of meaning naïvely on the old narrow self, inflating the separate ego or persecuting it, and thereby evade the more complex and often painful emergence of the individuated self that is in dialogue with the whole.

Such an emergence requires attending to the claims and communications of the larger cosmos of the unconscious. A painstaking cultivation of self-knowledge must be undertaken to avoid succumbing to mere projection. Discriminating such events requires a self-critical awareness of unconscious tendencies towards narcissistic distortion by which random or peripheral events are continually transformed into signs of an egocentric universe. No less crucial is the development and balanced interplay of multiple faculties of cognition—empirical, rational, emotional, relational, intuitive, symbolic. A capacity for acute yet balanced discernment has to be forged, founded not only on an alertness to meaningful pattern but also on a disciplined mindfulness of the larger whole within which the individual self seeks orientation.

Today, a half century after Jung's original formulation of the principle of synchronicity, with both the concept and the phenomenon now so widely recognized, one can discern a typical sequence and progression in the nature of synchronistic events and responses. The first stage is usually marked by the experience of various ambiguously suggestive coincidences and patternings that may seem somewhat remarkable, curious, or even vaguely uncanny, but can still be regarded as perhaps merely fortuitous or subjective, and are therefore usually ignored and forgotten. Eventually, there may occur one or more especially powerful synchronicities, unambiguous in their coincidental force and precision of patterning, that have a revelatory effect on the individual and mark a decisive threshold in his or her psychological and spiritual development. Not infrequently, synchronicities of this category occur in association with births, deaths, crises, and other major turning points in life. On occasion, there may take place a sudden convergence of many such synchronicities, intricately interconnected, occurring in close proximity or in rapid succession, and having the effect of an overpowering epiphany of new meaning and purpose in the life of the individual.

Over time, however, after this threshold has been crossed, a new attitude toward synchronicities often emerges as their frequency and character come to seem part of life's pervasive intelligence and artistry—less a paradigm-shifting revelation of a new order of reality and more a continuing source of meaning and orientation with which to participate in life with greater sensitivity and intelligence. A disciplined alertness to significant pattern in the outer world as well as inner begins to develop as an essential aspect of living a more conscious life. The occurrence of synchronicities is seen as permitting a continuing dialogue with the unconscious and the larger whole of life while also calling forth an aesthetic and spiritual appreciation of life's powers of symbolically resonant complex patterning.

Although Jung himself did not explicitly describe this later stage in his principal monograph on synchronicity, it is evident from many scattered passages in his writings and from the recollections and memoirs of others that he both lived his life and conducted his clinical practice in a manner that entailed a constant attention to potentially meaningful synchronistic events that would then shape his understanding and actions. Jung saw nature and one's surrounding environment as a living matrix of potential synchronistic meaning that could illuminate the human sphere. He attended to sudden or unusual movements or appearances of animals, flocks of birds, the wind, storms, the suddenly louder lapping of the lake outside the window of his consulting room, and similar phenomena as possessing possible symbolic relevance for the parallel unfolding of interior psychological realities. For the woman who had the dream of the golden scarab, the next day's synchronistic visitation through the window was dramatically transformative, whereas the same event for Jung represented a striking but not uncharacteristic example of the meaningful patterning of inner and outer events to which he had long before learned to be attentive.

In sharp contrast to the modern world view, Jung ceased to regard the outer world as merely a neutral background against which the human psyche pursued its isolated intrasubjective quest for meaning and purpose. Rather, all events, inner and outer, whether emanating from the human unconscious or from the larger matrix of the world, were recognized as sources of potential psychological and spiritual significance. From this perspective, not only the individual psyche and not only humanity's collective unconscious but all of nature supported and moved the human psyche towards a larger consciousness of purpose and meaning.[4] Each moment in time possessed a certain tangible character or quality which pervaded the various events taking place at that moment.

It seems, indeed, as though time, far from being an abstraction, is a concrete continuum which contains qualities or fundamentals which can manifest themselves in relative simultaneousness in different places and in a parallelism which cannot be explained, as in cases of simultaneous appearance of identical thoughts, symbols, or psychic conditions. . . . Whatever is born or done at this particular moment of time has the quality of this moment of time."[5]

Central to Jung's understanding of such phenomena was his observation that the underlying meaning or formal factor that linked the synchronistic inner and outer events—the formal cause, in Aristotelian terms—was archetypal in nature. Building on insights from Freud, and drawing from the classical Platonic philosophical vocabulary and from esoteric traditions, Jung had long regarded and defined archetypes as the fundamental governing principles of the human psyche. On the basis of his own analyses as well as those of others, not only of a diverse range of clinical phenomena but also of the art, myths, and religions of many eras and cultures, Jung had come to view archetypes as innate symbolic forms and psychological dispositions that unconsciously structure and impel human behavior and experience at both the personal and collective level. They are "self-portraits" of the instincts and render human experience meaningful according to certain timeless universal patterns or forms: Light and Dark, Birth and Death, Rebirth, the Hero, the Great Mother, the Child, the Trickster, the Shadow, Good and Evil, Eros and Logos, Feminine and Masculine, as well as more specifically personified and culturally inflected forms such as Aphrodite, Oedipus, Dionysus, Prometheus, Saturn, Shakti, Kali, Shiva, Wotan, Isis, and Sophia. Another major category of the archetypes comprises the mathematical principles of number and geometric form, as in the Pythagorean-Platonic tradition, and traditional sacred forms such as the mandala, the circle, and the cross. All these principles were seen as possessing a primordial, mythic, and numinous character grounded in the deepest layers of the psyche and expressing a collective unconscious shared by all human beings.

For most of his career, Jung worked and wrote within the modern Cartesian-Kantian philosophical framework of a basic division between the human subject and the objective world, and thus tended to restrict archetypes to the interior world of the human psyche. His view of archetypes in the early and middle periods of his career was generally equivalent to Kant's notion of a priori forms and categories: They were inherited psychological structures or dispositions that preceded and shaped the character of human experience but could not be said to transcend the human psyche. In his later work, however, and most explicitly in the context of his analysis of synchronicities, Jung moved towards a conception of archetypes as autonomous patterns of meaning that inform both psyche and matter, providing a bridge between inner and outer: "Synchronicity postulates a meaning which is a priori in relation to human consciousness and apparently exists outside man." Jung's later work thus intimated the ancient understanding of an ensouled world, of an *anima mundi* in which the human psyche participates and with which it shares the same ordering principles of meaning. Jung noted parallels between synchronistic phenomena and the Chinese understanding of the Tao, the ancient Greek conception of the cosmic sympathy of all things, the Hermetic doctrine of microcosm and macrocosm, the medieval and Renaissance theory of correspondences, and the medieval concept of the preexistent ultimate unity of all existence, the *unus mundus* (the unitary world).[6]

In each case of synchronicity, Jung discerned an underlying archetypal coherence that linked the otherwise unconnected events, informed the larger field of meaning, and gave to the time of the synchronicity's occurrence a specific fundamental quality. In the first case cited above, for example, the symbolically charged image of the golden scarab expressed the archetypal principle of rebirth and renewal, visible in the Egyptian myth of the Sun-god who in the netherworld during the night sea journey changes himself into a scarab, then mounts the barge to rise again reborn into the morning sky at dawn. In Egyptian religion, the mythic journey of the Sun mediated the spiritual journey of the soul, providing the individual with a transformative symbolic pattern of descent and renewal, death and rebirth.

The case of the stopped watch, by contrast, was pervasively informed by the complex archetype of Saturn-Kronos, the *senex* principle, a central symbol and figure in the Western cultural tradition from the ancient Greek and Hellenistic era through the Middle Ages and Renaissance.[7] In this synchronicity, the Saturn archetype was visible not only in all the concrete details involving time, but also in the intricately interrelated themes of stoppage and being stuck (in both mind and watch), of opposition and rejection, error, fault, correction, judgment and self-judgment, the superego. Each element and stage of the event suggested another dimension of the Saturn principle's multivalent spectrum of meanings: the precise meeting time, the task at hand, the problem to be solved, the pronouncement of judgments, the strife of disagreement, the attempt to bring an end to the task, the careful checking and comparing of the time, the act of negation and criticism first directed outward towards the other and then inward towards the self, the self-correction followed by repetition, engaging the problem again and trying this time to get it right. Finally, the overarching themes, deciding the fate of the manuscript, judging the legacy of the deceased, death as the stopping of time: all characteristic expressions of Saturn and the senex discernible within the hour of the meeting.

Because synchronicities seemed to reflect and embody the same archetypal forms that Jung and many others came to see as basic underlying principles of the human psyche, the occurrence and recognition of such meaningful coincidences gave a crucial new dimension to the archetypal perspective. The empirical conformity between the event occurring in the external world and the archetypal quality of the internal state of consciousness suggested that the active archetype could not be localized as an exclusively subjective intrapsychic reality. Rather, both psyche and world, inner and outer, were informed by the archetypal pattern and thereby united by the correlation. It was specifically the experiential potency of this spontaneous archetypal resonance that seemed to act as a healing solvent on the hardened polarities—between self and world, subject and object, conscious and unconscious—of the person experiencing the synchronicity.

> The collective unconscious surrounds us on all sides. . . . It is more like an atmosphere in which we live than something that is found *in* us. . . . Also, it does not by any means behave merely psychologically; in the cases of so-called synchronicity it proves to be a universal substrate present in the environment rather than a psychological premise. Wherever we come into contact with an archetype we enter into relationship with transconscious, metapsychic factors.

This development in Jung's thought thus constituted a major shift in his understanding of the religious situation confronting the modern psyche. From early in his career, Jung saw both the psychological and the spiritual path of the modern self as requiring a sustained direct encounter with the archetypal unconscious. Here lay the possibility not only of deeper psychological self-awareness but also of spiritual transformation, permitting an engagement with those numinous realities that could profoundly heal the psyche and provide it with an orienting purpose and transcendent meaning. Throughout most of his writings this engagement was understood as taking place within what Jung essentially regarded as the sacred circle of the human psyche. Eventually, however, Jung's many years of studying synchronicities moved him to recognize this engagement as something that is enacted within the larger sacred circle of nature as a whole. In this perspective, not just the interior depths of the human psyche but also the interior depths of nature itself supports the unfolding of human spirituality and each person's struggle towards individuation.[8]

The recognition of synchronicities' potential metaphysical implications not only suggested a transformation in the psychology of religion; it represented a critical step towards bridging the schism between religion and science in the modern era so long embodied in the seemingly unbridgeable chasm between psyche and world. As the physicist Victor Mansfield has written, speaking for many: "I have encountered too many synchronistic experiences, both in my life and that of others, to ignore them. Yet these surprisingly common experiences pose tremendous psychological and philosophical challenges for our world view. They are especially troubling experiences for me as a physicist trained within the culture of scientific materialism." With these implications in mind, both philosophical and psychological, Jung's student and close associate Marie-Louise von Franz stated in an interview late in her life that "the work which has now to be done is to work out the concept of synchronicity. I don't know the people who will continue it. They must exist, but I don't know where they are."

Despite synchronicities' enigmatic and often readily dismissed character, it was with such humble clues that Jung began to open up the possibility of a fundamental redefinition of both the modern religious situation and the scientific world picture, beyond the closed universe of the spiritually aspiring psyche encompassed by a disenchanted world. Recalling the diagram illustrating the modern world view, the existence of synchronicities implied that the large outer circle representing the world could no longer be seen as a definitively meaningless void. The dynamic relationship between different dimensions of being—both between the human self and the encompassing world and between consciousness and the unconscious—had to be reconceived. It appears to have been Jung's growing recognition of the magnitude of these implications for the modern world view that impelled him to labor so strenuously, even courageously, to bring critical awareness of the phenomenon of synchronicity into the intellectual discourse of the twentieth century.[9]

The psychological and spiritual quest of the modern self now extended beyond an exclusively subjective, intrapsychic horizon, for that quest took place within the matrix of a world that evidently possessed an intrinsic capacity for expressing and supporting meaning and purpose. Subtly and tenuously, the larger context within which the modern psyche pursued its search for wholeness had begun to shift.

The Archetypal Cosmos

So it comes to pass that, when we pursue an inquiry beyond a certain depth, we step out of the field of psychological categories and enter the sphere of the ultimate mysteries of life. The floorboards of the soul, to which we try to penetrate, fan open and reveal the starry firmament.

—Bruno Schulz

Over the years, many researchers have taken a special interest in the problem of coincidences, precisely because such events could be interpreted as evidence that the world possesses more underlying unity, order, and meaning than the modern mind has assumed. Not unlike the anomalous situation that confronted Newtonian physics in the late nineteenth century with the Michelson-Morley experiment that measured the speed of light, synchronicity represented a phenomenon that, simply put, should not have been occurring, at least not in a random, purposeless universe. Yet the problem has remained ambiguous, for although coincidences are often personally significant, they tend to resist objective assessment. Only if such phenomena were in some sense public and pervasive rather than private and exceptional—only if the archetypal patternings were more universally discernible and associated more widely with collective experience and the world at large rather than sporadically with isolated special cases—could the suggestion of a deeper order be effectively substantiated in a way that could influence the cultural world view.

One special, highly controversial class of synchronicities, however, did appear to resemble this description. In the course of his career Jung's attention was increasingly drawn to the ancient cosmological perspective of astrology, which posits a systematic symbolic correspondence between planetary positions and the events of human existence. Here was the thesis, widely accepted in most other cultures as well as in earlier eras of the West, that the universe is so ordered that the movements and patterns of the heavens are synchronously correlated with the movements and patterns of human affairs in such a manner as to be both intelligible and meaningful to the human mind. Jung began to examine astrology as early as 1911, when he mentioned his inquiries in a letter to Freud.

("My evenings are taken up very largely with astrology. I make horoscopic calculations in order to find a clue to the core of psychological truth. Some remarkable things have turned up. . . .") The interest gradually developed into a major focus of investigation, and in his later years Jung devoted himself with considerable passion to astrological research. "Astrology," he stated, "represents the sum of all the psychological knowledge of antiquity." Though his published writings presented varying and at times ambiguous views of the subject over the course of his life, it is evident that insights from his astrological studies influenced many of his most significant theoretical formulations in the final, extraordinarily fruitful phase of his life's work (archetypal theory, synchronicity, philosophy of history). It is also clear from reports from his family and others close to him that in his last decades he came to employ the analysis of birth charts and transits as a regular and integral aspect of his clinical work with patients in analysis.[10]

Of course, astrology has not been held in high esteem during most of the modern era, for a variety of compelling reasons. Certainly its popular expressions have seldom been such as to inspire confidence in the enterprise. More fundamentally, astrology could not be reconciled with the world picture that emerged from the natural sciences of the seventeenth to nineteenth centuries, wherein all natural phenomena, from the motion of planets to the evolution of species, were understood in terms of material substances and mechanistic principles that functioned without purpose or design. Nor could it prevail against that tendency of the modern mind, established during the Enlightenment, to uphold its own rational autonomy and to depreciate earlier thought systems that seemed to support any form of primitive *participation mystique* between the human psyche and a world endowed with pregiven structures of meaning. One can appreciate Jung's reluctance to make more public the extent of his use of astrology. In the context of twentieth-century beliefs and the dominance of scientific thinking, he had already pressed the boundaries of intellectual discourse about as far as could be sustained.

Like most products of a modern education, I myself long viewed any form of astrology with automatic skepticism. Eventually, however, influenced not only by Jung's example but also by a number of colleagues whose intellectual judgment I had reason to trust, I came to think that some essence of the astrological thesis might be worth investigating. Several factors contributed to my interest. Once I moved past the usual disparagements of the conventional accounts, I noticed that the history of astrology contained certain remarkable features. It seemed curious to me that the historical periods during which astrology flourished in the West—classical Greek and Roman antiquity, the Hellenistic era in Alexandria, the High Middle Ages, the Italian Renaissance, the Elizabethan age in England, the sixteenth and early seventeenth centuries in Europe generally—all happened to be eras in which intellectual and cultural creativity was unusually luminous. The same could be said of astrology's prominence during the centuries in which science and culture were at their height in the Islamic world, and so too in India. I thought it curious as well that astrology had provided the principal foundation for the earliest development of science itself, in the ancient civilizations of Mesopotamia, and that its intimate bond with astronomy had played a significant role in the evolution of Western cosmology for two thousand years, from its Greek origins through the pivotal period of the Copernican revolution. I was also impressed by the high intellectual caliber of those philosophers, scientists, and writers who in one form or another had supported the astrological thesis, a group that to my surprise turned out to include many of the greatest figures of Western thought: Plato and Aristotle, Hipparchus and Ptolemy, Plotinus and Proclus, Albertus Magnus and Thomas Aquinas, Dante, Ficino, Kepler, Goethe, Yeats, Jung.[11]

Beyond these several historical factors, I was also impressed by a number of commonalities between that ancient thought system and the new conception of reality currently emerging in many fields out of the postmodern matrix: the affirmation of the multidimensional nature of reality, the complex holistic understanding of part and whole in all phenomena, the recognition of an "ecology of mind" in nature, the new discernment of subtle dimensions of order in seemingly random natural processes, the openness to sources of knowledge and traditions of thought beyond those sanctioned by conventional modern rationality, the acknowledgment of the spiritual dimension of existence, the appreciation of the role of symbolic, mythic, and archetypal meaning in human experience. Unlike its mechanistic modern predecessor, the emerging paradigm provided a general conceptual framework that in many respects was not inherently incompatible with the astrological perspective.

But what especially stimulated and, in the end, compelled my reconsideration of astrology was, as in Jung's case, the unexpected results of research I myself decided to undertake. I believe now that only this direct encounter with empirical data that one has personally investigated can effectively serve to overcome the extreme resistance that virtually every person educated within the modern context must initially experience towards astrology. Despite the parallels with the other emerging theories and perspectives just mentioned, and despite its perhaps noble ancient lineage, astrology has for too long represented the very antithesis of modern thought and cosmology to permit most educated individuals today to approach astrology effectively in any other way. Of all "new paradigm" perspectives and theories, astrology is the most uncomfortably beyond the prevailing paradigm boundary line, the most likely to evoke immediate scorn and derision, the most apt to be known more through its caricature in the popular media than through its serious research, journals, and scholarship. Above all, astrology is that perspective which most directly contradicts the long-established disenchanted and decentered cosmology that encompasses virtually all modern and postmodern experience. It posits an intrinsically meaning-permeated cosmos that in some sense is focused on the Earth, even on the individual human being, as a nexus of that meaning. Such a conception of the universe uniquely controverts the most fundamental assumptions of the modern mind.

For just this reason, astrology has long been uncompromisingly opposed, often with vehement intensity, by most contemporary scientists. As they frequently point out, if astrology were in any sense valid, the very foundations of the modern world view would be placed in question. Its inherent absurdity has been regarded as so self-evident as to be beyond discussion: Astrology is the last lingering vestige of primitive animism, a strangely enduring affront to the objective rationality of the modern mind.

These are formidable obstacles confronting anyone considering this perspective and method of inquiry. Yet human knowledge constantly evolves and changes, sometimes in quite unexpected ways. What is unequivocally rejected in one age may be dramatically reclaimed in another, as happened when the ancient heliocentric hypothesis of Aristarchus, long ignored by scientific authorities as valueless and absurd, was resurrected and vindicated by Copernicus, Kepler, and Galileo. Widespread or even universal conviction at any given moment has never been a reliable indication of the truth or falsity of an idea. I could not dogmatically rule out the possibility that there was more to astrology than the modern mind had assumed.

After learning the rudiments of how to calculate natal charts, I directed my attention to a curious phenomenon of which I had heard reports circulating among professionals in the mental health field, corroborating an observation that Jung also had made. The reports concerned planetary "transits," which are alignments formed between the current positions of the orbiting planets and the planetary positions at an individual's birth. Beginning with a small sample and then steadily augmenting it, I found to my considerable astonishment that individuals engaged in various forms of psychotherapy and transformational practices showed a consistent tendency to experience psychological breakthroughs and healing transformations in coincidence with a certain category of planetary transits to their natal charts, while periods of sustained psychological difficulty tended to coincide with a different category of transits involving other planets. The consistency and precision of these initial correlations between clearly definable psychological states and coinciding transiting alignments seemed too significant to be explained by chance. Yet given currently accepted views of the universe, such correlations simply should not have been happening. What especially drew my attention was the inexplicable fact that the character of the observed psychological states corresponded so closely to the supposed meanings of the relevant transiting and natal planets as described in standard astrological texts. For there to be any consistent correlations at all was obviously puzzling; for the correlations also to match the traditional meanings of the planets was startling.

As I investigated further, it soon became apparent that the nature of the planetary correlations was far more complex than my initial observations concerning a simple dichotomy between positive and negative psychological states had led me to believe. A deeper understanding of astrological principles, combined with recent theoretical advances in depth psychology, particularly from the archetypal and transpersonal schools, gave me a glimpse into a much larger range of correlations between planetary movements and human experience. These findings impelled me to step back and approach the research task in a more fully prepared and systematic manner. I decided to examine the history and principles of astrology in earnest by reading carefully through the canon of major astrological works, from Ptolemy's summation of classical astrology, the *Tetrabiblos*, and Kepler's *On the More Certain Fundamentals of Astrology*, to modern texts by Leo, Rudhyar, Carter, Ebertin, Addey, Harvey, Hand, Greene, and Arroyo.[12] I studied planetary ephemerides—astronomical tables that list the positions of the Sun, Moon, and planets for any given day and year in terms of degrees and minutes of celestial longitude as measured along the zodiac—until I could decipher the changing planetary patterns and alignments with some facility. Because this was before the advent of personal computers, I learned to make fairly quickly the numerous calculations necessary for constructing accurate natal charts, showing the exact planetary positions at a person's birth, and for determining other basic astrological indicators such as transits. The mathematics required for these operations, I discovered, is relatively simple. But more important, and more revealing, I found the symbolic principles associated with the planets at the core of the astrological tradition unexpectedly easy to assimilate, since they proved to be surprisingly similar—indeed, essentially identical—to the archetypes of modern depth psychology familiar from the work of Freud and Jung and their successors in archetypal and transpersonal psychology.

Equipping myself in this manner, I first made an intensive examination of my own natal chart and the charts of forty to fifty other individuals I knew well, attempting to ascertain whether a significant correlation existed between the planetary positions at birth on the one hand and the personal character and biography on the other. Keeping in mind the suggestibility inherent in such assessments, I was nevertheless deeply impressed by the range and complex precision of the empirical correspondences. It was as if an uncommonly gifted depth psychologist, after long acquaintance with my own or another individual's life and personality, had determined the archetypal dynamics operative in that person's biography and then constructed an appropriate planetary diagram to match—though in reality this diagram represented the actual positions of the planets at the time of that person's birth.

This certainly would have been striking in itself, yet even more extraordinary were the correlations between specific transits and the timing of major events and psychological conditions. Expanding upon my initial observations, I observed that the continuously moving planets as listed in the astronomical tables consistently seemed to cross, or transit, the planetary positions in the birth chart in coincidence with times in a person's life that in archetypal terms were uncannily appropriate. In each instance the particular meaning and character of significant life experiences closely corresponded to the postulated meaning of the planetary transits occurring at that time. The more systematically I examined the two sets of variables—planetary positions and biographical events—the more impressive were the correspondences.

Yet there were also problems and discrepancies. A considerable portion of the astrological tradition was so vague, overspecific, or quaintly irrelevant as to make useful correlations unobtainable. I came to suspect that a number of conventional astrological tenets were no more than inherited ad hoc formulae that had been gradually solidified into established doctrine, elaborated, and passed down over the centuries much like the epicyclical accretions of medieval astronomy. Certainly much astrological theory and practice entirely lacked critical rigor. It seemed to me that considerable waste, misdirection, and even harm occurred as a result of many astrological teachings and consultations.

Nevertheless, a certain core of the astrological tradition—above all, the planetary correspondences with specific archetypal principles, and the importance of major geometrical alignments between the planets—appeared to have a substantial empirical basis. As time passed, I applied the same mode of analysis to the lives of more and more persons in a widening circle of inquiry, with equally illuminating results. The more exact the available data and the more deeply familiar I was with the person or event, the more compelling were the correspondences. Both the quantity and the quality of positive correlations made my initial skepticism difficult to sustain. The coincidence between planetary positions and appropriate biographical and psychological phenomena was in general so precise and consistent as to make it altogether impossible for me to regard the intricate patterning as merely the product of chance.

I should clarify that the focus of this research was not the astrology of the fortune-teller and the newspaper columns. It bore no resemblance to sun-sign horoscope predictions. In contrast to my previous uninformed impression of the subject, the mode of inquiry that gradually emerged was, I discovered, an intellectually demanding method of analysis, mathematically precise and even elegant in form, that used all the planets and their shifting geometrical alignments with each other, and that required a constant reciprocal interaction between archetypal insight and empirical rigor. Moreover, an essential characteristic of this analysis was that it did not predict specific events or personality traits. Rather, it articulated the deeper archetypal dynamics of which events and traits were the concrete expression. This it seemed to do with astonishing precision and subtlety.

Compared with the more rigid determinism and literalism that characterized much of the astrological tradition, the evidence I encountered pointed to a rather different understanding of astrological "influence" on human affairs. This newer understanding better recognized the critical significance of both the particular context and the participatory human role, and it challenged the possibility and appropriateness of specific concrete prediction. A key to this emerging perspective, I came to realize, was the concept of archetype as developed by Jung, taking into account not only its complex Platonic, Kantian, and Freudian background but also its more recent evolution in depth psychology through the work of James Hillman, Stanislav Grof, and others. Only as I more fully appreciated the multidimensional and multivalent nature of archetypes—their formal coherence and consistency that could give rise to a plurality of meaning and possible manifestation—did I begin to discern the precise nature of astrological correlations.

The archetypes associated with specific planetary alignments were equally apt to express themselves in the interior life of the psyche as in the external world of concrete events, and often both at once. In addition, any particular manifestation of a given archetype could be "positive" or "negative," benign or destructive, admirable or ignoble, profound or trivial. Closely linked yet entirely opposite polarities contained in the same archetypal complex could be expressed in coincidence with the same planetary configuration. Individuals with the same alignment could be on either the acting or the receiving end of the same archetypal gestalt, with altogether different experiential consequences. Which of all these related multivalent possibilities occurred seemed to be determined largely by contingent circumstances and individual response rather than by anything observable in the birth chart or planetary alignments per se. My eventual conclusion was that the archetypal principles at work in these correlations were powerful but radically participatory in nature. That is, though they represented enduring, structurally decisive forms or essences of complex meaning, and were clearly discernible underlying the flux and diversity of the observed phenomena, these principles were also both fundamentally shaped by many relevant circumstantial factors and co-creatively modulated and enacted through human will and intelligence.

Because of this distinctive combination of dynamic archetypal multivalence and sensitivity to particular conditions and human participation, I gradually came to recognize that, contrary to its traditional reputation and deployment, such an astrology is not concretely predictive but, rather, *archetypally* predictive. Compared with, for example, the aims and modus operandi of various forms of intuitive divination and clairvoyance, with which astrology in earlier eras was often systematically conjoined, the essential structure of this emerging astrological paradigm appeared to be focused not on the prediction of specific concrete outcomes but rather on the precise discernment of archetypal dynamics and their complex unfolding in time.[13] This understanding greatly clarified for me numerous long-standing issues surrounding astrology, such as the question of fate versus free will, the problem of identical planetary configurations coinciding with concretely different though archetypally parallel phenomena, and the fundamental inadequacy of statistical tests for detecting most astrological correlations.

In essence, astrology seemed to offer a singularly valuable kind of insight into the dynamic activity of archetypes in human experience—indicating which ones were most operative in a specific instance, in what combinations, during which periods of time, and as part of what larger patterns. In providing such a perspective, this emerging development of the astrological tradition can be seen as essentially continuing and deepening the depth psychology project: namely, to make conscious the unconscious, to help free the conscious self from being a puppet of unconscious forces (as in acting out, projection, inflated identification, drawing towards one as "fate" what is repressed or unconscious, and so forth). Such an astrology appeared to possess a unique capacity for mediating a heightened level of communication and coordination between consciousness and the unconscious, with "the unconscious" now suggestive of considerably larger dimensions than originally conceived—less exclusively personal, less subjective, more cosmically embedded. It provided this mediation, however, not by spelling out anything in a literalistic predictive manner, but rather by disclosing intelligible patterns of meaning whose very nature and complexity—multivalence, indeterminacy, sensitivity to context and participation, and a seemingly improvisatory creativity—were precisely what made possible a dynamically co-creative role for human agency in participatory interaction with the archetypal forces and principles involved.

As the evidence itself pointed in this direction, I eventually extended my research to encompass various categories of historical and cultural phenomena. Compared with the psychotherapeutic data and biographical material involving nonfamous individuals on which I initially had focused, the timing and character of historically significant events and the biographical data of major cultural figures presented the advantage of being publicly verifiable, so that planetary correspondences were more open to rigorous evaluation. Beyond this methodological concern, the possibility that the larger historical process might itself possess some intrinsic order relative to planetary cycles and universal archetypes seemed especially deserving of investigation. Evidence for such an order would obviously have serious implications in many fields—history, cosmology, philosophy, psychology, ethics, religion. I therefore took the basic principles for which the earlier correlations had given support and began a systematic study in this larger domain of research.

Together with many colleagues and students, I have now steadily pursued this research for three decades. What I have found far surpassed my expectations. Much remains a mystery, and certainly much will always remain a mystery, but I have become convinced, after the most painstaking investigation and critical assessment of which I am capable, that there does in fact exist a highly significant—indeed a pervasive—correspondence between planetary movements and human affairs, and that the modern assumption to the contrary has been erroneous. The evidence suggests not that the planets themselves *cause* various events or character traits, but rather that a consistently meaningful empirical correspondence exists between the two sets of phenomena, astronomical and human, with the connecting principle most fruitfully approached as some form of archetypally informed synchronicity.

In the following chapters I set forth several of the major categories of evidence with which I personally have been concerned, and I discuss their broader implications. I have striven to present this material to readers new to the field in such a way that it is at once readily comprehensible, manageable in size, and representative of the whole, even though the accumulated evidence from which the present sampling is drawn comprises many thousands of meticulously analyzed correlations. This larger body of research has been the subject of many lecture courses and seminars I have taught over the past decade in graduate programs in psychology, philosophy, and cultural history. A systematic treatment of this research will require more than a single book. Yet it seemed desirable to set forth first a preliminary survey of evidence that would give the interested reader a general sense for the nature of the observed correspondences.

Many critics will of course object to the entire project of this book. Anything astrological, they will say, must be both simplistic and absurd. Having once held that opinion myself, I now believe that such an indiscriminate rejection is virtually always based on personal and cultural prejudice rather than conscientious inquiry. I can sympathize with such a prejudice, and I appreciate its background. For myself, however, a sustained examination of the evidence has been decisive. I believe that the open-minded reader who sincerely seeks to discover the potential validity and value of this perspective and method of analysis and who carefully examines the evidence—above all, the evidence pertaining to his or her own life and fields of personal expertise, which that person is especially able to assess—will be as impressed as I continue to be with the striking character and precision of the correlations. The method of analysis described in the following chapters is highly democratic: It is not unlike the telescope in Galileo's time, through which any interested person could observe the new body of evidence supporting the Copernican hypothesis. Every reader with a modest degree of preparation can take the principles set forth in this book, focus on those experiences and events that are most personally significant in his or her life, and determine whether the archetypal astrological understanding offers a larger perspective, sheds new light, brings deeper meaning, provides greater intelligibility.

To help the reader make an informed judgment on these matters is one of the principal purposes of this book. In the following chapters, therefore, I present both the basic technical knowledge necessary to begin the exploration and illustrative examples of correlations in history and in the lives of significant cultural figures. These examples are presented as information perhaps interesting and instructive in itself but also as an aid in developing, or awakening, what Hillman has called "an archetypal eye": that form of imaginative intelligence, implicit and potential in all of us, that is capable of recognizing and discriminating the rich multiplicity of archetypal patterns in the intimate microcosm of one's own life as well as in the great events of history and culture. After this survey of evidence, I briefly address its implications and suggest a philosophical and cosmological framework within which it might most cogently be integrated.

III

Through the Archetypal Telescope

My guide and I entered through that hidden path to make our way back into the shining world. And with no time for rest, we climbed upward—he first, I following—until, through a round opening, I saw those things of beauty that Heaven holds. It was thence, at last, we came forth to see again the stars.

—Dante
The Divine Comedy

The Evolving Tradition

A strology in its most general definition rests on a conception of the cosmos as a coherent embodiment of creative intelligence, purpose, and meaning expressed through a constant complex correspondence between astronomical patterns and human experience. The various celestial bodies are regarded as possessing an intrinsic association with specific universal principles. Both these principles and their astronomical correspondences are seen as ultimately grounded in the nature of the cosmos itself, thereby integrating the celestial and terrestrial, macrocosm and microcosm. As the planets move through their cycles, they form various geometrical relationships with each other relative to the Earth within the larger cosmic environment. These alignments are observed to coincide with specific archetypally patterned phenomena in human lives. From the beginning of Western astrology, such an understanding was closely associated with the original Greek conception of *kosmos*, a word first applied to the world as a whole by the Pythagoreans to convey a characteristically Greek synthesis of intelligent order, beauty, and structural perfection.

The astrological tradition initiated by the Greeks in Alexandria in the Hellenistic era, during the centuries immediately before and after the birth of Christ, was embedded in a classical world conception deeply influenced by Pythagorean and Platonic thought. It had earlier roots in ancient Mesopotamian celestial observations from at least the beginning of the second millennium BCE, and was shaped by ancient Babylonian, Egyptian, and Persian cultural influences. The first known natal chart, or horoscope, dates from about 400 BCE (the time of Socrates and Plato). The astrological perspective and method that emerged in the following centuries was closely associated with the scientific disciplines of Greek astronomy, mathematics, and medicine, with the esoteric streams of thought that informed the mystery religions and Hermetic literature of classical antiquity, and with major philosophical and religious movements such as Neoplatonism, Aristotelianism, Stoicism, and Gnosticism. As an overarching view of the universe and the cosmic position of the human being, astrology was singularly pervasive in the classical era; it transcended the boundaries of science, religion, and philosophy.[1] It subsequently influenced Christian, Islamic, and Jewish thought and played a central role in the art, literature, and cultural ethos of the European

High Middle Ages and Renaissance. Because of this extraordinary diversity in its origins and the succession of its later environments, astrology was constantly being reconceived according to the different intellectual and cultural contexts in which it flourished.

Yet at the heart of all these various inflections, the implicit cosmological metastructure within which the Western astrological tradition developed can be described as essentially Pythagorean-Platonic in character: that is, the cosmos is understood to be pervasively informed and integrated through the active presence of a universal ordering principle, at once mathematical and archetypal in manifestation, whereby the celestial bodies and their cyclical patterns possess a symbolic significance that is intelligibly reflected within the human sphere. Over the centuries, diverse schools, interpretations, and frameworks arose that continually reshaped and transformed this underlying perspective, positing different views concerning the nature and extent of cosmic influence, the relative balance of celestial constraint and human freedom, the question as to whether planets are indications or causes, and, in the case of the long-influential Aristotelian-Ptolemaic model, the possibility of a more physically causal determinism produced by the celestial spheres.

From its Mesopotamian and Egyptian origins to its subsequent Hellenistic synthesis in the classical era, the history of Western astrology can, in very general terms, be seen as having moved from a more fluid astral divination (focused on intuiting the will of the celestial gods and responding to this perception through appropriate action, ritual, and supplication for divine favor) to an increasing emphasis on systematic observation of the geometric regularities of astronomical movements, the application of universal principles of interpretation, and eventually the formulation of elaborate rules for concrete prediction. This gradual process of "rationalization" (in Weber's sense) was combined in later antiquity and the medieval period with an increasingly mechanistic view of celestial causality, which in turn became linked with a more rigid determinism.[2] A similar evolution took place in India after the conquests of Alexander the Great brought Greek culture to Asia; Vedic astrology was shaped both by the Mesopotamian-Hellenistic tradition and by India's own distinctive religious and social legacies in a manner that has continued to the present.

In Europe, in the wake of the Enlightenment of the late seventeenth and eighteenth centuries, astrology virtually disappeared from scholarly discourse and the world view of the educated. Lingering principally in the form of popular astrological almanacs, it underwent a gradual revival during the nineteenth century with the growing European interest during the Romantic period in esoteric traditions and later in theosophy. Finally, in the course of the twentieth century, a widespread rebirth of astrology took place, beginning in England and spreading to North America and the rest of Europe. The astrology that emerged was informed by goals and theoretical assumptions that often differed from those of the ancient and medieval periods in fundamental ways. In general, its character was more individualistic and psychological—emphasizing internal reality over external, self-understanding over concrete event-prediction, symbolic interpretation over literal, and participatory engagement over passive fatalism. Accompanying this shift of character has been the gradual rise within the astrological community of a discourse of critical philosophical reflection and the questioning of many traditional astrological assumptions and tenets.

Numerous factors have played a role in this recent trend. Increased access to precise astronomical data and the discovery of the outer planets have deeply affected astrological practice and theory. So also has the enormous increase in the available data, with incomparably more individual birth charts, biographies, and historical periods having now become the basis for a collaborative development of accepted principles of interpretation. No less important have been broader cultural changes affecting general intellectual presuppositions and the modern psychological character. These changes include a larger commitment to and experience of individual autonomy, a deepened sense of interiority and the value of psychological reflection, a more complex grasp of symbolic cognition and interpretive multivalence, a more critical understanding of the mutual implication of inner and outer realities, and a deeper recognition of the participatory character of human experience. Associated with this shift is also an increased awareness of the multidimensional and multicausal nature of all phenomena, combined with an appreciation of the irreducible indeterminacy of life's unfolding.

The widespread emergence of a more psychologically sophisticated astrology in the second half of the twentieth century, with Jung and Dane Rudhyar the key figures, represents the dominant historical trend, but an important peripheral development at this time was a new interest from outside the field in statistical tests of astrological hypotheses. Of these, the most significant were the massive studies conducted by the French statisticians Michel and Françoise Gauquelin over a forty-year period beginning in the 1950s. The widely discussed "Mars effect" first observed by the Gauquelins and since replicated by other research groups demonstrated a highly significant statistical correlation of Mars located on either the eastern horizon or the zenith at the birth of prominent athletes. Similar correlations with planetary position were found at the birth of eminent leaders in other fields: Saturn for scientists, Jupiter for politicians, and the Moon for writers, all correctly corresponding to the traditional astrological principles and character traits associated with those particular celestial bodies.[3] In 1982, after extensive examination of the Gauquelin research, Hans Eysenck, a prominent academic psychologist unsympathetic to astrology (and famous for his criticism of psychoanalysis for its lack of statistical support), published with his coauthor David Nias a summary of their conclusions:

We feel obliged to admit that there is something here that requires explanation. However much it may go against the grain, other scientists who take the trouble to examine the evidence may eventually be forced to a similar conclusion. The findings are inexplicable but they are also factual, and as such can no longer be ignored; they cannot just be wished away because they are unpalatable or not in accord with the laws of present-day science. . . . Perhaps the time has come to state quite unequivocally that a new science is in process of being born.

The positive results of the Gauquelin studies and their replication by others presented a robust challenge on science's own terms to the scientific dismissal of astrology. Yet, paradoxically, statistical studies have added relatively little to the astrological understanding, and they appear to be methodologically inadequate for entering into the archetypal frame of reference central to the astrological tradition. The larger resurgence of astrology during these decades has continued to be qualitative rather than quantitative in its practice and research, reflecting its sources in the Western astrological tradition and contemporary depth psychology rather than experimental science and behaviorism. Common to the two approaches, however, has been an underlying impulse in the past half century, from both within and outside of the astrological discipline, that has moved astrology into a more direct engagement with the mainstream modern world view.[4]

Causality and Correlation

In the modern era, with the dominant Cartesian-Newtonian paradigm in the background of all thought and discourse on the subject, considerable confusion has been produced by the conventional scientific attempt to interpret—and thus reject the possibility of—astrological correspondences within a modern mechanistic cosmological framework. In effect, the Cartesian-Newtonian standpoint led to a single simple question that, within its framework, was regarded as decisive for the issue of astrology's validity: How can the planets influence events on the Earth if no physical forces have been observed that could cause those events? This question was so defining for the mainstream scientific mind that even well-replicated statistical evidence that supported astrological tenets could not affect the intensity of its resistance. To a great extent the question of physical planetary influence reflected the residual strength of materialist and mechanistic assumptions in contemporary scientific thought, even after the conceptual shifts introduced by quantum physics. Physical forces represented the only kind of relationship that could be imagined to exist between celestial bodies and human life. This approach to astrology also, less obviously, reflected certain lingering literalist and mechanistic tendencies in the astrological tradition itself that made it vulnerable to a reductionist critique after the ancient Ptolemaic-Aristotelian cosmology was rejected and replaced by Newtonian science.[5] Above all, however, the modern dismissal of astrology reflected the virtually universal modern conviction that the cosmos was disenchanted.

Given the nature of the evidence now known, it is difficult to imagine any physical factor that could serve as the ultimate source or medium of the observed astrological correlations. At least on the basis of the principal categories of data I have examined, it seems to me highly unlikely that the planets send out physical emanations, like electromagnetic radiation, that causally influence events in human life in a mechanistic way so as to produce the observed correlations. The range of correspondences between planetary positions and human existence is just too vast and multidimensional—too manifestly ordered by structures of meaning, too suggestive of creative intelligence, too vividly informed by aesthetic patterning, too metaphorically multivalent, too experientially complex and nuanced, and too responsive to human participatory inflection—to be explained by straightforward material factors alone. Given as well the consistent nature of correlations involving the Sun, the Moon, and all the planets of the solar system from Mercury and Venus to Neptune and Pluto, irrespective of their size or distance from Earth, any causal factor resembling gravitational influence seems to be equally improbable.

I believe that a more plausible and comprehensive explanation of the available evidence would rest on a conception of the universe as a fundamentally and irreducibly interconnected whole, informed by creative intelligence and pervaded by patterns of meaning and order that extend through every level, and that are expressed through a constant correspondence between astronomical events and human events. Such a view is concisely reflected in the Hermetic axiom "as above, so below," which describes a universe all of whose parts and dimensions are integrated into an intelligible whole. In the perspective I am suggesting here, reflecting the dominant trend in contemporary astrological theory, the planets do not "cause" specific events any more than the hands on a clock "cause" a specific time. Rather, the planetary positions are *indicative* of the cosmic state of archetypal dynamics at that time. The words of Plotinus, the most influential philosopher of later classical antiquity, speak directly to this understanding:

> The stars are like letters which inscribe themselves at every moment in the sky. . . . Everything in the world is full of signs. . . . All events are coordinated. . . . All things depend on each other; as has been said, "Everything breathes together."

Instead of the linear causal mechanisms of matter and force assumed in a Newtonian universe, the continuous meaningful coincidence between celestial patterns and human affairs seems rather to reflect a fundamental underlying unity and correspondence between the two realms—macrocosm and microcosm, celestial and terrestrial—and thus the intelligent coherence of a living, fully animate cosmos. The postulation of a systematic correspondence of this kind implies a universe in which mind and matter, psyche and cosmos, are more pervasively related or radically united than has been assumed in the modern world view.

As for the relevance of causality in understanding astrological correlations, it seems that a fundamentally new kind of causality must be posited to account for the observed phenomena. Rather than anything resembling the linear mechanistic causality of the conventional modern understanding, what is suggested by the evidence is an archetypal causality that in crucial respects possesses Platonic and Aristotelian characteristics, yet is far more complex, fluid, multivalent, and co-creatively participatory than previous conceptual models—whether from physics, philosophy, or astrology—have been able to accommodate.

Free Will and Determinism

Because the question of free will and determinism has long been the most existentially and spiritually critical issue in all discussions of astrology, I will offer a few preliminary remarks here.

There is no question that a substantial part of the Western astrological tradition supported a relatively deterministic interpretation of cosmic influence (a tendency even more marked in Indian astrology). For numerous schools and theorists of ancient and medieval astrology, the horoscope revealed a person's destined fate, and the celestial powers governed human lives with a more or less rigid sovereignty. The widespread reemergence of Western astrology in the course of the twentieth century, however, arising in a new context and at a different stage in the West's cultural and psychological evolution, brought with it a deeply transformed vision of both the human self and the nature of astrological prediction. The most characteristic attitude among contemporary astrologers holds astrological knowledge to be ultimately emancipatory rather than constricting, bringing a potential increase of personal freedom and fulfillment through an enlarged understanding of the self and its cosmic context.

In this view, knowing the basic archetypal dynamics and patterns of meaning in one's birth chart allows one to bring greater awareness to the task of fulfilling one's authentic nature and intrinsic potential, as in Jung's concept of individuation. The more accurately one understands the archetypal forces that inform and affect one's life, the more flexibly and intelligently responsive one can be in dealing with them. To the extent that one is unconscious of these potent and sometimes highly problematic forces, one is more or less a pawn of the archetypes, acting according to unconscious motivations with little possibility of being a co-creative participant in the unfolding and refining of those potentials. Archetypal awareness brings greater self-awareness and thus greater personal autonomy. Again, this is the basic rationale for depth psychology, from Freud and Jung onward: to release oneself from the bondage of blind action and unconsciously motivated experience, to recognize and explore the deeper forces in the human psyche and thereby modulate and transform them. On the individual level, astrology is valued for its capacity to articulate which archetypes are especially important for each person, how they interact with each other, and when they are most likely to be activated in the course of each life.

But in addition to the psychological evolution of the modern self with its increased sense of dynamic autonomy and self-reflective interiority, perhaps the most significant factor in the emerging emancipatory understanding of astrology is a deepening grasp of the nature of the archetypal principles themselves, the subject to which we now turn.

Archetypal Principles

The concept of planetary archetypes, in many respects the pivotal concept of the emerging astrological paradigm, is complex and must be approached from several directions. Before describing the nature of the association between planets and archetypes, however, we must first address the general concept of archetypes and the remarkable evolution of the archetypal perspective in the history of Western thought.

The earliest form of the archetypal perspective, and in certain respects its deepest ground, is the primordial experience of the great gods and goddesses of the ancient mythic imagination. In this once universal mode of consciousness, memorably embodied at the dawn of Western culture in the Homeric epics and later in classical Greek drama, reality is understood to be pervaded and structured by powerful numinous forces and presences that are rendered to the human imagination as the divinized figures and narratives of ancient myth, often closely associated with the celestial bodies.

Yet our modern word *god,* or *deity* or *divinity,* does not accurately convey the lived meaning of these primordial powers for the archaic sensibility, a meaning that was sustained and developed in the Platonic understanding of the divine. This point was clearly articulated by W. K. C. Guthrie, drawing on a valuable distinction originally made by the German scholar Wilamowitz-Moellendorff:

> *Theos,* the Greek word which we have in mind when we speak of Plato's god, has primarily a predicative force. That is to say, the Greeks did not, as Christians or Jews do, first assert the existence of God and then proceed to enumerate his attributes, saying "God is good," "God is love" and so forth. Rather they were so impressed or awed by the things in life or nature remarkable either for joy or fear that they said "this is a god" or "that is a god." The Christian says "God is love," the Greek "Love is *theos,*" or "a god." As another writer [G. M. A. Grube] has explained it: "By saying that love, or victory, is god, or, to be more accurate, a god, was meant first and foremost that it is more than human, not subject to death, everlasting. . . . Any power, any force we see at work in the world,

which is not born with us and will continue after we are gone could thus be called a god, and most of them were."

In this state of mind, and with this sensitiveness to the superhuman character of many things which happen to us, and which give us, it may be, sudden stabs of joy or pain which we do not understand, a Greek poet could write lines like: "Recognition between friends is *theos.*" It is a state of mind which obviously has no small bearing on the much-discussed question of monotheism or polytheism in Plato, if indeed it does not rob the question of meaning altogether.

As the Greek mind evolved, by a process sometimes too simply described as a transition from myth to reason, the divine absolutes ordering the world of the mythic imagination were gradually deconstructed and conceived anew in philosophical form in the dialogues of Plato. Building on both the Presocratics' early philosophical discussions of the *archai* and the Pythagorean understanding of transcendent mathematical forms, and then more directly on the critical inquiries of his teacher Socrates, Plato gave to the archetypal perspective its classic metaphysical formulation. In the Platonic view, archetypes—the Ideas or Forms—are absolute essences that transcend the empirical world yet give the world its form and meaning. They are timeless universals that serve as the fundamental reality informing every concrete particular. Something is beautiful precisely to the extent that the archetype of Beauty is present in it. Or, described from a different viewpoint, something is beautiful precisely to the extent that it participates in the archetype of Beauty. For Plato, direct knowledge of these Forms or Ideas is regarded as the spiritual goal of the philosopher and the intellectual passion of the scientist.

In turn, Plato's student and successor Aristotle brought to the concept of universal forms a more empiricist approach, one supported by a rationalism whose spirit of logical analysis was secular rather than spiritual and epiphanic. In the Aristotelian perspective, the forms lost their numinosity but gained a new recognition of their dynamic and teleological character as concretely embodied in the empirical world and processes of life. For Aristotle, the universal forms primarily exist *in* things, not above or beyond them. Moreover, they not only give form and essential qualities to concrete particulars but also dynamically transmute them from within, from potentiality to actuality and maturity, as the acorn gradually metamorphoses into the oak tree, the embryo into the mature organism, a young girl into a woman. The organism is drawn forward by the form to a realization of its inherent potential, just as a work of art is actualized by the artist guided by the form in the artist's mind. Matter is an intrinsic susceptibility to form, an unqualified openness to being configured and dynamically realized through form. In a developing organism, after its essential character has been fully actualized, decay occurs as the form gradually "loses its hold." The Aristotelian form thus serves both as an indwelling impulse that orders and moves development and as the intelligible structure of a thing, its inner nature, that which makes it what it is, its essence. For Aristotle as for Plato, form is the principle by which something can be known, its essence recognized, its universal character distinguished within its particular embodiment.

The idea of archetypal or universal forms then underwent a number of important developments in the later classical, medieval, and Renaissance periods.[6] It became the focus of one of the central and most sustained debates of Scholastic philosophy, "the problem of universals," a controversy that both reflected and mediated the evolution of Western thought as the locus of intelligible reality gradually shifted from the transcendent to the immanent, from the universal to the particular, and ultimately from the divinely given archetypal Form (*eidos*) to the humanly constructed general name (*nomina*). After a final efflorescence in the philosophy and art of the High Renaissance, the concept of archetypes gradually retreated and then virtually disappeared with the modern rise of nominalist philosophy and empiricist science. The archetypal perspective remained vital principally in the arts, in classical and mythological studies, and in Romanticism, as a kind of archaic afterglow. Confined to the subjective realm of interior meaning by the dominant Enlightenment world view, it continued in this form latent in the modern sensibility. The radiant ascent and dominance of modern reason coincided precisely with the eclipse of the archetypal vision.

Between the triumph of nominalism in the seventeenth century and the rise of depth psychology in the twentieth, philosophy brought forth a weighty development, Kant's Copernican revolution in philosophy, that subsequently had major consequences for the form in which the archetypal perspective eventually reemerged. With Kant's critical turn focused on discovering those subjective interpretive structures of the mind that order and condition all human knowledge and experience, the a priori categories and forms, the Enlightenment project underwent a crucial shift in philosophical concern, from the object of knowledge to the knowing subject, that has influenced virtually every field of modern thought.

It was not until the turn of the twentieth century that the concept of archetypes, foreshadowed by Nietzsche's vision of the Dionysian and Apollonian principles shaping human culture, underwent an unexpected renascence. The immediate matrix of its rebirth was the empirical discoveries of depth psychology, first with Freud's formulations of the Oedipus complex, Eros and Thanatos, ego, id, and superego (a "powerful mythology," as Wittgenstein called psychoanalysis), then in an expanded, fully articulated form with the work of Jung and archetypal psychology. Jung, as we have seen, drawing on Kant's critical epistemology and Freud's instinct theory yet going beyond both, described archetypes as autonomous primordial forms in the psyche that structure and impel all human experience and behavior. In his last formulations influenced by his research on synchronicities, Jung came to regard archetypes as expressions not only of a collective unconscious shared by all human beings but also of a larger matrix of being and meaning that informs and encompasses both the physical world and the human psyche.

Finally, further developments of the archetypal perspective emerged in the postmodern period, not only in post-Jungian psychology but in other fields such as anthropology, mythology, religious studies, philosophy of science, linguistic analysis, phenomenology, process philosophy, and feminist scholarship. Advances in understanding the role of paradigms, symbols, and metaphors in shaping human experience and cognition brought new dimensions to the archetypal understanding. In the crucible of postmodern thought, the concept of archetypes was elaborated and critiqued, refined through the deconstruction of rigidly essential-ist "false universals" and cultural stereotypes, and enriched through an increased awareness of archetypes' fluid, evolving, multivalent, and participatory nature. Reflecting many of the above influences, James Hillman sums up the archetypal perspective in depth psychology:

> Let us then imagine archetypes as the deepest patterns of psychic func-tioning, the roots of the soul governing the perspectives we have of our-selves and the world. They are the axiomatic, self-evident images to which psychic life and our theories about it ever return. . . . There are many other metaphors for describing them: immaterial potentials of structure, like invisible crystals in solution or forms in plants that sud-denly show forth under certain conditions; patterns of instinctual be-havior like those in animals that direct actions along unswerving paths; the *genres* and *topoi* in literature; the recurring typicalities in history; the basic syndromes in psychiatry; the paradigmatic thought models in sci-ence; the worldwide figures, rituals, and relationships in anthropology.
>
> But one thing is absolutely essential to the notion of archetypes: their emotional possessive effect, their bedazzlement of consciousness so that it becomes blind to its own stance. By setting up a universe which tends to hold everything we do, see, and say in the sway of its cosmos, an archetype is best comparable with a God. And Gods, religions some-times say, are less accessible to the senses and to the intellect than they are to the imaginative vision and emotion of the soul.
>
> They are cosmic perspectives in which the soul participates. They are the lords of its realms of being, the patterns for its mimesis. The soul cannot be, except in one of their patterns. All psychic reality is governed by one or another archetypal fantasy, given sanction by a God. I cannot but be in them.
>
> There is no place without Gods and no activity that does not enact them. Every fantasy, every experience has its archetypal reason. There is nothing that does not belong to one God or another.

Archetypes thus can be understood and described in many ways, and much of the history of Western thought has evolved and revolved around this very issue. For our present purposes, we can define an archetype as a universal principle or force that affects—impels, structures, permeates—the human psyche and the world of human experience on many levels. One can think of them in mythic terms as gods and goddesses (or what Blake called "the Immortals"), in Platonic terms as transcendent first principles and numinous Ideas, or in Aristotelian terms as immanent universals and dynamic indwelling forms. One can approach them in a Kantian mode as a priori categories of perception and cognition, in Schopenhauerian terms as the universal essences of life embodied in great works of art, or in the Nietzschean manner as primordial principles symbolizing basic cultural tendencies and modes of being. In the twentieth-century context, one can conceive of them in Husserlian terms as essential structures of human experience, in Wittgensteinian terms as linguistic family resemblances linking disparate but overlapping particulars, in Whiteheadian terms as eternal objects and pure potentialities whose ingression informs the unfolding process of reality, or in Kuhnian terms as underlying paradigmatic structures that shape scientific understanding and research. Finally, with depth psychology, one can approach them in the Freudian mode as primordial instincts impelling and structuring biological and psychological processes, or in the Jungian manner as fundamental formal principles of the human psyche, universal expressions of a collective unconscious and, ultimately, of the *unus mundus*.

In a sense, the idea of archetypes is itself an archetype, an *archē*, a continually shape-shifting principle of principles, with multiple creative inflections and variations through the ages as diffracted through different individual and cultural sensibilities. In the course of that long evolution, the archetypal idea seems to have come full circle, arriving now in its post-synchronicity development at a place very closely resembling its ancient origins as cosmic *archai* but with its many inflections and potentialities, as well as new dimensions altogether, having been unfolded and explored.

We can thus conceive of archetypes as possessing a transcendent and numinous quality, yet simultaneously manifesting in specific down-to-earth physical, emotional, and cognitive embodiments. They are enduring a priori structures and essences yet are also dynamically indeterminate, open to inflection by many contingent factors, cultural and biographical, circumstantial and participatory. They are in one sense timeless and above the changing flux of phenomena, as in the Platonic understanding, yet in another sense deeply malleable, evolving, and open to the widest diversity of creative human enaction. They seem to move from both within and without, manifesting as impulses, emotions, images, ideas, and interpretive structures in the interior psyche yet also as concrete forms, events, and contexts in the external world, including synchronistic phenomena. Finally, they can be discussed and thought of in a scientific or philosophical manner as first principles and formal causes, yet also be understood at another level in terms of mythic *personae dramatis* that are most adequately approached or apprehended through the powers of the poetic imagination or spiritual intuition. As Jung noted about his own mode of discourse when discussing the archetypal content of psychological phenomena:

> It is possible to describe this content in rational, scientific language, but in this way one entirely fails to express its living character. Therefore, in describing the living processes of the psyche, I deliberately and consciously give preference to a dramatic, mythological way of thinking and speaking, because this is not only more expressive but also more exact than an abstract scientific terminology, which is wont to toy with the notion that its theoretic formulations may one fine day be resolved into algebraic equations.

Planetary Archetypes

The astrological thesis as developed within the Platonic-Jungian lineage holds that these complex, multidimensional archetypes governing the forms of human experience are intelligibly connected with the planets and their movements in the heavens. This association is observable in a constant coincidence between specific planetary alignments and specific archetypally patterned phenomena in human affairs. It is important for what follows that we understand the nature of this correspondence between planets and archetypes. It does not appear to be accurate to say that astrologers have in essence arbitrarily used the mythological stories of the ancients about the gods Jupiter, Saturn, Venus, Mars, Mercury, and the rest to project symbolic meaning onto the planets, which are in actuality merely neutral material bodies without intrinsic significance. Rather, a considerable body of evidence suggests that the movements of the planets named Jupiter, Saturn, Venus, Mars, and Mercury tend to coincide with patterns of human experience that closely resemble the character of those planets' mythical counterparts. That is, the astrologer's insight, perhaps intuitive and divinatory in its ancient origins, appears to be fundamentally an empirical one. This empiricism is given context and meaning by a mythic, archetypal perspective, a perspective that the planetary correlations seem to support and illustrate with remarkable consistency. The nature of these correlations presents to the astrological researcher what appears to be an orchestrated synthesis combining the precision of mathematical astronomy with the psychological complexity of the archetypal imagination, a synthesis whose sources seemingly exist a priori within the fabric of the universe.

Here is where the distinction between the ancient philosophical (Platonic) and the modern psychological (earlier Jungian) conceptions of archetypes becomes especially relevant. Whereas the original Jungian archetypes were primarily considered to be the basic formal principles of the human psyche, the original Platonic archetypes were regarded as the essential principles of reality itself, rooted in the very nature of the cosmos.[7] What separated these two views was the long development of Western thought that gradually differentiated a meaning-giving human subject from a neutral objective world, thereby locating the source of any universal principles of meaning exclusively within the human psyche. Integrating these two views (much as Jung began to do in his final years under the influence of synchronicities), contemporary astrology suggests that archetypes possess a reality that is both objective and subjective, one that informs both outer cosmos and inner human psyche, "as above, so below."

In effect, planetary archetypes are considered to be both "Jungian" (psychological) and "Platonic" (metaphysical) in nature: universal essences or forms at once intrinsic to and independent of the human mind, that not only endure as timeless universals but are also co-creatively enacted and recursively affected through human participation. And they are regarded as functioning in something like a Pythagorean-Platonic cosmic setting, i.e., in a cosmos pervasively integrated through the workings of a universal intelligence and creative principle. What distinguishes the contemporary astrological view is the additional factor of human co-creative participation in the concrete expressions of this creative principle, with the human being recognized as itself a potentially autonomous embodiment of the cosmos and its creative power and intelligence.

In Jungian terms, the astrological evidence suggests that the collective unconscious is ultimately embedded in the macrocosm itself, with the planetary motions a synchronistic reflection of the unfolding archetypal dynamics of human experience. In Platonic terms, astrology affirms the existence of an *anima mundi* informing the cosmos, a world soul in which the human psyche participates as a microcosm of the whole. Finally, the Platonic, Jungian, and astrological understandings of archetypes are all complexly linked, both historically and conceptually, to the archetypal structures, narratives, and figures of ancient myth. Thus Campbell's famous dictum:

> It would not be too much to say that myth is the secret opening through which the inexhaustible energies of the cosmos pour into human cultural manifestation.

So also Jung: "I hold Kerényi to be absolutely right when he says that in the symbol the *world itself* is speaking."[8]

For conceptual clarity, then, when we consider the meaning and character of each planetary archetype in the following chapters, it will be useful to understand these principles in three different senses: in the Homeric sense as a primordial deity and mythic figure; in the Platonic sense as a cosmic and metaphysical principle; and in the Jungian sense as a psychological principle (with its Kantian and Freudian background)—with all of these associated with a specific planet. For example, the archetype of Venus can be approached on the Homeric level as the Greek mythic figure of Aphrodite, the goddess of beauty and love, the Mesopotamian Ishtar, the Roman Venus. On the Platonic level Venus can be understood in terms of the metaphysical principle of Eros and the Beautiful. And on the Jungian level Venus can be viewed as the psychological tendency to perceive, desire, create, or in some other way experience beauty and love, to attract and be attracted, to seek harmony and aesthetic or sensuous pleasure, to engage in artistic activity and in romantic and social relations. These different levels or senses are distinguished here only to suggest the inherent complexity of archetypes, which must be formulated not as literal concretely definable entities but rather as dynamic potentialities and essences of meaning that cannot be localized or restricted to a specific dimension.

Finally, alongside this essential *multidimensionality* of archetypes is their equally essential *multivalence*. The Saturn archetype can express itself as judgment but also as old age, as tradition but also as oppression, as time but also as mortality, as depression but also as discipline, as gravity in the sense of heaviness and weight but also as gravity in the sense of seriousness and dignity. Thus Jung:

> The ground principles, the *archai,* of the unconscious are indescribable because of their wealth of reference, although in themselves recognizable. The discriminating intellect naturally keeps on trying to establish their singleness of meaning and thus misses the essential point; for what we can above all establish as the one thing consistent with their nature is their manifold meaning, their almost limitless wealth of reference, which makes any unilateral formulation impossible.

This discussion is directly relevant to the outcome of our earlier consideration of free will and determinism in astrology. If I may summarize that thesis in a single statement: It seems to be specifically the multivalent potentiality that is intrinsic to the planetary archetypes—their dynamic indeterminacy—that opens up ontological space for the human being's full co-creative participation in the unfolding of individual life, history, and the cosmic process. It is just this combination of archetypal multivalence and an autonomous participatory self that engenders the possibility of a genuinely open universe. The resulting cosmological metastructure is still Pythagorean-Platonic in essential ways, but the relationship of the human self and the cosmic principles has undergone a metamorphosis that fully reflects and integrates the enormous modern and postmodern developments.

Our philosophical understanding of archetypes, our scientific understanding of the cosmos, and our psychological understanding of the self have all undergone a profound evolution in the course of history, and they have done so in complexly interconnected ways at each stage in this development. Our *experience* of all these has evolved, century by century, and thus our theories have as well.

The Planets

Wisdom is knowing in depth the great metaphors of meaning.
—C. G. Jung

There are ten planetary archetypes. Seven of these were recognized in the classical astrological tradition and correspond to the seven celestial bodies of the solar system visible to the unaided eye (Sun, Moon, Mercury, Venus, Mars, Jupiter, Saturn); the other three correspond to those planets discovered by telescope in the modern era (Uranus, Neptune, and Pluto).[9] The astrological tradition has long held that when astronomy was originally united with astrology, the ancients named the visible planets according to each one's intrinsic archetypal character, that is, according to the ruling mythic deity of which the planet was the visible manifestation. The earliest surviving Greek text that named all the known planets is the Platonist dialogue the *Epinomis*, which explicitly postulated a cosmic association between the planets and specific gods, speaking of them as cosmic powers and visible deities.[10] Written in the fourth century BCE as an appendix to Plato's last work, the *Laws* (and composed either by Plato himself or a close disciple), the *Epinomis* affirmed the divinity of the planets and then went on to introduce the specific Greek name for each planet according to the deity which that planet was understood to be "sacred to"—Hermes, Aphrodite, Ares, Zeus, Kronos. These Greek gods were cited as corresponding to the equivalent Mesopotamian deities whose names had long been associated with the planets by the already ancient astrological tradition inherited from Babylonia. In turn, in later centuries these planets became known in Europe and the modern West by the names of their Roman equivalents: Mercury, Venus, Mars, Jupiter, and Saturn.

It will be useful here as a preliminary summary to set forth the specific archetypal meanings and qualities associated with each planet. As Jung recognized, however, the meanings of archetypes cannot be reduced to simple definitions as if they were literal concrete entities whose basic essence could be exhausted once and for all with a neat algebraic formula:

A kind of fluid interpenetration belongs to the very nature of all archetypes. They can only be roughly circumscribed at best. Their living meaning comes out more from their presentation as a whole than from a single formulation. Every attempt to focus them more sharply is immediately punished by the intangible core of meaning losing its luminosity. No archetype can be reduced to a simple formula. It is a vessel which we can never empty, and never fill. . . . It persists throughout the ages and requires interpreting ever anew. The archetypes are the imperishable elements of the unconscious, but they change their shape continually.

An archetypal principle is thus not so much defined as evoked. It is better conveyed through a wide range of examples that collectively illustrate and suggest the enduring intangible essence that is variously inflected through the archetype's diverse embodiments. In the following chapters I have adopted this mode of presentation—a kind of self-presentation by the archetypes through their embodiments—as the one most appropriate to the nature of the principles and data we will be exploring. With these caveats and qualifications in mind, the following brief summary can serve as a starting point for the more extensive descriptions and analyses to come.

Each archetypal principle can express itself in both positive and problematic form. Each can express itself in the context of the individual life and psyche or on a collective level. Each has a potential for both feminine and masculine inflections beyond the specific gender of the Greco-Roman mythic figure associated with the planet or luminary in question. For all the planets, both those known to the ancients and those discovered in the modern era, the body of evidence we will be examining points to the existence of *transcultural* archetypal principles that inform and encompass the observed synchronistic patterns of meaning. The specific mythic deities of the more local cultural mythologies, such as the Greek or Roman, appear to represent particular inflections of these transcultural archetypes. The Greco-Roman figures and narratives are resonant with significance for the Western cultural imagination but ultimately seem to be best understood as culturally specific embodiments of more universal archetypal principles.

Sun: the central principle of vital creative energy, the will to exist; the impulse and capacity to *be*, to manifest, to be active, to be central, to radiate, to "shine"; to rise above, achieve, illuminate, and integrate; the individual will and personal identity, the seat of mind and spirit, the animus, the executive functions of the self or ego, the capacity for initiative and purposeful assertion, the drive for individual autonomy and independence; directed and focused consciousness and self-awareness, the centrifugal expression of the self, the trajectory of self-manifestation, ascent and descent; the ruler of the day sky, of the clearly visible, the single source of luminosity that overcomes the encompassing darkness, the monocentric; *yang;* the part that contains the whole *in potentia;* Sol and all solar deities, the archetypal Hero in its many forms.

Moon: the matrix of being, the psychosomatic foundation of the self, the womb and ground of life; the body and the soul, that which senses and intuits, the feeling nature; the impulse and capacity to gestate and bring forth, to receive and reflect, to relate and respond, to need and to care, to nurture and be nurtured, the condition of dependence and interdependence; the diffusely conscious and the unconscious, the anima, the immanent, the centripetal, the home, the fertile source and ground; the cycle of manifestation, the waxing and waning, the eternal round; the ruler of the night sky, of the diffusely visible and the invisible, multiple sources of luminosity within the encompassing darkness, the polycentric; *yin;* the whole that contains the part *in potentia;* Luna and all lunar deities, the Great Mother Goddess, together with aspects of the Child (*puella, puer*), constituting the relational matrix of life.

Mercury: the principle of mind, thought, communication, that which articulates the primary creative energy and renders it intelligible; the impulse and capacity to think, to conceptualize, to connect and mediate, to use words and language, to give and receive information; to make sense of, to grasp, to perceive and reason, understand and articulate; to transport, translate, transmit; the principle of Logos; Hermes, the messenger of the gods.

Venus: the principle of desire, love, beauty, value; the impulse and capacity to attract and be attracted, to love and be loved, to seek and create beauty and harmony, to engage in social and romantic relations, sensuous pleasure, artistic and aesthetic experience; the principle of Eros and the Beautiful; Aphrodite, the goddess of love and beauty.

Mars: the principle of energetic force; the impulse and capacity to assert, to act and move energetically and forcefully, to have an impact, to press forward and against, to defend and offend, to act with sharpness and ardor; the tendency to experience aggressiveness, anger, conflict, harm, violence, forceful physical energy; to be combative, competitive, courageous, vigorous; Ares, the god of war.

Jupiter: the principle of expansion, magnitude, growth, elevation, superiority; the capacity and impulse to enlarge and grow, to ascend and progress, to improve and magnify, to incorporate that which is external, to make greater wholes, to inflate; to experience success, honor, advancement, plenitude, abundance, prodigality, excess, surfeit; the capacity or inclination for magnanimity, optimism, enthusiasm, exuberance, joy, joviality, liberality, breadth of experience, philosophical and cultural aspiration, comprehensiveness and largeness of vision, pride, arrogance, aggrandizement, extravagance; fecundity, fortune, and providence; Zeus, the king of the Olympian gods.

Saturn: the principle of limit, structure, contraction, constraint, necessity, hard materiality, concrete manifestation; time, the past, tradition, age, maturity, mortality, the endings of things; gravity and gravitas, weightiness, that which burdens, binds, challenges, fortifies, deepens; the tendency to confine and constrict, to separate, to divide and define, to cut and shorten, to negate and oppose, to strengthen and forge through tension and resistance, to rigidify, to repress, to maintain a conservative and strict authority; to experience difficulty, decline, deprivation, defect and deficit, defeat, failure, loss, alienation; the labor of existence, suffering, old age, death; the weight of the past, the workings of fate, character, karma, the consequences of past action, error and guilt, punishment, retribution, imprisonment, the sense of "no exit"; pessimism, inferiority, inhibition, isolation, oppression and depression; the impulse and capacity for discipline and duty, order, solitude, concentration, conciseness, thoroughness and precision, discrimination and objectivity, restraint and patience, endurance, responsibility, seriousness, authority, wisdom; the harvest of time, effort, and experience; the concern with consensus reality, factual concreteness, conventional forms and structures, foundations, boundaries, solidity and stability, security and control, rational organization, efficiency, law, right and wrong, judgment, the superego; the dark, cold, heavy, dense, dry, old, slow, distant; the *senex*, Kronos, the stern father of the gods.

The above seven archetypal principles correspond to the seven celestial bodies known to the ancients and constituted the foundation of the astrological tradition from its prehistoric origins through the early modern era. These principles were well established in their basic character from the beginning of the classical Western astrological tradition in the early Hellenistic era, from around the second century BCE onward, and their meanings continued to develop and be elaborated through later antiquity, the medieval era, and the Renaissance not only in astrological practice and esoteric writings but in the art, literature, and evolving religious and scientific thought of the larger culture.

Of the seven, Saturn was the most distant, slowest-moving planet visible to the naked eye, and its complex of meanings directly reflected that status: the ruler of boundaries and limits, of finitude and endings, of distance, slowness, age, time, death, and fate. Many ancients, such as the Gnostics and initiates of the mystery religions, believed that beyond Saturn existed another realm ruled by a greater, more encompassing deity, a domain of freedom and immortality beyond the constraints of fate and death. As we move to a brief summary of Uranus, Neptune, and Pluto, of their discovery and their observed archetypal qualities, we move in time from the ancient to the modern, and in space from the orbit of Saturn to the much larger regions of space circumscribed by these three outlying planets, evocatively described by Rudhyar as "ambassadors of the galaxy."

Compared with the planets known to the ancients, with their Greco-Roman mythological associations and corresponding astrological meanings, the names and meanings of the three planets discovered by telescope in the modern era present a very different situation. Uranus, Neptune, and Pluto were named by modern astronomers without any archetypal correspondences in mind. They therefore inherited no archetypal meanings sanctioned by ancient tradition, meanings that were in turn affirmed, refined, and elaborated by continuing observations over many centuries. This circumstance formed the starting point for an unexpectedly fruitful line of research whose results inform the following chapters. Based on the astrological research community's expanding body of empirical correlations for all the planets, many insights and clarifications concerning the relationship between the planets' given astronomical names and their observed archetypal meanings have now emerged. While correlations involving the ancient planets out through Saturn consistently suggest a definite coherence between the planets' inherited mythological names and the observed synchronistic phenomena, correlations involving the outer three planets point to archetypal principles that in crucial respects differ from or radically transcend their astronomical names.

Uranus: For millennia, the Sun and Moon, Mercury, Venus, Mars, Jupiter, and Saturn formed what the ancients considered to be an absolute cosmic structure of moving celestial bodies reflecting the primordial forces that governed human affairs. Then in 1781 the astronomer and musician William Herschel, while conducting an exhaustive survey of the heavens using a telescope of his own design, suddenly observed an object that was not an ordinary star. The object turned out to be the first planet to be discovered since antiquity. Herschel's stunning discovery immediately transformed the dimensions of the known solar system, the new planet being twice as far from the Sun as Saturn. It also presented an unprecedented challenge to the astrological tradition. The ancient seven-planet hierarchy circumscribed by Saturn had been irrevocably disrupted, with no established archetypal meaning for the new planet. Contemporary skeptics viewed its discovery as having placed the last nail in the coffin of a discredited astrology whose demise had been caused by the Scientific Revolution and proclaimed by the Enlightenment.

Astronomers considered several names for the new planet. Herschel first proposed the name Georgium Sidus in honor of his sovereign patron, George III of England. The French, no doubt unenthusiastic about the planetary deification of an English monarch, used the name Herschel. In the end, in keeping with the planets known to the ancients, the pantheon of classical mythology was called upon. The German astronomer Johann Elert Bode had suggested the name Uranus in the year of its discovery, and it was this name that eventually received international acceptance. The logic for naming the new planet Uranus seems to have been straightforward: The mythological Ouranos was the father of Kronos (Saturn) and thus corresponded to the location of the new planet beyond Saturn in the heavens, just as Saturn was both the father of Jupiter in mythology and the name of the next planet beyond Jupiter in the heavens. Ouranos was also the god of "the starry sky," as Hesiod called him, thus providing what seemed to be an especially apt name for the new planet. Astrologers adopted the name Uranus as well, but the meaning they eventually came to attribute to the new planet was generally different in character from that of the mythological Ouranos.

Since at least the turn of the twentieth century, the unanimous consensus among astrologers is that the planet Uranus is empirically associated with the principle of change, rebellion, freedom, liberation, reform and revolution, and the unexpected breakup of structures; with sudden surprises, revelations and awakenings, lightning-like flashes of insight, the acceleration of thoughts and events; with births and new beginnings of all kinds; and with intellectual brilliance, cultural innovation, technological invention, experiment, creativity, and originality. In addition to the occurrence of sudden breakthroughs and liberating events, Uranus transits are linked to unpredictable and disruptive changes; hence the planet is often referred to as the "cosmic trickster." Another set of themes associated with Uranus is a concern with the celestial and the cosmic, with astronomy and astrology, with science and esoteric knowledge, and with space travel and aviation. With respect to personal character, Uranus is regarded as signifying the rebel and the innovator, the awakener, the individualist, the dissident, the eccentric, the restless and wayward. These various qualities are considered to be so pronounced in persons born with a prominent Uranus and expressed so conspicuously in a person's life during Uranus transits that there seems to have been no significant disagreement among astrological authorities for at least the past century that these characteristics reflect the archetypal nature of the planet Uranus.

Most of these observed qualities, however, are not especially relevant to the Greek mythic figure of Ouranos. There is nothing in the mythological Ouranos's character suggestive of the capacity or impulse for change, rebellion, liberation, awakening, or inventiveness. The tenor of the myth is entirely different: Ouranos is the primordial god of the heavens, found in many mythologies, whose relationship to the Earth goddess Gaia forms part of the Greek creation myth. Ouranos's role in that myth is not to initiate rebellion and change but to resist it. Where the mythological Ouranos encountered a revolt by his progeny and was overthrown, the astrological Uranus is regarded as quite the opposite: that which rebels and overthrows. Most of the other qualities believed by astrologers to be associated with the planet Uranus—freedom, unpredictability, suddenness, speed, excitement, stimulation, restlessness, experiment, brilliance, originality, individualism, and so forth—have no plausible counterparts in the myth of Ouranos. The important exception among the qualities and themes attributed to Uranus is the concern with the cosmic and celestial, with space and space travel, and with astronomy and astrology, all of which well fit Ouranos's nature as the god of the "starry sky." Aside from this crucial parallel, however, unlike the planets known to the ancients, the planet Uranus does not closely correspond in its mythological name with the larger range of its observed astrological meanings. In most respects, the naming appears to have risen from the conventional logic of late eighteenth-century astronomers, not from the intuitive archetypal insight that is traditionally assumed to have played a role in the naming of the ancient planets.

Remarkably, however, all of the archetypal qualities associated with the new planet do fit another figure in Greek mythology with extraordinary precision: Prometheus, the Titan who rebelled against the gods, helped Zeus overthrow the tyrannical Kronos, then tricked the new sovereign authority Zeus and stole fire from the heavens to liberate humanity from the gods' power. Prometheus was considered the wisest of his race and taught humankind all the arts and sciences; in a later tradition, Prometheus was the creator of humankind and thus held a special relationship to humanity's fate from the beginning. Every major theme and quality that astrologers associate with the planet Uranus seems to be reflected in the myth of Prometheus with striking poetic exactitude: the initiation of radical change, the passion for freedom, the defiance of authority, the act of cosmic rebellion against a universal structure to free humanity of bondage, the urge to transcend limitation, the creative impulse, the intellectual brilliance and genius, the element of excitement and risk. So also Prometheus's style in outwitting the gods, when he used subtle stratagems and unexpected timing to upset the established order. He too was regarded as the trickster in the cosmic scheme. The resonant symbol of Prometheus's fire conveys at once a rich cluster of meanings—the creative spark, the catalyst of the new, cultural and technological breakthrough, brilliance and innovation, the enhancement of human autonomy, sudden inspiration from above, the liberating gift from the heavens, the solar fire and light, lightning and electricity both literal and metaphoric, speed and instantaneousness, incandescence, sudden enlightenment, intellectual and spiritual awakening—all of which astrologers associate specifically with the planet Uranus.

Even the major theme of the astrological Uranus that *was* clearly relevant to the mythological Ouranos—the association with the heavens, the cosmic, the astronomical and astrological, "the starry sky"—can be recognized as essential to the Promethean myth, visible in Prometheus's role as teacher of astronomy and science to humankind, his quest to steal the fire from the heavens, and his concern with foresight, prediction, and esoteric understanding in defiance of the established order. The same theme is evident in the essential Promethean impulse to ascend and liberate from all constraints, to break free from the weight and slowness of gravity, and, more generally, to move humankind into a fundamentally different cosmic position in relation to the gods.

The extant astrological literature does not reveal the precise basis originally used to determine Uranus's astrological meaning in the course of the nineteenth century, when astrologers were few and texts rare. Texts from the beginning of the twentieth century imply that consensus on the basic themes and qualities had already been achieved some time before. It is possible that the unique (and, indeed, Promethean) character of the planet's discovery itself had suggested the nature of the principle involved: the sudden breakthrough from the heavens, the unexpected and unprecedented nature of the event, the crucial involvement of a technological invention (telescope), the radical disruption of astronomical and astrological tradition, the overthrow of past limits and structures. However, the earliest nineteenth-century texts to discuss Uranus in detail referred mainly to certain qualities in persons born with Uranus prominently placed (inventiveness, independence, eccentricity, proneness to sudden unexpected changes), implying that the study of natal charts had served as the principal basis for arriving at a definition.

More recent astrological sources suggested that the historical period of the planet's discovery in the late eighteenth century was relevant to its archetypal meaning, reasoning that the discovery of the physical planet in some sense represented an emergence of the planet's corresponding archetype into the conscious awareness of the collective psyche. In this regard the parallels with Uranus's astrological meaning were certainly clear: The planet's discovery in 1781 occurred at the culmination of the Enlightenment, in the extraordinary era that brought forth the American and French Revolutions, the Industrial Revolution, and the beginning of Romanticism. In all these coinciding historical phenomena, the figure of Prometheus is of course readily evident as well: the championing of human freedom and individual self-determination, the challenge to traditional beliefs and customs, the fervent revolt against royalty and aristocracy, established religion, social privilege, and political oppression; the Declaration of Independence and the Declaration of the Rights of Man, *liberté* and *egalité*; the beginnings of feminism, the widespread interest in radical ideas, the rapidity of change, the embrace of novelty, the celebration of human progress, the many inventions and technological advances, the revolutions in art and literature, the exaltation of the free human imagination and creative will, the plethora of geniuses and culture heroes. Here too were the Romantic poets with their great paeans to Prometheus himself. If the age of Uranus's discovery is to be given an archetypal characterization, none seems more appropriate than "Prometheus Unbound."

I have taken more time here in explicating the case of Uranus in the midst of these otherwise brief initial summaries of the planetary meanings because it was my early study of this planet and the significant discrepancies between its given mythological name and its subsequently observed archetypal associations that set in motion many of the conceptual clarifications and research directions that formed the background of the present book.[11] The parallels with the mythic figure of Prometheus were sufficiently suggestive that I began a systematic examination of Uranus in natal charts, in transits, and in historical cycles to see whether such an archetypal identification or association deepened my understanding of the relevant phenomena. The parallels also suggested to me the importance of carefully thinking through the relationship between planets and archetypes, between the given mythological names and the observed astrological meanings, and, more generally, between the empirical evidence of synchronistic correlations and an archetypal dimension of being to which the correlations appeared to point.

Neptune: In 1846, on the basis of unexplained aberrations in the observed orbit of Uranus, the French mathematician Urbain LeVerrier posited the existence and position of a planet beyond Uranus whose gravitational influence was pulling Uranus out of its calculated orbit. The new planet was immediately discovered in the predicted position by the German astronomer Johann Galle in 1846 and named Neptune after the god of the sea.[12] In the ensuing decades, astrologers again gradually arrived at a surprisingly universal consensus on the principal qualities and themes observed to coincide with the new planet's position in natal charts and transits.

Neptune is associated with the transcendent, spiritual, ideal, symbolic, and imaginative dimensions of life; with the subtle, formless, intangible, and invisible; with the unitive, timeless, immaterial, and infinite; with all that which transcends the limited literal temporal and material world of concretely empirical reality: myth and religion, art and inspiration, ideals and aspirations, images and reflections, symbols and metaphors, dreams and visions, mysticism, religious devotion, universal compassion. It is associated with the impulse to surrender separative existence and egoic control, to dissolve boundaries and structures in favor of underlying unities and undifferentiated wholes, merging that which was separate, healing and wholeness; the dissolution of ego boundaries and reality structures, states of psychological fusion and intimations of intrauterine existence, melted ecstasy, mystical union, and primary narcissism; with tendencies towards illusion and delusion, deception and self-deception, escapism, intoxication, psychosis, perceptual and cognitive distortions, conflation and confusion, projection, fantasy; with the bedazzlement of consciousness whether by gods, archetypes, beliefs, dreams, ideals, or ideologies; with enchantment, in both positive and negative senses.

The archetypal principle linked to Neptune governs all nonordinary states of consciousness as well as the stream of consciousness and the oceanic depths of the unconscious. Characteristic metaphors for its domain include the infinite sea of the imagination, the ocean of divine consciousness, and the archetypal wellspring of life. It is in a sense the archetype of the archetypal dimension itself, the *anima mundi,* the Gnostic pleroma, the Platonic realm of transcendent Ideas, the domain of the gods, the Immortals. In mythic and religious terms, it is associated with the all-encompassing womb of the Goddess and with all deities of mystical union, universal love, and transcendent beauty; the mystical Christ, the all-compassionate Buddha, the Atman-Brahman union, the union of Shiva and Shakti, the *hieros gamos* or sacred marriage, the *coniunctio oppositorum;* the dreaming Vishnu, *maya* and *lila,* the self-reflecting Narcissus, the divine absorbed in its own reflection; Orpheus, god of artistic inspiration, the Muses; the cosmic Sophia whose spiritual beauty and wisdom pervade all.

Considered as a whole, these themes, qualities, and figures suggest that the name Neptune is both apt and inadequate in denoting a mythological figure embodying the planet's corresponding archetypal principle. On the one hand, central to the observed characteristics is an underlying symbolic association with water, the sea, the ocean, streams and rivers, mists and fogs, liquidity and dissolution, the amniotic and prenatal, the permeable and undifferentiated. In this regard, one thinks of the many oceanic and watery metaphors used to describe mystical experience, the all-encompassing ocean of divine consciousness of which our individual selves are but momentarily separate drops, the ceaselessly flowing all-informing Tao whose waterlike fluidity evades all definition, the primordial *participation mystique* of undifferentiated awareness, the mists of prehistory, the amniotic fetal and infantile state of primary fusion, the oceanic realms of the imagination, the fluid nature of psychic life generally: the flow and stream of consciousness, the influx of inspiration, the fog of confusion, drowning in the treacherous deep waters of the unconscious psyche, slipping into madness or addiction, surrendering to the flow of experience, dissolving into the divine union, the cleansing waters of purity and healing, melted ecstasy, and so forth. One thinks here, too, of Freud's reference to the "oceanic feeling": "a sensation of 'eternity,' a feeling as of something limitless, unbounded—as it were, 'oceanic'. . . . it is the feeling of an indissoluble bond, of being one with the external world as a whole." Equally relevant is William James's image of a transcendental "mother-sea" of consciousness with which the individual consciousness is continuous and of which the brain essentially serves as a sieve or filtering conduit.[13]

On the other hand, in virtually all other respects the original mythological character of the Roman Neptune and the Greek Poseidon—tempestuous, violent, belligerent, often ill-tempered and vengeful (thus resembling most of the other Greco-Roman patriarchal warrior gods)—is deeply incongruent with the complex set of qualities and themes that have been consistently observed in connection with the planet Neptune and that are more accurately reflected in the mystically unitive deities and archetypal figures cited above. Nevertheless, as with Uranus's mythological association with the starry heavens and air, so also with Neptune's association with the sea and water: the name given to the new planet was indeed poetically accurate with respect to the mythological location and element associated with that deity, perhaps a reflection of synchronistic factors playing a role in the astronomers' intuition and choice of names.

As with the period of Uranus's discovery in 1781, the discovery of Neptune in 1846 coincided with a range of synchronistic historical and cultural phenomena in the immediately surrounding decades, and more generally in the nineteenth century, that are distinctly suggestive of the corresponding archetype. These include the rapid spread of spiritualism throughout the world beginning in the late 1840s, the upsurge of utopian social ideologies at the same time, the rise of universalist and communitarian aspirations in both secular and religious movements, the full ascendancy of Idealist and Romantic philosophies of spirit and the imagination, the widespread cultural influence of Transcendentalism, the new popular interest in both Eastern mystical and Western esoteric traditions, and the emergence of theosophy. Here too could be cited the rise of the recreational use of psychoactive drugs in European bohemian circles, the beginning of the chemical and pharmaceutical industries, and the invention of anesthetics. The invention and cultural impact of photography and the early experiments in motion pictures, as well as the new aesthetic spirit of Impressionism and Post-Impressionism, were characteristic of the Neptune archetype in its association with image, reflection, subjectivity, illusion, and multiple realities. The growing focus on the unconscious, dreams, myths, hypnosis, and non-ordinary states of consciousness in the decades after Neptune's discovery is also suggestive of the archetype. So also was the distinct collective emergence of a more socially compassionate humanitarian sensibility that was expressed in the public attitudes, social legislation, art and literature of the Victorian era and the nineteenth century generally (the novels of Dickens and Stowe, Tolstoy and Dostoevsky, the abolition of slavery and serfdom, the movements and laws to limit child labor and other cruelties of industrial capitalism, the first laws abolishing capital punishment, the wave of foundings of societies for the protection of animals, the growing role of women in shaping social policy, the beginning of modern nursing through the work of Florence Nightingale, the spread of care for the sick and wounded in war, the first Geneva Convention, the founding of the International Red Cross, etc.).

Pluto: On the basis of discrepancies observed in the orbit of Neptune and aberrations yet unexplained in the orbit of Uranus, the existence of a further planet was posited by the American astronomer Percival Lowell, which led to its discovery in 1930 by Clyde Tombaugh. After much consideration among many alternatives, the new planet was named Pluto, god of the underworld. Observations of potential correlations with Pluto by astrologers in the subsequent decades suggested that the qualities associated with the new planet in fact bore a striking relevance to the mythic character of Pluto, the Greek Hades, and also to the figure of Dionysus, with whom Hades-Pluto was closely associated by the Greeks. (Both Heraclitus and Euripides identified Dionysus and Hades as one and the same deity.) Closely analogous to Freud's concept of the primordial id, "the broiling cauldron of the instincts," and to Darwin's understanding of an ever-evolving nature and the biological struggle for existence, the archetype associated with the planet Pluto is also linked to Nietzsche's Dionysian principle and the will to power and to Schopenhauer's blind striving universal will, all these embodying the powerful forces of nature and emerging from nature's chthonic depths, within and without, the intense, fiery elemental underworld. Again, as with both Uranus and Neptune, so also in Pluto's case the mythological domain and element associated with the new planet's given name appear to be poetically accurate, but here the archetypal parallels between the mythic figure and the observed qualities are especially extensive.

Beyond these ancient Greco-Roman figures (Pluto, Hades, Dionysus) and cognate modern European concepts (Freudian id, Darwinian nature, Schopenhauerian will, Nietzschean will to power and Dionysian impulse), the archetype associated with the planet Pluto also encompasses a number of major deities outside the Western context, such as the Hindu deity Shiva, god of destruction and creation, and Kali and Shakti, goddesses of erotic power and elemental transformation, destruction and regeneration, death and rebirth.

To summarize the consensus of contemporary astrologers: Pluto is associated with the principle of elemental power, depth, and intensity; with that which compels, empowers, and intensifies whatever it touches, sometimes to overwhelming and catastrophic extremes; with the primordial instincts, libidinal and aggressive, destructive and regenerative, volcanic and cathartic, eliminative, transformative, ever-evolving; with the biological processes of birth, sex, and death, the cycle of death and rebirth; with upheaval, breakdown, decay, and fertilization; violent purgatorial discharge of pent-up energies, purifying fire; situations of life-and-death extremes, power struggles, all that is titanic, potent, and massive. Pluto represents the underworld and underground in all senses: elemental, geological, instinctual, political, social, sexual, urban, criminal, mythological, demonic. It is the dark, mysterious, taboo, and often terrifying reality that lurks beneath the surface of things, beneath the ego, societal conventions, and the veneer of civilization, beneath the surface of the Earth, that is periodically unleashed with destructive and transformative force. Pluto impels, burns, consumes, transfigures, resurrects. In mythic and religious terms, it is associated with all myths of descent and transformation, and with all deities of destruction and regeneration, death and rebirth: Dionysus, Hades and Persephone, Pan, Medusa, Lilith, Innana, Isis and Osiris, the volcano goddess Pele, Quetzalcoatl, the Serpent power, Kundalini, Shiva, Kali, Shakti.

With respect to Pluto's discovery, the synchronistic phenomena in the decades immediately surrounding 1930, and more generally in the twentieth century, include the splitting of the atom and the unleashing of nuclear power; the titanic technological empowerment of modern industrial civilization and military force; the rise of fascism and other mass movements; the widespread cultural influence of evolutionary theory and psychoanalysis with their focus on the biological instincts; increased sexual and erotic expression in social mores and the arts; intensified activity and public awareness of the criminal underworld; and a tangible intensification of instinctually driven mass violence and catastrophic historical developments, evident in the world wars, the holocaust, and the threat of nuclear annihilation and ecological devastation. Here also can be mentioned the intensified politicization and power struggles characteristic of twentieth-century life, the development of powerful forms of depth-psychological transformation and catharsis, and the scientific recognition of the entire cosmos as a vast evolutionary phenomenon from the primordial fireball to the still-evolving present.

In retrospect, the discoveries of Uranus, Neptune, and Pluto appear to have coincided with the emergence of three fundamental archetypes into collective human experience in a newly constellated form, visible in major historical events and cultural trends of the eighteenth century (Uranus), the nineteenth (Neptune), and the twentieth (Pluto). The centuries of their discoveries in each case appear to have brought forth in the evolution of human consciousness the rapid development and radical heightening of a distinctive set of qualities and impulses that were also systematically observable in precise natal and transit correlations involving those specific planets for individuals and eras throughout history. Although the astrological tradition developed on the basis of the seven ancient celestial bodies and their inherited meanings, much of the evidence we will be examining involves alignments of these three outer planets whose corresponding archetypal principles appear to be particularly relevant for illuminating the deeper transpersonal and collective patterns of human experience.

The discoveries in the past several years of small planet-like objects in the Kuiper Belt beyond Pluto, probably the remnants of a very early stage in the evolution of the solar system, are too recent for adequate assessments to have been made concerning possible empirical correlations or their potential significance. The resulting reclassification of Pluto as a dwarf planet does not affect the archetypal meaning that astrologers have consistently observed to coincide with its movements. However, the newly discovered bodies appearing at the beginning of the new millennium, with their unusual and vast orbits and ambiguous astronomical status, serve well to remind both astronomers and astrologers of the still-expanding horizon of our knowledge of our own solar system.

We turn now to the basic theoretical principles by means of which astrologers have observed and interpreted correlations between planetary movements and the archetypal patterns of human experience.

☉	Sun	♃	Jupiter
☽	Moon	♄	Saturn
☿	Mercury	♅	Uranus
♀	Venus	♆	Neptune
♂	Mars	♇	Pluto

Planetary Symbols

Figure 5

Forms of Correspondence

It is a peculiar fact that every major advance in thinking, every epoch-making new insight, springs from a new type of symbolic transformation.

—Suzanne K. Langer
Philosophy in a New Key

As the astrological tradition developed, the observed correspondence between planetary movements and the patterns of human affairs took a number of forms, of which three are now considered most essential:

The natal chart: The positions of the planets relative to the time and place of an individual's birth are regarded as bearing a significant correspondence to that person's life as a whole, reflecting the specific archetypal dynamics and relationships expressed in his or her specific psychological tendencies and biography.

Personal transits: The positions of the planets at any given time in relation to their positions at an individual's birth are regarded as bearing a significant correspondence to the specific experiences of that person at that time, reflecting a dynamic activation of the archetypal potential symbolized in the natal chart.

World transits: The positions of the planets relative to the Earth at any given time are regarded as bearing a significant correspondence to the prevailing state of the world, reflecting the state of collective archetypal dynamics visible in the specific historical and cultural conditions and events of that time.

In all three forms of correspondence, the particulars of the planetary interaction—which planets are involved and how they are geometrically aligned with each other—are considered to be the most important determining factors in understanding the corresponding human phenomena. These three forms of correspondence can be understood as different expressions of Jung's basic principle of qualitative time cited earlier, in which time is "a concrete continuum which contains qualities or fundamentals which can manifest themselves in relative simultaneousness in different places and in a parallelism which cannot be explained, as in cases of simultaneous appearance of identical thoughts, symbols, or psychic conditions. . . . Whatever is born or done at this particular moment of time has the quality of this moment of time." In this view, time is characterized not only by quantity, as in the conventional scientific understanding, but also by quality, the latter as tangible as the former is measurable.

From an astrological perspective, the planetary archetypes constitute a kind of Olympian pantheon of fundamental principles governing the ever-shifting qualitative dynamics of time. The birth of any being or phenomenon—whether a person, a work of art, a cultural movement, an historical phenomenon, a nation, a community, or any other organism or creative emergence—is seen as reflecting and embodying the archetypal dynamics implicit at the time of birth, and creatively unfolding those dynamics over the course of its life. In Jung's words, "We are born at a given moment, in a given place, and we have, like celebrated vintages, the same qualities of the year and of the season which saw our birth."

A birth chart or natal chart (horoscope) is a geometrical portrait of the heavens from the perspective of the Earth at the moment of an individual's birth. The Sun, Moon, and planets are positioned around the chart to reflect their positions around the Earth when the person was born. For example, where the symbol for the Sun is located in the chart reflects the time of day at which the person was born. If one were born at dawn, the Sun would be shown rising on the left side of the chart near the eastern horizon, called the Ascendant; if one were born at noon, the Sun would be at the top of the chart, called the Midheaven or MC (*Medium Coeli*). A birth at sunset, with the Sun on the western horizon, would be shown with the Sun on the right side of the chart at the Descendant; a midnight birth would be shown with the Sun at the base of the chart, the IC (*Imum Coeli*).

Thus the natal chart of a person born at dawn at the time of a Full Moon would show the Sun positioned at the Ascendant on the left and the Moon at the Descendant on the right, reflecting the Sun's rising in the east and the Moon's setting in the west, as in Figure 6. If Jupiter had been high overhead at the time of birth, it would be shown near the Midheaven.

The principal difference between a natal chart and the astronomical reality it portrays is that the natal chart has two dimensions rather than three and does not reflect the varying distances of the Sun, Moon, and planets from the Earth. As a simplified schematic diagram, its primary purpose is to convey accurately the exact pattern of angular relationships existing at a given moment between the celestial bodies and the Earth in the larger cosmic environment.

Personal transits to the birth chart can be depicted by placing outside the circle of the chart the celestial positions of the transiting planets in the sky at any given time, so as to clarify their current geometrical alignments with the natal planetary positions shown inside the circle. The nature of those patterns—

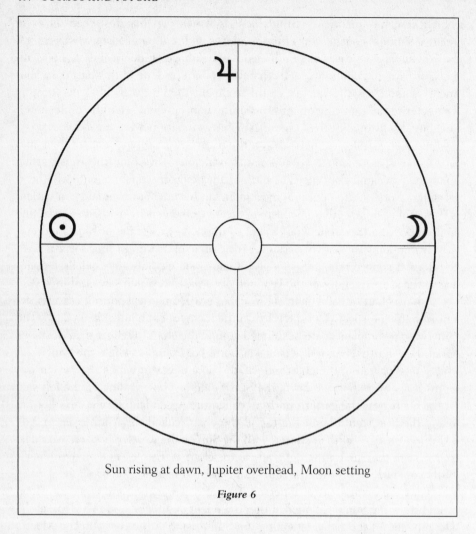

Sun rising at dawn, Jupiter overhead, Moon setting

Figure 6

which planets and how they are positioned—appears to correlate in a strikingly consistent way with the archetypal character of the individual's experiences at that time. Each planet or luminary has a different length of orbit; consequently, each body's transits are of a proportionately different duration. Transits of the Moon last several hours; transits of the Sun, Mercury, Venus, or Mars last several days; transits of Jupiter and Saturn last several months; and transits of Uranus, Neptune, and Pluto last several years.

World transits, like a birth chart, represent the planetary positions with respect to the Earth at a given moment. The most significant correlations in this category involve long-term cyclical alignments of the outer planets coinciding with distinct archetypal patterns in collective historical and cultural phenomena, with a duration of many months or years at a time.

The archetypal potential symbolized by the planetary alignments at any given moment is thus observed both in the collective dynamics and cultural phenomena that occurred at that time (world transits) and in the lives and personalities of individuals who were born at that time (natal charts). These individuals then embody and unfold that dynamic potential in the course of their lives, and the timing of this unfolding development is observed to coincide with the continuing planetary movements of the world transits as these form specific geometrical relationships (personal transits) to the natal planetary positions. In essence, the precise interaction between the world transits and the natal chart at any given moment constitutes the individual's current personal transits.

From this perspective, each person and each period of time is informed by multiple archetypal forces in dynamic interplay. The research set forth in the following chapters involves the examination of correlations between particular planetary alignments (transits) and what appears to be the simultaneous activation of corresponding archetypal complexes in specific individual lives and historical periods. I use the term "complex" here (in the noun form, as when discussing a particular "archetypal complex") to signify a coherent field of archetypally connected meanings, experiences, and psychological tendencies—expressed in perceptions, emotions, images, attitudes, beliefs, fantasies, and memories, as well as in synchronistic external events and historical and cultural phenomena— all of which appear to be informed by a dominant archetypal principle or combination of such principles. An archetypal complex can be conceived of as the experiential equivalent of a force field or a magnetic field in physics, producing an integrated pattern or gestalt out of many diverse particulars. Any given archetypal complex always contains problematic and pathological shadow tendencies intertwined with more salutary, fruitful, and creative ones, all of which inhere *in potentia* in each complex.

Cycles and Aspects

In the course of every planetary cycle as viewed from the Earth, each planet moves into and out of certain significant alignments or geometrical relationships with respect to every other planet. These alignments are called *aspects*. The presence of an aspect between planets is regarded as indicating a distinct mutual activation and interaction of the corresponding planetary archetypes. That is, when two planets enter into a specific geometrical relationship (measured in degrees of celestial longitude along the zodiacal circle of the ecliptic), the two corresponding archetypes are observed to be in a state of heightened dynamic interaction and concrete expression in human affairs. This was for Kepler the most fundamental and empirically validated principle in astrology:

> Experience, more than anything else, gives credibility to the effectiveness of aspects. This is so clear that it can be denied only by those who themselves have not tried them.

That power that makes the aspects effective [is] a reflection of God, who creates according to geometric principles, and is activated by this very geometry or harmony of the celestial aspects.

Five such alignments were recognized by the Greeks as most significant. They are now referred to as the *major aspects:*

> Conjunction (0°)
> Opposition (180°)
> Trine (120°)
> Square (90°)
> Sextile (60°)

The conjunction and opposition—the "axial" alignments—represent the two climaxes of every planetary cycle. For example, the New Moon each month is formed by the Moon's conjunction with the Sun, the Full Moon by its opposition to the Sun. The other major aspects represent significant intermediate points in the unfolding cycle. Generally speaking, the conjunction, opposition, and two squares—together constituting the "quadrature" aspects—are regarded as indicating a more dynamic and potentially critical ("hard") interaction between two planetary archetypes. The two trines and two sextiles that occur during each cycle are seen as reflecting a more intrinsically harmonious and confluent ("soft") interaction.

The forming of a major aspect between two planets is seen as coinciding with a significant mutual activation of the two corresponding archetypes, and the nature or vector of that interaction reflects which specific aspect has been formed. Both the astrological tradition and contemporary research suggest that it is especially the hard-aspect quadrature alignments in any given cycle (conjunction, opposition, squares) that coincide with highly dynamic archetypal tendencies and decisive concrete events reflecting that dynamism. By contrast, the soft aspects (trines and sextiles) are regarded as reflecting harmonious and potentially generative states of being in which those principles are fully present and mutually activated but in a manner that is generally less challenging, less dynamically evident, and less likely to be correlated with stressfully constellated concrete events.

As the planets move close to and then away from exact alignment, the concrete archetypal expression of the aspect is observed to gradually intensify until exactitude is reached and then diminish gradually afterwards in a wavelike continuum, with the general shape of a bell curve. To be considered "in aspect," two planets must be positioned within a certain range of degrees of exactitude. This range of degrees on each side of exactitude within which the alignment is considered to be archetypally operative is called an *orb.* The specific orb varies according to aspect (a conjunction having a wider orb than a sextile) and also varies

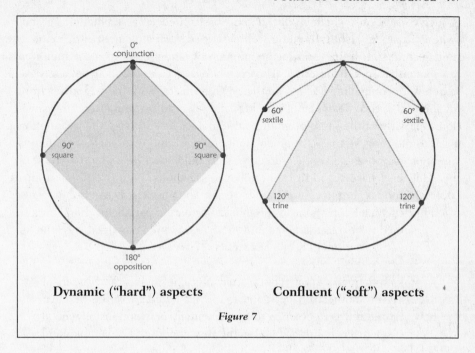

Dynamic ("hard") aspects   **Confluent ("soft") aspects**

Figure 7

according to the form of correspondence involved (aspects in natal charts and world transits having wider orbs than aspects in personal transits).

Generally speaking, in the theoretical framework outlined here, the most important astronomical factors to know are which planets are in major aspect, which aspects are involved, and how close to exact are the alignments.

These few concepts and principles—the three basic forms of correspondence, the five major aspects, and a progressively deepening understanding of the specific meanings of the ten planetary archetypes—formed the essential theoretical structure for the research surveyed in this book. Though many other factors, such as the twelve zodiacal signs (Aries through Pisces) and the twelve diurnal sectors of the chart called houses, play a significant role in both traditional and contemporary astrological practice, I consistently found that it was correlations involving the major planetary aspects in natal charts, personal transits, and world transits that seemed to represent the fundamental core of the astrological perspective and offered the most cogent and clarifying path of entry into this field of study.[14]

Yet beyond the specific principles outlined above, perhaps the most essential element in the research paradigm was the basic nature of my approach to the evidence and the possibility of discovering significant correlations. This approach emerged only after I had encountered what was in effect a critical mass of such correlations, which produced in my basic intellectual orientation a gestalt switch or paradigm shift, as Kuhn well described such a change: in this case, a fundamental shift from a starting assumption of randomness to the assumption of a potential underlying order. The correlations I came upon in my early research were compelling enough on their own terms to move me tentatively from my initial skeptical dismissal of astrology and to set in motion a fuller investigation. But without the more profound epistemological shift from the assumption of a cosmic process that is fundamentally random and meaningless to the assumption of a potential subtle orderedness, I would never have glimpsed most of the evidence I have set forth in the following chapters. One is unlikely to discover what one is certain cannot possibly exist. The physicist David Bohm recognized just this fatal constraint in the modern scientific paradigm: "Randomness is . . . assumed to be a fundamental but inexplicable and unanalyzable feature of nature, and indeed ultimately of all existence." However,

> what is randomness in one context may reveal itself as simple orders of necessity in another broader context. . . . It should therefore be clear how important it is to be open to fundamentally new notions of general order, if science is not to be blind to the very important but complex and subtle orders that escape the coarse mesh of the"net" on current ways of thinking.

Whatever the field of inquiry, attempting to assess a phenomenon with a methodology that is based on the firm underlying assumption that the phenomenon does not exist has proved itself to be a singularly inadequate strategy, at once self-fulfilling and self-limiting. For the the present research, critical rigor was necessary, but so also was a certain openness of mind and spirit, and patience to allow authentic patterns and deeper meanings to emerge with time and further observation.

The other essential factor making possible the present research was a technical one. In the course of the past thirty years, because of rapid advances in computer technology and the development of increasingly sophisticated programs for the calculation of planetary positions over long periods of time, I was gradually able to gain access to precise astronomical data for all the planets extending for many centuries into the past: first the twentieth and nineteenth centuries, then the earlier modern period going back to the Renaissance, then the medieval era, and finally classical antiquity.[15] For myself as well as for many other researchers, these technical advances created a gradually opening horizon extending back in time further and further as the years passed and the research progressed. Compared with the situation facing previous generations of researchers, the sudden availability of such extensive accurate planetary data permitted us to investigate many significant cultural figures and historical events that had long been inaccessible to such analysis.

Personal Transit Cycles

In the following chapters, we will examine correlations for all three forms of correspondence: natal charts, personal transits, and world transits. Although natal chart analysis has been the basis for most modern astrological research and practice, and although study of my own and others' birth charts was certainly crucial in my growing recognition of astrology's possible validity, it was the analysis of personal transits that first fully compelled my attention. The study of personal transits is particularly illuminating because it involves the precise correlation of life events with two sets of astronomical factors: planetary positions currently in the sky and planetary positions in the individual's natal chart, the one set aligning with the other, each with their own specific archetypal meanings depending on which planets are involved. If both the timing of a particular life event and its archetypal quality are found to correlate with the appropriate planetary transits across the appropriate natal planetary positions, the possible implications can more readily be assessed.

Awakenings, Rebellions, Breakthroughs: The Uranus Cycle

The transits of the Sun, the Moon, and the inner planets—Mercury, Venus, and Mars—are fast-moving and brief in duration. The five outer planets move more slowly, and their transits can last several months or years. It is these that hold the most significance for biographical research. Surprisingly, considering the longer astrological tradition, the first set of correlations I observed that alerted me to the potential importance of personal transits centered not on one of the planets known to the ancients that had always been part of the astrological tradition, but rather on the planet Uranus, the first one discovered by telescope in the modern age.

With what still now seems to me stunning regularity, I found that transiting Uranus in the sky happened to be in precise geometrical alignment with planets in individuals' natal charts during the periods in which those individuals underwent major biographical shifts having an underlying character of sudden change, creative awakening, and unexpected disruption of established life structures: psychological turning points and breakthroughs, radical changes in philosophical perspective, periods of intensified innovation and discovery, acts of rebellion against various personal or societal constraints, and the like. Uranus transits last about three years. After the first several cases in which I had noted such a correlation in the lives of persons well known to me, I began a systematic examination of hundreds of such cases. The coinciding events and experiences were not at all literally identical, nor, given their concrete variety of expression, were they susceptible to statistical measurement, yet the underlying common set of qualities could be readily discerned. Equally significant, those qualities closely matched the consensus of the modern astrological tradition concerning the archetypal meaning associated with the planet Uranus.

In many of these cases, transiting Uranus had formed an exact alignment to the individual's natal Sun, and in these cases the periods of rapid change and creative breakthrough seemed especially linked with an awakening of the individual self that radically changed and sometimes liberated the sense of personal identity. Such a transit can occur at different times of life for different individuals, depending on the specific astronomical situation in each case. One person might undergo the transit of Uranus conjunct Sun, for example, early in life, even in early childhood; another might do so much later, in her fifties, thereby providing a very different biographical context in which the corresponding archetypal complex could emerge. Despite the numerous differences in age and biographical context, however, I found that an archetypal commonality was readily evident, with the occurrence of various events and experiences possessing a distinctly Promethean character.

An especially noteworthy pattern of correlation I observed occurred when transiting Uranus formed a major aspect to the position of Uranus itself in an individual's natal chart. As we will see, all individuals undergo the sequence of major geometrical alignments of Uranus to its own natal position at approximately the same ages. I found that each such alignment appeared to coincide with periods in which there was evident a greater than usual potential for sudden radical shifts and breakthroughs of various kinds. This pattern of apparent archetypal activation in coincidence with the Uranus transit cycle became particularly clear when I began to examine in detail the biographies of major cultural figures with whose lives and works I was familiar.

For example, I discovered that when Galileo made his first telescopic discoveries between October 1609 and March 1610 and then quickly wrote and published *Sidereus Nuncius* ("The Starry Messenger"), which heralded the truth of the Copernican theory and caused a sensation in European intellectual circles, he had the identical personal Uranus transit that René Descartes had in 1637 when he published his equally epoch-making *Discourse on Method*, the manifesto of modern reason and the foundational work of modern philosophy. Moreover, this also happened to be the same transit Isaac Newton had in 1687 when he published the *Principia*, the foundational work of modern science.

In all three cases, the transit that coincided with these pivotal periods was

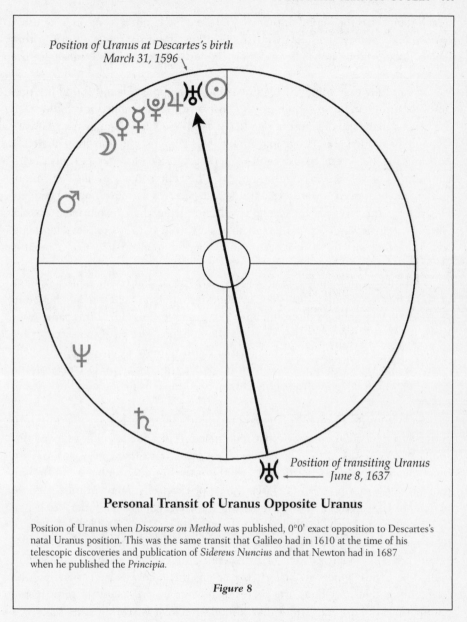

Position of Uranus at Descartes's birth March 31, 1596

Position of transiting Uranus — June 8, 1637

Personal Transit of Uranus Opposite Uranus

Position of Uranus when *Discourse on Method* was published, 0°0' exact opposition to Descartes's natal Uranus position. This was the same transit that Galileo had in 1610 at the time of his telescopic discoveries and publication of *Sidereus Nuncius* and that Newton had in 1687 when he published the *Principia*.

Figure 8

Uranus reaching the exact halfway point, 180°, in its full cycle around the birth chart, i.e., the point of opposition to the degree of celestial longitude that Uranus occupied at the individual's birth. This is referred to as "transiting Uranus opposite natal Uranus" (or simply, "Uranus opposite Uranus"). One can think of it as the "Full Moon" point of the personal Uranus transit cycle. It is the one time in a person's life that Uranus has reached the midpoint of its eighty-four-year orbit since his or her birth. The duration of this transit is approximately three years, which represents the period during which transiting Uranus is within 5° of exact opposition alignment with its own natal position, the usual range, or orb, within which I observed archetypal correlations in hard-aspect personal transits of the outer planets.[16]

In carefully examining the historical and biographical data, I found the precision of timing in these various cases consistently remarkable. One could track the development and the crest of significant creative achievement, personal breakthrough, or sudden life-change in each biography against the transiting planetary positions for the several months and years on each side of the exact transit, with a result that closely resembled the shape of a bell curve in a wavelike continuum as the transit moved towards exactitude and afterwards moved apart. Galileo, Descartes, and Newton, for example, all completed their revolutionary works when the transit was at its mathematical peak, within 1° to 2° of exact alignment, something that with this transit occurs altogether for approximately twelve months in the course of an entire lifetime.

I found that this same transit was regularly present at comparable moments of sudden breakthrough, discovery, innovation, rebellion, and radical change in the lives of other major cultural figures. For example, Freud had this same transit in 1895–97, the years that brought the sudden wave of discoveries in his thought that gave birth to psychoanalysis, the beginning of his systematic self-analysis, and the beginning of his writing of *The Interpretation of Dreams*—the period of which he later wrote, "Insight such as this falls to one's lot but once in a lifetime."

A close examination of this period of Freud's life reveals the rapid intensification of intellectual creativity that took place during the specific years of this transit. Uranus was in the opposition phase of its transiting cycle, within 5° of exact alignment with its position at Freud's birth, from November 1894 to September 1897, moving into its closest range of exact alignment in the 1895–96 period. In the spring of 1895, Freud and his colleague Josef Breuer published *Studies on Hysteria*, the final chapter on psychotherapy by Freud being that with which it is customary to date the beginning of psychoanalysis. On July 24, 1895, Freud first fully analyzed one of his dreams, the "dream of Irma's injection." Called by Ernest Jones an "historic occasion," this date was later memorialized by Freud as that on which "the secret of dreams was revealed" to him. In the summer of 1895, Breuer wrote that "Freud's intellect is soaring at its highest. I gaze after him as a hen at a hawk."

During this period Freud postulated the latent wish-fulfillment function of dreams, formulated the distinction between primary and secondary mental processes, and developed his views on the sexual etiology of neurosis, the existence of infantile eroticism, and the nature of the conscious ego with its resistance to the instincts. These years also brought the first mention of the fundamental concepts of compromise formation, overdetermination, the return of the repressed, and erotogenic zones. According to Jones, "Freud was in his most revolutionary stage, both intellectually and emotionally." *The Interpretation of Dreams*, the foundational work of psychoanalysis on which he labored for the rest of the decade, was according to Freud "finished in all essentials at the beginning of 1896." The term "psychoanalysis" was first used in a paper completed on February 5, 1896. In the spring of 1897, Freud first began developing his conception of the Oedipus complex. In the summer of 1897, spurred by his own psychological unrest as well as by his emerging understanding of the psyche, Freud commenced his self-analysis, generally considered the critical turning point of his intellectual and psychological evolution.

In the case of Jung, the same transit occurred in coincidence with the famous juncture in 1914–17 that brought the major personal and intellectual turning point of his life as well. These were the years of Jung's most intensive and systematic self-analysis, which constituted a period of psychological transformation and breakthrough precisely parallel to Freud's, out of which Jung emerged with his fundamental concepts of the collective unconscious, the Self, the process of individuation, the transcendent function, and the internal objectivity of psychic reality. Near the end of his life, in *Memories, Dreams, Reflections*, Jung spoke of this period as the most crucial in his career, as the source of virtually all his subsequent scientific and psychological insights:

> The years when I was pursuing my inner images were the most important in my life—in them everything essential was decided. It all began then; the later details are only supplements and clarifications of the material that burst forth from the unconscious, and at first swamped me. It was the *prima materia* for a lifetime's work.

Similar transits involving the major-aspect alignments of the Uranus-Uranus transit cycle took place with Einstein and the theory of relativity, Darwin and the theory of natural selection, Kant and his Copernican revolution in philosophy, and in many other figures of scientific and intellectual innovation for whom we have sufficiently precise historical data.[17] But again I must emphasize the larger complexity and multivalent patterning in the data, even beyond the important differences between the individual natal charts involved. Not only were other overlapping transits involving other planets often relevant in throwing light on the character and timing of the events in question, but the Uranus-opposite-Uranus transit on its own terms coincided with a far wider range of significant phenomena than the above examples suggest. Yet within that diversity this transit consistently marked periods in which defining events and experiences took place bearing the same basic archetypal character of experiment and change, creative breakthrough, sudden awakening, disruption of the status quo, defiant rebellion against established structures, and the like.

For example, this same Uranus transit was taking place in the case of Rosa Parks in 1955 when by refusing to leave her seat on the bus in Montgomery, Alabama, she set in motion the American civil rights movement. The sudden decisive act of defiance, the disturbance of social conventions, the resulting radical change in life experience from then on—though in this case historic in outcome—all these qualities were characteristic of this particular transit.

This was also the same transit that Betty Friedan had in 1962–63 when, after five years of writing, she published *The Feminine Mystique*, launching the modern feminist movement:

> My answers may disturb the experts and women alike, for they imply social change. But there would be no sense in my writing this book at all if I did not believe that women can affect society, as well as be affected by it; that, in the end, a woman, like a man, has the power to choose, and to make her own heaven or hell.

Again, in all these cases—Rosa Parks, Betty Friedan, Freud, Jung, Galileo, Descartes, Newton, and the numerous individuals who experienced psychotherapeutic transformations, personal breakthroughs and turning points—the particular biographical events certainly can be seen to have differed in various ways, in character, intensity, and consequences, and are not statistically measurable as identical phenomena, yet a coherent underlying archetypal pattern seems clearly evident.

It is possible that after a cursory review of a few such correlations, one could reasonably conclude that these coincidences merely reflect the fact that the Uranus cycle's 180° opposition transit takes place during a period in individuals' lives—at some point, varying from person to person, during the late thirties and early forties—when a kind of peak of creative vitality could often be expected anyway. I repeatedly considered that possibility, but a combination of several interconnected factors argued against discounting the correlations as inconsequential coincidences. First, the acute precision of the correlations between the transiting alignment and the relevant events, down to the exact degree and month, was impressive, even uncanny, particularly since the character of the correlated events fit so precisely the astrological meaning of the specific planet involved. Second, different Uranus transits occurring at different times of life coincided with phenomena having the same archetypal character, but the specific phenomena varied according to which aspect or cyclical alignment was involved. They further varied according to which natal planet was being transited (a Uranus transit to natal Venus, for example, tended to coincide with a different category of sudden change, awakening, or disruption from that of a Uranus transit to Mercury or to Mars).

Finally, as I examined the lives of a much larger range of individuals beyond the well-known figures just cited and the cases of psychological breakthrough I initially encountered, I found that the Uranus-opposite-Uranus transit regularly coincided with a period of life in which inner experience and external events presented a distinct quality that, while differing in important respects from these more dramatic turning points, nevertheless strongly suggested the active presence of the same Promethean archetypal principle. The specific three-year span of this transit coincided with striking frequency with that period of life popularly referred to as the midlife crisis, or midlife transition. A certain existential restlessness, a suddenly intensified desire to break free from the existing structures of one's life—career, daily work, marriage, community, accustomed personal identity and social persona, belief system, and so forth—was typical at this time. So also was a greater than usual boldness in taking risks, an urge to explore new horizons, a readiness to forgo previous commitments and responsibilities. Moreover, equally frequent during this transit were events having an unpredictable, disruptive character, events whose ultimate effect—bringing about sudden shifts in one's life circumstances and existential structures—was similar to that of the self-initiated kind. The awakenings that coincided with this transit might be expansively uplifting or intensely difficult. Yet the underlying archetypal principle appeared to be the same whether the events were unanticipated or self-initiated, and whether their eventual outcome was destabilizing and problematic or liberating and creative.

Often the coinciding events during this transit reflected *all* of these qualities, as several of the examples above suggest. Neither Freud nor Jung especially sought out or welcomed the challenging psychological states that emerged for them at this time, yet both the intellectual fruits and the internal growth that resulted from this period constituted significant breakthroughs that unfolded throughout the rest of their lives. The impulses and actions taken during this transit by Rosa Parks or Galileo were both personally and culturally liberating, but their effect was also to initiate a succession of highly challenging, destabilizing events in their lives and their world.

Similarly, the individual's attitude towards the coinciding phenomena varied considerably. The external changes and even the internal impulses might be enthusiastically embraced or simply coped with. They might be actively nurtured and developed or strenuously opposed and suppressed. No specific form of event or response seemed foreordained, nor was any specific outcome. What was consistent was the underlying archetypal quality of sudden or rapid significant change, novelty from within or without, experiment, uncertainty, and unexpected shifts in life circumstances or personal vision. The common denominator appeared to be the constellation of a state of being in which one's domain of experience was suddenly pressed beyond the accustomed status quo towards new horizons, irrespective of whether the previous condition was viewed as providing stable security or oppressive constraint.

The case of Betty Friedan during this transit is instructive, as it involves both personal and collective dimensions closely interwoven. On the one hand, exemplifying one side of the archetypal pattern, *The Feminine Mystique* represented in itself a major creative breakthrough—both personal and societal, as well as both intellectual and psychological—that mediated a sudden shift of perspective and new existential possibilities. On the other hand, the specific focus of the book was on the very issues whose emergence in individual lives regularly coincided with this transit but that were here addressed on a larger societal scale: "the problem with no name," the increasing restlessness of modern women experiencing the confinement of traditional patriarchal social structures. The book gave voice to, as it helped catalyze, a newly conscious desire in women to break free from established social roles to explore a larger range of activities and avenues for self-realization. Thus both the restless condition Friedan addressed and diagnosed in *The Feminine Mystique* and the creative breakthrough represented by her writing the book illustrate two of the most characteristic patterns I observed with this transit.

Considered on its own, apart from any other correlations, the coincidence between this stage of potential transition or transformation in many individuals' lives and the Uranus opposition transit would have been suggestive but of course hardly decisive. What made it more compelling was its being embedded in a much larger interconnected pattern of correlations involving the same planet and the same archetypal principle. For example, before the opposition point of the Uranus cycle in each individual's life there is an earlier period in which Uranus reaches the first quadrature alignment, or dynamic hard aspect, of its cycle—the 90° square, which occurs midway between birth and the 180° opposition just discussed. This Uranus-square-Uranus transit coincides with a three-year period in the late teens and early twenties when youthful rebellion and striving for independence is typically at a peak. Again, as with the opposition point of the same cycle, a radically heightened emancipatory impulse appears to be consistently catalyzed during these years, one that impels youth to make its first fundamental break from structures established or upheld by the previous generation. The restless striving for unconstrained autonomy that increases in strength throughout the teen years, as expressed in acts of social rebellion and unpredictable changes of behavior, is fully catalyzed and empowered during this period and reaches a climax. Both the encounter with and the impulse to experiment with new forms of experience, new perspectives, new relationships, and new fields of action are rapidly accelerated and intensified.

That the majority of college students and senior high school students are undergoing this transit was at least archetypally congruent with the fact that universities and high schools so often serve as a kind of hotbed of rebellious, liberating, creative, impulsive, and disruptive behavior and ideas. So also in youths of the same age on the street (or, increasingly in the United States, in prison). Equally suggestive were the frequent spontaneous connections that psychologists and sociologists make between these two periods of life—the square and the opposition of the Uranus cycle—often referring to the midlife crisis period as a "second adolescence." In both these periods, individuals seemed to feel driven to break out of conventional structures imposed by society, family, or their own psyche to experiment and explore, to seek greater freedom, creative self-expression, new ideas, and new horizons. Moreover, in coincidence with these self-initiated events and newly emergent impulses, an equally prominent tendency in both periods is the occurrence of unpredictable, destabilizing, and disruptive events.

In highly creative individuals, one can often recognize quite specific developmental connections between the two periods involved. For example, in the case of Newton, the square and opposition points of the Uranus cycle precisely coincided with the two famous periods of his life that brought forth his most important scientific achievements. From January 1664 to December 1666, Uranus was at the 90° point of its cycle, within 5° of exact alignment. It was precisely during the years 1664 to 1666, when he was in his early twenties, that Newton laid most of the foundations for his later work: developing the binomial theorem and the calculus, performing advanced research in optics, and deriving the inverse square relation for planetary motion. This was the period when, according to Newton's own account, the incident of the falling apple took place. As the historian of science D. T. Whiteside observed, "In two short years, summer 1664 to October 1666, Newton the mathematician was born, and in a sense the rest of his creative life was largely the working out, in calculus as in his mathematical thought in general, of the mass of burgeoning ideas which sprouted in his mind on the threshold of intellectual maturity." Newton himself wrote of this period, "I was in the prime of my age for invention and minded Mathematics and Philosophy more than at any time since."

Thus a perfect symmetrical pattern was visible in the larger trajectory of Newton's life: These early discoveries, which were the necessary forerunners of the *Principia*, occurred when Uranus had moved 90° from its position at Newton's birth, while the *Principia* itself, containing his formulation of the three laws of motion and the law of universal gravitation, was published when Uranus had moved exactly 90° further, to form the 180° opposition.

These and many correlations like them suggested to me the possibility that there existed in each life a significant archetypal connection and continuity between events that coincided with the successive major alignments of the Uranus transit cycle. The nature of the evidence seemed to indicate the existence of a constant correlation between the Uranus transit cycle and activations of an archetypal principle having a Promethean character—emancipatory, rebellious, inventive, unpredictable, mediating sudden change and new realities—visible in the specific quality and timing of these various events and breakthroughs. Numerous other factors, such as the specific planets forming aspects to Uranus in the natal chart and the presence of other concurrent transits, were also relevant for assessing the exact character and timing of these correlations. Apart from the Uranus-Uranus cycle, many comparable events with these same qualities coincided with transits in which Uranus was transiting another important point in the natal chart (e.g., transiting Uranus conjunct natal Sun, as when James Joyce wrote *Ulysses*, beginning in 1914), or in which another outer planet in the sky was transiting natal Uranus (e.g., transiting Pluto conjunct natal Uranus, as when Thomas Jefferson wrote the Declaration of Independence in June 1776).[18] Yet the Uranus-Uranus transit cycle on its own terms appeared to represent an especially significant cyclical pattern for what seemed to be an unfolding Promethean impulse.

With the full 360° Uranus cycle taking eighty-four years to complete itself, the life trajectory of many individuals does not afford the possibility of comparable correlations during the period when Uranus reaches conjunction with its original position at the person's birth (a transit referred to as the "Uranus return"). However, among those just cited, Freud lived to his eighty-fourth year, and just as Uranus reached the point of conjunction in the summer of 1938, when he was suddenly compelled by the Nazis' takeover in Austria to move to London for what turned out to be the last months of his life, he wrote his brilliant, succinctly definitive summary of psychoanalytic theory, *An Outline of Psychoanalysis*. His last book, the celebrated *Outline* was in effect a synopsis of his life's work. Moreover, this same period also saw the completion and publication of his *Moses and Monotheism*, a work of personal summation as well, both because it had so long occupied his attention and because it analyzed the revolutionary cultural figure with whom Freud had identified throughout his life.

Similarly, Jung lived to the age of eighty-five. When the Uranus cycle in his life reached the 360° point of completion, with transiting Uranus having moved into conjunction with its natal position from 1957 to 1960, Jung composed his celebrated life summary, *Memories, Dreams, Reflections*. Thus both Freud and Jung wrote summations of their life's revolutionary work precisely during the period coincident with Uranus's conjunction to itself at the end of its cycle.

A clear sequential pattern is thus visible in both cases: In Freud's life, the 180° halfway point of the Uranus cycle that occurred in 1895–97 coincided with his period of major breakthrough—the beginning of his self-analysis, his formulation of the basic concepts of psychoanalysis, and the start of his writing his foundational work, *The Interpretation of Dreams*—and the 360° point of the cycle's completion coincided with his lifework summations, the *Outline of Psychoanalysis* and *Moses and Monotheism*. In Jung's life, the same symmetrical pattern was visible, with the halfway point of the Uranus cycle during the 1914–17 period coinciding with the seminal turning point of his life both intellectually and psychologically (as he later described in *Memories, Dreams, Reflections*), and the cycle's completion coincided with the writing of *Memories, Dreams, Reflections* itself, his life summary.[19]

Similarly suggestive patterns of the full cycle were evident at the collective level. For example, if one considers the birth of the United States to be July 4, 1776, the signing of the Declaration of Independence, the full Uranus cycle was completed eighty-four years later when the Civil War began, in April 1861, within 1° of exact alignment. This dramatic period in the history of the United States brought what Abraham Lincoln called "a new birth of freedom" to a nation conceived in liberty but until then deeply oppressed, compromised, and corrupted by the institution of slavery. Similarly, the next Uranus cycle was completed in the life of the United States in the mid-1940s. This Uranus return reached exact alignment one week before D-day in June 1944, as the Allies began the liberation of Europe from the Nazis, and continued through 1945 in coincidence with the successful end of World War II, the emergence of the United States as a dominant power in the world, and the founding of the United Nations.

The Structural Unfolding of Life: The Saturn Cycle

Another planetary transit cycle in which distinctive archetypal correlations can be easily recognized in individual biographies is the Saturn cycle, approximately twenty-nine and a half years in length. All individuals go through the first Saturn return transit from about the age of twenty-eight through age thirty, a three-year period in the course of which a characteristic complex of biographical events and experiences seems to occur with remarkable consistency.[20] During these years individuals tend to experience their lives as distinctly coming to the end of an era—bringing the years of youth to a close and initiating the person, in an often challenging way, into the principal period of mature activity in the world in engagement with the established social order.

In examining many hundreds of individual biographies, I observed that during the years from age twenty-eight to thirty, a tangibly different, usually more serious posture towards life, work, long-term goals, security, parents, tradition, and established social structures tended to emerge. At this time, the wider aspirations and wanderings of youth seemed to undergo a transformation, becoming focused on and grounded in concrete practicalities and particular commitments: vocational, relational, intellectual, psychological, spiritual. Significant relationships often came to an end, and others of enduring consequence began. Modes of being that had characterized the preceding years were now outgrown and decisively left behind as no longer appropriate, or ineluctably taken away by changing life circumstances. The consequences of past actions and events tended to emerge and require assimilation, and a growing tendency to engage in serious self-reflection and biographical retrospection was typical.

In coincidence with the Saturn return transit, the challenging realities of life and death, time and aging, loss and adversity, work and responsibility became dominant concerns in a distinctly different manner from how these same realities were experienced in one's teens or twenties. Equally characteristic during this three-year transit was a definite sense of existential compression or contraction, generally accompanied by obstacles, limitations, and frustrations of various kinds—financial, physical, relational—and often including a definite encounter with human mortality, finitude, and fallibility. For some, the years of this transit near age thirty marked a psychological transformation that brought an end to the more creative, adventurous, open-minded and free-spirited youthful self and the establishment of a more rigidly conservative, constrained, and risk-averse personality identified with the status quo and unquestioned conventional values. By contrast, many others seemed to resolve this archetypal transition through the strenuous forging of a synthesis of the aspiring, creative impulses of youth with the structuring, stabilizing, disciplining, foundation-building impulses of maturity.

In either case, the often noted, fairly easily recognizable difference between individuals who are over thirty from those younger than thirty seemed to be associated with the decisive emergence in just these years of personal qualities and life circumstances whose common qualities all seemed to be comprehensible in terms of the Saturn archetype being potently constellated at that time.[21] The following description by Gertrude Stein, from her early work *Fernhurst*, well describes a characteristic form of the life transition that consistently coincides with the Saturn return period:

> It happens often in the twenty-ninth year of life that all the forces that have been engaged through the years of childhood, adolescence and youth in confused and ferocious combat range themselves in ordered ranks—one is uncertain of one's aims, meaning and power during these years of tumultuous growth when aspiration has no relation to fulfillment and one plunges here and there with energy and misdirection during the storm and stress of the making of a personality until at last we reach the twenty-ninth year, the straight and narrow gateway of maturity and life which was all uproar and confusion narrows down to form and purpose and we exchange a great dim possibility for a small hard reality.
>
> Also in our American life where there is no coercion in custom and it is our right to change our vocation so often as we have desire and opportunity, it is a common experience that our youth extends through the whole first twenty-nine years of our life and it is not until we reach thirty that we find at last that vocation for which we feel ourselves fit and to which we willingly devote continued labor.

In researching hundreds of biographies to examine the nature of each individual's life trajectory, I regularly observed that the succeeding three decades—the person's thirties, forties, and fifties—could be seen in retrospect to have been decisively shaped by the structural transformations that took place during the first Saturn return transit between the ages of twenty-eight and thirty. One's first symphony is composed and first public concert takes place (Beethoven); one's major professional association is established (Shakespeare becomes a member of the Globe's company of players and their chief playwright); one's pivotal career appointment is received (Ficino as head of the Platonic Academy of Florence, Luther as teacher of biblical theology at Wittenberg, Kepler as Imperial Mathematician in Prague, Galileo as professor of mathematics in Padua, William James as lecturer in science at Harvard); one's first significant achievement occurs (Marie Curie discovers radium and polonium, Niels Bohr formulates his theory of atomic structure); one's first significant public recognition takes place (Newton is elected to the Royal Society, Georgia O'Keeffe has her first exhibition at Alfred Stieglitz's gallery, Duke Ellington begins his five-year engagement at the Cotton Club); one's first major public act takes place that defines one's subsequent career (Demosthenes's first major speech before the Athenian Assembly, Martin Luther King's participation and arrest in a protest against racial segregation in Atlanta).

Other biographical patterns with a comparable archetypal character were equally evident during these years of the Saturn return, age twenty-eight to thirty, as for example the tendency to take on a new level of personal responsibility and achieve a new degree of personal independence (Margaret Fuller becomes editor of the Transcendentalist journal *The Dial*; Abigail Adams, with her husband John away in public service for most of a decade, raises their family and runs household, farm, and business largely by herself from age twenty-nine, establishes her own independent sensibility and finds her own voice in writing her letters). Or one leaves the wanderings of youth to enter one's mature calling ("The irresponsible days of my youth are over," Tennessee Williams wrote of the moment, age twenty-nine, when he received a telegram in Mexico from the Theatre Guild that requested him to return to New York for his first Broadway production). One's first film is directed (Truffaut's *The 400 Blows*, Godard's *Breathless*, Fellini's *Luci del Varietà*, Buñuel's *Un Chien Andalou*); one's first mature work is produced (Kafka writes *The Judgment* and *The Metamorphosis*, F. Scott Fitzgerald writes *The Great Gatsby*, Camus writes *The Myth of Sisyphus* and *The Stranger*, Saul Bellow writes *The Dangling Man*, Allen Ginsberg writes *Howl*); one establishes one's public persona (Aurore Dupin employs the nom de plume George Sand and publishes her first novel *Indiana*, Samuel Clemens publishes his first literary work, *The Celebrated Jumping Frog of Calaveras County*, under the nom de plume Mark Twain). Or one meets the mentor or model for one's subsequent development (Augustine meets Bishop Ambrose, Melville befriends Hawthorne, Freud studies with Charcot, Jung begins correspondence with Freud, Pablo Neruda encounters Federico García Lorca). Or one moves to the location and cultural milieu in which one's life work will begin to unfold (Leonardo moves to Milan to work in the court of Duke Ludovico Sforza, Rousseau moves to Paris and meets Diderot and the encyclopedists, Gertrude Stein moves to Paris and establishes her salon at 27 rue de Fleurus).

The Saturn return transit generally coincided with what might be called a period of biographical crystallization, visible not only in external events such as those just cited but also in a certain solidifying of the individual's psychic constitution and establishing of the basic structure of the personality. William James believed that after age thirty a person's character was "set in plaster." Yet depending on the individual's specific response to the pressures and circumstances of these critical years, this maturation and solidification could actually entail a new level of personal autonomy and self-reliance that had been unattainable in the years just before, a new confidence grounded in self-knowledge and the sense of having found one's direction or purpose. Many factors seemed relevant for understanding the variability among the experiences of different individuals during this period, including differences in how the person led his or her life before the transit and differences between the birth charts of the individuals involved.

On occasion, the achievement of maturational independence and individuation seemed to inhibit or close down the sources of creativity that were previously accessible in youth, as if the spontaneous influx from a kind of creative wellspring could not survive the transition into maturity. With certain highly creative young artists, the crystallization of personality and maturational pressures of the Saturn return period resulted in an individuation that both climaxed and effectively ended the more freely experimental creativity of their twenties (a creativity that typically began during the Uranus square Uranus transit of the late teens and early twenties). A notable example of this pattern is the case of the four Beatles: John Lennon, Paul McCartney, George Harrison, and Ringo Starr. After the period of brilliant group creativity sustained through their twenties, from 1962 to 1969, the four musicians decisively moved away from each other in the course of their Saturn return transits, preferring individual songwriting, bringing forth their first solo albums, and establishing marital relationships that precluded the close creative bond of the preceding years. The work the four men produced during their respective Saturn return periods between age twenty-eight and thirty, which began in 1968 and extended into the early 1970s, marked the climax of their creative lives, as embodied both in their extraordinary final albums as Beatles (the double *White Album, Let It Be, Abbey Road*) and in the first solo albums that each produced. After the age of thirty, their individual efforts seldom attained the creative brilliance of their youth, as if that particular form of creativity had flourished best as a kind of spontaneous collective influx through the group mind of the young Beatles, and ceased to thrive after the assimilation of the Saturn principle of maturity, separation, self-reliance, and serious engagement with the realities of the individual life associated with the period of the Saturn return.

I found that individual variations in the experiences during this period also closely corresponded with the other outer-planet transits that happened to coincide with the Saturn return, transits that varied from person to person according to their uniquely configured natal chart. (Only a transit of a planet to its own natal position happens to everyone at approximately the same time of life, as with the cycles of transiting Uranus to natal Uranus and of transiting Saturn to natal Saturn that we have been discussing.) The specific quality of the events and responses that occurred during an individual's Saturn return seemed to be affected by the distinctive character of the archetypal principles associated with these other coinciding planetary transits.

Such a case is vividly exemplified in the life of William James, whose Saturn return transit happened to coincide with the once-in-a-lifetime transit of Uranus opposite natal Sun, a transit that I observed consistently coincided with periods of sudden personal emancipation and creative breakthrough with a sense of self-awakening or self-liberation. When James was in his twenty-ninth year, he experienced a crisis of depression and anxiety that reached nearly suicidal intensity. This emotional crisis was closely linked with his sustained philosophical struggle with the nature of free will and determinism, both scientific and theological. He experienced this struggle at a personal level in the form of a general sense of oppressive existential constraint and moral impotence. One day while reading the work of the French philosopher Charles Renouvier on free will, James suddenly saw his way clear to a resolution of the crisis, deciding that "my first act of free will shall be to believe in free will." From this pivotal moment can be traced the subsequent unfolding of James's life and thought, with his distinctive life-long philosophical commitment to human freedom, individual autonomy, creative unpredictability, and pragmatic flexibility in response to an indeterminate open universe.

> Human freedom is . . . a special case of universal indeterminism. My future, though continuous with my past, is not determined by it. Just so the future of the world; although it grows out of the total past, it is not a mere result of that past. If I am creative—that is, if human freedom is effectual—then the world is creative, if for no other reason than that I am part of the world. What is constant in my behavior is the result of habits which never entirely lose their flexibility. In the same way the constancies charted by the laws of science are only more inveterate habits.

James's case exemplifies a distinctive synthesis of the two different archetypal impulses at work in correlation with the two transits. On the one hand, we see the characteristic biographical tendencies of the Saturn return period: the occurrence of a personal crisis involving an encounter with mortality, a general sense of existential contraction and enforced maturational development, a life decision establishing an enduring personal commitment and philosophical perspective, the crystallization of lifelong character traits, and the occurrence of a pivotal development establishing the direction of one's career (his appointment as lecturer at Harvard). On the other hand, the outcome of this period also bore the distinctive archetypal character of the Promethean themes and qualities typical of a major Uranus transit to the natal Sun: the sudden personal emancipation from a constraining reality, a new and unexpected sense of freedom of the self, a newly awakened capacity for the active assertion of the individual will, the discovery of a path of self-expression liberating one's creativity, and a new experience of creative indeterminacy in the world itself.

I found that a similarly decisive threshold of transformation, with similar individual variability, consistently coincided with the *second* Saturn return transit one full Saturn cycle later. Taking place during a three-year period approximately between the ages of fifty-seven and sixty, the period of the second Saturn return was typically marked by some form of culmination, completion, or cyclical closure of the processes and structures that had been established during the first Saturn return three decades earlier, including one's work and career, significant relationships, and basic existential attitudes. Again, a deep encounter with the limits and mortal realities of human existence was typical (as expressed, for example, in Tolstoy's great novella *The Death of Ivan Illich*, written during his second Saturn return). An acute awareness that the end of life was now closer than its beginning characteristically intensified existential concerns about what one's life had accomplished, what values had been served, whether one's current commitments reflected the reality of the finite time remaining. The entire spectrum of motifs and tendencies associated with the Saturn archetype again seems to be constellated during this moment in life coincident with the completion of the planet Saturn's orbit: age, mortality, gravity of concern, self-judgment, duty, worldly status, work and value, endings of things, the passing of an era, a decisive maturational threshold.

The approach of the age of sixty generally seemed to mark a fundamental moment of biographical transformation with a quality suggestive of cyclical completion, life review, and structural reconfiguration in certain respects not unlike the first Saturn return. In this later period, however, the completion and reconfiguration was taking place *after*, at the other end of, the thirty-year cycle of adult activity and responsibility in the world. It mediated the transition into what in traditional societies would be called the status of elderhood, whether this transition connotes simply age and the consequences of time and life's labors or a notably new level of societal responsibility, well-earned respect, personal gravitas, or wisdom grounded in long experience. Often the character of this period suggested the theme of reaping what had been sown, for better or worse. A new stage of life was beginning, at once older and yet also, sometimes, lighter—as if a task has been completed, a burden lifted, an obligation discharged—a cycle of Saturn completed. Both Saturn return periods seemed to function as a kind of constricting birth canal that bodied forth the next stage of life.

Before and after these cyclical conjunction periods of the Saturn cycle near the ages of thirty and sixty is a further noteworthy pattern of correlations involving the ongoing sequence of quadrature alignments in the personal Saturn transit cycle after birth and after each conjunction—the square, the opposition, and the next square followed by the subsequent conjunction. These quadrature aspects occur in intervals approximately every seven to seven and a half years, and last for about a year each time. The first Saturn-square-Saturn transit takes place near the age of seven; the opposition transit takes place around age fourteen to fifteen; the next square sometime between twenty-one and twenty-three.

After the first Saturn return at the age of twenty-eight to thirty, the cycle begins again, continuing in approximately seven-year intervals throughout life.

I found that these transits marked with an almost clocklike regularity periods of critical transformation, maturational crises, pivotal decisions, and biographical contractions and stresses of various kinds. Transformative encounters with authority, with limitations, with mortality, and with the consequences of past actions were highly characteristic. Different forms of separation from parental, familial, or social matrices often occurred, requiring a new level of existential self-reliance, inner authority, maturity and competence, individuation, concentration of energies, and consolidation of resources, and bringing a fundamental realignment of one's life and character. Distinct patterns were often visible connecting one Saturn quadrature alignment period with another—seven years later, or fourteen to fifteen years later, or twenty-eight to thirty years later.

I have seldom researched a biography for which I had sufficiently detailed records of the major inner and outer events in a person's life where I did not find the above patterning readily visible. What made these correlations impressive to me was the precision with which their character matched the archetypal principle with which the planet Saturn has always been associated in the astrological tradition. Equally striking was the way in which the additional qualities specific to each unique case consistently matched the other planets specifically involved by transit in that individual's life during those particular periods. In each instance, the basic Saturnian archetypal qualities and events that were characteristic of the Saturn alignment periods seemed to be given more specific inflections and further qualitative nuances in close correspondence with the other planetary archetypal principles being constellated at that time.

Archetypal Coherence
and Concrete Diversity

The same archetypal principles and patternings that were evident in the study of personal transits were equally evident in the study of natal charts. I found the interconnected coherence of these different forms of correspondence an especially important factor in assessing the evidence. With respect to the two planets we examined in the last chapter, for example, I noticed that individuals who were born with *Uranus* prominently positioned (as in a major aspect to the Sun) tended to display in their lives and personalities a certain family of archetypally related characteristics: rebelliousness, impatience with conventional constraints or traditional structures, originality and inventiveness, erratic and unpredictable behavior, susceptibility to frequent sudden changes in life, restless seeking of one's own path in life, incessant striving for freedom and the new, habitual desire for unusual or exciting experiences, and the like. By contrast, individuals born with *Saturn* similarly positioned showed equally distinct tendencies towards caution, conservatism, awareness of limits and constraints, a heightened sense of the weight and significance of the past, grounded realism, sternness and discipline, the maturity of long experience, a potential for pessimism and rigidity, and so forth.

Percy Bysshe Shelley, for example, was born with a conjunction of *Uranus* with the Sun. Throughout his life, Shelley personally embodied and expressed an overriding impulse towards freedom, radical change, and unconstrained personal autonomy. He identified himself with the forces of social revolution and called for the birth of a new era to bring the liberation of humanity from all sources of oppression. His life and work were marked by creative originality and a certain spontaneous striving for heroic individualism. His relationships and the trajectory of his life were characterized by many sudden changes and unexpected breaks, and an almost compulsive flouting of social conventions and inconstancy of commitment that left several casualties in their wake. Shelley's emphatic alignment of his own personal identity and self-image with the Promethean impulse can especially be seen in his having written the poetic drama *Prometheus Unbound*, the preeminent work in modern literature devoted to the figure of Prometheus.

By way of simple contrast, we might compare Shelley with his close contemporary Arthur Schopenhauer, who was born with a conjunction of *Saturn* with the Sun. Schopenhauer's philosophical perspective was dominated by a profound sense of life's constraints, suffering, and mortality. In his vision, humanity was imprisoned in a world of ceaseless struggle, pain, and ultimate defeat. Whereas Shelley's life and work can be seen as devoted toward the liberation of the self, Schopenhauer called for a sterner confrontation with life's problematic realities and an ascetic denial of the self to permit its transcendence from the painful struggle of existence. Whereas Shelley's personality and biography were marked by a constant quest for the new and unexplored, a striving for new horizons of experience, whether in modes of self-expression, in relationships, or in the quest for a future age of human freedom, Schopenhauer's personality and biography were marked rather by a brooding solitude, constant fear of the unexpected, and a kind of radiant pessimism.

The two men's personal transits are equally suggestive. Schopenhauer's principal work, *The World as Will and Idea*, was written and published during his first Saturn return. "A man reaches the maturity of his reasoning powers and mental faculties hardly before the age of twenty-eight," Schopenhauer wrote many years later. Shelley wrote *Prometheus Unbound* in 1818–19 earlier in his twenties in exact coincidence with his Uranus-trine-Uranus transit. He never experienced the Uranus-opposite-Uranus transit, as he drowned at the age of twenty-nine, during his Saturn return.

Schopenhauer's life also embodied another theme regularly seen in the case of those born with Sun-Saturn aspects, a tendency to experience personal recognition in the world and a sense of individual self-realization (corresponding to the Sun) only in later years, after the passage of time, the reaching of a more mature age, and the experience of rejection and long solitude (corresponding to Saturn). When Schopenhauer published his masterwork, *The World as Will and Idea*, at age thirty, the book was almost entirely ignored and his lectures at the University of Berlin, which he purposely scheduled at a time that conflicted with those of his far more famous philosophical opponent Hegel, went largely unattended. Schopenhauer withdrew in resentment to a life of solitude. In his early sixties, after years of further writing and publishing, he brought forth his more accessible collection of essays and aphorisms, *Parerga und Paralipomena*, from which time his name became widely known throughout Europe and his ideas began to exert a major influence on the culture. For the last decade of his life, until his death at age seventy-two, he enjoyed considerable fame and recognition. In a sense Schopenhauer seemed to see all of life through the lens of the Sun-Saturn archetypal complex and generalized his experience into a universal principle: "The nobler and more perfect a thing is, the later and more slowly does it come to maturity."

By contrast, Shelley's creative unfolding and recognition by his peers took place from an early age and at an accelerated pace throughout his brief life. He had already written *The Necessity of Atheism* at age eighteen while still at Oxford, for which he was promptly expelled, in exact coincidence with his Uranus-square-Uranus transit. Thus he began his own final decade of life, a shooting star of precocious literary creativity, incessant change, intensely nonconformist living, and free-spirited thought. Shelley seemed to identify with a principle of creative freedom that defied limitation and transcended death: "I change, but I cannot die."

Although the sharp contrast of the Shelley-Schopenhauer comparison is instructive, I must emphasize that any given archetypal complex that coincides with a specific natal alignment or personal transit could be embodied in an extraordinary diversity of ways while still remaining clearly recognizable as manifestations of the same underlying principles. Not every person born with a Sun-Uranus conjunction precisely resembles Shelley, nor are all those born with Sun-Saturn conjunctions just like Schopenhauer. In many other individuals born with one or the other of these two configurations, I found that their lives and personalities indeed reflected the corresponding archetypal complex in ways that could readily be discerned, yet each did so in a manner unique to that individual. A Sun-Uranus natal aspect might be found in the birth chart of a leading feminist pioneer or a free-wandering irresponsible missing parent, a major scientific innovator or a harmless eccentric, a celebrated cultural liberator or a lifelong juvenile delinquent (indeed, in some cases, both at once). A Sun-Saturn natal aspect might be found in a person noted for maturity of judgment, discipline, self-reliance, and comfort with solitude or in a person prone to depression, loneliness, and rigidity. The evidence suggested that each individual drew out different and often multiple elements of the archetypal complex in accordance with the varying cultural and biographical circumstances in each case. Many factors appeared to influence these differing expressions of the same complex, including what seemed to be the unique and unpredictable creative response of each individual in assimilating that particular complex. This diversity in archetypal manifestation was observable in every category of natal aspect or personal transit I examined.[22]

That a given natal aspect can coincide with the expression of a specific archetypal complex in a virtually limitless variety of forms is, I believe, not only characteristic of all astrological correspondence but essential to it. Again, underlying this observation seems to be the principle that astrological patterns are not concretely predictive but rather archetypally predictive. While I found that a given planetary alignment tended to coincide with a visible activation of the corresponding archetypal complex, the specific character of the final result did not appear to be predetermined in any way by the existence of that aspect. Two different persons might be born with the same planetary alignment, but for one person the intrinsic power and quality of the archetypal stimulus might be considerably greater or more profound than for the other, and that difference was not necessarily discernible in the natal chart. Or the archetype might express itself in one way rather than another (as compulsive rebelliousness, for instance, rather than innovative brilliance), both being equally appropriate to the specific archetype in question. From this perspective, the investigation of major cultural figures was valuable not because they alone were born with the aspects in question, which they were not, nor because their particular cultural achievement represented the likely outcome of a particular natal aspect, but rather because their lives and characters expressed specific archetypal traits in an especially conspicuous and publicly assessable manner.

The combination of archetypal coherence and concrete diversity in the evidence appeared to be fundamental and irreducible. It simultaneously precluded attempts at statistical proof or disproof while it permitted a field for authentic human autonomy. Within these deeper structures of unfolding archetypal meaning, a kind of improvisatory cosmic autonomy seemed to express itself, both *in response to* and *through* the autonomous acts and decisions of the individual person (much in the way William James described human freedom as ultimately rooted in and reflective of the universe's indeterminacy). The natal chart appeared to indicate something like the underlying archetypal chordal structures of life, while the transits suggested the tempo and rhythmic structure of its unfolding. What was not indicated was the unique melody, the specific manner of creative realization that the individual life ultimately enacted within and by means of those archetypal structures.

Over many years of research, I found that the robustness of the specific archetypal principles associated with the planets became more decisively evident as I continued to expand the body of data. Perhaps most telling was the fact that the archetypal principles were even more precisely visible as the particular data under analysis became more challengingly specific. Consider, for example, two people who were born not simply with the same planetary alignment but on the same day of the same year, and who thus had in their respective natal charts virtually all of the same planetary configurations in common.

Charles Darwin and Abraham Lincoln, for example, are most interesting in this respect: The two men were born on February 12, 1809, within twelve hours of each other. One was born to wealth and privilege in imperial England, the other into poverty and deprivation in the American wilderness. Over the years I have studied many such cases, and I consistently found that such exactly contemporaneous individuals tended to express, in their lives and psychological propensities, all of the relevant archetypal dynamics in ways that were concretely different yet on another level were nevertheless deeply parallel and analogous. To illustrate these parallels, it will be helpful here to list briefly a number of the natal alignments shared by the two men, along with the corresponding psychological tendencies and biographical themes.

Lincoln and Darwin were both born with a relatively rare five-planet config-uration of Mercury simultaneously in different major aspects with the four outer-most planets, Saturn, Uranus, Neptune, and Pluto. Considered separately, each of these specific aspects I regularly observed as occurring in the birth charts of individuals who possessed a distinctive constellation of personal qualities and tendencies. These qualities and tendencies seemed to embody different inflec-tions of the archetypal principle associated with Mercury, which comprises all that concerns mind, thought, information, communication, articulation, language, learning, study, analysis, and so forth. While the specific concrete form taken by each of these several archetypal complexes varied considerably in the many indi-viduals who shared a particular aspect, each concrete instance was precisely, though differently, expressive of the same archetypal principles.

In Lincoln and Darwin, both born with a configuration involving all five planets, these several archetypal complexes were all simultaneously visible, often in subtle interaction with each other. I will explore the technical specifics else-where; for the present it is sufficient to note that among the characteristic traits and biographical circumstances I regularly found associated with these aspects, especially noteworthy were the following: educational circumstances that were constraining, inadequate, or discouraging (Mercury-Saturn); self-critical intel-lectual rigor combined with unusual economy and clarity of expression and a tendency to remain silent for long periods (Mercury-Saturn); a certain mental stubbornness or tenacity in slowly pondering seemingly intractable problems over extended lengths of time (Mercury-Saturn); a tendency to think with acute, pene-trating intensity that in exceptional cases reflected the possession of a powerful, driven intellect (Mercury-Pluto); an unusual capacity for strategic thinking and cunning, shrewd analysis of underlying or hidden motivations (Mercury-Pluto) often combined with close, detailed observation (Mercury-Saturn); a desire to penetrate below superficial levels of understanding to grasp deeper princi-ples and operative forces (Mercury-Pluto); a drive to develop a facility for effec-tive and even compelling communication, written or spoken, intended to influ-ence and transform the opinions of others (Mercury-Pluto); a tendency to think in ways that dissolve previously established structures and boundaries, and to intuit, usually after sustained periods of mental confusion and amorphous day-dreaming, larger unities underlying apparently separate and divergent phenomena (Mercury-Neptune); and a heightened impulse for conceiving or entering into ideas and perspectives that defy conventional views and assumptions (Mercury-Uranus) and that often elicit intense negative judgment, criticism, and sarcastic attack (Mercury-Saturn with Mercury-Pluto).

Darwin and Lincoln were also born with a Jupiter-Pluto conjunction, an as-pect found in the birth charts of individuals possessing a stronger than usual drive or capacity for personal leadership or cultural power, whether intellectual, moral, or political. In addition, they were born when Uranus was in a trine as-pect with Pluto, which regularly coincided with significant concern with or active participation in major revolutionary or emancipatory movements of some kind.

Finally, the two men were both born with a Saturn-Neptune conjunction, which I often found associated with an acute sensitivity to the suffering and sorrow of life, whether experienced by oneself or others; more than the usual concern with death and its spiritual implications; and potential tendencies towards persistent melancholy or depression, insomnia, and difficult-to-diagnose chronic psychosomatic symptoms. Such individuals frequently experienced an enduring response to poignant emotional loss of some kind and a pervading sense of being haunted by guilt or responsibility for tragic events. This same aspect was also associated with individuals whose philosophical outlook showed an emphatic tendency towards skeptical realism, which ranged in character from, on the one hand, agnosticism or atheism to, on the other, a critical attitude towards conventional religious belief combined with a serious, sometimes somber spiritual vision of life of a highly pragmatic, this-worldly nature.

As has been well documented, the biographies of both Lincoln and Darwin exhibited each of these characteristics and themes in conspicuous ways. Yet they did so in quite different contexts, with differing inflections, and with altogether different historical consequences. The identical archetypal dynamics seemed to play themselves out with great specificity and potency in both cases, but in divergent forms and circumstances. The educational constraints, the mental habits, the intellectual power, the silences and long ponderings, the gravity of thought and expression, the capacity and inclination to think outside conventional structures of belief, the strenuously developed gifts for writing and persuasive communication were all strikingly similar in essence. So too their shared skepticism about a personal afterlife, and their tendencies to depression and despair. Both tragically lost their mothers in childhood (Darwin at age eight, Lincoln at nine), losses exacerbated in both cases by their fathers' inability to provide emotional and spiritual comfort to their bereaved children. Both men suffered the equally tragic loss of their own young children when they themselves were fathers. Both were haunted by a sense of responsibility for the deaths of others, both were unusually sensitive to the suffering and death of others (in both cases including that of animals), and both abhorred slavery. The shared seriousness of their respective moral visions, their this-worldly focus and somber realism, their impulse for cultural leadership, their active participation in major revolutionary and emancipatory events: Each of these particular qualities evident in their life and personality appeared to represent the concrete embodiment of a broader field of qualitative potentials and tendencies, which in turn were intelligible in terms of more fundamental archetypal complexes that were inflected by and through the particular biographical and historical contexts.

I should also emphasize here that birth charts did not appear to carry anything like a pregiven moral vector: There were no planetary configurations or any other factors in a birth chart that correlated with whether a person turned out to be on balance a good or evil person, noble or ignoble. Charlie Chaplin and Adolf Hitler had very similar natal charts, born as they were only four days apart in April 1889 with many, though not all, of their principal planetary configurations remaining in alignment during the brief period that encompassed their births. Both shared a particular combination of several different planetary aspects, each of which I found consistently associated with a specific archetypal complex and field of qualitative potentials. Again, the concrete form these several complexes took in individual cases showed considerable diversity while still exhibiting common underlying archetypal patterns.

Without entering into all the specific planetary alignments in Chaplin's and Hitler's birth charts, let me simply note here that typical expressions of the particular archetypal complexes associated with these aspects included idiosyncratic and sometimes virtuosic skills of communication; proneness to nervous agitation; harsh life experiences such as sustained poverty and isolation; susceptibility to displays of anger; problematic relationships with authorities combined with dictatorial controlling tendencies; a strong inclination toward personal eccentricity; marked artistic impulses or interests; unusually charged libidinal or romantic ardor combined with a tendency to experience rejection or frustration; inclination towards erotic relationships with unusually young or emotionally immature partners; and an impulse to experience or create dramatic illusions capable of powerfully moving audiences. Again, both men embodied all these particular characteristics with considerable specificity (even to the point of Chaplin's impersonating Hitler in *The Great Dictator*, with brilliant acuity and to the latter's intense annoyance), but how radically different the moral vector in each case, and how different the consequences.

Whatever the relationship of the moral character to the archetypal dimension—and, like Jung, I believe it is a profound and complex one—the vector of that character does not seem to be in any way prefigured in the natal chart. Many diverse factors appear to play determining roles in shaping how an archetypal complex is concretely embodied: cultural, historical, ancestral, familial, circumstantial. To these must be added such factors as individual choice and degree of self-awareness, as well as, perhaps, karma, grace, chance, and other unmeasurables. Gender alone seems to play a considerable role. Reflecting an intricate interplay of biological and cultural factors, a particular archetypal complex expressed in a woman's life, as well as personality often appears to be inflected and embodied differently from the same archetypal complex in the life and personality of a man born at the same time. At least some of these differences seem to be intensified in direct proportion to the extent to which patriarchal structures are dominant in the society into which the individual is born. A woman living in contemporary Afghanistan or Nigeria has sharply different potential for the expression and embodiment of specific archetypal tendencies from those of a woman living at the same time in Scandinavia or California. Context is crucial.

All these considerations underscore the central feature of the entire body of evidence I examined and what is perhaps the most critical factor in understanding the phenomenon of planetary synchronicities: the extraordinary empirical display of archetypal constancy and concrete diversity in every category of planetary correlations. I repeatedly marveled at the strikingly coherent patterns of both unity and multiplicity of archetypal meaning that unfolded in biographical and historical phenomena in systematic coincidence with the patterns of planetary alignments. The characteristic manner in which both the constancy and the multivalence were evident in the data in subtle and intricate interplay was, it seemed to me, consistently remarkable.

But given the considerable range of possible manifestation observed for any given archetypal complex associated with a specific planetary configuration, the question arises: With such diversity, how genuine are the archetypal categories? This of course evokes that critical issue that has dominated the history of Western philosophy: the problem of universals. Upon its outcome rest enormous stakes, not only epistemological but cosmological. Are the archetypal categories rooted in something beyond our local projections? Or are they merely arbitrary constructions of the categorizing mind? Are they perhaps no more than figments of the metaphorical imagination?

Only a range of data and a depth of research commensurate with the profundity of these issues can provide the possibility of their resolution, and in the following chapters I have set forth an initial survey of evidence that I believe may help do so. If I may anticipate here: after intensive analysis of a much larger body of evidence during the past thirty years, I have become fully persuaded that these archetypal categories are not merely constructed but are in some sense both psychological *and* cosmological in nature. They provide a comprehensive conceptual structure that makes intelligible the complexities of human experience in a manner unmatched by any other approach I have encountered. The existence of constantly diverse inflections of the same archetypal principles seems to reflect a dynamic indeterminacy of formal patterning in the nature of things that permits the simultaneous coexistence of both meaningful coherence and creative unpredictability in human life.

In the categories of evidence discussed above, for example, I found that an individual's undergoing a specific transit, such as Uranus opposite natal Uranus or a Saturn return, did not entail any absolute pregiven constraints upon what external events or internal changes might unfold at that time in the person's life. Nor did an individual's having been born with a particular planetary aspect, such as Sun conjunct Uranus or Mercury square Saturn, entail any pregiven constraints concerning the concrete form the various relevant qualities or tendencies would take in that person's life and psychic constitution. Yet in each case I found that the archetypal principles associated with the relevant planets provided a lucid perspective of pattern, order, and coherence for understanding the manifold complexity of many themes central to that specific individual's personal character and unfolding biography. Radically different embodiments of a given archetypal complex appeared to be equally possible, as multiple potentialities and "tendencies to exist" (to use the phrase familiar from quantum physics), while they still remained faithful in underlying ways to the deeper principles involved.

Yet in philosophical terms, how can a principle be at once so multivalent and still maintain its underlying identity in all its expressions? This question directs us to the very heart of the archetypal perspective, with its roots in the Platonic Forms of classical philosophy and in the gods of the ancient mythic imagination. In particular, it compels us to engage what the philosopher J. N. Findlay has called the archetypal Forms' intrinsic capacity for "elastic and variable identity," "iridescent variation of aspect," and "differentiation without difference." Their very essence lies in this multiform potentiality, from which is elicited the unique particular that is creatively actualized within the unfolding stream of life. In this perspective, every individual being is a locus of many interpenetrating archetypal forms and forces, each of which permeates and influences the whole in such a way that each archetypal presence affects all the rest in its characteristic manner. Each individual, moved by countless interacting factors, draws out and creatively enacts a unique inflection and embodiment of the many archetypal principles that inform his or her being. Nor is the situation static, for a particular archetypal field can be more strongly constellated at certain periods in a person's life in coincidence with transits to the corresponding natal aspects. It can also be affected by the presence of other important archetypal factors that are concurrently activated. As a method for discriminating and clarifying these many complexities, the astrological perspective was, I found, able to provide a uniquely precise insight into which archetypes were most likely to be dominant in a person's life, in what larger archetypal combinations, and during which times of life.

Assessing Patterns of Correlation

The challenge inherent in any attempt to examine and assess evidence for planetary correlations arises from the inescapable reality that no single correlation between an individual's personality and birth chart, nor any single correlation between a specific biographical event and a specific personal transit, could in itself ever constitute decisive evidence for the astrological hypothesis. Nor even could any group of such correlations, though certainly the larger the group and the more vivid the correspondences, the more suggestive the evidence. Ultimately, however, I found that it was the enormously vast and ever-increasing body of observed correlations involving all the planets—each with its specific corresponding archetypal complex of meaning, with the planetary alignments coinciding again and again with strikingly appropriate events, personality characteristics, and precise timing—that taken in its entirety constituted a highly coherent and compelling body of data.

Yet the narrative exposition of such evidence presents considerable difficulty. The larger body of correlations must be approached simultaneously as a whole yet also as comprising many interconnected particulars, each requiring nuanced attention. One can assess any particular natal aspect or transit only in the context of a much larger set of data—all the major transits in a particular individual's life, for example, or all the major aspects in the natal chart, with these compared and contrasted with the same transits and same natal aspects for many other individuals. Yet while it is ultimately the larger whole of data that is required to evaluate the significance of any single correlation, in practice one can examine or set forth only one correlation at a time, gradually building up a larger foundation and context for assessing each new particular. It is a challenge not unlike that facing Darwin in *The Origin of Species*: He had to set out one by one the examples of evidence for natural selection that he had observed over the preceding three decades, no one of which considered on its own would be probative—a task made all the more formidable because the implications of his evidence seemed to contradict the most well-established assumptions of his age.

In our situation, before we can recognize or assess a correlation we must have a working knowledge of the planetary archetypes that form our interpretive lens. For this, not only do we require a basic understanding of each planetary archetype's specific complex of meanings on its own terms; we also need to be able to recognize the way those meanings are combined and mutually inflected when two such archetypes are linked, corresponding to an alignment between two planets. The nature of the data—cultural, historical, biographical, existential, aesthetic—is such that it cannot be assessed by simple quantitative methods of analysis, inserted into a statistical protocol, and mechanically quantified. The data's significance must be judged both individually and as an entirety, with all of our cultural and psychological sensibilities brought into the equation. ·

What is especially required is an ability to recognize multivalent archetypal patterns and underlying coherencies in a wide range of very different personalities and biographies, historical events, and cultural epochs. The ability for such discernment is a developed human skill, a cultivated mode of vision and understanding that cannot be reduced to a computer algorithm and impersonally deployed in a double-blind study with controls. As Hillman has emphasized, even a purely clinical psychological approach is inadequate: "An archetypal eye . . . is difficult to acquire through focus upon persons and cases. This eye needs training through profound appreciation of history and biography, of the arts, of ideas and culture." The method used in this research is essentially both a science and an art—both mathematical and interpretive, rational and aesthetic—in an intricate synthesis.[23]

Over many years of research, I examined in detail the biographies of a considerable range of culturally significant individuals—Nietzsche and Jung, Virginia Woolf and Mary Shelley, Beethoven and Wagner, Dostoevsky, Tolstoy, Einstein, Picasso, Churchill, Gandhi, Martin Luther King, Rachel Carson, Harriet Beecher Stowe, Byron, Goethe, and hundreds of others. Only with such a substantial data base could an inquiry of this kind be effectively pursued. Working with such iconic cultural figures provided two further important advantages: First, their biographies and personal characters were well known and well documented. Equally important, individuals who have made major cultural contributions or whose historical influence has been significant are, in certain respects, paradigmatic. The shape and force of their lives and characters, the sharp contours and decisive vector of their biographies, render more discernible their essential qualities. Such individuals are more conspicuous embodiments of archetypal tendencies that are present in varying degrees in everyone, and thus potential correlations can more readily be judged.

To a great extent the analysis of individual biographies pertains to the first two forms of astrological correspondence I listed above in the chapter on forms of correspondence: natal charts and personal transits. However, as we begin to explore planetary correlations with the patterns of human experience in the following chapters, it will be helpful for several reasons to examine in some depth a category of evidence associated more widely with collective experience and the world at large: namely, world transits. Historically, world transits represented the earliest form of astrological observation. Whereas modern astrology, reflecting the humanistic individualism of the modern era, has been principally concerned with the analysis of individual natal charts and personal transits, the most ancient forms of astrology were based rather on the study of astronomical correspondences with events of collective significance. To my considerable surprise, I found that with this category of correlations—cyclical alignments of the outer planets with each other that coincided with major historical events and widespread cultural phenomena—it was possible to assess the presence and relative significance of correlations just as readily as with natal and personal transit analysis of famous individuals, but with specific added advantages.

With the study of individual natal charts, one can always ask how, despite the impressive agreement between the planetary positions and the individual's life and personality, did this same natal aspect or personal transit correlate with the lives of countless others who were also born with it? Ten, twenty, even a thousand compelling examples would only be a drop in the ocean of the larger class of individuals born with that aspect or undergoing that transit. But when we look also at world transits, we can examine the chronology of the human community, its collective biography, as it were. In such a study, one can focus on entire cultural epochs and the collective experience of many individuals at once, comprising a wider distribution of phenomena at a particular time for evaluating correlations with the concurrent planetary alignments. The specific years and decades at issue involve many events and many lives coalescing within a certain general zeitgeist, which can more easily lend itself to critical assessments and historical comparisons. By contrast with the details of individual biographies, the character and cultural significance of major historical eras tend to be more widely known, better documented, and more open to straightforward evaluation. They either obviously fit the postulated archetypal meanings of the current planetary alignments, or they do not.

In the following four sections, therefore, I have set forth an initial survey of four different cycles of world transits involving specific combinations of the outer planets, each with its own distinctive archetypal character and each with its specific length and frequency. In terms of the major alignments formed by the planets in these cycles, I have further restricted this initial survey to an examination of only the major dynamic aspects: first the conjunctions and oppositions (the two axial alignments), and later the squares midway between them. By focusing on just the major dynamic aspects of four world transit cycles of the outer planets as measured against the chronology of history, I believe we may enter more quickly and deeply into the nature of the archetypal astrological perspective and assess more readily its validity.

In the following chapters I have focused principally on the history and figures of the Western cultural tradition, as it is this history that I know well enough to make historical judgments with some degree of confidence. It also happens to be an unusually vast, diverse, and complex cultural tradition for which precise historical data is especially extensive and accessible. Where possible and relevant, however, I have cited significant events in the histories of non-Western cultures, especially in more recent periods, and I look forward to future collaboration with scholars in these traditions to pursue more detailed analyses on that broader canvas.

Although most people first encounter serious astrology through readings given by others of their own natal chart and personal transits, many factors in such analyses have actually served to sustain the estrangement of the modern mind from the astrological perspective. The elaborately complicated principles of interpretation and often arcane terminology employed in most conventional astrological analyses, compounded by the subjectivity and suggestibility involved in receiving such analyses, especially in the early stages of inquiry, have contributed to a situation in which many thousands of individuals privately believe that astrology may indeed "work," but they do not know how to assess that possibility for themselves. They cannot see how to bring such a perspective into coherence with the dominant modern scientific world view nor how to communicate their insights in any way that others might find plausible.

Throughout the modern era, an opaque veil over the archetypal cosmos has been effectively maintained by a potent combination of diverse factors, including the disenchanted cosmology of the modern age, the dubious pronouncements of the daily newspaper horoscope columns, the armored resistance of skeptics who do not deeply examine what they zealously reject, the baroque jargon of much astrological discourse, the naïvely uncritical perspectives and frequently harmful predictive practices of many contemporary astrologers, and a vague uneasiness about the seemingly deterministic and fatalistic implications of an astrologically governed universe. I have come to believe, however, that because of the important theoretical and technological advances in the field that have emerged in our time, a careful examination of historical correlations with the cycles of the outer planets can allow the modern mind to explore and assess the astrological perspective with a rigor and depth that has not previously been possible.

That said, I nevertheless believe that an individual who wishes to make a genuinely rigorous assessment of the possible validity and value of astrology must in the end have sufficient knowledge to be able to recognize the most significant structures of meaning in a natal chart, and be able to calculate and interpret personal transits. These are not difficult skills to master, and there is no adequate substitute for a direct encounter with the depth and consistency of these archetypal patternings, based above all on a sustained examination of natal and transit correlations in the context of one's own biographical history and ongoing life experience. In preparation for such a study, I believe that a survey of major planetary cycles within the context of history and culture can provide a uniquely helpful beginning to the reader's journey of exploration into this remarkable realm.

IV

Epochs of Revolution

And life itself told me this secret: "Behold," it said, "I am that which must overcome itself again and again."

—Friedrich Nietzsche
Thus Spoke Zarathustra

From the French Revolution
to the 1960s

I was encouraged to examine the possible existence of historical correlations with planetary cycles when I encountered a number of highly suggestive patterns in which certain cyclical alignments between the outer planets coincided with major historical events and cultural trends of a distinctive character, as if the specific archetypes associated with those planets were emerging on the collective level in periodic cycles. In astronomical terms, these world transits consist of major extended alignments between two or more of the outer planets (Jupiter, Saturn, Uranus, Neptune, and Pluto). Rather than personal transits of a planet in the sky to a planetary position in an individual natal chart, as with the examples cited earlier, world transits are configurations between two or more planets concurrently aligned with each other in the sky—alignments relevant to the entire world, so to speak, rather than to a specific individual. These alignments, such as conjunction or opposition, can last a year or more, and in cases involving any of the three outermost planets with each other (Uranus, Neptune, and Pluto), even a decade or longer.

However, compared with ancient astrology, which appears to have been strongly divinatory in character and based on a considerably smaller body of astronomical observations, the situation that has now emerged provides a radically different as well as greatly expanded basis for research in the area of collective historical correspondences. The discovery of the three outermost planets by telescope in the modern period, combined with the gradual but eventually universal consensus in the astrological community on the empirical correlation of those planets with specific archetypal principles, has dramatically opened up new horizons for research and understanding. Scarcely less significant is the development of computer technology and programming, as well as continued improvements in historical scholarship, which have brought an extraordinary increase in the accuracy and extent of both astronomical and historical data for many centuries into the past. All these factors have produced a very different context for such research. Correlations that in earlier eras were entirely impossible to examine or even imagine are now suddenly visible and open to critical assessment.

The archetypal meanings of the three outermost planets seem to have been derived principally from correlations observed in the study of individual natal charts and personal transits, and of synchronistic historical phenomena in the specific eras in which those planets were discovered. When I applied those meanings to this entirely different category of phenomena—analyzing periods of history when the outer planets were in major alignment in the sky and thus, theoretically, when the corresponding archetypes were most activated in the collective psyche—I was deeply impressed by the empirical correlations. These extended alignments of the outer planets consistently seemed to coincide with sustained periods during which a particular archetypal complex was conspicuously dominant in the collective psyche, defining the zeitgeist, as it were, of that cultural moment. The dominant archetypal complex was always discernibly composed of the specific archetypal principles associated with the relevant aligned planets, as if those archetypes were interacting, merging, and mutually inflecting each other in highly visible ways.

One of the first such instances was the decade of the 1960s. By all accounts the Sixties were an extraordinary era. Intense, problematic, and seminal, the entire decade seems to have been animated by a peculiarly vivid and compelling spirit—something "in the air"—an elemental force apparent to all at the time, that was not present in such a tangible manner during the immediately preceding or subsequent decades, and that in retrospect still sets the era apart as a phenomenon unique in recent memory. Early in the course of my research I noticed that during the entire period of this decade, specifically from 1960 to 1972, there took place a conjunction of two outer planets, Uranus and Pluto, that occurs relatively rarely. Indeed, this was the only conjunction of these planets in the entire twentieth century.

Because of the great distance of both planets from the Sun and Earth, the Uranus-Pluto cycle is one of the longest of all planetary cycles and, because of Pluto's eccentric orbit, is variable in duration. Conjunctions and oppositions between Uranus and Pluto, the two axial alignments, occur only once each per century, with each such alignment lasting approximately twelve years, when the two planets are within 15° of exactitude.[1] To recapitulate briefly the nature of the archetypal principles associated with these two planets: The planet Uranus appears to be correlated with events and biographical phenomena suggestive of an archetypal principle whose essential character is Promethean: emancipatory, rebellious, progressive and innovative, awakening, disruptive and destabilizing, unpredictable, serving to catalyze new beginnings and sudden unexpected change. The planet Pluto, by contrast, is associated with an archetypal principle whose character is Dionysian: elemental, instinctual, powerfully compelling, extreme in its intensity, arising from the depths, both libidinal and destructive, overwhelming and transformative, ever-evolving. On the collective level, the archetypal principle associated with Pluto is regarded as possessing a prodigious, titanic dimension, empowering, intensifying, and compelling whatever it touches on a massive scale.

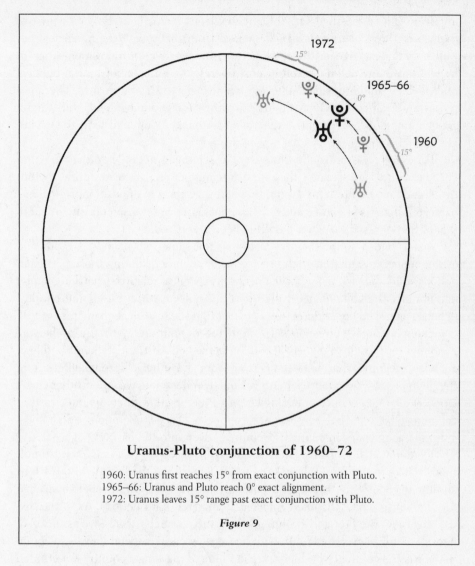

Uranus-Pluto conjunction of 1960–72

1960: Uranus first reaches 15° from exact conjunction with Pluto.
1965–66: Uranus and Pluto reach 0° exact alignment.
1972: Uranus leaves 15° range past exact conjunction with Pluto.

Figure 9

When I applied these specific archetypal meanings to an examination of the historical periods that coincided with the sequence of major alignments of the Uranus-Pluto cycle, it was immediately apparent that not only were these two archetypal principles each conspicuously active in the collective psyche in these particular eras; they were also in some sense combining with each other—acting upon each other, mutually inflecting and synergistically merging. The resulting archetypal complex seemed to express itself quite dramatically during those specific historical eras in which Uranus and Pluto were in axial alignment, as evidenced by such phenomena as widespread radical social and political change and often destructive upheaval, massive empowerment of revolutionary and rebellious impulses, and intensified artistic and intellectual creativity. Other distinctive themes of these historical periods included unusually rapid technological advance, an underlying spirit of restless experiment, drive for innovation, urge for freedom in many realms, revolt against oppression, embrace of radical political philosophies, and intensified collective will to bring forth a new world. These impulses and events were typically mixed with massive demographic shifts and a general ambiance of fervent, often violent intensity combined with the excitement of moving rapidly towards new horizons.

For example, Uranus and Pluto were in alignment not only during the entire decade of the 1960s, when they were in conjunction, but also during the entire decade of the French Revolution when they were in opposition, from 1787 to 1798. This was of course an era whose character was conspicuously similar to that of the 1960s, to which it has often been compared.

Again, had it simply been a matter of the same two planets, Uranus and Pluto, happening to be in such precise major alignment during those particular periods, and not being in such alignment during eras of relative social and cultural equilibrium, the coincidence would have been at best interesting and curious. What so provoked my attention was the fact that the historical character of these coinciding periods corresponded exactly, even profoundly, to the archetypal meanings for those two planets according to the consensus of standard astrological texts, meanings that had been derived from altogether different sources from the phenomena I was now examining. Equally remarkable was the further correlation of alignments of the ongoing Uranus-Pluto cycle with comparable historical periods of epochal revolutionary upheaval, social liberation, and radical cultural change in each century I examined, deep into the past.

Certainly at first glance there would seem to be no two eras more tumultuously alike in such a similarly sustained manner than the decade of the 1960s and the decade of the French Revolution. A pervasive spirit of rebellion against the "Establishment," the *ancien régime,* dominated both periods. As in the Sixties, so also in the French Revolutionary era there was the aggressive assertion of new freedoms in every realm. In both decades an entire generation was swept up in the passions of the era, which were not limited to a single country but erupted simultaneously and independently in many different places in both hemispheres, in a seeming tidal wave of revolts and revolutions, marches, demonstrations, strikes, riots, insurrections, street fighting and barricades, protest movements, independence movements, liberation movements, and calls for radical change. The widespread sense of awakening to a new consciousness of freedom, bringing the birth of a new age, was nearly identical in the two eras and was repeatedly articulated in terms that eloquently conveyed the epochal significance of the historic drama taking place during these decades.[2]

The word "revolution" itself, so often heard in the 1960s and so emblematic of its spirit, first came into wide use in the 1790s in its present meaning of sudden radical change of an overwhelming nature, bringing into being a fundamentally new condition.³ Innumerable allusions, explicit or otherwise, were made in the press and the popular culture of the Sixties that directly connected the spirit and violent revolutionary impulses of that era with those of the French Revolution, as in the lyrics to *Street Fighting Man* by the Rolling Stones:

> *Hey! said my name is called disturbance*
> *I'll shout and scream, I'll kill the king, I'll rail at all his servants.*⁴

The massive upsurge of the revolutionary impulse during these two eras was not only or even principally a political phenomenon, for it expressed itself in every aspect of cultural life: in the music heard, the books read, the ideas discussed, the ideals embraced, the images produced, the evolution of language and fashion, the radical changes in social and sexual mores. It was visible in the incessant challenge to established beliefs and widespread embrace of new perspectives, the movements for radical theological and church reform and antireligious revolt, the drive towards innovation and experiment that affected all the arts, the sudden empowerment of the young, the pivotal role of university communities in the rapid cultural shift. And it was evident above all in the prodigious energy and activism of both eras, the general impulse towards extremes and "radicalization" in so many areas, the suddenly intensified will to construct a new world.

Yet of course in the larger historical context the similarity of these two periods was actually not unique, and as I examined the planetary tables further, I soon found that the precise coincidence of this particular planetary cycle with both the 1960s and the French Revolutionary era was in fact part of a much larger pattern. For it turned out that cyclical alignments of Uranus and Pluto—specifically the conjunction and opposition (the two axial alignments, equivalent to the New Moon and Full Moon alignments of the Sun and Moon in the lunar cycle but on a much larger and longer scale)—consistently occurred in close coincidence with periods in past centuries that were marked by equally extraordinary widespread and sustained social upheavals and radical cultural change, in an apparently systematic manner extending back in time for as far as we have adequate historical records.

For example, since the French Revolution, there were only two other periods when Uranus and Pluto were in conjunction or opposition alignments. Both of these eras stand out as clearly defined by historical events and cultural trends bearing this same highly charged character of massive change and revolution, innovation and upheaval. The first of these alignments took place in the mid-nineteenth century, from 1845 to 1856. This was coincident with the wave of revolutionary upheavals that took place in almost every capital of Europe in 1848–49: Paris, Berlin, Vienna, Budapest, Dresden, Baden, Prague, Rome, Milan. Again one sees the sudden eruption of a collective revolutionary impulse affecting an entire continent with mass insurrections, the emergence of radical political and social movements, revolts for nationalist independence, and the abrupt overthrow of governments throughout Europe. As many historians have said, it was in fact the climax of the revolutionary impulses that were set in motion by the French Revolution. A striking convergence of other archetypally relevant events also occurred during the years of this alignment: among many that could be cited, Karl Marx and Friedrich Engels wrote *The Communist Manifesto*, Henry David Thoreau wrote *On the Duty of Civil Disobedience*, Frederick Douglass and Harriet Tubman led antislavery efforts in the United States, and the women's rights movement began with Elizabeth Cady Stanton and Susan B. Anthony.

Throughout Europe during the years of this conjunction, major artists and intellectuals engaged in revolutionary activities and radical ideas. Beginning in 1845 Dostoevsky entered into revolutionary circles in St. Petersburg first with the radical critic Belinski and then through his involvement in 1848 with the anticzarist utopian Petrashevski circle. Mikhail Bakunin participated in the revolutionary agitations of 1848 in succession in Germany, Austria, and France, and developed his theory of revolutionary anarchism. Wagner, influenced by Bakunin, took part in the 1849 revolution in Dresden and then wrote *Art and Revolution* in exile in Switzerland.

Moreover, this was the same period in which comparable upheavals took place in China (the nearly simultaneous Taiping and Nian rebellions), Japan (the revolutionary dismantling of the long-established Tokugawa social order with the forced opening to the West), India (the intensive British incursions leading to the Sepoy Mutiny), and the Ottoman Empire (catalyzed by the Crimean War): a remarkable clustering of events in less than a decade when sudden "revolts either from above or from below," in the words of the historian William McNeill, "symbolized the irremediable collapse of the traditional order of each of the major Asian civilizations" and permanently transformed the global ecumene. McNeill sums up "the remarkable coincidences which funneled so great a change in world history into the space of less than ten years":

> Thus in each of the great Asian civilizations, revolt either from above or from below rather suddenly discredited or subverted old ways and values; and, in each instance, disruptive influences were enormously stimulated by contacts and collisions with the industrializing West. Indeed, it seems scarcely an exaggeration to say that within the decade of the 1850's the fundamental fourfold cultural balance of the ecumene [Europe, the Middle East, China, India], which had endured the buffets of more than two thousand years, finally gave way. Instead of four (or with Japan, five) autonomous though interconnected civilizations, a yeasty, half-formless, but genuinely global cosmopolitanism began to emerge as the dominant reality of the human community.

The second such alignment of Uranus and Pluto since the French Revolution was the opposition that took place during the decade that spanned the turn of the twentieth century, from 1896 to 1907—again, a period characterized by intense political and social ferment, with the widespread emergence of radical movements and a wave of revolutionary upheavals, drastic social changes, and massive demographic shifts throughout the world. A sudden proliferation of progressive and radical labor movements occurred in this period throughout Europe and North America. These included the near-simultaneous founding of each of the major socialist parties in England, the United States, Russia, and France—all taking place between 1900 and 1905—and also the Industrial Workers of the World, the Menshevik Party, and the Bolshevik Party under Lenin and Trotsky that marked the beginning of modern Communism, all between 1903 and 1905.

This was also the critical period for the emergence of both the militant women's movement and the black civil rights movement, with the founding of the Women's Social and Political Union in 1903, the International Woman Suffrage Alliance in 1904, and the Niagara Movement in 1905. In France the entire period of 1896–1907 was dominated by the long upheaval of the Dreyfus Affair, which convulsed the nation in ways markedly similar to the upheavals that occurred in France during the three other Uranus-Pluto alignments cited above (these included the sustained unleashing of violent passions, conflicts over reform, and defiance of established authority, as in Émile Zola's famous *"J'accuse"* open letter to the president of France) and which resulted in the unification and empowerment of left-wing movements in French politics. And here again an extraordinary number of leaders and advocates in the area of progressive and radical social transformation emerged and flourished during this period, from mainstream progressive reformists like Theodore Roosevelt and William Jennings Bryan to more radical figures such as Eugene Debs, Emma Goldman, Rosa Luxemburg, Beatrice and Sidney Webb, George Bernard Shaw and other Fabians, H. G. Wells, Emmeline Pankhurst, Jane Addams, Upton Sinclair, Ida Tarbell, Lincoln Steffens, W. E. B. Du Bois, Theodor Herzl, and Georges Sorel, among many others. From civil rights and feminism to journalism and economic reform, the writings and actions of this wave of reformers and radical leaders at this time exerted a decisive influence on the social and political life of the twentieth century.

As with the other axial Uranus-Pluto periods, during this same span of years occurred comparable epoch-making events throughout the world: the Boxer Rebellion in China of 1898–1900 and the rapid rise of revolutionary Chinese nationalist movements; the *Potemkin* mutiny and Russian revolution of 1905–06, which brought the beginning of the violent upheavals that culminated in the overthrow of the czar twelve years later; a wave of nationalist revolts in India, Turkey, Persia, and the Austro-Hungarian Empire; the beginning of the long civil disobedience movement of the Indians in South Africa led by Gandhi; and the founding of other seminal nationalist independence movements such as the World Zionist Organization in 1897 and the Sinn Fein party in Ireland in 1902.

It was as if an immense wave of revolutionary energy swept through the world at the turn of the twentieth century, producing in many nations and in many spheres of activity a profusion of movements pressing for freedom, change, and reform. Taken together, these and many other events of a similar character constituted a decisive watershed for the emergence of modern progressivism, radicalism, equal rights, and independence movements with significant consequences for the ensuing century, many of which came to a climax in the 1960s during the next conjunction of Uranus and Pluto.

In the course of examining thousands of historical events and cultural phenomena over the years, I found that archetypally relevant events consistently began to coincide with conjunctions and oppositions of the outer planets when the planets first moved within approximately 20° of exact alignment, gradually increasing in frequency and intensity and then, after exactitude was reached, decreasing in a wavelike continuum. From the time the planets reached 15° of exact alignment, the archetypal complex appeared to be fully active, with the frequency and intensity of observed correlations especially robust. For purposes of simplicity and clarity, in the detailed survey of the evidence presented in these chapters, the years I have specified for each period as coinciding with outer-planet conjunctions and oppositions reflect the smaller 15° orb. Beyond that point, however, was a penumbral range, up through about 20°, during which correlations could regularly be observed that I will cite and specify as such when relevant.

I should also clarify here that the periods coinciding with these alignments did not mark years in which the characteristic historical events and cultural trends suddenly turned on and then off, when the alignment was over, like bivalent light switches. Rather, the periods in question seemed to represent times when continuing, usually long-developing trends came to a boil, as it were; when a certain heightened stimulus or concrete fruition brought specific categories of cultural phenomena to conspicuous expression, causing those tendencies to emerge more explicitly and dramatically into the collective consciousness. From that more decisive point of inception or climax, those cultural tendencies then continued to unfold in diverse ways in subsequent years and decades after the alignment was over.

In general, the observed correlations suggested something more like fluidly interpenetrating quantum wave patterns rather than discrete atomistic Newtonian events. The dynamics appeared to be complex, holistic, and probabilistic rather than simple, linear, and reductively deterministic. The correlations were most intelligible if they were regarded not as mechanistically causal in character but rather as multidimensionally archetypal and synchronistic.

Synchronic and Diachronic
Patterns in History

T he relevant archetypal patterns of historical events and cultural activity coincident with these planetary alignments were both synchronic and dia-chronic in nature, a dual form of patterning that was strikingly consistent throughout the larger body of evidence. The *synchronic* patterns involved those cases where many events of the same archetypal character took place simultane-ously in different cultures and individual lives in coincidence with the same alignment, such as simultaneous revolutions or simultaneous scientific break-throughs occurring independently in separate countries and continents. The *dia-chronic* patterns, by contrast, involved cases where events taking place during one alignment had a close archetypal and often historical association with events occurring during preceding and subsequent alignments of the same planets in such a way as to suggest a distinct unfolding cycle.

The periods of these alignments of Uranus and Pluto were thus related not only in terms of the general archetypal character that they had in common but also by their sequential dynamism. Relevant historical trends and cultural move-ments seemed to undergo a sharply intensified development during each of these specific periods in what appeared to be a continuously unfolding but cyclically "punctuated" evolution. Such diachronic patterns were clearly evident in corre-lation with the Uranus-Pluto alignments of the past several centuries in a number of areas of modern cultural history, such as feminism and the women's move-ment, the abolitionist and civil rights movements, and philosophies of political revolution and radical social change, among others.

Feminism and Women's Movements

Historians of feminism and women's movements will immediately recognize the pivotal importance of the four specific eras that coincided with the sequence of consecutive Uranus-Pluto axial alignments of the past two hundred fifty years, as if the evolution of the struggle for women's rights had been decisively impelled forward in distinct stages each of which began in exact coincidence with these specific periods of planetary alignment.

The earliest significant emergence of modern feminism took place during the Uranus-Pluto opposition of the French Revolutionary period (1787–98). In

England, this period brought the publication in 1792 of the first great feminist document and manifesto, Mary Wollstonecraft's *A Vindication of the Rights of Woman* ("I do not wish them to have power over men, but over themselves"). In France, women at many levels of society played significant roles in the revolutionary upheaval, from the Belgian courtesan and revolutionary street orator Théroigne de Méricourt to radical aristocrats such as Madame de Staël and Madame Roland whose salons became influential centers of political debate and activity. Demands to honor women's "inalienable rights" were made to the Assembly by Olympe de Gouges and were supported by the women's political organization *Amis de la Vérité*, which argued for women's education, civil rights, and freedom for divorce.

The next major stage developed during the immediately following Uranus-Pluto conjunction of 1845–56, with the emergence of the women's suffrage movement in the United States under the leadership of Elizabeth Cady Stanton, Lucretia Mott, Lucy Stone, and Susan B. Anthony. At this time the first Women's Rights Convention was held at Seneca Falls, New York, in 1848, after which women's rights meetings were held regularly. At this time Stanton formulated the first organized demand for women's suffrage, while in England Harriet Taylor wrote *The Enfranchisement of Women*. During this same conjunction, Margaret Fuller wrote *Woman in the Nineteenth Century*, the first major work of American feminism; Lucretia Mott published *Discourse on Women*, which argued for educational equality for women; Amelia Bloomer began the first prominent women's rights newspaper; and Sojourner Truth delivered her famous "Ain't I a Woman?" speech before a women's rights convention in Akron, Ohio. Near the end of the conjunction period, Walt Whitman opened his epoch-making *Leaves of Grass* in 1855 with the proclamation:

> *I am the poet of the woman the same as the man,*
> *And I say it is as great to be a woman as to be a man.*

The women's suffrage movement then reached its next, more militant and international stage during the immediately following Uranus-Pluto opposition of 1896–1907, which was marked by a wave of militant suffragist activity and such seminal events as the delivery to British parliament in 1902 of a 37,000 signatory petition demanding women's right to vote, the founding of the Women's Social and Political Union in England in 1903 under the leadership of Emmeline Pankhurst, the founding of the International Woman Suffrage Alliance in 1904, and the political reorganization of the National American Woman Suffrage Association by Carrie Chapman Catt beginning in 1905. In the following year, the term "suffragette" was first used. Also in 1906 Emma Goldman cofounded and edited the anarchist monthly *Mother Earth*. During the same alignment, galvanized by Nannie Helen Burroughs's speech "How the Sisters are Hindered from Helping" to the National Baptist Convention, the largest African-American women's organization, Women's Convention, was founded. Also published during this period was Charlotte Perkins Gilman's *Women and Economics* of 1898, calling for economic freedom and social equality for women—a book widely influential and internationally translated at the time but then unread for several decades until it was rediscovered by feminists in the 1960s. On other fronts, Marie Curie in France became in 1903 the first woman to receive the Nobel Prize, while in London from 1905 the Bloomsbury Group emerged as Virginia Woolf and her circle of artistic and intellectual pioneers broke free of Victorian social codes. At the end of the alignment period in 1906, Susan B. Anthony died; in her final public speech she asserted her famous motto: "Failure is impossible."

Finally, the immediately following conjunction of 1960–72 coincided with perhaps the most dramatic stage in this evolution, with the decisive widespread emergence of feminism and the women's liberation movement, impelled by the publication of Betty Friedan's landmark work *The Feminine Mystique* in 1963 (five million copies were sold by 1970), the founding of the National Organization for Women in 1966, the beginning of radical feminism with the founding of New York Radical Women and Redstockings in 1968–69, the writing of *Our Bodies, Ourselves* by the Boston Women's Health Collective in 1969, the founding of the Women's Action Alliance in 1971, and the work of many individual writers and activists such as Doris Lessing, Kate Millett, Germaine Greer, and Gloria Steinem, all contributing to innumerable advances initiated on many fronts in those years.

In examining cyclical sequences of a specific cultural stream, I observed two typical patterns. One took the form of dense clusterings of events and figures that shared a specific archetypal character—in this instance a sharply intensified impulse towards emancipation and empowerment—all appearing in close coincidence with the period of a particular alignment, followed by an intervening period in which such phenomena were diminished in number and intensity. This less active period would last until the next cyclical alignment, which would coincide with a new clustering of events and figures of the same archetypal character that bore a clear historical relationship to the earlier epoch. The quiescent intervening period resembled a stage of gestation, with the cultural impulse undergoing a kind of invisible subterranean development until the next alignment period brought forth a resurgence of the phenomenon, but now in a new form that reflected the intervening historical influences and the new cultural context.

In the second typical pattern, the period of dense clustering during the original alignment was followed in subsequent years by a continuing and sometimes even increasing appearance of related cultural phenomena. In these cases, the alignment period seemed to act as a decisive catalyst for the cultural impulse in question, which would continue developing unabated after the alignment period was over, coming to fruition in significant ways or taking new forms. These subsequent developments and transformations, as we will see, consistently coincided with other planetary alignments whose different archetypal character closely corresponded to the nature of the development (successful and expansive milestones when Jupiter aligned with Uranus, for example, and more problematic, constricting developments, or structuring and solidifying ones, when Saturn was involved). When, however, the next major Uranus-Pluto alignment occurred, another sustained catalyzing period took place, marked by another dense clustering of archetypally relevant cultural phenomena bearing a clear historical relationship to the preceding Uranus-Pluto alignment. We will be able to observe these two basic forms of sequential patterning throughout the evidence presented below. With the history of feminism as with the other cultural phenomena we are examining, the larger interplay of correlations will emerge as our survey encompasses the other planetary cycles.

Abolitionist and Civil Rights Movements

A parallel pattern of cyclical stages of accelerated development occurred in an entirely different emancipatory struggle during these same centuries, the long movement for the freedom and civil rights of African-Americans. During the Uranus-Pluto alignment of 1787–98, that of the French Revolution, there simultaneously emerged in Britain, the United States, and France the first widespread public call for the abolition of slavery, with the appearance of enormously popular petitions against the slave trade, the founding of the Abolition Society in England led by Thomas Clarkson (1787), the Free African Society in Philadelphia (1787), the Society of the Friends of the Blacks in France (1788), and the publication of the widely read autobiography of the freed slave Olaudah Equiano (1789), which was the first English-language indictment of slavery. In addition, this same period saw the publication of William Blake's engravings of slave life (1796), which strongly influenced all subsequent abolitionist iconography; the successful revolution of Haitian slaves under the leadership of Toussaint L'Ouverture (1791–94); the abandonment of the slave trade by Denmark (1792), the first nation to do so; and the French Revolutionary government's freeing of slaves in all French colonies (1794), the first instance of such an emancipation.

Similarly, the immediately following Uranus-Pluto alignment of 1845–56 coincided with the peak of abolitionist activism in the United States, which was marked by the influential activity of Frederick Douglass, the publication of his autobiography (1845) and his antislavery newspaper the *North Star* (from 1847), the flourishing of the Underground Railway through the work of Harriet Tubman (who escaped from slavery in 1849) among many others, the electrifying preaching of Sojourner Truth against slavery and on behalf of women's rights, the publication of her autobiography (1850), Emerson's many public lectures against slavery, popular uprisings by both blacks and whites in the North against the Fugitive Slave Act (1850–54), the publication of Harriet Beecher Stowe's immensely influential *Uncle Tom's Cabin* (1852), and the militant antislavery activity of John Brown and his followers (from 1855). This same period also saw the founding of the Free Soil (1848) and Republican parties (1854), the latter joined by Lincoln, which brought abolitionist views into the mainstream of American politics and eventually precipitated the Civil War.[5] It was during this period as well that Liberia proclaimed its independence (1847), the first African colony to do so.

This cyclical sequence then continued during the immediately following Uranus-Pluto opposition alignment of 1896–1907, first with the rise of Booker T. Washington and his call for moderate social and educational reform for blacks, and then with the first emergence of organized black protest in the United States under the leadership of W. E. B. Du Bois, which was marked by the founding of the Niagara Movement in 1905 by Du Bois and twenty-nine other black intellectuals and which called for full political, social, and civil rights for all African-Americans. Du Bois published at this time his influential *The Souls of Black Folk* (1903), which began the intellectual revolt against accommodationism. During the period of this same alignment, there took place the first Pan-African Conference in London (1900), which supported the struggle for the freedom of all peoples of African descent, and the founding of the Congo Reform Association by Edmund Morel in England, supported by many major cultural figures such as Arthur Conan Doyle, Mark Twain, and Booker T. Washington, to protest colonialist atrocities in the Belgian Congo (1904).

And finally of course, the period of 1960–1972, that of the most recent Uranus-Pluto conjunction, brought a culmination of the movement for black civil rights with the activities of Martin Luther King Jr., Malcolm X, and Bayard Rustin, among many other leaders; such organizations as the National Association for the Advancement of Colored People (which emerged directly from the Niagara Movement of the previous alignment) and the Student Nonviolent Coordinating Committee; the Freedom Riders and the great multitude of sit-ins, demonstrations, and marches; the passage of the Civil Rights Acts of 1965 and 1968; the rise of the black power movement and the founding of the Black Panthers; the writings and speeches of James Baldwin, Stokeley Carmichael, Angela Davis, Eldridge Cleaver; and a host of other events, actions, and writings that reflected the climactic nature of the 1960s for this movement. Comparable phenomena took place throughout the continent of Africa at this time, from the dramatic resistance activities of Nelson Mandela and the African National Congress in South Africa to the insurrections, independence movements, and achievement of indigenous African control over European colonial powers that occurred in most of the nations of sub-Saharan Africa during this decade.

Perhaps the paradigmatic statement of this powerful collective impulse during the 1960s was Martin Luther King's historic speech in front of the Lincoln Memorial at the March on Washington in 1963, where King gave prophetic voice to the long evolutionary struggle (Pluto) for liberation, awakening, and freedom (Uranus):

I have a dream that one day this nation will rise up and live out the true meaning of its creed: "We hold these truths to be self-evident: that all men are created equal." I have a dream that one day on the red hills of Georgia the sons of former slaves and the sons of former slaveowners will be able to sit down together at a table of brotherhood. I have a dream that one day even the state of Mississippi, a desert state, swelter- ing with the heat of injustice and oppression, will be transformed into an oasis of freedom and justice. I have a dream that my four children will one day live in a nation where they will not be judged by the color of their skin but by the content of their character. . . . With this faith we will be able to work together, to pray together, to struggle together, to go to jail together, to stand up for freedom together, knowing that we will be free one day.

This will be the day when all of God's children will be able to sing with a new meaning, "My country, 'tis of thee, sweet land of liberty, of thee I sing. Land where my fathers died, land of the pilgrim's pride, from every mountainside, let freedom ring." And if America is to be a great nation, this must become true. So let freedom ring from the prodi- gious hilltops of New Hampshire. Let freedom ring from the mighty mountains of New York. Let freedom ring from the heightening Alleghe- nies of Pennsylvania! Let freedom ring from the snowcapped Rockies of Colorado! Let freedom ring from the curvaceous peaks of California! But not only that; let freedom ring from Stone Mountain of Georgia! Let freedom ring from Lookout Mountain of Tennessee! Let freedom ring from every hill and every molehill of Mississippi. From every moun- tainside, let freedom ring.

When we let freedom ring, when we let it ring from every village and every hamlet, from every state and every city, we will be able to speed up that day when all of God's children, black men and white men, Jews and Gentiles, Protestants and Catholics, will be able to join hands and sing in the words of the old Negro spiritual, "Free at last! Free at last! Thank God Almighty, we are free at last!"

Nonviolent Civil Disobedience

The great historical dramas of both of these enduring movements for social change and human freedom thus appeared to follow a consistent pattern of cyclical peaks that precisely coincided with the periods of the Uranus-Pluto alignments. These in turn appeared to be particular manifestations of a more general cyclical pattern in which a collective impulse of emancipation and radi- cal change was activated and empowered in many areas simultaneously in just these periods. Yet the connections between these eras were often even more spe- cific. For example, the philosophy and tactics of nonviolent civil disobedience employed by Martin Luther King and others in the Sixties' civil rights and anti-war movements were inspired above all by the example of Mohandas Gandhi. During the Uranus-Pluto opposition that immediately preceded the conjunction of the 1960s, Gandhi first developed and employed his civil disobedience philosophy of *satyagraha* ("truth force" or "holding to truth") in the struggle for Indian rights in South Africa in 1906 in response to his being thrown off a "whites only" train car.

Gandhi was influenced, as was King later, by the political writings of Leo Tolstoy, whose influence on radical reform and revolutionary movements in Russian society and personal defiance of the Russian state and church were at their peak in these same years, 1896–1907. This cyclical pattern reached back still further, for it was during the Uranus-Pluto conjunction just before this (1845–56) that Thoreau wrote and published in 1849 his seminal essay *On the Duty of Civil Disobedience*, which described his brief imprisonment for refusing, on anti-slavery grounds, to pay a tax levied by the U.S. government to support its war against Mexico. Thoreau's essay directly influenced first Tolstoy, then Gandhi, then King. This lineage of descent in the evolution of civil disobedience—Thoreau, Tolstoy, Gandhi, King—is of course well known. What is surprising—and what should not happen so consistently—is the precise correlation with the Uranus-Pluto cycle, a correlation replicated in so many other archetypally related historical and cultural phenomena.

Radical Socialism

A comparable pattern occurred in the evolution of radical socialist theory. Thus Marx and Engels's *Communist Manifesto* of 1848 and the origins of revolutionary Marxist socialism coincided precisely with the Uranus-Pluto conjunction of the 1845–56 period. The next decisive step in that evolution—the emergence of Lenin and Trotsky, the founding of the Bolshevik Party, and the formulation of Marxist-Leninist philosophy in Lenin's manifesto *What Is To Be Done?*—exactly coincided with the immediately following Uranus-Pluto opposition of 1896–1907.

Finally, during the following conjunction of 1960–72, there took place the most massive upsurge and dissemination of radical socialist and Marxist-Leninist doctrines, which influenced revolutionary movements throughout the Third World and student activists and intellectuals throughout the West, and brought unprecedentedly widespread popularity to Marxist-inspired revolutionary leaders and theorists such as Che Guevara, Ho Chi Minh, Mao Zedong, Fidel Castro, Frantz Fanon, Jean-Paul Sartre, and Herbert Marcuse. This period brought yet another influential Marxist manifesto, Mao's "Little Red Book," the bible of the tens of thousands of young Chinese Cultural Revolutionaries during these years. In a different spirit, the liberation theology movement was born in Latin America during this same conjunction, through the work of Gustavo Gutiérrez and Leonardo Boff, who sought to combine Marxist principles of social revolution and historical consciousness of structures of economic oppression with incarnational Christian ideals of justice, community, and compassionate engagement with the plight of the poor.

Nor was this cyclical pattern limited to these last three alignments, for it was during the French Revolution and the 1790s, the period of the Uranus-Pluto opposition just before these, that alongside the revolutionary leaders Danton, Marat, Saint-Just, and Robespierre there emerged the first major theorist of revolutionary socialism, François-Noël Babeuf, the leader of the Conspiracy of the Equals that attempted to overthrow the Directory and press the French Revolution to bring full economic equality as well as political equality to the masses. In 1794 Babeuf founded *Le Tribun du Peuple*, the first journal that advocated socialist views, and formulated a doctrine of class war and the revolutionary role of the working class that became fundamental to the Marxist theory of revolution which emerged during the following Uranus-Pluto conjunction of 1845–56. Similarly, the radical anarchist and libertarian views of Proudhon, Bakunin, and Herzen—all formulated precisely during the period of the latter conjunction—were principally anticipated by William Godwin's *Enquiry Concerning Political Justice*. Godwin's celebrated work was published in 1793 during the French Revolutionary alignment; in its lucid and passionate summary of both the radical beliefs that had contributed to the Revolution and those then emerging from it, the book exerted immense influence on the intellectual life of the age and of the century to come—especially during subsequent Uranus-Pluto alignments.

The English Revolution and Radical Reformation

If we take another step back into history and look at the Uranus-Pluto cycle during the centuries preceding the French Revolution, we find a clear continuation of the same pattern. The Uranus-Pluto opposition immediately prior to that of the French Revolution took place from 1643 to 1654, in close coincidence with the great wave of revolutions and rebellions that swept Europe in the mid-seventeenth century, and in particular with virtually the entire period of England's major revolutionary watershed: the English or Puritan Revolution (referred to in its own century as "The Great Rebellion"). This was yet again an era of extraordinarily intense, widespread, and sustained social upheaval, political radicalism, and countercultural vitality, essentially the English equivalent of the French Revolution, which it influenced and anticipated.

As in the four alignment periods just discussed, here too the same themes appear with remarkable consistency: the successive waves of rebellion against the established order, year after year of political and social chaos, the proliferation of radical movements and ideas that deeply affected the subsequent course of Western history. Here again was the collective empowerment of a many-sided impulse to make over the world in radically new ways, with the sudden emergence of innumerable revolutionary groups and dissenting factions—radical Puritans, Independents, Roundheads, Levellers, Diggers, Quakers, Ranters, Fifth Monarchy Men, Adamists, among many such radical sects that flourished during just those years—resulting in, as the title of Christopher Hill's well-known history described it, "the world turned upside down." Here again was the call for an overthrow of royal tyranny and the forced abdication and execution of the king—Charles I during this Uranus-Pluto alignment of the 1640s thus meeting the same fate that would befall Louis XVI during the following opposition of the 1790s (and, less the execution, Louis-Philippe during the following conjunction of the 1840s).

It was in the years of this alignment, 1643–54, that there emerged the seminal appeal to such characteristically emancipatory ideas as the sovereignty of the people, representative government, natural rights, a written constitution, equality of representation, freedom of the press, religious toleration, and the superiority of rational debate over theological dogma and historical tradition for political decision-making—all this producing, in Hill's words, "so great an intellectual revolution that it is difficult for us to conceive how men thought before it was made." It was of course these ideas that directly anticipated the revolutionary ideals that would later be instituted during the following Uranus-Pluto opposition of 1787–98, one cycle later, in the U.S. Constitution (1787–88) and the French Declaration of the Rights of Man and the Citizen (1789). These same principles would in turn inform the ideals and movements that emerged with new force and in new contexts precisely during the three subsequent Uranus-Pluto alignments: the revolutionary 1845–56 period, the turn of the twentieth century, and the 1960s.

Moreover, as historians have often remarked, with much the same wonder and puzzlement with which they contemplated these later periods of widespread simultaneous revolutions that erupted independently in many nations (constantly appearing in these restrained and sober historical analyses are such phrases as "astonishing," "virtually incredible," "utterly baffling"), what happened in England in the 1643–54 era curiously coincided with a wave of rebellions and upheavals that swept the rest of Europe and Asia during just those same years.[6] In France once again there occurred another sustained period of revolt and political turmoil—the five-year series of Fronde uprisings by the parlements and the nobility which took place from 1648 to 1653—the most significant rebellion against royal sovereignty in France until Uranus and Pluto were again in opposition during the French Revolution. Here again, barricades were thrown up in Paris, amid mass riots and street fighting, as part of a larger cyclical pattern—in exact coincidence with Uranus-Pluto alignments—of comparable mass street insurrections in Paris in July 1789, Paris in February 1848, and Paris in May 1968.

In Russia during the same years as the Fronde revolts, there occurred a five-year mass uprising by the serfs (1648–53), while also during this alignment the Cossacks revolted to gain Ukrainian independence from Poland, the Irish rebelled against England, Portugal revolted against Spain, and the long and influential struggle of the Netherlands for political liberty was finally achieved and ratified in the Treaty of Münster (1648). Throughout the continent of Europe, "rebellion was everywhere in the air." Nor were these upheavals limited to Europe; in Asia during this same period, sustained and massive rebellions in China brought about the collapse of the Ming dynasty (1644), after three centuries' rule, and the rise of the Manchu dynasty. The latter would begin its own fall two centuries later with the Taiping Rebellion during the Uranus-Pluto conjunction of the 1845–56 period.

Again, as one moves yet further back in history, one finds fully comparable periods of extraordinary social upheaval, rebellion, and political transformation coincident with the Uranus-Pluto cycle. For example, the opposition preceding that just cited took place during the years 1533 to 1545, the most tumultuous and radical period of the Reformation as it swept through Europe: armed insurrections, the anarchistic revolt in Münster by the Anabaptists and their militant establishment of a "communist state" under John of Leiden, Henry VIII's epochal schism of England from Rome and the Catholic Church, and the adoption of the Reformation in Geneva, Württemberg, Brandenburg, Saxony, Denmark, Norway, Sweden, and Finland.

To mention here just two examples from classical antiquity, the period of Spartacus's massive rebellion of slaves and the dispossessed against the Roman state in 73–71 BCE, the largest and most sustained such insurrection in ancient history, took place during the Uranus-Pluto conjunction of 74–65, the same era in which Julius Caesar began his rise to power. And still earlier, the conjunction of 328–318 BCE coincided with the period of profound cultural and political upheaval that transformed the ancient world, from Greece and Egypt to Persia and India, in the wake of Alexander the Great's conquests and the beginning of the Hellenistic era.

Scientific and
Technological Revolutions

One of the most interesting and challenging characteristics of the historical correlations with the Uranus-Pluto cycle is the occurrence of distinctive cyclical developments exactly like those cited above in altogether
separate, seemingly independent—but in archetypal terms clearly related—areas
of human endeavor during precisely the same periods and with the same degree
of cyclical definition. For example, the entire sequence of Uranus-Pluto alignment periods in the modern era that we have been examining in terms of revolutionary social and political phenomena happened to be eras marked by equally
significant scientific and technological revolutions and advances—thus involving
breakthroughs, revolutions, radical social changes, and emancipatory impulses
of an entirely different category. Again, it appeared as if during these specific
historical periods, a multivalently comprehensive archetypal complex—a Promethean principle at once emancipatory and innovative, scientific-technological
and social-political—were being activated and empowered in many areas of human
activity simultaneously. This coincidence of scientific-technological and social-
political phenomena, repeated so precisely during each alignment period, is difficult to explain in conventional sociological terms, though it makes perfect sense
from an archetypal point of view: in this light, the various phenomena reflected
a collective empowerment (Pluto) of the Promethean impulse (Uranus), a dynamic evolutionary drive pressing both individuals and societies towards radical
change, freedom, and innovation on many levels simultaneously.

In the area of technological advance, the period of the most recent Uranus-
Pluto conjunction, 1960–72, brought an especially dramatic technological breakthrough and achievement, the American and Russian space programs that climaxed
in the Apollo 11 Moon landing in 1969. The entire arc of this momentous series
of space flights, from the first expeditions by Yuri Gagarin and Alan Shepard in
1961 through the last of the Moon landings in 1972, took place precisely within
the 15° time-span of the Uranus-Pluto conjunction. Here was the titanic empowerment of Promethean technological genius, the restless quest for new horizons, the defiance of gravity, the epochal breakthrough beyond ancient limits,
the penetration into celestial space, "stealing fire from the heavens."

This correlation with epochal breakthroughs in the technology of human flight was in fact part of a larger pattern, for it was exactly during the immediately preceding Uranus-Pluto opposition of 1896–1907 that the initial development of the airplane took place, when the Wright brothers achieved their first successful powered flight near Kitty Hawk, North Carolina, in 1903. Coincidentally, several other experiments in powered aviation took place independently during this same opposition, almost simultaneously in several parts of the world, including the invention of the first rigid airship, the Zeppelin, in 1900. Of these, it was Wilbur and Orville Wright who succeeded in accomplishing, in the careful terms of historians of aviation, "the first power-driven heavier-than-air machine in which humans made free, controlled and sustained flight."

Nor were these diachronic achievements in aviation and space flight isolated technological advances in their times, for both these periods, 1960–72 and 1896–1907, were pervasively marked by an extraordinary acceleration of technological developments, breakthroughs, and their proliferation in many areas simultaneously. The turn of the twentieth century saw such dramatic advances not only in the development of the airplane but also of the automobile, radio, motion picture technology, chromatography, the cathode ray tube, and the photoelectric cell, among many other technological advances; and the 1960s brought a comparable multitude of advances in computer technology, microelectronics, biochemistry, agriculture, industrial and medical technology, jet aviation, and space satellite technology, all with deeply transforming consequences for twentieth-century life.

Again, these too were part of much longer cyclical patterns in which Uranus-Pluto alignments in earlier centuries precisely coincided with periods of sustained major technological advance and transformation. Thus we see the rapid development and global proliferation of the telegraph, railroads, and steamships during the Uranus-Pluto conjunction of the 1845–56 period, when the collective self-awareness of that era's unprecedented technological progress was displayed at the famous Great Exhibition and Crystal Palace in London in 1851 and at the Paris International Exposition of 1854.

The two immediately preceding Uranus-Pluto alignments presented a similar pattern of historically consequential technological advances and milestones. In the 1787–98 French Revolutionary period, Eli Whitney's invention of the cotton gin in 1793, his pioneering of mass production techniques, the automation of grain milling, and the widespread mechanization of the textile industry caused a radical transformation of the American and British economies and accelerated the spread of the Industrial Revolution. The actual beginnings of the Industrial Revolution can be precisely traced to the immediately preceding conjunction of 1705–16, when the combination of Thomas Newcomen's invention of the first practical steam engine in 1705–11 and Abraham Darby's discovery in 1709 of the utility of coal for iron-smelting furnaces began the age of steam, coal, and iron.

Finally, going back to the first Uranus-Pluto conjunction of the modern period, that of 1450–61, we find that it was just these years that brought Gutenberg's epoch-making development of the movable-type printing press—the necessary precondition for the Reformation, Scientific Revolution, and Enlightenment. This was the same conjunction that coincided with the fall of Constantinople (1453) and the resulting mass emigration of scholars to the West from the collapsing Byzantine Empire that played such a crucial role in precipitating the Renaissance.

The history of scientific revolution and advance displayed the same remarkable pattern of close correlation with the Uranus-Pluto cycle. Copernicus's *De Revolutionibus*, the epochal starting point of the Scientific Revolution, was published in 1543 during the same Uranus-Pluto opposition that coincided with the radical Reformation (1533–45). (This was the alignment immediately following that of Gutenberg's press invention just cited.) Here we see as well the synchronic nature of these correlations, not only in the social-political realm but within the realm of science itself: Historians of science have often noted the coincidence that Vesalius's *De Humani Corporis Fabrica*, which founded modern anatomy and began a revolution in biology and medicine just as Copernicus began one in astronomy, was published in the same year, 1543, as *De Revolutionibus*.

Here too we see the diachronic patterning in clear evidence: Historians of science have also often noted that virtually no significant advances were made in the Copernican revolution for almost half a century after 1543, not until Kepler and Galileo embraced the heliocentric hypothesis—which took place in exact coincidence with the next Uranus-Pluto conjunction after the publication of *De Revolutionibus*, that of 1592–1602. During this period the entire Scientific Revolution was decisively propelled forward as Galileo began his revolutionary studies in the laws of motion (from 1592). Kepler experienced his initial sudden illumination concerning the geometrical harmonies of the planetary orbits (1595) that led to the writing of his first work, *Mysterium Cosmographicum* (1595–96), the first fully committed Copernican treatise since *De Revolutionibus* that expanded the mathematical arguments for the heliocentric theory. Kepler then moved to Prague and began his seminal work with Tycho de Brahe's unprecedentedly accurate astronomical observations, which provided the essential empirical basis for the heliocentric theory (1600). William Gilbert published his revolutionary *De Magnete* (1600), which in turn influenced Kepler's theories on the physical dynamics of the solar system. And finally, Francis Bacon began his long series of influential writings that declared the need for a radically new philosophy for a new age—empirical, pragmatic, scientific, no longer constrained by fruitless veneration for past authorities—beginning with *Temporis partus masculus* ("Child of the Time," 1602–03) and followed by *The Advancement of Learning* (1605).

Significant advances in scientific thought, of course, did not take place exclusively during such periods; the patterns were far more complex and nuanced than that, and here, as with the other phenomena we have been discussing, the Uranus-Pluto cycle was not the only relevant one. (As we will see later, the much shorter and more frequent Jupiter-Uranus cycle, for example, coincided with extraordinary consistency with an ongoing cyclical pattern of scientific and other intellectual and cultural breakthroughs that unfolded in between as well as in coincidence with the Uranus-Pluto alignments.) Yet keeping this caveat in mind, there was nevertheless an unmistakable tendency for these long and relatively rare Uranus-Pluto alignments to coincide with sustained widespread advances in science that had an especially epochal and revolutionary character.

For example, after the two alignments just cited, the immediately following opposition of 1643–54 that coincided with the English Revolution also coincided closely with the Cartesian mechanistic revolution that radically transformed the scientific understanding in the mid-seventeenth century. This was marked by the publication of Descartes's *Principles of Philosophy* in 1644–47 and the work of Hobbes, Boyle, Pascal, and others beginning at this time, which definitively overthrew the Aristotelian framework and established the necessary foundation for the Newtonian synthesis.

Similarly, the immediately following Uranus-Pluto opposition one full cycle later, which coincided with the French Revolution, also precisely coincided with the revolution in modern chemistry that was marked by the publication of Lavoisier's *Elements of Chemistry* in 1789 *and* the revolution in modern geology that was marked by the publication of James Hutton's *A Theory of the Earth* in 1795, both during this same alignment.

The next such alignment, the conjunction of 1845–56 that coincided with the wave of revolutions and upheavals throughout Europe and Asia discussed earlier, also coincided with the period in which Charles Darwin, after years of work on the theory, began at last in 1855 to write his book on natural selection that described his theory of evolution. As we shall examine later, he did not make his theory public until 1858 (just as Jupiter conjoined Uranus in the sky), when he received the famous letter from Alfred Russel Wallace containing the latter's independent formulation of the same theory, which he had developed during his years of research in South America and Borneo from 1848 onwards.

Remarkably, it was during the immediately preceding Uranus-Pluto opposition of the 1790s that Darwin's grandfather Erasmus Darwin in England (1794), Goethe in Germany (1794–95), and Geoffroy Saint-Hilaire in France (1795) all independently developed evolutionary theories on the origin of species that constituted the immediate precedents to Darwin's and Wallace's theory. This coincidence was noted by Darwin himself in *The Origin of Species*: "It is rather a singular instance of the manner in which similar views arise at about the same time, that Goethe in Germany, Dr. Darwin in England, and Geoffroy Saint-Hilaire in France, came to the same conclusion on the origin of species in the years 1794–95." Moreover, also in France, Lamarck began developing *his* evolutionary theory some time between 1794 and 1802. Finally it was also during the

1790s alignment that Malthus wrote and published, in 1798, his *Essay on the Principle of Population* with its theory of the necessary relation of human population growth to food supply, which when Darwin read it several decades later provided him with the crucial idea he required for solving the problem of the mechanism of natural selection.

Returning to the 1845–56 conjunction, now in physics rather than biology, it was during this same period just cited for Darwin that Hermann von Helmholtz formulated the principle of conservation of energy, in 1847. Helmholtz's analysis proved that mechanical work, heat, and electricity were all different forms of the same physical substrate, a conclusion considered by many scientists to be the most important physical discovery of the nineteenth century. During this same conjunction, William Kelvin and Rudolf Clausius in 1850–51 formulated the second law of thermodynamics, and in 1854 Clausius formulated the concept of entropy, from which he famously extrapolated to the conclusion that the universe is heading toward thermal annihilation. Also during this same period, James Clerk Maxwell began the work on electromagnetic fields that transformed modern physics. This was marked by the first in his series of papers on the subject, "On Faraday's Lines of Force" (1855), the seed for which was Michael Faraday's paper "Thoughts on Ray Vibrations" (1846), published at the beginning of the same alignment.

The period of the next such Uranus-Pluto alignment at the turn of the twentieth century, 1896–1907, brought both of the major revolutions of modern physics: quantum mechanics, initiated by the work of Max Planck (1900), and relativity theory, initiated by Albert Einstein (1905). It was during this same period that Freud commenced a comparable revolution in psychology with the founding of psychoanalysis and the publication of *The Interpretation of Dreams* (1899–1900). This extraordinary period, which saw the emergence of the many radical and emancipatory political movements and upheavals cited earlier, as well as the invention of the airplane and many other technological advances, also brought the discovery of the electron by J. J. Thomson, the discovery of radioactivity by Becquerel and the Curies, and the founding of the science of genetics by William Bateson and others, among many other significant scientific advances at that time.

Finally, the most recent Uranus-Pluto conjunction of 1960–72 coincided with another remarkable wave of revolutionary scientific developments: the plate tectonics revolution in geology initiated by Harry Hess's seminal paper on seafloor spreading (1962); Benoit Mandelbrot's invention of fractal images (1962); Edward Lorenz's seminal first paper on chaos theory (1963); the ascendancy of big bang cosmology by the discovery of background cosmic radiation by Penzias and Wilson, the first definitive evidence for the expansion of the universe from a hotter and denser primordial state (1964–65); the discovery of quarks by Gell-Mann and Zweig (1964); the formulation of Bell's theorem of nonlocality (1964); the emergence of systems theory, epitomized in von Bertalanffy's *General System*

Theory (1968); and the formulation of the Gaia hypothesis by James Lovelock (1968) and the endosymbiotic theory by Lynn Margulis (1969). During this same period emerged what has been called "a second Darwinian revolution" in evolutionary biology, the joining of geneticists and naturalists in the forging of an evolutionary synthesis, combined with Stephen Jay Gould's and Niles Eldredge's theory of punctuated equilibria (1972). This period also brought the rapid development of ecological thought that began with Rachel Carson's epoch-making *Silent Spring* of 1962, followed by the work of Gregory Bateson, Arne Naess, and many others. In addition, in the philosophy of science, the very concept of "scientific revolution" was given a radically new formulation and influential analysis in this period with Thomas Kuhn's 1962 masterwork *The Structure of Scientific Revolutions*, which in itself commenced a paradigm-shifting revolution in twentieth-century thought.

Again, there would seem to be no apparent necessary relationship between social-political revolution and scientific-technological revolution and thus no reason why the two should regularly coincide with each other so consistently during the exact same historical periods.[7] Yet from an archetypal perspective, a definite underlying coherence connects the two categories of phenomena—a coherence of meaning, of formal causality rather than of efficient causality. Of course, what is most intellectually challenging within the context of current cosmological assumptions is the possibility that this synchronistic archetypal coherence in historical phenomena also bears a systematic correspondence with planetary movements.

Certainly, considered one by one, none of the many correlations we have so far examined represents a significant challenge. It is rather their cumulative character, as well as their archetypal precision, that is difficult to disregard. I found that virtually identical diachronic and synchronic patterns in close coincidence with the sequence of Uranus-Pluto alignment periods were also readily discernible for several other important categories of historical and cultural phenomena. Historians and specialists in the relevant disciplines will recognize striking correlations between the specific periods of these alignments and eras marked by such archetypally appropriate developments as unusually rapid modernization and secularization of society; epochal shifts in the rise and fall of imperial powers and dynasties and turning points in world history that mark tectonic shifts in the global balance of power; periods bringing the rise of nationalism simultaneously in various countries and continents; eras of mass immigrations and demographic shifts; and periods bringing major historical developments in mass communication, sudden increases in the power of the press, and the struggle to establish freedom of the press—all of these correlations consistently suggestive of cyclical patternings comparable to those we have been exploring.[8]

Other archetypally relevant eras that coincided with cyclical alignments of Uranus and Pluto include historical periods that brought the sudden rise and empowerment of countercultures and youth cultures; eras marked by the emergence and flourishing of historically significant bohemian and countercultural districts, communities, and demimondes (the Left Bank, Bloomsbury, Soho, Greenwich Village, Haight-Ashbury, Berkeley, Harvard Square); eras that had a decisive formative effect on contemporary youths who later brought forth further developments of the specific impulses associated with that period (e.g., the influence of Schiller's writings and the French Revolutionary ideals on the young Beethoven in Austria in the 1790s, or the same era's impact on the young Wordsworth and Coleridge in England,[9] and also on the young Hegel, Schelling, and Hölderlin in Germany, all with enduring consequences for later developments in modern culture); periods that brought the rapid emergence and proliferation of ecological, environmental, and nature-oriented movements of various kinds; and eras marked by cultural trends and movements advocating sexual revolution and erotic emancipation in society and the arts.

THE URANUS-PLUTO CYCLE

Axial alignments since 1450

15° orb		Exact alignment <1°
1450–1461	conjunction	1455–56
1533–1545	opposition	1538–40
1592–1602	conjunction	1597–98
1643–1654	opposition	1648–49
1705–1716	conjunction	1710–11
1787–1798	opposition	1792–94
1845–1856	conjunction	1850–51
1896–1907	opposition	1901–02
1960–1972	conjunction	1965–66

Dates given represent first and last times planets were positioned within stated orb. 20° orb adds one to two years before and after dates given for 15°.

Awakenings of the Dionysian

In these last-cited phenomena, we begin to recognize an essential characteristic of the archetypal correlations that we have not yet identified. With each planetary correlation, whether involving a natal aspect, a personal transit, or a world transit, I found that an alignment between two or more planets consistently indicated a *mutual activation* of the corresponding archetypes, each one acting upon the other in its characteristic way. In the survey above, I have mainly been discussing the eras of Uranus-Pluto alignments in terms that can perhaps most simply be understood as the Plutonic-Dionysian archetype, associated with the planet Pluto, intensifying and empowering on a massive scale the Prometheus archetype of rebellion and freedom, creativity, innovation, and sudden radical change, all associated with the planet Uranus. This way of approaching the phenomena essentially focuses on one vector of archetypal activity—Pluto acting upon Uranus, so to speak: Pluto→Uranus.

However, these same periods can also be understood and further illuminated if we consider as well the *converse* archetypal dynamic operating in the various historical events and cultural phenomena coincident with these same alignments: that is, if we not only consider the Pluto archetype as intensely compelling and empowering the Promethean impulse in these eras but also consider the Prometheus archetype as suddenly and unexpectedly liberating the elemental forces of the Plutonic-Dionysian impulse: Uranus→Pluto. For in any given archetypal complex that is constituted by two or more planetary principles, each principle seems simultaneously to *act* and *be acted upon* in the relevant phenomena, each one doing so in accordance with its own specific archetypal character. The Promethean principle associated with the planet Uranus appears to act by suddenly liberating or awakening that which it touches, with unexpected, innovative, disruptive, and emancipatory consequences, while the Plutonic-Dionysian principle appears to act by compelling, empowering, and intensifying what it touches, with profoundly transformative and sometimes overwhelming, destructive consequences.

With these considerations in mind, I found that many of the most distinctive cultural and historical phenomena during the periods of Uranus-Pluto alignments could be recognized in terms of this second vector of archetypal dynamism, *from* the Promethean, acting *upon, towards,* and *through* the Dionysian-Plutonic: Uranus→Pluto. This vector was immediately visible, for example, in the extraordinarily consistent sudden awakenings and emancipation of the erotic dimension of life in the Uranus-Pluto periods we have been examining, as expressed in the social mores, arts, and leading philosophical and psychological ideas that emerged in those eras.

Thus we recall of course the 1960s and early 1970s, with the tremendous sudden upsurge and liberation (Uranus) of the erotic (Pluto) during that decade and its immediate aftermath, the "sexual revolution" in all its forms—the radical loosening of sexual restraints in social mores, the reclamation of the body and the celebration of sensuous experience, the personal striving for erotic liberation, the "free love" of the hippies and flower children, the countless Dionysian festivals of music and dance, the mass "happenings" and Acid Tests, the exuberant sexual unconstraint of the burgeoning alternative press and underground comics, the emancipation of women's sexuality impelled by the feminist revolution and the new availability of reliable contraception, the beginning of gay liberation, the publication of widely read advice books from *Sex and the Single Girl* in 1962 to *The Joy of Sex* in 1972. In this same era there arose intensified interest in the psychological perspectives derived from Freud advocating greater sexual freedom, with new widespread attention to the ideas of Wilhelm Reich, D. H. Lawrence, and William Blake, and the rise of theorists and proponents of erotic liberation such as Herbert Marcuse, Norman O. Brown, Germaine Greer, Monique Wittig, and Mary Daly.

The entire period was marked as well by a new sexual explicitness in drama, literature, music, dance, film. One thinks, for example, of the gradual crescendo of eroticism from Federico Fellini's *La Dolce Vita* of 1960 to his *Satyricon* of 1969, or the great popularity of the erotically charged music and powerful Dionysian theater of Mick Jagger and the Rolling Stones, Jim Morrison and the Doors, Jimi Hendrix, Janis Joplin, Cream, The Who, Led Zeppelin, the Velvet Underground, and many similar performers and groups. One recalls the era's prevailing spirit of passionate energy and wild abandon, the polymorphously orgiastic quality of the decade. All these specific qualities strongly suggest the presence of an archetypal complex constituted by the Promethean and Dionysian principles in synthesis—especially if we can divest these transcultural archetypal principles of their gendered Hellenic inflection, holding in our minds, for example, the clear association of Dionysus-Pluto with the great Indian mythic figures of Kali and Shakti, goddesses of erotic power and elemental transformation, death and rebirth, destruction and creation.

The unmistakable cultural ambiance which pervaded the decade of the Sixties, a zeitgeist whose prevailing quality combined a mass awakening of emancipatory and creative impulses with a titanic eruption of elemental and libidinal forces, was talked about, celebrated, criticized, feared. Attempts were made to suppress it, attempts were made to sustain it indefinitely. It dominated people's experience at the time, just as it now dominates retrospective views of that era. In a sense, the 1960s seemed to unleash the force of a great collective Oedipal impulse, catalyzing a vast wave of erotically motivated rebellion against the repressive structures of established authority. The driving force of so much of the decade's most characteristic activities and sentiments appeared to be the attempt to overthrow any limitations to libidinal satisfaction, whether social or political, artistic, intellectual, psychological, or somatic. Again, if we move beyond the masculine inflection of these resonant Hellenic symbols to understand them at their most general, transgendered level, the Oedipus impulse and complex can be recognized as essentially a manifestation of two distinct archetypes—the rebellious Promethean and the erotic Dionysian—acting in close conjunction and mutual activation.

Nor was the liberation of the Dionysian in the 1960s limited to that archetype's erotic or libidinal side, for the same decade was characterized by an equally powerful eruption of the volcanic, violent, and destructive elemental energies associated with the Dionysian-Plutonic-Kali principle. Moreover, the expression of these energies was consistently and directly linked throughout this period to the Promethean cause of revolutionary change and political liberation. Here was the tremendous mass violence unleashed by the Cultural Revolution in China, the repeated eruption of violence and fiery destruction in African-American communities in the inner cities of the United States, the wave of assassinations, the unprecedentedly intensive decade-long destruction of Vietnam, the self-immolating protesters in Prague and Saigon, the unprecedented increase of violence in the cinema—*Bonnie and Clyde, The Wild Bunch, A Clockwork Orange*—the extreme turmoil and violence portrayed daily in the television news, the persistent impulse towards violent fury on both sides in the antiwar demonstrations, the pervasive "heat" of the period.

I found that viewing the 1960s as a collective manifestation of an archetypal synthesis of Prometheus and Dionysus seemed to afford a perspective that was not only historically accurate and precise but also aptly multivalent and comprehensive. It provided a wealth of insight, both through assimilating the manifold meanings of the two archetypes and through recognizing the dynamic mutuality of their interaction. In the complex interplay of those two archetypal principles the historical character and pervading spirit of the 1960s seemed to be expressed with a kind of concise and profound clarity.

So too I found a similar deepening of understanding of the 1787–98 French Revolutionary period. We have so far discussed this era mainly as the Prometheus archetype of liberation and radical change being intensely compelled and empowered by the Pluto-Dionysus principle. But if we reorganize our vision to take account of the converse side of this archetypal dynamic—that is, the Prometheus principle's suddenly awakening and liberating the elemental energies of the Plutonic-Dionysian—an entirely different yet equally fundamental dimension of the French Revolutionary period becomes intelligible: its spectacular synthesis of emancipatory innovation and mass violence. Here again, as in the 1960–72 period, we see the specifically destructive element of the Dionysus archetype, yet we see it always inextricably linked with Promethean themes of freedom and rebellion—the many mass insurrections that convulsed Paris and much of France throughout the decade, the repeated massacres, the regicide, the thousands of executions at the guillotine, the Reign of Terror, the bloodshed and fury, the unbounded irrational rage of the radicals attempting to remake the world, the decapitated heads carried about on pikes in front of cheering mobs, the overwhelming social chaos and political turmoil.

As in the 1960s, here too was the experience of sudden and sustained cataclysmic upheaval, an awakening of volcanic forces that precipitated the collapse of the established order. Here again erupted a sudden collective wave of disinhibition, a return of the repressed, that unleashed primordial destructive forces in close association with liberatory and rebellious impulses. The apocalyptic orgy of killing in the September Massacres of 1792 and the Reign of Terror of 1793–94 had their counterparts in the 1960s with the countless atrocities of the Chinese Cultural Revolution, the vast destruction of Tibet, Vietnam, Cambodia, Laos, Indonesia, the My Lai massacre, the Manson murders, Altamont, Hell's Angels. The various extremist groups in revolutionary France such as the Jacobins, the Indulgents, and the Enragés had their counterparts in many similar radical factions of the Sixties, such as the Red Guards, the Black Panthers, and the SDS Weathermen, with their own Days of Rage.

Both of these Uranus-Pluto decades brought forth repeated outbursts of mass emotion of great intensity. Whether violent or libidinous, the dominant archetypal complex in each of these periods seemed to constellate sudden sustained outbursts of nonspecific emotional intensity and elemental power that informed and compelled human activity and experience on a mass scale. Nor was this upsurge of intensified mass emotion in the French Revolutionary epoch limited to the violent and aggressive, for visible here as well was an elemental upwelling of *fraternité,* the third of the French Revolution's sovereign trinity of values. The powerful wave of feeling that overcame the Legislative Assembly in July 1792 at the height of the democratic period of the Revolution, when the deputies suddenly surrendered their antagonisms and commenced embracing and kissing each other in tears of deep emotion, and that swept through Paris generally in 1792 had its counterparts in such events as the San Francisco Summer of Love in 1967 or the Woodstock music festival in 1969.

So also with the upsurge of the erotic and sensuous in both decades. The sexual liberation of the 1960s had its counterparts in the 1790s in the new erotic poetry of Goethe, in Blake's redemptive embrace of sexual desire and sensual ecstasy linked to divine creative power and imaginative freedom, in the bared breasts and diaphanous gowns of radical aristocratic women in Paris, in Casanova's memoirs of amorous intrigues and exploits, in the unleashed violent sexuality of the Marquis de Sade's novels. Nearly identical cultural phenomena were emphatically conspicuous in the 1960s—and often involved the rediscovery, appropriation, and further creative development of the 1790s' precedents, as with the celebrated and controversial 1960s' play and film *Marat/Sade*, in which the impulse of violent revolution (personified by Jean-Paul Marat) and the impulse of violent eroticism (personified by the Marquis de Sade) discharge themselves in tense dramatic dialogue.[10]

We see the same rediscovery and reappropriation of the 1790s' cultural mood in the 1960s' enthusiastic turn to Blake, with his titanic exaltation of "Energy"—erotic, creative, emancipatory—in rebellion against the shackles of church and state, commerce and industry, mechanistic materialism and positivist empiricism. Numerous aphorisms from *The Marriage of Heaven and Hell* vividly reflect the common ethos of the two Uranus-Pluto periods, the 1790s and the 1960s, at once Promethean and Dionysian, celebrating passion unbound and defying all arbitrary limits to life's creative exuberance:

> Energy is Eternal Delight.
>
> The roaring of lions, the howling of wolves, the raging of the stormy sea, and the destructive sword are portions of eternity too great for the eye of man.
>
> When thou seest an Eagle, thou seest a portion of Genius. Lift up thy head!
>
> Joys impregnate. Sorrows bring forth.
>
> The head Sublime, the heart Pathos, the genitals Beauty, the hands & feet Proportion.
>
> Those who restrain desire, do so because theirs is weak enough to be restrained.
>
> He who desires but acts not, breeds pestilence.
>
> Sooner murder an infant in his cradle than nurse unacted desires.
>
> You never know what is enough unless you know what is more than enough.
>
> The road of excess leads to the palace of wisdom.
>
> Damn braces: Bless relaxes.
>
> Exuberance is beauty.

Again, both Uranus-Pluto decades seem to have been characterized by a sustained eruption of the Promethean and Dionysian principles in combination, with all the complexities of those two archetypes in conspicuous mutual inter-action. Blake himself was born in 1759 when Uranus and Pluto were in an exact square alignment (with his Sun in conjunction with Pluto), this being the Uranus-Pluto quadrature aspect immediately preceding the opposition of the French Revolutionary period. I repeatedly observed a distinct pattern in which historically significant individuals who played crucial cultural roles in subse-quent Uranus-Pluto eras were born during earlier eras when the same two plan-ets were in alignment. Especially of interest in this context is the seminal figure of Jean-Jacques Rousseau.

The Liberation of Nature

Born at the very heart of the preceding Uranus-Pluto conjunction period of the early eighteenth century, in 1712 when the alignment was nearly exact, Rousseau was also born when both the Sun and Moon were aligned in close major aspect to the Uranus-Pluto conjunction. This was the conjunction that coincided with the beginning of the Industrial Revolution and that immediately preceded the opposition alignment of the French Revolution. The sequence of consecutive Uranus-Pluto alignments precisely paralleled Rousseau's central role in bringing forth from within himself and then articulating so many of the principal themes that opened the cultural vision and sensibility in the very directions that came to climactic expression in the French Revolution: the emancipatory fervor ("Man was born free, and everywhere he is in chains"), the intense communal feeling, the liberation of deep emotion, the quest for individual autonomy and self-dependence, the affirmation of a natural religious feeling, the belief in the natural goodness of the human being, the liberation from the oppressive doctrine of Original Sin, the recognition of the corrupting influence of civilization's web of pretense and vain ambition. The very slogan *"Liberté, Egalité, Fraternité"* was Rousseau's.

All these themes and values transmitted by Rousseau shaped the evolving intellectual and cultural climate that burst forth in the 1790s, affecting not only the France of the revolutionaries but the Germany of Schiller and Schelling, Hölderlin and Hegel, and the England of Blake, Wordsworth, and Coleridge. It was this same Rousseauian complex of impulses and aspirations that surged forth again in new inflections and in unprecedentedly widespread form in the countercultural ideals and zeitgeist of the 1960s. The quest for personal freedom, joy in the intimate communion with nature, the elevation of the feelings of the heart over the dictates of mere calculating rationality, the developed conscience recognized as the true voice of nature, the inviolability of personal ideals against the pressures of society and the state, the democraticizing of social mores, the valuing of simplicity and authenticity, the affirmation of ordinary life, the critique of modern society for its stimulation of spurious needs and wasteful consumption, the appreciation of the natural child's spontaneous intelligence, the call for radical educational reform—all these and more derived from the eloquent pen and troubled heart of Rousseau.

It happened that all the major works in which Rousseau set forth these themes and values, from *The Discourse on the Origin and Foundations of Inequality Amongst Men* of 1755 to *Émile* and *The Social Contract* of 1762, were written and published during the Uranus-Pluto square that occurred exactly midway between the conjunction of his birth and the opposition of the French Revolution, the same square alignment during which Blake was born. An exactly similar pattern is visible in Rousseau's friend and contrasting counterpart amongst the French philosophes, Denis Diderot, who embodied and guided the more secular and rationalist side of the eighteenth-century Enlightenment's long quest for intellectual and cultural emancipation.

Like Rousseau, Diderot was born during the Uranus-Pluto conjunction at the beginning of the century, in 1713, just one year after Rousseau.[11] Then, precisely during the entire period of the square alignment from 1751 onward, he edited and brought forth volume after volume of the *Encyclopédie*, not only an enormous compendium of treatises that forwarded the modern mind's growing scientific understanding of nature but also, in Jacques Barzun's words, "the tremendous storehouse of fact and propaganda that swept Europe and taught it what 'reason,' 'rights,' 'authority,' 'government,' 'liberty,' 'equality,' and related social principles are or should be." And as with Rousseau, it was precisely when the Uranus-Pluto cycle reached its next axial alignment during the French Revolution in 1787–98 that Diderot's great didactic enterprise found dramatic fruition in both the social-political and the scientific-technological revolutions of that decade. Rousseau and Diderot essentially represent two poles of the archetypal complex we are examining, each of which is emancipatory and revolutionary but with different emphases and consequences (Marat and de Sade representing two poles of this same complex as well, in darker hues).

Thus the two Uranus-Pluto alignments periods we have been examining, the French Revolutionary epoch and the 1960s, were notable for the conspicuous presence of both Promethean and Dionysian phenomena at the same time, not just one or the other: the call for freedom but also a revelation of nature, intellectual awakening but also an eruption of feeling and instinct, radical change but also heightened eros, creative innovation and experiment but also destruction and upheaval. I found especially suggestive the evidence for the complex *mutual interaction* of the two archetypes, their inextricable synthesis—self-dependent freedom *with* the affirmation of nature, liberation *with* sexuality, rebellion *with* violence, innovation and change *with* overwhelming intensity, all on a massive scale. Of course what was especially suggestive and challenging was the further coincidence that these two principles happened to be the specific planetary archetypes associated with the two planets that were in alignment during just those particular eras.

When I considered major events that took place beyond the European context in the French Revolutionary period, I recognized strikingly similar archetypal dynamics at work in other parts of the world as well. Thus, for example, in Tahiti and other islands of the South Pacific, a sudden liberating and awakening of the Dionysian took place for many British sailors and other European travelers during this period of 1787 to 1798, as they experienced for the first time the revelation of Polynesian eroticism and freer sexual mores than those permitted by European custom and long-established patterns of Christian sexual inhibition. (Appropriately it had been Diderot, born during the preceding conjunction, who had notably extolled the Polynesian peoples' sexual freedom, which he believed made them both physically and spiritually healthier than Europeans subject to their society's unnatural sexual constraints.) Conversely, during this same period the indigenous peoples of the Pacific islands, from Tahiti to Hawaii, as well as in Australia and New Zealand experienced a tremendous cultural upheaval and the start of the eventual destruction of their societies as a consequence of the sustained penetration of their world by Europeans that began at this time.

If we look at the two intervening Uranus-Pluto axial alignments that occurred between the French Revolutionary epoch and the 1960s, we see remarkably similar archetypal dynamics at work. At the turn of the twentieth century, during the 1896–1907 Uranus-Pluto opposition, we see again the sudden rise of widespread movements for sexual emancipation in many centers in Europe and the United States; the rise of bohemian communities from Montmartre to Greenwich Village; the neopagan nature, free love, and youth movements in Germany and Switzerland; the influx of European bohemians into California and the beginnings of the West Coast counterculture; the women's emancipation movements that called for the spread of contraceptive methods and sexual freedom; the new artistic celebration of the primitive and the primordial, as in the paintings of Picasso; the new freedom of physical expression, as in the electrifying performances of the young American dancer Isadora Duncan as she gave birth to modern dance. The influence of Duncan at this time was immense, not only in the world of dance, ballet, and the theater but on culture and society generally, her free-spiritedness in life and her originality in art galvanizing European as well as American audiences. In Max Eastman's words:

All who have escaped in any degree from the rigidity and prissiness of our once national religion of negation owe a debt to Isadora Duncan's dancing. She rode the wave of revolt against Puritanism; she rode it, and with her fame and Dionysian raptures drove it on. She was—perhaps it is simplest to say—the crest of the wave, an event not only in art but in the history of life.

In the intellectual domain during these same years, we see the first widespread awakening of interest in the writings and Dionysian philosophy of Nietzsche, which in turn influenced the work of many artists at this time, from Isadora Duncan's dance and the titanic symphonic works of Richard Strauss and Gustav Mahler to the philosophical plays of George Bernard Shaw (*Man and Superman*). We see the same archetypal complex at work as well in the rise of philosophies that combined social and political revolution with the necessity of violence, as in the writings during these years of Lenin and Georges Sorel. Simultaneously during this same period occurred sustained and repeated acts of mass violence, in China, India, France, and the Austro-Hungarian Empire, revolutionary movements that advocated violent overthrow of existing institutions, and, much as in the 1790s and 1960s, a wave of assassinations by anarchists of national leaders— the president of the United States, the king of Italy, the empress of Austria, the king and queen of Serbia.

An especially paradigmatic expression of the theme of Dionysian awakening in both the intellectual and the psychological domains was Freud's seminal articulation of the instinctual unconscious in just these years of 1896 to 1907. We have cited this correlation above in the cyclical patterning of major scientific and intellectual revolutions coincident with Uranus-Pluto alignments. Here I wish to focus on the converse archetypal dynamic that was evident in the rapid emergence of psychoanalysis in this period. This period encompassed Freud's writing of both *The Interpretation of Dreams* (from 1896 to 1900) and *Three Contributions to the Theory of Sexuality* (1905), the initial rise of the psychoanalytic movement when Freud was joined by Abraham, Adler, Jung, Rank, Ferenczi, and the rest of the early pioneers (1900–07), and, not least, the host of Freud's discoveries at this time: the Oedipus complex, the sexual etiology of neurosis, the erotogenic zones, the existence of infant sexuality, the resistance of the conscious ego to the unconscious instincts, the return of the repressed, and many related concepts and insights.

In all of these, the theme of Promethean liberation of the Dionysian can be discerned on many levels. In terms of intellectual history, Freud's achievement can be recognized as the rationalist Enlightenment's entrance into the Plutonic underworld of the instinctual unconscious, the revelation of the "broiling cauldron of the instincts." It represented an epochal Promethean awakening to—as well as of—the Dionysian id. On the cultural level, the same theme was visible in the enduring social consequences of Freud's work, both in its liberation of the scientific study of sexuality from the long-established cultural taboos against which he himself had to contend and in its pivotal role in the radical transformation of modern attitudes towards sexuality generally. On the psychodynamic level, the theme was visible in psychoanalysis's recognition of the principle of catharsis and abreaction, the therapeutic imperative to release repressed instinctually charged memories to free the psyche and body from neurotic fixations, thereby bringing the suppressed unconscious energies to conscious awareness and expression. Freud himself underscored the specifically Promethean-Plutonic mythical character of his work in the powerful epigraph from Virgil with which he chose to begin his magnum opus, *The Interpretation of Dreams*: "If I cannot bend the Gods above, then I will move the Infernal regions."

Again, the central role of the Oedipus complex in Freud's life and work, which he first recognized in 1897, during this opposition, can be understood as a precise synthesis of the two archetypal principles, the Promethean and the Dionysian—the rebellion against tyrannical authority and the impulse for erotic fulfillment—that were at work in so many cultural phenomena at this time. Significantly, Freud was himself born at the end of the preceding Uranus-Pluto conjunction of 1845–56, with his Sun positioned directly between Uranus and Pluto.[12] In another striking cyclical pattern, it was Freud's disciple Wilhelm Reich who carried forth with such passion the project of Dionysian liberation to release the orgasmic energies locked within the psychosomatic structures of muscular and character armoring, blockages that he regarded as directly contributing to the authoritarian psychology of fascism and totalitarianism. Reich was born in 1897, the same year in which Freud discovered the Oedipus complex. It was during the next Uranus-Pluto conjunction, that of the 1960s, that Reich's work became most influential and the Reichian project of sexual liberation was impelled and empowered on a collective scale.

If we then move back to the preceding Uranus-Pluto conjunction, that of 1845–56, when Freud was born, we see again the same striking constellation of cultural phenomena suggesting a widespread collective emergence and awakening of the Dionysian principle. Amidst the violent turmoil and great revolutionary movements of this era—radical socialist, nationalist independence, anarchist, abolitionist, women's suffrage, civil disobedience—we also find a simultaneous eruption and liberation of the elemental and erotic. This phenomenon was evident during these years in the rise of intentional communities in the United States that combined religious unorthodoxy with sexual experiment. It was similarly apparent in the powerful Dionysian music of Wagner and Liszt, in the eruption of dark eros and the urban underworld in Baudelaire's *Les Fleurs du mal* then being written, and in Flaubert's realistic exploration of adultery and bourgeois marriage in *Madame Bovary* (both *Les Fleurs* and *Madame Bovary* being prosecuted for immorality upon publication in 1857, before the same judge in Paris). We see it in the revelation of Polynesian eroticism and sexual freedom that Herman Melville's first novel, *Typee*, brought to startled American and British readers at that time. This was the same period in which the explorer and linguist Richard Burton entered deep into the cultures and sexual underworlds of India and the Middle East, which provided him with the basis for his translations of the *Kama Sutra* and the *Arabian Nights*. And we recognize the entire complex of Promethean and Dionysian themes in the poetry of Walt Whitman—the buoyant erotic and democratic emancipation, the open embrace of the future, the liberated individual embodying within himself the variegated mass of all humankind—these several themes interweaving and emboldening each other:

I am large. I contain multitudes.

One's Self I sing, a simple separate person,
Yet utter the word Democratic, the word En-Masse.

Of physiology from top to toe I sing,
Not physiognomy alone nor brain alone is worthy for the Muse, I
 say the form complete is worthier far,
The Female equally with the Male I sing.

O Life immense in passion, pulse, and power,
Cheerful, for freest action form'd under the laws divine,
The Modern Man I sing.

Urge and urge and urge,
Always the procreant urge of the world.

If anything is sacred the human body is sacred . . .

A woman waits for me, she contains all, nothing is lacking,
Yet all were lacking if sex were lacking. . . .
Sex contains all, bodies, souls,
Meanings, proofs, purities, delicacies, results . . .
All hopes, benefactions, bestowals, all the passions, loves, beauties,
 delights of the earth. . . .

Give me now libidinous joys only,
Give me the drench of my passions. . . .

The awakening to nature's pulse and power during this period was expressed as much in the spheres of science and philosophy as it was in poetry. On the one hand, the Darwinian evolutionary developments described earlier possessed a powerfully Promethean character (Pluto→Uranus), as a revolution of thought and a liberation from confining tradition and ignorance. On the other hand, if we shift to the other archetypal vector, we can also recognize the theory's distinctly Dionysian character, its liberation of the Plutonic (Uranus→Pluto). The reality of nature's encompassing power in the larger scheme of things, the ceaseless striving of evolutionary forces, the driving libidinal and aggressive urges for sexual reproduction and species preservation, the struggle for survival, nature red in tooth and claw—to all this the modern mind was now awakened, often startlingly so, much as it was again by Freud's instinctual unconscious during the following Uranus-Pluto opposition.

Yet even here, in the theory of natural selection and in the phenomena it depicted, these Plutonic themes of biological evolution, instinctual drives, and the struggle for survival were always tightly linked with specifically Promethean motifs embedded in the principle of variation itself: the random appearance of sudden mutations in a species, the creative emergence of unpredictable biological innovation—the evolutionary trickster, as it were, the innovative rebel against the species norm, the eccentric chance offspring that, under ever-changing circumstances, unexpectedly survives. Again, the complex synthesis of the two archetypal principles seemed to unfold on many levels simultaneously.

Moreover, during the period of this same conjunction, a closely related epochal shift in the history of European thought took place with the widespread dissemination after 1851 of Schopenhauer's philosophy of the primordial will that drives the forces of nature and shapes all human motivation from the depths. In many ways the closest parallel in philosophy to the scientific theory of Darwin, Schopenhauer's vision in turn inspired both Nietzsche and Freud, whose formulations of the will to power and the Dionysian principle in the one case and the instinctual unconscious and the id in the other have the Schopenhauerian will as their crucial precedent. Schopenhauer was born at the start of the preceding Uranus-Pluto opposition of the French Revolutionary period.[13] Nietzsche was born at the beginning of this Uranus-Pluto conjunction, and Freud was born at its end.[14] In turn, moving forward, both Nietzsche's and Freud's theories began to come to cultural attention during the immediately following opposition, that of 1896–1907.

Schopenhauer's philosophy also deeply influenced both Wagner and Mahler by its conception of music and artistic genius as uniquely capable of directly portraying the primal forces of the will in nature. This influence was most explicitly expressed in the music that emerged from the two composers during those two consecutive Uranus-Pluto eras: Wagner's *Tristan und Isolde* and *Der Ring des Nibelungen* in the 1850s and Mahler's Third Symphony and its successors in the 1896–1907 period.

The entire period of the conjunction was pivotal for both Wagner's musical development and his cultural influence as his controversial operas first made their way through Europe, his polemical writings were widely debated, and his genius was recognized. During the first half of the conjunction, from 1844 to 1848, Wagner composed *Tannhäuser*, with its orgiastic bacchanale and sonic depiction of overwhelming instinctual forces, and *Lohengrin*. After his participation in the political revolutions of 1848–49, he devoted himself for the next several years to a deep rethinking of the entire creative process by which music, myth, and narrative drama could be integrated into one powerful artistic expression, drawing on classical Greek tragedy as the most realized instance of a complete art form. Out of this crucible, he commenced work in the 1850s on the epic *Ring* cycle, interrupting it in 1857 to compose *Tristan*, his masterpiece of insatiable erotic passion—works that constituted both a revolution in the history of music and a vivid expression of the Schopenhauerian will.

It was during the immediately following Uranus-Pluto opposition of 1896–

1907 that Isadora Duncan, invited by Wagner's widow Cosima, famously performed the bacchanale from *Tannhäuser* at Bayreuth. Significantly, Duncan often proclaimed that the sources of her artistic inspiration were specifically Wagner, Nietzsche, and Whitman, and ultimately the power and forms of nature itself.

At the beginning of this same Uranus-Pluto alignment, in 1896, Mahler wrote a letter to a friend describing the composition of his Third Symphony with words that well convey his own experience of the compelling intensity of a larger will grounded in the depths of nature driving the force of artistic creativity:

> I am working on a large composition. Don't you know that this demands one's whole personality, and that one is often so deeply immersed in it, that it is as if one were dead to the outside world? Now, imagine a work of such scope that the whole world actually is reflected in it—one becomes, so to speak, only an instrument upon which the universe plays . . . My Symphony will be something that the world has never heard before! In this score, all nature speaks and tells such deep secrets . . . I tell you, at certain places in the score, a quite uncanny feeling takes possession of me, and I feel as if I had not created this myself.

Mahler's phrases and experience call to mind not only Nietzsche and Schopenhauer but also the influential philosophy of nature that emerged in German thought and culture precisely during the preceding Uranus-Pluto opposition of the 1790s, one full cycle earlier. From Goethe's studies and writings on the metamorphosis of plants (from 1791) and Schiller's writings on the poet's dynamic relationship to nature (from 1794) to Schelling's series of works on *Naturphilosophie* (from 1797), there emerged the immensely influential Romantic conception of nature as dynamic self-activity, ceaselessly striving to realize itself, to bring forth the infinite within the finite, with the human being as its vessel of awakening consciousness. This stream of thought deeply influenced the thought of Hegel during the period of this alignment, the formative years in his philosophical development. This was the same Uranus-Pluto alignment that coincided with the sudden simultaneous emergence of independent evolutionary conceptions of nature, anticipating Darwin, in the work of Goethe, Erasmus Darwin, Geoffroy Saint-Hilaire, and Lamarck. And again we see the theme of both scientific revolution and awakening to the dynamic evolution of the Earth in Hutton's seminal work of 1795 during this same alignment, *A Theory of the Earth*, the foundation of all modern geology.

In many of these examples, we are revisiting cultural and intellectual developments that we earlier examined in terms of the Prometheus principle of revolutionary awakenings being driven and empowered by the Plutonic (Pluto→Uranus), but which we can now perceive as reflecting the converse archetypal dynamic of the Prometheus principle's suddenly awakening the collective psyche and scientific mind to new dimensions of the Dionysian-Plutonic forces of nature, evolutionary processes, and instinctual drives (Uranus→Pluto). This sequential pattern of artistic and intellectual awakenings to the elemental forces of nature and chthonic evolutionary processes is again clearly evident on many fronts during the most recent Uranus-Pluto conjunction, that of the 1960–72 period.

In addition to the sudden eruption and pervasive presence of the Dionysian impulse in the music, dance, film, theater, and literature of the Sixties, we find a distinctive complex of Promethean-Dionysian themes expressed in a different form in the sciences during these years. It was visible in the rapid theoretical developments and intensified focus concerning the evolutionary roots of human behavior and anatomy evident in such widely discussed works of that decade as Konrad Lorenz's *On Aggression*, Robert Ardrey's *The Territorial Imperative*, and Desmond Morris's *The Naked Ape*, and in the development of sociobiology in those years by Edward O. Wilson and others. We see it as well in the emergence of the evolutionary synthesis forged by geneticists and naturalists, the "second Darwinian revolution" in evolutionary biology, and again in Gould's and Eldredge's theory of punctuated equilibria. The motif of chthonic awakening is similarly evident in the Earth sciences during these same years, with the plate-tectonics revolution that built on Wegener's concept of continental drift from the beginning of the century. Catalyzed in 1960 by Hess's theory of sea-floor spreading, the plate-tectonics revolution gradually unfolded during this alignment, as crucial confirming experiments were formulated by Vine and Matthews in 1963 ("equal in importance to any formulated in the geological sciences in this century") and successfully carried out in the immediately following years. The latter developments in turn appeared to be part of a larger intellectual awakening in this period to the Earth as a living, dynamic, self-transforming system. Many other scientific and philosophical developments of these years, such as those related to chaos theory, complexity theory, and systems theory, reflect similar themes suggestive of this same archetypal complex. Again, a paradigmatic expression of these themes was Lovelock's proposal in 1968 of what became known as the Gaia hypothesis, which conceived of the entire Earth as a living, self-regulating planetary ecosystem.

Indeed, throughout the 1960–72 period of the Uranus-Pluto conjunction, we see evidence of a widespread awakening to the claims of nature and a liberation of nature's voice, beginning with the rapid emergence of ecological awareness initiated by Rachel Carson near the start of the conjunction in 1962. In the summer of 1969, in the midst of the most intense period of antiwar activism, teach-ins, and student rebellion, planning began for Earth Day, a national grassroots protest on behalf of the environment. Both a symbol and a collective expression of the rising ecological awareness, Earth Day took place in 1970, with over twenty million demonstrators and the participation of thousands of schools and local communities. In the same year Greenpeace was founded. Finally, near the end of the conjunction period, in 1972, a further stage was marked by the emergence of deep ecology as formulated by the Norwegian philosopher Arne Naess. Naess's philosophy of biocentrism set forth a new ethic, embracing plants and animals as well as human beings, that he believed was necessary for human societies to live in harmony with the natural world on which they depend for survival and well-being. Once again we see a diachronic pattern with the preceding Uranus-Pluto conjunction period one cycle earlier, 1845–56, which brought forth Thoreau's writing and publication of *Walden, or Life in the Woods*. Here Thoreau's articulation of other characteristic Uranus-Pluto themes, such as radical individualism and social rebellion, was embedded in perhaps the most seminal of all works calling for humanity's reawakening to the voice of nature, epitomized in his dictum, "In Wildness is the preservation of the world."

Unleashing the Forces of Nature

In the category of historical and cultural phenomena we have been exploring, we see cyclically patterned archetypal variations, with seemingly endless creativity, on the theme of liberating or awakening to the forces of nature—the creative powers of nature and life, erotic libido and sexuality, the Freudian instinctual unconscious and the id, the Nietzschean will to power and the Schopenhauerian universal will, the Darwinian biological forces of evolution and the chthonic geological forces of the Earth. We have seen other forms as well, as in that sudden liberation of creative forces in the peoples of previously repressive societies that has so often accompanied revolutionary emancipations, as in the 1640s in England, in the 1790s throughout Europe, and in the 1960s throughout the world. Even going back as far as the Uranus-Pluto conjunction of the 1450s and the development of the Gutenberg press, we see another version of this theme: the unprecedented unleashing of both historical forces and the creative forces of the human spirit that took place in the wake of the printing press, which proved to be a crucial precondition for many of the most important cultural and technological developments of the modern era. And we have seen the more problematic expression of this archetypal motif in the unleashing of mass political violence and mob behavior during all of these alignments.

If we now review the entire category of technological revolutions we earlier surveyed, we can recognize this same archetypal theme as having been played out in yet another form: namely, a more literal Promethean unleashing of the forces of nature, with immense consequences that are still unfolding. Thus the Uranus-Pluto conjunction of 1705–16 coincided with the invention of the steam engine and the discovery of the use of coal for iron-smelting furnaces that began the Industrial Revolution and the age of steam, coal, and iron. The following conjunction of 1845–56 coincided with the discovery of petroleum oil as a fuel, a discovery that began the petroleum age whose cultural, ecological, and geopolitical consequences are still unfolding. And the following opposition of 1896–1907 coincided with the birth of the nuclear age with the discovery of radioactivity in uranium, the isolation of radium and polonium, and Einstein's $E = mc^2$ formulation.

Each of these inventions and discoveries in turn played a role in major technological and industrial developments that coincided with subsequent Uranus-Pluto periods, suggesting the same kind of diachronic cyclical patterning we have observed in other areas. Restricting ourselves here to the axial alignments: as discussed earlier, the steam-driven and coal-driven Industrial Revolution rapidly accelerated first in the 1790s and then more potently and globally in the 1845–56 period with the proliferation of railroads and steamships and the widespread mechanization of industry. In turn, the opposition of 1896–1907 coincided precisely with the oil-fueled proliferation of automobiles (from twenty-five produced in the United States in 1896 to twenty-five thousand in 1905) and of motorbuses, motorcycles, trucks, electricity plants, and the first airplanes. The same period brought both the discovery of vast oil deposits in Texas and the beginning of oil exploration in the Middle East (both in 1901). Finally, the period of the most recent conjunction of the 1960s brought the rapid proliferation of nuclear power plants throughout the world, the rise of global jet aviation, and the deployment of the titanic energy and power required for space travel, all made possible by the technological discoveries of the preceding Uranus-Pluto alignments.[15]

Here again we are taking the same developments we earlier analyzed in terms of epochal scientific and technological revolutions, understood as the Plutonic empowerment of the Promethean principle of intellectual breakthrough and radical change (Pluto→Uranus). And we are shifting our perception to recognize the converse archetypal dynamic in which Promethean technological innovation and human ingenuity unleash the Plutonic forces of nature (Uranus→ Pluto).

All these phenomena represent the concrete embodiment of Bacon's dictum that "Knowledge is power," another form of Prometheus unbound and empowered. Bacon himself, we will recall, began his philosophical writings that were inspired by the knowledge/power imperative under the Uranus-Pluto conjunction of 1592–1602. During this same conjunction occurred the birth of Descartes, the other major philosophical progenitor of the modern scientific-technological will to power.

Religious Rebellion and
Erotic Emancipation

Historically, both radical religious reform and rebellion against religious authority and tradition have been consistently in evidence during Uranus-Pluto alignment periods. These took many forms, some as the sudden rise of pressure for change from within, as with the unprecedentedly reformist Second Vatican Council called by Pope John XXIII in 1962 "to open the window" of the Catholic Church to the fresh winds and spirit of the time. Other expressions of the same theme were more radical and antagonistic, as with the French Revolutionary abolition of the worship of God in 1793, when the churches of Paris were closed and public reading of the Bible was forbidden. The Bishop of Paris publicly abjured the Catholic religion and declared that only Liberty and Equality should henceforth be worshipped in France.

On November 10, 1793, a Festival of Reason was declared, and the cathedral of Notre Dame was plundered and then ritually dedicated to the cult of Reason. Before an immense and joyful crowd, an actress from the Paris opera was selected to represent the Goddess of Reason. After being embraced by the president, she was paraded in glory through the thronged streets to the cathedral, where she was enthroned on the high altar, crowned as Deity, and worshipped by all present. Stirred by the demonstrations, the Convention two weeks later outlawed the Bible and any expression of the Christian religion under penalty of death. Parish churches were reopened as Temples of Truth and Reason, and Christianity was replaced by "natural religion." In this period marriage was no longer under the Church's authority, and divorce was legalized. The Revolution's systematic attempt to dechristianize French society and establish a new religion of Reason and Humanity continued for over three years until religious freedom was instituted in 1797, but with the Roman papacy still regarded as an enemy of the Revolution. In 1798, near the end of the opposition, the French military expelled Pope Pius VI from Rome and put him in prison, where he died. Thus during the span of this alignment period, the Revolution's early anticlericalism moved through increasing degrees of secularism to a stringent atheism, and finally to a legalization of religious freedom combined with an attack on the Roman papacy, all in the service of a new religion of liberty, reason, and nature.

We see this same motif of rebellion against religious orthodoxy again during the following conjunction of the mid-nineteenth century at the philosophical level of high culture. Amidst the social and political revolutions of the period (including another Pope Pius, IX, being compelled by revolutionary forces to leave Rome, in 1848), a powerful emancipatory impulse in the religious context expressed itself with the wave of religious skepticism that swept the European intellectual world in the 1840s and 1850s in the wake of the ideas of Schopenhauer, Marx, and Engels, as well as David Friedrich Strauss, Ludwig Feuerbach, and George Eliot, among others. This shift in the culture's philosophical vision in turn influenced Darwin and later Nietzsche. Similarly, another comparable wave of religious doubt, philosophical innovation, and intensified secularist impulses in Western culture emerged during the following Uranus-Pluto axial alignment of 1896–1907 in association with the enormous social and political, technological, scientific, and artistic shifts that marked those years at the turn of the twentieth century. Related movements, pressures, and disruptions were evident in China, Japan, India, Russia, and the Middle East during both of these periods and again in the 1960s in a clear diachronic sequence.

Yet in all of these periods and in many of the clearly Promethean phenomena just cited, the Dionysian element was regularly implicated. In each of the Uranus-Pluto eras, we see a volatile synthesis in which rebellion against religious authority and dogma is closely linked to a suddenly awakened collective impulse for erotic emancipation. Such a synthesis of the two motifs, erotic and religious, was notably visible in the French Revolution's Festival of Reason after the ceremonies in the cathedral of Notre Dame, as the excited populace danced wildly in the cathedral sanctuary, women bared their breasts and men disrobed, and couples engaged freely in sexual intercourse in the sacristy. The entire parade through the streets, with its *carnivale* atmosphere and the playfully transgressive crowds cheering on the magnificent carriage that brought the Goddess to the cathedral, is strikingly redolent of the ancient ceremonial procession of the Dionysian chariot.

At the same moment as these extraordinary events in France, Blake in England was proclaiming a remarkably similar combination of religious rebellion and erotic freedom. The opening declaration of *The Marriage of Heaven and Hell*, written in this same year of 1793, announces that synthesis with Blake's characteristically apodictic assurance:

All Bibles or sacred codes have been the causes of the following Errors:
    1. That Man has two real existing principles Viz: a Body & a Soul.
    2. That Energy, call'd Evil, is alone from the Body, & that Reason, call'd Good, is alone from the Soul.
    3. That God will torment Man in Eternity for following his Energies.
But the following Contraries to these are True:
    1. Man has no Body distinct from his Soul for that call'd Body is a

portion of Soul discern'd by the five Senses, the chief inlets of Soul in this age.
2. Energy is the only life and is from the Body and Reason is the bound or outward circumference of Energy.
3. Energy is Eternal Delight.

Blake continues the argument with aphorisms pungent in their defiance of conventional religion and morality yet imbued with a biblical resonance:

> Prisons are built with stones of Law, Brothels with bricks of Religion. . . .
> The pride of the peacock is the glory of God.
> The lust of the goat is the bounty of God.
> The wrath of the lion is the wisdom of God.
> The nakedness of woman is the work of God.

And then a prophecy:

> The ancient tradition that the world will be consumed in fire at the end of six thousand years is true, as I have heard from Hell. For the cherub with his flaming sword is hereby commanded to leave his guard at the tree of life, and when he does, the whole creation will be consumed and appear infinite and holy whereas it now appears finite & corrupt. This will come to pass by an improvement of sensual enjoyment. But first the notion that man has a body distinct from his soul is to be expunged.

Similar patterns of liberation and the awakening of the Dionysian principle in human affairs were evident for Uranus-Pluto alignments from earlier centuries before the French Revolution, such as the period of tumultuous upheaval and widespread revolutionary developments that dominated the 1643–54 period at the time of the English Revolution, exactly one full cycle before the period of Blake's *Marriage of Heaven and Hell* and the French Revolution. Amidst the multitude of radical political parties that emerged at this time, there was a simultaneous upwelling of emancipatory social movements in which the erotic dimension was decisively prominent, visible in the religious "enthusiasts" who celebrated the divinity of nature and the natural human instincts, communal love, equality of the sexes in relationships as well as in religion and politics, the sacredness of sexuality, and, like Blake, the affirmation of nudity and the naked human body as reflecting the original divine glory of the human being.

In a different spirit but with a comparable emancipatory influence on subsequent social developments and erotic expression, it was during this same Uranus-Pluto alignment that John Milton argued for both the religious importance and the legal necessity of divorce to free deeply incompatible partners from the lifelong prison of an unhappy marriage in *The Doctrine and Discipline of Divorce* of

1644. This issue arose with increasing force during subsequent Uranus-Pluto alignments and came to its most emphatic and widespread expression in the radical social changes that began during the conjunction of the 1960s.

And moving back one more cycle, similar cultural phenomena reflecting these same motifs were yet again evident during the immediately preceding Uranus-Pluto opposition of the Radical Reformation, in 1533–45, in phenomena that included the hedonistic orgies and polygamy of the Münster Anabaptists, with their antinomian anarchism and communization of property, and Henry VIII's divorce-driven schism from the Roman Catholic Church that brought the Reformation to England and a vast shift towards the secularization of society.

The combined drive for religious and sexual freedom was often expressed in Uranus-Pluto eras not only through radical rejection but also through sustained efforts for liberal reform. For example, the synthesis of religious and erotic emancipation in the 1960s was evident in the growing movement in the Catholic Church in the wake of the Second Vatican Council towards the acceptance of contraception. This fundamental change in traditional Church policy was ultimately rejected by the Roman hierarchy but was overwhelmingly embraced in practice by much of the Church laity from that decade onwards, thus creating a significant fissure between the hierarchy and the people—between the "head" of the Church and its "body"—with rippling effects in other areas of religious doctrine and increasing tendencies towards nonconformity by both laity and clergy.

More generally during these same years of the 1960s and after, in virtually all the major religions worldwide, countless multitudes of individuals left or largely ignored their inherited faith. While many factors impelled this exodus, a central one for many was an explicit or implicit rebellion against the sexually repressive moral codes of the established religious traditions that, in the highly secular and psychologically transformed zeitgeist of the 1960s, seemed pathologically constricting and contrary to the free and wholesome expression of nature's healthy instincts.

Here we begin to see the remarkably rich and complex interplay of the mutually activated archetypal forces during such eras, in which different manifestations of the same multivalent principles, Promethean and Dionysian, set in motion other manifestations of the same principles in an intensifying spiral of causes and effects. To unpack just one example: In the 1960s, the technological breakthrough that brought forth the contraceptive pill and led to its widespread use also empowered, and in certain respects made possible, the sexual revolution, freeing both women and men from constraints, fears, and enduring responsibilities that previously inhibited sexual activity. In turn, the use of contraceptive methods gave women a new freedom of choice between the pursuit of career and marriage, encouraged postponement of marriage for both men and women—since they were no longer required to marry to fulfill their sexual longings—and dramatically increased the frequency of both premarital and extramarital sexual relations with a resulting increase in the number of divorces as well.

All these developments in turn supported and strengthened personal autonomy in social behavior and morality. They also engendered major changes and disruptions in the social fabric, evident in widespread defiance by youths of traditional parental and community authority and the emergence of an intensely polarized "generation gap" that simultaneously arose in the political sphere. Especially notable was the heightening of sexual expression that increasingly pervaded and impelled the rock music of the era, the art form that was both most emblematic and most formative of the emerging countercultural zeitgeist. Rock music's synthesis of Promethean and Dionysian impulses—unprecedentedly empowered on a mass scale by technological advances, both through electronic amplification and through its virtually global dissemination by radio and recordings—was in turn expressed in a wave of mass concerts and festivals of music and dance in enormous rituals of art, eros, and transformation.

As mentioned above in the Catholic context, unfettered expression of sexual impulses also encouraged a new disregard of long-established religious prohibitions, which in turn reinforced the larger movement of the era towards religious experiment and the rejection of orthodox belief. The new individualism and new freedom from religious constraint augmented a broader tendency towards intellectual and moral independence of all kinds and accelerated the dismantling of a wide range of internal and external structures of social restraint, with many unforeseen consequences that unfolded in the subsequent decades.

This delineation of a cascading sequence of causes and effects certainly simplifies the reality. The Promethean technological breakthrough that made possible the contraceptive pill did not by itself cause the libidinal disinhibition in the culture, signs of which were already evident from the beginning of the decade in many cultural phenomena, such as popular films, music, and literature, before the widespread adoption of the pill. Rather, I believe that the technological innovation should be seen as a synchronistic and powerfully synergistic factor in a much larger, more complex, multicausal historical process in which the two principles, Promethean and Dionysian, potently interacted and mutually catalyzed each other at many levels, thereby producing an accelerating proliferation of causes and effects.

Filling in the Cyclical Sequence

In all these phenomena involving the synthesis and mutual activation of these two archetypal impulses, we see clear suggestions of the two different forms of patterning in correlation with the Uranus-Pluto cycle: a synchronic pattern, in which a single alignment coincides with a multiplicity of archetypally related events in different locations and different areas of activity that occur independently yet in close temporal proximity; and a diachronic pattern, in which a series of cyclical alignments over the course of several centuries coincides with a distinct sequence of significant events that forms a meaningful progression for a specific movement or in a specific area of activity. As I continued the historical research, I found that these two general types of patterning repeatedly emerged with each of the planetary cycles I examined, in an astonishing variety of forms yet with rigorous archetypal consistency. Both types of patterning were also visible, and were rendered both more comprehensive and more tightly coherent, when I included the intervening square alignments in the unfolding planetary cycle.

For simplicity's sake, in reviewing the distinctive pattern of correlations for the Uranus-Pluto cycle, I have restricted our attention almost entirely to just the two axial alignments, the conjunction and opposition, the two climaxes of the ongoing 360° cycle. A more detailed analysis would include careful examination of historical and cultural phenomena that coincided with the intervening square alignments and filled in the full quadrature sequence. I mentioned earlier the Uranus-Pluto square that occurred midway between the conjunction at the births of Rousseau and Diderot and the opposition of the French Revolution, which coincided with all of Rousseau's seminal works and with Diderot's *Encyclopédie*, both of which found powerful expression in the events and ideals of the Revolution during the immediately following Uranus-Pluto quadrature alignment and in subsequent alignment periods. A similar pattern can be recognized with the birth of Blake during that same square, followed by the outpouring of his revolutionary works during the 1790s, and then the upsurge of his influence in later Uranus-Pluto periods, especially in the 1960s. Also during this same square alignment were born both Mary Wollstonecraft and William Godwin, two of the most crucial figures in British thought of the French Revolutionary period. So too both Robespierre and Danton, pivotal figures in the French Revolution itself.

All five of these individuals were born in the 1756–59 period when the Uranus-Pluto square alignment was closest to exact. Here we can clearly discern an unfolding diachronic sequence of archetypally and historically related events during these three successive quadrature alignments of the eighteenth century that climaxed in the French Revolutionary period.

We can perceive the same pattern in the immediately following sequence of quadrature alignments. The Uranus-Pluto square that occurred halfway between the opposition of the French Revolution and the conjunction of the 1848 revolutions took place between 1816 and 1824. These were the years when the two planets were within 10° of exact alignment, the usual range within which I observed the coincidence of archetypally relevant events with the square aspect (the alignment reached exactitude in 1820–21). This eight-year period precisely coincided with the great wave of Latin American revolutions that brought independence in rapid succession to Argentina (1816), Chile (1817), Colombia (1819), Mexico, Venezuela, Costa Rica, El Salvador, Guatemala, Honduras, Panama, Santo Domingo (all in 1821, when the alignment was exact), Brazil and Ecuador (1822), and Peru (1824). What appears to be the bell-shaped curve of an archetypal wave pattern of a suddenly empowered Promethean principle expressing itself in collective human activity and historical events, here unmistakably centering on 1820–21, is again readily discernible.

Moreover, in Europe during this same period occurred a wave of revolutions and revolts in Spain, Portugal, Italy, and France, intense ferment against the Habsburg Empire throughout central and eastern Europe, and the beginning of the long war for Greek independence from the Turks. Lord Byron, who died during this period in 1824 while supporting the fight for Greek independence, was born in 1788 at the start of the immediately preceding Uranus-Pluto opposition of the French Revolutionary period (with the Sun in alignment with both Uranus and Pluto, and with Venus in nearly exact conjunction with Pluto). Byron's life and his iconic embodiment of both erotic emancipation and, at its end, the struggle for political freedom vividly suggest the presence of the Promethean and Dionysian impulses in close interaction. His charismatic embodiment of this archetypal combination exerted an enduring cultural influence, asserting itself repeatedly during subsequent Uranus-Pluto alignments in a wide range of forms, from leaders of the 1840s–50s nationalist struggles like Mazzini and Mickiewicz to cultural figures such as Baudelaire and Oscar Wilde, and on finally to the 1960s and Mick Jagger.[16]

So also with Percy Bysshe Shelley, all of whose mature work was produced in the years of the Uranus-Pluto square between 1816 and 1822, when he drowned in a storm off the coast of Italy a month before he turned thirty. Like Byron, Shelley was born during the French Revolutionary opposition, in 1792 (with the Sun and Venus in close alignment with both Uranus and Pluto), his birth occurring in the same summer that brought the wave of fraternal ecstasy which suddenly overtook the French legislature and the population of Paris. The constellation of commitments that inspired Shelley throughout his life—to social justice and political revolution, to individual liberty, to the creative freedom and power of the poet, to rebellion against confining religious orthodoxy, and to romantic freedom and erotic emancipation—all reflect the characteristic themes of the Promethean-Dionysian complex. Many of these themes were particularly embodied in his poetic masterwork, *Prometheus Unbound*, written in 1820 when the Uranus-Pluto square alignment was exact.[17]

In turn, figures who were crucial in subsequent Uranus-Pluto periods were born in this period of the 1816–24 square. Frederick Douglass, Harriet Tubman, and Susan B. Anthony were all born during this square and brought forth their liberating achievements in coincidence with the immediately following conjunction of 1845–56. An especially paradigmatic example is Karl Marx, born in 1818 during the Uranus-Pluto square, whose life and work were devoted with a kind of elemental intensity to the cause of mass revolution and emancipation that first fully emerged during the conjunction of the 1845–56 period. ("Prometheus is the noblest saint and martyr in the calendar of philosophy," Marx wrote in his doctoral dissertation.) Again, the Uranus-Pluto square that coincided with the birth of Marx and also of Engels, and that coincided as well with the revolutionary wave in Latin America and Europe, was the intervening quadrature alignment that took place exactly halfway between the Uranus-Pluto opposition of the French Revolution and the conjunction of the 1848 revolutions—the two periods whose dynamic historical and evolutionary connection Marx played such a central role in articulating.

This sequence of the three quadrature alignments from the French Revolution to the mid-nineteenth century was in turn part of the larger ongoing Uranus-Pluto cycle that brought forth subsequent waves of revolutionary, radical socialist,

---

THE URANUS-PLUTO CYCLE

Intervening square alignments

10° orb		Exact alignment <1°
1489–1507	*square*	1496–1500
1563–1570	*square*	1566–67
1620–1627	*square*	1623–24
1674–1683	*square*	1678–80
1749–1764	*square*	1755–58
1816–1824	*square*	1820–21
1873–1880	*square*	1876–77
1928–1937	*square*	1932–34
2007–2020	*square*	2012–15

15° orb adds one to three years before and after dates given for 10°.

and Marxist movements and events, as we have seen and explored earlier in these chapters: the rise of Lenin and Trotsky, the founding of the Bolshevik and the major socialist parties, and the beginning of the Russian revolutionary epoch during the following opposition of 1896–1907; and the worldwide wave of radical socialist, Marxist, and independence movements during the conjunction of the 1960s. The only Uranus-Pluto square of the twentieth century occurred halfway between these last-cited alignments, through most of the tumultuous decade of the 1930s (within 10° orb from 1928 to 1937). This alignment coincided with the period of heightened tension, violence, and struggle when the upsurge of Marxist and radical socialist movements in both the masses and cultural elites was especially widespread and international.

Characteristic of this tendency were the dramatic developments in Spain during the 1930s, from the election of the Socialist Party and its anti-Church policies to the rise of the Popular Front and the Spanish Civil War. In the United States, a wave of major labor strikes such as the historic Flint auto workers strike of 1936–37 resulted in the empowerment of labor unions throughout the country. On the religious side, the radical reform movement led by Dorothy Day and the Catholic Worker flourished during the 1930s, similar in spirit to the liberation theology movement that would emerge in the 1960s during the conjunction. We can also recognize the precise diachronic patterning coincident with the sequence of twentieth-century Uranus-Pluto alignments in the often-noted cyclical awakening of progressivism and social-political reform in the United States, spurred from both below and above, in the 1900s during the presidency of Theodore Roosevelt, in the 1930s during the presidency of Franklin Roosevelt, and in the 1960s during the presidencies of Kennedy and Johnson.

Indeed in many fields during the 1930s we can recognize the characteristic radical changes and paradigm shifts we have seen during earlier Uranus-Pluto alignments. In the intellectual sphere, economic upheavals throughout the world during the 1930s engendered revolutionary economic theories, above all those of John Maynard Keynes, set out in his *General Theory of Employment, Interest and Money*, which transformed economic decision-making for the rest of the twentieth century. In philosophy, the rise of existentialism, with its concerns with human freedom, metaphysical skepticism, and social emancipation, began during the 1930s as well, especially through the work of Jean-Paul Sartre and Simone de Beauvoir, whose long relationship as well as teaching and writing careers commenced during this alignment. In feminism, the period of this Uranus-Pluto square coincided with not only the emergence of Beauvoir in France but also the publication in England of Virginia Woolf's influential feminist milestone *A Room of One's Own*. In the history of protest music, it was during the 1930s that Woodie Guthrie, riding freight trains and traveling on the open road amidst the mass migration of Dust Bowl refugees, began his career as a composer and performer of folk songs protesting social injustice, which in turn inspired Bob Dylan and the protest music of the 1960s.

Many other cultural phenomena of the twentieth century show a similar sequential progression in coincidence with the three Uranus-Pluto dynamic alignments of that century, as in the distinct cyclical awakenings of a Promethean-Dionysian impulse expressed in widespread intensified cultural creativity and libidinal dynamism. In popular culture, for example, during the decade centered on 1900 with its Uranus-Pluto opposition, we see the emergence of jazz in New Orleans from the dynamic interplay of ragtime, blues, folk songs, church music, and marching-band music (this period also bringing the birth of the first generation of jazz giants like Louis Armstrong and Duke Ellington). In turn, the Uranus-Pluto square of the 1930s coincided with the wave of propulsive energy that surged through popular culture as swing and the big bands swept the country from Harlem to Los Angeles and brought an unexpected eruption of physicality, rhythmic potency, and improvisatory freedom in music and dance, as well as new social pressures for racial integration. And this was succeeded by the Dionysian-Promethean explosion during the conjunction of the 1960s that discharged itself in the jazz, rock, and dance of the popular culture of that epoch. A comparable pattern can be noted in the history of psychoanalysis, with its awakening to the power of the id and the sexual instincts: its initial emergence in the works of Freud and his first followers during the Uranus-Pluto opposition at the turn of the century, its rapid widespread embrace by intellectuals during the square of the 1930s, and its mass dissemination and radicalization during the conjunction of the 1960s.

Also suggestive of this archetypal combination was the unleashing of elemental forces and the violent rise of mass movements and collective actions of many kinds that took place in the 1930s—fascist, communist, socialist, the mass Nuremburg rallies, *The Triumph of the Will*, the Hitler Youth, the upsurge of Aryan neo-paganism, the power of the criminal underworld and gangsterism, the mass strikes and demonstrations, the many forced mass emigrations and cultural disruptions throughout the world at this time. Widely read works such as Freud's *Civilization and Its Discontents* and Ortega y Gasset's *Revolt of the Masses* (both 1930) reflected these concerns and developments. So also did Jung's famous 1936 essay *Wotan*, which diagnosed the rise of Hitler and Nazism overtaking Germany as an eruption of an archaic force within the German psyche personified by the ancient Teutonic mythological figure of Wotan, "a god of storm and frenzy, the unleasher of passions and the lust of battle. . . . A god has taken possession of the Germans and their house is filled with a 'mighty rushing wind.'" In this dangerous state the German nation was like a "raving berserker tearing himself free from his bonds. A hurricane has broken loose in Germany, while we still believe it is fine weather."

The unleashing of nature's elemental forces was evident in other ways as well during the Uranus-Pluto square of the 1930s, and in a close diachronic pattern with the preceding opposition of the 1896–1907 period. It was during these years that physicists first split the atom (John Cockroft and E.T.S. Walton, 1932), achieved the first nuclear fission (Enrico Fermi, 1934), proposed creating a chain reaction that would lead to the "liberation of nuclear energy for power production and other purposes through nuclear 'transmutation' " (Leo Szilard, 1934), and began conducting the research that led to the development of weapons of mass destruction. Prophetically, in 1903, during the preceding Uranus-Pluto opposition, the physicist Ernest Rutherford made the "playful suggestion that, could a proper detonator be found, it was just conceivable that a wave of atomic disintegration might be started through matter, which would indeed make this old world vanish in smoke." Twenty-nine years later, during the Uranus-Pluto square in 1932, using a linear accelerator built in Rutherford's own Cavendish Laboratory, Cockcroft and Walton split the atom.

The diachronic patterns involving the intervening Uranus-Pluto square alignments sometimes extended back over several centuries. For example, Che Guevara, who fought in revolutionary movements throughout Latin America, was born during the Uranus-Pluto square of the 1928–37 period, exactly one cycle after the great wave of Latin American revolutionary movements of liberation during the Uranus-Pluto square of 1816–24. In the background of that epoch of revolutions against Spain and Portugal, and reflecting a different motif of the same archetypal complex, the initial 1492 "discovery" of America by Christopher Columbus in service to the Spanish crown coincided with the Uranus-Pluto square of the 1490s. Indeed, all four of Columbus's journeys to the New World, the signing of the Treaty of Tordesillas that divided the newly discovered lands between Spain and Portugal (1494), John Cabot's reaching North America (1497), Vasco da Gama's reaching India (1498), and Pedro Cabral's reaching Brazil (1500) all took place during the long Uranus-Pluto square that extended from 1489 to 1507 (unusually long because of Pluto's speed during those years in comparison with that of Uranus). This epochal awakening of the European mind to the existence of new worlds, combined with the unprecedented centrifugal thrust of European power beyond its own continent, began the enormous upheaval that, like a centuries-long hurricane, swept through and overwhelmed the indigenous peoples, flora, and fauna of those many lands.

The eruption of a collective will to power during Uranus-Pluto eras can also become concentrated and embodied in a single powerful figure, a world-historic political-military conqueror or tyrant driven as if by a force of nature: One of the most striking diachronic sequences of this cycle is the coincidence of Uranus-Pluto alignments with the emergence of just such figures: Alexander the Great during the conjunction of 328–318 BCE, Julius Caesar during the conjunction of 74–65 BCE, Charlemagne during the opposition of 766–82, Genghis Khan during the conjunction of 1196–1206, Tamerlane during the opposition of 1390–1400, Peter the Great during the conjunction of 1705–12, Napoleon during the opposition of 1787–98, Hitler, Mussolini, Stalin, and Mao during the square of the 1930s, with Mao and his cult of personality reaching its apex during the conjunction of the 1960s. Many other such figures of lesser power but with similar impulses and characteristics—dictators, conquistadors, tyrants, strongmen—arose over the centuries during periods of Uranus-Pluto alignments.

The Individual and the Collective

Throughout the evidence, I continually observed the importance of attending both to the full quadrature cycle and to the birth of particularly significant individuals whose lives expressed the characteristic archetypal complex associated with that cycle. For example, considering the just-cited set of milestones in global exploration, I noticed that Columbus himself was born in 1451 during the immediately preceding Uranus-Pluto conjunction that began that quadrature cycle—the same conjunction that coincided with Gutenberg's development of the printing press and the fall of Constantinople that helped catalyze the Renaissance in Italy. With Columbus and his subsequent epoch-making expeditions, so also in numerous other cases, I found that the work or achievement of an individual born during one alignment of a planetary cycle, the archetypal character of which he or she embodied in an especially paradigmatic way, consistently took place and often suddenly found new life in close coincidence with subsequent alignments of the same planets.

Restricting ourselves to individuals we have already been discussing, and to the one cycle of Uranus-Pluto quadrature alignments that extended from the beginning of the eighteenth to the middle of the nineteenth century, we can recognize a kind of archetypal clockwork in the unfolding sequence of correlations. The four alignments mark a precise succession of historically crucial Promethean figures who were born during one alignment and whose cultural contribution flourished in close coincidence with subsequent ones: Thus Rousseau and Diderot are born during the conjunction and flourish precisely during the period of the following square; Blake, Wollstonecraft, Godwin, Robespierre, and Danton are born during that square and flourish during the period of the following opposition, that of the French Revolution, when also the ideas of Rousseau and Diderot become powerfully influential. Byron and Shelley and Schopenhauer are born then, carry forth that energy, and flourish during the following square that in turn coincides with the births of Marx, Engels, Frederick Douglass, Harriet Tubman, George Eliot, Whitman, Baudelaire, Dostoevsky, and Melville. That cycle ends with the conjunction of the mid-nineteenth century and the births of Nietzsche and Freud—and an influx of births of other pivotal figures of cultural rebellion, artistic revolution, heroic individualism, and erotic emancipation such as Rimbaud, Oscar Wilde, Van Gogh, and Gauguin, as well as such alternative embodiments of the empowered Prometheus as the paradigmatic inventors and experimenters Edison and Tesla.

Similarly, with respect to still other Promethean themes, the conjunction of 1705–16 that coincided with the births of Rousseau and Diderot also coincided with the births of the equally Promethean eighteenth-century figures David Hume and Benjamin Franklin: Hume, the most radical British philosopher of the century and an avatar of the Enlightenment's project of intellectual emancipation from orthodox beliefs; Franklin, another iconic figure of the Enlightenment whose lifetime of scientific, technological, and political activity speaks to the sustained presence of an empowered Promethean impulse, as concisely suggested in the famous epigram by Turgot: "He snatched the lightning from the skies and the sceptre from tyrants."[18]

This lineage of epochal Prometheans continues as we move back through the cyclical alignments. At the beginning of the immediately preceding Uranus-Pluto opposition, which coincided with the English revolutionary era, occurred the birth of Newton, the climactic figure of the Scientific Revolution, in 1643. The immediately previous conjunction is that of 1592–1602, at the heart of which in 1596 occurred the birth of Descartes. What entire epochs of intellectual and cultural revolution did in subsequent centuries—sweeping away great superstructures of established thought and tradition—Descartes commenced in the crucible of his mind and writings. As the historian Jules Michelet famously observed, "The Revolution of 1789 had begun with the *Discourse on Method*."

Descartes's birth occurred in the same conjunction period that brought the wave of scientific breakthroughs of Galileo and Kepler, Tycho and Gilbert, cited earlier. This conjunction of 1592–1602 also precisely coincided with the great period of brilliant cultural creativity of the Elizabethan age that saw the near-simultaneous emergence of Shakespeare, Bacon, Spenser, Marlowe, and Jonson.[19] Focusing here on Shakespeare, we see the familiar Uranus-Pluto themes and qualities in the sudden eruption of creative power and dramatic intensity in this first decade of his career as he brought forth a new play on average every six months, beginning precisely with the start of this conjunction. We are so accustomed to what now seems like the timeless existence of the full Shakespearean canon that it takes an effort to put this astounding creative torrent into perspective: A full-bodied complex Shakespearean play emerged from his pen on average every six months, two a year, four every two years, eight in four years, and so on. This tremendous empowerment of the creative impulse and sustained creative intensity represents the archetypal vector of Pluto→Uranus. Simultaneously, the specific narrative themes and qualities of character in these works display the characteristic motifs of Uranus→Pluto: the liberation and creative expression of the deep forces of eros and instinct; all the dazzling dramas of the human will in violent struggle and unleashed passion from *Richard III* and the other histories to *Julius Caesar* and *Hamlet*; the free-spirited eroticism of *The Taming of the Shrew* and *A Midsummer Night's Dream*; the great Rabelaisian figure of Falstaff (remarkably, Rabelais himself produced his masterwork *Gargantua and Pantagruel* in coincidence with the preceding Uranus-Pluto opposition of 1533–45). So too Shakespeare's poems of passion and sensuality, beginning with his immensely popular first published poem *Venus and Adonis* (published during his Saturn return), which ran through six editions in nine years in exact coincidence with the years of this conjunction.

More generally, with their unprecedented articulation of self-willed and self-reflective personalities who engage the full range of life's dramatic tensions and crises, we see in Shakespeare's works a creative emergence of the modern self no less influential and liberating and, in crucial respects, incomparably more complex and whole than the extremely potent form of the modern self mediated by Descartes, who was born at the very time Shakespeare's career was fully emerging in 1595–96. Shakespeare himself was born during the immediately preceding Uranus-Pluto square alignment in April 1564. Two months earlier during the same square, in February 1564, Galileo was born, he too a titan of the early modern self, a powerful agent of cultural awakening and of defiant struggle against orthodox belief and traditional authority.

Moving back one more cycle to the opposition of the first Uranus-Pluto cycle of the modern age, the alignment of 1533–45 coincided with the publication of Copernicus's *De Revolutionibus*, the work that commenced the entire Promethean awakening of the Scientific Revolution and the Enlightenment. Finally, if we move back to the beginning of this cycle at the dawn of the modern age, the conjunction of 1450–61, besides the epoch-making development of the Gutenberg press, the great cultural shift from Byzantium to Renaissance Italy, and the birth of Columbus, we find that this same conjunction also coincided with the birth of Leonardo da Vinci in 1452. Here again we can recognize so many of the characteristic motifs associated with this planetary cycle—the compelling drive towards creative innovation, the incessant impulse to experiment and explore, to discover the new, to liberate the human being from previously established limits. We see the distinctive signs of this archetypal complex expressed in Leonardo's extraordinary individualism, his assertion of the autonomous will in such widely diverse fields of action, his voracious appetite for scientific research, his lifelong concern with the forces of nature and with geology, biology, physiology, hydrodynamics, aeronautics, engineering, mechanics. It is visible too in his prophetic anticipation of so many technological advances of the future, to be used for good or ill, from airplanes and space travel to weapons of mass destruction. Above all, we recognize this archetypal complex in Leonardo's epochal embodiment in his own person of the sudden, radical evolutionary advance of the species. A kind of liberation of the titanic occurs in and through Leonardo, one that is evident as much in his technological imagination as in his almost superhuman creative drive.

As we have seen throughout this survey, all these themes evident in Leonardo's life and work were played out again and again in history, conspicuously and with dramatic intensity, in each era that coincided with Uranus-Pluto align-ments. In an individual such as Leonardo, it is as if all the ongoing, subcon-sciously developing creative powers and evolutionary forces of nature condensed and particularized themselves for a time in one person—as, in a sense, they did in each of the many seminal figures discussed in these chapters—to compel and drive forward the collective transformation of the whole. Such an impulse, again, seems unmistakably reflective of the Promethean and Dionysian principles in a dynamic interpenetrating synthesis.

If we reconsider the long sequence of Uranus-Pluto eras, we can now recog-nize that besides all the distinctive themes and impulses we have already noted—social and political revolutions, erotic emancipation, scientific and technological revolutions—we can also discern the correlation of this cycle with historical peri-ods of tremendously heightened creativity seemingly affecting every realm of hu-man activity and indeed making possible the many other manifestations and motifs just mentioned. Again, this appears to reflect the dynamic vector of the Plutonic archetype driving and empowering the Promethean: Pluto→Uranus. As with the spectacular burst of creativity and cultural influence sustained between 1962 and 1970 by the Beatles and Dylan and scores of other suddenly creatively empowered musicians, it was as if all the arts and sciences in the 1960s had been given a rocket boost of creative *shakti* that paralleled the titanic technological, social, and political explosion of the decade—a creative power capable of hur-tling human beings around the Earth and into space, within and without. So too the preceding opposition at the turn of the twentieth century with its great surge of creative breakthroughs in the arts and sciences—Einstein and Planck, Freud and Jung, Mahler and Stravinsky, Cézanne and Picasso, Mann and Rilke, William and Henry James, Isadora Duncan, among so many others—again in close con-cert with the revolutionary changes and emancipatory movements then taking place throughout the world in the social, political, and technological realms, all taking flight, as it were, along with the Wright brothers.[20]

Even in the cultural life of a single country we can recognize the potency of this archetypal patterning. The Uranus-Pluto conjunction of 1845–56 coincided precisely with the most intensely creative moment of nineteenth-century Ameri-can culture, with Emerson at his peak, traveling throughout the country giving over eighty lectures a year, which became the essays of *Representative Men* and *The Conduct of Life*, riding far and wide on the proliferating railroads and deliv-ering his emancipatory message that celebrated the creative power and heroic nobility of the self-reliant individual embedded in a universe of deeper mean-ings. During this period, Thoreau was at Walden, Melville and Hawthorne were writing their masterworks, Whitman brought forth *Leaves of Grass*, and Marga-ret Fuller wrote her pathbreaking criticism, called for recognition of women's equality and rights to self-fulfillment, and joined the struggle for liberty in Italy. In these same years of the 1840s and 1850s, an equally brilliant creative wave and the rise of a new cultural spirit was taking place in Europe, with the emergence of Wagner, Baudelaire, Flaubert, the Brontës, Dostoevsky, Tolstoy, many of these individuals also embedded in the surging revolutionary movements and ideas of those same years.

No less vivid an illustration of this pattern is the extraordinary epoch of em-powered creativity in the preceding Uranus-Pluto opposition of the 1790s and French Revolution, visible above all in the great Romantic emergence in litera-ture and the arts, philosophy and science at that time: Blake, Wordsworth and Coleridge, Goethe and Schiller, Hölderlin and Novalis, the Kant of the later critiques, Hegel in his crucial formative period, Fichte, Schelling, the Schlegels, Mozart and Haydn at their peak, the dramatic arrival of the young Beethoven in Vienna with the unprecedented power and improvisatory freedom of his piano performances—the nineteenth-century equivalent of the electrifyingly powerful performances of the young Hendrix as he arrived in London during the conjunc-tion of the 1960s.

If we then move back in history all the way to classical antiquity to see whether comparable correlations are evident—recalling en route the conjunc-tion of the Elizabethan era and the sudden brilliant emergence of Shakespeare, Bacon, Spenser, Marlowe, and the rest—we find that the Uranus-Pluto conjunc-tion period of the classical Greek era (one cycle before the conjunction that co-incided with Alexander the Great's conquests and the birth of the Hellenistic age) took place in the period from 443 to 430 BCE. These years were precisely the height of the Periclean age in Athens, when Pericles as the uncrowned king from 443 to 429 pressed for radical democratic reform and presided over the most culturally and intellectually creative era of the century, when the Parthenon was built, from 447 to 432, when Socrates emerged at the start of his long career (age twenty-seven to forty in the period of the conjunction), when the Sophists brought to Athens their liberating secularist critical thinking and the birth of hu-manistic education, the *paideia,* and when Sophocles, Euripides, Anaxagoras, Democritus, Leucippus, and Hippocrates flourished.

In this extraordinary litany of sequential bursts of cultural creativity and awakening, we can recognize that one of the most strikingly consistent charac-teristics in all these individuals, eras, and cultural phenomena is a certain un-leashed or awakened *titanic* quality. Whether we are considering paradigmatic individuals born in Uranus-Pluto periods such as Leonardo and Galileo, Blake and Byron, Wollstonecraft and Douglass, Marx and Nietzsche, or distinctive cul-tural expressions of these eras such as the poetry of Whitman and the songs of Dylan, the music of Wagner and the Rolling Stones, the writings and theories of Rousseau and Schopenhauer, Darwin and Freud, or the eras themselves such as the Periclean age and the Elizabethan, the French Revolutionary epoch and the 1960s, in all these periods, figures, and cultural phenomena we can readily see this distinctive titanic quality—titanic impulse for change, titanic intensity and creativity, titanic struggle and defiance—so appropriate for an archetypal synthesis of the Promethean and Dionysian principles. These eras and figures seem to be the vessels for a sudden upsurge of elemental creative forces from nature's depths that catalyze and accelerate the evolutionary transformation of human life.

It seems to me remarkable how many of the great works of literature that especially embody this tendency towards creative power, titanic depths, and violent forces—the plays of Shakespeare, the poetry and prophecies of Blake, the novels of Dostoevsky, Melville's *Moby Dick*, Jung's prophetic *Answer to Job*, to name a few of the most notable—were written by individuals *born* during Uranus-Pluto periods and were very often *created* during the next quadrature alignment of the same planets. It is as if such works of the creative imagination reflect the unleashing of an elemental dramatic power much like their eras as a whole. Characters such as Ahab and Lear and the Karamazovs break forth from the page or the stage to compel our visceral attention, as if a kind of volcanic force from the depths of the human spirit is being bodied forth before our eyes.

Interestingly, the births of all five of the just-named authors took place during Uranus-Pluto *square* alignments, as the square in particular seems to correlate with a certain high tension wrought by the combined archetypal principles, Promethean and Dionysian, that emphasizes the clashing extremity of the dynamic forces that have been activated. Such heightened tension appears to be especially demanding of some kind of dramatic embodiment and articulation. It presses intensely and urgently towards the possibility of a larger resolution. We see this same depth and dynamic tension in the novels and poetry of Mann and Rilke; both were born in the same year as Jung, 1875, during the same Uranus-Pluto square alignment, and in both cases their works, like Jung's, first emerged in coincidence with the following opposition of 1896–1907. So too Isadora Duncan, born during the same square alignment as Jung, Mann, and Rilke, and bringing forth her revolution during the same opposition at the turn of the century. These same qualities are strongly evident as well in such historically crucial works as Mary Wollstonecraft's *Vindication of the Rights of Woman* of 1792 and *The Autobiography of Frederick Douglass* of 1845. Both Wollstonecraft and Douglass were born during Uranus-Pluto square alignments, and their great works were published during the immediately following Uranus-Pluto axial alignments.

As with these many iconic expressions of the individual will and imagination, so too the same power and drama—intellectual, emotional, elemental—are consistently conspicuous in the collective life and historical events of the great sequence of Uranus-Pluto eras we have examined. In our own life and time, even several decades later, whether we are now twenty years old or seventy, the most recent Uranus-Pluto conjunction period of the 1960s continues to exert its titanic effects—emancipatory, revolutionary, violent, creative, erotic, disruptive, destabilizing, driving ineluctably towards the future, awakening to the new.

Yet as Dostoevsky and Melville, Shakespeare and Jung all explored so penetratingly, this awakened titanic impulse is also dangerous in the intensity and potential destructiveness of its unleashed energies, and in its potential self-destructiveness. Here we encounter one of the deep challenges and ambiguities of this archetypal complex. When we consider many of these titanic Promethean figures and epochs, it is evident that the combination of the Promethean and Dionysian principles often seemed to express itself not only through the intensification, empowerment, and violent eruption of the Promethean but also through the *destruction of* the Promethean, which burns itself out in the flames of its own intensity, in the exigencies of its own archetypal drama. This potential outcome reflects the deep ambiguity of the Dionysian-Plutonic-Kali principle, which is at once empowering and intensifying, violent and destructive, transformative and regenerative.

Thinking of Byron and Shelley, for example, or many comparable figures of the 1960s, we cannot help noticing that one of the most conspicuous features of Uranus-Pluto eras is the frequency of premature death, often by violence or mishap, of so many young Promethean figures in the crucial moment of their life drama. For the Sixties brought not only the decisive empowerment of many Promethean figures and impulses but also their destruction: paradigmatic political figures such as Che Guevara, Malcolm X, Martin Luther King, and the Kennedys, as well as leading artists of the counterculture such as Jimi Hendrix, Janis Joplin, and Jim Morrison. A similar pattern is evident in the French Revolutionary epoch: the violent deaths of Marat, Danton, Robespierre, Saint-Just—most still in their twenties and thirties, as was also true in the 1960s. Sometimes this archetypal drama took place more internally and psychologically, or in a complex interaction with the outer world, as in the lives of Rousseau, Nietzsche, Wilde, Rimbaud, and Van Gogh, all born during Uranus-Pluto conjunctions.

Given this distinct archetypal pattern, it is remarkable that Aeschylus, the titanic creator of classical tragedy and the author of the prototypical drama of titanic defiance, *Prometheus Bound*, was born during a Uranus-Pluto alignment, the opposition immediately preceding the conjunction of the Periclean age. As both Aeschylus and Jung knew, in the complex relationship between humankind and the gods, everything is at stake.

For the very drama we see unfold with all these Promethean individuals, we see as well in entire Promethean eras. The eruptive emancipatory intensity and extremity of the French Revolutionary epoch, or the English revolution before it, or later the 1848 revolutions and the 1960s, all in some way brought about a kind of self-immolation of the entire epoch. The unleashed forces of destruction and self-destruction—and the unleashed forces of violent conservative reaction—deeply compromised and complicated the emancipatory and creative impulses of all those eras, even as those impulses continued to live and develop in the ensuing decades. No less problematic and consequential were the unleashed energies of violent power in the already powerful during just these eras: the United States in Vietnam, Athens in the Peloponnesian War, Revolutionary France in its

Napoleonic explosion, modern civilization itself in its vast technological potency and destructiveness.

All these observations suggest the immense historical and individual responsibility presented by these powerful forces in the collective psyche and in ourselves. For what has happened in the past is not past, but lives within us.

A Larger View of the Sixties

After many years of closely studying the correlations set forth in the preceding chapters, as well as the evidence for correlation patterns involving the other outer planetary cycles, I gradually gained the distinct impression that in some sense everything that occurs during one alignment is implicitly present and contributing to every subsequent one, as if it were a single continuing and cumulative historical development. This appeared to be true not just in the life of an individual person during successive alignments of the same cycle but also in the collective life of a culture, as if indeed the entire culture were a single individual being. It seemed to me that whatever was achieved, experienced, suffered through, painfully or joyfully brought forth during one cyclical alignment somehow remained present and causally efficacious (in both the Aristotelian and Whiteheadian senses) during the following alignments of the cycle, making possible and informing new developments. Something like this dynamic continuity was clearly evident in the various lines of development that linked, for example, the English revolutionary epoch of the seventeenth century to the French revolutionary epoch of the eighteenth century, on to the revolutions of 1848 and the mid-nineteenth century, to the many revolutionary developments at the turn of the twentieth century, and finally to the 1960s, in all the areas we have examined: feminism and women's rights, antislavery and civil rights, progressive and radical social thought and political movements, technological and scientific revolutions, erotic emancipation, and the unleashing of the forces of nature, of violence and destruction, and of self-destruction.

Thus each era, each event, each cultural phenomenon, and each individual life that coincided with a specific planetary alignment seemed to me best regarded not in isolation but rather as having been deeply shaped by and carrying forth within it what happened in preceding alignment periods of that cycle—and also, as we will see, by what occurred in preceding alignment periods of other planetary cycles that are associated with very different archetypal principles and complexes. This seemed to be true even if what was achieved or struggled with took place in the seclusion of an isolated individual life or local society or subculture, unbeknownst to the life of the larger world. One feels when looking at these many historical and cultural phenomena that what is worked out and brought forth at each moment is never lost, nor is it truly isolated in its individual or local context. Rather at some deeper level it participates and endures in a much larger collective unfolding.

These ongoing archetypal developments affect all of us, not just those born under those particular alignments—some obviously more dramatically than others, but everyone is in some way carrying the whole within them. We all have those archetypal principles and complexes living within us, in varying forms and combinations with other archetypal impulses—much in the same way that we all have those planets in our birth charts, in endlessly diverse configurations— and these archetypal impulses carry vast streams of historical experience.

From this point of view, it is as if everyone who was born *after* the 1960s actually in some way *lived through* the 1960s. They bear within themselves the effects of that era, they know its conflicts and struggles, its truths and revelations. In some sense this knowledge lives subconsciously within them. They then enter new eras with all those impulses and forces existing potently within them, both the epochal resolutions from the earlier era *and* all that is deeply unresolved. So too do we all, with respect to all the preceding centuries of alignments and human experience.

These reflections are, of course, all anticipated by Jung's understanding of the collective unconscious, but the evidence set forth in this book introduces a certain specificity, and perhaps a more explicit cosmic ground, to the Jungian perspective.[21] It vividly indicates in great detail the ongoing cyclical awakenings and activations of a particular archetypal impulse in human affairs, showing its dynamic continuity and its specific timing over the centuries. It allows a new potential for historical self-awareness and conscious archetypal participation. All this is made possible by the hypothesis, or the understanding, that *the planetary movements have significance:* that is, they bear an intelligible correspondence to particular archetypal principles, and their unfolding cyclical patterns are closely associated with the unfolding cyclical patterns of human affairs.

Just as everything that happened in the 1960s depended on, and carried within it, what happened in the earlier Uranus-Pluto eras, so also is this true now with the continuing dynamic presence of the "Sixties" in subsequent decades up through the present moment. The great worldwide awakening of feminism and the women's liberation movement that surged forth in the 1960s, that expanded tremendously in the following years, and continues ever-strengthening and growing today utterly depended on, and bore within it, what had been struggled through and achieved by the militant suffragists of the 1900s, by the women's rights pioneers of 1848, by Mary Wollestonecraft and the French Revolutionary women of the 1790s. When Dylan sang with his tongue on fire in the 1960s, he drew on all the freedom-crying, times-changing singers and poets that came before him, and the power of his prophetic voice in those years has continued to shape the cultural ethos through each subsequent decade. So also with Martin Luther King and the civil rights movement, Rachel Carson and the ecology movement, the progressive political movements, the scientific and technological advances, the evolution of literature and the other arts.

And so also with the unleashed titanic forces of nature—of technological power, of instinctual and libidinal freedom, and of radical rebellion whether in the form of revolutionary violence or a sublimated will to power that brings a more profound and integrated transformation of society and self.

Of course much of what I am saying here is already widely accepted, sometimes to the point of truism, but again the evidence we have been examining provides a certain detailed specificity of dynamic connections, both historical *and* archetypal, and also a detailed specificity of both the timing and the archetypal character of these developments that is available to us in no other manner. I believe that this specificity of detail and cyclical patterning radically enhances our understanding of cultural evolution as a vast historical development that is shaped by dynamic archetypal forces, powers that move within a collective psyche that is in turn rooted in and expressive of a cosmic ground.

During the same Uranus-Pluto alignment in the fifth century BCE that coincided with the birth of the Promethean tragedian Aeschylus, the early Greek philosopher Xenophanes articulated for the first time the idea of an underlying progress in human affairs that was dependent on the human quest for truth and the unfolding of time: "The gods did not reveal, from the beginning, all things to us; but in the course of time, through seeking, human beings find that which is the better. . . ."[22]

Thus it was this unexpected combination of so many factors—the strikingly close fit between the historical phenomena and the relevant archetypal principles, the precise timing, the inexplicable simultaneity of such phenomena in widely dispersed locations, and the coherent patterning of major archetypally related events and figures in coincidence with cyclical alignments over long periods of time—that in their totality seemed to me to require a fresh assessment of the ancient astrological vision of the universe, far beyond what conventional modern explanations could provide. I found compelling the subtlety and comprehensiveness of the archetypal astrological method, in which superficially unrelated phenomena of different categories could be integrated on a deeper conceptual level and thereby illuminated. Employing this perspective and this mode of analysis seemed to bring forth a continuing fountain of surprising insights into a wide range of cultural phenomena and cyclical patterns in history that I would not otherwise have come upon.

Let us now turn our attention to historical correlations of a different cycle of the outer planets, shorter in duration and more frequent than the Uranus-Pluto cycle but no less striking in its archetypal patternings. I found that as I expanded my research to encompass a larger spectrum of phenomena of different themes and qualities, and as a more comprehensive picture emerged of the ongoing multiple planetary cycles—sequential, interweaving, and overlapping with respect to each other—the complex archetypal patterns of human history were more fully illuminated and made more richly intelligible.

V

Cycles of Crisis and Contraction

Waves of anger and fear
Circulate over the bright
And darkened lands of the earth. . . .

—W. H. Auden
"September 1, 1939"

World Wars, Cold War,
and September 11

We will now examine the planetary cycle of Pluto with *Saturn*, which in important respects bears a resemblance to the Uranus-Pluto cycle. The nature of this resemblance seems to reflect the activated presence of the archetypal principle associated with the planet Pluto in both cycles. But *how* the Pluto archetype is activated during Saturn-Pluto alignment periods (Saturn→Pluto) and, conversely, what second archetypal principle is empowered and intensified by the Pluto archetype (Pluto→Saturn), presents an altogether different picture.

While the Uranus-Pluto periods consistently coincided with widespread revolutionary upheaval, intensified emancipatory impulses, and radical cultural innovation, the successive quadrature alignments of the Saturn-Pluto cycle coincided with especially challenging historical periods marked by a pervasive quality of intense *contraction*: eras of international crisis and conflict, empowerment of reactionary forces and totalitarian impulses, organized violence and oppression, all sometimes marked by lasting traumatic effects. An atmosphere of gravity and tension tended to accompany these three-to-four-year periods, as did a widespread sense of epochal closure: "the end of an era," "the end of innocence," the destruction of an earlier mode of life that in retrospect may seem to have been marked by widespread indulgence, decadence, naïveté, denial, and inflation. Profound transformation was a dominant theme, as with the Uranus-Pluto cycle, but here the transformation was through contraction, conservative reaction, crisis and termination.

Both the First World War and the Second World War began in precise coincidence with virtually exact hard-aspect alignments of Saturn and Pluto, in August 1914 and September 1939, respectively. The most recent Saturn-Pluto alignment occurred in precise coincidence with the events of September 11, 2001, the destruction of the World Trade Center in New York and the attack on the Pentagon in Washington, and the many events set in motion in its wake. In the first half of September 2001, Saturn and Pluto were within 2° of exact opposition. (In that same period, a Full Moon configuration of the Sun in exact opposition to the Moon formed a rare and extraordinarily precise "grand cross" with Saturn and Pluto, with the two oppositions—Sun to Moon, Saturn to Pluto—

both 90° square to each other.) Many astrologers had speculated, both in print and in private, about what might take place during this alignment, including the strong possibility of terrorism.[1] Within moments of the attacks on the World Trade Center and the Pentagon on September 11, virtually every astrologer in the country knew that the forces symbolized by the Saturn-Pluto alignment, an alignment that had coincided in the past with so many grim periods of historical crisis and contraction, had erupted.

The vivid complex of qualities, emotions, and meanings connected with those grave events—the beginning of the two world wars, September 11 and its aftermath, and many other such events during the periods of Saturn-Pluto alignments—fits with remarkable precision the synthesis of archetypal principles associated with those two planets in combination, expressed in their most extreme form, both negatively and positively: profoundly weighty events of enduring consequence; violence and death on a massive scale; the irrevocable termination of an established order of existence; collective intensification of division, antagonism, and hostility; the deployment of massive, highly disciplined, carefully organized destructive power; and a widespread sense of victimization and suffering under the impact of cataclysmic and oppressive forces of history.

More generally, this archetypal complex tended to constellate a widespread sense that one's life was determined and constrained by large impersonal forces of many kinds—historical, political, military, social, economic, judicial, biological, elemental, instinctual—too powerful and dominant to be affected by the individual self. This sense of vulnerability was in turn regularly matched by a drive for power, control, and domination. Sometimes the two sides of this larger gestalt were constellated simultaneously in two opposing persons or groups, one predatory, the other victimized. Yet just as often the two sides were constellated simultaneously within the same person, group, or nation, each part of the complex unconsciously eliciting the other. Experiences of deep humiliation caused by violence, violation, and defeat were thus often accompanied by a compensatory need to prove one's steely strength, invulnerability, and capacity to retaliate with lethal potency.

Saturn-Pluto alignment periods are also characterized by displays of personal and collective determination, unbending will, courage and sacrifice; by intensely focused, silent, strenuous effort in the face of danger and death; by a deepening capacity for moral discernment born from experience and suffering; and by the transformation and forging of enduring structures, whether material, political, or psychological.

The events of September 11 constituted an extraordinary human tragedy and represented a dark and consequential moment in human history. This was especially true for the people of New York and the United States, but because the searing images of the event were instantly transmitted throughout the world, the impact of the attack was to a great extent felt by people everywhere. The events drew forth a powerful sustained response in the following weeks and months—

emotional and existential, political and military, morally reflective. Horrific violence was visited upon many other peoples during this alignment period—Iraq,
Afghanistan, Israel and Palestine, Spain, Chechnya, Sudan, Kenya, Turkey, Saudi
Arabia, Morocco, Bali—some directly connected with the September 11 events,
some as part of a synchronic wave of terror and death that marked the years
of this alignment. In all these respects, the events of September 11 and their
aftermath resembled other periods of great historical gravity, and with remarkable consistency those periods coincided with the quadrature alignments of the
Saturn-Pluto cycle.

As an archetypal principle, Saturn has long been associated with a complex
of meanings that, while multivalent and diverse, nevertheless possess a certain
easily discernible coherence and consistency: the hard structures and limitations
of material reality and mortal existence, contraction and constraint, deprivation
and negation, division and conflict, gravity and gravitas, necessity and finality, the
endings of things. Saturn presses things to their conclusion and defines them
in their finitude. It expresses itself in such existential realities as aging and maturity, dying and death, labor and duty, suffering and hardship, the weight of time
and the past, the wisdom of experience. It governs authority, solidity, security, re-
liability, established tradition, the status quo, order and system, that which endures and sustains.

The Saturn archetype encompasses all that involves boundaries and limits.
It defines and grounds, constricts and solidifies. It expresses itself in discipline
and control, rigor and rigidity, repression and oppression. It rules judgment, guilt,
the consequences of past actions, error and fault, defeat and failure, deflation
and decline, depression and sorrow. Saturn is, in Nietzsche's phrase, the "spirit
of gravity," both heavy and dark. In Freud's terms, it is the "reality principle," the
delays and resistances to gratification, the obstacles and diminishments presented by life's exigencies. Saturn is the conveyer of the hard truth: naked, un-
adorned, instructive, sobering, often painful. It is the bottom line, the workings
of necessity, the inevitable and inescapable.

In major aspects between two planets of which one is Saturn, the corresponding phenomena suggest that the Saturn archetype tends to combine itself
with the second principle in such a way as to express its characteristic qualities
and themes of contraction, realism, division, deprivation, materiality, hardship,
judgment, strict authority, and so forth, but in this case through and by means of
the archetypal principle associated with Pluto. With hard aspects in particular,
the Saturn principle tends to bring out the problematic potential of whatever it
touches while in other respects opposing or negating that second planetary principle. Its archetypal influence seems also to be one of moving events towards
critical and defining junctures.

Just as during *Uranus*-Pluto alignments the archetypal principle associated
with Pluto appeared to empower and intensify the Promethean impulse of rebellion, innovation, radical change, and the urge for freedom, with epochally

transformative and sometimes destructive consequences, so too during *Saturn-Pluto* alignments the Plutonic principle seemed to empower and intensify each of the above-mentioned Saturnian tendencies and qualities to an often overwhelming degree and on a massive scale. Besides this intensifying and empowering influence, the Pluto archetype also appeared to add into the larger complex its own distinctive qualities involving instinctual and elemental forces, titanic power and violent intensity, violation and destruction, chthonic and underworld depths, and evolutionary transformation.

With these archetypal principles in mind, we can begin to observe the extraordinary consistency with which periods of profound historical gravity, crisis, and contraction coincided with successive major alignments of the Saturn-Pluto cycle. As with the Uranus-Pluto cycle examined in the preceding chapters, the evidence again suggested striking correlations involving the sequence of consecutive conjunction and opposition alignments. For the sake of simplicity and clarity, when reviewing the distinctive pattern of correlations for the Uranus-Pluto cycle, I restricted our attention through much of that initial analysis to the two axial alignments, the conjunction and opposition, bringing in the square alignment only in the later sections. Here we will include from the beginning the full sequence of the four quadrature alignments of Saturn and Pluto in their ongoing cycle. Again, these alignments are the conjunction (0°), the opposition (180°), and the two intervening squares (90°), which are collectively known as the "major hard aspects." These are equivalent in the lunar cycle to the New Moon, the Full Moon, and the two intervening positions, the waxing First Quarter and waning Last Quarter. The orb for the years given in all these chapters for conjunctions and oppositions of outer-planet world transits is approximately 15°, with a penumbral range up to 20°, while the orb for the intervening squares is somewhat smaller, approximately 10°, with a proportionately smaller penumbra.

The first Saturn-Pluto conjunction of the twentieth century coincided with the immediate buildup to and eruption of World War I in 1913–16, first moving to exact alignment during the three months of August, September, and October of 1914, when most of the nations of Europe in rapid succession declared war on each other and mobilized their immense armies to begin the horrific slaughter of the following months and years throughout the conjunction period and beyond.

In turn, the immediately following first square, in 1921–23, coincided with the decisive emergence of fascism and totalitarianism in Europe marked by Mussolini's coming to power in Italy, Stalin's seizure of the Communist party machinery in the Soviet Union, and the beginning of Hitler's rise in Germany leading to the beer hall putsch in Munich.

The next such alignment, the opposition that extended from 1930 to 1933, coincided with worldwide economic crisis and the rapid ascendancy of Nazism in Germany and the beginning of Hitler's dictatorship, the rise of Japanese militarism and the invasion of Manchuria and China, and the intensified dominance of Stalin's totalitarian control in the Soviet Union, his policies of forced collectivization, and the beginning of his mass starvation of over seven million Ukrainians.

Finally, the closing square coincided precisely with the beginning of World War II in 1939–41, first moving to 1° of exact alignment in August and September of 1939 as Germany invaded Poland. This alignment continued through the darkest period of Nazi dominance in Europe, the blitzkrieg, the fall of France and most of the other nations of western and northern Europe, the harrowing Battle of Britain, the massive German invasion of the Soviet Union, Hitler's formulation of the Final Solution, and the beginning of the Holocaust.

It was also in this period—August 1939, when the alignment was first exact—that Einstein, fearful of German nuclear research, signed the fateful letter to Roosevelt urging the U.S. government to develop an atomic bomb (which he later considered "the greatest mistake" of his life). The Manhattan Project began in the ensuing months during this alignment.

This cyclical pattern of diachronically related historical events possessing the same archetypal character began again with the immediately following conjunction of these two planets, which occurred in 1946–48 in precise coincidence with the beginning of the Cold War, the establishment of the Iron Curtain, and the domination of Eastern Europe by the Soviet Union. Both terms—"Iron Curtain" and "Cold War"—first emerged at this time, each highly characteristic of the archetypal complex associated with the Saturn-Pluto cycle: the rigid impenetrable boundary separating implacable enemies, the armored state of permanent hostility, the relentlessly frigid geopolitical climate, the atmosphere of historical darkness and gravity, the sustained global condition in which catastrophic destructive power was simultaneously poised and held in check by the fear of mutual annihilation.[2]

The period of this conjunction brought a wave of events strongly suggestive of this archetypal complex: the beginning of the global nuclear arms race, the beginning of U.S. atomic bomb testing in the South Pacific, the escalation of systematic Cold War espionage and the smuggling of atomic secrets to the Soviet Union, the succession of communist takeovers and establishment of totalitarian governments in Albania, Yugoslavia, Bulgaria, Hungary, Romania, and Czechoslovakia, the Berlin blockade crisis with the Soviet Union and Western allies in sustained intense confrontation, the rapid ascendancy of communism under Mao in China, the communist takeover of North Korea, the founding of NATO, the establishment of the CIA, and the rise of the anticommunist Cold War establishment and mentality in the United States. It was also during this conjunction, in 1948, that apartheid was instituted in South Africa with the rise to power of the right-wing Afrikaner National Party.

The successive cyclical conjunctions of these two planets occur approximately every thirty-one to thirty-seven years, depending on Pluto's orbital position and speed. In the sequence of Saturn-Pluto alignments during the twentieth century, we can observe how the three successive conjunctions coincided with defining events and decisions that established an enduring historical foundation upon which causally related developments would then unfold for several decades afterward. In broad terms, the first conjunction of the twentieth century that coincided with the onset of the First World War in 1914 essentially marked the commencement of the twentieth century's "Thirty Years' War" that engulfed Europe and then the world, critically unfolding from that point through the Second World War in close association with the successive quadrature aspects of those two planets during those three decades (1914–45).

In turn, the second Saturn-Pluto conjunction of the century coincided precisely with the beginning of the Cold War in 1946–48, which unfolded in a similar manner and was closely correlated with that cycle's successive quadrature alignments. The following square of 1955–57 coincided with the Soviet Union's reoccupation of Hungary, its crushing of dissent in Poland, and intensified threats against the West by Khrushchev ("History is on our side. We will bury you!"). The midpoint of this cycle, the opposition of 1964–67, coincided precisely with the start of the U.S. war in Vietnam and its rapid escalation. The following square of 1973–75 brought the U.S. defeat in Vietnam and the takeover by communist regimes in South Vietnam, Laos, and Cambodia.

The concluding alignment of this cycle, the last conjunction of Saturn and

---

THE SATURN-PLUTO CYCLE

Quadrature alignments since 1914

15° orb for conjunctions and oppositions
10° orb for squares

Exact alignment <1°

August 1913–June 1916	*conjunction*	October 1914–May 1915
October 1921–October 1923	*square*	January–October 1922
January 1930–October 1933	*opposition*	February–December 1931
March 1939–March 1941	*square*	June 1939–April 1940
June 1946–September 1948	*conjunction*	July–August 1947
December 1954–October 1957	*square*	December 1955–October 1956
March 1964–January 1968	*opposition*	April 1965–February 1966
May 1973–May 1975	*square*	August 1973–June 1974
December 1980–October 1984	*conjunction*	October 1982–July 1983
March 1992–January 1995	*square*	March 1993–January 1994
June 2000–April 2004	*opposition*	July 2001–June 2002
November 2008–August 2011	*square*	November 2009–August 2010
January 2018–December 2021	*conjunction*	December 2019–January 2020

For conjunctions and oppositions, 20° orb generally adds two months before and after dates given for 15°, occasionally up to eleven months. Likewise, for squares, 15° orb adds two to eleven months before and after dates given for 10°.

Pluto in the twentieth century, began in late 1980 and extended from 1981 through most of 1984. At this time the global nuclear arms race, the escalation of Cold War antagonism, and widespread fear of nuclear apocalypse reached its climax during the first Reagan administration and the final years of the pre-Gorbachev Soviet Union under Brezhnev, Andropov, and Chernenko. During the period of this conjunction, the global situation was marked by massively increased defensive armoring, rigidly established boundaries, hostile separation, mutual demonization (e.g., Reagan's calling the Soviet Union an "evil empire" and "the focus of evil in the modern world"), intensive military buildups, and repressive military action and state-sponsored terrorism in many parts of the world, including Central and South America, the Middle East, and Afghanistan. Characteristic events of these years included the activities of death squads in El Salvador and Guatemala, the intensification of apartheid in South Africa, the militant ascendancy of Islamic extremists in Central Asia, and the West-supported rise of military aggression by Saddam Hussein in Iraq.

This same cycle is also clearly visible in and closely correlated with the series of Middle East crises and Arab-Israeli wars that began with the period of Middle Eastern war and terrorism in 1946–48 out of which was founded modern Israel in Palestine during the Saturn-Pluto conjunction at the start of the Cold War. This was followed in almost clocklike fashion by the consecutive sequence of wars in the Middle East: the Suez War of 1956 (square), the Six Days' War in 1967 (opposition), the Yom Kippur War in 1973 (square), and Israel's invasion of Lebanon in 1982 (conjunction). This last alignment, the conjunction of 1981–84, coincided as well with the sustained massive slaughter of the Iran-Iraq War, the Falkland War between Britain and Argentina, and the depths of the Soviet war in Afghanistan that led to the rise of the Islamic jihadist movement, fueled by clandestine U.S. support. The entire sequence of the Middle East wars just cited occurred in uncannily close coincidence with the sequence of quadrature alignments between Saturn and Pluto. This pattern has continued unabated during the most recent Saturn-Pluto opposition, both with the United States–led Iraq War in 2003 and the sustained Israel-Palestine crisis of 2000–04, with its traumatic cycle of suicide bombings and retaliatory repression.

A parallel pattern is evident in correlation with the same cycle during the same period for India and Pakistan, beginning with India's independence and partition in 1947–48 and the massive destruction that occurred at that time, the assassination of Gandhi by a Hindu extremist, and the deaths of millions in the unleashed sectarian violence. The quadrature correlations again continued in succession up through the most recent Saturn-Pluto opposition, which coincided with the Kashmir crisis, nuclear standoff, and repeated acts of mass violence and retribution between Hindus and Muslims in 2000–04.

Thus the first Saturn-Pluto cycle of the twentieth century correlated closely with the world wars and the second with the Cold War. The events that have coincided with the successive quadrature aspects of the third, though we are still in the middle of it, have up to this point closely correlated with the phenomenon of international terrorism and the ensuing war on terror. The conjunction of 1981–84 discussed above in relation to the Cold War and the Middle East wars also coincided with the initial terrorist bombings of the U.S. embassy in Beirut and of U.S. and French barracks in Lebanon (which have been called the most consequential terrorist acts before the World Trade Center attack that occurred under the following opposition). This same conjunction of 1981–84 also coincided with a sudden wave of other major terrorist acts (in Northern Ireland, France, Iran, the Philippines, Central America), assassinations (Anwar Sadat in Egypt, Indira Gandhi in India, Benigno Aquino in the Philippines), and assassination attempts (Pope John Paul II, Ronald Reagan) in many parts of the world. In turn, the following Saturn–Pluto square of 1992–94 exactly coincided with the first World Trade Center bombing, Osama bin Laden's first call for a jihad against America, and the coming to power of the Taliban in Afghanistan.

Finally, the most recent opposition coincided with the full emergence of international terrorism and the war on terror with the events of September 11, 2001, and the many measures of repression, retribution, government-sponsored violence, and further acts of terrorist response that followed in their wake.[3] The alignment first reached exactitude in August-September 2001, in coincidence with the destruction of the World Trade Center and the attack on the Pentagon, followed by the U.S. invasion of Afghanistan; and its final pass to within 3° of exactitude occurred in March 2003 in coincidence with the invasion of Iraq and its "shock and awe" tactics of overwhelming destruction. The long period of violence and terror in Iraq that continued after the invasion, which included the abuse and torture of Iraqi prisoners by U.S. military and paramilitary personnel and gruesome beheadings and suicide bombings by Islamist and Iraqi resistance forces, began in coincidence with the later stages of the Saturn-Pluto opposition in 2003–04. This phase of the transit included the terrorist bombings in Madrid and the prisoner abuse and torture scandal of Abu Ghraib, which emerged as the alignment approached the final 15° point. In a parallel with the larger cyclical unfolding of geopolitical structures and historically consequential events, the United States' invasion of Iraq was also widely viewed as bringing an end to the postwar world order that had been based on the multilateral Western European–American alliance and its fundamental support of the United Nations. Parallel developments in terror, retaliation, oppression, and conservative empowerment took place in these same years in Russia under Putin, where continuing violent conflict with Chechnyan insurgents served as justification for a more general neo-Stalinization of Russian political life.

Remarkably, the age of modern terrorism is widely considered to have begun in 1946 with the bombing of the King David Hotel by Zionist radicals, in coincidence with the Saturn-Pluto conjunction of 1946–48 that also coincided with the beginning of the Cold War. Such historically defining Saturn-Pluto cycles

consistently took place in earlier centuries, such as the conjunction that occurred in 1618 at the beginning of the original Thirty Years' War that started in
that year and soon spread throughout Europe. All of the continent was ravaged
by a state of nearly continuous, unprecedentedly brutal warfare for thirty years,
until 1648, precisely coincident with the next Saturn-Pluto conjunction one full
cycle later—as also happened in the thirty-year period encompassing World War
I and World War II in the twentieth century.

Another such defining conjunction was that of 1348–51 that coincided with
the eruption and spread of the Black Death, which similarly devastated Europe
and set in motion cultural and economic shifts that permanently transformed
European life in the late medieval period. The Black Death, or bubonic plague,
began in China in 1333 in coincidence with the preceding Saturn-Pluto opposition and reached a climax in Europe in the 1348–51 period during the conjunction. A comparable pattern can be discerned in the AIDS epidemic, which
first widely emerged and was identified during the Saturn-Pluto conjunction of
1981–84, and which reached pandemic proportions worldwide, especially in Africa, during the following Saturn-Pluto opposition of 2000–04.

Whenever adequate historical records were available, I found that the simultaneous occurrence of multiple categories of diverse but archetypally connected
events during Saturn-Pluto alignments occurred consistently throughout history.
To take one example of such a synchronic wave, the first Saturn-Pluto conjunction of the thirteenth century took place during the years of 1210–13. Much like
the first conjunction of the twentieth century in 1914–16, wars and mass violence pervaded much of Europe during the period of this alignment, driven by
conflicts between the Roman Catholic Church and the Holy Roman Empire
and by the efforts of Pope Innocent III to extirpate heretics and infidels and sub-
jugate the political enemies of the Church. In these same years the peace-loving
Cathars in southern France were persecuted and burned at the stake as part of
the Albigensian crusade. In 1212, during the same period, the Children's Crusade set out for the Holy Land; the result was the loss of approximately fifty
thousand children, many kidnapped by slave dealers. In Asia during the same conjunction, in 1211–12, the Mongol conqueror Genghis Khan began his massive
invasion of China.

The correlation of the Saturn-Pluto cycle with genocide, ethnocide, and
mass killings is striking: In the past century these include the mass killings of
the Armenians by the Ottoman Turks during the conjunction of 1914–15, the
death of millions of kulaks under Stalin that began during the opposition of
1930–33, Hitler's conceiving of the Final Solution and the mass killing of Jews
that began during the square of 1939–41, the slaughter of nearly a million In-
donesians by the right-wing military regime in 1965–66, the Khmer Rouge's killing of over a million Cambodians that began during the square of 1973–75, the
death squads in El Salvador and Guatamala during the conjunction of 1981–84,

the mass killings in Bosnia and Rwanda during the square of 1992–94, and, most recently, the deaths of hundreds of thousands of Sudanese in the Darfur region at the hands of their own government during the conjunction of 2000–04.

Finally, one example of many from classical antiquity is the Saturn-Pluto conjunction that coincided with the most intensive period of the barbarian invasions of the Roman Empire, those of 410–12 by the Huns, Vandals, and Visigoths. Led by Alaric the Visigoths sacked Rome, burning and pillaging the ancient world's most powerful city, in August 410, when Saturn and Pluto were 2° from exact alignment—strikingly suggestive of a parallel with the terrorist destruction in New York, the modern world's most powerful city, on September 11, 2001, when the same two planets were again 2° from exact alignment.

Historical Contrasts and Tensions

A consistent theme of Saturn-Pluto alignment periods was that of widespread conservative, reactionary, or repressive empowerment, in precise agreement with the archetypal principles associated with these two planets—the Plutonic empowering and intensifying of the Saturn impulse towards conservative reaction or repression. For example, the most recent Saturn-Pluto conjunction during the 1981–84 period coincided with both the first Reagan administration and the last years of the old regime of the Soviet Union under Brezhnev, Andropov, and Chernenko. These specific years brought a nearly universal ascendancy of conservatism, in distinctly different forms yet nevertheless showing clear commonalities. This took place not only in the United States and the Soviet Union (visible, for example, in the Kremlin's imprisonment of dissidents like Sakharov and Sharansky at this time) but also in Britain under Margaret Thatcher and, in more extreme dictatorial forms, in Poland under General Jaruzelski (bringing martial law and the repression of the Solidarity movement), in Chile under General Pinochet, in Panama under Manuel Noriega, in Iraq under Saddam Hussein, and in the Philippines under Ferdinand Marcos, among many others.

Similarly, in the religious context, this same period established a new era of conservatism in the Roman Catholic Church under Pope John Paul II and the rise to power in the Vatican of the conservative Opus Dei organization, in sharp contrast to the radical reformer Pope John XXIII who oversaw the Second Vatican Council during the Uranus-Pluto conjunction of the 1960s. More generally, the period of the Saturn-Pluto conjunction during the early 1980s brought the decisive emergence and empowerment of religious fundamentalism throughout the world—Christian (both Catholic and Protestant), Jewish, Islamic, Hindu. Again, each of these conservative or reactionary ascendancies possessed its own character highly distinct from the others, each one defining itself as radically opposed to others mentioned, but the underlying archetypal parallels between them are nonetheless evident. As with the Uranus-Pluto cycle discussed in the preceding chapters, this remarkable combination of archetypal multivalence and coherence during the same planetary alignment—here, sharply different forms

of the empowered conservative or reactionary impulse—was altogether characteristic of such synchronic patterns for outer-planet cycles.

We can readily discern the vivid difference in the underlying spirit of the
various historical periods coinciding with these two different planetary cycles if
we examine the acute contrast between the most recent *Saturn*-Pluto conjunction period, that of 1981–84, and the most recent *Uranus*-Pluto conjunction period, that of 1960–72. Where the 1960s had brought a decisive widespread
empowerment of the emancipatory, innovative, destabilizing, revolutionary impulse that produced liberal reform or radical change in virtually every area of human activity—religion, politics, sexuality, civil rights, human rights, feminism,
environmentalism, the arts—the first half of the 1980s brought an equally decisive empowerment of the conservative, reactionary, or repressive impulse in the
same areas. In the United States, a systematic backlash against the various
movements that dominated the 1960s was evident at this time. The Equal Rights
Amendment for women's rights was defeated. New federal policies that opposed
affirmative action were instituted by the Reagan administration. Antienvironmental policies that opened national forests to clear-cutting and federal lands
to oil drilling were initiated and enforced, and previously established limits on
industrial pollution were removed. Identical tendencies were visible during the
same years in Britain under the Thatcher administration and in many other
countries throughout the world. Again, in the first half of the 1980s, Pluto's principle of intensification and empowerment seems to have been potently united
with the archetypal principle of contraction and conservatism associated with
Saturn, just as it had been with the archetypal principle of emancipation and innovation associated with Uranus in the 1960s.

While the archetypal complex associated with Uranus-Pluto alignments
consistently expressed itself in the form of radical liberatory and revolutionary
impulses, Saturn-Pluto alignments tended to coincide with the emergence of
"radical conservatism." The common factor in both tendencies, the *radical* com-
ponent in each complex, seems to reflect the characteristic quality and vector
given to any complex by the presence of the Pluto archetype. The nature of the
Plutonic-Dionysian principle is to press towards greater intensity, to the extreme,
to be compelling, deep—radical as *radix*, root, grounded in the depths, drawing
on the power of the underworld, driving whatever it touches to an overwhelming
potency that has a compulsive, destructive, even self-destructive potential.

But what happens when two planetary cycles associated with such different
archetypal complexes coincide or overlap during the same period? I found that
when the shorter-period alignments of the Saturn-Pluto cycle (three to four
years in length) coincided with longer-period alignments of the Uranus-Pluto cycle (generally twelve to thirteen years), as took place in the middle of both the
1960s and the French Revolutionary period, complicated archetypal tensions
were strongly in evidence. A sustained three-planet configuration of this kind,
when Saturn opposed the Uranus-Pluto conjunction, occurred during the critical

period of 1964–67 (extending partly into 1968). These years coincided not only with the outbreak and escalation of the war in Vietnam under Lyndon Johnson but also with widespread urban riots and violent civil disturbances throughout the United States (Los Angeles, Detroit, Newark, and over 120 other cities), as well as the Cultural Revolution in China under the Red Guards, among many other similar phenomena in those critical years throughout the world from Central and South America to Africa and Indonesia.

In such periods there seemed to be constellated a dynamic tension, dialectic, and synthesis of the three distinct archetypal complexes: the more revolutionary, rebellious, innovative impulse associated with Uranus in various compromise formations with the more limiting, contracting, and controlling impulse associated with Saturn, with both impulses empowered and intensified, often violently, by the principle associated with Pluto. Alignments of these three planets in hard aspect were consistently associated with periods of intensified emancipatory and revolutionary activity as well as intensified efforts at order, control, conservative reaction, and repression, all combining to produce a state of extreme tension and crisis. The schisms both in society—generational, political, cultural—and in the world tended to be exacerbated, as in the "generation gap" that emerged during this period in the 1960s (the Who's *My Generation*, 1965, "Hope I die before I get old"). More generally, it was in these years that there arose the "culture wars" that still drive the tense divisions within the social and political body of the United States.

Especially problematic in such eras was the extreme intensification of both widespread revolutionary upheaval and violent authoritarian repression in a tightly bound dialectic, mutually activating each other. Sometimes these opposing impulses were present simultaneously in the same political movement or historical phenomenon, often with catastrophic consequences, as with Mao's Red Guards during the Chinese Cultural Revolution, who rampaged through the countryside in a destructive frenzy of repressive "revolutionary" activity.

When these same two cycles overlapped during the French Revolution to form another such multi-planet alignment of Saturn, Uranus, and Pluto, this configuration took place in 1793–96 in precise coincidence with the Reign of Terror. Again, this was an era that was simultaneously intensely revolutionary and intensely repressive, as in the dictatorial powers arrogated by the Committee of Public Safety led by Danton and then Robespierre with his "revolutionary puritanism." Unprecedentedly rigid control over the nation was attempted through a regime of conformity and fear. Neighbors and family members were pressured to inform on each other, and there were hurried trials for the accused and death sentences for those found guilty. Women's societies were suppressed, and leading women of the revolution such as Olympe de Gouges were imprisoned and then guillotined. In less than one year between September 1793 and July 1794, over 25,000 suspected enemies of the revolution were beheaded by guillotine in the public squares, including finally Danton and Robespierre themselves. The entire period of the triple alignment was marked by scarcely imaginable massive social turmoil, orgies of unbridled violence, and the killing of hundreds of thousands of the French people by its own revolutionary army. The later part of this same period of the three-planet alignment brought the conservative Thermidorean Reaction, which in revulsion against the Terror undid many of the democratic reforms of the earlier part of the Revolution and initiated a period of retribution against the radicals. Here too can be seen a further expression of the two opposing tendencies, revolutionary and conservative, producing a tense compromise formation.

Besides the configuration of the mid-1960s, there was one other period in twentieth-century history when these three planets—Saturn, Uranus, and Pluto—moved into an alignment constituted entirely by hard aspects. This took place from late 1929 to 1933, when the longer Uranus square Pluto that lasted through most of the 1930s was joined at its start by Saturn in what is called a T-square formation (formed by two planets in 180° opposition and a third planet in 90° square alignment with both). The three planets first moved into an exact midpoint configuration, with Uranus halfway between Saturn and Pluto within 1°, in late October 1929 in precise coincidence with the Wall Street stock market collapse on October 29, "the blackest day in stock market history," which precipitated the first stage of the Great Depression and helped to set in motion the tumultuous political upheavals that unfolded throughout that decade.[4] The longer Uranus-Pluto square then continued on through the Thirties, coinciding with that decade's widespread social and political turmoil, catalyzing of mass movements, rise of radical political philosophies and parties, intensified labor unrest, student strikes and demonstrations, unleashed mob violence, and mass immigrations.

The convergence of all three planets in hard aspect in the 1929–33 period appeared to be correlated with historical events that reflected the characteristic themes of all three relevant planetary cycles: the *Saturn-Pluto* cycle, with its intensification of authoritarian and totalitarian impulses, mass hardship, economic failure, and the other phenomena discussed in the present section; the *Uranus-Pluto* cycle, with its sustained social and political unrest, mass movements, empowerment of radical political programs, and mass demographic shifts, which we observed in the preceding chapters; and a cycle we have not yet examined, *Saturn-Uranus*.

Historical periods in which Saturn and Uranus moved into dynamic aspect were marked by certain distinctive themes that were readily intelligible in terms of the archetypal principles associated with these two planets: the exacerbation of tensions between authority and rebellion, order and freedom, structure and change. Often the two archetypal principles combined and interpenetrated in contradictory ways: repressive revolution, erratically unpredictable authority, and so forth, as evident during the Terror in revolutionary France and the Cultural Revolution in communist China just mentioned. Especially frequent with this cycle were crises and the sudden collapse of structures, crashes and accidents, grim awakenings, and sudden breakdowns, whether political, economic, or psychological.

Such phenomena regularly coincided with hard-aspect alignments of the Saturn-Uranus cycle; with the additional presence of Pluto in the more rare three-planet configuration, an especially massive, overwhelming, sometimes catastrophic dimension was typically constellated. In the 1929–33 period, the widespread political and economic destabilizations (Saturn-Uranus) suddenly catalyzed a full range of characteristic Saturn-Pluto phenomena: widespread financial failure, poverty, and traumatic personal hardship on a vast scale throughout the world, plus the rapid ascendancy of authoritarian and totalitarian forces—in Germany, the empowerment of Hitler and his anti-Semitic policies after the collapse of German liberalism and the Weimar government; in the Soviet Union, intensified repression by Stalin and the immense disaster imposed on the Ukraine by his policies of compulsory collectivization, mass starvation, gulag imprisonment, exile, and the forced displacement of millions; the aggressive assertion of fascist militarism in Italy and Japan; and the rise of fascist and communist political movements that pressed for power in many other countries. Economists are still unable to adequately account for the sudden mass collapse in 1929–33 that shook the world's structures to their foundations and had so many long-term consequences. It was also during this period that the first splitting of the atom occurred, in 1932 at the Cavendish Laboratory, which represents another form of structural breakdown with the sudden release of titanic energy, also with consequences that extended far into the future. This was the only T-square of Saturn, Uranus, and Pluto in the twentieth century.

I found that individuals born during this configuration in this critical period of 1929–33, as also during the similar three-planet alignment of the 1964–67 period, seemed to experience with special acuity the challenges and tensions of these dynamically interacting forces in the course of their lives. In an extremely varied range of ways, the circumstances of their lives seemed to require them to hold the tension and negotiate a highly complex clash of opposites, sometimes (as with Mikhail Gorbachev and Boris Yeltsin, both born when the T-square was near exact in 1931) on a large scale and with enduring consequences.

One other important category of historical phenomena that should be mentioned here comprises the many instances in which events that occurred during a longer *Uranus-Pluto* alignment set in motion powerful forces that later, after that alignment was over, suddenly reached a crisis or breaking point, a critical collapse of structures, precisely when *Saturn* moved into hard aspect with Uranus. Often this sequence took the form of emancipatory or dissident forces emerging on a wide scale during the earlier Uranus-Pluto alignment, then subsequently producing a violent schism in the body politic. For example, the sustained wave of intensified abolitionist activity and related political and social developments during the Uranus-Pluto conjunction of 1845–56—the activities of Frederick

Douglass, Harriet Tubman, Sojourner Truth, and John Brown, the Underground Railway, Harriet Beecher Stowe's *Uncle Tom's Cabin*, the founding of the Free Soil and Republican parties that brought the rise of Lincoln—all led to the Civil War, which began in precise coincidence with Saturn's movement into exact square with Uranus in 1861, immediately after the election of Lincoln. Not only are the characteristic Saturn-Uranus themes of sudden crisis, political breakdown, structural destabilization, and national schism visible here; so also is the peculiar combination of rebellious (Uranus) and repressive (Saturn) impulses that coalesced in the slaveholding Confederate states, which specifically sought and proclaimed freedom (Uranus) from the Union to maintain their systemically oppressive (Saturn) mode of life.

A similar sequential pattern is visible in the sequence of events that led to the Russian Revolution. The Uranus-Pluto opposition of 1896–1907 which we examined earlier coincided with a sustained surge of radical impulses and activities in Russian political life, including Lenin's seminal manifesto of violent revolution to be led by an elite vanguard of the proletariat, *What Is To Be Done?* of 1902, the founding of the Bolshevik party by Lenin in 1903, and the first Russian Revolution of 1905–06. These developments led directly to the Bolshevik Revolution and the Russian civil war, which began just as Saturn moved into close opposition to Uranus in November 1917 (and in the immediate aftermath of the Saturn-Pluto conjunction of 1914–16 and the first years of World War I with their disastrous effect on Czarist Russia).

Certain distinctive themes were visible in the Bolshevik Revolution and in the character of the resulting Soviet Union that uncannily fit what one might expect in a problematic synthesis of the two archetypal principles associated with Saturn and Uranus: the emancipatory impulse intricately interlocked with the impulse for authoritarian control, which engendered one of the most rigid political structures in history yet was heralded as a new bulwark of freedom and defended in the name of revolution. Many of the glaring contradictions in the Soviet style of government—the erection of implacable barriers to keep the citizens firmly liberated, the ubiquitous censorship to ensure the propagation of only truly revolutionary ideas, the totalitarian dictatorship to realize the ultimate freedom of the people—suggest the uneasy and unresolved integration of the two opposing principles.

Considering his critical role in these developments, it is remarkable that Karl Marx himself was born with Saturn, Uranus, and Pluto all in hard aspect. This three-way archetypal complex can be seen in the marked tension and often unconscious compromise formations in Marx's personality and thought between the rebellious, innovative, emancipatory impulse of Uranus with the Saturnian principle of control, rigidity, structure, repression, and authority—with the two principles merging in self-contradictory and problematic ways, and with both compelled and empowered with Plutonic titanic intensity. Marx therefore was born with the same category of configuration that coincided with the several periods we have examined above—the time of the French Revolutionary Terror and Committee on Public Safety in the mid-1790s, the tumultuous period of political and economic breakdown and crisis of the 1929–33 period, and the era of the Chinese Cultural Revolution under Mao beginning in the mid-1960s—all eras when the characteristic motifs and contradictory impulses present in Marx's thought were acted out on an immense collective scale.

Conservative Empowerment

Returning now to the Saturn-Pluto cycle on its own terms, we can examine more closely the diachronic patterning of historically significant events coinciding with the successive conjunctions, then with the intervening squares and oppositions. The events of the 1981–84 conjunction period—the wave of conservative and reactionary empowerment throughout the world and the climactic intensification of the Cold War antagonism between the two superpowers—can be recognized as closely related to the events of the immediately preceding Saturn-Pluto conjunction of 1946–48 at the beginning of the Cold War. During the earlier alignment, the emergence of the Iron Curtain and the Soviet domination of Eastern Europe was met in the United States by the establishment of the many enduring anticommunist and Cold War political and military structures that characterized the American response to that state of sustained global crisis and tension. These included the founding of the Central Intelligence Agency, the National Security Council, and the Department of Defense; the formulation of the containment policy in George Kennan's influential paper in *Foreign Affairs* and the assertion of the Truman Doctrine; the intensification of the anticommunist hearings by the House Un-American Activities Committee (HUAC) that led to the McCarthy era, the establishment of the Hollywood blacklist, and widespread anticommunist witch hunts, among many other comparable phenomena reflective of this archetypal complex.

Remarkably, George Orwell wrote *1984*, his dark vision of totalitarian oppression and control, during the Saturn-Pluto conjunction of 1946–48, and placed it in a year, 1984, that happened to coincide with the very next Saturn-Pluto conjunction one full cycle later. Orwell's writing of the book was driven by his growing fear and conviction that not only had a Cold War (his coinage) begun against totalitarianism but that in this critical period of the later 1940s, during the conjunction, the Western democracies were losing it.

These two periods of 1946–48 and 1981–84 that coincided with the two successive Saturn-Pluto *conjunctions* bear a close historical and archetypal connection to the period of the intervening *opposition* of the same two planets in 1964–67. In the United States, for example, in 1964 Barry Goldwater—against the larger trend of the decade—effectively initiated the gradual grassroots rise of the Republican right that culminated in the election of Reagan at the following Saturn-Pluto conjunction. (Yet even Goldwater, in his own, highly conservative inflection of the 1960s' zeitgeist, gave voice to the dominant impulse of that decade archetypally associated with the Uranus-Pluto conjunction—extreme intensity in the service of freedom—with his famous declaration, "Extremism in the defense of liberty is no vice.") During the same opposition, in 1966, Reagan began his political ascent by winning the California governorship in a landslide and immediately afterwards took action to suppress student protests and the free speech movement at the University of California at Berkeley. Similarly reflective of the turn to the right during these same years in the 1964–67 period was the rise of a widespread "white backlash" movement against black civil rights gains. So also was the Johnson administration's move to the right, as expressed in the decision to escalate the Vietnam War from 1964–65 on. In the Soviet Union, the more liberalizing Khrushchev was replaced in 1964 by the more conservative Brezhnev, whose regime lasted precisely until the next Saturn-Pluto conjunction in 1982.

This cyclical pattern of conservative empowerment in the United States extended to the most recent Saturn-Pluto alignment, the opposition of 2000–04. The period of this alignment began with the contested presidential election and Supreme Court decision that brought to power the younger Bush and the Republican right just as the opposition first moved within 15° in the fall of 2000. The subsequent further empowerment of the Bush administration and the Republican right in the immediate aftermath of the events of September 11, 2001, and the systematic intensification of their efforts on behalf of a more extreme conservative agenda coincided precisely with the Saturn-Pluto opposition's reaching exactitude. The period of greatest conservative empowerment, including the U.S. invasion of Iraq in March 2003, coincided with the following two years when Saturn and Pluto were positioned in closest alignment. George W. Bush was himself born during the Saturn-Pluto conjunction of 1946 that coincided with the start of the Cold War.

During all the Saturn-Pluto periods we have been examining, such as 1981–84 or 2000–04 when the two planets were last in conjunction and opposition, we can observe how consistently these specific eras bring forth the emergence of a widespread strengthened resolve to reestablish "traditional values," with broad social and political support. Various movements tend to arise that are devoted to "restoring a solid moral foundation," to reempower "the moral majority," to "bring back family values." For example, in the United States, whereas the decade of the 1960s during the Uranus-Pluto conjunction exalted progressive, radical, and revolutionary thinkers, the 1981–84 period and again the more recent 2000–04 period coincident with the Saturn-Pluto alignments brought into prominence and power a wave of conservative and neoconservative thinkers. Whereas the 1960s brought a wave of rebellion against established structures and values, a rebellion that was embraced by an enormous segment of the population, the 1981–84 and 2000–04 periods brought a conservative move-ment demanding law and order that was equally widely embraced. The entire decade and dominant ethos of the 1960s became the frequent target of moral condemnation by prominent figures of the 1981–84 period, as with Margaret Thatcher's characteristic dismissal of the Sixties when she was prime minister in 1982: "Fashionable theories and permissive claptrap set the scene for a society in which old values of discipline and restraint were denigrated."

During Saturn-Pluto periods such as 1981–84 or 2000–04, conservative empowerment regularly expressed itself through social and legal constraints and judgments (Saturn) against sexuality (Pluto), such as legislative and administra-tive attempts to limit contraceptive technologies, abortion rights, premarital sex, and same-sex marriage. During both periods, government funding was cut off for scientific research and international public health programs that were viewed by conservatives as encouraging sexual irresponsibility. Sexual abstinence and monogamy were affirmed as social and religious ideals. Nature itself seemed to conspire in the archetypal shift from the 1960s to the early 1980s, when the emergence of the AIDS epidemic during the Saturn-Pluto conjunction of 1981–84 brought what was widely called at that time an "end to the sexual revolution" and the era of sexual experiment and freedom that had emerged during the Uranus-Pluto conjunction and Dionysian awakening of the 1960s. Such charac-teristic Saturn-Pluto themes as mass suffering, disease, death, and fear arose at this time in relationship to sexuality, as did a resulting conservative transforma-tion of social mores with the establishment of new structures of inhibition and control, both internal and external.

Another important characteristic set of Saturn-Pluto themes emerged at this time in the collective psyche in the widespread rise of fundamentalist interpreta-tions and denunciatory moralistic judgments of the epidemic as God's righteous punishment of sin and licentiousness. This phenomenon closely resembled the emergence of widespread views throughout medieval Europe concerning the Black Death or bubonic plague as the manifest embodiment of God's punitive wrath during the Saturn-Pluto conjunction of 1348–50.

Similar interpretations of contemporary historical events reappeared during the Saturn-Pluto conjunction of the 2000–04 period, such as Christian funda-mentalist claims about the true cause of the attacks on the World Trade Center in New York on September 11. Religious leaders such as Jerry Falwell and Pat Robertson stated that the attacks were God's righteous punishment for the moral corruption and licentiousness of the targeted city, which symbolized the sins committed by secular America, liberals, gays, and feminists. These assess-ments were in certain respects nearly identical in terminology and in archetypal character to Islamic fundamentalist views of the same events, including those that inspired jihad terrorists. Comparable phenomena can be recognized in ear-lier historical epochs, such as the ancient interpretations, both pagan and Christian, of the barbarian sack of Rome as reflecting the punitive wrath of the gods or God against a faithless people.

The archetypal contrast between the Uranus-Pluto era of the 1960s and the two Saturn-Pluto periods of the early 1980s and the early 2000s was equally evident in the dominant popular attitudes in those periods towards patriotism. In the United States, for example, whereas the 1960s brought widespread and fervent resistance by American citizens against the U.S. government throughout the decade, by contrast the 1981–84 and 2000–04 periods brought a widespread and equally fervent resurgence of traditional American patriotism that was pervasively visible in the display of flags, performance of ceremonies, and expression of popular attitudes. Often the intensified patriotic impulse and an intensified conservative law-and-order impulse were tightly amalgamated into one phenomenon, or one was appropriated by the other, as in the Patriot Act in the 2001–04 period. Passed hurriedly by the U.S. Congress in the immediate wake of the September 11 attacks and overseen by the Christian fundamentalist attorney general, John Ashcroft, the act established as "vital security measures" a degree of governmental jurisdiction that was regarded by many observers as having legitimized an incursion on civil liberties so problematic that references were widely and repeatedly made to Orwell's *1984* and the shadow of Big Brother state control over the private lives and freedoms of citizens. The tendency towards hypervigilance and armored boundaries associated with the Saturn-Pluto archetypal complex was evident in the collective experience of the 2001–04 period in many ways, as in the extreme intensification of air travel security, the constant warnings of heightened alerts to catastrophic threats, and the widespread popularity of aggressively oversize, quasi-military vehicles such as SUVs and Hummers. (The armored tank itself was first conceived and produced during the Saturn-Pluto conjunction of 1914–15.)

The intervening quadrature alignments of the full cycle suggest further signs of the same pattern. For example, in the American political context, the most recent Saturn-Pluto square alignment took place in 1992–94 (halfway between the conjunction of the early 1980s with the first Reagan administration and the opposition of the 2000–04 period with the first administration of the younger Bush). This period coincided precisely with the intermediate ascendancy of conservativism that was embodied in the Republican-dominated Congress elected in 1994, with Newt Gingrich as speaker of the house and with the "Contract with America" as its manifesto. The same Saturn-Pluto square coincided with an unmistakable wave of other events in the United States and throughout the world that reflected the characteristic patterns of this archetypal complex, such as the apocalyptic siege of the fundamentalist Branch Davidians in Waco, Texas; the Rodney King beating trial and the subsequent riots in Los Angeles; the ambush of American soldiers in Mogadishu by Somalian warlords, the most violent and disastrous U.S. combat firefight since Vietnam; the Bosnian crisis and ethnic cleansing in Yugoslavia and the first concentration camps in Europe since World War II; and the beginning of the Rwanda crisis and massacres. All these events took place during the same Saturn-Pluto alignment of 1992–94 that coincided with the several events cited earlier for this period with regard to international terrorism—the coming to power of the fundamentalist Taliban in Afghanistan, bin Laden's call for a jihad against the United States, and the first World Trade Center bombing. As was typical with these Saturn-Pluto hard-aspect alignments, the general ambiance of a pervasive contraction in human affairs was palpable and widespread.

Many other themes related to this archetypal complex were characteristically heightened during all these alignments: increased calls for moral rigor and social constraints, censorship and repression, puritanical standards of conduct, severe punitive judgments (such as the increased use of the harsh Shariah laws in the Islamic world or the imposition of the death penalty in the United States), and wars against enemies perceived and described as evil. The remarkable correlation of many of these quadrature alignment periods with worldwide economic depressions, recessions, and hardship (1921–23, 1929–33, 1946–48, 1973–75, 1981–84, 2000–2004) should also be noted. More generally, this cyclical pattern seemed to coincide with a widespread sense, both individual and collective, of being severely constricted or threatened by larger forces in life, by hostile powers, by poverty or lack of resources, by the legacy and errors of the past, and by the punitive judgments and oppressive power of established authority.

Equally visible during Saturn-Pluto alignments was the unfolding of events that possessed a distinct ambiance of grave wrongdoing, moral and political scandal, public guilt and humiliation, trial and judgment, crime and punishment. The Nuremberg trials of the Nazi war criminals during the Saturn-Pluto conjunction in the 1946–48 period was an especially grave and historically consequential but altogether characteristic example of this tendency. Émile Zola's famous "J'accuse" open letter to the president of France denouncing the anti-Semitic injustices perpetrated by the war department during the Dreyfus scandal, which forced a new trial and the revelation of the extent of military and governmental corruption, was written during the Saturn-Pluto opposition of 1898–99.

The most recent Saturn-Pluto alignment, of 2000–04, coincided with the wave of scandals in the Roman Catholic Church, whose hierarchy was accused of systematically covering up crimes by sexually abusive priests. This crisis brought widespread critical reflection on the shadow side of the Church's hierarchically imposed strictures concerning human sexuality, the compulsory celibacy of priests, the male domination of the hierarchy, and the subordinate religious status of women. The numerous church closings and declarations of bankruptcy in the wake of the scandals, trials, and settlements were similarly reflective of the same archetypal field. In the same period occurred a wave of major corporate and financial scandals, involving systematic criminal practices by the executives and administrators of Enron, Halliburton, WorldCom, Vivendi, Harken Energy, and the New York Stock Exchange, among many others in the United States, with similar events in Russia, Italy, France, Mexico, the United Nations, and elsewhere. These phenomena reflected the characteristic Saturn-Pluto theme of crime and punishment, of Saturnian judgment against Plutonic transgressions, whether of greed, power, sexuality, or political corruption.[5]

The most dramatic scandal in U.S. political history, the Watergate scandal and the resulting Senate hearings and forced resignation of Nixon, coincided precisely with the Saturn-Pluto square of 1973–75. This was the quadrature alignment immediately following the opposition that coincided with the start of the Vietnam War. Significantly, this same alignment in 1973–75 also coincided with the U.S. defeat in Vietnam (widely perceived by Americans as humiliating and traumatic, both characteristic qualities of the Saturn-Pluto archetypal complex) as well as the OPEC oil embargo and worldwide energy crisis, which resulted in global economic recession and had major geopolitical ramifications that unfolded in the following years.

Moreover, other events highly characteristic of the Saturn-Pluto cycle and archetypal complex during this same period included the right-wing military coup in Chile, supported by the CIA, that brought General Pinochet to dictatorial power, the Greek military junta's invasion of Cyprus, the devastating famine in Ethiopia, India's first nuclear weapon test, the Yom Kippur War in the Middle East, the sustained U.S. air-bombing of civilians in Cambodia, and the beginning of the genocidally destructive Khmer Rouge regime under the dictator Pol Pot. Again, a widespread sense of profound historical contraction and crisis during the period of this alignment was acutely palpable.

As with George W. Bush beginning in the 2000–04 period, it is typical of such eras that individuals born during Saturn-Pluto alignments—such as Henry Kissinger, born during the square in 1923—are politically empowered and play significant roles in historical events at that time, as Kissinger did in an extraordinary number of the just-cited historical events: Vietnam, Cambodia, the Middle East, Chile. Similarly, Donald Rumsfeld and Dick Cheney, the two men who played the most powerful role in U.S. foreign policy under Bush beginning during the 2000–04 Saturn-Pluto opposition, were born during the two Saturn-Pluto quadrature alignments that occurred between those of Kissinger's birth and Bush's—Rumsfeld during the opposition in 1932, Cheney during the following square in 1941, both with their Sun aligned with the Saturn-Pluto configuration.

Just as any single period of a Saturn-Pluto alignment consistently brought a multiplicity of concurrent events reflecting the characteristic themes of this archetypal complex, so also I found that single, especially paradigmatic events during such alignment periods tended to embody a multiplicity of the relevant archetypal themes, all coming together in complex compromise formation to constitute the peculiar character of that event. For example, in the following remarkable diachronic sequence, we see at once the public accusation of grave wrongdoing, solemn trial and judgment, fundamentalist denunciation and prohibition, and intensive assertion of conservative or reactionary authority with highly inhibiting and repressive consequences. Thus the Roman Inquisition's heresy trial and execution of Giordano Bruno exactly coincided with the Saturn-Pluto opposition of 1600. During the immediately following Saturn-Pluto conjunction, in 1616, the Vatican declared the Copernican theory "false and erroneous" and placed the *De Revolutionibus* on its list of books prohibited for all Roman Catholics, the *Index Librorum Prohibitorum*. The very next Saturn-Pluto axial alignment, the opposition in 1632–33, exactly coincided with the Roman Inquisition's summons, trial, and condemnation of Galileo and the Vatican's placement of Galileo's *Dialogue Concerning the Two Chief World Systems* on the Index of forbidden books. All three epochal events involving the Inquisition and Church heresy trials, censorship, and condemnation took place precisely in coincidence with the consecutive sequence of Saturn-Pluto axial alignments— 1600, 1616, and 1632–33—all three of these alignments being exact in those specific years.

It was under an earlier such Saturn-Pluto alignment, in 1543 (the year *De Revolutionibus* was published and Copernicus died), that the Spanish Inquisition burned Protestants at the stake for the first time and Pope Paul III in Rome instituted the *Index Librorum Prohibitorum*. This distinctive theme of the Saturn-Pluto archetypal complex was visible on both sides of the Protestant-Catholic divide: During the immediately preceding Saturn-Pluto opposition of 1534–36, Henry VIII in England imprisoned Thomas More, his scholarly friend and lord chancellor, for refusing to recognize him as head of the English Church (1534) and a year later had him beheaded (1535).

It was during this same alignment that John Calvin—who was himself born during the first Saturn-Pluto square of the century—published his *Institutes of the Christian Religion*, with its doctrines of humanity's innate moral depravity after the Fall, God's predestination of the majority of humankind to eternal damnation, and the consequent need for severe strictures on human thought and action to ensure moral rectitude and dogmatic correctness. During this same period under Calvin's influence Protestant reformers took over the government of Geneva: Catholic priests were imprisoned, the altars were stripped and sacred images destroyed, citizens were fined for not attending sermons, and a regime of strict moral censorship commenced. During the immediately following Saturn-Pluto conjunction in 1553, the Spanish physician astrologer and theologian Michael Servetus—who had criticized Calvin's *Institutes* and opposed the doctrines of original sin and innate human depravity, instead affirming the presence of God in all creation—was arrested in Geneva at Calvin's behest for heresy and burned at the stake. Widespread revulsion at Servetus's execution helped catalyze the birth of religious tolerance in Europe.

Remarkably, Saturn and Pluto were also in opposition from 28 to 31 CE, the years to which many biblical historians assign the period of Jesus's trial and crucifixion. Characteristic themes of the Saturn-Pluto cycle are also clearly evident in the spirit of profound moral urgency, gravity, judgment, calls for repentance, and apocalyptic end-time expectations that pervade the New Testament accounts of the teachings of both Jesus of Nazareth and his exact contemporary, John the Baptist, whose ministry began in 28–29, "in the fifteenth year of Tiberius Caesar."

Looking back even further, we find that Saturn and Pluto were also in hard aspect in 399 BCE, the year of Socrates's trial and death in Athens, when he was condemned for "impiety and corruption of youth" through his philosophical teachings. Here again, as with Giordano Bruno's trial and burning at the stake in 1600, the Church's condemnation of Copernicanism in 1616, and Galileo's trial under the Inquisition in 1633, the coincidence of the Saturn-Pluto cycle with historically weighty events reflecting the motif of trial, judgment, condemnation, and the punitive assertion of conservative or reactionary authority formed an especially consistent pattern.

Splitting, Evil, and Terror

One of the most important, mysterious, and potentially useful characteristics I regularly observed in all categories of correlations was a persistent commonality—yet also a deep ambiguity—between interior experiences and external events during the same alignment. The archetypal complex involved seemed to be equally relevant for understanding both subjective and objective manifestations, and often the boundary between these categories was difficult to ascertain.

For example, alignments of the Saturn-Pluto cycle, including the most recent one coincident with the events of September 11 and their aftermath, seemed to correlate not only with events whose overwhelming gravity, danger, oppressiveness, and moral darkness were vivid actualities, but also with an equally pronounced tendency on the part of the collective psyche to spontaneously constellate and project those shadow qualities with unusual potency. This characteristically took such forms as interpreting the world exclusively as a war between good and evil, perceiving and uncompromisingly enforcing simplistic dichotomies, seeing others as morally or mortally dangerous threats, and identifying particular individuals or states as evil enemies. An eruption of ancient resentments and enmities often occurred, as did a pronounced tendency towards both scapegoating and feeling victimized by specific identified groups.

Such phenomena were typically accompanied by the establishment of rigid defensive boundaries and repressive political structures that were justified by the need for "vital security," often combined with "preemptive" offensive aggression against real or perceived enemies. Deliberate and highly organized acts of mass destruction consistently coincided with Saturn-Pluto quadrature aspects and often were justified as representing a necessary response to matters of life-and-death urgency, national survival, a need for more territory, the perceived enemy's hostile intentions or past actions, or the special destiny of the invading nation to make war now to create a world of peace later. One regularly sees at such times a peculiar close association and mutual empowerment between bellicose right-wing forces within established governments and fundamentalist terrorist forces outside them, both of which support mass killing as a strategic necessity in their mortally opposed yet mutually implicated world views. The overwhelming nature of a trauma suffered by a nation or a people can convince it that its positions and actions are morally unassailable, as with the Bush administration and much of the American public after September 11, 2001, or as in the psychology that has often governed the state of Israel, born during the Saturn-Pluto conjunction of 1946–48 in the shadow of the Holocaust. Alternatively, the gravity of what is at stake, such as eternal salvation or the historical necessity of humanity's movement towards utopian equality, as we will see later with Augustine and Marx, is regarded as justifying the use of authoritarian power and repression in the service of defeating the evil one, the bourgeois enemy, the pagan, the heretic, the dissident, the ever-insidious threat of ideological and moral corruption.

Often during these alignments there emerged a strong identification, either by a leader or by the group or nation, with a God of righteous vengeance and ruthless justice whose will and judgment cannot be questioned. A posture of moral absolutism was asserted with a conviction that one's own motivations were self-evidently aligned with the forces of good in the world. During Saturn-Pluto alignments, as the collective psyche began to be gripped by such archetypal perceptions and shadow impulses, leaders who expressed and exacerbated this complex tended to arise, sometimes catalyzing entire nations into acting out the aroused impulses in often devastating ways. Religious symbols closely intertwined with authoritarian impulses potently manipulated public opinion. Characteristic of such periods was a call for crusades, jihads, and holy wars against the evil enemy.

For example, the First Crusade, of Christians in Europe against Muslims in the Middle East, coincided precisely with the Saturn-Pluto opposition of 1097–99, climaxing in the infamous massacre of Jerusalem in July 1099 as the planets reached exact alignment. Similar perceptions, claims, and actions were evident during the most recent Saturn-Pluto opposition of 2000–04, from both sides of the war on terror, with leaders' references to crusades and jihads (Bush, bin Laden), and repeated claims to represent God's authority in the battle against the ruthless evil enemy—a "war of opposing fundamentalisms." A similar constellation of mutual demonization and righteous retribution was evident in the Israeli-Palestinian conflict of the same years with its incessant cycle of suicide bombings and lethal counterattacks and repression.

Especially virulent forms of this complex were visible in the emergence of white supremacist and Aryan racist movements during alignments of the Saturn-Pluto cycle. Saturn and Pluto were in opposition in 1865–67 at the time of the foundings of both the Ku Klux Klan and the Knights of the White Camelia— supremacist groups cloaked with a religious conviction that asserted white racial superiority and the insidious threat of black political and sexual empowerment— which brought terror and lynchings to blacks throughout the American South for many decades after the Civil War. The Final Solution to exterminate the Jews was conceived and began to be executed by Hitler and the Nazis during the Saturn-Pluto square of 1939–41.

This archetypal gestalt seemed therefore to reflect an epistemologically ambiguous interplay between the two multivalent principles associated with Saturn and Pluto. On the one hand, there was the perception, projection, or eruption of threatening subversive elements—infidels, heretics, terrorists, savages, inferior races, barbarians, criminals, subversives, perverts, evildoers. All these can be regarded as representing the archetypal Plutonic "underworld" in several senses: instinctual, psychological, sociological, theological. On the other hand, this perception of dire threat was matched by a compensatory empowerment of conservative, repressive, or reactionary forces in complex combination and compromise formations. Such an empowerment often brought about the authoritative implementation of methods and activities (war, torture, enslavement, legalized murder, extermination, weapons of mass destruction, manipulative deception and propaganda) that in other contexts or as used by others would be regarded by the same parties as something to be morally condemned and prohibited.

The psychodynamics underlying this interplay was insightfully depicted by Freud in his understanding of the superego's complex relationship to the id. The superego, as the internal principle of conscience, moral judgment, and instinctual constraint, carries in itself the fear of punitive retribution from the introjected parental authority. Freud recognized that the superego was not only repressive and punitive *against* the instinctual drives of the id, but was also energetically informed and impelled *by* the id—unconsciously from below, as it were, even when it perceived the nefarious threat to be from the outside. The psychological consequence could sometimes take the form of obsessive-compulsive and cruel, sadistic tendencies, directed either internally against the self or externally against others, often both. This conception of the superego (archetypally associated with Saturn) and the id (with Pluto) was formulated by Freud precisely during the Saturn-Pluto square of 1921–23 in his book *The Ego and the Id*, published in 1923.

Highly characteristic of Saturn-Pluto historical periods in psychoanalytic terms was an intensified dialectic on the collective level between the repression of the id and the "return of the repressed," often in a covert form. The periods of such alignments seemed to coincide with an emphatically increased tendency towards psychological "splitting"—for example, tending to view oneself as entirely identified with the good and the other entirely with evil. Closely associated with this mechanism of defense was an equally powerful tendency towards "othering": the intense objectification of other subjects. This objectification, when combined with the projection or experience of evil and shadow qualities, tended to impel such emotions as violent suspicion, terror, hatred, revenge, fanaticism, and murderous cruelty.

Such behavior and impulses seemed to be made psychologically possible by establishing or experiencing an absolute boundary (Saturn) between the self and the other. The other—whether defined by nationality, religion, race, class, caste, gender, sexual orientation, belief system, or any other category—was then perceived as radically separate and alien, sometimes as subhuman and unworthy of life. During these Saturn-Pluto alignment periods, frequent references were made to vile beasts, predatory animals, swine, filth, demons, devils, cancers, viruses, vermin, rodents, moles, reptiles, vipers, swamps, lairs, hunting down animals or smoking them out, exterminating a pestilence, and the like—all reflecting Plutonic themes.

The Freudian insight into the superego's hidden dual relation to the id can be deepened by the Jungian perspective in which the shadow, possessing the ego but projected onto the other, enacts its cruelty against the object of its wrath with all the insidious destructiveness it perceives in the other and denies in itself. In theological terms, evil subtly appropriates the motivations of the soul that identifies itself exclusively with God and the good, and that then performs its dark actions in self-deceiving but absolute confidence that it is morally obliged to act thus against such a manifest evil. Thus the God-fearing parent cruelly punishes the wayward child "for its own sake." The Inquisitor tortures and burns at the stake a person whose beliefs are perceived to differ dangerously from his own. The committee of public safety, the department of covert activity, gathers its information, trains its death squads, undermines elections, foments and assassinates to make certain that good prevails in the world.

The psychological orientation associated with the Saturn-Pluto complex often constellates a compulsion for an Ahab-like obsessive pursuit of an evil that must be rooted out at any cost. Remarkably, Herman Melville, who explored this complex with such memorable profundity, was born during the first Saturn-Pluto conjunction of the nineteenth century (1819), and wrote *Moby Dick* precisely one cycle later during the immediately following Saturn-Pluto conjunction (1850–51).

> Ever since that almost fatal encounter, Ahab had cherished a wild vindictiveness against the whale, all the more fell for that in his frantic morbidness he at last came to identify with him, not only all his bodily woes, but all his intellectual and spiritual exasperations. The White Whale swam before him as the monomaniac incarnation of all those malicious agencies which some deep men feel eating them, till they are left living on with half a heart and half a lung. That intangible malignity which has been from the beginning, to whose dominion even the modern Christians ascribe one-half of the worlds; which the ancient Ophites of the east reverenced in the statue devil;—Ahab did not fall down and worship it like them; but deliriously transferring its idea to the abhorred white whale, he pitted himself, all mutilated against it. All that most maddens and torments; all that stirs up the lees of things; all truth with malice in it; all that cracks the sinews and cakes the brain; all the subtle

demonisms of life and thought; all evil, to crazy Ahab, were visibly personified, and made practically assailable in Moby Dick. He piled upon the whale's white hump the sum of all the general rage and hate felt by his whole race from Adam down; and, then, as if his chest had been a mortar, he burst his hot heart's shell upon it.

Thus acts the suicide bomber, the witch burner, the whip-wielding slavemaster and the cross-burning klansman, the monomaniacal dictator and the righteous leader whose divinely authorized task is to rid the world of evil he knows is so uniquely and malignantly embodied in another person or race. With this absolute conviction of ineluctable destiny and righteousness, just before the final battle with the abhorred object of his obsession, Ahab declared: "This whole act's immutably decreed. . . . I am the Fates' lieutenant; I act under orders."

Moby Dick and Nature's Depths

One of the most remarkable sequences of synchronicities I have ever observed was a dramatic convergence of events involving Melville, *Moby Dick*, and the two planetary cycles we have been examining in this book. As we have seen, Melville was born in 1819 when Saturn and Pluto were in conjunction, and also when the Uranus-Pluto square was occurring, which corresponds to that powerful combination of conflicting complexes and impulses that we observed in Marx, who was born during the same alignments, and in several especially critical historical periods such as the mid-1960s and mid-1790s. In Melville and *Moby Dick*, we can recognize the potent interaction between these two archetypal complexes: on the one hand, the Uranus-Pluto themes of the awakening and eruption of nature's forces in the whale, the unleashing of the instinctual id in Ahab his act of titanic defiance and the titanic power and creative intensity of the book *Moby Dick* itself; and on the other hand, the Saturn-Pluto themes of punitive retribution *against* nature and relentless obsession with projected evil, the cauldron of the instincts within Ahab driving his compulsion for vengeance with inexorable force.

Eleven days after Melville was born, in August 1919, the whaleship *Essex* departed from Nantucket for the southern Pacific Ocean, where it was attacked by an eighty-foot whale and sunk. According to the account later published by the *Essex*'s first mate, Owen Chase, the whale rammed the ship deliberately and repeatedly with "fury and vengeance" until it had destroyed and sunk the ship. The twenty surviving whalers were forced to spend the next ninety-three days unprotected and starving in rowboats in the open ocean, where most of them eventually died. This fateful voyage, from its departure through the ramming and sinking of the ship by the whale fifteen months later, took place during the same Saturn-Pluto conjunction and Uranus-Pluto square of Melville's birth. The titanic forces of nature embodied in the whale, a vivid expression of the Plutonic principle of nature's elemental power, mass, and instinct, can here be seen as suddenly awakened and erupting in a most unexpected manner, as is characteristic of the Uranus-Pluto complex. Yet the whale that turned upon and destroyed the *Essex* has also become, like both Moby Dick and Ahab, the Saturnian agent of judgment, punishment, retribution, and death—precisely reflective of the Saturn-Pluto complex.

Growing up unaware of this dramatic event that occurred so near his birth, Melville in his early twenties signed on to a three-year whaling voyage, which took him to the same area of the South Pacific as the scene of the *Essex*'s sinking. While on that voyage, he happened to meet the son of Owen Chase, the *Essex*'s first mate, who loaned him a copy of the father's original narrative. Melville was deeply affected by reading "the wondrous story upon the landless sea," as he later wrote, "and so close to the very latitude of the shipwreck."

Exactly one full Saturn-Pluto cycle after Melville's birth and the sinking of the *Essex*, during the very next conjunction of those two planets in 1850–51, Melville wrote and published *Moby Dick*. Amazingly, just as Melville was completing his book, in August 1851, with the Saturn-Pluto conjunction within 4° of exact alignment, the whaleship *Ann Alexander* was rammed and sunk by an enraged sperm whale it had been pursuing in the same waters in which the same fate had befallen the *Essex* over thirty years earlier—to this day the only two well-documented cases of such an event. Melville was stunned when he learned of the great coincidence.

Moreover, as we may recall, the publication of *Moby Dick* and the sinking of the *Ann Alexander* coincided with not only the Saturn-Pluto conjunction but also the Uranus-Pluto conjunction of 1845–56 we earlier examined—the three planets in a triple conjunction, the only such triple conjunction in the past two hundred years. The extraordinary elemental power of *Moby Dick*, its sudden liberation of the dark and volcanic, the unleashing of the forces of nature in both the whale and the human creative imagination, fully possessed Melville as he worked on the novel. Writing hour after hour through the day without stopping for food, alternately on fire with energy and weary from the immense expenditure, he cried out:

> Give me Vesuvius's crater for an inkstand! Friends, hold my arms! For in the mere act of penning my thoughts of this Leviathan, they weary me, and make me faint with their outreaching comprehensiveness of sweep, as if to include the whole circle of the sciences, and all the generations of whales, and men, and mastodons, past, present, and to come, with all the revolving panoramas of empire on earth, and throughout the whole universe. . . . Such, and so magnifying, is the virture of a large and liberal theme! We expand to its bulk. To produce a mighty book, you must choose a mighty theme.

All these figures and events—Melville's life and creative imagination, the narrative and themes of *Moby Dick*, the titanic figure of Ahab, the killing of whales, and whales that kill the killers of whales—profoundly reflect the character of the two archetypal complexes we have been examining here, Saturn-Pluto and

Uranus-Pluto. I was considerably struck by the extraordinary synchronistic patterning in which two of the events, Melville's birth and *Moby Dick*'s publication, coincided with the successive Saturn-Pluto and Uranus-Pluto alignments so precisely: These were the *only* two conjunctions of Saturn and Pluto in the first seventy years of the nineteenth century, and the *only* two hard-aspect alignments of Uranus and Pluto in that same period. But when I later discovered that both of those events also coincided with such rare and symbolically evocative sinkings of whaleships by whales, events that were so uncannily relevant to both Melville's entire life and his masterwork, yet were also so precisely appropriate to the archetypal complexes associated with the rare coinciding planetary alignments— in all these events and coincidences, one succeeding another with relentless coherence, I felt that an intensity of synchronistic power had erupted through the acts of nature itself that was genuinely numinous in its elemental potency. "Some certain significance lurks in all things," wrote Melville in *Moby Dick*.

As we know, Jung paid special attention to the sudden or unusual movements of nature for their potential synchronistic significance, whether of wind and water or of birds, insects, fish, and other animals. But these events and coincidences just recounted, the whaleship-sinkings, the births of Melville and *Moby Dick*, and the cosmic movements and archetypal patternings with which they all so precisely coincided, suggest a form of synchronistic orchestration in nature that, by comparison with the golden-scarab insect that entered Jung's window while his patient recounted her dream, are awe-inspiring in their epic magnitude. Such powerful patterning, working at so many levels of the human and natural worlds, strongly intimates the possibility that an *anima mundi,* an archetypally informed depth of interiority, lies within "all things"—in the depths of the human psyche and in the depths of nature. Melville's mighty work was something more than a human artifact: It represented the upsurging force of nature itself, imbued with dark and numinous significance. Elemental forces of meaning and purpose upwelled from the oceanic depths, twice in the whales, and twice in human forms, in the births of Melville and his book. These extraordinary double synchronicities in the human and cetacean realms are, on their own terms, sufficiently astonishing to compel deep reflection. Yet somehow precisely linked to and uniting all these events and coincidences is the great macrocosm itself, the planetary movements in the vast starry sky high above the ocean of whales and men, all reflecting a profundity of significant pattern and mysterious purpose in the depths of all things.

Historical Determinism,
Realpolitik, and Apocalypse

To maintain a modicum of simplicity and clarity in what for many readers may be their first entrance into the archetypal astrological perspective and mode of analysis, I have generally focused on just one theme at a time for any given phenomenon, and emphasized some themes at the expense of others, in a way that conveys only a portion of the true complexity of the larger body of data. Since we are concentrating entirely on the dynamic, or hard, quadrature aspects of the Saturn-Pluto cycle, the evidence presented has been heavily weighted to the more challenging, problematic, and dark dimensions of this complex. Moreover, we have been centering our attention mainly on the great drama of history and culture, where the ordeals and crises of collective humanity are writ large and where paradigmatic individuals embody and express the forces and struggles of the whole. In doing so, we have been able to glimpse more directly the full magnitude and power of the archetypal dimension expressing itself in human affairs.

If, however, we were to examine each individual born with Saturn-Pluto aspects or who is undergoing Saturn-Pluto transits (either world transits or personal transits), we would see many examples of equally characteristic but far less intense embodiments of the same archetypal principles. And were we to examine the confluent, or soft, aspects of this cycle as well, the trines and sextiles, we would see the many ways in which these two principles regularly come together in more easily harmonious, mutually supportive, and intrinsically strengthening ways: for example, a well-developed capacity for sustained effort and discipline, a spontaneous facility for containing and focusing intense energies, the balanced and effective organization of power, a certain spirit of well-earned personal authority and gravitas, extraordinary solidity of character, perceptive moral judgment, deeply established enduring structures of all kinds, and the like. Using one example to stand for many: George Kennan, born with the Saturn-Pluto trine in 1904, represented a paradigmatic expression of these qualities, embodied in his well-known personal gravitas and authoritative influence, as well as his depth of historical-psychological insight and moral conviction. The characteristic qualities of the Saturn-Pluto complex were precisely articulated in Kennan's summary statement from the famous *Foreign Affairs* article of 1947 that would guide

American Cold War strategy against Stalin: "In these circumstances it is clear that the main element of any United States policy toward the Soviet Union must be that of long-term, patient but firm and vigilant containment." Equally reflective was Kennan's role as intellectual architect of the Marshall Plan that helped rebuild postwar Europe.[6]

Moreover, contrary to much of the astrological tradition, I found that even hard aspects between two planets often coincided with a full embodiment of the positive potentialities of the relevant archetypes—though typically only after considerable effort, whether individual or collective, had been expended in the integration of the different impulses involved in the challenging dialectic. The present discussion, therefore, must be recognized as only an introduction to and a fragment of a considerably larger and more complex reality. It offers an entrance to the larger body of evidence that, while accurately reflective of the archetypal dynamics correlated with this planetary cycle, illuminates only a part of the full spectrum of manifestations that regularly accompany such alignments. Yet the analysis pursued in these pages possesses the advantage of highlighting some of the most significant and distinctive characteristics and themes of this powerful archetypal complex. Given the particular character of these two principles— both of them potentially challenging and serious, sometimes in the extreme—our focus on the hard aspects in the context of history and influential cultural figures permits a sharper rendering of the essential qualities associated with this planetary combination.

Just as Melville's work vividly reflected many archetypal themes and psychological mechanisms characteristic of the Saturn-Pluto complex, so also with the work of Franz Kafka, who was born in 1882 during the very next Saturn-Pluto conjunction after Melville's *Moby Dick*, and who wrote his paradigmatic works *The Trial* and *In the Penal Colony* in 1914 exactly one cycle later during the Saturn-Pluto conjunction immediately after that. It is striking that these four consecutive Saturn-Pluto conjunctions so precisely coincided with the succession of births and major works of these two literary and psychological masters, both deep explorers of the very archetypal complex with which this planetary cycle is so consistently associated. With surreal precision, Kafka depicted the characteristic Saturn-Pluto motifs of judgment and guilt, cruel punishment, claustrophobic bureaucracy and totalitarian confinement. In work after work, in stories, novels, and his own diary, he portrayed the relentless imprisonment of consciousness wrought in the heart of both tyrant and victim, both pursuer and pursued, who are sometimes the same individual.

Especially relevant here is one of the last stories Kafka wrote, *The Burrow*, in which a determined mole, using his head as a sledgehammer, spends every waking minute obsessively digging and fortifying an elaborate maze of tunnels and defenses to protect him from the predatory beast he is certain awaits him outside his underground fortress. All the powers of a hyperacute reason are placed in the service of that task as he ceaselessly constructs in his mind the countless ways his invisible enemy will at any moment be able to surprise and kill him. A brilliantly sustained parable of the ego's incessant fear of an all-encompassing dangerous world, one whose constant peril lies as much in the depths of one's own psyche and the fear of death as in the outer environment, *The Burrow* was written in 1923 just before Kafka's own death, during the same Saturn-Pluto square in which Freud wrote *The Ego and the Id*.

On the collective level, the characteristic tendencies of the Saturn-Pluto complex towards perceiving and constellating danger, subversive threat, and malefic shadow elements in a rigidly polarized world view were typically accompanied by an increased perception of the inevitability of conflict and war, whether expressed on the level of mass psychology or of elaborate rational analysis. The underlying conviction of the inevitability of conflict and war has found philosophical expression in such paradigmatic works of political thought as Thomas Hobbes's *Leviathan*, with its vision of humanity's natural condition as a state of "war of all against all," or more recently Samuel Huntington's *The Clash of Civilizations*, with its view of the world's geopolitical future as ineluctably shaped by historically determined enmity between religiously and culturally defined blocs of humanity, such as Islam and the West. Both of these works were written in precise coincidence with Saturn-Pluto alignments (the conjunction of 1648–50 and the most recent square of 1992–94, respectively). In turn, such works tended to be revived, widely referred to, and affirmed as authoritative in subsequent periods of Saturn-Pluto alignments, as in the aftermath of September 11, 2001. A related form of the same archetypal gestalt was the perception of civilization or history as moving towards inevitable decline, as in Oswald Spengler's *The Decline of the West*, largely written during the Saturn-Pluto conjunction of World War I.[7]

An unflinching realism and gravity of perspective tied to a vision of inevitable conflict or decline—whether authentic and empirically justified or subjectively distorted and self-fulfilling—was a dominant theme of this archetypal complex. The word *realpolitik*, for example, first entered the English language from the German during the Saturn-Pluto conjunction of 1914. Many of the themes cited above can be recognized in the political philosophy, foreign policy decisions, and covert activities of Henry Kissinger, who was born in 1923 during the immediately following Saturn-Pluto square that also coincided with Kafka's *The Burrow*. Characteristic of certain forms of the Saturn-Pluto realpolitik perspective and ethos is Kissinger's response to Congress to criticism he received for having the CIA actively foment resistance among the Kurds against Saddam Hussein in 1975 (during another Saturn-Pluto square) and then suddenly abandoning them when his diplomatic strategy changed, which resulted in the slaughter of thousands of Kurdish people: "Covert activities should not be mistaken for missionary work." Comparable actions and statements reflecting a realpolitik perspective could be cited for Donald Rumsfeld and Dick Cheney, often involving the same figures and geographical areas, and again in coincidence with the Saturn-Pluto cycle.[8]

Civilization and Its Discontents

An extraordinary number of the archetypal tendencies discussed here were evident, in a distinct inflection that proved immensely consequential, in the work and vision of Karl Marx, whom we will consider now in greater detail from the perspective of his natal Saturn-Pluto aspect. In our earlier discussion of the three-planet combination of Uranus and Saturn with Pluto, we saw how the tension and compromise formations between the Saturn principle of control and authority and the Uranus principle of rebellion and freedom were prominent in Marx's philosophy and character, with Pluto intensifying both impulses. (His statement that "Prometheus is the noblest saint and martyr in the calendar of philosophy" well represents the heightened sense of Prometheus Bound that is frequently found associated with the Saturn-Uranus archetypal complex.) Marx was born in 1818 during the first Saturn-Pluto conjunction of the nineteenth century—the same one as Melville—and presents many of the symptoms characteristic of the Saturn-Pluto complex. Like Melville, Marx was born with both the Uranus-Pluto square alignment, as we saw in our study of that cycle, and the Saturn-Pluto conjunction, and in each of these titanic figures both of the archetypal complexes we have been examining in these chapters were conspicuously in evidence. In a sense, *Das Kapital* was Marx's *Moby Dick*, with capitalism in the targeted role of the white whale, to be destroyed with all the obsessive power and will that could be mobilized in a task of such metaphysical and historical urgency.

All of Marx's work was in the service of an overarching framework of mass revolution on behalf of an emancipatory cause, corresponding with his close natal Uranus-Pluto square. Yet within that framework, such characteristic themes of the Saturn-Pluto complex as absolute determinism and inevitability, rigidly polarized conflict, oppression and dictatorship were all dominant in Marx's philosophical vision. We see the positive side of the complex in his penetrating analysis of and sensitivity to the shadow side of nineteenth-century capitalism, the extreme social injustice and human alienation inherent in the economic systems and societies of his time. This sensitivity was intensified as he articulated his analysis of the master-slave relationship, his recognition of the continual reappearance throughout history of structures of oppression, his vision of the crushingly inhuman prison in which so many human lives were enclosed, the enslavement and impoverishment of workers under capitalism, and the ubiquitous power of the oppressor over the oppressed.

The larger range of Saturn-Pluto themes was embodied and elaborated in such Marxist doctrines as the ultimate determinism of all structures of society and belief by economic and material factors, the ineradicable contradictions of bourgeois social relations, the necessity of class conflict and struggle, the inevit-able unfolding of the dialectic of history, and the need for an intervening dic-tatorship of the proletariat to destroy all remnants of bourgeois society. More generally, the complex was evident in a certain authoritarian rigidity and dog-matism in the Marxist philosophy and sensibility, driven by a kind of titanic force of will.

Yet we begin to see the extraordinary range of archetypal multivalence in the Saturn-Pluto correlations when we compare Marx's expression of an emphati-cally atheistic historical vision with an equally paradigmatic theological vision of history. For many of precisely these same archetypal themes—determinism and the overpowering nature of the forces governing and constraining human life, rigidly polarized conflict, intensely negative moral judgment of humanity's cur-rent condition, the need for unbending will to counter and repress the forces of darkness—were acutely expressed, though with entirely different inflections and intentions, in the religious ideas and enduring legacies of Saint Augustine and John Calvin.

The most influential theologians of Catholicism and Protestantism, respec-tively, Augustine and Calvin were both born with Saturn and Pluto in square alignment. In both cases, their personal conceptions of human destiny took the form of grave moral judgment shaped by a vivid sense of humanity's deep cor-ruption, the power of evil in the world, and the inborn guilt of the human soul. Other themes that precisely reflected this archetypal complex include both theologians' lifelong emphasis on the encompassing threat of eternal damnation, the need for rigorous suppression of sexuality and unregenerate instinct, God's overwhelming and implacable omnipotence, and the theological certainty of predestination.

The dominant archetypal motifs of an individual's life and work consistently seemed to find paradigmatic expression at the time of planetary alignments that were archetypally consonant with those specific themes, and when correspond-ing external events shaped both the individual's personal outlook and the larger cultural zeitgeist. Many of the themes just cited were articulated, with lasting in-fluence on the Western religious imagination, in Augustine's monumental work *The City of God*. There he set forth his vision of history as a dramatic battle be-tween the two invisible societies of the elect and of the damned, the city of God and the city of the world, climaxing in the Last Judgment. The powerful vision of *The City of God* seems to have been especially inspired and pervaded by the archetypal complex associated with the Saturn-Pluto cycle: the perception of human existence as bound and driven by overwhelming forces, the moral and mortal gravity of the human condition, Manicheaen cosmic dualism, the endur-ing power of evil and satanic subversion, the anticipation of eschatological fi-nality and judgment, hell and damnation. Augustine conceived and began writing *The City of God* during the first Saturn-Pluto conjunction of the fifth century, in 410–12. This was the same conjunction that coincided with the massive barbarian incursions and the sack of Rome by Alaric and the Visigoths, awareness of which deeply shaped Augustine's historical understanding and the vision set forth in *The City of God*.

Thus we can recognize here both the diachronic and synchronic patterning that I found so pervasive in studying planetary correlations with cultural and historical phenomena. Diachronically, as we saw with Kafka and Melville above, Augustine was born during one Saturn-Pluto alignment and wrote the work that especially reflects that complex during a subsequent one. Synchronically, the period that brought forth that work was marked by the simultaneous occurrence of significant historical events bearing the same archetypal character as the work itself.

As it happens, the correlation was more complexly precise than this, for Augustine was himself born with not only Saturn and Pluto in hard aspect but also Uranus and Pluto—like both Marx and Melville—with the characteristic titanic conflict and violent intensity, inner and outer, that so consistently coincided with this three-planet configuration. Moreover, these same three planets were again in hard aspect in the 410–12 period (the shorter Saturn-Pluto conjunction of those years occurring near the end of the longer Uranus-Pluto square of 406–13) in the period of immense upheavals in the late Roman Empire produced by the barbarian incursions and the sack of Rome, when Augustine began *The City of God*. Both the drama of Augustine's life and character and these historic upheavals and traumas closely reflect the archetypal forces of the two planetary cycles we have been examining, Uranus-Pluto and Saturn-Pluto, in tense and often violently destabilizing interaction.

We see a closely analogous pattern over a millennium later in Hobbes's milestone of early modern political philosophy, *Leviathan*, with its similar obsession with violent social disorder, its perception of nature as a state of perpetual war, and the consequent need for absolute authoritarian control by a sovereign ruler (Hobbes's call for absolute monarchy substituted for Augustine's call for the sovereign authority of the Church). *Leviathan* was written in 1648–50 under the impact of the Thirty Years' War just ending and the execution of King Charles I during the political turmoil of the revolutionary epoch of the English Civil War. This coincided with both the Saturn-Pluto conjunction of 1647–50 and the longer Uranus-Pluto opposition of 1643–55 during the English revolutionary epoch, which we examined earlier.

Like Augustine's *City of God*, therefore, the period that brought forth Hobbes's influential historical vision was one of those—like that of the barbarian incursions and sack of Rome in 410–12, the Reign of Terror in 1793–95, the 1929–33 period of global economic and political collapse and fascist empowerment, and the 1964–67 period of violent revolutionary insurgency, oppression, and upheaval throughout the world—when Saturn, Uranus, and Pluto were all in hard-aspect alignment with each other. All of these periods were marked by an extraordinarily intense, violent, even cataclysmic clash of opposing forces.

There is one other major work whose historical vision is strikingly similar to *Leviathan* and *The City of God* in both cultural influence and archetypal character, Freud's late work *Civilization and Its Discontents*, published in 1930 when Saturn was opposite Pluto. It was especially in the two works of Freud's cited in this chapter, *The Ego and the Id* and *Civilization and Its Discontents*, that this particular archetypal dynamic associated with the Saturn-Pluto complex was most dominant in Freud's work—one at the individual level, the other at the collective—and those two works coincided precisely with the successive Saturn-Pluto hard aspects following the conjunction of World War I. In both works, Freud emphasized the intense conflict and intricate interaction between the id and the superego, between Pluto and Saturn, whether played out on the battlefield of the ego and the individual life or the battlefield of civilization and history.

Thus here again, as in *The City of God* and *Leviathan*, the historical vision set forth in *Civilization and Its Discontents* was informed by a perception of life as dominated by inevitable conflict, struggle, and the overwhelming power of impersonal forces. Moreover, like the earlier works by Augustine and Hobbes, this work coincided with not only the Saturn-Pluto cycle but also the Uranus-Pluto cycle, at one of those relatively rare times when all three planets had moved into mutual hard aspect. Freud's book was deeply influenced by the terrible impact of the First World War, which coincided with the Saturn-Pluto conjunction, and was written and published against the backdrop of the rapid rise of Nazism during the opposition point of that same cycle, the 1929–33 period when Uranus was in square to both Saturn and Pluto. Thus like *The City of God*'s relation to the barbarian invasions and sack of Rome, and *Leviathan*'s relation to the Thirty Years' War and the upheavals of the English Civil War, so *Civilization and Its Discontents* was shaped by the historically traumatic events coincident with the Saturn-Pluto cycle, with the added intensity and conflict contributed by the emancipatory impulses and unleashing of titanic forces associated with the Uranus-Pluto cycle.

The archetypal complex connected with this three-planet combination corresponds closely to both the philosophical tenor of the three works and the times in which they were born: the revolutionary turmoil, the threat of catastrophic collapse of established structures, the violent unpredictability of life, the inevitability of conflict between forces of disruption and forces of order, and thus the need for firm or even absolute control of unconstrained instinct and rebellious elements lest civilization be lost to licentiousness, war, and chaos. With these three paradigmatic historical visions before us, we can perhaps recognize the family resemblance between works produced in widely separated eras and in altogether different genres yet during identical planetary alignments and reflecting identical archetypal dynamics. On the one hand, Freud's *Civilization and Its Discontents* is an analysis explicitly in the tradition of Hobbes, with its view of humanity's natural state as an instinctually violent condition of anarchy and war, and thus the need for strict socially imposed constraints to prevent endless catastrophe. Yet on the other hand, at a deeper level of the archetypal imagination, the work reflects the tradition of Augustine, with its variation on the Manichaean view of life as an eternal battle between light and dark—but expressed in the Freudian terms of a battle between Eros and Thanatos, love and hate, the drive of life and the drive of death and destruction.

In Freud's vision, this eternal conflict is interwoven with and complicated by the perpetual battle between civilization and nature's instincts by which human society is both driven and threatened. All human instinct and desire (Pluto), whether libidinal or aggressive, is forever necessarily constrained and frustrated by the needs of civilization and the cultural superego (Saturn), with the outcome of humankind's fate perilously uncertain (much as in Augustine's vision, though in certain respects from an almost opposite perspective). For Freud, the survival of humanity depends on civilization's suppression of erotic passion and destructive aggression, a never successful but always necessary coercion that results in incurable misery. The human condition is thus an insoluble predicament.

In popular culture, Freud's analysis in *Civilization and Its Discontents* of the libidinal instincts as frustrated by the constraints of civilization was given iconic embodiment in the Rolling Stones' *(I Can't Get No) Satisfaction*, recorded in early 1965 and listened to endlessly by millions during the Saturn opposition Uranus-Pluto alignment in 1965–67. Throughout the song, the dominant Promethean-Dionysian impulse of the 1960s towards erotic emancipation and release is simultaneously expressed in defiance of convention and yet with equal force held in check by the empowered Saturnian principle. The characteristic Saturnian motifs appear in the song on several levels at once: in the repeated experiences of sexual rejection, in the mind-numbing vapidity of commercial advertisements and the conformist society they epitomize, and in the bass-heavy simplistic regularity of the music itself. The two opposing archetypal complexes, Uranus-Pluto and Saturn-Pluto, are locked in tense confrontation, at once tautly balanced and rhythmically discharged through the sledgehammer repetition of the Dionysian complaint. The sustained popular success of *Satisfaction* can be viewed in part as a natural consequence of its articulating so directly and emphatically an archetypal conflict at the very moment that the collective psyche was experiencing a heightened tension between just those opposed forces.

Remarkably, *Civilization and Its Discontents* of 1930 and *Satisfaction* of 1965 coincided with the only two times in the twentieth century that the three relevant planets—Saturn, Uranus, and Pluto—were all simultaneously in hard-aspect alignment with each other. The two celebrated works, each in its own idiosyncratic and eloquent manner, precisely embodied the Dionysian-Promethean impulse for erotic liberation that is relentlessly inhibited by the cultural superego and rigid constraints of the Saturn-Pluto complex.

In addition to Augustine, Hobbes, and Freud, there is a fourth major figure whose most influential work, with notably similar themes and character, involved the identical sequence of correlations with the two cycles we have been examining. While the resonances with Hobbes and Augustine can be discerned in Freud's historical vision, in the more immediate background was Schopenhauer's conception of a blind striving will or energy that dominates life and impels all human desire and instinct. Schopenhauer was born in 1788 at the start of the Uranus-Pluto opposition of the French Revolutionary epoch, as discussed earlier, and at the end of the Saturn-Pluto conjunction of 1785–88 (whose severe economic depression and widespread famine helped precipitate the French Revolution). Moreover, he published his major work, *The World as Will and Idea*, in 1818 during the immediately following Saturn-Pluto conjunction—the one that coincided with the births of Marx and Melville—which happened also to be the very next time Uranus was in quadrature alignment with Pluto, as discussed above with Marx and Melville. Again, it seems that when these two planetary cycles, Uranus-Pluto and Saturn-Pluto, overlap, with a corresponding activation of the two powerful archetypal complexes, the human effort to assimilate and articulate the titanic clash of the forces involved regularly seems to bring forth especially potent and influential works of the individual and cultural imagination.

Schopenhauer's philosophy vividly reflects both the Uranus-Pluto and the Saturn-Pluto archetypal complexes, not simply as two separate themes but rather with the two closely integrated in a potent synthesis. In Schopenhauer's vision, the ceaselessly striving universal will to live is an irresistible impulse that grips human existence and produces struggle, competition, and unsatisfiable cravings whose inevitable frustration produces constant misery. The will constantly seeks to perpetuate itself through us by using our never-satisfiable desires and drives without our conscious awareness as mere devices and strategies to fulfill its endless goal of propagation and self-preservation—in certain respects a nineteenth-century philosophical anticipation of sociobiology, which was itself founded during the Saturn-Pluto square of 1973–75 with the publication of Edward O. Wilson's *Sociobiology*. (This was the Saturn-Pluto alignment that began just as the Uranus-Pluto conjunction of the 1960s and early 1970s ended, the period that coincided with Watergate and the height of Kissinger's geopolitical activity, among many other archetypally related phenomena cited earlier.)

In Schopenhauer's perspective, the primordial will pervasively shapes and reifies our perceptions, our ideas, our world. Yet the Saturnian dimension of this reality and philosophy asserts itself not only in the imprisoning and frustrating power of the Plutonic will, but also in Schopenhauer's doctrine of the "denial of the will." For in his view, only through the ascetic denial of this all-consuming will to live, constraining its power through self-knowledge or transcending it through art, can one attempt to find some equilibrium amidst the pervasive pain of existence. All these themes were driven by the conviction, so reflective of the Saturn-Pluto complex, that no philosophy or religion that fails to face the dark, genuinely evil nature of the world as it is actually experienced by living beings can pretend to be adequate or valid. Thus Schopenhauer pushed the European mind as never before to recognize the immense suffering of all life, not only human but animal, and the animal in the human. He brilliantly confronted the cruelty of the widespread Christian belief in a punitive God who would create a world in which only a tiny minority would be saved and the vast majority condemned to eternal suffering, and compared this to the actual hell of life on Earth and the actual cruelty of human beings in their treatment of other humans and animals. He relentlessly demanded a confrontation with the shadow side of existence and an engagement with those depths of one's being—instinctual, irrational, wild, blind, overpowering—that did not fit neatly into the light-filled optimisms of Enlightenment rationalism, shallow versions of Romantic idealism, or conventional Christianity.[9]

I consistently observed that perspectives which emphasized the darkly problematic aspects of existence—intense struggle, suffering and death, the relentless tension of opposing forces, and more generally the overwhelming power of impersonal forces determining human life—emerged with extraordinary regularity during periods of Saturn-Pluto alignments, as did philosophical and religious visions of a highly dualistic or apocalyptic character. Given the Manichaean overtones of Freud's and Augustine's works, it is striking that Saturn and Pluto were in conjunction in the years 243–45 CE when Mani, the founder of Manichaeism itself in ancient Persia, first proclaimed his ascetic religion of cosmic dualism in which all existence is determined by a universal battle between the good forces of Light and the evil, chaotic forces of Darkness, with Light identified with God, and Darkness identified with matter and embodiment.

Similarly, the rise to power of the fiery fundamentalist preacher Savonarola in Florence, where he denounced the vanity and corruption of Renaissance culture and initiated a strict moral reform under the threat of eternal damnation and imminent apocalypse, began during the Saturn-Pluto square of 1490–92. Here again both the *synchronic* and the *multivalent* nature of these correlations was strikingly visible. For this was the same Saturn-Pluto alignment that coincided with the start of what turned out to be in many respects the apocalyptic transformation of the Western hemisphere that began when Columbus reached the Bahama Islands on October 12, 1492. This event coincided both with the Saturn-Pluto square and with the long Uranus-Pluto square of the 1490s cited earlier for the era of initial European penetration to the West and to India by the navigators and explorers of Spain and Portugal.

Moreover, it was also in 1492 that King Ferdinand in Spain conquered Granada and expelled the Moors, thus completing the long crusade against Islam in Europe, immediately after which the Spanish Inquisition expelled the Jews from Spain. Over fifty thousand Jewish families were ordered to leave the country within four months of the Inquisition's edict "for the honor and glory of

God," thereby forcing into motion a vast migration of Jewish refugees not unlike the one that began during the similar configuration of Saturn, Uranus, and Pluto in the 1930s.

Apocalyptic Scenarios

I must emphasize again the extent to which such archetypal correlations transcended simple dichotomies of subjective and objective, of distorted projection versus accurate discernment. When a powerful archetypal field was constellated, the domain of its influence was not merely intrapsychic. The widespread conviction that human individuals live lives that are helplessly bound in the grip of overwhelming impersonal, destructive, or dark forces, a conviction that consistently emerged during Saturn-Pluto alignments (including the most recent, that of 2000–04), often arose on the basis of strongly suggestive evidence. It is true that such alignments also coincided regularly with a religious belief that the end of the world was imminent. Yet apocalyptic and doomsday scenarios also emerged during such alignments in sober political and military analyses, even in the natural sciences and with considerable empirical support.

For example, the "nuclear winter" scenario of the probable fallout from nuclear war was hypothesized by Carl Sagan and other scientists during the Saturn-Pluto conjunction of 1981–84, when the widespread experience of a nuclear "sword of Damocles" hanging over the world reached a climax during the first Reagan administration. In those years the tremendous nuclear buildup on both sides of the Atlantic, in preparation for "nuclear overkill," reached what was recognized by many to be genuinely apocalyptic proportions, and gave rise in the collective psyche to pervasive fears of nuclear holocaust in a Manichaean battle between the superpowers. Widespread anxiety concerning the possibility of "triggering World War III," the drawing of many historical parallels with the disastrous beginning of World War I (which had occurred during the same planetary alignment, the Saturn-Pluto conjunction, two cycles earlier), the widely seen television program of nuclear catastrophe, *The Day After*, were all expressive of this activated archetypal field during that period. These themes and concerns were similarly embodied at this time in the intense antinuclear activism and apocalyptic warnings of Helen Caldicott and the Physicians for Social Responsibility as well as in Jonathan Schell's influential *The Fate of the Earth*, all during the same alignment. Again, it is true that these fears and images of a nuclear Armageddon catalyzed the fundamentalist imagination, but such anxieties were nearly universal at the time, among the reasonable and the unreasonable alike, and helped drive the Cold War to its conclusion.[10]

During the most recent Saturn-Pluto alignment in 2003, the U.S. Department of Defense produced the widely discussed scientific report "An Abrupt Climate Change Scenario and Its Implications for U.S. National Security: Imagining the Unthinkable" on the possible effects of abrupt changes in the global climate if global warming continues. Drawing on empirical data and computer models, like the nuclear winter scenario of the preceding conjunction, the report suggested that catastrophic consequences could result for much of the world in the next two decades—worldwide flooding, mega-droughts, freezing cold, famine, and endemic war and chaos—a warning that reflected the same Saturn-Pluto themes in its rendering of an apocalyptic future as the fundamentalist literature of the same period. The widely viewed film *The Day After Tomorrow* of 2004 presented a cinematic version of a global warming catastrophe, remarkably paralleling the character and cultural effect of *The Day After* of 1983 with its rendering of nuclear catastrophe during the immediately prior Saturn-Pluto conjunction.

Paradoxically, alignments of the Saturn-Pluto cycle have coincided not only with the intensified collective awareness of dire threats to the human species and to the planetary biosphere, but also with another frequent expression of the same archetypal complex in an almost opposite form: namely, the intensification of strenuous antienvironmental efforts, particularly in the United States, on the part of corporate and political establishments. Here a characteristic combination of predatory materialism and a relentless impulse for control and domination over nature strongly suggests the presence of the negative Saturn-Pluto complex. Equally suggestive is the frequently observed association of antienvironmental policies with conservative social and political views, fundamentalist religious beliefs, and corporate pressures for regulatory autonomy and increased profits. The systematic empowerment of antienvironmental forces and policies took place with unusual intensity during the most recent Saturn-Pluto opposition of 2001–04 under the first Bush-Cheney administration, as it did during the preceding Saturn-Pluto conjunction of 1981–84 under the first Reagan administration, especially through the policies of the Secretary of the Interior James Watt.

Here too the synergy working between different forms of this archetypal complex is evident, as the Republican constituencies that elected Reagan and the younger Bush included many fundamentalist Christians with explicitly apocalyptic expectations that similarly reflected the Saturn-Pluto complex in one of its possible inflections. The cultural ascendancy of individuals and groups that hold apocalyptic beliefs, whether in the manner of fundamentalist preachers like Savonarola in 1490–92 and David Koresh of the Branch Davidians in 1992–93 or politicians influenced by fundamentalism like Reagan in 1981–84 and Bush in 2001–04, coincided consistently with periods of Saturn-Pluto alignments. Apocalyptic attitudes were regularly interconnected with antagonistic or indifferent attitudes towards nature and the present world, which encouraged policies of exploitation or destruction that at once ratified the sense of religious separation from nature and served to hasten the anticipated apocalypse.[11]

The War Between Man and Nature

The Saturn-Pluto planetary cycle and archetypal complex appears to be closely associated with many phenomena and tendencies in which the "war between man and nature" is a central theme. Freud's battle between the superego and the id, Hobbes's conflict between a controlling government authority and nature's state of endless war, Augustine's and Calvin's obsessive drive to negate the claims of instinct and repress sexuality, related motifs of world rejection in Puritanism and fundamentalist Christianity, apocalyptic beliefs, punitive asceticism and body hatred, fear of or disgust towards sexuality, fear of nature's elemental power, the impulse to dominate or avenge oneself on nature, whale hunting and big-game hunting, corporate devastation of the environment, the objectification of nonhuman nature, certain forms of mechanistic science and industrial technology— are all diverse expressions of this archetypally constellated tension.

Each of the terms in the familiar phrase "the war between man and nature" reflects presuppositions that are usually unconscious and are rooted in themes central to the Saturn-Pluto complex: the metaphor of "war," with its implication of an established state of ongoing intentional mutual mass violence and murderous antagonism; the narrow masculine heroic symbolization implicit in "man," used to represent the larger human condition and human community, this long-conventional term in Western and modern thought deeply grounded in and dependent upon its implied gendered exclusivity; and finally "nature" itself as a distinct substantive noun, a defined and objectified entity that is at some level essentially separate from and antagonistic to "man," with the unconscious image of a powerful and threatening Mother Nature lurking in the background.

Several characteristic motifs of the Saturn-Pluto complex are visible in this archetypal "war": first, a focus on those aspects of nature that are harsh, punishing, problematic, constricting and depriving, overpowering, mortally threatening; second, the fear of nature producing a compensatory need to defend against, control, defeat, punish, or destroy nature; third, an emphasis on predatory and murderous instincts in both human beings and the rest of nature; fourth, a tendency to draw a sharp and rigid boundary between man and nature in such a way as to see the latter as radically "other," inferior, unconscious, soulless, insensitive to pain, incapable of suffering, bestial, subhuman, and self-evidently undeserving of the rights and respectful treatment as would be merited by a human being; fifth, in a scientific variant, the impulse to objectify and constrain nature to master it (vividly embodied in Francis Bacon, born with the Saturn-Pluto square), often combined with a belief in nature's ultimate calculability and absolute causal determinism (as in the paradigmatic figure of the Enlightenment scientist–mathematician Pierre-Simon Laplace, born with the Saturn-Pluto conjunction); and sixth, in counterpoint to all of the above, an ecological perspective dominated by a view of nature as the victim of ruthless human exploitation: objectified, dissected, imprisoned, factory-farmed, clear-cut, cruelly experimented upon, devastated, made extinct. (Thus Schopenhauer: "One might say with truth, Mankind are the devils of the earth, and the animals the souls they torment.")

Natal hard aspects involving Saturn and Pluto are regularly found, for example, in the charts of individuals with a pronounced impulse to kill wild animals, such as big-game hunters like Ernest Hemingway and Theodore Roosevelt, or leaders of organizations like the National Rifle Association such as Charlton Heston. (Historically, the close relationship between European imperial ambitions for dominance in Africa and Asia and demands by European elites for ever-expanding access to territories for big-game hunting is also relevant to this archetypal complex.) Sometimes, however, as with the three whaleships, the *Essex*, the *Ann Alexander*, and the *Pequod* in *Moby Dick*, the tables are turned.

The theme of nature's destructive and elemental power, and the need for extreme feats of human fortitude in response, can be seen in the case of the Shackleton expedition to Antarctica during the Saturn-Pluto conjunction of 1914–16. The expedition's ship, *Endurance*, became entrapped in the pack ice of the Antarctic Weddell Sea and then crushed by the ice pressure. For nearly two years the twenty-eight men were stranded in relentless cold and dark with little shelter or food before finally making their harrowing escape. Jack London, born with the Saturn-Pluto square, repeatedly explored identical themes in his writings, as in his memorable short story *To Build a Fire*. The starkly realistic film *Quest for Fire*, produced during the Saturn-Pluto conjunction 1981–82, wordlessly depicted the primordial life of Ice Age humans in a state of nature that constantly threatened individual and group survival, was brutally indifferent to human existence, and required acts of desperate courage and extreme physical stamina merely to endure.

Conversely, this same planetary cycle and archetypal complex was closely associated with both eras and individuals possessed by a pronounced sense of nature's ruthless exploitation by human activity—rapacious corporate treatment of the environment, the destruction of the subtle balance of nature, cruelty to animals, and so forth—with the felt need to take decisive action in response. The Society for the Prevention of Cruelty to Animals, for example, was founded during the Saturn-Pluto opposition of 1866, the one immediately following the conjunction coincident with the publication of *Moby Dick*. Similarly, Rachel Carson, the mother of the modern environmental movement, was born during the first Saturn-Pluto square of the twentieth century, in 1907. The Australian moral philosopher Peter Singer, the founder of the animal rights movement and the International Association of Bioethics, was born during the Saturn-Pluto conjunction of 1946. Singer's *Animal Liberation*, the seminal work in this field, which grew out of developments during the 1960s' Uranus-Pluto conjunction, was written and published in coincidence with the Saturn-Pluto square of 1973–75. The Endangered Species Act of 1973 was passed by the U.S. Congress during the same alignment. The very first law in the United States protecting endangered species was passed in 1966 during the immediately preceding Saturn-Pluto opposition.

Both of the two most recent Saturn-Pluto axial alignment periods, 1981–84 and 2000–04, brought not only the empowerment of antienvironmental administrations and policies but also a marked intensification of environmentalist commitment and a rapid increase in membership in major ecological organizations.

The perceived empowerment and depredations of the one side catalyzed and galvanized the will of the other to defend and protect. Both sides were informed and driven by the same highly activated archetypal complex but in diametrically opposite ways. During the latter period, there was decisively constellated in the collective psyche a set of interconnected Saturn-Pluto motifs: a sharply heightened consciousness of nature's inherent limits, the accelerating reality of the mass extinction crisis, the potential exhaustion of the Earth's resources that threatened to destabilize international relations and cause devastating wars, and the looming possibility of severe climate change that would lead to catastrophe.

A concise reflection of several such themes is the widely read book by the geologist and evolutionary biologist Jared Diamond, *Collapse: How Societies Choose to Fail or Succeed*, written during the most recent Saturn-Pluto opposition of 2000–04. Examining the histories of a wide range of extinct civilizations, Diamond analyzed the ways in which societies, blinded by fixed cultural assumptions, determine their own fate and destroy themselves through systematic mismanagement of natural resources that leads to a general ecological collapse.

At the same time Diamond was writing *Collapse*, a very different concise statement of Saturn-Pluto themes was issued by the U.S. Air Force Space Command, under the leadership of Donald Rumsfeld. The Space Command's *Strategic Master Plan 2004 and Beyond* declared its mission to attain ultimate warfare advantage and global military dominance by achieving "ownership" of space, which would provide the capability for launching an instant attack against any location on the Earth: "A viable prompt global strike capability, whether nuclear or non-nuclear, will allow the US to rapidly strike high-payoff, difficult-to-defeat targets from stand-off ranges and produce the desired effect." But, the *Master Plan* warned, "we cannot fully *exploit* space until we *control* it." (Emphasis in original.)

As with all archetypal complexes, it seems that both sides of the larger Saturn-Pluto gestalt are always carried within its dynamic interplay, as polar complements that are mutually implicated and that together constitute the larger complex. This observation represents an essential element of the archetypes' multivalent potentiality—and thus the corollary human choice and responsibility—that is intrinsic to the perspective and the correlations set forth in this book. Here one thinks of the moral realism, expressed in a vivid Saturn-Pluto metaphor, in this utterance by Melville's old black cook on the *Pequod*: "If you gobern de shark in you, why den you be angel; for all angel is not'ing more dan de shark well goberned."

Moral Courage, Facing the Shadow, and the Tension of Opposites

It is always necessary to remind ourselves of the complex nature of these archetypal principles and the multivalent potential of their concrete enactments. In particular, it is important to call attention here to the profoundly noble dimension of the Saturn-Pluto archetypal gestalt that was evident in many of these phenomena and that was equally expressive of the principles involved. For alignments of Saturn and Pluto regularly seemed to coincide with the calling forth, both individually and collectively, of unusually sustained effort and resolution, intense focus and discipline with minimal resources, and exceptional courage and acts of will in the face of extreme danger, hardship, death, and moral darkness. The firefighters and police who ascended the World Trade Center towers after the terrorist attacks in 2001 are paradigmatic examples. So too are Churchill and the British when they stood alone against the overwhelming dominance of Nazi Germany in the dark days of 1939–41.

Another example was the situation of committed environmentalists and indigenous peoples who confronted the grim realities of mass species extinction, habitat destruction, global warming, and the Earth's vast ecological crisis, all unfolding and accelerating at the same moment as government and corporate antienvironmental forces, especially in the United States, were unprecedentedly empowered and their policies became dominant beginning in the 2000–04 period. The experience of confronting, and perhaps achieving, what absolutely *must* be accomplished in the face of overwhelming, apparently insurmountable obstacles and resistance—as in the virtually inexpressible experience of a mother in hard labor at excruciating stages of the birth process, or Sisyphus's persevering against all hope to push the massive boulder up the mountain— seems to be close to the heart of the Saturn-Pluto archetypal complex.

As dark and problematic as was its shadow, this archetypal complex seemed equally capable of constellating actions, transformations, and enduring social-political consequences involving extraordinary moral determination as well as sheer physical and volitional effort. Whether for good or ill, such periods seemed to coincide consistently with a collective sense of stern purposefulness and determination, a galvanizing of the will against overwhelming odds, grim resolution in the face of extreme danger. Acts of personal or societal self-denial, intense hard labor, sustained commitment to an arduous task, and a radical deepening of gravitas in the collective psyche were typical.[12]

A frequent theme of correlations with this cycle was the sustained mobilization of collective will and resources to meet a life-and-death emergency, as was visible in the September 11 catastrophe. A paradigmatic example was the American and British airlift in response to the Soviet blockade of West Berlin during the Saturn-Pluto conjunction of 1948, in which thousands of aircraft flew in 4,500 tons of food and supplies every day for over a year to prevent the two million residents of West Berlin from succumbing either to starvation or Soviet occupation. All of these themes were archetypally relevant—the sustained fortitude and disciplined organization and deployment of massive resources on the one hand, the threat of starvation and oppression on the other, in a darkly encompassing atmosphere of mortal danger and grave geopolitical consequences—each reflecting a different dimension of the Saturn-Pluto complex.

Equally characteristic of this archetypal complex was the task of rebuilding out of the rubble of destruction, as in the deployment of the Marshall Plan and the vast rebuilding of Europe after World War II during the conjunction of 1946–48. A more recent expression of this same theme was the herculean labor of clearing and cleaning the immense mass of destruction at Ground Zero, the site of the World Trade Center in Manhattan, restoring structures, and stabilizing the deep underground foundations and containments destroyed or threatened by the collapse.

During these same alignments, many less dramatic and less extreme versions of all these tendencies—rebuilding from the ashes of destruction, coping with apparently insurmountable problems, the sustained mobilization of resources and will in situations of mortal crisis, the courageous encounter with danger or evil, facing death and intense suffering, unflinching realism of judgment, relentless discipline—were evident in other contexts and were expressed on a smaller scale, in more personal and private circumstances, and with less graphic intensity.

We see during Saturn-Pluto alignments a greatly increased collective tendency to confront the moral shadow of humanity. This was visible, for example, during the conjunction of the 1946–48 period, when the world for the first time faced the full horror and evil of the Holocaust, with the Nuremberg trials of the Nazi war criminals, the showing of films of the Nazi concentration camps taken at the end of the war, and the publication of the first books about the camps. The atmosphere at those trials of grave moral and legal judgment, of the confrontation with horrific evil, of "man's inhumanity to man" were all highly characteristic of this archetypal gestalt.

That same Saturn-Pluto conjunction also coincided with widespread public assimilation of and reflection on the American dropping of atomic bombs on Hiroshima and Nagasaki, as articulated, for example, in John Hersey's powerful

1946 account, *Hiroshima*.[13] In a lecture at the Massachusetts Institute of Technology during this conjunction in 1947, J. Robert Oppenheimer, the head of the Manhattan Project which produced the bomb, expressed this emerging dark awareness with an Augustine-like confession of collective moral responsibility and fall: "In some sort of crude sense which no vulgarity, no humour, no overstatement can quite extinguish, the physicists have known sin; and this is a knowledge which they cannot lose." Together, the Holocaust and the atomic bombings brought forth a wave of intensive moral reflection on the dark reality of human cruelty and violence, the horror of mass death and suffering, and the nature of individual and collective moral responsibility and guilt in the face of such events. This same phenomenon was again evident in the period after September 11, 2001, in the extraordinary outpouring of moral reflection on the human capacity for evil and violence, and on the dark side of both religious fundamentalism and Western economic triumphalism.

Another wave of moral deliberation on these same themes, and on the nature of war and the violent deployment of unilateral power in an interdependent world, occurred in the period just before and after the Bush administration's decision to invade Iraq in March 2003 during the later part of the same Saturn-Pluto opposition. During the immediately preceding opposition, in 1964–67 during the escalation of the United States' war in Vietnam, there occurred a similar emergence of collective moral judgment against the Johnson administration's war policies and what was regarded by many as unprovoked military aggression and destruction being visited upon many innocent people. In both cases during these two consecutive Saturn-Pluto oppositions, the actions taken by those in power, with motivations and tactics very much reflective of this archetypal complex, commenced a long, unanticipated (by those in power) cycle of chaotic violence, suffering, and destruction.

During the 2000–04 opposition period there also took place major Nuremburg-like trials before the World Court in The Hague for war crimes that had taken place in Bosnia and Rwanda during the preceding square of Saturn-Pluto in 1992–94. This period also coincided with the international revulsion against the torture and sexual humiliation of prisoners by the United States in Iraq, which brought widespread calls for judgment and the prosecution of the guilty. A similar dynamic was evident in the Bush administration's sanctioning of cruelly abusive treatment of prisoners in Guantánamo Bay, Cuba, in the wake of the war in Afghanistan, its rejection of the international human rights standards defined by the Geneva Convention, and its clandestine exporting of suspects to other countries to be interrogated and tortured.

The archetypal dynamic at work in these phenomena—from Nazism and the Nuremburg trials to the Vietnam War, September 11, and the war in Iraq— is complex. The two principles combine in multiple ways within the same phenomenon: The Saturn-Pluto complex is at once the tyranny exerted by terrorism (the Pluto→Saturn vector) and also the grimly determined effort to oppose and obliterate terrorism (the Saturn→Pluto vector). It is also the tyranny of a society imprisoned by its own antiterrorist fears, controls, and rigidities, like the obsessive mole in Kafka's *The Burrow*. And it is a state that is willing to murder thousands of innocent people to effect its implacable purpose of exterminating the evil enemy. The mobilization of structures of power against evil often moves the agents of that power, when possessed by their shadow, into the grip of the very forces they perceive so vividly in the enemy.

In one sense, the negative Saturn and Pluto principles synergistically combine in the various events and acts being confronted: the trauma and crisis of war, the efficiently organized violence and deployment of vast destructive power, the victimization of the powerless, the mass death and end of innocence. We also see the negative Saturn principle acting against an at least partly projected Plutonic principle, the evil without, and simultaneously being driven by inner Plutonic impulses, as in Freud's sadistic superego: the deployment of violence and terror under the guise of moral rightness, a just cause, God's will, national security, law and order—the harsh repression by an established government, the objectifying of the other, the radical splitting between good self and evil enemy.

Yet in another sense, in the ensuing drama of critical moral reflection, we see the Saturnian conscience standing in judgment against the Plutonic forces of war and unleashed instincts, reflecting a positive expression of the superego countering and judging the id: confronting and naming the inhuman cruelty and violence, the bestial evil, the holocaustal and nuclear horror, the ethnic cleansing, the predatory imperialism. Finally, the Pluto archetype gives intensity and depth to Saturn's judgment, profundity to its moral assessment. It empowers the impulse to penetrate to an underlying, foundational hard truth, a moral confrontation with the self or other, sometimes on a mass scale. The positive and negative manifestations of the same complex are inextricably intertwined. All these dimensions of the archetypal dialectic, all these distinct embodiments of both a Saturn→Pluto vector and a Pluto→Saturn vector, are working simultaneously in the phenomena we are examining.[14]

We see this complexity embodied in an especially paradigmatic form in the great figure of Augustine, the originator of so much that shaped the Western spirit and forged its conscience. Writing during the death throes of the western Roman Empire and classical civilization, Augustine was painfully aware of the cruelty, evil, and suffering that human beings inflict on each other. He saw the ravages of war and mass violence, rape, murder, and corruption that so pervaded his age. He shrewdly dissected the psychological processes by which small decisions lead to enduring habits, which in turn forge ineluctable chains binding the human spirit. In his own dramatic spiritual journey, Augustine brought a relentless intensity of moral judgment to bear on his own soul and life, always in the service of forging a deeper relationship to the God of absolute goodness and light he so fervently loved. Yet it was this very luminosity of the divine and the transcendent that by contrast placed the human being and the created world in such deep shadow.

In view of the great diversity with which revelations of the divine have been experienced by human beings over the millennia, I found it of considerable interest that when Augustine had his powerful conversion experience in the garden of Milan in September 386, Saturn was square Pluto in the sky—just as it was at his birth, precisely one full cycle earlier—having moved at that time to within 2° of exact alignment. The entire character of Augustine's famous conversion experience as he later described it in the *Confessions*, from the acute physical torment produced by the extremity of his interior conflict to the specific message conveyed by the words from Paul's Letter to the Romans that produced Augustine's revelatory transformation, bear the unmistakable signs of a highly activated Saturn-Pluto complex.

As his ordeal that dramatic day reached a climax of intensity, Augustine groaned and thrashed about in a frenzy of spiritual agony, tearing his hair out and battering his forehead. He felt imprisoned by his base instincts and frustrated beyond words by his incapacity to turn his will in the chaste spiritual direction he wished. Finally, after hearing a child's voice mysteriously repeating *"Tolle, lege, tolle, lege"* ("Pick up and read"), in desperation he took in hand the nearby book of Paul's epistles, opened it at random, and read in silence the first passage upon which his eyes fell: "Not in reveling and drunkenness, not in debauchery and licentiousness, not in quarreling and jealousy. Instead, put on the Lord Jesus Christ, and make no provision for the flesh, to gratify its desires" (Romans, 13:13–14). With those fatefully relevant words, he "did not want to read further, there was no need to. For as soon as I reached the end of this sentence, it was as though my heart was filled with a light of confidence and all the shadows of my doubts were swept away."

The scriptural passage that opened the way for the subsequent unfolding of Augustine's spiritual life—and the spiritual life of those millions of Catholics and Protestants who would be shaped by his experience in the following fifteen hundred years—was one that seemed to speak a decisive judgment against the sinful futility of his past life and called upon him to turn away from his submission to licentiousness to surrender to the absolute transcendent purity of God's will. Augustine's failing struggle with his own will and instincts, his sense of being enslaved by physical desires, the excruciating birth-labor frenzy of his interior ordeal: all these classic expressions of the Saturn-Pluto archetypal complex were suddenly resolved in a powerful numinous experience.

Augustine also had at this time a once-in-a-lifetime personal transit of Neptune crossing in exact conjunction with his natal Pluto. As we will see later when we discuss Dostoevsky, this is a transit that I found frequently coincided with unusually intense imaginative and spiritual experiences (Pluto→Neptune), in exceptional cases marked by an overwhelming numinosity. Often these experiences constituted a dialectic of some kind between the biological-instinctual (Pluto) and the spiritual-imaginal (Neptune) dimensions of existence, between nature and spirit, as the two interpenetrated in an experience at once visceral and numinous.

The elemental potency of that day's spiritual resolution to Augustine's long ordeal never left him. The terms of that resolution were pervaded by an overpowering sense of a divine light of goodness that was sharply opposed in character to the shadows of his own bodily passions. The negation of his erotic instincts, the characterization of sexuality as a kind of enslavement, the affirmation of a higher morality as based upon a life of sexual constraint, the continuing presence of remorse and guilt in his inner life—all suggest that this dominant Saturn-Pluto complex in Augustine's psyche and biography was strongly constellated, but now with all the elemental force of an overpowering spiritual transformation.

Throughout his stormy interior journey, Augustine had been drawn to religious and philosophical positions, such as Platonism and Manichaeism, that were marked by a dualistic depreciation of the physical body and the natural world in favor of a transcendent spiritual purity. This profound polarity, so characteristic of many of the Axial Age religions across much of the ancient world, was one that Augustine, by all accounts the most complexly self-reflective person of his age, seems to have experienced as an especially acute tension of opposing impulses within himself. When his spiritual crisis finally reached its breaking point, the resolution he experienced was a decisive affirmation of one side of the polarity and an equally emphatic negation of the other. The many implications inherent in that negation—his theological views of the body, nature, sexuality, women, conception and birth; his understanding of evil, guilt, original sin, hell, damnation, predestination; his commitment to the absolute authority of the Church, his dualistic vision of history, his image of God and redemption—all seem to have reflected his personal resolution of conflicts and themes that are deeply associated with the Saturn-Pluto archetypal complex.

The spiritual power and potent dualism of Augustine's conversion produced an authoritative structure of religious belief and psychological attitude that permeated the subsequent evolution of the Western spirit. The inward conflict between opposing drives that precipitated his conversion experience was directly passed on to future generations of striving Christians in the form of a continuing impossible tension between the spiritual quest and the sexual instincts. Underlying and informing this continuing legacy was the larger tension Augustine experienced between the transcendent divine and the embodied human, with the interior struggle, guilt, and morally tinged polarization between the sexes that this tension undergirded.

We turn now to Jung, in whose work and sensibility the sustained, penetrating contemplation of the human shadow was so strongly marked. Like Augustine, Jung himself was born with Saturn and Pluto in square aspect, within 1° of exact alignment. Throughout his life, Jung stressed the critical need for the modern self to become aware of its shadow, which he named, recognized as an archetypal principle, and examined in the traumas of twentieth-century history: the shadow of European civilization, the shadow of modern man, the shadow of modern technology, the shadow of patriarchy and masculine one-sidedness, the shadow of Christianity, the shadow of the conscious ego, the shadow within each individual. "It is indeed no small matter to know of one's own guilt and one's own evil, and there is certainly nothing to be gained by losing sight of one's shadow. . . . Without guilt, unfortunately, there can be no psychic maturation and no widening of the spiritual horizon." For Jung, even the evolving God (or God-image) of the biblical tradition has been compelled to encounter and assimilate his own shadow in the course of his coevolving relationship with the human self. In *Answer to Job*, his most historically incisive and consequential work from the last years of his life, Jung wrestled with the Yahweh of stern omnipotence and apocalyptically violent retribution—like Augustine and Calvin, like Melville, like Job himself—as if in an historical lineage of powerful prophetic encounters with the Saturn-Pluto dimension of the divine.

The very notion of the shadow as Jung conceived it represents an intricate synthesis of the two planetary principles: from Saturn, the motifs of judgment, guilt and shame, suppression and repression, splitting and separation, denial, the inferior, that which is regretted and negated; and from Pluto, those aspects of the self that constitute its "underworld," the instincts, the dark depths of the personality, the animal-like, the often ruthless and ugly, serving impulses for power, domination, lust, and other drives yet also representing that healthy instinctuality from which healing, wholeness, and a higher consciousness can ultimately emerge.

The frequent tone in Jung's writings of intense moral urgency and historical gravity was highly characteristic of this archetypal complex, as was his tendency towards sternness of judgment. So also was his continuing emphasis on the fateful determining power of the archetypal unconscious over human life and history, beyond any assumed control of the rational self, if not attended to, differentiated, articulated, made conscious. At times, Jung's sensitivity to this power of archetypal forces to shape and dominate human life from the depths of the collective unconscious, and his awareness of the powerful apocalyptic tendencies at work in twentieth-century history, almost overwhelmed his belief in the capacity of the individual self to be the "makeweight that tips the scales," "that infinitesimal unit on whom a world depends."

Many of the themes that we see in Jung involving moral gravity and histori-cal judgment, guilt and responsibility, the power of fate and determinism, divine omnipotence and the existence of evil can also be recognized in other figures we have discussed in these chapters on the Saturn-Pluto complex, from Augustine to Calvin to Schopenhauer, who deeply affected Jung in his formative years.[15] But in Jung these themes took a new form of psychologically complex reflection, with new possibilities for moral and historical evolutionary development. Espe-cially relevant to this new psychological potential is Jung's central recognition that the shadow contains sources of vital energy whose suppression in the un-conscious contributes to its destructive, distorting, and corrupting character, yet whose integration permits its regenerative and creative potential to be released.

There was another crucial motif in Jung's life and thought that clearly re-flected the Saturn-Pluto archetypal complex in a manner different from that of facing the shadow, though in the end highly relevant to that very task. This was the importance Jung gave to the challenge of fully engaging the inevitable con-flict of opposing forces in life, of holding the often unbearable tension of oppo-sites in the psyche, even to the point of its feeling like a crucifixion. Here we see the Saturn principle of tension, polarity, contradiction, and conflict intensified to titanic proportions by the Plutonic principle, sometimes constellating an experi-ence of agonizing pain, either psychological or physical, as we saw in Augustine. What seems to have made this tension of opposites both so dominant and so fraught with what seemed to Jung impossible complexity in his own psyche and biography was the additional factor, evident throughout his work, of the Prome-thean impulse towards emancipation and change (Uranus) being simultaneously *bound by* yet *working through and by means of* this unbending conflict of oppos-ing forces (Saturn-Pluto).

Like Augustine, Schopenhauer, Marx, and Melville, Jung was born with both Saturn-Pluto *and* Uranus-Pluto in hard aspect (in Jung's case this was in a T-square configuration, with Saturn and Uranus in opposition, and Pluto square to both). Again, in the lives of these several individuals who were born with all three planets in hard-aspect configuration, and also in the historical periods in which such three-planet alignments have occurred, I found this planetary com-bination to be associated with an especially challenging archetypal dynamic in which the entire range of conflicts that characterize the dialectic between the Promethean principle and the Saturnian—between change and resistance to change, future and past, creative unpredictability and ineluctable order, freedom and oppression, disruption and stability, innovation and tradition, *puer* and *senex*—tended to be intensified to the extreme. The period of the mid-1960s, the last time these three planets were all in hard aspect with each other (Saturn opposite the Uranus-Pluto conjunction), provides us with an easily recalled ex-ample of this complicated archetypal dialectic, with that era's extraordinary so-cial and political turmoil, and the many deep schisms that emerged in those years that continue to influence American society and the global community.

Yet in Jung, as in other individuals or eras with this alignment, I found that the presence of the Promethean principle as a third factor in the Saturn-Pluto complex of overwhelmingly intensified conflict appeared to provide not only a further problematic dimension to the conflict that increased its seemingly impossible challenge, but also a new possibility for creative resolution of the antagonistic polarities. On the one hand, it produced a situation in which the impulse for change and freedom was simultaneously activated yet bound and imprisoned by the Saturn-Pluto complex, a state of "Prometheus Bound": Saturn/Pluto→Uranus. On the other hand, in keeping with its archetypal nature, the Promethean principle also appeared to provide a certain potentiality of unexpected liberation *by means of* and *through* the titanically intensified and ineluctable conflict: Uranus→Saturn/Pluto. Remarkably, Shelley wrote *Prometheus Unbound*, in which Prometheus is finally liberated in the dramatic unfolding of just such an archetypal dialectic, in 1820 when just this configuration occurred—the same triple Saturn-Uranus-Pluto alignment that coincided with the births of Melville and Marx, whose work similarly engaged this dialectic.

At its most profound, this resolution to the archetypal tension of opposites seemed to occur not by means of a successful one-sided identification with one pole that somehow eventually defeated the other, as happened with, for example, Marx and Augustine (labor *over* capital, or spirit *over* nature), but rather—as Jung so often emphasized—by sustaining the tension that relentlessly pulled at one from both sides. By strenuously maintaining fidelity to each of the opposing principles—conscience *and* instinct, superego *and* id, individual *and* community, tradition *and* innovation, masculine *and* feminine, conscious *and* unconscious, fate *and* free will, or whatever other polarity is present—there then may arise, though with no assurance of when or how, the sudden resolution of the tension and a deep structural transformation, despite the apparently irresolvable imprisonment and darkness of the current polarized condition.

As regards the long historical evolution of the Western psyche and spirit, these two paradigmatic figures, Jung and Augustine, were born with nearly identical configurations of the three planets we have been studying, and in their lives and thought they worked with highly similar archetypal dynamics and tensions. Because Jung came at a much later stage of the immense historical development in which Augustine stood nearer the beginning, he was able to draw upon what had been suffered through, discovered, and forged over the intervening centuries. This long development included the increasing incarnational movement towards the natural world and the body as represented in their various, often conflicting ways by so many protagonists of the later Western spiritual tradition, Rousseau, Goethe, Schopenhauer, Darwin, Nietzsche, and Freud, among many others. In this task Jung also benefited by the crucial influence of the extraordinary women in his life, above all Emma Jung and Toni Wolff.

Supported and impelled by this enormous historical development as well as these enduring relationships, Jung was able to engage and work through in a new way many of the sharp polarities presented to him by both the Christian tradition and the modern mind, and to confront, as much as he was able, the shadow within Christianity, within the modern mind, and within himself. With considerable courage and fortitude, he also attempted to sustain the tension of opposites in the larger human condition, and to bring forth a new and different resolution to the spiritual demands of the modern age. Hence we see Jung's immense labors and genuinely titanic struggles with the great cultural schisms of his and our time, to integrate the opposites between science and religion, spirit and nature, inner and outer, feminine and masculine.

When he was seventy years old, Jung movingly articulated just this archetypal drama and dynamic in a letter to a woman who experienced herself as trapped between conflicting demands of career and family:

> Dear Frau Frobe,
> . . . There can be no resolution, only patient endurance of the opposites which ultimately spring from your own nature. You yourself are a conflict that rages in itself and against itself, in order to melt its incompatible substances, the male and the female, in the fire of suffering, and thus create that fixed and unalterable form which is the goal of life. Everyone goes through this mill, consciously or unconsciously, voluntarily or forcibly. We are crucified between the opposites and delivered up to the torture until the "reconciling third" takes shape. Do not doubt the rightness of the two sides within you, and let whatever may happen, happen. The apparently unendurable conflict is proof of the rightness of your life. A life without inner contradiction is either only half a life or else a life in the Beyond, which is destined only for angels. But God loves human beings more than the angels.
> With kindest regards,
> C.G. Jung

Here, in the depth of authority and solidity of character that permeates these words, we see a further theme often evident in individuals born with Saturn-Pluto configurations. The experience of having suffered through an intense confrontation with the opposites and its relentless contradiction and inward compression, combined with a deep encounter with the shadow dimension of oneself and of existence, can sometimes result in a profound existential authority that communicates itself in the work and personality of such an individual. We see this in Jung, we see it in Augustine, we see it also in Melville and Marx. Depending on the extent of the confrontation and the depth of the resolution, the resulting qualities can be expressed as a rigid dogmatism and driven authoritarianism or as the authentic gravitas of a wisdom forged through suffering, time, and experience.

The same year that brought the birth of Jung, 1875, also brought the birth of

Rainer Maria Rilke, who was born with the same T-square between the three planets Saturn, Uranus, and Pluto. Remarkably, Rilke engaged precisely the same dialectic we have seen in Jung: the long psychological and spiritual challenge of struggling with and sustaining the tension of life's opposites to bring forth the new creation, the poetic birth, the divine child. Near the end of his life, after many years of deep striving and patient waiting for the inspiration that finally and fully graced him in the *Duino Elegies,* Rilke wrote the famous words that speak so directly to this challenge, with a vision virtually identical to Jung's, hard-won and epiphanic:

> *Take your well-disciplined strengths*
> *and stretch them between two opposing poles.*
> *Because inside human beings*
> *is where God learns.*

Paradigmatic Works of Art

The archetypal dimension is expressed in especially vivid and tangible form in the realm of art. Throughout our survey, we have seen the Saturn-Pluto cycle and archetypal complex associated with such themes as harsh oppression and constraint, crime and punishment, sin and judgment, trauma and retribution, rigid control and dark consequences, intensely challenging contradictions and tensions, the depths of shadow and moral discernment. I found that these same themes were consistently visible when I examined the creation of literary works produced during periods of Saturn-Pluto alignments. Orwell's *1984*, Melville's *Moby Dick*, and Kafka's *The Trial*, cited earlier, each eloquently reflective of this archetypal domain, were all written when Saturn and Pluto were in conjunction. I found that these correlations were part of much larger synchronic and diachronic patterns involving other paradigmatic works of literature equally reflective of the same archetypal field.

Thus Mary Shelley published *Frankenstein*, her prophetic Gothic masterpiece that depicted the monstrous shadow of the technological will to power, during the Saturn-Pluto conjunction of 1818—during the same year and conjunction that Schopenhauer published *his* dark masterwork of blind struggling will, *The World as Will and Idea*. During the immediately following Saturn-Pluto conjunction of 1850, Hawthorne published *The Scarlet Letter*, his powerful rendering of Puritan judgment and guilt, dark secrets and sexual transgression, scapegoating and public humiliation, unforgiving hardness and obsessive pursuit—this being the same conjunction that coincided with the writing and publication of Melville's *Moby Dick*. During the immediately following Saturn-Pluto opposition of 1865–67, Dostoevsky wrote and published *Crime and Punishment*, one of the supreme explorations of this archetypal domain. The immediately following Saturn-Pluto opposition in 1898–99 coincided with Conrad's *Heart of Darkness*, which depicted the horrific cruelty and evil of European exploitation of Africans in the jungles of the Congo ("the horror, the horror").

T. S. Eliot's classic poem of modernist pessimism, *The Waste Land*, was written during the Saturn-Pluto square in 1921–22. John Steinbeck's epic of human hardship, oppression, and endurance, *The Grapes of Wrath*, was published in 1939 during the immediately following square. During that same alignment of

1939–41 that coincided with the start of World War II, Albert Camus wrote both *The Stranger* (finished May 1940) and *The Myth of Sisyphus* (finished February 1941). Camus himself, so strongly identified with the figure of Sisyphus, and the author of other major works such as *The Fall* and *The Plague* that confronted the dark, inescapable, and morally problematic aspects of human existence, was born in November 1913 at the beginning of the Saturn-Pluto conjunction that coincided with the start of World War I. Similarly, Arthur Miller, whose plays consistently dealt with grave issues of moral conscience and oppressive social forces, was born during that same Saturn-Pluto conjunction, in 1915, and wrote the paradigmatic American tragedy *Death of a Salesman* in 1948 during the very next Saturn-Pluto conjunction—the same alignment that coincided with Orwell's writing of *1984*.

The common archetypal spirit, ambiance, and motifs that unite these many disparate works are easily recognizable and are all clearly associated with the Saturn-Pluto complex. These works are iconic in part precisely because of the eloquent intensity with which they articulated and embodied the profound and mysterious themes of this many-sided archetypal complex. Equally expressive were major works in other arts, such as the music composed during such alignments. For example, during the same Saturn-Pluto opposition of 1865–67 as Dostoevsky's *Crime and Punishment*, Mussorgsky composed his dark symphonic poem *Night on Bald Mountain*, which depicted the satanic rites of the Witches' Sabbath. This was the same alignment that coincided with the founding of the Ku Klux Klan, with its own dark rituals of burning crosses, death, hatred, and terror.[16]

Igor Stravinsky was born during the Saturn-Pluto conjunction in 1882 (the same one as Kafka) and composed *The Rite of Spring* in 1913 at age thirty when transiting Saturn crossed his natal Saturn-Pluto conjunction (hence during his Saturn return as well). Both the music of *The Rite of Spring* and its riot-torn premiere were prophetic of the eruption of destructive forces that would devastate European civilization during the Saturn-Pluto conjunction world transit of 1913–16. A few months later in 1914 during that same conjunction, Gustav Holst's darkly titanic opening movement of *The Planets* gave a more militaristic embodiment to the same primordial energy, in vivid anticipation of the totalitarian armies that would march, kill, and die across Europe in the three decades that started within a few weeks of Holst's completing the composition.[17] More recently, in 1967 Jim Morrison and the Doors' iconic song of apocalyptic descent and the eruption of murderous instinct, *The End*, coincided with the Saturn-Pluto opposition of 1964–67 and the American war in Vietnam.

A different expression of the mid-Sixties' combination of the Uranus-Pluto revolutionary impulse with the Saturn-Pluto complex was Bob Dylan's epoch-making *Like a Rolling Stone*, recorded in 1965. The intensity of stark judgment expressed with incantatory power that was heard again and again by millions seemed to serve as an initiatory catalyst for the era, moving it towards a harder existential maturity from a prelapsarian state of unconscious presumption and inauthenticity. Dylan's searing words and voice invoked such characteristic Saturn-Pluto themes as the end to naïveté and inflated privilege, the hard fall, the outcast, poverty and exile, the urban wilderness, relentless realism, the necessary descent into the fate of common humanity:

> How does it feel . . .
> To be on your own
> With no direction home
> Like a complete unknown
> Like a rolling stone?

So also in the other arts. In the history of film, Ingmar Bergman's stark, black-and-white masterpiece *The Seventh Seal*, an archetypal portrayal of the human encounter with death, was made during the immediately preceding Saturn-Pluto square of 1956. In the history of painting, an especially iconic example of this archetypal complex of themes, which coincided with the Saturn-Pluto opposition of 1536, is Michelangelo's *The Last Judgment*, with its powerful evocation of the fall into the underworld of damnation, mass suffering, absolute helplessness in the face of overwhelming divine condemnation.

Reflecting the same archetypal domain is Jonathan Edwards's most famous sermon, *Sinners in the Hands of an Angry God*, with its classic Calvinist portrayal of human corruption and God's omnipotence. Its vivid rendering of the damnation that awaits those who are not among the elect, with the sinner clinging like a spider to God's outstretched hand above the pit of hell, was delivered to his concerned Northampton congregation in July 1741 when Saturn and Pluto were within 1° of exact square alignment. This was exactly the same aspect—Saturn square Pluto—with which Calvin was born over two centuries earlier, and with which Augustine was born a thousand years before that—the two theologians most crucial in forging the metaphysical framework that underlay Edwards's vision of sin, hell, divine judgment, and the human condition.

Many of the most characteristic theological and psychological features of Puritanism, with its roots in Augustine and Calvin, can be recognized as direct expressions of the Saturn-Pluto archetypal complex in a peculiarly enduring and potent synthesis: the intensified forging of the moral consciousness, emerging from an inward struggle with opposing impulses and often self-contradictory theological doctrines; a view of God that combines extremely strict and punitive moral judgment with divine omnipotence and unquestionable goodness; the doctrine of predestination and the absolute determinism of God's will over all humanity; the pervasive consequences of the Fall, the inborn corruption of every human being because of Adam's original sin; the resulting loss of free will and incapacity of the human will on its own to choose other than sin; the eternal damnation that awaits the unelected majority of humankind; the cruelty of

God's divine retribution. All these constitute a doctrine that Calvin described as *horribilis,* to suggest both the terrifying and the awe-inspiring. Further expressions of the same complex in Puritanism are its characteristically negative judgment of sexuality and the rigorous suppression of the erotic and other natural instincts, including any activities suggestive of frivolity, sensual pleasure, and self-indulgence.

All of these themes find their most absolute expression in the ancient and medieval theological conception of hell, which can be understood as an exact synthesis of specific archetypal aspects of the two principles. On the one hand, from Saturn hell receives the motifs of finality and judgment, death and guilt, retribution, punishment and imprisonment, the consequences of error and sin, the strictures of divine law, the pervading experience of defeat and failure, suffering and affliction, separation and loneliness, bondage and constraint, the confinement to darkness and deprivation. On the other hand, reflecting the domain of Pluto, hell is the supreme embodiment of the fiery underworld. Hell's vividly Plutonic motifs include the unleashed instincts both human and divine, the demonic, the bestial, the scatological, decadence and decay, the grotesque, boundless horror, the ravenous flames of the chthonic depths. Here too can be seen Pluto's characteristic tendency towards extreme intensification of whatever archetype it interacts with, here serving to intensify all the Saturnian qualities to absolute and overwhelming extremes—horrific punishment, unspeakable suffering, absolute imprisonment, bottomless guilt, the relentless burden of infinitely extended time, eternal death, the end without end.

The most powerful depiction of hell in modern literature is the celebrated sermon from James Joyce's *A Portrait of the Artist as a Young Man.* In general, other archetypal dynamics are more prominent in Joyce's work, particularly ones associated with the Jupiter-Uranus-Neptune configuration of his birth. However, the familiar motifs of the Saturn-Pluto complex are given a richly expansive imaginative realization in the famous third chapter of the *Portrait,* which was published in 1914–15 during the Saturn-Pluto conjunction coincident with the beginning of World War I. The Irish Catholic preacher's vivid description of eternal damnation, heard in a state of terror by the young student stricken with sexual guilt, explores with exquisite precision and a darkly sublime eloquence every dimension of hell's eternal physical and spiritual agony. The solemn portrait of horror that unfolds is a summation of all the sermons on hell that had ever been given from ancient and medieval times to the moment of Joyce's rendering:

> Now let us try for a moment to realize, as far as we can, the nature of that abode of the damned which the justice of an offended God has called into existence for the eternal punishment of sinners. Hell is a strait and dark and foul-smelling prison, an abode of demons and lost souls, filled with fire and smoke. The straitness of this prison house is expressly designed by God to punish those who refused to be bound by

His laws. In earthly prisons the poor captive has at least some liberty of movement, were it only within the four walls of his cell or in the gloomy yard of his prison. Not so in hell. There, by reason of the great number of the damned, the prisoners are heaped together in their awful prison, the walls of which are said to be four thousand miles thick: and the damned are so utterly bound and helpless that, as a blessed saint, Saint Anselm, writes in his book on similitudes, they are not even able to remove from the eye a worm that gnaws it. . . .

Our earthly fire . . . no matter how fierce or widespread it may be, is always of a limited extent; but the lake of fire in hell is boundless, shoreless and bottomless. It is on record that the devil himself, when asked the question by a certain soldier, was obliged to confess that if a whole mountain were thrown into the burning ocean of hell it would be burned up in an instant like a piece of wax. And this terrible fire will not afflict the bodies of the damned only from without, but each lost soul will be a hell unto itself, the boundless fire raging in its very vitals. O, how terrible is the lot of those wretched beings! The blood seethes and boils in the veins, the brains are boiling in the skull, the heart in the breast glowing and bursting, the bowels a red-hot mass of burning pulp, the tender eyes flaming like molten balls.

And yet what I have said as to the strength and quality and boundlessness of this fire is as nothing when compared to its intensity, an intensity which it has as being the instrument chosen by divine design for the punishment of soul and body alike. It is a fire which proceeds directly from the ire of God, working not of its own activity but as an instrument of Divine vengeance. As the waters of baptism cleanse the soul with the body, so do the fires of punishment torture the spirit with the flesh. Every sense of the flesh is tortured and every faculty of the soul therewith: the eyes with impenetrable utter darkness, the nose with noisome odours, the ears with yells and howls and execrations, the taste with foul matter, leprous corruption, nameless suffocating filth, the touch with redhot goads and spikes, with cruel tongues of flame. And through the several torments of the senses the immortal soul is tortured eternally in its very essence amid the leagues upon leagues of glowing fires kindled in the abyss by the offended majesty of the Omnipotent God and fanned into everlasting and ever-increasing fury by the breath of the anger of the Godhead. . . .[18]

Here too could be cited iconic works brought forth by artists at the time they underwent personal Saturn-Pluto transits, such as Dante's *Inferno*, the ur-text of all subsequent renderings of hell, and Jean-Paul Sartre's *No Exit*, his modern existentialist version of hell where the condemned can never escape a self-tormenting state of endless interpersonal cruelty. So also works of artists who were themselves born during Saturn-Pluto alignments, such as Albrecht Dürer's classic woodcut of darkness and peril *Knight, Death, and the Devil* (anticipating both the themes and the aesthetic of Bergman's *The Seventh Seal*); Goethe's *Faust*, with its Mephstophelean tempter from hell who is the destructive "spirit who always negates"; Henry James's study of self-imprisoning obsession, *The Beast in the Jungle*; Frida Kahlo's many vivid paintings of death, extreme pain, and relentless constraint; and Arthur Miller's dramatic depiction of the Salem witch trials, *The Crucible*.

The characteristic upsurge of religious conservatism that coincides with Saturn-Pluto alignments often manifests in books and films that emphasize the aspects of Christian tradition that invoke the suffering and crucifixion of Christ, the darkness of the world, guilt and judgment. One of the most widely viewed and intensely discussed films of the most recent Saturn-Pluto opposition was *The Passion of the Christ*, produced and directed by Mel Gibson, who was himself born with Saturn and Pluto in hard aspect.[19] Many characteristic motifs of this archetypal complex were evident both in the film and in its larger cultural influence: the brutal realism, the confrontation with death, torture, excruciating suffering, judgment and execution, the crucifixion motif, the moral darkness and hatred, the continuing weight of the past, the conservative religious sensibility that was both expressed and empowered by the film, the religious divisiveness between Jews and Christians that was experienced in its wake, the atmosphere of grave accusation both within the film and against the film.

On occasion a work of art will portray a character whose qualities and motivations are so potently rendered as to become a kind of archetype in itself, to which actual individuals of similar qualities will be compared. Victor Hugo, for example, born with the Saturn-Pluto opposition, brought forth in *Les Misérables* an epic rendering of many Saturn-Pluto themes—vast human suffering and striving, crime and punishment, imprisonment and entrapment in a system of overwhelming social injustice—and a character who stands as an epitome of relentless persecutorial obsessiveness, Inspector Javert. Over a century later, the similarly relentless prosecutor Kenneth Starr in his obsession with the sexual transgressions of Bill Clinton was often compared to Javert. Starr was himself born with the Saturn-Pluto conjunction (in a quadruple conjunction with the Sun and Mercury). In these cases we can recognize the id-driven superego so characteristic of the Saturn-Pluto complex. Another literary precedent frequently cited by commentators during the Starr prosecution was Hawthorne's *The Scarlet Letter*—again, published under the same Saturn-Pluto conjunction as *Moby Dick* with its own obsessed persecutor Captain Ahab.

It is typical of artists born during Saturn-Pluto alignments to express many different facets of that archetypal complex in work after work, as if compelled to explore new possible inflections not yet fully enacted and embodied. Alfred

Hitchcock, for example, who was born in 1899 during the Saturn-Pluto opposition, brought forth an extraordinary succession of meticulously wrought films—*The 39 Steps*, *Sabotage*, *Suspicion*, *Spellbound*, *Notorious*, *I Confess*, *Dial M for Murder*, *Rear Window*, *Vertigo*, *North by Northwest*, *Psycho*, *The Birds*—that addressed a specific spectrum of motifs all associated with the Saturn-Pluto complex: mortal danger, extreme fear, murder, guilt, the hidden dark depths of human existence, sinister plots, helpless entrapment, horror and terror.[20]

The same year, 1899, and the same Saturn-Pluto opposition that coincided with the birth of Hitchcock also coincided with the birth of Ernest Hemingway, whose many novels and stories were equally emblematic of this complex, though they took a somewhat different range of inflections. Hemingway's lifelong concern with (and attraction to) war, death, killing, the grim brutality of life, and unflinching realism in the face of death and life's harshness are all suggestive of the Saturn-Pluto archetypal gestalt. Yet another side of the same complex is vividly expressed in Hemingway's late novel, *The Old Man and the Sea*, by the old fisherman's brave, unbending determination despite extreme hardship in a long battle with sharks, nature's elements, and death. Here too was the characteristic Saturn-Pluto theme, notable in Camus as well, of the inevitability of human defeat in an indifferent universe, yet also, like Sisphysus, the dignity of stoic endurance in the face of that dark truth.

In writers and artists born during Saturn-Pluto alignments like Hemingway and Hitchcock, I found that the creative work, the personality, and the life all tended to reflect the relevant archetypal motifs in an immediately recognizable manner, though, as always, in a multivalent diversity of forms. An especially poignant example is that of Franz Kafka, born in 1883 during the conjunction immediately preceding the opposition just cited for Hitchcock and Hemingway. Kafka's creative imagination seemed to serve as a lifelong stage upon which the characteristic motifs of this archetypal complex were enacted to an extreme, not only in those works already cited such as *The Trial*, *In the Penal Colony*, and *The Burrow*, but also in *The Judgment*, *The Metamorphosis*, *The Castle*, and *A Hunger Artist*, among many others. The titles themselves evoke many of the Saturn-Pluto themes—trial, judgment, punishment, imprisonment, torture, self-starvation, unspecified yet all-encompassing guilt—which are all portrayed with measured lucidity. Behind their particular renderings loomed a pervasive sense of the futility of the human condition before the incomprehensibility of God: "The state in which we find ourselves is sinful, quite independently of guilt . . . Only our concept of time makes it possible for us to speak of the Day of Judgment by that name: in reality it is a summary court in perpetual session."

We also know that the external circumstances of Kafka's life conspicuously reflected such motifs as well: his tyrannically critical and punitive father, the stultifying constraints of his work in the government bureaucracy, the oppressive confinement of Jewish life in Prague. These in turn paralleled the drama and tone of his inner life and personality, which are movingly depicted in his diaries:

the private hell of his ruthless self-judgment, his feelings of intolerable humiliation and impotence, his sense of helplessness against his father's overpowering
patriarchal domination. Contemplating the full gestalt of Kafka's life and work,
one would be hard-pressed to conceive of an overarching principle of order and
meaning more apt than the Saturn-Pluto archetypal complex in its capacity to
bring all the diverse motifs we recognize as quintessentially reflective of Kafka's
universe—as "Kafkaesque"—into a coherent unity. Whether he was depicting
the insanely pointless and diabolically defeating procedures of a totalitarian bureaucracy or an internal prison of relentless shame and self-disgust, his imaginative world possessed a pervasive consistency easily discerned by every reader. It
was saturated with a particular ambiance and spirit that was diffracted in multiple yet deeply coherent ways, with nightmarish clarity and intensity.[21]

While it was in Kafka's art rather than his external circumstances that the
full depths of the many archetypally relevant themes were explored, even here the
ambiguity between inner and outer realities again arises. For the highly wrought
character of Kafka's imaginative vision prophetically anticipated such all-too-real
historical developments as totalitarianism and the Holocaust, which were associated with the same archetypal complex and the same planetary cycle as it unfolded after his death. This prophetic and anticipatory dimension of art has often
been noted (as in Oscar Wilde's well-known statement, so acutely prophetic of
his own life: "Life imitates Art far more than Art imitates Life"). Yet the consistent coincidence of works of art and the events they anticipate with different
alignments of the same archetypally appropriate planetary cycle presents a new
dimension to the mystery of the creative imagination.

W. H. Auden, for example, who was born in 1907 with Saturn square Pluto,
wrote *September 1, 1939,* the poem that was widely circulated beginning on
the day of the World Trade Center attacks with a sense of wonder at its prophetic relevance. The poem itself was written during a Saturn-Pluto square exactly one full cycle after the birth of Auden. Saturn and Pluto were 1° from exact
alignment on the day commemorated in its title, when Nazi Germany invaded
Poland—just as the same two planets were again in nearly exact alignment on
the fateful September 11 of 2001.

> *Waves of anger and fear*
> *Circulate over the bright*
> *And darkened lands of the earth,*
> *Obsessing our private lives;*
> *The unmentionable odour of death*
> *Offends the September night. . . .*
>
> *What huge imago made*
> *A psychopathic god:*
> *I and the public know*

What all schoolchildren learn,
Those to whom evil is done
Do evil in return. . . .

Into this neutral air
Where blind skyscrapers use
Their full height to proclaim
The strength of Collective Man,
Each language pours its vain
Competitive excuse:
But who can live for long
In an euphoric dream;
Out of the mirror they stare,
Imperialism's face
And the international wrong . . .

Defenceless under the night
Our world in stupor lies. . . .[22]

Even without such uncanny specificity, an implicit collective awareness of the close archetypal kinship between such eras occurs consistently—books written, films produced, historical references spontaneously cited in essays and conversations—with of course no conscious knowledge that the same planetary alignment took place in both cases. While it is the parallel concrete details that are called attention to, it is the unspoken but potent archetypal identity and kinship between such eras that often underlies what is recognized and evoked. As discussed earlier, such spontaneous associations were widely in evidence during the 1981–84 period of climactic Cold War antagonism, when many observers anxiously recalled the similarly grave geopolitical tensions and crises that brought forth World War I during the same alignment in 1914. So also, in a different spirit of revolutionary upheaval and radical change, with the 1960s, the 1848 revolutions, the French Revolution, and other Uranus-Pluto eras we discussed in earlier chapters. Yet the occurrence of such spontaneous linkings is far more pervasive and remarkable than these particular connections between large-scale historical events might suggest.[23]

Often the unconscious resonance between such periods in an individual's personal life serves as a creative catalyst, as with experiences that are undergone earlier in an artist's life during one alignment and then given artistic embodiment at the time of the next such alignment. Joseph Conrad, for example, wrote *Heart of Darkness* in two months during the Saturn-Pluto opposition of 1898–99 (the one during which Hitchcock and Hemingway were born). The story was closely based on his deeply disturbing experience of witnessing atrocities in the Belgian Congo in 1890 during the exactly preceding Saturn-Pluto square. There he confronted the horrific consequences of European policies of imperial colonization of the "dark continent" that were promulgated in particular by Belgium's King Leopold II in 1889 during the same alignment. This was the same alignment that coincided with the battle of Wounded Knee, the 1890 massacre by the U.S. cavalry of three hundred unarmed Sioux men, women, and children in their encampment in South Dakota. This event marked the end of the last major Native American resistance to white settlement of the American continent.

In turn, the publication of *Heart of Darkness* in England in 1898 and the United States in 1899 during the immediately following Saturn-Pluto opposition played a major role in the emerging public debate on the dark reality of Western imperialism as it was reflected in European atrocities and systematic abuses in the Congo ("the most powerful thing ever written on the subject").[24] A parallel example of the same cultural phenomenon was the publication of Harriet Beecher Stowe's immensely influential *Uncle Tom's Cabin* during the Saturn-Pluto conjunction of 1852. It sold an unprecedented 300,000 copies within the year in the United States alone, going through 120 printings, and with comparable numbers of books sold abroad. Stowe's graphic descriptions of the cruelty of slavery were viewed by many, including Lincoln, as having played a crucial role in catalyzing the antislavery sentiment in the North that led to the Civil War. In the following letter written to Stowe by a friend, one glimpses both the power of the book's immediate effect on readers during that conjunction and the dual aspect of the Saturn-Pluto complex—the horrific suffering and oppression of slavery on the one hand, and the depth of moral passion and judgment in response:

My Dear Mrs. Stowe,

I sat up last night until long after one o'clock, reading and finishing "Uncle Tom's Cabin." I could *not leave* it any more than I could have left a dying child; nor could I restrain an almost hysterical sobbing for an hour after I laid my head upon my pillow. I thought I was a thoroughgoing abolitionist before, but your book has awakened so strong a feeling of indignation and of compassion, that I seem never to have had *any* feeling on this subject till now. But what *can* we do? Alas! Alas! what can we do? This storm of feeling has been raging, burning like a very fire in my bones all the livelong night, and through all my duties this morning it haunts me—I cannot away with it. Gladly would I have gone out in the midnight storm last night, and, like the blessed martyr of old, been stoned to death, if that could have rescued these oppressed and afflicted ones. But that would avail nothing. And now what am I doing? Just the most foolish thing in the world. Writing to you, who need no incitement; to you, who have spun from your very vitals this tissue of agony and truths; for I know, I feel, that there are burning drops of your heart's best blood here concentrated. To *you,* who need no encouragement or sympathy of mine, and whom I would not insult by praise—oh, no, you stand on too high an eminence for praise; but methinks I see the prayers of the poor, the blessings of those who are ready to perish, gathering in clouds about you, and forming a halo round your beloved head. And surely the tears of gentle, sympathizing childhood, that are dropping about many a Christian hearthstone over the wrongs and cruelties depicted by you so touchingly, will water the sod and spring up in bright flowers at your feet. And better still, I know—I see, in the flushing cheek, the clenched hand and indignant eye of the young man, as he dashes down the book and paces the room to hide the tears that he is too proud to show, too powerless to restrain, that you are sowing seed which shall yet spring up to the glory of God, to the good of the poor slave, to the enfranchisement of our beloved though guilty country.

Like so many in the antislavery movement, Harriet Beecher Stowe was deeply shaped by her Puritan religious background with its Calvinist and Augustinian roots. Her father and seven brothers were Congregational ministers, as were her husband and her son, and throughout her life Stowe's writing was driven by a moral passion that sought to instruct and reform, correct and edify, with literature as her pulpit. Like a healthy superego, the highly developed moral conscience that Puritanism helped forge can be seen as the positive form of the Saturn-Pluto archetypal complex, here associated with the religious experience of an all-powerful deity identified with absolute good governing a moral universe. The shadow side of the same complex can be recognized in the oppressive cruelty of the pathological superego, the internal slavemaster, the obsessive-compulsive neurotic structure, the life-denying puritanical conscience, the relentless compulsion for order, control, judgment, and inhibition. On the religious level, these themes are often associated with theological doctrines of primordial guilt, predestination, last judgment, and eternal damnation, and with the biblical portrait of apocalyptic vengeance and punitive tyranny embodied in the omnipotent Jehovah. (Thus Jung's distinctive combination of intense moral judgment and confrontation with the shadow side of the Judaeo-Christian God expressed in *Answer to Job*, with Jung gravely judging God's shadow.)[25] It is at this archetypal level that we can observe that paradoxical association of the merciless slavemaster, the inquisitional torturer, and the terrorist with absolute religious convictions and self-justifications, as they identify with the implacable righteousness of a deity—whether Jehovah or Allah—whose rigid boundaries and harsh judgments are absolute. Drawing on other resources in the biblical tradition and the evolving collective psyche, Stowe was able to assimilate from her Puritan Christian background the benign conscience-forging qualities of the Saturn-Pluto complex while recognizing and confronting the latter's shadow in the institution of slavery.

Similarly, Melville's *Moby Dick* was written and published at precisely the same time and during the same Saturn-Pluto conjunction as *Uncle Tom's Cabin*.

It too was shaped by the Puritan sensibility that Melville explored so penetratingly not only in the character of Ahab but in the novel's unfolding drama from its opening sermon to its apocalyptic climax. Both Stowe and Melville were born with Saturn and Pluto in hard aspect (in 1811 and 1819, respectively, during the successive square and conjunction), and both these works and their authors reflect the deep archetypal complexity of the Saturn-Pluto gestalt, and of Puritanism and the biblical religions generally. Completing this trinity of Saturn-Pluto masterworks of nineteenth-century American literature is Hawthorne's *The Scarlet Letter*, another paradigmatic exploration of the Puritan sensibility that was, remarkably, published in coincidence with the same Saturn-Pluto conjunction (1850–52) as *Moby Dick* and *Uncle Tom's Cabin*.

In their characters, plots, and moral vision, these three exactly synchronous novels exemplify the multiple, intersecting ways in which the Saturn-Pluto complex can be present in a single phenomenon. With Stowe, that complex was simultaneously visible, first, in her portrait of the sadistically tyrannical overseer Simon Legree; second, from the opposite side of the gestalt, in her rendering of the cruel suffering of the slaves; and third, in the intensity of her own moral passion, revulsion, and judgment. Similarly, in Melville's *Moby Dick*, the Saturn-Pluto complex was diffracted and diversely embodied in the extraordinary character of Ahab, in the figure of the whale as both victim and destroyer, and in Melville's own penetrating moral and psychological insight. So also in Hawthorne's *The Scarlet Letter*, where the same complex is simultaneously embodied in the obsessive persecutory character of Roger Chillingworth, in Hester Prynne's experience as both moral outcast and helpless victim, and in the depth of Hawthorne's own moral and psychological vision.

The polarized manifestations of a single archetypal complex during the same alignment can also be seen in the immediate historical context of Stowe's decision to write *Uncle Tom's Cabin*. She was especially driven to undertake the task by the passage of the Fugitive Slave Act by Congress in 1850 during this same Saturn-Pluto conjunction. The act made it a crime for citizens of free states to aid enslaved people who had escaped from slave states. The Fugitive Slave Act aroused widespread moral debate in the North on its legal enforcement of the "rights" of slaveowners to have runaway slaves arrested and returned to the South for punishment and continued enslavement.[26] The legalized empowerment of oppression, the compelling artistic rendering of that oppression from both sides of the slavery experience, the intense public encounter with and overwhelming response to that portrait, and finally the profound moral judgment against slavery's evil and cruelty—all reflect different yet intricately interconnected expressions of the Saturn-Pluto gestalt.

A comparable instance of this constellation of themes, which echoed Hawthorne's *The Scarlet Letter*, was visible during the most recent Saturn-Pluto opposition, between 2002 and 2004, in the decision by a Nigerian court under Islamic

Shariah law that condemned a young woman to death by stoning for adultery, the worldwide horror against that decision and judicial practice, and the collective pressure that was exerted on the Nigerian government to spare the woman's life.

Whether it is Stowe's *Uncle Tom's Cabin* and the Fugitive Slave Act or Hawthorne's *The Scarlet Letter* and Shariah adultery judgments (or, in another category, Melville's *Moby Dick* and the sinking of whaling ships by whales), the evidence suggests that specific archetypal gestalts become broadly constellated in the collective psyche in coincidence with specific planetary alignments, and that these are visible, both synchronically and diachronically, both in the artistic and philosophical expressions of a culture and in concrete historical events. Often, the two categories are closely linked. We have seen the same pattern in many other cases cited above, such as Augustine's *The City of God*, Conrad's *Heart of Darkness*, Freud's *Civilization and Its Discontents*, and Auden's *September 1, 1939*.

The Final Solution was conceived by Hitler and began to be deployed by the Nazis during the Saturn-Pluto square of 1939–41. The making or release of the most culturally influential films about the Holocaust coincided with extraordinary consistency with the following quadrature alignments of the Saturn-Pluto cycle. The sequence began during the Saturn-Pluto conjunction of 1946–48 with the public showing of the original documentary footage of the Nazi concentration camps, which with the Nuremberg trials of the same period first exposed the world to the full reality of the Holocaust's horror. This was followed in subsequent decades by Resnais's classic documentary *Night and Fog*, Lumet's *The Pawnbroker*, Pakula's *Sophie's Choice*, Lanzmann's *Shoah*, and Spielberg's *Schindler's List*, all produced in coincidence with Saturn-Pluto alignments.[27] The most recent such alignment, the Saturn-Pluto opposition, coincided with the making and release in 2002 of the most recent major Holocaust film, Polanski's *The Pianist*.

The characteristic spirit and aesthetic of the Saturn-Pluto complex, as well as the clear diachronic relationship to earlier historical events in the same cycle, are powerfully embodied in the Vietnam War Memorial in Washington that was designed by Maya Lin in 1981 and dedicated in 1982 in coincidence with the Saturn-Pluto conjunction of 1981–84 during the first Reagan adminstration. Here too is visible the diachronic pattern: the Vietnam War itself began—with fateful decisions made in that same city—during the immediately preceding Saturn-Pluto opposition of 1964–67. The memorial, with its immense solemnity and dark gravitas, its mute judgment on the war and on all war, its meticulous commemoration of death and suffering—57,692 names of Americans killed or missing in action in that war, etched in black granite—is itself an eloquent, enduring icon of the many historical and archetypal themes we have been examining.

This striking cyclical patterning continued during the most recent Saturn-

Pluto opposition, when in 2002, at the same time that the first steps were being taken in the design of the World Trade Center Memorial, and as the Jewish Holocaust Memorial was being constructed in Berlin, Maya Lin began working on a large memorial for the extinct species of the world.

The Dynamics of Tragedy

I should emphasize that not only world transits and natal aspects but also personal transits involving the Saturn-Pluto combination were highly relevant in examining these distinctive archetypal patterns. In such cases, like those of Dante's *Inferno* and Sartre's *No Exit* mentioned above, I found that the same archetypal complex we have been examining on the collective level tended to be constellated in the life and experience of an individual during the particular months or years that he underwent a personal transit of Pluto crossing his natal Saturn, or of Saturn transiting his natal Pluto. While most individuals are not born with Saturn and Pluto in hard aspect, everyone undergoes not only the collective epochs of Saturn-Pluto cyclical alignments discussed in these chapters but also periods in their personal lives when they undergo personal Saturn-Pluto transits. These periods are characterized by highly similar phenomena, except that they are more locally constellated within the life experience of the individual. For artists and writers, the archetypal complex can be visible in their internal world and creative work, in external biographical events—or both.

An especially dramatic example of the latter is Oscar Wilde, who was at the height of his creative powers in 1893–95 when transiting Uranus reached the opposition point of its cycle in his life, 180° from the position it had been in at his birth. Again, this was the same personal transit Galileo had when he turned the telescope to the heavens, Freud and Jung when they had their psychological and intellectual turning points, Betty Friedan when she wrote *The Feminine Mystique*, Rosa Parks when she refused to move from her bus seat, and so forth—a transit that typically coincided not only with major creative breakthroughs but also pivotal events of rebellious, unpredictable, and disruptive character. For Wilde, it was during this three-year personal transit that he composed his comic masterpiece, *The Importance of Being Earnest*, in a burst of creativity during August and September 1894 when the transit was virtually exact.[28] A few months later during this transit in early 1895, Wilde had both *An Ideal Husband* and *The Importance of Being Earnest* playing simultaneously on the London stage to great critical and public acclaim.

However, the year of 1895 also coincided with the beginning of a long once-in-a-lifetime personal transit of Pluto in conjunction with Wilde's natal Saturn. Simultaneously, in a convergence of personal transits that made the transiting situation even more rare, Saturn in 1895 moved into opposition to Wilde's natal Pluto in a shorter, twelve-month-long personal transit. Thus the same two planets, Saturn and Pluto, were involved in each transit—one as transiting planet,

the other as natal—which I found consistently coincided with a heightened intensification of what appeared to be a doubly activated archetypal complex. Precisely as these two transits converged in the period from February to May 1895,
in a series of fateful, partly self-initiated events, Wilde sued the Marquess of
Queensbury, the father of Wilde's lover Lord Alfred Douglas, for libel, as a result
of which he was himself brought to trial for his homosexual practices, found
guilty, and sentenced to hard labor in prison for two years.

The trial, verdict, and commencement of his prison sentence took place
precisely as these two transits converged. Publicly humiliated, his health and
spirit broken by the imprisonment, his plays shut down and declared unpro-
duceable, Wilde left England upon his release for Paris, where he lived in im-
poverished exile until he died in 1900—all precisely during the longer transit of
Pluto conjoining his natal Saturn. From this period came his final somber works,
The Ballad of Reading Gaol, a study of a prisoner condemned to death, and *De
Profundis*, his moving apologia and cri de coeur. As one example of the many
poignant expressions of the Saturn-Pluto archetypal complex evident in these
late works, in *De Profundis* Wilde reserved for himself the sternest judgment, for
his betrayal of his rare spiritual and imaginative gifts through his choice to abandon himself to what he had come to regard as years of mindless dissipation and
promiscuity unworthy of the cultural role he should have fulfilled.

> I must say to myself that I ruined myself, and that nobody great or small
> can be ruined except by his own hand. . . . This pitiless indictment I
> bring without pity against myself. Terrible as was what the world did to
> me, what I did to myself was far more terrible still. I was a man who
> stood in symbolic relations to the art and culture of my age. I had re-
> alised this for myself at the very dawn of my manhood, and had forced
> my age to realise it afterwards. Few men hold such a position in their
> own lifetime, and have it so acknowledged. It is usually discerned, if
> discerned at all, by the historian, or the critic, long after both the man
> and his age have passed away. With me it was different. I felt it myself,
> and made others feel it.
>
> The gods had given me almost everything. But I let myself be lured
> into long spells of senseless and sensual ease. I amused myself with
> being a flaneur, a dandy, a man of fashion. I surrounded myself with the
> smaller natures and the meaner minds. I became the spendthrift of my
> own genius, and to waste an eternal youth gave me a curious joy. Tired
> of being on the heights, I deliberately went to the depths in the search
> for new sensation. What the paradox was to me in the sphere of thought,
> perversity became to me in the sphere of passion. Desire, at the end, was
> a malady, or a madness, or both. I grew careless of the lives of others. I
> took pleasure where it pleased me, and passed on. I forgot that every lit-
> tle action of the common day makes or unmakes character, and that

therefore what one has done in the secret chamber one has some day to cry aloud on the housetop. I ceased to be lord over myself. I was no longer the captain of my soul, and did not know it. I allowed pleasure to dominate me. I ended in horrible disgrace. There is only one thing for me now, absolute humility.

A different example of a creative writer suffering extremely oppressive—and mortally threatening—judgment with the same personal transit is that of Salman Rushdie, who was born during the Saturn-Pluto conjunction of 1947. In 1989, when the Ayatollah Khomeini of Iran issued the fatwa, or death sentence, for the blasphemy he accused Rushdie of having committed in writing *The Satanic Verses*, published that year, Rushdie was undergoing the once-in-a-lifetime personal transit of Pluto in a square to his natal Saturn-Pluto conjunction. This transit had begun during the immediately preceding years when he was writing *The Satanic Verses*, many of whose themes reflect the characteristic motifs of the Saturn-Pluto archetypal complex.

As compared with the world transit cycle of Saturn-Pluto alignments we have been examining, in personal transits of the same planets the relevant phenomena occur specifically in the individual context rather than the collective. Yet ultimately such transits can also leave a mark on the larger cultural psyche. Such an influence can occur even when that transit does not coincide with dramatic external events visible to others, as with Wilde or Rushdie, but is instead reflected more potently in the inner life, which in a creative artist tends to be readily discernible in the dominant themes and spirit of the work produced during these years.

To give just one example: If, as most Shakespeare scholars believe, William Shakespeare was born in April 1564, we know that the one time in his life that he underwent a personal transit of Pluto in hard aspect to his natal Saturn was from 1599 to 1607. According to scholars' best estimates, this period precisely coincides with the years in which all the major Shakespearean tragedies were written and first performed, beginning with *Julius Caesar* in 1599–1600 (when the transit first reached 5° from exact alignment, the usual outer orb for personal transits), followed by *Hamlet* in 1600–01 (as the planets reached 3° from exact), then *Othello*, *King Lear*, and *Macbeth* in 1604–06 (the years the transit was most exact, within 1°). Even Shakespeare's comedies of this period, *All's Well That Ends Well* and *Measure For Measure* (1602–04), are traditionally called the "dark comedies." As the Pluto-Saturn transit moved to its last stages in 1606–07, at 3° past exact, *Antony and Cleopatra* was produced.[29] (As happened with Wilde as well, Shakespeare's long personal transit of Pluto to natal Saturn was twice as long as the same transit would be in our own time; this difference in duration is because Pluto was farther from the Sun and therefore moved slower during those eras.)

Many of the principal themes of the Saturn-Pluto complex discussed in these pages are expressed by Shakespeare in just these plays in profoundly archetypal form: the sustained exploration and articulation of the shadow side of human existence, the deep engagement with moral darkness, the constant focus on death and the significance of mortality, the concern with the fate of human beings caught in the grip of intractable contradictions. The dominant motifs—murderous ambition, jealousy and revenge, crime and retribution, the stain of guilt that cannot be removed, the horror of self-willed catastrophe, the overwhelming loss and suffering—are all reflective of the Saturn-Pluto gestalt. Throughout the sequence of the great tragedies, human life and death are viewed with the most extreme gravity. Immediately after this transit was over, Shakespeare's plays distinctly shifted in theme and spirit as he assimilated the tragic vision to the tragicomic romances of his final creative years: *Cymbeline*, *The Winter's Tale*, and *The Tempest* in 1609–11, plays that are highly characteristic of the Uranus-Neptune and Jupiter-Uranus alignments that occurred at that time and represent the two cycles we will explore next.

Remarkably, an exactly parallel correlation can be observed in Dante's life and work. Based on his own birth information given in *La Divina Commedia*, Dante underwent the same long, once-in-a-lifetime personal transit of Pluto square natal Saturn in the years between 1304 to 1316, centering on the eight-year period 1306–13. The years that he was writing the *Inferno* and the *Purgatorio* precisely coincide with this once-in-a-lifetime transit whose archetypal character corresponds so vividly to those two poems and the specific domains they portray. According to the widely accepted estimates of Giorgio Petrocchi, Dante composed the *Inferno* beginning in 1304 but mainly during the years 1306 to 1308, and he composed the *Purgatorio* from 1308 to 1312. In 1316, soon after the Pluto-Saturn transit was over, he began the *Paradiso*.[30] As we will see, the timing and the archetypal character of the Uranus-Neptune and Jupiter-Uranus cycles were highly relevant to the entire writing of *La Divina Commedia* and the expansive poetic-spiritual character of its vision.

Forging Deep Structures

As the foregoing chapters suggest, the positive potential of the archetypal complex associated with Saturn-Pluto alignments seemed to be inextricably intertwined with confronting its negative manifestations: moral discernment and wisdom born from difficult experience and suffering; fortitude and courageous acts of will in the face of darkness, evil, danger, and death; a capacity for sustained effort and determination; disciplined control of intense energies both inner and outer. Generally speaking, the Saturn-Pluto complex appeared to press the psyche, individual or collective, towards the forging of a deeper and stronger structure of moral consciousness. The superego forged could be rigid, pathological, and prone to projection and splitting, or represent a profound moral advance, a lasting deepening of conscience and critical self-awareness. When well integrated, it could bring forth a more penetrating understanding of the complexities of human motivation both in oneself and others, with a resulting strength of moral purpose in a world of grave drama where weighty consequences are at stake. We see this multivalence well embodied in the famous final words of Joyce's *A Portrait of the Artist as a Young Man*, when the young protagonist, Stephen Dedalus, ultimately rejects the narrow theological vision of sin and eternal damnation of his childhood religion to engage, with equal moral gravity, his calling to be an artist:

> Amen. So be it. Welcome, O life! I go to encounter for the millionth time the reality of experience and to forge in the smithy of my soul the uncreated conscience of my race. . . . Old father, old artificer, stand me now and ever in good stead.

I found that individuals born with Saturn and Pluto in hard aspect often seemed to be possessed of an underlying sense that they were living lives with special moral responsibilities, sometimes with the heavy burden of history on their shoulders. Such a tendency was evident in the biographies of many of the figures we examined above, such as Augustine or Marx, Harriet Beecher Stowe or Jung. A contemporary example is the theologian and ecologist Thomas Berry, born in 1914 during the same Saturn-Pluto conjunction that coincided with

World War I and with Joyce's *A Portrait of the Artist* just cited. In his influential writings and lectures, Berry expressed a vision of human history and evolution that synthesized many of the themes we have examined as characteristic of the Saturn-Pluto complex: the confrontation with the moral shadow of human activity, the acute concern with modern civilization's obsessive commercial-industrial exploitation and plundering of the natural world, the decimation of indigenous peoples and the mass extinction of species, the recognition of deep evolutionary structures and the ending of vast evolutionary epochs, and the experience of the dark periods of history as crucibles of transformation. Throughout Berry's analysis, as in these passages from his culminating book, *The Great Work* (published when he was eighty-four during his Uranus return transit), can also be found a view of human existence as ordered by weighty collective responsibilities, enormous generational tasks, and larger forces of destiny that assign us roles and labors beyond our conscious choosing:

> History is governed by those overarching movements that give shape and meaning to life by relating the human venture to the larger destinies of the universe. Creating such a movement might be called the Great Work of a people. . . . The Great Work now, as we move into a new millennium, is to carry out the transition from a period of human devastation of the Earth to a period when humans would be present to the planet in a mutually beneficial manner.
>
> The Great Work before us . . . is not a role that we have chosen. It is a role given to us, beyond any consultation with ourselves. We are, as it were, thrown into existence with a challenge and a role that is beyond any personal choice. We did not choose. We were chosen by some power beyond ourselves for this historical task. The nobility of our lives, however, depends upon the manner in which we come to understand and fulfill our assigned role.

This same spirit and vision of history was evident on a collective level during many eras of Saturn-Pluto alignments, as in the most recent such period, 2000–04. The zeitgeist is affected by a characteristic mood, one of confronting a dark epoch, of carrying the heavy burden of history with special moral responsibilities, and is often tinged with a sense that fate or larger forces determine one's life. In retrospect it was often possible to see that such periods of crisis and gravity, in history and in personal lives, served ultimately to build enduring moral-psychological and social-political foundations for the future. The deprivations, losses, and hard labors of these periods pressed individuals and societies out of an old form of life and into a new one, though during these alignments the new was often not readily visible, while the grim realities of hardship and oppression, contraction and decline were conspicuously in evidence.

All the events and experiences coincident with both of the cycles we have examined so far, Uranus-Pluto and Saturn-Pluto, display the deep bivalent ambiguity of the archetypal principle associated with Pluto, at once destructive and regenerative. These polar tendencies are especially clearly reflected in Dionysus in the Greek pantheon and in Kali and Shiva of the Indian pantheon, sovereign deities of the death-rebirth mystery. In the Saturn-Pluto cycle specifically, the combination of this powerful Plutonic archetype with the Saturn principle of hard contraction, critical endings, mortal finality, and grave turning points consistently marked what appeared to be the death contractions of history. Yet paradoxically, at another level less obvious to the empirical eye of the moment, this complex also seemed to bring about the inexpressibly hard labor of the *birth* contractions of history: the throes and travails of deep transformation, the destruction of an old order, and the forging of what became the enduring foundation and structure of a new evolutionary development.

Perhaps something like this deeper process could be discerned in the most recent such alignment period, when in the winter of 2002–03 the longer Saturn-Pluto opposition coincided with shorter alignments of Jupiter with Uranus and Neptune in succession, cycles associated with a very different, more expansively rebellious and idealistic spirit. The unprecedented worldwide wave of protest demonstrations in February 2003 against the Bush administration's drive for preemptive war against Iraq, a spontaneous coordination of tens of millions of marchers in Australia, New Zealand, Asia, Europe, and North America, represented a virtually global moral judgment against unprovoked war. The historic confrontation of diametrically opposed values and wills, the unarmed people on the world's streets versus a military superpower pressing for war, produced a clash of immensely potent forces "like two behemoth icebergs colliding in the North Atlantic." Whatever its short-term outcome, this enormous nonviolent statement of principled democratic resistance against the destructive use of power by established governments was indicative of a longer-term moral evolution within the collective psyche: the gradual forging of a collective conscience against the perceived moral shadow of a powerful governing authority. The difference between the international public response to the call for war in 2003 from that of 1914 could not be more vivid. The multitude of marches across the planet seemed to reflect a kind of collective individuation process in the global psyche of which both Jung and Gandhi would no doubt be proud—as would, in their several ways, Thoreau, Tolstoy, and King (all figures whose words and ideals were repeatedly cited in the period leading up to the marches). Despite the vast "shock and awe" destruction and suffering unleashed just weeks afterwards, the deeper moral structure in the collective consciousness that these marches reflected was not destroyed but will go on to express itself again and again, because it is not limited to any one individual or group of individuals who might be silenced, imprisoned, or killed. The forging has been slowly and gradually, often painfully, taking place on some other level of the ever-evolving human spirit, where it will endure.

I believe we can approach a deeper understanding of these and many other important developments, including our own moment in history, if we now examine the remarkable correlations and archetypal character of two other planetary cycles to which our discussion points.

VI

Cycles of Creativity and Expansion

There are a thousand paths that have never yet been trodden. . . . Humanity and humanity's earth are still unexhausted and undiscovered. Watch and listen, you solitaries! From the future come winds with a stealthy flapping of wings; and good tidings go out to delicate ears.

—Friedrich Nietzsche
Thus Spoke Zarathustra

Opening New Horizons

Historians and psychologists have long wrestled with the mysterious phenomenon of individuals and societies becoming swept up into particular ways of perceiving their reality and acting on the basis of those highly charged perceptions. The evidence we have been examining suggests that at certain times the constellation of a powerful archetypal complex can so dominate and inform every dimension of experience, both internally and externally, that the individual or society thus affected sees the world entirely through its compelling lens and acts accordingly. It is as if at different times of life or history one has entered into a different imaginative and emotional universe with its own distinct parameters, assumptions, and ambiance. The contrast between the two periods can be as vivid as that between, say, *Macbeth* and *Much Ado About Nothing,* or between *The Seventh Seal* and *The Sound of Music.*

Again, as James Hillman well described, "One thing is absolutely essential to the notion of archetypes: their emotional possessive effect, their bedazzlement of consciousness so that it becomes blind to its own stance. By setting up a universe which tends to hold everything we do, see, and say in the sway of its cosmos, an archetype is best comparable with a God." Indeed, the very image of God and the divine as experienced and articulated by different individuals and in different eras appears to be profoundly affected by the archetypal complexes that are then most constellated and active. Whether in religion or art, in personal biography or the great events and epochs of history, it is this archetypal dimension of experience that gives life its depth of meaning and informs the shifting contours of its unfolding drama. Yet it is precisely this subtle power to shape and reinforce our conscious perceptions and beliefs that holds such danger.

This power is not, however, simply a matter of inner distortions and perceptual filters by which different archetypal gestalts merely produce different inner states of being. The drastic difference in spirit and vision between Oscar Wilde's *The Importance of Being Earnest* and his *De Profundis* three years later was not caused simply by an inner shift, a change of mood. Nor was the difference in American attitudes towards national security issues before and after September 11, 2001. Decisive outer events took place that set in motion the archetypal complex. Yet even where the causal factors are not so self-evident, external events and interior attitudes tend to mirror each other. This mirroring of inner and outer, observed repeatedly by all of us in the course of life, seems to reflect their underlying coherence as two mutually implicated manifestations of a larger reality. The world in some sense conspires with our inner states, and vice versa. "Fate" plays a hand, with the occurrence of precisely appropriate synchronistic phenomena both affecting and reflecting the state of consciousness. One is seldom simply imagining things.

That is the great ambiguity that pervades so many of the phenomena we are examining. Archetypally informed perceptions of the world can be simultaneously "realistic" and yet highly partial, biased, and self-fulfilling in such a way as to render one increasingly blind to other realities and potentialities. These perceptions lead to assumptions and convictions that subtly move us to act one way rather than another, and elicit further confirmation of the initial perception, further enforcement of the initial event. Soon, in a complexly dynamic interaction with the environment, one has established an enduring structure of reality that is strongly determinative for the future, such as a state of "war against terror" that is fought by terror, a perpetual cycle of violence and repression, bombings and retribution, fear and hostility. Or, as during the Cold War, a state of global nuclear peril in an ever-worsening Manichaean schism driven by mutual demonization and worldwide hostile activity. Or in religion: a state of metaphysical fear and judgment, sin and guilt, heretics and inquisitions, expectations of apocalypse, eternal damnation, the soul's predestined fate in the hands of an angry God, the world sharply divided between the born again and the unredeemed, between good and evil, with all the social and psychological consequences of such beliefs. Or even in science: a state of empirically validated cosmic disenchantment, with the genetically programmed human being existentially isolated in a meaningless, purposeless universe, the inexplicably solitary locus of intelligence and idiosyncratic spiritual aspiration in a vast cosmos of random processes signifying nothing.

Thus the arising in us of an archetypal complex can serve as a window to a universe, indeed a door and a pathway, but it can also serve as an enclosing wall, an impermeable boundary and barrier that effectively creates a limit to our universe of possibilities. Only a critical awareness of that potential boundary, and an act of the imagination to transcend it, can open the horizon of our universe. I have found that such an awareness is mediated most effectively by a recognition of the dominant archetypal complexes and dynamics of a given time, whether for an individual or an entire civilization, and that this recognition is extraordinarily enhanced by a knowledge of what planets are in alignment at what time and for how long, an informed understanding of which can provide a crucial, irreplaceable perspective on the shifting archetypal dynamics of life.

In this sense, even when the correlations observed involve the gravest and darkest matters, the archetypal astrological perspective points to the possibility of an unexpected liberation from certain otherwise implacably confining conditions. This emancipatory potential has three different interrelated elements:

First, by providing nuanced, clarifying insight into which archetypal complexes are likely to be constellated in an individual or a society, as well as when, such a perspective can open up a new potential for *critical reflection and self-awareness*—a new possibility of transcending one's unconscious immersion in the moment, and thus a crucial degree of autonomy in relation to the powerful forces at work in the individual and collective psyche.

Second, such ongoing insight provides one with an edifying sense of the *relativity of every state of being* in which one finds oneself, whether a state of mind, a stage of life, or an historical epoch: "This too shall pass"—both the grievous and the glorious—and however persuasive the current archetypal gestalt appears to be, it is not the whole story.

Finally, apart from the particulars of the planetary and archetypal patterning, the very recognition that such correlations exist at all, and that they continue to exist with such extraordinary consistency and elegant complexity, can nurture a profound awareness of the human condition as one of *embeddedness and creative participation in a living cosmos of unfolding meaning and purpose*.

Such reflections started to inform my thinking as I came to grips with the expanding body of correlations, both individual and collective, that I encountered as my research progressed. My understanding of historical events and cultural phenomena was especially transformed and unexpectedly opened as I began to explore the planetary cycle we will next examine.

We have so far surveyed two cycles of the outer planets. It remains for me a source of continuing amazement that archetypal patterns of striking clarity and definition, each with its distinct and appropriate character, were evident in historical and cultural phenomena for every one of the ten planetary cycles involving the five outer planets and their combinations. Perhaps the most dazzling of these were the major alignments of the relatively short Jupiter-Uranus cycle, with each conjunction lasting approximately fourteen months.

As with the other planets known to the ancients, the archetypal significance of the planet Jupiter seems to have been established in the earliest origins of the classical astrological tradition. Linked with specific qualities of the corresponding mythic figure—the Greek deity Zeus, the king of the Olympian gods, the Babylonian Marduk, the Roman Jupiter—it received as well certain symbolic amplifications that emerged in the various contributing traditions: Platonic, Hermetic, Arabic, medieval and Renaissance. Throughout this historical development, Jupiter has been associated with the principle of expansion and magnitude, providence and plenitude, liberality, elevation and ascendancy, and with the tendency to experience growth and progress, success, honor, good fortune, abundance, aggrandizement, prodigality, excess and inflation. It also has a frequent association with the realm and aspirations of culture, especially high culture: high principle, higher learning, breadth of knowledge, liberal education, cultured erudition, a wide and encompassing vision. In general, it seems to impel a movement towards encompassing greater wholes and enlarging one's world, embracing higher principles of order, higher orders of magnitude, broader horizons of experience.

When Jupiter and a second planet enter into cyclical alignment, the coinciding events suggest Jupiter's archetypal influence to be one of magnifying and supporting the second planetary archetype with an expansive, elevating quality—"crowning" it, as it were—granting it success, honoring it, bringing it to fruition, mediating its positive unfolding, its growth, its fulfillment, its enrichment, its cultural ascension, with a definite potential for excess and inflation.

In the Jupiter-Uranus cycle, all these tendencies seemed to interact in an especially vivid manner with the principle we have seen associated with the planet Uranus—the archetypal complex encompassing sudden radical change, creative breakthrough, rebellion against constraints and the status quo, the impulse for freedom and the new, sudden openings and awakenings, a tendency to constellate the unexpected and disruptive, and so forth. The specific nature of these two planetary principles was such that their archetypal interaction seemed to have a mutually stimulating effect that was highly synergistic. An expansively and buoyantly energizing quality characterized such eras, one that often engendered a certain creative brilliance and the excitement of experiencing suddenly expanded horizons.

In world transits, the cyclical alignments of Jupiter and Uranus correlated consistently with condensed waves of celebrated milestones of creative or emancipatory activity across many fields. The conjunction of the two planets occurs approximately every fourteen years. During each of these, as well as during the intervening oppositions, decisive crests of remarkably synchronous breakthroughs and innovations appeared to take place within a brief period of time in many areas of human activity. The evidence suggested that the continuing long-term cultural developments that we saw associated with the longer Uranus-Pluto cycle (and with other longer outer-planet cycles we have yet to examine, such as Uranus-Neptune) consistently burst forth in a more frequent cyclical efflorescence in coincidence with the Jupiter-Uranus alignments. These cyclical waves of creative and emancipatory cultural activity occurred either as intervening crests between the longer, less frequent Uranus-Pluto alignments or as climactic moments during or just after the period of the longer alignment.

As with the personal transits of Uranus cited earlier, I found that here too, on the collective level, when I closely investigated the exact dates of specific cultural phenomena of this character, I could track the frequency and quality of significant creative and liberating breakthroughs, achievements, and new beginnings in the culture as a whole against the shifting planetary positions in the months and years on each side of the exact alignment, with a result that closely resembled the shape of a bell curve as the two planets, Jupiter and Uranus, moved towards exactitude and then moved apart. Although events of this kind frequently took place when Jupiter and Uranus were in close alignment in all major aspects, I found as the research progressed that the most vivid synchronistic and sequential patterns were evident in the succession of axial alignments—conjunctions and oppositions—with the relevant events tending to occur in a wavelike continuum during a period when the two planets were within approximately 15° of exact aspect. Not only synchronic patterns of simultaneous expressions of cultural creativity, rebellion, and awakenings but also extraordinarily precise diachronic patterns of closely related events across a series of consecutive alignments were consistently evident in close correlation with this planetary cycle.

Convergences of
Scientific Breakthroughs

E arly in my research I was alerted to the possibility of a cyclical pattern in history that correlated with the Jupiter-Uranus cycle when I noticed that a number of famous coincidences in the history of science, when two or more scientists virtually simultaneously brought major discoveries into the public arena, also happened to coincide with a Jupiter-Uranus conjunction.

One of the first instances I came upon, one often cited by historians of science, was when Kepler and Galileo independently made public within a few months of each other their separate discoveries that confirmed the Copernican theory of the solar system. In the summer of 1609 Kepler published in Prague his revolutionary work *Astronomia Nova*, which introduced his first two laws of planetary motion (stating that the planets moved in elliptical orbits with speeds based on equal areas swept out in equal times), thereby resolving the problem of the planets that astronomers had struggled with for two millennia. In that same summer Galileo made the first public demonstration of the telescope (in front of the Venetian Senate); then in Padua, between October 1609 and January 1610, he turned his telescope to the heavens for the first time and discovered the "unbelievably numerous" individual stars of the Milky Way, the craters on the Moon, the spots on the Sun, the four satellites of Jupiter, the phases of Venus, and other celestial phenomena that he found supported the Copernican hypothesis. On March 12, 1610, he published *Sidereus Nuncius* ("The Starry Messenger"), the epoch-making account of his observations (this entire period also coinciding with Galileo's personal transit of Uranus opposite natal Uranus cited earlier). The combination of the two events—the publication of Kepler's mathematical findings and Galileo's telescopic discoveries—provided the scientific world with a dramatic concurrence of evidence that effectively supported the heliocentric theory, brought it to widespread public attention, and laid the foundations for the eventual success of the Copernican revolution. Jupiter and Uranus were in close conjunction (less than 5°) at the time of both publications, having been within 15° of each other in the fourteen-month period from April 1609 to June 1610.

Jupiter and Uranus were again in conjunction in the fourteen-month period from November 1899 through December 1900. It has often been pointed out that this moment at the turn of the twentieth century marked the coincidental beginning of two of the century's most important intellectual revolutions, psychoanalysis and quantum theory. Psychoanalysis was brought to public notice by the publication in Vienna of Freud's *The Interpretation of Dreams* (published November 1899, dated 1900), and it was in two meetings of the German Physical Society in Berlin in the autumn of 1900 that Max Planck introduced his groundbreaking hypothesis that radiant energy is emitted or absorbed in discrete quanta, thereby initiating the twentieth-century revolution of quantum physics.

Appropriate to its own theory, quantum physics has progressed not in continuous fashion but rather in two major quantum leaps, one at its birth in 1900 with Planck, the second, at its coming to maturity, in 1927. Jupiter and Uranus were again conjunct in the extraordinary fourteen-month period from March 1927 to April 1928 when Niels Bohr, Werner Heisenberg, and their colleagues brought the quantum physics revolution begun by Planck to a culmination, both individually and in interaction at the historic October 1927 Solvay congress in Brussels. It has been said that in 1927 the pace of discovery in theoretical physics was perhaps greater than in any other year in the history of science. The resulting synthesis was, in the words of the intellectual leader of the congress, Bohr, the result of "a singularly fruitful cooperation of a whole generation of physicists," who included Schrödinger, Born, de Broglie, Pauli, Dirac, Planck, and Heisenberg. During the period of this conjunction, from March 1927 through April 1928, both of the two major revolutionary axioms of quantum mechanics, Heisenberg's principle of indeterminacy and Bohr's principle of complementarity, were formulated and made public. Moreover, this same conjunction in 1927 coincided with one of the most significant milestones in modern cosmology, as the Belgian astrophysicist Georges Lemaître proposed at this time the first expanding-universe cosmology and articulated a mathematical superstructure for what became the big bang theory of the origin of the universe. During the same alignment Alfred North Whitehead delivered the Gifford Lectures of 1927–28, which became the basis for *Process and Reality* and process philosophy, the last major metaphysical system of modern philosophy.

Jupiter and Uranus were also in conjunction at the time of the famous series of events that led to the first public announcement of the theory of evolution by Darwin and Alfred Russel Wallace in July 1858—a different form, though equally momentous and fruitful, of joint scientific breakthrough. Although Darwin had privately formulated the theory of evolution in his notebooks in September 1838 (when transiting Uranus was within 1° of exact trine to his natal Uranus), he did not make his findings public for nearly twenty years; instead he gradually accumulated evidence and developed the theory in relative isolation. Then on June 18, 1858, he unexpectedly received from Wallace, who was in the Malay Archipelago, a letter containing a statement of the theory of evolution which Wallace had conceived independently in virtually identical form. As a result of this letter and the urgings of Darwin's colleagues, a joint paper by

Darwin and Wallace was read before the Linnean Society of London on July 1, 1858, announcing the theory. Immediately afterward during this conjunction, Darwin commenced writing his magnum opus, *The Origin of Species*, the foundational work of modern biology.

It was these several convergences of scientific discoveries that entered the public awareness during Jupiter-Uranus conjunctions—Kepler and Galileo in 1609–10, Darwin and Wallace in 1858, Freud and Planck in 1900, Bohr, Heisenberg, Lemaître, Whitehead, and the rest in 1927—that first suggested to me the existence of a larger pattern. At this early point in my research, I would probably not have noticed these correlations except for the combination of their being such well-known turning points in the history of science and the striking appropriateness of the events for the archetypal meanings ascribed to Jupiter and Uranus: the successful fruition and cultural elevation (Jupiter) in a sudden, unexpected manner of the impulse for creative breakthrough and radical change (Uranus). In each case, it was as if the Promethean principle in the collective psyche had suddenly received an expansive amplification and fulfillment, and an unexpected cultural affirmation and ascendancy.

This initial impression was considerably heightened when I turned my attention to a different category of Promethean historical phenomena, in the social and political sphere. There I soon discovered that equally visible in coincidence with the Jupiter-Uranus cycle were sudden, often brilliantly successful, and later widely celebrated upwellings of a collective impulse for social and political emancipation, innovation, and rebellion.

THE JUPITER-URANUS CYCLE

Axial alignments since 1775

15° orb		Exact alignment <1°
March 1775–April 1776	*conjunction*	June 1775
January 1782–November 1783	*opposition*	March–December 1782
August 1788–October 1789	*conjunction*	June–July 1789
February 1796–March 1797	*opposition*	April 1796–March 1797
October 1802–July 1804	*conjunction*	September 1803
June 1809–April 1811	*opposition*	May 1810
December 1816–February 1818	*conjunction*	November 1817
July 1823–April 1825	*opposition*	September 1823–June 1824
December 1830–January 1832	*conjunction*	March 1831
October 1836–July 1838	*opposition*	September 1837–July 1838
March 1844–May 1845	*conjunction*	February 1845
November 1850–October 1852	*opposition*	October 1851
July 1857–March 1859	*conjunction*	May 1858
December 1864–October 1866	*opposition*	February–December 1865

July 1871–September 1872	*conjunction*	May–June 1872
February 1879–February 1880	*opposition*	March 1879–January 1880
September 1885–November 1886	*conjunction*	August 1886
June 1892–March 1894	*opposition*	April–May 1893
November 1899–January 1901	*conjunction*	October 1900
June 1906–July 1907	*opposition*	August 1906–June 1907
December 1913–January 1915	*conjunction*	February–March 1914
October 1919–August 1921	*opposition*	September 1920–May 1921
March 1927–April 1928	*conjunction*	June 1927–January 1928
October 1933–September 1935	*opposition*	January–October 1934
July 1940–August 1941	*conjunction*	May 1941
December 1947–January 1949	*opposition*	February–November 1948
June 1954–August 1955	*conjunction*	September 1954–May 1955
May 1961–February 1963	*opposition*	March–December 1962
August 1968–November 1969*	*conjunction*	November 1968–July 1969
May 1975–March 1977	*opposition*	April 1976
November 1982–December 1983	*conjunction*	February–October 1983
June 1989–July 1990	*opposition*	August 1989–May 1990
November 1996–December 1997	*conjunction*	February 1997
September 2002–August 2004	*opposition*	August–September 2003
March 2010–April 2011	*conjunction*	May 2010–January 2011
October 2016–September 2018	*opposition*	December 2016–October 2017

20° orb generally adds one month before and after dates given for 15°, occasionally up to nine months. In the case of oppositions and, more rarely, conjunctions that move in and out of 15° orb for twenty-three months, the 20° orb always adds only one month before and after.

*For 1968–69 and the triple Jupiter-Uranus-Pluto conjunction, see note 3, p. 522.

Social and Political
Rebellions and Awakenings

The most consistent pattern I observed was the close coincidence of these Jupiter-Uranus alignment periods with the opening months of a longer-term process, as if the particular archetypal impulse associated with this cycle acted as a sudden initiatory catalyst for such phenomena: Jupiter's principle of expansion and growth supporting the Promethean impulse of new beginnings. Jupiter and Uranus were in conjunction during the exact fourteen months coincident with the beginning of the American Revolution in 1775–76. On April 19, 1775, precisely one month after the conjunction had first moved within 15° of alignment, the War of Independence started when British soldiers were met by armed American rebels at Lexington with whom they exchanged fire, the "shot heard round the world." The succession of months during the Jupiter-Uranus conjunction closely coincided with the development of the revolution: in March 1775, the first month of the conjunction, Patrick Henry's "Give me liberty or give me death" speech at the Virginia convention that advocated militant opposition to the British; in April the battles at Lexington and Concord; in May the first American victory with the capture of Fort Ticonderoga, and the meeting of the Second Continental Congress in Philadelphia led by Thomas Jefferson, Benjamin Franklin, and John Adams; in June the appointment of George Washington as commander in chief of the revolutionary army, followed by the battle of Bunker Hill; in July the Congress's formal Declaration of Causes of Taking Up Arms; from that summer through the following spring Washington's organizing and training of the American army; in January 1776 the publication of *Common Sense*, Thomas Paine's manifesto against British royal power in the American colonies that mobilized public opinion behind the revolutionary cause and sold half a million copies in the colonies in a few weeks. In March 1776, Washington's army forced the main British contingent to evacuate Boston, thus winning the first decisive round in the War of Independence. The conjunction reached the final 15° point in late April 1776, and 20° in late May. As Mars moved into conjunction with Uranus in early June, Jefferson began to compose the Declaration of Independence.

Exactly one full cycle and fourteen years later during the immediately following conjunction the fall of the Bastille took place and the French Revolution began, with Jupiter and Uranus just 2° from exact conjunction on July 14, 1789. As with the start of the American Revolution, the entire period of this Jupiter-Uranus conjunction, from August 1788 to October 1789, coincided closely with the major events that commenced the French Revolution: in August 1788 the forced agreement by the French crown to call together the Estates-General, which set into motion the series of events that led to the revolution; in September the popular reaction against the parlement's decision to have the estates meet separately; in December the crown's decision to enlarge the Third Estate; in January 1789 the publication of the Abbé Sieyès's influential pamphlet "What is the Third Estate?"; in the spring of 1789 the gradual erosion of social order in the countryside; in April the rural and urban riots; in May the meeting of the Estates-General; in June the declaration of the National Assembly by the Third Estate and the Oath of the Tennis Court. After the storming of the Bastille prison in July and the Declaration of Rights of Man and the Citizen in August, the Assembly began in September to plan the new government. Finally, as the conjunction approached the final 15° point in early October 1789, the king and royal family were forced during the mass riots and marches of the October Days to move from Versailles to Paris, where they could be watched; the Assembly then moved to Paris as well, initiating the most radical phase of the revolution as Uranus and Pluto moved into closer opposition. The long revolutionary epoch then unfolded in exact correlation with the longer-term Uranus-Pluto alignment through most of the 1790s, as discussed earlier.

Compared with the more local revolution of the American colonies during the Jupiter-Uranus conjunction in 1775–76, the tumultuous era of the French Revolution was virtually worldwide, with the just-cited events of the 1788–89 Jupiter-Uranus conjunction serving as a catalyst for a sustained epoch of revolutionary violence and intensified emancipatory impulses that, as we have observed, regularly coincided with Uranus-Pluto alignments.

Just as both axial alignments of the Uranus-Pluto cycle—conjunctions and oppositions—consistently coincided with archetypally relevant historical and cultural phenomena, so also with the Jupiter-Uranus cycle. The consecutive axial alignments again revealed clear signs of a coherent sequential patterning in which the events of one conjunction were closely associated both with events of the opposition that followed and with those of the next conjunction, which completed the cycle. Such diachronic patterning was readily visible, for example, in the full Jupiter-Uranus cycle of alignments that unfolded in the 1770s and 1780s. The American Revolution, having begun in coincidence with the Jupiter-Uranus conjunction of 1775–76, was successfully concluded and the new nation's independence was formally ratified with the signing of the Treaty of Paris seven years later during the immediately following Jupiter-Uranus opposition of 1782–83.[1] The fulfillment of the quest for independence, the joy of emancipatory success, the expansive victory achieved by the rebellion all closely fit the characteristic archetypal complex associated with Jupiter and Uranus.

In turn, it was precisely during the fourteen months of the immediately following Jupiter-Uranus conjunction in 1788–89 that the new American government commenced operations, the ratified Constitution was put into effect, the first national elections were held, George Washington was inaugurated as first president, and the Bill of Rights was introduced in Congress—all in exact coincidence with the start of the French Revolution and the fall of the Bastille. The close historical connections and reciprocal causal factors that link the American and French Revolutions are further suggestive evidence of the diachronic pattern linking the successive alignments.

The *synchronic* nature of correlations with the Jupiter-Uranus cycle was as striking as the diachronic. For example, during the same spring of 1789 that the Revolution was first erupting throughout the countryside in France, the famous mutiny on HMS *Bounty* took place in the South Pacific, on April 28, led by Fletcher Christian against Captain William Bligh on the return voyage from Tahiti. Thus the same Jupiter-Uranus conjunction of 1789 that coincided with the fall of the Bastille also coincided with the mutiny on the *Bounty*, the two revolts taking place within a few weeks of each other, though on opposite sides of the globe.

In contemplating the causal factors that might make intelligible this kind of coincidence, I recognized that much, though certainly not all, of the other concurrent revolutionary activity in Europe and elsewhere during the Jupiter-Uranus conjunction in 1789 and afterwards—the Belgian revolution, the West Indies slave revolts, the Polish revolution, the Irish rebellion, the wave of radical thought in England and Germany—could plausibly be attributed to the direct influence and inspiration of the events in France. But the *Bounty* set sail from England for the South Pacific in late 1787, many months before the French Revolution emerged, and there had been no contact with Europe for over a year and a half by the time the mutiny occurred. That the most famous instance of rebellion in maritime history, the mutiny on the *Bounty*, took place at the same time as the most famous instance of rebellion in political history—the storming of the Bastille that began the French Revolution—yet thousands of miles away with no possible communication between the participants represented the kind of coincidence that supported Jung's concept that a powerful archetypal gestalt can emerge in the collective psyche and influence human affairs with no conventional causal connection. The further coincidence of these archetypally connected events with the Jupiter-Uranus conjunction in the sky at that time, the same alignment that coincided consistently with other cultural milestones of a successful Promethean character, suggested that such collective archetypal emergence might well take place in continuous correlation with planetary cycles.

As the Bastille correlation also suggests, on those occasions when these shorter alignments of the Jupiter-Uranus cycle coincided with the longer and less frequent alignments of the Uranus-Pluto cycle cited above—that is, when all three planets, Jupiter, Uranus, and Pluto, moved into alignment, as at the time of the Bastille revolt—the concurrent events tended to be especially dramatic, widespread, and consequential. In little more than fifty days in July and August 1789 in coincidence with this multiple alignment, the long-established and seemingly insuperable ancien régime in France largely collapsed. It was as if the characteristic burst of rebellious buoyancy, expansive cultural innovation, emancipation and awakening that tended to coincide with the short-lasting Jupiter-Uranus alignments served here as a successful activating catalyst for the more sustained, driven, and often violent revolutionary impulse associated with the longer-lasting Uranus-Pluto alignment that began at this time and continued through most of the 1790s.

A remarkably parallel unfolding of events happened as well in the *Bounty* mutiny. To this day the overpowering emotions and motives that compelled Fletcher Christian and the other seamen to suddenly rebel remain something of a mystery. With the success of that revolt began the long, intense, erotically charged, and murderously violent drama on Pitcairn Island in the course of the 1790s that overtook the mutineers and the Tahitian women and men who accompanied them—all happening on an island that was utterly isolated from the rest of the world, far from Europe and the violent upheaval that was taking place there at precisely the same time during the long Uranus-Pluto alignment. The result was a kind of laboratory case of a continuing synchronous emergence of parallel events totally isolated from each other yet reflecting the same archetypal complexes.[2]

In the past century, there was one time that Jupiter, Uranus, and Pluto were in a triple conjunction: 1968–69. During that entire two-year period, the three planets were closer to each other than at any other time in the twentieth century.[3] This was of course the extraordinary moment at the climax of the Sixties that brought the peak and full amplitude of that decade's characteristic trends and events, in an unprecedented collective outburst of rebellions, demonstrations, and strikes throughout the world. The protest movement was then at its height, and student revolts disrupted scores of colleges and universities, Columbia, Harvard, San Francisco State, among many others. The period encompassed by this triple conjunction brought the seminal Events of May in Paris, the powerful Tet insurgency in Vietnam, the tumultuous protests in Chicago at the Democratic National Convention, the ensuing trial of the Chicago Eight, the Weathermen's Days of Rage, the People's Park riots in Berkeley, the black American track champions at the Olympic Games in Mexico City standing on the medal podium with black-gloved fists raised in support of civil rights and black power, the founding of the militant American Indian Movement, and the Stonewall uprising in New York, among many other comparable events. The American-European "counterculture"—the term was invented during those months—entered its most exuberant phase. The Woodstock music festival took place, one of a wave of such mass festivals in these months that were impelled by an extraordinarily rich eruption of creativity in music and the other arts. Radical ideas in many fields were widely discussed and acted upon, as if a boiling point in the decade's creative turmoil had suddenly been reached.

Indeed, this period of the triple conjunction in 1968–69 coincided with a wave of cultural, technological, and scientific breakthroughs suggestive of a powerful archetypal emergence taking place in many other historically significant respects as well. Especially dramatic, in July 1969, was the successful culmination of the Sixties' space flight program with the Apollo 11 Moon landing. After a decade in which over fifteen billion man-hours were expended on the project and after three days traveling a quarter of a million miles through space, with a final dangerous passage that almost forced the aborting of the mission as Neil Armstrong had to take manual control of the landing module, the astronauts touched down on the Moon with twenty seconds of fuel remaining—the first time in history that human beings had broken free of the Earth's gravitational field and landed on another celestial body: "Houston. Tranquillity Base here. The Eagle has landed." Remarkably, at the time of the landing, the Moon was in a one-day quadruple conjunction with the Jupiter-Uranus-Pluto alignment.

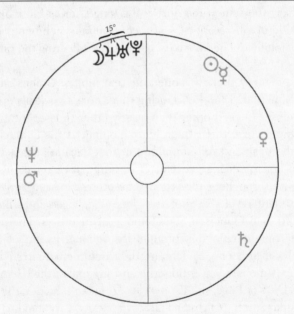

Apollo Moon Landing
July 20, 1969, 4:18 PM EDT, Cape Canaveral, Florida

Jupiter-Uranus-Pluto triple conjunction of 1968–69, with Moon in quadruple conjunction on date of Moon landing. Jupiter-Uranus separation is 0° 04'. Uranus-Pluto separation is 7° 41'. The entire quadruple conjunction is within 15° of exactitude.

Figure 10

Many other events occurred and new movements and ideas arose during the period of the triple conjunction that still influence contemporary society and thought. The famous public presentation by Douglas Engelhart of Stanford Research Institute in December 1968 ("still the most remarkable computer-technology demonstration of all time"), before an electrified audience in San Francisco of a thousand computer scientists and engineers, demonstrated the first working model for the future of personal computing: instantaneous long-distance sharing of complex digital information, display editing and word processing, the mouse, the cursor, windows, hypertext linking, email, shared-screen teleconferencing, and the underlying philosophy of using computers for radically enhancing individual and collective human intelligence. Nine months later the first successful transmission of the prototype for the Internet took place at UCLA. During this same period of the triple conjunction there occurred the first public presentation of what is now known as the Gaia hypothesis by James Lovelock at a meeting of the American Astronautical Society, the famous "Earth-rise" photograph taken by the Apollo 8 astronauts from the Moon on Christmas Eve 1968 ("the most influential environmental photograph ever taken"), the founding of the Earth Day project by Gaylord Nelson to catalyze global ecological awareness, and the beginning of radical ecology with the publication of Edward Abbey's *Desert Solitaire*.

This period also brought the beginning of gay liberation with the Stonewall uprising, and the emergence of radical feminism with the founding of New York Radical Women (who introduced the process of sharing stories that became known as consciousness-raising). During the same period occurred the first national women's liberation conference in Chicago, the founding of the radical feminist group Redstockings (which introduced the slogans "Sisterhood is powerful" and "The personal is political"), and the founding of the Boston Women's Health Book Collective, which produced the landmark feminist work *Our Bodies, Ourselves*. Elisabeth Kübler-Ross's *On Death and Dying* began the revolution in care of the dying and helped establish the hospice movement. Richard Alpert, just returned from India as Ram Dass, began his career as spiritual teacher and gave the public lectures that became the basis for the countercultural classic *Be Here Now*. Transpersonal psychology was founded by Stanislav Grof and Abraham Maslow in the United States, and archetypal psychology was founded by James Hillman and his circle in Switzerland.

Finally, this same period saw the publication of a wave of books that both reflected and helped catalyze the cultural and countercultural impulses of the time: Theodore Roszak's *The Making of a Counter Culture* (which originated the term), Kate Millett's *Sexual Politics*, Norman Mailer's *The Armies of the Night*, Eldridge Cleaver's *Soul on Ice*, Carlos Castañeda's *The Teachings of Don Juan*, Tom Wolfe's *The Electric Kool-Aid Acid Test*, Buckminster Fuller's *Operating Manual for Spaceship Earth*, Herbert Marcuse's *An Essay on Liberation*, Kurt Vonnegut's *Slaughterhouse-Five, or The Children's Crusade*, Fritz Perls's *Gestalt*

Therapy Verbatim, Jürgen Habermas's *Knowledge and Human Interests*, and Stewart Brand's *The Whole Earth Catalog*, among many others. There were few areas of human experience and activity that were not affected by the distinctive archetypal atmosphere and energy of the time, and few individuals who in retrospect do not regard that period as having been a powerful turning point in their lives.

There was another extraordinary occasion in the recent past that involved a rare multi-planet convergence coinciding with the Jupiter-Uranus cycle—in this instance with Neptune rather than Pluto. This was the last Jupiter-Uranus opposition of the twentieth century, which took place precisely during the astonishing fourteen-month period from June 1989 through July 1990 that brought the unexpected wave of demonstrations for freedom by hundreds of thousands of people across Eastern Europe, precipitating the collapse of communism throughout the continent and the fall of the Iron Curtain. Building on decades of courageous dissident acts and underground emancipatory movements, the sudden wave of liberation took place within weeks, beginning in Poland and the Baltic states and rapidly spreading through East Germany, Czechoslovakia, Hungary, Bulgaria, and Romania, bringing the fall of the Berlin Wall, the Velvet Revolution in Prague, and the election of Václav Havel. These same months also brought the release of Nelson Mandela and the turning of the tide against apartheid in South Africa.

The distinctive and nearly universal emotion of the time—sudden and unexpected euphoric liberation—was highly characteristic of the Jupiter-Uranus archetypal complex. It was an emotion and a liberation felt not only by the millions of people in the nations that underwent the surprisingly peaceful and rapid revolutionary change, but also by the billions around the world who sensed the end of the Cold War with its oppressive state of constant global nuclear tension and danger hovering over the human community. This Jupiter-Uranus alignment occurred in the early part of the long Uranus-Neptune conjunction of 1985–2001. As we will see later, the presence of a different outermost planet in this multiple configuration—Neptune, rather than Pluto as in 1968–69 or 1788–89—closely corresponded with the notably different archetypal inflection in this most recent instance compared with the other two historic periods of sudden radical change and emancipation.

Quantum Leaps and Peak Experiences

O f all planetary cycles the Jupiter-Uranus cycle presented perhaps the most richly abundant and brilliantly elaborate sequential patterning in the cultural and historical record. The expansive and elevating archetypal impulse associated with Jupiter seemed to interact in an unusually dynamic, mutually enhancing, and readily visible manner with the emancipatory and innovative principle of sudden radical change associated with Uranus. Major alignments of these two planets coincided with a consistent cyclical unfolding of successful creative milestones and liberating events in every field of human endeavor with whose history I was sufficiently familiar to evaluate significant correlations. The patterns of this archetypal complex were especially evident in the area of high culture—the arts and sciences, philosophy and the humanities, the history of ideas—but by no means exclusively so. It was also a planetary cycle and archetypal combination consistently associated with the timing of widespread private personal breakthroughs involving a sense of sudden happy awakening, new beginnings, unexpected good fortune, extraordinary expansion of consciousness, psychological rebirth, joyful intellectual epiphanies, radically extended horizons, and events often described by those experiencing them as "quantum leaps" and "peak experiences."

It is typical of the aesthetic precision and metaphoric coherence of these correlations that the original quantum leap—the emission or absorption of blackbody radiation in indivisible quanta of energy, Planck's innovative formulation that began the quantum physics revolution—first came to public attention during a Jupiter-Uranus conjunction, that of 1900.[4] This was the same conjunction that coincided with the publication of Freud's *Interpretation of Dreams*, which initiated the psychoanalytic revolution.

Similarly, the term "peak experiences"—coined by Abraham Maslow to signify especially elevating experiences that bring to the individual a sense of radically heightened understanding, happiness, and aliveness—came out of two personal experiences, one intellectual and the other emotional, that Maslow had during the Jupiter-Uranus conjunction of 1927–28. This was coincidentally the same conjunction that occurred at the climax of the quantum physics revolution that was marked by Bohr's principle of complementarity, Heisenberg's principle of indeterminacy, and the Solvay congress of October 1927.

Celebrated milestones in the history of science coincided with the Jupiter-Uranus cycle with extraordinary consistency. For example, the opposition alignment that immediately preceded the conjunction just cited coincided with the famous moment of triumph for Einstein's general theory of relativity in November 1919, when the Royal Society in London heard Arthur Eddington and Frank Dyson's stunning report of the eclipse calculations that confirmed Einstein's prediction of the bending of light in a gravitational field. The high drama of that event is worth recalling here in this context, not only because it so well exemplifies the archetypal dynamic at work during these alignments, but also for the people who were there and the poignant presence of Newton's image in the background, symbolizing the transfer of sovereignty from a long-established world view to a radically new one.

> It was not until the afternoon of Thursday, November 6, 1919, that the Fellows of the Royal and the Royal Astronomical Societies met in Burlington House to hear the official results of the two eclipse expeditions. . . . The aim of the operation had been to test Einstein's theory, and unofficial news of the results had been rumbling round the scientific world for weeks. Here, if nowhere else, men were aware that an age was ending, and the main hall of the Society was crowded. J. J. Thomson, now President of the Royal Society, James Jeans, and Lindemann were present. So were Sir Oliver Lodge and the mathematician and philosopher Alfred North Whitehead. All were agitated by the same question. Were the ideas upon which they had relied for so long to be found wanting? "The whole atmosphere of tense interest was exactly that of the Greek drama," wrote Whitehead later. "We were the chorus commenting on the decree of destiny as disclosed in the development of a supreme incident. There was dramatic quality in the very staging— the traditional ceremonial, and in the background the picture of Newton to remind us that the greatest of scientific generalizations was now, after more than two centuries, to receive its first modification. Nor was the personal interest wanting: a great adventure in thought had at length come safe to shore."

> Thomson rose to address the meeting, speaking of Einstein's theory as "one of the greatest achievements in the history of human thought," and then pushing home the full measure of what relativity meant. "It is not the discovery of an outlying island but of a whole continent of new scientific ideas. . . . It is the greatest discovery in connection with gravitation since Newton enunciated his principles."

Here we see not only the successful (Jupiter) scientific breakthrough (Uranus) but also the grand cultural honoring (Jupiter) of an unexpected revolutionary change in human thought (Uranus), both themes precisely reflective of the archetypal principles associated with the two planets in alignment. We also see a third archetypally appropriate theme, one that is frequent with this alignment, that of the sudden and unexpected expansion of intellectual and cosmological horizons to radically new dimensions.

In the succeeding months under this alignment, through 1920 and into 1921, Einstein's achievement and the theory of relativity were celebrated with what was for a scientific theory unprecedented media attention and public excitement. Einstein was declared the greatest genius who ever lived, and the theory of relativity was for the first time widely acclaimed by the scientific community and disseminated to the larger public. Einstein himself was born when Jupiter and Uranus were in close opposition alignment exactly three cycles earlier, and in certain respects his life and work can be seen as a paradigmatic embodiment of the Jupiter-Uranus archetypal complex—the supremely successful intellectual breakthrough, the astonishing leap of the scientific imagination beyond the established structures of time and space, the scarcely conceivable sudden shift in the nature of reality, the celebrated and honored rebel genius—Prometheus crowned king, as it were, in all these respects.

The Jupiter-Uranus complex appears to be associated with the experience of breakthroughs of all kinds, joyful Promethean moments of discovery, sudden ascents, unexpected insights that expand one's world, the "Aha!" experience. The history of technological breakthroughs is closely associated with Jupiter-Uranus axial alignments: the discovery of electromagnetic induction (1831), the invention of the telegraph (1844), the invention of the electric lightbulb (1879), the first radio broadcast (1920), the first sound motion picture (1927), the first television transmission (1927), the first Internet transmission (1969). During the Jupiter-Uranus opposition of 1976, Steve Wozniak and Steven Jobs constructed their first personal computer.

Especially notable is the history of aviation and space flight, in which the characteristic Jupiter-Uranus impulse to defy limits, to transcend gravity, to move upward and outward into freedom and expansive space, is particularly clearly embodied. Thus Jupiter and Uranus were in alignment at the time of the first recorded human flight of any kind, the balloon launching by the Montgolfier brothers in France in the late eighteenth century. The Montgolfiers invented the hot-air balloon in November 1782. After months of experiments they launched the first balloon with a human passenger in Paris on October 15, 1783, the first recorded instance in which a human being physically left the earth. Both of these events—the invention and the launching—occurred during the Jupiter-Uranus opposition of 1782–83, the alignment halfway between 1776 and 1789 that coincided with the Treaty of Paris ratifying the independence of the

American colonies, which was signed in the same city one month before the successful launching.

Benjamin Franklin, who was himself born during the first Jupiter-Uranus conjunction of the eighteenth century, in 1706, was in Paris during just this period representing the new nation. In a letter of July 1783 to Sir Joseph Banks, president of the Royal Society, the seventy-seven-year-old Franklin wrote of the future of science, technology, and human progress with that tone of expansive optimism and joy in discovery that is so characteristic of the Jupiter-Uranus combination:

> I am pleas'd with the late astronomical discoveries made by our Society. Furnish'd as all Europe now is with Academies of Science, with nice instruments and the spirit of Experiment, the progress of human knowledge will be rapid, and discoveries made of which we have at present no conception. I begin to be almost sorry I was born so soon, since I cannot have the happiness of knowing what will be known a hundred years hence.
>
> I wish continued success to the labours of the Royal Society, and that you may long adorn their chair, being with the highest esteem,
>
> Dear Sir, your most obedient and most humble servant,
>
> B. Franklin
>
> [P.S.] Dr Blagden will acquaint you with the experiment of a vast Globe sent up into the air, much talk'd of here at present, and which if prosecuted may furnish means of new knowledge.

Similarly, the first aviation experiments by the Wright brothers took place in October 1900 during the Jupiter-Uranus conjunction of that year, with their first flight in a glider at Kitty Hawk, North Carolina (this was the same conjunction that coincided with the beginnings of quantum physics and psychoanalysis). Jupiter and Uranus were again in conjunction in May 1927 when Charles Lindbergh made the first solo airplane flight across the Atlantic from Long Island to Paris in *The Spirit of St. Louis* (the same conjunction as that of the Bohr-Heisenberg and Solvay congress milestones in quantum physics).

And Jupiter and Uranus were yet again in alignment at the beginning of the history of space flight. The first space flights by Yury Gagarin and Alan Shepard coincided with the opposition of 1961–62.[5] It was during this same alignment, on May 25, 1961, that President John F. Kennedy made his epoch-making call for the United States to achieve a manned Moon landing within the decade.

> I believe that this nation should commit itself to achieving the goal, before this decade is out, of landing a man on the Moon and returning him safely to the Earth. No single space project in this period will be more impressive to mankind, or more important for the long-range

exploration of space; and none will be so difficult or expensive to accomplish.[6]

To summarize: The Uranus-Pluto conjunction spanned the entire period of the 1960s' space program. Its beginning coincided with the moment when Jupiter first moved into opposition alignment with this Uranus-Pluto conjunction. Its climax, the Apollo 11 Moon landing in 1969, coincided with the moment Jupiter moved into triple conjunction with Uranus and Pluto. The "giant leap for mankind" is a paradigmatic instance of the theme of quantum leaps and peak experiences, which here took place on an enormous collective global level. The scientific, technological, and human feat of flying to the distant Moon, landing, then returning safely to the Earth—unprecedented, spectacular, and before that decade scarcely conceivable—constituted both a quantum leap in human evolution and a peak experience engendered in the six hundred million people who witnessed the event worldwide.[7]

Three weeks later occurred the Woodstock music festival, which was attended by nearly half a million people and was in many ways both the emotional and artistic climax of the Sixties' countercultural ethos. The two events so close in time, the Moon landing and Woodstock, represent the same powerful archetypal complex though with very different inflections: the Jupiterian principle of elevation and expansion, largeness, success, grandeur, and joy combined with the Promethean impulse of innovation, creativity, rebellion, breakthrough, and defiance of constraints; with both of these titanically empowered and intensified by the Plutonic principle, which is also associated with events that have a mass, epochal, and evolutionary character.

It is most striking that both of these paradigmatic events took place in the summer of 1969 precisely during the only triple conjunction of Jupiter, Uranus, and Pluto in the twentieth century. The three planets at that time were in fact at their closest, most exact alignment since the birth of René Descartes in 1596. Remarkably, Descartes was born with the Sun in a quadruple conjunction with Jupiter, Uranus, and Pluto. This is perhaps as vivid a cosmic portrait as one can imagine for the declarer of the birth of the modern self in all its radiant solar glory, powerfully centered identity, and emancipatory confidence. "Everything must be thoroughly overthrown for once in my life," Descartes's declaration in the first of his *Meditations*, could well have been said by the better part of a generation in 1968–69.

From Copernicus to Darwin

Because of the specific character of the two principles associated with Jupiter and Uranus, their archetypal interaction seemed to have an expansively synergistic quality that translated itself into waves of creative brilliance and successful experiments that were remarkably apparent as soon as one examined the relevant periods and cultural data. The distinctive character of their historical correlations made the underlying patterns seem in the course of research to leap out at one, as if in a burst of awakening. The effect was very different from that of examining the sequence of the Saturn-Pluto cycle, as in the last section, where the unfolding patterns of grave historical crises and contractions sometimes seemed to present themselves with a dark and heavy inevitability, as if the workings of fate and destiny were executing their implacable judgments before one's eyes. Each archetypal complex seemed to rule its own universe: Not only did it inform the events and eras coincident with the corresponding planetary alignment, it also permeated the experience of researching and recognizing its characteristic manifestations and even the language and rhetorical modes used for its description and analysis. Like celestial bodies whose presence structure the very geometry of their surrounding space, these archetypal principles governed and pervaded their domains.

The Scientific Revolution

Let us return to Michelet's comment that "the Revolution of 1789 had begun with the *Discourse on Method*." Amazingly, Jupiter and Uranus were in conjunction not only in 1789 but also in 1637, the year Descartes's *Discourse on Method* was published with its epoch-making *cogito*.[8] This was the third Jupiter-Uranus conjunction following the one that coincided with Descartes's birth. The sequence of correlations for these four successive conjunctions is typical of the systematic sequential patterning of cultural breakthroughs that coincided with this planetary cycle.

The conjunction of 1595–96, when Descartes was born, also coincided with the crucial turning point in the life and work of Kepler. It was in July 1595 that Kepler experienced the sudden illumination of the geometrical harmonies of the planetary orbits that set in motion his long and arduous research that at last led triumphantly to his discovery of the laws of planetary motion. During this same conjunction he wrote his first major work, *Mysterium Cosmographicum*, the first work since the *De Revolutionibus* to develop and extend the mathematical arguments in favor of the Copernican theory, and the first work of modern science to demand physical explanations for celestial phenomena.

The next Jupiter-Uranus conjunction, fourteen years later, was the one of 1609–10 cited at the start of this section that coincided with the publication of both Kepler's *Astronomia Nova*, which made public his revolutionary laws of planetary motion, and Galileo's *Sidereus Nuncius*, which announced his epoch-making telescopic discoveries. The following conjunction in 1623–24 continued the sequence, coinciding with the publication of Galileo's celebrated *Assayer* (October 1623), which contained his influential exposition of the new scientific method and view of physical reality that formed the foundation of modern science. It was in this book that Galileo made his famous statement that "the Book of Nature is written in mathematical characters," first distinguished between primary (measurable) and secondary qualities of matter, and asserted the superiority of investigation to authority. Moreover, it was during this same conjunction that Galileo began his great Copernican treatise, *On the Two Chief World Systems*, the book that precipitated the conflict with the Catholic Church.

During the immediately following conjunction of 1637–38, Descartes published not only his *Discourse on Method*, the foundational work of modern philosophy, but also his *Geometry*, the founding work of modern analytic geometry that first introduced the Cartesian coordinates and the use of algebra to solve geometrical problems. Moreover, during this same conjunction Galileo published his last and greatest work, summing up his life's research in experimental science, the *Dialogue Concerning Two New Sciences*, which was smuggled out of Italy and published in Holland.

During the following opposition of 1644, Descartes published his most comprehensive work, the *Principia Philosophiae*, and during the following conjunction in 1651, Thomas Hobbes published his magnum opus, *Leviathan*. Finally, fourteen years later, Jupiter and Uranus were again conjunct, from January 1665 to February 1666. This was the crucial moment when Isaac Newton at age twenty-two, during his personal Uranus-square-Uranus transit, left Cambridge University for his home in Lincolnshire and began the spectacular eighteen-month period of intellectual creativity that laid the foundations for his later discoveries in mathematics and physical science: he discovered the general binomial theorem, invented differential and integral calculus, made his first astronomical discoveries, and performed the most advanced experimental research of his age in the science of optics. It was during this period that the incident of the falling apple occurred according to Newton's later account. Not unlike the comment made about 1927, one would not be far off in saying that in 1665 the pace of discovery in theoretical physics was possibly as great as any other year in the history of science.

The eventual fruition of those breakthroughs—Newton's formulation of the concept of universal gravitation and his writing of the *Principia*—took place in close coincidence with the Jupiter-Uranus opposition of 1685–86. This Jupiter-Uranus alignment in the sky, a world transit, coincided with Newton's once-in-a-lifetime personal transit of Uranus opposite Uranus, discussed earlier: Jupiter and Uranus both crossing his natal Uranus at the same time. This was in fact the same extraordinary convergence of personal and world transits that happened with both Galileo and Descartes and indeed also with Einstein, when in each case the Jupiter-Uranus world transit precisely coincided with the individual's Uranus-opposite-Uranus personal transit.

Remarkably, if we look back a century earlier to the very beginning of the Scientific Revolution, we find that Jupiter and Uranus were also in conjunction in 1540–41 at the time that Copernicus finally decided after many years of hesitation to publish his *De Revolutionibus*. He was persuaded to do so by his closest student, Rheticus, who at this time brought forth the first published account of the Copernican heliocentric theory, the *Narratio Prima* ("First Report"), in two editions, at Gdansk in 1540 and at Basel in 1541. Simultaneously, during the fourteen months of this 1540–41 conjunction, Vesalius wrote the bulk of his *De Humani Corporis Fabrica*, which marked the beginning of the modern scientific revolution in biology and medicine.

This particular alignment at the Copernican birth was an example of a Jupiter-Uranus conjunction coinciding with the longer Uranus-Pluto cycle (this was also the period of the Radical Reformation). Thus a form of the rare triple-planet axial configuration we saw with the Apollo Moon landing in 1969—which was, in a sense, the epochal climax of the Scientific Revolution—also happened to take place at the very beginning of the Scientific Revolution. In this case, rather than a triple conjunction, as in 1968–69, the Jupiter-Uranus conjunction was here aligned in opposition to Pluto—this being the same configuration that occurred in 1789 at the start of the French Revolution.

The Eighteenth and Nineteenth Centuries

The Jupiter-Uranus cycle was in fact the most reliable correlative factor for the timing of major intellectual events that occurred between Descartes's *Discourse* and the Revolution of 1789. For example, if we examine the history of European thought in the Enlightenment, focusing especially on those works that prepared the ground for the democratic revolutions at the end of the eighteenth century, we look to the contributions of the French philosophes—Voltaire, Montesquieu, Diderot, Rousseau. Along with the *Encyclopédie* (whose serial publication was spread out over the entire period of the Uranus-Pluto square of the midcentury and after), the most crucial works of the philosophes were the *Philosophical*

Letters by Voltaire, *The Spirit of Laws* by Montesquieu, and *The Social Contract* and *Émile* by Rousseau. Remarkably, all four of these books were published in precise coincidence with consecutive Jupiter-Uranus conjunctions at fourteen-year intervals: the *Philosophical Letters* in 1734, *The Spirit of Laws* in 1748, and *The Social Contract* and *Émile* both in 1762. These years coincided precisely with the three successive Jupiter-Uranus conjunctions of the mid-eighteenth century.

If we then look across the Channel to the major figures of the English Enlightenment who were contemporary with the French philosophes—Pope, Hume, Gibbon, Adam Smith—we find the same pattern. Alexander Pope's *Essay on Man* (reprinted over sixty times in France before 1789) was published during the conjunction of 1734, the same year as Voltaire's *Philosophical Letters*. David Hume's principal philosophical work, *Enquiry Concerning Human Understanding*, was published during the conjunction of 1748, the same year as Montesquieu's *The Spirit of Laws*. And both Edward Gibbon's *The History of the Decline and Fall of the Roman Empire* and Adam Smith's *The Wealth of Nations* were published during the conjunction of 1775–76, at the beginning of the American Revolution.

Nor did the sequential pattern cease there. The Jupiter-Uranus conjunctions immediately following the above sequence precisely coincided with the crucial milestones in the history of political and economic philosophy marked by the series of seminal works and analyses, at fourteen-year intervals, by Bentham (1789), Ricardo (1817), Tocqueville (1831), Marx and Engels (1844–45), and John Stuart Mill (1859).[9] Moreover, in the history of science in the decades during and after the American and French Revolutions, a parallel sequence of consecutive major breakthroughs and publications marked the revolution in modern chemistry, again precisely in coincidence with the Jupiter-Uranus cycle of every fourteen years: the crucial experiments by Priestley and Lavoisier that led to the overthrow of the phlogiston theory and the birth of modern chemistry (1775–76); Lavoisier's *Traité élémentaire de chimie* ("Elementary Treatise on Chemistry"), the foundation text of modern chemistry (1789); and Dalton's construction of the first table of atomic weights and first statement of the atomic theory of matter (1803).

Further: Faraday's historic experiments that demonstrated his discovery of electromagnetic induction took place during the Jupiter-Uranus conjunction of 1831. During this same conjunction, Charles Darwin embarked on his historic voyage to South America and the Galápagos Islands on HMS *Beagle*. During the next conjunction, of 1844–45, Darwin wrote his first summary of the theory of natural selection, the first version of what became *The Origin of Species*, a two-hundred-page manuscript that he shared only privately (much like Copernicus with his first summation of the heliocentric theory, the *Commentariolus*). Exactly fourteen years later in coincidence with the next conjunction came Darwin's and Wallace's announcement in 1858 of the theory of evolution and Darwin's writing of *The Origin of Species* itself. And fourteen more years and one cycle later, in coincidence with the Jupiter-Uranus conjunction of 1871–72, Darwin published *The Descent of Man.*

Parenthetically, following up on our earlier discussion of Darwin's and Lincoln's nearly identical birth charts: The year 1858, which first brought public attention to Darwin and his theory of evolution during this Jupiter-Uranus conjunction after the joint announcement at the Linnean Society in London, also first brought Lincoln and his views on slavery to national prominence as a result of the famous Lincoln-Douglas debates, when Lincoln's articulate opposition to the extension of slavery in the United States became widely known throughout the country. Lincoln received the nomination for U.S. Senator that began his campaign on June 16, 1858. Darwin received the crucial letter from Wallace that set into motion the public dissemination of his theory on June 18, 1858.

Returning to the history of science, it was during the immediately following Jupiter-Uranus opposition in 1865 that James Clerk Maxwell published his landmark paper "A Dynamical Theory of the Electromagnetic Field," which was the culmination of the revolution in nineteenth-century physics that had begun with Faraday's experiments during the conjunction of 1831. (Coincidentally, Maxwell himself was born during the latter conjunction in the same month Faraday announced to the Royal Society the results of these experiments, which became the basis for Maxwell's work in formulating the equations that underlay the theory of electromagnetic fields.)

Finally, it was during that same Jupiter-Uranus opposition of 1865 that Gregor Mendel announced his discovery of the laws of heredity, which gave Darwin's and Wallace's evolutionary hypothesis—announced during the immediately preceding conjunction—the genetic mechanism it required for its theoretical completion. However, this announcement by the Austrian monk-scientist, which occurred at two meetings of the Natural Science Society in Brno, Moravia, in February and March 1865, went virtually unnoticed. The revolutionary discoveries were entirely ignored by the scientific community for several decades until suddenly, in 1900, during the Jupiter-Uranus conjunction of that year, Mendel's work was simultaneously rediscovered by three European botanists—de Vries, Correns, and von Tschermak—who, working independently (in Amsterdam, Tübingen, and Vienna, respectively), conducted experiments that verified Mendel's theory and synchronistically published separate reports to that effect in a single two-month period. During the same year and conjunction, the English biologist William Bateson also discovered Mendel's work, translated his paper into English, and named the new science of genetics.

Music and Literature

The evidence of sequential correlations discussed in these chapters suggests that major cyclical alignments of the outer planets coincide with a mutual activation of the corresponding archetypal principles, but rather than simply signifying a mechanical "switching on" of the specific archetypal gestalt and then a "switching off" when the transit is over, each alignment seems to represent a more complex and subtle unfolding of archetypal wave patterns. The evidence suggests that each alignment in a particular planetary cycle coincides with a period in which the corresponding archetypal complex manifests itself in a definite, readily discerned manner—it "registers," it expresses its meaning, it brings forth its essence into the collective psyche with a conspicuous clustering of archetypally appropriate events—but then after the alignment is over, the same impulse continues to develop. It endures, it evolves, it goes through changes, sometimes below the surface, sometimes above. It undergoes constant modification under the impact of new archetypal influences as the ongoing and ever-shifting cyclical alignments with other planets occur, and as individuals undergo their personal transits and creatively respond to and enact in their particular ways the larger archetypal forces at work.

Then when the original two planets again come into major cyclical alignment, there takes place another conspicuous activation of the relevant archetypal complex, with the occurrence of cultural and historical phenomena that are clearly related to earlier periods of the same cycle. But this new activation takes place in such a way that everything that has unfolded since the last cyclical alignment has in the meantime been absorbed and is now newly expressed by the new cyclical upwelling of that archetypal complex. We saw suggestions of such a process of ongoing archetypal evolution with, for example, the Uranus-Pluto cycle and the great emancipatory movements and Dionysian awakenings that cyclically unfolded in the modern era. We saw this again with the Saturn-Pluto cycle and its sequential correlation with the world wars and Cold War, and with collective moral confrontations with the shadow side of existence. And it is evident in the historical developments cited here as well, from social and political liberation to scientific revolutions and artistic creativity.

Whatever field of human activity I turned my attention to, once I grasped the template provided by the Jupiter-Uranus cycle, the coinciding patterns of creative breakthroughs and cultural milestones were surprisingly clear. In the field of music, for example, I immediately examined the case of Beethoven's *Eroica*, his Third Symphony, this being perhaps the most explicitly and expansively Promethean work in the history of classical music—revolutionary in spirit, in conception, and in historical impact. I found that Beethoven composed the *Eroica* exactly during the Jupiter-Uranus conjunction of 1803. This was the first conjunction after that of 1788–89 and the start of the French Revolution, whose ideals directly inspired the great composition. In turn, Beethoven began the composition of the magnificently expansive and exalting Ninth Symphony during the immediately following conjunction fourteen years later, in 1817.

When I looked back to the work that most fully anticipated the *Eroica*—Mozart's last symphony, the aptly named *Jupiter* Symphony in C Major (K.551)—I found that this had in fact been composed during the 1788–89 Jupiter-Uranus conjunction exactly one full cycle before the *Eroica*. Moreover, during this same conjunction, Haydn had composed his *Oxford* Symphony (No. 92 in G Major), which has itself been called Haydn's "Eroica" because of the new creative freedom it displayed, beyond the classical constraints of earlier symphonies. The *Oxford* began a new stage in Haydn's musical evolution that unfolded through the 1790s with his series of London symphonies, which with Mozart's last three symphonies represent the summit of orchestral composition before the *Eroica*.

The diachronic patterning of these two consecutive conjunctions (1788–89 and 1803) that link Mozart and Haydn to Beethoven is suggestive of the more complex picture of archetypal evolution I just described above. These were the two Jupiter-Uranus conjunctions that took place at the beginning and end of the French Revolutionary period. One could say that what separated Mozart and Haydn's late symphonies from Beethoven's *Eroica* and its successors was the Uranus-Pluto opposition of the 1790s and all it represented. In archetypal terms, it was precisely the radical intensification of Promethean and Dionysian qualities in dynamic interplay that marked the dramatic evolution from Mozart and Haydn to Beethoven—the heightened emancipatory drive, the titanic will to creative freedom, the intensity of turmoil and sudden unpredictable shifts, the unleashing of elemental forces, the awakening of nature's depths, the sweeping mass movement of energies, the transformative power—the same qualities that marked the entire French Revolutionary epoch. As Wagner would later put it, Beethoven was "a Titan, wrestling with the Gods."

Remarkably, when I looked to the history of classical music after the *Eroica* to that work which exerted a comparably revolutionary influence on the second half of the nineteenth century—Wagner's *Tristan und Isolde*—I found that this seminal work too was composed precisely during a Jupiter-Uranus conjunction (the same conjunction, centered on the year 1858, that coincided with the

Darwin-Wallace announcement of the theory of evolution and Darwin's writing of *The Origin of Species*).[10] Indeed, in a pattern that closely resembled the one just noted with the *Eroica*, Wagner's *Tristan und Isolde* coincided with the Jupiter-Uranus conjunction that occurred immediately after the Uranus-Pluto conjunction of 1845–56, this being the very next Uranus-Pluto axial alignment after Beethoven and the French Revolutionary period.

Again, like the *Eroica*, *Tristan*'s extraordinary elemental power seemed to embody and carry forth the combination of Promethean and Dionysian archetypal energies—at once titanic and emancipatory, instinctual and revolutionary—that had been catalyzed during the years of the Uranus-Pluto period and influenced Wagner's inner development and musical aspirations, just as had occurred with Beethoven during the Uranus-Pluto alignment of the 1790s. Moreover, in the same year that Wagner began composing *Tristan und Isolde*, Baudelaire published the equally revolutionary *Les Fleurs du mal*. The coincidence has been noted by others: "That Wagner as harmonist initiated a new era is a commonplace of musical history; some historians are even inclined to regard *Tristan* as the beginning of modern music, just as Baudelaire's *Les Fleurs du mal* marked the beginning of modern literature. The coincidence of date is amazing."[11]

A remarkably similar pattern was visible with Stravinsky's *The Rite of Spring*, whose famous premiere in Paris took place in 1913 just as the Jupiter-Uranus conjunction reached the 20° point. Once again, this was the first Jupiter-Uranus conjunction to occur after the Uranus-Pluto opposition of the early twentieth century—the very next axial alignment after that just cited for Wagner—and again the characteristic Uranus-Pluto theme of a revolutionary awakening of Dionysian energies was vividly embodied. We can see the brilliantly creative *Rite of Spring* (and the audience's response at its premiere) both as bringing to new expression the unleashed orgiastic and chthonic forces of nature (Uranus-Pluto), and as anticipating the devastating destruction and epoch-ending trauma of the coming world war (coincident with the Saturn-Pluto conjunction that also was then just beginning, exactly one cycle after the Saturn-Pluto conjunction of Stravinsky's birth).

As these examples suggest, both the exact timing and the archetypal character of the correlations of major milestones in the history of classical music were considerably more complex than can be summarized as a simple correspondence with the Jupiter-Uranus cycle. Not only the multiplicity of ongoing and overlapping planetary cycles of the world transits but also the personal transits of the composers were consistently relevant. For example, Stravinsky underwent a once-in-a-lifetime personal transit of Pluto conjoining his natal Sun during the years 1909 to 1913, the period in which he composed *The Rite of Spring* and the similarly Dionysian works *The Firebird* (1910) and *Petrushka* (1911). After this period of primordial intensity, Stravinsky's work took on a decidedly more restrained character as he entered into his neoclassical and serialist phases. He never again composed works having the same inspired violently eruptive potency as those of the *Rite of Spring* period.

An important factor in assessing all such correlations was not simply the fact of a creative breakthrough but also the specific quality and spirit of the musical works in question. It is true that the Jupiter-Uranus cycle coincided with remarkable regularity with creative breakthroughs and historic milestones in music as in many other fields. But equally evident, works that were composed and premiered during these relatively brief alignments tended to reflect, like the overall cultural ethos of that moment, certain qualities that were highly suggestive of the Jupiter-Uranus archetypal complex itself, such as an especially high-spirited, celebratory, exuberant creative spirit. Thus Bach's Brandenburg Concertos, with their exhilarating virtuosity and vigor, a crowning achievement of the Baroque era, were brought forth during the Jupiter-Uranus conjunction of 1720–21. This too took place just after a longer Uranus-Pluto conjunction, the one before the opposition of the French Revolution, thus forming an exact cyclical sequence with the correlations cited above involving Mozart and Haydn, Beethoven, Wagner, and Stravinsky.

If we now turn to the history of literature, the 1720–21 period of the Jupiter-Uranus conjunction that brought Bach's Brandenburg Concertos also coincided with Jonathan Swift's commencing his great satire, *Gulliver's Travels*. Alignments of the Jupiter-Uranus cycle regularly coincided with creative works in which astonishing magnitude or a surprising expansion of conventional size limits played a role. This can be understood as an expression of the Uranus→ Jupiter dynamic vector, with the Promethean impulse suddenly liberating Jupiter's archetypal impulse towards largeness and expansion and giving it creative embodiment in surprising ways. Beethoven's *Eroica* was of course a classic example in the musical field in its unprecedented expansion of the size of the required orchestra, the length of each movement, and the length of the entire symphony— not to mention the magnitude of the sound itself—in all of these respects, far beyond the limits established by Mozart and Haydn. We see a very different creative inflection of this same theme of astonishing size in Swift's *Gulliver's Travels*, both in the Lilliputians' experience of suddenly encountering the wondrously gigantic Gulliver and, conversely, in Gulliver's own amazed experience of astounding size in Brobdingnag, the land of giants.

In the history of literature, which has so many significant authors and works and constitutes so large a database, both the synchronic and the diachronic patterns are especially rich and ramified. Each Jupiter-Uranus axial alignment consistently coincided with an unusual multiplicity of creative milestones in literature, and subsequent alignments of the same planets coincided with similar waves of literary creativity whose close archetypal and historical connection with the preceding alignments strongly suggested the existence of ongoing cyclical patterns of creative breakthrough.

For example, when I investigated a literary epoch well-known for its sustained revolutionary character, the first two decades of the twentieth century, I examined possible correlations with the Jupiter-Uranus cycle involving those several writers who together brought about the radical transformation of modern literature at that time: Joyce, Proust, Kafka, Yeats, Pound, Eliot, Stein, Lawrence, and Woolf. The Jupiter-Uranus conjunction that occurred in that general time period was within 15° of exactitude, typically the period of greatest archetypal intensity, in the fourteen months centered on the year 1914 that extended from December 1913 to January 1915.

When I reviewed the relevant biographies for this brief period, it was quickly clear that these specific fourteen months were pivotal for virtually every one of those writers, bringing the simultaneous emergence of an extraordinary number of landmark works in twentieth-century literature. After years of solitary writing and artistic development, Joyce published both of his first works, *The Dubliners* and *A Portrait of the Artist as a Young Man*, during these months. At this same time he began his masterpiece, *Ulysses* (completing it seven years later at the following Jupiter-Uranus opposition). T. S. Eliot moved from the United States to England at this time, the turning point in his career, and began his fertile association with Ezra Pound. Pound, who discovered and began the serial publication of Joyce's *A Portrait of the Artist* that year, also discovered Eliot's first major poem, *The Lovesong of J. Alfred Prufrock*, that same year of 1914, published the first anthology of Imagist poetry, *Des Imagistes*, and, with Wyndham Lewis, began the Vorticist magazine *Blast*. In the same year William Butler Yeats published his *Responsibilities and Other Poems*, which similarly reflected the new modernist aesthetic, while Gertrude Stein published her most explicitly "cubist" volume of poems, *Tender Buttons*. Wallace Stevens published his first poems that year, while Robert Frost published *North of Boston*, which contained many of his best-known poems, such as *Mending Wall* and *The Death of the Hired Man*. D. H. Lawrence published his first volume of short fiction, *The Prussian Officer and Other Stories*, while also writing in these months the first of his greatest novels, *The Rainbow*. Franz Kafka during these same months wrote his first major novel, *The Trial*. And in the month just before the 15° point of the conjunction was reached, in November 1913, Marcel Proust published at his own expense the first volume of his masterpiece, *À la recherche du temps perdu* (*Remembrance of Things Past*).

This striking synchronic pattern can be recognized as part of a longer *diachronic* pattern of coherently related correlations with this cycle. For example, with respect to the development of the modernist novel, during the immediately preceding Jupiter-Uranus conjunction of 1900 (coincident with Freud's *The Interpretation of Dreams* and Planck's quantum physics discovery), Henry James wrote *The Ambassadors* (begun in the summer of 1900, completed the following spring). This and its two successors, *The Wings of the Dove* and *The Golden Bowl*, anticipated the formal and thematic innovations of twentieth-century fiction that would soon be fully exploited in the work of Joyce and Proust, and later in the work of Virginia Woolf and William Faulkner.

During the conjunction immediately *after* the two just cited, that of 1927–28 (coincident with the Bohr-Heisenberg quantum physics synthesis and Lemaître's expanding-universe theory), Virginia Woolf published *To the Lighthouse*, her greatest novel, while in the same months William Faulkner began his extraordinary succession of major works, writing *Sartoris*, the first of his long series of Yoknapatawpha County novels, then, still during this conjunction, beginning *The Sound and the Fury*, the first of his masterworks and perhaps his greatest novel.

The history of the modernist novel thus suggests a diachronic pattern of development that closely correlates with the first three Jupiter-Uranus conjunctions of the twentieth century, which in retrospect can be seen to have coincided with the inception or publication of the most significant and pivotal works in that literary revolution: James's *The Ambassadors* as the major precursor, Proust's *Remembrance of Things Past* and Joyce's *Ulysses* (and, in a different strain of modernism, Kafka's *The Trial*) as the fully achieved first-generation works, and Woolf's *To the Lighthouse* and Faulkner's *The Sound and the Fury* as the next generation.

Comparable patterns were visible in whatever literary epoch I examined. For example, major milestones in the history of English literature from Spenser to Milton took place in precise coincidence with the major milestones of the Scientific Revolution noted earlier involving Kepler, Galileo, Descartes, and Newton. During the conjunction of 1595–96, Edmund Spenser published his masterpiece, *The Faerie Queen*; William Shakespeare's *Sonnets* were first published during the immediately following conjunction of 1609–10; the First Folio edition of Shakespeare's plays was published during the next conjunction of 1623–24; during the following one of 1637–38 was published John Milton's *Lycidas*, one of the greatest poems in the English language; and during the conjunction of 1665–66, Milton completed his masterpiece, *Paradise Lost*. Continuing the sequence, *Paradise Regained* was published during the following opposition of 1671–72, as was Milton's final masterwork, *Samson Agonistes*.

So also with the beginnings of the English novel in the eighteenth century: When I checked the publication dates for the pioneering works in this form by Henry Fielding, Samuel Richardson, and Tobias Smollett, I found that two had published their greatest novels—*Tom Jones* by Fielding, *Clarissa* by Richardson—and Smollett had published his first novel, *Roderick Random*, all during a single fourteen-month period between January 1748 and February 1749 when Jupiter and Uranus were in conjunction. During the immediately preceding Jupiter-Uranus opposition, centered on the year 1741, both Richardson and Fielding had published *their* first novels, *Pamela* by Richardson and *Joseph Andrews* by Fielding.

Again, it is important to consider the underlying character and spirit of the work in question as much as its status as a cultural icon of innovation or achievement. In Fielding's *Tom Jones*, for example, as in many other artistic works and cultural phenomena coincident with the Jupiter-Uranus cycle (e.g., the *Eroica*, the celebrated revolutionary awakenings of 1775–76 and 1789, the countercultural efflorescence of 1968–69, the euphoric 1989 fall of communism in Eastern Europe), one can readily discern in the hero and narrative of such a work the characteristically prodigal spirit of the Jupiter-Uranus archetypal complex: robustly adventurous, untrammeled, ebullient, generous, excessive, at once admirably principled and blithely transgressive, constantly opening out to new horizons. Such a spirit reflected an essential dimension of the underlying Jupiter-Uranus archetypal complex whose emergence in the collective life of the culture during these alignments seemed to constellate a certain widespread adventurous vitality and enhanced creative inspiration, which in turn brought forth these cyclical waves of innovative works.

The general picture with respect to the history of literature is thus one in which the axial alignments of the Jupiter-Uranus cycle coincided consistently with many concurrent milestones of creative innovation, events that were part of larger continuities that formed serial patterns in coincidence with the preceding and subsequent alignments of the same planets. Striking diachronic patterns coincident with the Jupiter-Uranus cycle are in fact readily apparent in the history of Western literature from the Renaissance to the present. Again, it is not that such events suddenly and exclusively happened during these alignment periods, with no connection to the events and activities of the intervening years. Rather, there seemed to occur a kind of cresting of the wave of ongoing literary activity and cultural creativity in general correlation with those periods. That cresting is visible in the numerous publications or inceptions of significant and revolutionary works that occurred during the alignments, as well as in distinct clusterings in several other similar categories of events such as the beginnings of influential movements, new genres, and creative associations between major literary figures. The entire set of correlations appears to form an intelligible pattern of cyclically related cultural phenomena that bear the precise archetypal qualities associated with Jupiter and Uranus.

Often a particular Jupiter-Uranus conjunction period brought forth a work that marked the beginning of a sustained series of such works by a major author that took their basic character from the one that had appeared in coincidence with the conjunction. One example is that of Faulkner, who started his long sequence of Yoknapatawpha County novels during the Jupiter-Uranus conjunction of 1927–28 with *Sartoris* and *The Sound and the Fury*, the first in the series of masterpieces that rapidly followed (*As I Lay Dying, Sanctuary, Light in August*, and the rest). Another case is that of Thomas Hardy, who began his long series of Wessex novels with *Under the Greenwood Tree* during the conjunction of 1871–72 and followed it with *Far from the Madding Crowd, The Return of the Native, The*

Mayor of Casterbridge, Tess of the D'Urbervilles, and his other novels that focused on the people and landscape of southwest England.

During the same conjunction of 1871–72, Émile Zola initiated his twenty-novel experiment in naturalism, the *Les Rougon-Macquart* cycle of novels that documented life in the French Second Empire, with the publication of *La Fortune des Rougon.* Likewise, it was during the conjunction of 1900 that Colette published the first of her Claudine series of novels. During the same conjunction, as mentioned above, Henry James commenced his final and most complex phase of work with *The Ambassadors,* which was followed by *The Wings of the Dove* and *The Golden Bowl,* the three novels forming a coherent whole both formally and philosophically. The following conjunction of 1913–14 brought the first volume of Proust's multivolume *Remembrance of Things Past* (whose final volume was published in 1927 in coincidence with the next conjunction).

During the one Jupiter-Uranus conjunction I left out in the above sequence, yet another memorable series of fictional works was initiated when Arthur Conan Doyle wrote, in March and April of 1886, the first Sherlock Holmes story, *A Study in Scarlet.*[12] Moreover, in the cycle just before this, Lewis Carroll published *Alice's Adventures in Wonderland* and its sequel, *Through the Looking-Glass,* in exact correlation with the successive Jupiter-Uranus alignments of 1865 and 1872. After decades of writing, Tolkien commenced publication of his *Lord of the Rings* trilogy during the conjunction of 1954–55, with all three volumes published in those two years. During the same conjunction J. D. Salinger began his final Glass-family phase with *The New Yorker*'s publication of *Franny* in January 1955, followed by *Zooey; Raise High the Roof Beam, Carpenters; Seymour: An Introduction;* and *Hapworth, 16, 1924,* which were all published over the next decade and similarly formed a coherent artistic and philosophical whole.[13] During the immediately following conjunction of 1968–69, Patrick O'Brian published *Master and Commander,* the first in his twenty-volume series of Aubrey-Maturin historical novels set in the Napoleonic Era. During the same conjunction, in a different genre, Carlos Castañeda's series of Don Juan books commenced with *The Teachings of Don Juan.* Many other comparable examples could be cited. During the most recent Jupiter-Uranus conjunction of 1997, J. K. Rowling published the first of the Harry Potter series, *Harry Potter and the Philosopher's Stone.*

The common denominator in many of these patterns of literary creativity was the precise correlation of the Jupiter-Uranus cycle with new beginnings of many kinds: the first published work of a major author, the first of a major series of closely connected works, the first of a new genre, and so forth. Dostoevsky, Tolstoy, and Melville, for example, all wrote or published their first works or first novels in coincidence with Jupiter-Uranus conjunctions or oppositions, as did Jane Austen, Mary Shelley, Dickens, Thackeray, Gogol, Mark Twain, George Eliot, Henry James, Zola, Colette, Conrad, London, Dreiser, Mann, Kafka, Joyce, Thomas Wolfe, Evelyn Waugh, Jorge Luis Borges, Gabriel García Márquez, and earlier, at the dawn of the novel, Fielding, Richardson, and Smollett. So also the first works by poets: Blake, Keats, Baudelaire, Auden, García Lorca, Wallace Stevens, Dylan Thomas, Derek Walcott, Allen Ginsberg. It was during the Jupiter-Uranus conjunction of 1858 that Emily Dickinson began to collect her poems into bound fascicles—the only form approaching publication of her poetry during her lifetime.

Iconic Moments and
Cultural Milestones

Correlations with the Jupiter-Uranus cycle involving other cultural phenomena, such as the histories of film, theater, painting, jazz, rock music, and the counterculture, and of specific fields of study such as anthropology, psychology, and philosophy, presented equally rich and instructive patterns of synchronic and diachronic events and milestones. To give a small indication here of some of these patterns: If asked to single out the three films that had the most significant impact on the evolution of the cinema, most film historians would choose D. W. Griffith's *The Birth of a Nation*, which is widely considered the single most influential work in the history of film, one whose many technical and aesthetic innovations established the vocabulary of the new art; *The Jazz Singer*, with Al Jolson, the film with synchronized sound that revolutionized the motion picture industry and marked the birth of the sound era; and Orson Welles's *Citizen Kane*, a landmark in the history of sound film, with its mastery of many technical and artistic innovations that influenced subsequent filmmaking much as *The Birth of a Nation* did in the silent era. These three films precisely coincided with the three consecutive Jupiter-Uranus conjunctions of the first half of the twentieth century: *The Birth of a Nation* was made during the conjunction of 1914, premiering in early 1915; *The Jazz Singer* coincided with the next conjunction, its celebrated premiere taking place in October 1927 (the same month as the Bohr-Heisenberg Solvay physics conference); and *Citizen Kane* coincided with the following conjunction, premiering in May 1941.

Each of these periods was highly significant for the history of film in many other regards. The sequence of Jupiter-Uranus axial alignments in the twentieth century coincided closely both with specific masterworks that represented climactic milestones of the preceding years' developments and with the beginnings of new movements and genres that unfolded in succeeding years. The conjunction of 1940–41 that coincided with *Citizen Kane*, for example, also coincided with the birth of Italian neorealism in the films and published manifestos at that time of Rossellini, de Sica, and Visconti. The very next conjunction of 1954–55 coincided with another extraordinary wave of film milestones with the simultaneous emergence of both Bergman and Fellini as leading directors; the birth of the French *Nouvelle Vague* with the manifestos and first experiments of Truffaut, Godard, Varda, and Resnais; and the emergence of the British Free Cinema movement led by Lindsay Anderson, Karel Reisz, and Tony Richardson.

The immediately following conjunction of 1968–69 (the triple conjunction with Pluto) coincided with an explosion of innovative and influential works in virtually every national cinema and genre, both by established directors (Fellini, Bergman, Visconti, Bresson, Buñuel, Godard, Truffaut, Antonioni, Bertolucci, Polanski, Pasolini, Rohmer, Chabrol, Tati, Varda, Wajda, Anderson, Nichols, Kubrick) and by an extraordinary wave of new directors who brought forth their first films (Scorsese, Spielberg, Woody Allen, Rafelson, Mazursky, Fosse, Bogdanovich, Pakula, Newman, Herzog, Fassbinder). Equally notable during this last alignment at the end of the 1960s was the wave of so many films that reflected revolutionary or countercultural themes or that centered on rebel heroes or antiheroes, from *The Graduate, Easy Rider, Alice's Restaurant, Medium Cool*, and *Midnight Cowboy* to *The Conformist, Adalen 31, If*, and *Z*.

I will address elsewhere with more precision and thoroughness the remarkable clarity of the patterns in film history revealed by this cycle, as well as their interweaving complexity and many nuances, as these patterns provided a new dimension of understanding for the historical development of film in the twentieth century. The major milestones of twentieth-century comedy, for example, were closely correlated with the Jupiter-Uranus cycle, from Charlie Chaplin's first films and his invention of the Tramp during the conjunction of 1914 to the first Monty Python broadcast during the conjunction of 1969. Identical patterns are evident for the history of jazz, from Louis Armstrong's epoch-making Hot Five and Hot Seven recordings and Duke Ellington's five-year engagement that began at the Cotton Club during the conjunction of 1927–28, through the first recordings of Billie Holiday, the emergence of Benny Goodman's and Count Basie's big bands, and the sudden rise of swing, all occurring during the opposition centered on 1934, to the beginnings of the bebop revolution, when Charlie Parker and Dizzy Gillespie played with Lester Young, Kenny Clarke, Charlie Christian, and Thelonious Monk at Minton's Playhouse and Monroe's Uptown House during the conjunction of 1940–41, and then the emergence of cool jazz with Miles Davis's "Birth of the Cool" recordings during the following Jupiter-Uranus opposition in 1948.

So also the history of rock music, beginning with the following conjunction: Remarkably, all five of the recordings that marked the birth of rock and roll took place during the fourteen months of the Jupiter-Uranus conjunction in 1954–55: Elvis Presley's first record (*That's All Right*, July 1954), Bo Diddley's first record (*Bo Diddley*, May 1955), Chuck Berry's first record (*Maybelline*, July 1955), Buddy Holly's first recordings (eleven demo songs, released posthumously), and Bill Haley and the Comets' performance of *Rock Around the Clock* in the 1955 film

Blackboard Jungle.[14] It was also in early 1955 that Ray Charles recorded the seminal *I've Got a Woman*, often called the birth of soul music, a synthesis of gospel with rhythm and blues.

The following Jupiter-Uranus opposition, of 1962, coincided with the first recordings of Bob Dylan and the Beatles and the formation of the Rolling Stones, the three dominant creative forces in the musical culture of the Sixties. This synchronisitic creative emergence was part of a wave of cultural milestones that catalyzed many of the key movements of the 1960s and the longer Uranus-Pluto conjunction of that decade.[15]

The following triple conjunction of Jupiter, Uranus, and Pluto in 1968–69 coincided with what was in certain respects the climax of the classical era of rock, a twenty-four month period that brought a virtual Niagara Falls of creativity and many of the most celebrated works of this genre: all three of the Beatles' final albums (the double *White Album*, *Abbey Road*, and *Let It Be*), the Rolling Stones' *Beggar's Banquet* and *Let It Bleed* (including the songs *Sympathy for the Devil*, *Street Fighting Man*, *Midnight Rambler*, and *Gimme Shelter*), Dylan's *John Wesley Harding* and *Nashville Skyline*, Hendrix's *Axis: Bold as Love*, *Electric Ladyland*, and the titanic *Star-Spangled Banner* at Woodstock, the Who's rock opera *Tommy*, Cream's *Wheels of Fire* with Eric Clapton's masterful *Crossroads*, the Grateful Dead's *Live/Dead*, Big Brother and the Holding Company's *Cheap Thrills* with Janis Joplin, the Band's *Music from Big Pink* and *The Band*, the Incredible String Band's *The Hangman's Beautiful Daughter*, Van Morrison's *Astral Weeks*, John Mayall's *The Turning Point*, the birth of reggae in Jamaica with the Maytals' *Do the Reggay*, and Miles Davis's landmark jazz-rock fusion recordings *In a Silent Way* and *Bitches Brew*.

Equally noteworthy was the appearance in 1968–69 of an extraordinary wave of debut albums (and often the first two albums) by bands and solo artists whose music became central to the larger era and its legacy: Joni Mitchell, Crosby Stills and Nash, Neil Young, James Taylor, Leonard Cohen, Santana, the Allman Brothers, Led Zeppelin, Jeff Beck, Quicksilver Messenger Service, Creedence Clearwater, Blood Sweat and Tears, Procul Harum, Jethro Tull, Blind Faith, Fairport Convention, King Crimson, Genesis, Spirit, Yes, and many others.[16] Reflective of this creative outburst in the counterculture, sixteen mass music festivals, including Woodstock with its many musical triumphs, took place from the summer of 1968 through the summer of 1969, the average attendance at which was over one hundred thousand. No moment in the history of popular music is comparable to this period of the triple Jupiter-Uranus-Pluto conjunction, the only one of the twentieth century.

One can follow the ongoing sequence through subsequent Jupiter-Uranus alignments after the Sixties. For example, the opposition of 1975–76 coincided precisely with the emergence of both punk rock (Patti Smith, the Sex Pistols, the Clash, the Ramones) and new wave (Talking Heads, the Cars), as well as the founding of U2, the preeminent rock band of the following decades. During the following conjunction in 1983 the leading jam-rock band of these decades, Phish, was founded, and during the following opposition of 1989–90 Nirvana recorded its debut album, marking yet another new generational impulse in the history of rock music.

If, on the other hand, we look back again at the Jupiter-Uranus conjunction just before the Sixties, that of 1954–55, in terms of the themes of rebellion, creativity, and countercultural turning points so characteristic of this archetypal complex, hardly less remarkable than the synchronistic convergence of works that marked the birth of rock music at that time is the coincidence of this same conjunction with significant milestones in several other areas as well. The four-teen months from the summer of 1954 through the summer of 1955 brought the making or release of all three of James Dean's films—*East of Eden, Rebel Without a Cause,* and *Giant* (Dean died one month after the conjunction ended)—as well as Marlon Brando's *On the Waterfront.* These same months also coincided with the literary turning point of the Beat movement. Allen Ginsberg wrote *Howl,* the poetic manifesto of the Beats, in the summer of 1955. Jack Kerouac's *On the Road* was first published in an excerpt in *New World Writing* in April 1955 under the title "Jazz of the Beat Generation" (in the same issue was "Catch 18" by Joseph Heller, the first sign of what became *Catch-22*). In San Francisco, Lawrence Ferlinghetti began the City Lights bookstore poetry series, the first to publish works by the Beat poets, with the publication in July 1955 of his first volume of poems, *Pictures of the Gone World.* In Tangiers during these same months, William Burroughs began writing *Naked Lunch,* the work that with *Howl* and *On the Road* formed the classic triumvirate of Beat literature.

In these and many other correlations can be seen a tendency in both popu-lar culture and high culture for the events and figures that played roles during Jupiter-Uranus alignments to possess a certain mythologized, legendary aura, as they were again and again celebrated and invoked to the point that they became iconic in the cultural imagination: Galileo's first turning his telescope to the heavens, Newton's apple-falling epiphany of the universal law of gravity, the "shot heard round the world" at Lexington, Patrick Henry's "Give me liberty or give me death" speech, Paul Revere's ride to warn the countryside of the British approach, the fall of the Bastille, the mutiny on the *Bounty,* Beethoven's com-posing the *Eroica,* Byron's fighting for Greek independence, Nat Turner's slave rebellion in Virginia, Darwin's voyage on the *Beagle,* Emerson's *American Scholar* address (called by Oliver Wendell Holmes an "intellectual declaration of inde-pendence"), Samuel Morse's first electric telegraph transmission ("What hath God wrought?"), Thoreau's building his cabin at Walden Pond, the Lincoln-Douglas debates, Darwin's and Wallace's joint announcement of the theory of evolution, Thomas Edison's demonstration of the electric carbon-filament light ("the birthday of modern technological research," October 21, 1879), Pancho Villa's uprising in Mexico, Gandhi's first fast as a means of political demonstra-tion against British rule in India, the dramatic confirmation of Einstein's relativity theory, Charles Lindbergh's solo flight across the Atlantic, Neil Armstrong's stepping onto the Moon, the Woodstock music festival, the fall of the Berlin Wall and the Velvet Revolution, and so on.

To these could be added comparable moments from the history of sports, such as Babe Ruth's hitting sixty home runs in one season during the Jupiter-Uranus conjunction of 1927, or fourteen years later during the immediately following conjunction in 1941, Joe DiMaggio's setting his equally famous and still-standing record of getting a hit in fifty-six consecutive games. Or more recently, Tiger Woods's historic performance in winning the Masters golf tournament with a record-breaking score during the most recent Jupiter-Uranus conjunction in 1997.

A related category of cultural phenomena that show a far more than random correlation with the Jupiter-Uranus cycle comprises celebrated first meetings of major cultural figures that marked the beginnings of culturally significant personal associations that have become iconic in the collective imagination. Thus the first meeting of Freud and Jung at Freud's house in Vienna on March 3, 1907, when the two men spoke animatedly with each other for thirteen hours straight, took place during a Jupiter-Uranus opposition—the one immediately following the conjunction of 1900 and *The Interpretation of Dreams*. Other culturally influential associations that began in coincidence with Jupiter-Uranus alignments include those of Goethe and Schiller (1788), Wordsworth and Coleridge (1797), Keats and Shelley (1817), Chopin and Liszt (1831), Pushkin and Gogol (1831), Emerson and Thoreau (1837), Marx and Engels (1844), Verlaine and Rimbaud (1871), Van Gogh and Gauguin (1886), T. S. Eliot and Ezra Pound (1914), and Einstein and Bohr (1920), to name only a few.

Significant romantic associations were more likely to occur in coincidence with personal transits of the outer planets crossing the natal Venus, Moon, or Ascendant (and also, in the case of marriages and long-term committed relationships, with the personal Saturn transit cycle). Yet here too the Jupiter-Uranus world transit cycle was often relevant: Goethe scholars, for example, will recognize the periods of the two conjunctions that coincided with the beginnings of the American and French Revolutions (1775–76 and 1788–89) as also exactly coinciding with the beginnings of Goethe's two most important romantic relationships: the first with Charlotte von Stein, the second with Christiane Vulpius. Similarly, the famous first meeting of Petrarch with Laura in Avignon, on April 6, 1327, took place when Jupiter and Uranus were in opposition, transiting across his natal Sun. This proved to be the turning point in Petrarch's creative journey, with Laura serving as the queen of his poetic inspiration for the rest of his life.

A common theme in many of these correlations was that of the sudden and unexpected expansion of personal or cultural horizons. This expansion could be quite literal as well as intellectual, as when Galileo discovered a new and immensely expanded universe by turning his telescope to the heavens during the conjunction of 1610. So also during the conjunction of 1513, when the Spanish explorer Balboa became the first European to cross the Isthmus of Panama and, from the heights of the Darién mountain range, saw the magnificent vista of the Pacific Ocean. This moment was later commemorated by Keats in his first great sonnet, *On First Looking into Chapman's Homer*, which was itself published during yet another Jupiter-Uranus conjunction, that of 1816–17:[17]

> He stared at the Pacific—and all his men
> Looked at each other with a wild surmise—
> Silent, upon a peak in Darien.

In such instances we see that form of the Uranus→Jupiter vector in which the Uranus principle suddenly and unexpectedly opens up the Jupiterian experience of wider horizons, expanded experience, elevation and magnitude, a larger world. Captain James Cook's first voyage to Tahiti, New Zealand, and Australia during the Jupiter-Uranus opposition of 1768–69 is another example. The sudden expansion of horizons can be achieved by vertical as well as horizontal movement—the first balloon ascents, the first space flights, the first Moon landing. In the biographies of many cultural figures, the sudden expansion of horizons often took the form of major turning points in which the individual moved to a new environment where his or her creative work and personal life unfolded on a profoundly new level. Sometimes this was a journey or an extended stay at another place that in some way exerted a significant influence on the person's intellectual or artistic development. So it was with Darwin's long voyage to South America and the Galápagos Islands, begun during the conjunction of 1831, or Tocqueville's famous nine-month visit to the United States during that same conjunction in 1831 that became the basis for his prescient and still insightful *Democracy in America*. Here too could be cited Thoreau's building of his cabin at Walden Pond in 1845 during the immediately following conjunction. So also Voltaire's life-changing stay in England during the Jupiter-Uranus opposition of 1726–27, which profoundly affected his intellectual outlook and inspired him to bring the liberating aspirations of the Enlightenment he saw successfully embodied there to the Continent. His influential *Lettres Philosophiques* that contained these ideas was then published during the immediately following conjunction of 1734.

Often the suddenly expanded horizons took the form of a transformative encounter abroad with a specific individual or institution, as in Freud's pivotal stay in Paris during the conjunction of 1885–86 when he studied at the Salpêtrière with the neurologist Jean-Martin Charcot, who inspired Freud to change his life's work to the study of psychopathology and the unconscious. So too Joseph Campbell's transformative journey during the conjunction of 1927–28 to study in Paris and Munich, where he first encountered the work of Freud, Jung, Joyce, Mann, and Picasso, and conceived his understanding of the mythic foundations of human experience. Moreover, Campbell's similarly transformative year-long pilgrimage to India, Southeast Asia, and Japan took place precisely within the fourteen-month period of another Jupiter-Uranus conjunction, in 1954–55. James Hillman's major turning point occurred during the immediately following Jupiter-Uranus conjunction in April 1969 in London at the Warburg Institute, where his revelatory encounter with a tradition of classical polytheistic images and the larger Western cultural imagination helped inspire the birth of archetypal psychology.

Sometimes the sudden opening of new horizons took place through a book accidentally discovered, as when Nietzsche came upon Schopenhauer's *The World as Will and Idea* in a Leipzig bookstore during the Jupiter-Uranus opposition of 1865, which proved to be a crucial turning point in his intellectual life. At other times, a shift of geographic location and expansion of horizons was both literal and intellectual, as when Nietzsche, during the immediately following opposition of 1879 fourteen years later, left his university teaching career and began his great creative decade of wandering and writing in Switzerland, France, and Italy.[18]

> I am a wanderer and a mountain-climber. . . . I do not like the plains
> and it seems I cannot sit still for long. And whatever may yet come to
> me as fate and experience—a wandering and a mountain-climbing will
> be in it: in the final analysis one experiences only oneself.

In other instances, the shift of location to a new and more creatively stimulating setting was specific and long-term, as in Goethe's life-changing move to Weimar during the conjunction of 1775–76, or T. S. Eliot's equally consequential move, during the conjunction of 1914, to England, where his poetic gifts were catalyzed and his literary career unfolded.

As in the case of Eliot's joining Pound and other early modernists in London, an individual artist's move during a Jupiter-Uranus alignment often resulted in a developmentally decisive encounter with a larger milieu of creative artists, as in Chopin's move to Paris during the conjunction of 1831, where he met Liszt, Berlioz, Bellini, and Mendelssohn. Equally decisive was Van Gogh's move to Paris during the conjunction of 1885–86, where he met Gauguin, Toulouse-Lautrec, Pissarro, and Seurat. So also was Picasso's move to Paris fourteen years later during the next conjunction of 1900—where, during the immediately following Jupiter-Uranus opposition of 1906–07, he painted the first cubist masterpiece, *Les Demoiselles d'Avignon*, in many ways the pivotal work of twentieth-century art.

The High Renaissance

In general, I found well-defined correlative patterns in the history of Western thought and culture, the tradition with which I am most familiar, in every century for which we have historical records sufficiently precise and extensive to research a planetary cycle of such brevity. As one moves back into earlier eras, the density of cultural data gradually thins out, and is drastically attenuated once one moves into the centuries and millennia preceding the year 1500. It is thus of special interest to study the first conjunction after 1500, centered on the year 1513 (the planets actually first came within 15° orb in June 1512, moved in and out of orb through the rest of 1512–13, and finally left it in February 1514, an unusually long span for a Jupiter-Uranus conjunction). This period coincided with an extraordinary wave of events that in many ways seemed to mark a climax of the Italian High Renaissance.

In October-November 1512 Michelangelo's Sistine Chapel ceiling painting was completed and unveiled. In early 1513 he began to carve the *Moses* for the tomb of Pope Julius II. During the same period Raphael completed the great cycle of paintings for the Vatican Stanza della Segnatura and Stanza di Eliodoro that included *The School of Athens*, *Mount Parnassus*, and *The Triumph of the Church*. This was in fact the culminating period of the papacy of Julius II, the greatest art patron of the Renaissance, who was himself born during a Jupiter-Uranus conjunction five cycles earlier and who oversaw Michelangelo's and Raphael's achievements in the Sistine Chapel and the Vatican apartments. (Julius's other great legacy, the building of St. Peter's Basilica, which was then in progress, began under Bramante during the immediately previous Jupiter-Uranus opposition seven years earlier, its foundation stone having been laid in April 1506.) In Venice during this conjunction, Titian, who was just starting his long career, painted his famous Neoplatonic allegory, *Sacred and Profane Love*. In Germany at this same time Albrecht Dürer engraved his greatest works, the set of three masterpieces, *Saint Jerome in His Study*; *Knight, Death, and the Devil*; and *Melancholia I*, all in 1513–14.

Nor was this creative wave limited to the visual arts. Between the spring and autumn of 1513 Machiavelli began work on both of his masterpieces, *The Prince* and the *Discorsi*, the foundation works of modern political theory. Castiglione in the same year commenced his quintessential Renaissance work *The Book of the Courtier*, which after expanding and polishing it for fourteen years he finally sent to the publisher in early 1527 during the immediately following Jupiter-Uranus conjunction.

The conjunction of 1513 proved to be consequential as well for theology and religion. Martin Luther in Wittenberg during these same months began his famous series of lectures on the Psalms and Paul's Letter to the Romans that set forth his new understanding of salvation through faith alone in God's grace, thereby establishing the theological basis for the Reformation.

Moreover, historians of science believe that this period coincided with the writing and private distribution of Copernicus's *Commentariolus*, the short manuscript that contained the earliest description of his heliocentric theory, which he circulated to friends and colleagues. The first record we have of its existence is its having been listed in early 1514 in a scholar's library inventory, just three months after the conjunction reached the final 15° point. Copernicus scholars regard it as having most probably been written in 1512–13.

It is as if, five hundred years ago, some archetypal force pushed the modern self into being all at once—in art, religion, science, the Renaissance, the Reformation, the Scientific Revolution—and this brief period represented a kind of accelerated threshold of the larger phenomenon. Even in global exploration, it was in these same extraordinary months, in September 1513, that Balboa first sighted the Pacific Ocean, a literal, geographical form of unexpected awakening and the expansion to new horizons. Moreover, amidst all the synchronic events and cultural phenomena we have been noting, the diachronic patterning in global exploration is visible as well: It was during the immediately following Jupiter-Uranus opposition, in October and November 1520, that Ferdinand Magellan first traversed the strait at the southernmost tip of South America that links the Atlantic and the Pacific (bestowing the name Pacifica on the latter as he did so) in that expedition's historic first circumnavigation of the globe. And if we look in the other direction, it was exactly two cycles earlier, during the Jupiter-Uranus opposition of 1492, that Christopher Columbus set sail from Spain on the voyage that first took him to the New World.

Great Heights and Shadows

I n these diverse correlations so closely patterned in sequential coincidence with the Jupiter-Uranus cycle, we can recognize Jupiter's archetypal principle in its broadening and elevating cultural dimension—the expansion of intellectual and artistic horizons, with an inclination towards higher aspirations, high culture, the arts and sciences, philosophy, higher learning, broader understanding, breadth of cultural and intellectual vision, opening to other cultures and an expanded range of perspectives. We can also see Jupiter's association with an impulse for global expansions, heights, and glories of a more literal kind, as in the vast explorations of the transoceanic navigators. In turn, the Promethean archetypal principle associated with Uranus seems to catalyze and liberate this Jupiter impulse in unexpected, innovative ways, in many forms of human experience and endeavor, while simultaneously being successfully elevated and expanded (Jupiter) in its own emancipatory and creative tendency (Uranus). Thus we begin to see something of the richly complex archetypal dialectic that takes place between the two principles: both Jupiter→Uranus and Uranus→Jupiter. The two mutually activate, interpenetrate, and inflect each other, each in its characteristic way.

In the preceding chapters, we have seen many milestones in the history of freedom that coincided with the Jupiter-Uranus cycle, from the shot heard round the world and the fall of the Bastille to the fall of the Berlin Wall. This cyclical unfolding of successful expansions and flowerings of the Promethean impulse also regularly took the form of major breakthroughs that advanced human rights, such as the Declaration of the Rights of Man and the Citizen that was proclaimed in France during the conjunction in 1789, and the Bill of Rights that was introduced in the U.S. Congress in 1789 during the same conjunction. Similarly, Jupiter and Uranus were in opposition on August 1, 1838, the long-celebrated day on which all slaves in the British Empire were freed, that climaxed the abolitionist movement begun over fifty years earlier by William Clarkson. Jupiter and Uranus were again in opposition in 1865 when slavery was prohibited in the United States by the Thirteenth Amendment to the Constitution. The same two planets were again in opposition in 1893 when New Zealand became the first country to grant women the vote, and yet again in 1920 when the

336 COSMOS AND PSYCHE

long drive for women's suffrage in the United States culminated in the ratification of the Nineteenth Amendment.

To these could be added many other similarly paradigmatic events. In England, during the same opposition in 1865 that coincided with the ending of slavery in the United States, John Stuart Mill introduced in Parliament the first bill in English history that supported women's right to vote, another landmark in the struggle for the emancipation of women. The same opposition in 1920 that coincided with the granting of women's suffrage in the United States also coincided with the founding of the American Civil Liberties Union. The Universal Declaration of Human Rights was ratified by the United Nations during the Jupiter-Uranus opposition in 1948. The Helsinki Accords on Human Rights was signed during the Jupiter-Uranus opposition of 1975–76, "the crowning achievement of the era of détente." This milestone played a major role in galvanizing dissidents in the Soviet Union and other Eastern European countries in the years leading up to the collapse of the Iron Curtain, which in turn occurred exactly one cycle later during the immediately following Jupiter-Uranus opposition in 1989.

Again, such correlations with the Jupiter-Uranus cycle, in politics and human rights as in the arts and sciences, seemed to express in their manifold ways the specific archetypal synthesis of Jupiter and Prometheus: the expansion, growth, and success of the principle of freedom, revolution, and creative innovation. To adopt a Homeric manner of speaking (and if we can divest these mythic personifications of their masculine specificity), in such events Jupiter seemed to elevate and confer success upon Prometheus—the king of the Olympian gods, as it were, granting honor and triumph to the rebel and creative genius. Yet the archetypal interaction during the cyclical alignments of Jupiter and Uranus can be seen not only as one archetypal principle affecting the other, with each a separate entity, but also, perhaps more precisely, as the two principles permeating each other, becoming fully integrated, manifesting themselves as one composite principle—as if the two mythic figures, Prometheus and Jupiter, had joined and become one. We saw a similar phenomenon during Uranus-Pluto alignments, such as that of the 1960s or the French Revolution, when a composite archetypal figure of Prometheus-Dionysus seemed to be collectively constellated. In the case of Jupiter-Uranus alignments, it seems as if in these various creative and revolutionary breakthroughs, Prometheus himself *became* the Olympian sovereign Jupiter and was crowned king, to use the metaphor that suggested itself for the apotheosis of Einstein. The same image of Prometheus as crowned king might be invoked for the triumph of the Apollo Moon landing. In a sense, every creative breakthrough, every moment of successful rebellion, every unexpected expansion or happy awakening can be seen as an expression of this archetypal synthesis.

While the crowning of Prometheus is expressed in a multitude of ways in the correlations we have examined, at times the metaphor becomes unusually vivid, as in the case of the Statue of Liberty ("Liberty Enlightening the World"), a superb iconic embodiment of the Jupiter-Uranus archetypal complex in a single integrated form. In one statue, the two distinctive symbols of the two gods—Jupiter's elevating crown and Prometheus's liberating fire—are perfectly synthesized. Moreover, the Statue of Liberty embodies not only the Jupiter→Uranus vector, in the monument's celebrating and elevating to high honor the eternal human aspiration to freedom and enlightenment, but also the Uranus→Jupiter vector, which is expressed in the sheer astounding magnitude of the statue, the wondrous expansion of the Promethean Liberty to gigantic Gulliver-like dimensions: the Goddess of Liberty. In both its integrated dual symbolism and its astonishing size, the Statue of Liberty is perhaps the quintessential Jupiterian monument to the Prometheus archetype.

It would seem to be expressive of a high form of cosmic artistry that this grand gesture of freedom was erected and dedicated in New York Harbor precisely during the fourteen-month period of the Jupiter-Uranus conjunction of 1885–86—with France's gift to the United States commemorating the American and French Revolutions of a century earlier, both of which began in coincidence with their own Jupiter-Uranus conjunctions, the consecutive ones of 1775–76 and 1788–89.[19]

The vivid archetypal contrast between the Statue of Liberty, which was erected during a Jupiter-Uranus conjunction, and the Vietnam Memorial, which was erected during a Saturn-Pluto conjunction, is instructive. In a multitude of ways—their form and appearance, the spirit and character of their aesthetic, their symbolic meanings, and the historical events and eras they commemorate—the two monuments are paradigmatic expressions of their respective planetary cycles and the corresponding archetypal principles.

In view of this comparison and many similar correlations cited in the chapters devoted to these two cycles, one could say that the archetypal combination of Saturn and Pluto suggested a dominant quality of dark weightiness, a vector of downward depth, hard contraction, grim reality, death and loss, the enduring power and weight of the past; while alignments of Jupiter and Uranus seemed rather to coincide with phenomena that have a lighter, upward and expansive vector—the quest for the future, ascending to brilliant heights, sudden freedom, the expansion to new and unexpected worlds in creative joy.

Conversely, while events of the Saturn-Pluto cycle brought enduring structures and foundations, moral gravitas, depth of experience, solemnity and solidity, long-sustained deep tradition, the hard-earned wisdom of maturity, and the empowered *senex* principle, the Jupiter-Uranus tendency was often naïvely optimistic and unbounded, the *puer eternus,* the eternal child inflated and untrammeled in Icarus-like limitless ascending flight: Thus one sees associated with Jupiter-Uranus alignments the uncritical celebration of scientific and technological progress, the gleeful breaking of rules and limits, the prodigal lack of restraint of countercultural rebellion, the carnivals of excess, the fleeting euphoria of the newly liberated, the immoderate indulgences and flashy wealth of the nouveau riche, the glitz and dazzle of celebrity, the manic inventor claiming yet another incredible breakthrough.

Every archetypal complex has its shadow, as do the coinciding correlations. In the Jupiter-Uranus complex, it can indeed be easy to make light of the shadow of such happy superabundance. As Mae West, herself born with a Jupiter-Uranus opposition, said so well, "Too much of a good thing is wonderful." So speaks the irrepressible smiling Trickster in defense of Jupiter's grand domain of over-the-top plenitude, blithely free of inhibiting concerns and deploying the unexpected twist of humor to better celebrate the virtues of excess and unlimited good times. In the universe of the Jupiter-Uranus archetypal complex, shadows cannot be seen. Yet the world is not ruled by any one archetypal complex. The gods, said Schiller, never appear alone.

It sometimes happens that the two very different planetary cycles we have here been comparing, Saturn-Pluto and Jupiter-Uranus, unfold in such a way that they precisely overlap in a particular moment of history. We can then observe the telling ways in which the coinciding phenomena reflect the two distinct archetypal complexes working together. For example, in 1914 the first Saturn-Pluto conjunction of the twentieth century exactly coincided with the briefer Jupiter-Uranus conjunction of that year. In the summer and fall of 1914, both pairs of planets, Saturn-Pluto and Jupiter-Uranus, were aligned in their respective cyclical conjunctions during those fateful months when virtually all of Europe enthusiastically leapt into war. Excited national leaders and eagerly volunteering young men alike, inspired by boundless optimism and visions of patriotic and personal glory, set in motion the most horrific slaughter the world had ever seen, bringing to a dark end the age of European civilization's ascendancy. Two generations of unfulfilled creative genius were lost in the ensuing thirty years of global conflict.

Similar dynamics can be recognized in the unfolding of an individual life as well. Napoleon was born during a Jupiter-Uranus opposition (both planets were in close major aspect to Mars, associated with the archetypal principle of assertive action, aggression, and the warrior). After a long series of nearly unbroken brilliant military successes, Napoleon was at the height of his power in 1808–11 as transiting Uranus aligned with this configuration, conjoining his natal Jupiter and opposing natal Uranus (the same transits that Einstein had when his theory of relativity was corroborated and he was acclaimed the greatest genius who ever lived). The genius of war who emerged from the French Revolutionary epoch was not only the Emperor of France, having crowned himself in Notre Dame cathedral, but the most powerful man in Europe. He had risen from Corsican obscurity to the heights of of imperial grandeur. Like an ancient conqueror, he had crossed the Mediterranean to invade and conquer Egypt in the battle of the Pyramids. His empire included the Netherlands, Tuscany, parts of Germany, and the Illyrian Provinces. The kingdoms of Spain, Italy, Westphalia, and Naples were now vassal states ruled by his relatives. He was married to the daughter of the Austrian emperor, and his newborn son was the king of Rome. He considered himself the heir of Alexander and Charlemagne. No obstacles to the further expansion of his dazzling success seemed insuperable.

The next year, Napoleon invaded Russia, and as transiting Saturn moved into exact conjunction with his natal Pluto in the harsh Russian winter of 1812–13, his fortunes turned. In a fateful series of errors in judgment, military overextensions, and imperial overreach, Napoleon's empire began its fall. In June 1815, precisely when transiting Saturn had moved into square alignment with his natal Jupiter-Uranus alignment, Napoleon was defeated at Waterloo—the sudden fall from grace, the collapse of the inflation.

Some personal dramas take place on the public stage of history, witnessed and experienced by multitudes. Others unfold in the solitude of a life and work largely unknown to contemporaries, on an interior battlefield, yet are no less archetypal in intensity and magnitude. Perhaps no figure in Western thought more powerfully articulated the impulse of unbounded Promethean liberation than Friedrich Nietzsche, who was born in 1844 with Jupiter and Uranus in close conjunction. This was the same Jupiter-Uranus conjunction that coincided with Wagner's composition of *Tannhäuser*, the beginning of Marx's and Engels's collaboration and their first major works, Darwin's first exposition of his evolutionary theory, and Thoreau's building his cabin and living at Walden Pond. All these events and the Jupiter-Uranus conjunction occurred at the beginning of the longer Uranus-Pluto conjunction of the mid-nineteenth century in a broader version of the rare triple-planet conjunction that took a more exact form in 1968–69.[20]

Throughout his life, Nietzsche rebelled against, brilliantly critiqued, and broke free from one established cultural belief and philosophical assumption after another. When Jupiter and Uranus moved into opposition in 1879, he left the life of the nineteenth-century university professor for which he was so superbly educated but so painfully unfitted, and entered his ten years of wandering.

> For this is the truth: I have left the house of scholars and slammed the door behind me. Too long did my soul sit hungry at their table; I have not been schooled, as they have, to crack knowledge as one cracks nuts. I love freedom and the air over fresh soil; I would sleep on ox-skins rather than on their dignities and respectabilities. I am too hot and scorched by my own thought: it is often about to take my breath away. Then I have to get into the open air and away from all dusty rooms.

In a manner vividly reflective of the Jupiter-Uranus complex, Nietzsche was possessed by compelling metaphors of flight and ascent, ever striving towards radically new horizons and the opening of new worlds. In the climactic passage that ends *Daybreak*, written near the start of his years of wandering, he gives testimony with soaring eloquence to the aspirations he felt rising within him and within the human soul:

> We aeronauts of the spirit!—All those brave birds which fly out into the distance, into the farthest distance—it is certain! somewhere or other they will be unable to go on and will perch down on a mast or a bare cliff-face—and they will even be thankful for this miserable accommodation! But who could venture to infer from that, that there was *not* an immense open space before them, that they had flown as far as one *could* fly! All our great teachers and predecessors have at last come to a stop . . . it will be the same with you and me! *Other birds will fly farther!* This insight and faith of ours vies with them in flying up and away; it rises above our heads and above our impotence into the heights and from there surveys the distance and sees before it the flocks of birds which, far stronger than we, still strive whither we have striven, and where everything is sea, sea, sea!—And whither then would we go? Would we *cross* the sea? Whither does this mighty longing draw us, this longing that is worth more to us than any pleasure? Why just in this direction, thither where all the suns of humanity have hitherto *gone down?* Will it perhaps be said of us one day that we too, *steering westward, hoped to reach an India*—but that it was our fate to be wrecked against infinity? Or, my brothers. Or?—

Nietzsche was born with his Jupiter-Uranus conjunction in exact opposition to an equally close Mars-Mercury conjunction—the archetypal synthesis of the warrior and the thinker, the warrior whose sword is his pen, his words, his ideas. In Nietzsche's life and character, the Mars-Mercury archetypal complex was expressed in his consistently combative, forceful use of language, his incisive ideas, his sharp directness of statement, his constant close linking of thought and action. With his aphoristic style of writing, he felt like "an officer storming the barricades." He saw himself as serving the great imperative of his era to "prepare the way for a yet higher age, and assemble the force which that age will one day have need of—that age which will carry heroism into knowledge and *wage war* for the sake of ideas and their consequences. To that end many brave pioneers are needed now. . . ."

This synthesis of the Mars warrior and the Mercury thinker and writer was closely intertwined in Nietzsche with the unbounded Promethean impulse associated with Jupiter-Uranus: the impulse towards soaring freedom, the liberation of cultural and philosophical vision, the discovery of new worlds, the delight in uncertainty, the joy of victorious rebellion, the celebration of unfettered creative genius—all expressed in ideas and language (Mercury) at once assertive and forceful (Mars), brilliantly inventive and unexpected (Uranus), and expansively elevating and exalted, as if proclaimed from the top of a mountain (Jupiter).

Every individual is a meeting point of and vessel for many archetypal drives. With Nietzsche as with every other person discussed in this book, I found that the only way I could begin to grasp the rich complexity of the unique human being in archetypal astrological terms was to recognize the extent to which every specific natal aspect was embedded in a larger whole—the full natal chart—that encompassed all the planets, each uniquely and complexly configured with others in such a way that each relevant archetypal complex was shaped and inflected by every other such complex at work in the person's life and character. While in one sense Nietzsche's Jupiter-Uranus conjunction can be isolated and its distinctive archetypal complex recognized in his biography and ideas, in another sense that complex can be understood only if one takes into account the entire natal chart with its multiplicity of intersecting natal aspects. In the present work, for the sake of simplicity and clarity, I have focused the discussion on one planetary combination at a time. But a more adequate analysis must engage the larger complex of archetypal relationships that are always at work in every person's life, every event, and every cultural epoch.

In Nietzsche's birth chart as in his biography, it is clear that the central unifying archetypal complex and planetary configuration at work is his exact opposition of the Sun with Pluto—i.e., the 180° Full Moon moment of the Sun-Pluto cycle. It would not be an exaggeration to say that Nietzsche's embodiment of his Sun-Pluto configuration is a paradigmatic illustration of that aspect, with his unparalleled role as the heroic avatar of Dionysus in the history of Western thought. His lifelong identification with the Dionysian principle (even to the point of signing his last letters "Dionysus"), his commitment to the elemental forces of nature and the instincts ("To the discerning man, all instincts are holy"), his philosophical focus on and identification with the will to power ("Something invulnerable, unburiable is within me, something that rends rocks: it is called *my Will*"), his titanic power struggle with the entire civilization of which he was both vessel and antagonist, his repeated call for the *going down* of the courageous human being, like the Sun's descent into the Plutonic underworld darkness to permit a resurrection of greater life—all these reflect an extraordinarily compelling embodiment of the archetypal principles associated with the Sun and Pluto in dynamic interplay.

We see the same archetypal complex expressed in Nietzsche's identification with life as a state of ceaseless flux, evolving, transforming, dying and regenerating ("Behold, I am that *which must overcome itself again and again*"). We see it too in his consciousness of inward chaos and warfare among the instincts as essential to his creative essence:

One must have chaos inside oneself to give birth to a dancing star.

And in his celebration of struggle, strife, and danger as necessary for greatness of spirit:

For believe me!—the secret of realizing the greatest fruitfulness and the greatest enjoyment of existence is: to *live dangerously!* Build your cities on the slopes of Vesuvius! Send your ships out into uncharted seas! Live in conflict with your equals and with yourselves!

All these show the Sun→Pluto dynamic, the solar principle as it illuminates and heroically embodies the Plutonic principle, identifies with it, descends into it, is overcome by it and reborn through it:

And only where there are graves are there resurrections.

Yet equally vividly throughout Nietzsche's life we can also see the converse archetypal dynamic, Pluto→Sun, above all in the titanic intensification and empowerment of the will to *be,* to manifest, to radiantly give forth one's being and light into the world, to actualize to the fullest the individual heroic self, to *become* ("Become what you are!"). This archetypal vector *from* Pluto *towards* the Sun is also evident in Nietzsche's profound sense of an evolutionary drive at work within himself and in the human species to bring forth, through struggle, destruction, and transformation, a new form of human being, a new and more powerful self. He articulated this evolutionary impulse as he simultaneously identified his own self and being *as* a force of nature, becoming possessed, at times, by the Dionysian principle itself. This complex reciprocality of archetypal dynamic, each principle activating the other as in a recursive feedback loop, would come together in Nietzsche's central vision of the *Übermensch,* the ultimate embodiment of creative will and empowered selfhood that he sensed was emerging within him in anticipation of a larger development within humanity.

But Nietzsche's Sun-Pluto aspect was not simply given boundless free play and bold articulation, as if his only other natal configurations were the Jupiter-Uranus and Mercury-Mars conjunctions. For Nietzsche was also born with *Saturn* in a 90° square hard aspect to both the Sun and Pluto in a T-square configuration. The juxtaposition of these two larger natal configurations associated with such powerfully opposite archetypal vectors and qualities—the Jupiter-Uranus and the Saturn-Pluto, the two complexes we have been examining in this section and the one previous—precisely parallels the extraordinary tension of opposites that marked Nietzsche's life and thought. On the one hand, his impulse for unbounded creative freedom brought forth in him a certain gleeful lightness of spirit and a willingness to defy any limit he discerned as being no more than the arbitrary imposition of a constraining belief despite how culturally sanctioned and widely accepted that belief might be—traits clearly characteristic of the Jupiter-Uranus complex. Yet on the other hand, reflecting the Saturn-Pluto on his Sun, Nietzsche was possessed by an overwhelming sense of fate, the ineluctable power of necessity governing his life both positively and nega-

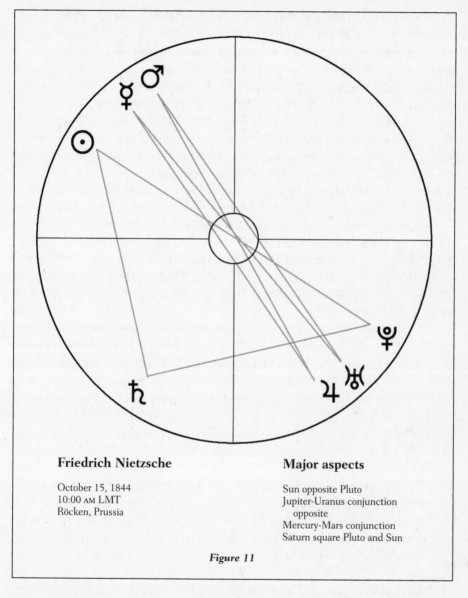

Friedrich Nietzsche

October 15, 1844
10:00 AM LMT
Röcken, Prussia

Major aspects

Sun opposite Pluto
Jupiter-Uranus conjunction
  opposite
Mercury-Mars conjunction
Saturn square Pluto and Sun

Figure 11

tively. He knew the prison of lifelong solitude, and of being almost completely unheard and unrecognized. He was preternaturally alert to the impoverishment of life produced by inherited codes and dogmas, the table of values hanging over every people that controls the herd but also produces mediocrity and kills healthy life. He discerned everywhere the crushing weight of history, habit, unconsciousness, and compulsion shackling the life force and passion inside the human being. For decade after decade, he himself suffered incessant illness, debilitating weakness, blinding headaches. "I have a subtler sense for signs of ascent and decline than any man has ever had, I am the teacher *par excellence* in this matter—I know both, I am both."

The multivalent Saturn-Pluto complex expressed itself with great potency in many other aspects of Nietzsche's character and vision as well. He felt compelled to gaze long and unflinchingly into the dark abyss of existence, the purposeless chaos that lay beyond all human constructs of order and value. He recognized nihilism as the inevitable price of a truly free mind, the price of one's fully embracing the human condition of life in a universe of random necessity devoid of meaning. He discerned the baser biological instincts that concealed themselves behind the metaphysical beliefs and moral pretenses of the human animal, which he judged with unprecedented acuity and harshness. Nietzsche's implied political philosophy, grounded in the will to power, possessed an unapologetically ruthless realpolitik character. He constantly focused on the nature of evil, its relation to the instincts, its culturally constructed character. At times he seemed to identify himself with evil and the "wicked," but in an ambiguous manner, sometimes with a certain playful insouciance, at other times with an intensely driven seriousness as if reflecting virtually a moral commitment to the amoral abyss within.

Yet Nietzsche also came to embrace and express another side of the Saturn-Pluto archetypal complex that was specifically directed *towards* the self, invoking Saturnian qualities to be deployed with Plutonic intensity. This was expressed in his repeated demand that one be capable of the most rigorous discipline, capable of unsparing hardness towards oneself, committed with unbending silent resolution to a solitary quest, willing to embrace every defeat and loss, to shoulder the heaviest burdens of life, to become one's *own* sternest judge and master: "He who cannot obey himself will be commanded."

> Can you furnish yourself with your own good and evil and hang up your own will above yourself as a law? Can you be judge of yourself and avenger of your law? It is terrible to be alone with the judge and avenger of one's own law. It is to be like a star thrown forth into empty space and into the icy breath of solitude.

As each year passed, Nietzsche engaged this struggle of opposing tendencies, between soaring boundless freedom and ruthless constraint and dark suffering, with increasing intensity. By the early 1880s, in book after book written "for free spirits" that were all virtually unread in their time, he had pushed the boundaries of his thinking as far into the skeptical and nihilistic crisis of the modern condition as anyone ever had. Saturn had now moved into an extremely rare triple conjunction in the sky with both Pluto and Neptune, the only such alignment in the modern era. It was at this moment that Nietzsche declared the irrevocable reality of the death of God: the destruction of the powerful projected

Being in "the beyond" who had presided over civilization and provided both its sustaining moral structure and its life-oppressing constraints. This death he recognized—again, the precise archetypal polarity and tension seems to have run through everything Nietzsche thought and wrote—as both a liberation and a dark, awesome, terrifying event:

> How have we done this? Who gave us the sponge to wipe away the entire horizon? What were we doing when we unchained this earth from its sun? Whither is it moving now? Whither are we moving? Away from all suns? Are we not plunging continually? Backward, sideward, forward, in all directions? Is there still any up or down? Are we not straying as through an infinite nothing? Do we not feel the breath of empty space? Has it not become colder? Is not night continually closing in on us?

It was an epochal turning point whose reality he knew had scarcely begun to register in the collective psyche but whose consequences he foresaw would be momentous, even catastrophic. At this furthermost frontier of reason, Nietzsche himself then underwent a sustained crisis, both philosophical and emotional, in which the humiliating failure of his romantic hopes for love with Lou Salomé played a central role. By December of 1882, he had become suicidal.

Then, just as transiting Uranus first reached the opposition point to his natal Jupiter-Uranus conjunction in January 1883, "as a result of ten absolutely fresh and cheerful January days," the long-building tension suddenly broke. An explosion of creative power overtook him, and *Thus Spoke Zarathustra* poured forth in an onrush of inspired clarity, pathos, and beauty. Nietzsche later described the state of inspiration that overcame him in a manner that, again, precisely reflected the two archetypal complexes in synthesis:

> Has anyone at the end of the nineteenth century a distinct conception of what poets of strong ages called *inspiration?* If not, I will describe it.—If one had the slightest residue of superstition left in one, one would hardly be able to set aside the idea that one is merely incarnation, merely mouthpiece, merely medium of overwhelming forces. The concept of revelation, in the sense that something suddenly, with unspeakable certainty and subtlety, becomes *visible,* audible, something that shakes and overturns one to the depths, simply describes the fact. One hears, one does not seek; one takes, one does not ask who gives; a thought flashes up like lightning, with necessity, unfalteringly formed— I have never had any choice. An ecstasy whose tremendous tension sometimes discharges itself in a flood of tears, while one's steps now involuntarily rush along, now involuntarily lag . . . a depth of happiness in which the most painful and gloomy things appear, not as an antithesis,

but as conditioned, demanded, as a *necessary* colour within such a superfluity of light. . . . Everything is in the highest degree involuntary but
takes place as in a tempest of a feeling of freedom, of absoluteness, of
power, of divinity. . . . This is *my* experience of inspiration; I do not
doubt that one has to go back thousands of years to find anyone who
could say to me "it is mine also."

Here we encounter in one vivid epiphany the precise synthesis of the two archetypal complexes in the closest possible interpenetration: an experience that is simultaneously deeply involuntary (Saturn-Pluto) yet paradoxically marked by an
exalted freedom (Jupiter-Uranus); an experience of the most painful and gloomy
(Saturn-Pluto) that appears within a superfluity of light and happiness (Jupiter-
Uranus), *not* as its antithesis but as *its necessary condition*. As Nietzsche wrote
after he finished *Zarathustra*:

You want if possible . . . *to abolish suffering*; and we?—it really does
seem that *we* would rather increase it and make it worse than it has ever
been! . . . The discipline of suffering, of *great* suffering—do you not
know that it is this discipline alone which has created every elevation of
mankind hitherto? That tension of the soul during misfortune which
transmits to it its strength, its terror at the sight of great destruction, its
inventiveness and bravery in undergoing, enduring, interpreting and exploiting misfortune; and whatever depth, mystery, mask, spirit, cunning
and greatness has been bestowed upon it—has it not been bestowed
through suffering, through the discipline of great suffering?

In the two years from January 1883 to January 1885, in coincidence with the
once-in-a-lifetime personal transit of Uranus crossing his natal Jupiter-Uranus aspect (essentially the same personal transit across their natal Jupiter-Uranus
aspects that Einstein and Napoleon underwent at their respective peak moments) and also in coincidence with the once-in-an-age world transit of the
triple Saturn-Neptune-Pluto conjunction in the sky, Nietzsche composed the
four parts of *Zarathustra*, as in a storm wind of freedom and power. The long-
held dialectical tension between the two great archetypal dominants in his
life—and in the collective psyche—now seemed to come together with volcanic
intensity in a creative synthesis that transcended each complex on its own yet
fulfilled them both at a higher level. The contradiction of opposites had reached
fever pitch and then erupted, bringing forth a prophetic testament that carried
the characteristic gravitas, authority, judgment, fatefulness, and power of the one
complex and the rebellious defiance, transcending freedom, lightness of spirit,
and creative joy of the other.

Here the will to power and its dominion over human life was both preserved
and radically reconceived: Through the heroic individual who possesses the

strength to master his passions rather than weaken or extirpate them, who has the courage to *overcome himself,* through such a person the universal Will in all its potent and fateful inevitability becomes the very instrument of freedom and brings forth the birth of a new form of being—the unconditionally life-affirming joyful creator who has become his own law, and who realizes within his own being the meaning of the Earth.

> You must be ready to burn yourself in your own flame: how could you become new, if you had not first become ashes?

Nietzsche confronted the inhibiting power of the dark *senex:*

> And when I beheld my devil, I found him serious, thorough, profound, solemn: it was the spirit of Gravity—through him all things are ruined. One does not kill by anger but by laughter. Come, let us kill the Spirit of Gravity.

He affirmed the creative miracle of the eternal *puer:*

> The child is innocence and forgetfulness, a new beginning, a sport, a self-propelling wheel, a first motion, a sacred Yes.

> I have learned to walk: since then I have run. I have learned to fly: since then I do not have to be pushed in order to move. Now I am nimble, now I fly, now I see myself under myself, now a god dances within me.

And finally:

> I flew, an arrow, quivering with sun-intoxicated rapture: out into the distant future, which no dream has yet seen, into warmer Souths than artists have ever dreamed of, there where gods, dancing, are ashamed of all clothes. . . . Where all becoming seemed to me the dancing of gods . . . where necessity was freedom itself, which blissfully played with the goad of freedom.

> O my Will! . . . Preserve me from all petty victories! Preserve and spare me for a great destiny! . . . That I may one day be ready and ripe in the great noontide . . . a bow eager for its arrow, an arrow eager for its star— a star, ready and ripe in its noontide, glowing, transpierced, blissful through annihilating sun-arrows. . . . Spare me for one great victory!

In all its titanic power and exalted grandeur, *Zarathustra* is at once a hymn to solitude and necessity and a manifesto of creative freedom and joy.

By my love and hope I entreat you: do not reject the hero in your soul!
Keep holy your highest hope! Thus spoke Zarathustra.

I will examine elsewhere the remaining years of Nietzsche's creative life and
its tragic denouement in the mental collapse of January 1889. To do so will require an understanding of archetypal complexes we have not yet explored, particularly the Saturn-Neptune and Neptune-Pluto combinations. Maintaining our
focus here on the Jupiter-Uranus complex, we can follow the subsequent cultural unfolding of *Thus Spoke Zarathustra*, where a remarkable pattern of similar
planetary correlations continued. In homage to Nietzsche's masterwork, Richard
Strauss composed the symphonic poem *Also Sprach Zarathustra* in 1896, precisely
when transiting Uranus moved into conjunction with his natal Jupiter, again, a
once-in-a-lifetime personal transit, *and* when transiting Saturn opposed his natal
Pluto. The startling synthesis of dark titanic power and soaring brilliance in its
opening passage, "Dawn," well conveys both its Nietzschean inspiration and the
corresponding archetypal forces. On a larger scale, we can also recognize the continuation of the longer Uranus-Pluto cycle and its archetypal complex: Nietzsche's birth at the start of the mid-nineteenth-century Uranus-Pluto conjunction
period and Strauss's composing of *Zarathustra* at the start of the immediately following Uranus-Pluto opposition in 1896 both reflected, in a cyclical sequence,
the theme of titanic struggle and liberation.

Finally, it was during the next Uranus-Pluto conjunction, when Jupiter and
Uranus were also in conjunction at the time of the triple conjunction with Pluto
in 1968–69—the only such alignment of the twentieth century, which brought
together the three planets that were conjoined more broadly in the preceding
century at Nietzsche's birth—that this powerful opening passage from Strauss's
Also Sprach Zarathustra first entered into broad public awareness when it accompanied the opening images of Stanley Kubrick's epic film *2001: A Space
Odyssey*. With its distinctive expression of such themes as sudden evolutionary
and technological breakthrough, "The Dawn of Man," unexpected radical expansion of consciousness, cosmic grandeur, and the prophecy of a coming birth of a
new form of human being, the film well embodied the archetypal symbolism of
the triple conjunction. This was the same 1968–69 alignment that coincided
with the Apollo Moon landing, the proposal of the Gaia hypothesis, the photograph "Earthrise," the climax of the Sixties' counterculture and its exuberant
celebration of creative freedom, and the rapid emergence of a conviction widely
shared throughout the world, evident in the social movements, music, writings,
and many other cultural phenomena of the time, that a new age was dawning.

Hidden Births

The flow of human activity and thought, needless to say, hardly stops and starts in lockstep accordance with planetary alignments. Many significant cultural phenomena take place every year and every decade. Yet it does indeed seem that with extraordinary consistency the conjunctions and oppositions of Jupiter and Uranus tend to coincide with a palpable intensification, a visible cyclic climax, of ongoing cultural creativity, liberation, and a sense of new beginnings, in both individual lives and the life of the human community. Each such alignment seems to serve as a punctuation point in the continuing cycle: as a culmination of what preceded it, a fruition of the creative processes of the immediate past, yet also a breakthrough into a new level of creativity that unfolds through the succeeding years—with revolutionary ideas entering public discourse, with long-germinating creative processes suddenly breaking the surface, with new works born and disseminated, new horizons explored, new associations begun, new movements initiated, new freedoms won, new understandings awakened.

Yet one of the less obvious characteristics of the correlations cited here is that the significance of many events that coincide with the Jupiter-Uranus world transit alignments was not visible at the time they occurred, nor in the immediately following years. In numerous instances that we have seen, the significance was indeed self-evident and widely recognized—the Moon landing, the fall of the Bastille, the fall of the Berlin Wall. But few people in 1858 realized the significance of Darwin and Wallace's joint paper on the theory of evolution when it was read before the Linnean Society. It received only a muted response at the time, and when it was published in the society's minutes the response was largely a critical one. Several months afterwards, when the president of the society summarized the events of the preceding year, he remarked with regret:

> The year which has passed . . . has not, indeed, been marked by any of those striking discoveries which at once revolutionise, so to speak, the department of science on which they bear.

The moment of cultural awakening, no matter how epochal, often occurs very quietly. Few if any besides Kepler realized the full significance of his *Astronomia Nova* in 1609–10, with its brilliant solution to the ancient problem of the planets and its mathematical confirmation of the Copernican heliocentric theory. Galileo himself, his own ambitions foremost in his consciousness, entirely failed to recognize the importance of Kepler's work. Kepler was being only partly rhetorical when he declared, "It can wait a century for a reader, as God himself has waited six thousand years for a witness."

For this reason it is difficult to speak with sufficient historical perspective about correlations with the more recent alignments of Jupiter and Uranus. Scarcely anyone during the conjunction in 1803 knew that Beethoven was composing the *Eroica*, let alone what it would signify for later generations. Even six years after the publication of Freud's *Interpretation of Dreams* during the conjunction of 1900, only 351 copies had been sold. The unassuming Jesuit priest Lemaître and his expanding-universe hypothesis were impatiently brushed aside and ignored in 1927 by all the distinguished physicists, including Einstein, at the famous Solvay congress. No one in 1962 recognized that Betty Friedan had just completed a book that would catalyze a social revolution. Few could have predicted that Rachel Carson in the same year had initiated a new epoch in ecological awareness and a movement of such planetary consequence.

Although Jupiter-Uranus alignments regularly coincided with creative and emancipatory beginnings, births of important works and movements and ideas, these beginnings were often, as it were, births in a stable, humble and remote from the centers of world power and attention—in privacy and solitude, in a quiet study, in a small meeting, in a notebook, alone on a mountain path, by a pond, inside an individual mind, the interior castle. They were often unrecognized at the time by the larger public, and sometimes they were unrecognized by anyone, even the creative agents themselves. Only later did the event or its significance become visible—indeed, sometimes much later, under a subsequent Jupiter-Uranus alignment, as with Mendel's long-ignored genetic discoveries. No one during the Jupiter-Uranus opposition in 1976 knew that two young men in a garage in California had begun the personal computer revolution. No one during the following Jupiter-Uranus conjunction in 1983 recognized that perestroika was being born when Mikhail Gorbachev, as the Soviet Union's chief agricultural expert, made his crucial visit to Canada that year, where he encountered the efficiency and productivity of North American farming and the open political style of the West and began his pivotal association with Aleksandr Yakovlev, then the Soviet ambassador to Canada, who became the principal theorist of perestroika and glasnost. Such correlations become visible only over time.

Judging by the evidence for all previous Jupiter-Uranus alignments, it is virtually certain that the majority of the most significant Promethean events coincident with the recent alignments are not yet known—something to keep in mind with the current (as of this writing) Jupiter-Uranus opposition, which began in the fall of 2002 and extends through the summer of 2004. Certainly many characteristic Jupiter-Uranus phenomena during this period are readily visible, such as the wave of breakthroughs in astronomy and space exploration, the worldwide demonstrations against the U.S. invasion of Iraq discussed earlier, the sudden popular enthusiasm for antiestablishment documentaries, and the intensified transformation of the Internet into a medium of progressive activism and dissemination of news and dissident opinion.[21] But as with most of the correlations discussed throughout these chapters on the Jupiter-Uranus cycle, from Descartes's *Discourse on Method* and the *cogito* in 1637 to the birth of rock and roll in 1954–55, many, perhaps most, of the major archetypally relevant cultural phenomena of the 2002–04 alignment will become visible and open to historical assessment only in the course of time as we gain sufficient distance from the age in which we live.

Perhaps it is appropriate to end this section on the Jupiter-Uranus cycle by mentioning that Pico della Mirandola's *Oration on the Dignity of Man*, with which we began this book, was itself composed exactly during the Jupiter-Uranus conjunction of 1486 at the dawn of the High Renaissance. The coincidence is both marvelous and altogether representative of the cycle. Universally recognized by modern scholars as epoch-making, Pico's manifesto was scarcely known in the year of its composition, since the meeting of philosophers for which it was written as the opening oration was prohibited by the Vatican from taking place. Yet with its stirring declaration of human freedom and boundless possibility in the cosmic adventure, with its optimism and creativity, and with its ultimate cultural success and legendary historical status, the *Oratio* vividly illustrates the central themes of the Jupiter-Uranus cycle and its corresponding archetypal complex, Prometheus crowned king:

> Thou, constrained by no limits, in accordance with thine own free will, in whose hand We have placed thee, shalt ordain for thyself the limits of thy nature. . . . We have made thee neither of heaven nor of earth, neither mortal nor immortal, so that with freedom of choice and with honor, as though the maker and molder of thyself, thou mayest fashion thyself in whatever shape thou shalt prefer.

VII

Awakenings of
Spirit and Soul

Our normal waking consciousness, rational consciousness as we
call it, is but one special type of consciousness, whilst all about it,
parted from it by the filmiest of screens, there lie potential forms of
consciousness entirely different. . . . No account of the universe in
its totality can be final which leaves these other forms of consciousness quite disregarded.

—William James
The Varieties of Religious Experience

Epochal Shifts of Cultural Vision

L et us now examine our fourth and final planetary cycle in this initial survey of world transits and historical correlations with collective cultural
phenomena. The Uranus-Neptune cycle is approximately 172 years in
length, the longest we have examined so far. Conjunctions and oppositions of
Uranus and Neptune last for relatively long periods, remaining within 15° orb
for approximately fourteen to nineteen years. In general, I found that the archetypal character of these historical periods was less concrete and tangible than
the other cycles we have been examining, yet their ultimate influence on subsequent human history was no less profound or enduring.

In the century and a half since Neptune's discovery, astrologers have come
to regard the archetypal principle associated with the planet as both all-
encompassing and vanishingly subtle in nature. It is considered to govern the
transcendent dimensions of life, imaginative and spiritual vision, and the realm
of the ideal. It rules the invisible and intangible ground of experience, shaping
awareness beyond the usual causal mechanisms. Its characteristic influence is
one of dissolving boundaries and structures, merging that which was separate. It
favors the unitive over the divided, the timeless over the temporal, the immaterial over the material, the infinite over the finite.

The Neptune archetype is also associated with illusion and delusion, deception and self-deception, confusion, ambiguity, projection, *maya*. It rules both the
positive and negative meanings of enchantment—both poetic vision and wish-
ful fantasy, mysticism and madness, higher realities and delusional unreality. It
informs all that is paradoxically united. It transcends and confuses attempts
to maintain strict boundaries, definitions, and dichotomies. It is the archetypal
principle of the multidimensional and the metaempirical, the metaphorical and
multivalent.

The Neptune principle has a special relation to the stream of consciousness
and the oceanic depths of the unconscious, to all nonordinary states of consciousness, to the realm of dreams and visions, images and reflections. It governs
myth and religion, poetry and the arts, inspiration and aspiration, the experience
of divinity, the numinous, the ineffable, the sacred and mysterious. Its domain is

that of meaning rather than matter, the symbolic rather than the literal. It is associated with the realm of soul and spirit, the transpersonal domain, the collective unconscious, the *anima mundi,* the archetypal dimension of life, the realm of the Platonic Ideas. More broadly, Neptune is regarded as that which ultimately governs all modes of consciousness, in the sense of encompassing all the gods and archetypes that inform and shape how one experiences the world, both outer and inner. It is also the archetypal principle that informs the preceding sentences—that makes possible any perspective or experience concerning "gods and archetypes," "the numinous," or "the *anima mundi.*"

In periods of Uranus-Neptune alignments, as with the other cycles involving Uranus we have examined, I observed that the Prometheus archetype again seemed to be clearly constellated in the collective psyche and evident in cultural phenomena. Its familiar qualities of accelerated change, sudden awakening, creative innovation, emancipation, rebellion, and disruption were easily visible, but in this case these qualities were active specifically in relation to the various archetypal themes and domains of experience associated with Neptune. The periods of Uranus-Neptune alignments were characterized not so much by great political or similarly concrete external changes as by pervasive transformations of a culture's underlying vision: widespread spiritual awakenings, the birth of new religious movements, cultural renaissances, the emergence of new philosophical perspectives, rebirths of idealism, sudden shifts in a culture's cosmological and metaphysical vision, rapid collective changes in psychological understanding and interior sensibility, certain forms of scientific paradigm shifts, new utopian social visions and movements, and epochal shifts in a culture's artistic imagination.

More problematical, these alignments also tended to coincide with periods of widespread spiritual and philosophical confusion and disorientation that were associated with the rapid dissolution of previously established structures of belief and certainty, and a greater than usual susceptibility to mass entrancements of various kinds. As with other configurations involving Uranus, there was consistently evident either an exciting, liberatory, awakening quality, accompanied by spontaneous creative innovation, or a disruptive, destabilizing quality produced by sudden unexpected radical change. But in either mode, those qualities were characteristically expressed in and through the domain of the collective imagination and cultural vision—spiritual, artistic, scientific, cosmological, philosophical, social—with a general tendency towards the idealistic, the poetic, the esoteric, and the mystical, often accompanied by a restless impulse for transcendence and spiritual illumination.

Let us begin this survey by citing a few paradigmatic historical examples. Regarding *the birth of new philosophical movements,* especially those of an idealist metaphysical character, Uranus and Neptune were in conjunction in the period from 412 to 397 BCE, the years of Socrates's most influential teaching in Athens during the final decade and a half of his life, including the entire period of Plato's study with him, his death, and the resulting birth of Platonism, indeed of the entire Western philosophical tradition whose source and wellspring are Socrates and Plato. Many characteristic features of subsequent alignments are evident in the philosophical vision that emerges from this period, such as the affirmation of a transcendent spiritual reality, the vision of the archetypal Ideas, the belief that death is a gateway to greater life, and the revelation of a superior realm of existence that informs and imbues human life with meaning and purpose.

In the area of *spiritual awakenings and the birth of new religions,* Uranus and Neptune were in opposition from 16 to 32 CE, a period historians generally consider to encompass the adult life and ministry of Jesus, his death, and the birth of the Christian religion. As we will see in the course of our survey, many characteristic features of other Uranus-Neptune alignments can be discerned here in a quintessential form: the charismatic influence of a spiritual teacher inspired and informed by a mystical awakening, the revelation of a new spiritual order and the sudden forming of a new relation to the divine, the belief that a greater divine reality has unexpectedly entered into human affairs with liberating consequences, the pentecostal influx of new spiritual powers and the ecstatic communion with divinity.

Where the Uranus-*Pluto* cycle of the 1960s, the French Revolutionary epoch, and other comparable periods such as that of the enormous Spartacus rebellion in Roman antiquity can be seen as coinciding with collective activations of the titanically empowered Prometheus, the Uranus-*Neptune* cycle appears to be correlated with the collective activation of a more spiritual Prometheus. The image of Jesus Christ that emerges from this period bears many of the distinctive Promethean motifs, though in an emphatically spiritual context and mode of manifestation—the divine rebel against the old order, the eternal liberator of humanity who brings the fire of divine grace from the heavens to emancipate humankind from its enslavement to death and sin, reopening the gates of paradise. As we will see, many other themes were visible in this era that would be characteristic of subsequent Uranus-Neptune alignment periods: the focus on miraculous and supernatural phenomena, sudden healings of both a physical and spiritual nature, the concern with redemption and spiritual rebirth, the widespread collective belief that a radically different reality would suddenly replace the present world order, the perceived dissolution of long-established limiting structures of reality and conventional laws of causation, the unexpected awakening to immortal life, the evoking of an ethic of universal compassion and the spiritual unity of humankind.

In the area of *cultural renaissances,* Uranus and Neptune were in conjunction from 1472 to 1486, the heart of the Italian Renaissance that saw the Florentine Academy's Platonic revival at its height during the reign of Lorenzo the Magnificent, when Marsilio Ficino wrote his eighteen-volume magnum opus, the

Theologia Platonica, developed his influential conception of Platonic love, disseminated the ideas of the Hermetic and other esoteric and mystical traditions, and published the first complete translation of Plato in the West. This same period saw Leonardo da Vinci begin his artistic career with *The Adoration of the Magi* and Botticelli paint both *Primavera* and *The Birth of Venus,* the quintessential symbol of the Renaissance's rebirth of archetypal beauty. This was the formative period for Erasmus, the paradigmatic Renaissance Christian Humanist. Especially emblematic of this archetypal complex, as the Uranus-Neptune conjunction entered its last year, Pico della Mirandola composed the *Oration on the Dignity of Man,* the manifesto of Renaissance Humanism.

At the time Pico's *Oration* was written, in 1486, there took place a rare triple conjunction of Jupiter, Uranus, and Neptune. We discussed above those elements of the *Oration* that reflected the Jupiter-Uranus archetypal impulse. In the context of the present cycle we can recognize several characteristic themes of the Uranus-Neptune archetypal complex: the numinous revelation of a newly autonomous form of human being; the fluid syncretism and interpenetration of many spiritual and philosophical traditions, often of an esoteric character; the renewal of classical antiquity and the ancient imagination; the creative revisioning of ancient myths and biblical texts; and the celebration of an image of the human being that is simultaneously Promethean and spiritual, divinely informed, and specially graced to fulfill its unique cosmic role.

As we saw in other planetary cycles, major outer-planet alignment periods coincided not only with archetypally relevant cultural phenomena but also with the births of individuals whose subsequent life and work embodied and carried forward the archetypal impulses associated with that specific planetary combination. During the Uranus-Neptune alignment of 1472–86 occurred the births of both Raphael and Michelangelo, paradigmatic embodiments of the High Renaissance artistic ideal, both of whom were inspired by a synthesis of Neoplatonic and Christian mysticism. This alignment also coincided with the births of both Copernicus and Luther, the two men who initiated, respectively, the great cosmological and religious paradigm shifts that launched the modern era.

During this alignment at the heart of the Italian Renaissance we can recognize the evidence for synchronic archetypal phenomena that occur across several categories of cultural experience simultaneously and affect the cultural imagination and sensibility in many areas: the arts, philosophy, religion, science. We can also see the characteristic tendency of these periods to dissolve the boundaries between domains, as in Leonardo (art and science), Ficino and Pico (philosophy and religion, scholarship and gnosis), and Botticelli and Raphael (art and philosophy). A vivid example of this synchronic multiplicity and interplay from the more recent past is the most recent Uranus-Neptune opposition, which took place at the beginning of the twentieth century.

In the cultural phenomena and events during the alignment that took place from 1899 to 1918, the characteristic themes of the Uranus-Neptune archetypal combination can be seen in virtually every category. Regarding a *major cultural shift in artistic vision,* this is the crucial period in painting and the visual arts for Picasso, Braque, Matisse, Mondrian, Duchamp, Kandinsky, and Klee, as well as the influential later work of Cézanne and Rodin. In literature, this is the pivotal period of radical change and experiment for Joyce, Proust, Mann, Rilke, Kafka, Yeats, Pound, T. S. Eliot, D. H. Lawrence, Gertrude Stein, Robert Frost, and Wallace Stevens. So too in music, for Stravinsky, Schönberg, and Scriabin, as well as dance, for Isadora Duncan, Nijinsky, and Diaghilev. The Uranus-Neptune alignment of this period precisely encompassed the many-sided birth of modernism in European and American culture.

We should note that this period of the Uranus-*Neptune* opposition significantly overlapped the Uranus-*Pluto* opposition of 1896–1907, whose many revolutionary social, political, cultural, scientific, and technological events and trends we examined earlier. Whenever there were such overlaps in planetary alignments, I consistently found distinct parallel expressions and syntheses of the two archetypal complexes in the coinciding historical phenomena. In a case such as this, where both alignments were so long, where the overlap was so sustained, and where one planet (Uranus) was in both cycles, the distinctions could sometimes be subtle, but were still clearly visible when seen in the light of the larger historical pattern.

Those elements and themes that the two cycles shared—heightened creativity, rapid and radical change and disruption, emancipatory shifts from previously established structures, sudden awakenings of various kinds, artistic and scientific innovation—were all associated with the planet Uranus. But, to take science as an example, the Uranus-*Pluto* cycle consistently coincided with epochal scientific revolutions that were associated with a definite collective intensification of the drive for intellectual innovation, technological empowerment, and evolutionary transformation, notably including, in the 1896–1907 period, the birth of the nuclear age—the discovery of radioactivity in uranium, the isolation of radium and polonium, and Einstein's formulation of the equivalence of mass and energy—as well as the development of the airplane, the automobile, and many other technological advances. By contrast, the Uranus-*Neptune* cycle tended to coincide with radical changes in the collective scientific imagination that had a more intangible metaphysical or epistemological dimension, dissolving previously established structures of belief concerning the nature of reality in a manner that often transcended the scientific field in which they began.

Thus the period in which the Uranus-Pluto and Uranus-Neptune oppositions overlapped at the beginning of the twentieth century coincided with the beginning of the great twin revolutions in modern physics, relativity theory and quantum physics. The two revolutions together constituted a larger paradigm shift that eventually informed and affected all the sciences and strongly shaped the cultural imagination of the twentieth century. As many cultural historians have pointed out, the parallels were many and profound between the artistic revolution brought forth by Cézanne, Picasso, Braque, Matisse, Joyce, Proust, Stravinsky, and Schönberg and the scientific revolution embodied in the work of Einstein, Planck, Bohr, and others, and in the long run the two revolutions were mutually influential and synergistic. In addition, we see in both these shifts another set of characteristic Uranus-Neptune themes: the dissolution of established perspectives and structures of reality, often in a manner that is confusing and disorienting, that introduces a plurality of simultaneous or overlapping realities and perspectives, and that brings into question fundamental assumptions about subjectivity and objectivity, the relative and the absolute, time and space, substance and process.

Periods of Uranus-Neptune alignments often coincided with *epochal shifts of cosmological vision,* catalyzed either by new astronomical data or by major leaps of the scientific imagination that bring forth a radically new conceptual framework. The entire sequence of events involved in Einstein's transformation of the modern cosmological vision took place in precise coincidence with the full duration of the long Uranus-Neptune opposition, and it is instructive to note the synchronistic unfolding of the relativity revolution and this planetary alignment. We can also discern here the characteristic Uranus-Neptune theme of the subversion of established reality structures associated with Saturn—absolute time, solid matter, gravity, and consensus reality. The revolution began when Uranus was in opposition to both Neptune and Pluto, during the time of the overlapping cycles, when in 1905 Einstein wrote and published the four papers that contained the special theory of relativity, the equivalence of mass and energy, the theory of Brownian motion, and the photon theory of light. In the next several years, as the Uranus-Pluto opposition ended and the Uranus-Neptune opposition approached exactitude (1906–10), the theory of relativity, largely ignored at first, gradually attracted the attention of Planck, Max Born, and other physicists who then gave lectures and published articles that described the theory and its implications. In 1907, Einstein produced a comprehensive paper on the theory of relativity, which included the general result that $E = mc^2$. In a series of lectures and papers from 1907 to 1910, Einstein's former mathematics teacher, Hermann Minkowski, introduced the concept of a single four-dimensional space-time continuum, reformulated the theory's mathematics, and noted that in the light of relativity the Newtonian theory of gravity was now inadequate. In 1911, Paul Langevin gave the famous lecture that set out the "twins paradox," in which, in sensational defiance of absolute time, a person traveling at a very high speed to a star and back will have experienced two years in the course of his voyage, while on Earth, where his twin remains, two centuries will have elapsed. In 1912 Planck's assistant, Max von Laue, wrote the first textbook on relativity.

In the meantime, in 1907 as the Uranus-Neptune opposition first reached exact alignment, Einstein had the crucial idea that set in motion the *general* theory of relativity when he recognized that if a person falls freely he will not feel his own weight. (Here we see the characteristic Promethean "defiance of gravity," but here expressed on the imaginative-cosmological level typical of Uranus-Neptune alignments, as compared with the Wright brothers' slightly earlier more literal and technologically empowered defiance of gravity by the development of the airplane when the Uranus-*Pluto* opposition was in orb, or as compared with the space flights of the Uranus-Pluto conjunction of the 1960s.) Einstein worked for the next several years during the Uranus-Neptune alignment until he was able to present the fully developed general theory in 1915, followed by the publication of an "Authorized Version" of the theory in 1916, which radically transfigured Newtonian gravitational forces into aspects of the curvature of the four-dimensional space-time continuum. In 1917, still during the alignment, Einstein wrote the paper "Cosmological Considerations in General Relativity," which introduced the now-confirmed cosmological constant and more generally opened up the field of cosmology, previously more a branch of metaphysics, to the new data and theories of physics and physical astronomy. In the same year, the first observational evidence that the universe was expanding was reported in a paper by the American astronomer Vesto Slipher.

Finally, in 1918, as the Uranus-Neptune alignment reached the 15° orb, Arthur Eddington, the leading exponent of Einstein's ideas, wrote his authoritative and influential summary "Report on the Relativity Theory of Gravitation." In 1919, with the ending of the war, Eddington organized the momentous eclipse expedition to test the theory's prediction that the Sun bent starlight. In November of that year, just as *Jupiter* moved into alignment with the Uranus-Neptune opposition (then at 16°), the joint meeting of the Royal Society and Royal Astronomy Society took place at which the electrifying announcement was made that the measurements confirmed Einstein's theory. As we discussed above, almost overnight and with increasing intensity during the entire Jupiter-Uranus alignment in 1920–21, both the fame of Einstein and the astounding cosmological revolution that challenged the very structure of reality for scientist and layperson alike unfolded in countless news articles, editorials, celebratory headlines, and public discussions. This last phase of the relativity revolution took place in the period when Uranus and Neptune were in the last stages of the alignment, between 15° and 20° past exactitude. Much as we saw in numerous instances in other planetary cycles, the cumulative archetypal developments that took place in the course of the entire Uranus-Neptune opposition period of the early twentieth century can be seen as reaching a climax as the alignment approached the 20° orb. The frequently intensified or climactic quality of the events and experiences that occur near the end of a long alignment period is suggestive of a sunset, with the latter's greater depth of light and fully saturated colors as the arc of the day's journey is completed. The movement of Jupiter into the alignment, should it occur at this stage, generally coincides with an additional quality of expansion, optimism, and success in the relevant events.

Regarding *epochal shifts in psychological understanding and interior sensibility,* this same period of overlapping major outer-planet alignments at the beginning of the twentieth century coincided with the cultural emergence of depth psychology in the work of Freud and Jung. The period in question spanned the publication of Freud's *The Interpretation of Dreams* in 1899–1900 through the publication of Jung's *Symbols of Transformation* in 1911–12, as well as the subsequent critical advances made by both men in the immediately ensuing years. Remarkably, it was during the period in which Uranus and *Pluto* were most closely in alignment (1896–1907) that Freud's more instinctually and biologically oriented psychology received its most significant impetus, one appropriate to the Dionysian-Plutonic archetypal complex (again, eloquently embodied in Freud's telling epigraph from Virgil for *The Interpretation of Dreams*, "If I cannot move the Gods above, then I will move the Infernal regions"). By contrast, Jung's more transpersonal, mythic, symbolical, and spiritually oriented psychology, including his early studies in astrology and esoteric traditions, as well as his seminal insights into the *coniunctio oppositorum* (conjunction of opposites) and the transcendent function, received its most significant impetus when Uranus was in close alignment exclusively with *Neptune* (1908–18).

The Uranus-Neptune cycle's correlation with the emergence of new philosophies that dissolved established assumptions and structures of belief, and in which a spiritual, idealist, or psychological dimension was central, was clearly visible in the work of many philosophers and psychologists during this 1899–1918 alignment. These included William James in the United States (*The Varieties of Religious Experience, A Pluralistic Mystic*), Henri Bergson in France (intuitionist metaphysics, creative evolution), Alfred North Whitehead in England (philosophy of mathematics in the Platonic-Pythagorean tradition, philosophy of science that formulated alternatives to materialism), Edmund Husserl in Germany (phenomenology), Benedetto Croce in Italy (idealistic aesthetics), Josiah Royce in the United States (ethical idealism, the "beloved community" of all humanity as the object of ultimate loyalty and source of ethical values), Richard Bucke in Canada (*Cosmic Consciousness*), and Frederic Myers in England (*Human Personality and Its Survival of Bodily Death*), whose concept of the subliminal Self would in turn influence William James.

In the area of *esoteric philosophy and mystical spirituality,* Rudolf Steiner began to publicly present his esoteric work in a stream of lectures and books at this time: *Mysticism at the Dawn of the Modern Age, Christianity as Mystical Fact, Knowledge of the Higher Worlds and Its Attainment, Theosophy, An Outline of Esoteric Science.* In 1913 Steiner founded the new form of theosophy that he called anthroposophy—"a path of knowledge leading the spiritual in the human being to the spiritual in the universe"—which emphasized the evolution of consciousness, the cosmic significance of the human being, moral and spiritual freedom, the conjoining of Christian esotericism with Hindu and Buddhist mystical streams, and the necessity of forging a "spiritual science" for the modern era:

There slumber in every human being faculties by means of which one can acquire for oneself a knowledge of higher worlds. Mystics, Gnostics, Theosophists—all speak of a world of soul and spirit which for them is just as real as the world we see with our physical eyes and touch with our physical hands.

During these same years in coincidence with this alignment, the work of artists such as Mondrian and Kandinsky was deeply influenced by their encounter with Theosophy. Art itself during this alignment was infused with a new sense of spiritual significance, whether in painting, in literature (Rilke, Joyce, Proust), or dance (Isadora Duncan: "Art which is not religious is not art, is mere merchandise").

It was also during this period that Martin Buber's influential turn to Hasidism took place. Sri Aurobindo's seminal reformation of Indian mystical thought began at this time as well, and the Indian philosopher and poet Rabindranath Tagore brought forth *Gitanjali*, his most celebrated work of mystical poetry. In each of these cultural streams—American pragmatism, European esotericism and idealism, Jewish spirituality, Indian mysticism—there emerged during this Uranus-Neptune alignment of 1899–1918 a creative, spiritually informed philosophical impulse that became deeply influential for the intellectual, artistic, and religious development of the twentieth century.

We see the theme of *spiritually inspired political activism* during this same alignment in Gandhi's development of *satyagraha* that began in 1906. Both Gandhi's philosophy of political resistance and Tolstoy's spiritually informed engagement with the political realm from the turn of the century, to which I drew attention in the context of the Uranus-*Pluto* cycle, are characteristic examples of the combined archetypal influences of these two cycles, which were then overlapping. The famous correspondence between Tolstoy and Gandhi on religion and nonviolent resistance to evil took place during the Uranus-Neptune alignment in the years 1909–10, just before Tolstoy's death. Focusing on just the Uranus-Neptune cycle, we can readily discern in the philosophy and strategy of nonviolent resistance the precise combination of the two archetypal principles associated with these two planets: with Uranus, freedom, rebellion, defiance of legal and political structures, resistance to oppression, creative and unpredictably nonconformist activity; with Neptune, social and spiritual idealism, the act of surrender in the service of a higher reality, universal compassion. Both Tolstoy and Thoreau, the two key nineteenth-century figures in the development of nonviolent resistance, were born during the preceding Uranus-Neptune conjunction of the 1814–29 period, and Gandhi was born during the intervening Uranus-Neptune square in 1869, midway to the opposition of the early twentieth century. All three figures stated that they were inspired by the ethical idealism expressed in the teachings and actions of Jesus, who flourished during the Uranus-Neptune alignment of 16–32.

The sequence and overlap of these two major cycles, Uranus-Neptune and Uranus-Pluto, at the beginning of the twentieth century can be seen to have co-incided with a more distinctly differentiated shift in the concerns and activities of significant cultural figures at this time. Just as the changing emphasis from Freud to Jung in early depth psychology closely coincided with the shift from the Uranus-Pluto opposition to the Uranus-Neptune opposition, so did a parallel shift in the lives and work of many of their contemporaries among the figures cited above. Each such shift reflected in its own way the characteristic motifs of the two archetypal complexes. For example, Sri Aurobindo was an active leader in the nationalist revolutionary political movement against British imperialism in India during the Uranus-*Pluto* opposition of 1896–1907. Arrested in 1908, he then underwent a series of transformative mystical experiences while in prison in 1908–09, in coincidence with the Uranus-*Neptune* opposition. During the re-mainder of that alignment, which continued for the next decade, Aurobindo es-tablished the Pondicherry Ashram in 1910 and there began his major works of mystical philosophy, *The Life Divine* and *The Synthesis of Yoga*, which were pub-lished serially from 1914.

Similarly, Martin Buber was active with Theodor Herzl in the Zionist politi-cal movement in Vienna in the Uranus-*Pluto* period, eventually becoming the editor of the official Zionist organ *Die Welt* in 1901. The Uranus-*Neptune* period exactly coincided with Buber's subsequent intensive study of Hasidism, which began in late 1903 and was followed by the publication of his first Hasidic books in 1906–09, his influential lectures on Judaism in Prague in 1909–11, and his beginning the composition of his masterwork, *I and Thou*, in 1916.

Finally, as regards *new art forms and new media of expression for the cultural imagination,* in the same period that saw the many revolutionary artistic develop-ments and figures already mentioned (Picasso, Stravinsky, Joyce, et al.), this same alignment of 1899–1918 was also the period that saw the emergence of motion pictures as a creative art form and a broad cultural influence. Motion pictures required technological advances for the production, projection, and dissemina-tion (Uranus) of their *maya*-like images (Neptune). Their cultural influence from that period onwards was on the one hand emancipatory, innovative, and disrup-tive of established modes of expression and social relations (Uranus) and on the other hand stimulating of the imagination, hypnotic, often escapist, and dissolv-ing of conventional structures of identity and reality (Neptune).

The remarkable coalescing of all these events and trends—in the arts, sci-ences, philosophy, psychology, politics, and spirituality—during the period of this 1899–1918 alignment precipitated a complex transformation of cultural ex-perience on many fronts, and brought the seeds of significant future changes in the collective psyche that are still unfolding.

THE URANUS-NEPTUNE CYCLE

Axial alignments since 600 BCE

15° orb   Exact alignment <1°

584–568 BCE (BC)	*conjunction*	576–575
499–482	*opposition*	493–488
412–397	*conjunction*	405–403
328–311	*opposition*	322–317
240–226	*conjunction*	234–232
157–140	*opposition*	150–146
69–55	*conjunction*	62–61
16–32 CE (AD)	*opposition*	22–26
104–117	*conjunction*	110–11
187–203	*opposition*	193–97
275–288	*conjunction*	281–82
358–374	*opposition*	364–68
446–458	*conjunction*	452–53
529–545	*opposition*	535–39
617–629	*conjunction*	632–24
700–716	*opposition*	706–10
788–800	*conjunction*	794–95
872–887	*opposition*	877–82
959–972	*conjunction*	964–66
1043–1059	*opposition*	1048–53
1130–1143	*conjunction*	1135–37
1213–1230	*opposition*	1219–24
1301–1314	*conjunction*	1307–08
1385–1402	*opposition*	1391–95
1472–1486	*conjunction*	1478–79
1556–1574	*opposition*	1563–67
1643–1658	*conjunction*	1649–50
1728–1746	*opposition*	1734–38
1814–1829	*conjunction*	1821–22
1899–1918	*opposition*	1906–10
1985–2001	*conjunction*	1992–93

20° orb adds two to three years before and after dates given for 15°.

Spiritual Epiphanies and the
Emergence of New Religions

As with the other outer-planet cycles already surveyed, both synchronic and diachronic patterns of striking clarity branched out from each of the periods cited in close coincidence with the succession of major cyclical alignments of Uranus and Neptune. For example, with respect to spiritual awakenings and the emergence of new religions since the birth of Christianity, Uranus and Neptune were again in alignment from 617 to 630, the exact period of the founding of Islam by Muhammad. Uranus and Neptune were 1° from exact conjunction in the year 622 at the time of the Hegira, the emigration to Medina, the "city of the Prophet," that marked the first year of the Muslim era. By 629, Muhammad was recognized as a prophet by Mecca, and by 630 Islam was dominant throughout Arabia.

In the Western context, the succession of major spiritual renewals that periodically pulsed through medieval and early modern Europe as well as colonial America coincided with the sequence of Uranus-Neptune conjunctions and oppositions over the centuries with extraordinary consistency. Often these religious movements were catalyzed by a powerful mystical awakening experienced by an individual who subsequently led or influenced the spiritual renewal. For example, the first Uranus-Neptune conjunction of the past millennium, which took place in 1130–43, coincided with the mystical vision that transformed the life of Hildegard von Bingen in 1141 and initiated her nearly forty years of spiritual leadership, artistic creativity, and influential writing on medicine, natural history, and theology:

> And it came to pass . . . when I was forty-two years and seven months old, that the heavens were opened and a blinding light of exceptional brilliance flowed through my entire brain. And so it kindled my whole heart and breast like a flame, not burning but warming . . . and suddenly I understood of the meaning of expositions of the books. . . .

It was during this same Uranus-Neptune conjunction, in 1136, that Saint Bernard of Clairvaux, the dominant figure of his age in European Christendom, began his *Sermons on the Song of Songs*, which set out the ideal of Christian aspiration in the mystical union with God in a state of infinite divine love. As with the other planetary cycles, I observed that these alignments also regularly coincided with the births of significant figures whose lives and cultural influence strongly reflected the characteristic archetypal themes. For example, during this same conjunction, in 1135 in the great metropolitan city of Córdoba in Moorish Spain, was born Moses Maimonides, whose philosophical synthesis of the Jewish religion and Greek rationalism provided a model for Thomas Aquinas's synthesis in a Christian context in the following century.

The immediately following Uranus-Neptune opposition of 1214–30 coincided with the widespread evangelical awakening led by Saint Francis of Assisi and Saint Dominic and the rapid dissemination throughout Europe of the Franciscan and Dominican orders. Here the characteristic archetypal themes of the Uranus-Neptune cycle were visible not only in the decisive spiritual quickening of the era but also in the Franciscans' and Dominicans' innovative dissolving of the boundaries between the lay world and the religious, bringing the dynamism of the Christian faith out of the cloister and into the world; in the more democratic forms of government within these religious orders that affirmed greater individual autonomy; in Francis's sense of universal compassion that extended to a mystical participation in nature as an expression of divinity, subverting traditional Christian tendencies towards a dualism of spirit and nature; and in Dominic's influential call for an awakening of scholarship and education that would better serve the dissemination of the Christian gospel and liberate both the intellect and the spirit by their interplay.

Appropriately, this same Uranus-Neptune alignment coincided with the birth of Thomas Aquinas (1225), who represented the climax of this spiritual-intellectual awakening of the High Middle Ages, and whose creative synthesis of the Christian gospel and Greek philosophy, of faith and reason—initially condemned by the Church for its innovations but eventually enshrined as canonical—was crucial for the subsequent evolution of Western thought. We can recognize the themes of the Uranus-Neptune archetypal complex here on several levels: again, the unexpected creative integration of realms previously kept rigidly separate by orthodox authority (religion and rationality, pagan thought and Christian belief, spirit and nature); again, the philosophical breakthrough of an idealist, metaphysical, spiritually informed character, but in a new, liberating form that affirmed the value of the natural world and the present life; again, the renewal and creative reformulation of the Platonic tradition, enriched by an encounter with Aristotle; and again, the rebellion against conservative or reactionary religious authority in the service of a new spiritual autonomy. Even Aquinas's mode of philosophical argumentation showed a liberating new self-reliance and independence from the previously heavy authority of the past: "Authority is the weakest source of proof," he wrote in *Summa Theologica*, anticipating the spirit of the Enlightenment.

The Uranus-Neptune archetypal complex is especially visible in Aquinas's philosophical affirmation of human autonomy (Uranus) within a universe ordered and pervaded by divinity and spirit (Neptune). This synthesis was achieved through Aquinas's articulation of what was in essence the mystical principle of participation, in which the human striving for freedom, autonomous intellectual development, and existential self-realization was seen not as a threat to the sovereignty of an aloofly separate God, but as an affirmation and expression of the divine will itself, with the finite human being participating in the infinite divine being from which humanity received its extraordinary capacities and essence. Whereas the dissolving of categorical boundaries and the mystical quality of this vision reflect the Neptune archetype, the elements of creative philosophical innovation, the striving for human freedom, and the openness to novelty in the universal order all reflect the presence of the Promethean principle associated with Uranus. It was this theological revolution, brought forth by Aquinas in the High Middle Ages, that established the necessary historical foundation for the emergence of the modern mind and the modern self—the birth of the modern from the medieval womb, achieved through an intellectual and spiritual reformation and synthesis of the Greek and Christian sources of the Western legacy.

The immediately following Uranus-Neptune conjunction of 1301–14 precisely coincided with the great wave of mystical fervor that swept through the Rhineland and central Europe in the early fourteenth century, and that was above all reflected in and influenced by the teachings of Meister Eckhart at that time. Eckhart's mystical understanding of the divine immanence in human experience was epitomized in his famous statement: "The eye by which I see God is the same eye by which God sees me: my eye and God's eye are one and the same—one in seeing, one in knowing, and one in loving." Many such statements, and his repeated assertion that the birth of Christ takes place in the present within the individual soul, as it did in history and as it does in eternity, strongly convey a synthesis of the mystical impulse associated with Neptune and the liberating subversiveness against orthodox structures associated with Uranus.

> Where is he who is born King of the Jews? Now concerning this birth, mark where it befalls. I say again, as I have often said before, that this birth befalls in the soul exactly as it does in eternity, neither more nor less, for it is the same birth: this birth befalls in the ground and essence of the soul. . . . God is in all things as being, as activity, as power.

In Italy this same alignment period coincided with Dante's composition of *La Divina Commedia*, the preeminent literary work of the medieval spiritual and artistic imagination, which Dante began in 1304–06 and continued writing through the entirety of the Uranus-Neptune conjunction and after until his death in 1321. In a vast synthesis of Christian faith, Thomist theology, Neoplatonic philosophy, medieval astronomy and astrology, classical epic, and the courtly troubador tradition of romantic poetry, all infused with his own mystical gnosis, Dante composed the one hundred cantos that climax in the *Paradiso* with the Beatific Vision of the Absolute. Here we can again observe the characteristic Uranus-Neptune correlation: Direct religious experience and illumination are combined with a rebellion against orthodox Church structures (as in Dante's encountering seven popes in the course of his journey through hell). Here too can be seen the theme of the Platonic-Pythagorean music of the celestial spheres (which we will see again in Kepler), whose cosmic motions are the expression of the divine creativity and beauty. Here also can be recognized the Uranus-Neptune complex's close association of divine creativity with the freedom of the human will:

> The greatest gift that God in His bounty made in creation, and the most conformable to His goodness, and that which He prizes the most, was the freedom of the will, with which the creatures with intelligence, they all and they alone, were and are endowed.

Another indication of the presence of this archetypal complex is Dante's creative synthesis of Christian mysticism with the courtly exaltation of romantic love and the divine feminine, with Beatrice as both his guide to paradise and the symbol of liberating spiritual revelation:

> Overcoming me with the light of a smile, she said to me: "Turn and listen, for not only in my eyes is Paradise."

Especially characteristic of the Uranus-Neptune gestalt is Dante's climactic mystical epiphany of the divine light and its universal omnipresence:

> O abounding grace, by which I dared to fix my look on the Eternal Light so long that I spent all my sight upon it! In its depths I saw that it contained, bound by love in one volume, that which is scattered in leaves through the universe, substances and accidents and their relations as it were fused together in such a way that what I tell of is a simple light. I think I saw the universal form of this complex, because in telling of it I feel my joy expand. Thus my mind, all rapt, was gazing, fixed, still and intent, and ever enkindled with gazing. At that light one becomes such that it is impossible for him ever to consent that he should turn from it to another sight; for the good which is the object of the will is all gathered in it.

Finally, we can observe in this epiphany one other frequent Uranus-Neptune motif, the experience of being suddenly illuminated in such a manner that the very heart of one's being is united with the cosmos and the divine in a sublime harmony:

Now my desire and will, like a wheel that spins with even motion, were revolved by the Love that moves the sun and the other stars.

The seminal years when Dante is believed to have begun the great epic were between 1304 and 1308, with 1306 singled out as when work on the poem became especially intensive. Dante underwent his Uranus-opposite-Uranus personal transit in 1304–07. In the pivotal year of 1306, there occurred a rare world transit triple conjunction of Jupiter, Uranus, and Neptune, a configuration that did not occur again until 1486 when Pico's similarly epoch-making *Oration on the Dignity of Man* was written.

Moreover, the period of this same Uranus-Neptune conjunction in 1301–14 coincided not only with the wave of Rhineland mysticism and the teachings of Meister Eckhart in Germany, and with Dante's composition of the *Divine Comedy* in Italy, but also, in Spain, with the first publication of the *Zohar*, the foundation text of the Kabbalah.

Finally, as regards the birth of significant individuals whose cultural role especially embodied the archetypal impulses associated with the Uranus-Neptune cycle, during this same alignment, in 1304, occurred the birth of Petrarch, the forerunner and prophet of the Italian Renaissance whose expression of spiritually informed poetic epiphany and cultural awakening was so influential. In Petrarch we can recognize several highly characteristic themes of the Uranus-Neptune complex. We see it in his restlessness with traditional definitions of the religious life and his urge to experience the spiritual and the sacred in new ways. It is expressed in his creative renewal of culture through a recognition of the classical ideals and achievements of the ancient past, and in his new appreciation and recovery of the Platonic tradition. And this archetypal combination is also evident in Petrarch's invention of new literary forms, his lifelong cultivation of the creative imagination, his spiritual idealization of romantic love, and his heralding of a new cultural epoch defined by new imaginative and spiritual values.

As we continue to follow the sequence of Uranus-Neptune axial alignments, we can again recognize *diachronic* developments in these several areas—religious awakening and rebellion, cultural renaissance, artistic and literary creativity involving spiritual and religious elements—in the events and births that coincided with the next opposition, that of 1385–1402. The preaching of the Bohemian religious reformer Jan Hus, a crucial precursor to the Reformation, began at this time, while in England the first English-language Bible was published, in 1388, which began that movement towards lay religiosity and vernacular translations of the Bible that had such a democratizing influence on European spirituality in the succeeding centuries. Geoffrey Chaucer, as was true of Dante and the *Divine Comedy* during the preceding conjunction, spent virtually the entire period of this alignment in the composition of *The Canterbury Tales*. In addition, the birth of many of the key early figures of the fifteenth-century Italian Renaissance took place in coincidence with this alignment: Donatello, Masaccio, Alberti, Nicholas of Cusa, Cosimo de Medici.

The next Uranus-Neptune conjunction was that of 1472–86 at the heart of the Italian Renaissance which we have already cited. Again, we see the theme of religious rebellion and awakening during the same alignment in the birth of Martin Luther, as well as of Zwingli, who led the Protestant Reformation in Switzerland. In the arts, this period brought the births of both Raphael and Michelangelo, who were distinguished not only for their artistic creativity and revelatory power but also for their heightened spiritual luminosity and Neoplatonic inspiration. The esoteric theme is visible in the coincidence of this conjunction with the works of Ficino and Pico that recovered and renewed ancient esoteric traditions and ideas, and also with the birth of Agrippa von Nettesheim, the author of the treatise *De Occulta Philosophia*, which exercised wide influence on Renaissance esoteric thought.

Uranus and Neptune were next in opposition from 1556 to 1574, the extraordinary period in the history of Spanish mysticism when both Saint Teresa of Ávila and Saint John of the Cross experienced their transformative epiphanies. Teresa wrote and published a detailed report of her mystical experiences in her autobiography (1562–65), founded the Discalced Carmelite spiritual order for nuns (1562), and began her association with John of the Cross, who started the same reformed order for friars (1568). In the same period John Knox, inspired by his experience of the Reformed theocracy in Geneva—"the maist perfyt schoole of Chryst that ever was in the erth since the dayis of the Apostillis"—initiated the Presbyterian religious movement in Scotland. In Jewish esotericism, this same alignment coincided with the years of Isaac ben Solomon Luria's revolutionary teaching of the Kabbalah in Jerusalem, which thereafter served as the foundation for Kabbalistic studies. At this same time the Elizabethan magus and scientist John Dee wrote his principal esoteric work, *Monas Hieroglyphica*, which set out the Kabbalistic and Hermetic philosophy of nature as a divinely inscribed Book whose language and deep mysteries can be comprehended by the initiated scholar.

Moving forward to the next axial alignment, the immediately following Uranus-Neptune conjunction in the mid-seventeenth century, from 1643 to 1658, coincided with Blaise Pascal's influential religious conversion experience as well as with the founding of the Quakers (the Religious Society of Friends) that emerged from George Fox's spiritual epiphany at this time. During these same years there occurred in England an especially widespread and energetic wave of other mystical, "enthusiastic," and millenarian religious movements. We may recall that this was also the period of the Uranus-*Pluto* opposition (1643–54) we examined earlier that coincided with the period of great social turmoil, violent rebellion, and political radicalism variously called the English or Puritan Revolution, the Civil Wars, and the Great Rebellion ("the world turned upside down"). The combination of the two distinct themes associated with these two planetary cycles—the spiritual awakening, religious enthusiasm, and esoteric-mystical-utopian tendencies of the Uranus-Neptune cycle and the violent political revolution, philosophical radicalism, and social turmoil of the Uranus-Pluto cycle—was clearly evident in the dramatic historical events and trends of that time. The many new or newly empowered groups that arose in this period—radical Puritans, Levellers, Quakers, Shakers, Diggers, Ranters, Muggletonians, Fifth Monarchy Men, Adamists, and others—were notable precisely for their combining radical political convictions with emancipatory religious beliefs in an unusually potent manner. They flourished exactly in the years of these overlapping cycles.

The next Uranus-Neptune opposition, from 1728 to 1746, coincided with the birth of Methodism in England under John Wesley and the simultaneous Great Awakening that swept through the American colonies, which began with the revival sparked by Jonathan Edwards in 1734 and expanded enormously with George Whitefield's evangelistic tour in 1740–42. (These two most concentrated bursts of religious revival exactly coincided with the Jupiter-Uranus conjunction and opposition of 1734 and 1740–41.) The title of Edwards's work of 1736—A Faithful Narrative of the Surprising Work of God—in which he defended the spiritual authenticity of the spontaneous religious conversions and the accompanying startling behavior that occurred in the 1734 revival, well conveys the two archetypal principles associated with Uranus and Neptune as they work in synthesis: the unexpected combined with the divine, the trickster combined with the sacred. Here too we can contrast the character of this longer Uranus-Neptune alignment of spiritual awakening at this time, 1728–46, with the shorter Saturn-Pluto square that took place within this long period in exact coincidence with Edwards's famous sermon of 1741, "Sinners in the Hands of an Angry God."

Many other themes relevant to the Uranus-Neptune archetypal complex were evident in the interconnected social, psychological, and religious impulses active in the American colonies during the Great Awakening of the 1730s and 1740s: the widespread loosening of ties between church and civil government, the new individual freedom to choose and intermingle with other denominations, the religious affirmation of psychological independence from parental authority and tradition. Especially consequential was the Great Awakening's generation of a widespread sense of spiritual optimism and cohesiveness in the American colonies, associated with a conviction that the young culture possessed a special spiritual status and glory as a new Israel that would lead the world towards a millennial transformation whose early arrival was eagerly expected.

Simultaneously in Europe, this same period of 1728–46 brought the birth of Hasidism and the teachings of Ba'al Shem Tov, its founder, which brought a new religious impulse into European Judaism. A diachronic Uranus-Neptune cyclical pattern is evident here, since Hasidism essentially brought the mystical Kabbalistic vision articulated during earlier alignments into widespread, socially embodied form. This in turn subsequently received a new creative expression in the work of Buber in coincidence with the Uranus-Neptune opposition of the early twentieth century one cycle later. Moreover, this same eighteenth-century alignment that coincided with the Great Awakening in America, the birth of Methodism in England, and the birth of Hasidism in Poland also coincided with Emanuel Swedenborg's major spiritual epiphany in Sweden that became the basis for his theosophical writings that would influence many in subsequent generations.[1]

This remarkable sequence continued with the immediately following Uranus-Neptune conjunction, from 1814 to 1829, which coincided with the founding of yet another major new religious movement, Mormonism, by Joseph Smith. It coincided as well with the birth of two founders of new religions, Bahaullah, the leader of the Baha'i faith, and Mary Baker Eddy, the founder of Christian Science. This era was also the height of the Second Great Awakening, which was marked by the rapid spread of revivalist Evangelicalism carried throughout the new American nation by traveling Baptist and Methodist preachers and emotionally charged camp revivals. This religious movement brought a new emphasis on the private stirrings of the heart, the individual emotional relationship to the divine, and reliance on Jesus as personal savior and moral exemplar. Such evangelical activism, growing from the time of the revolutionary 1790s and the Uranus-Pluto opposition, strengthened popular impulses towards religious liberty and a dynamic grassroots democratization of spirituality.

The empowerment of diverse local religious groups and charismatic preachers during the Second Great Awakening produced a centrifugal movement of religious authority away from the established churches and their more conservative theological doctrines and eventually led to a liberalizing movement in all Protestant churches in the United States in the 1810s and 1820s. Here again can be seen the characteristic signs of a synthesis of the two archetypal principles associated with Neptune and Uranus, the one spiritual, the other emancipatory. The sterner doctrines of Calvinism—predestination, innate depravity, salvation dependent on a stern God's arbitrary will—were increasingly displaced by a new belief in the universal possibility of salvation and regeneration through inner faith, devotional service, and the moral exercise of free will. This shift also reflected the liberalizing influences of the Enlightenment with its affirmation of human freedom and more benign conceptions of both nature and Deity. Equally encouraging of such tendencies was the mobile open society and optimistic individualism of the new American nation, which helped shape a new religious consciousness that focused on a combination of personal salvation and social reform. As the Second Great Awakening reached its full maturity in the late 1820s and after, a more intellectually developed and universalist form of the movement emerged in New England with Emerson and the Transcendentalists.

Finally, the following Uranus-Neptune opposition at the beginning of the twentieth century, from 1899 to 1918, which we examined above in terms of the birth of modernism and the many radical artistic, scientific, and philosophical shifts of that time, coincided not only with the spiritual and religious cultural phenomena evident in those years in the work of James, Jung, Buber, Gandhi, and Aurobindo but also with the spiritual awakenings of other figures who played a transformative role in twentieth-century religious life such as Yogananda, Meher Baba, and Krishnamurti. It was at the start of this alignment, in late 1899, that Rudolf Steiner underwent his pivotal mystical opening that culminated in his "standing in the spiritual presence of the Mystery of Golgotha in a most profound and solemn festival of knowledge," after which his life as an esoteric teacher began. This same alignment also coincided with the birth of yet another new religion, Pentecostalism, in 1906—with Islam and Mormonism, one of the fastest growing religions in the world today. The original Pentecostal event, it will be recalled, coincided with another Uranus-Neptune alignment nineteen hundred years earlier, at the birth of Christianity.

The description of the Pentecost in the Acts of the Apostles in the New Testament contains many of the most distinctive characteristics and themes of the Uranus-Neptune archetypal complex: the sudden collective spiritual awakening, the visions and prophesies, the faith healings and other surprising charismatic phenomena, the descent of the Holy Spirit's Promethean fire. Remarkably similar events seem to have been repeatedly constellated in close coincidence with the unfolding sequence of Uranus-Neptune cyclical alignments in subsequent centuries.

> And when the day of Pentecost was fully come, they were all with one accord in one place. And suddenly there came a sound from heaven as of a rushing mighty wind, and it filled all the house where they were sitting. And there appeared unto them tongues like as of fire, and it sat upon each of them. And they were all filled with the Holy Spirit, and began to speak with other tongues, as the Spirit gave them utterance. . . .
>
> . . . [T]his is that which was spoken by the prophet Joel: And it shall come to pass in the last days, saith God, I will pour out of my Spirit upon all flesh: and your sons and your daughters shall prophesy, and your young men shall see visions, and your old men shall dream dreams: And on my servants and on my handmaidens I will pour out in those days of my Spirit; and they shall prophesy: And I will show wonders in heaven above, and signs in the earth beneath. . . . (Acts 2:1–4, 16–19)

Utopian Social Visions

Throughout these same centuries I noticed a parallel pattern of historical and cultural phenomena, similarly coincident with the alignments of the Uranus-Neptune cycle, involving the emergence of utopian social visions and movements. Again, the underlying archetypal gestalt in this category can be recognized as a distinct synthesis of the two relevant principles: Uranus's Promethean impulse towards creative experiment and innovation, freedom, rebellion against the status quo, and a vector towards the future all complexly interacting with Neptune's idealism and hope, spiritual inspiration, intuitive vision, the dissolving of conventional boundaries and structures, and the imagination of a perfect harmony and unity to be realized in the human community.

For example, the earliest influential statement of a utopian social vision in the Western tradition was Plato's ideal communitarian republic that was to be overseen by philosopher rulers guided by the eternal Ideas. Outlined in *The Republic*, this vision emerged from Plato's philosophical awakening during the Uranus-Neptune conjunction at the turn of the fourth century BCE. Similarly, the first utopian work of the early modern period was Thomas More's *Utopia* with its Renaissance Humanist vision of a more ideal social order. More's work was the first to use the word "utopia," which, with typically Neptunian ambiguity and paradox, draws on Greek roots to mean both "good place" (*eu-topos*) and "no place" (*ou-topos*), a world at once ideal and imaginary—two distinct sides of Neptune's archetypal principle compressed into a single bivalent term. The sequence of axial alignments of the Uranus-Neptune cycle was closely correlated with the births of individuals who brought forth influential utopian works and visions, as with Thomas More's birth in 1478 with a nearly exact Uranus-Neptune conjunction. This was the conjunction that took place from 1472 to 1486—the period of the Florentine Platonic Academy and the revival of Platonism, of Ficino, Pico, Botticelli, and Leonardo, which also coincided with the birth of radical visionary reformers such as Luther and Copernicus.

Continuing this pattern, the immediately following Uranus-Neptune opposition of 1556–74 coincided with the birth of Francis Bacon, whose explicitly utopian *The New Atlantis*, along with his other major works like *The Advancement of Learning* and *Novum Organum*, set forth an immensely influential vision of a luminous future society in which science, technology, and the progress of knowledge would help humankind regain the paradise that had been lost in the Fall. In essence, Bacon integrated the buoyantly progressive spirit of the emerging Scientific Revolution with a Christian millennialist hope newly charged by the Protestant Reformation. On this basis he prophesied a scientific civilization whose radical improvement of humanity's material conditions would coincide with the attainment of the Christian millennium. Here, with considerable historical effect, were combined the religious, redemptive, idealistic, and visionary (Neptune) with the scientific, technological, inventive, and emancipatory (Uranus).

In the centuries following Bacon, I found that these several utopian themes, which variously brought together visionary idealism and spiritual inspiration with social-political emancipation and philosophical-scientific advance, arose repeatedly in close coincidence with the continuing Uranus-Neptune cycle. Such a pattern was clearly visible in the wave of utopian works and movements that emerged in the immediately following conjunction period of 1643–58 during the English Great Rebellion, or Puritan Revolution, and continued thereafter with the writings and the births of the leading utopian thinkers in the Western tradition—Condorcet, Fourier, Owen, Saint-Simon, Marx, Engels, Thoreau, and Tolstoy—in the sequence of alignments in the eighteenth and nineteenth centuries. The most recent Uranus-Neptune opposition of the early twentieth century coincided with both H. G. Wells's *A Modern Utopia* and Charlotte Perkins Gilman's feminist utopian *Herland*, and also with the birth, in 1904, of the behaviorist B. F. Skinner, the author of the most recent widely read utopian work, *Walden Two*, which again combined science and technology with utopian idealism and fantasy.

Many of the major utopian visions and experiments were inspired by explicitly religious ideals and sources. The influence of Judaic and Christian sources in particular on the utopian imagination was a complex one: While in some respects the Judaeo-Christian legacy worked against utopianism, because of the biblical stress on the necessity of God's intervention and the weakness of humanity's capacity for self-improvement, in other important respects it strongly supported the utopian impulse with concrete images of universal harmony and an underlying belief in the divinely willed movement of human history towards a future age of blessedness. One especially enduring source of inspiration was the teachings of Jesus in the New Testament on the Kingdom of Heaven and the description in the Acts of the Apostles of the state of communal unity and self-transcending love that suddenly emerged among the first Christians in the immediate aftermath of the Pentecost:

> And they continued steadfastly in the apostles' doctrine and fellowship, and in breaking of bread, and in prayers. . . . And all that believed were together, and had all things common. And sold their possessions and

goods, and parted them to all, as every person had need. And they, continuing daily with one accord in the temple, and breaking bread from house to house, did eat their meat with gladness and singleness of heart, praising God, and having favour with all the people. And the Lord added to the church daily such as should be saved. (Acts 2:42, 44–47)

Yet it is remarkable to witness the extent to which a quality of visionary hope and idealism of a virtually mystical luminosity can infuse the philosophical writings and awareness of an individual born during a Uranus-Neptune alignment who is entirely committed to a robust secularism defiantly free of all religious constraints. This visionary idealism of a future utopian fulfillment can thrive even in the face of great personal suffering and the most contradictory concrete evidence of human corruption and historical trauma. In this respect, the utopian faith of a thoroughly unbelieving Enlightenment philosophe can resemble the redemptive conviction of an ancient Christian martyr under Roman persecution.

Eloquent testimony to this capacity, which transcends not just religious affiliation but religion altogether, at least as conventionally understood, is offered by the Marquis de Condorcet, born in 1743 during the Uranus-Neptune opposition coincident with the Great Awakening. At the age of fifty, Condorcet wrote the most encompassing and exalted statement of the Enlightenment's progressive philosophy of history, the *Esquisse d'un tableau historique des progrès de l'esprit humain* ("Sketch for a Historical Picture of the Progress of the Human Spirit"), the "philosophical testament of the eighteenth century" bequeathed to the nineteenth century. In 1793, while hiding from the Jacobins' Committee of Public Safety, which had issued a warrant for his arrest, with only a few months before he would die in prison, Cordorcet wrote his great work. This was during the Terror and the darkest moments of the French Revolution of which he was so idealistic and articulate a supporter. In the *Esquisse*, Condorcet described the long journey of humanity as it progressed through many stages, gradually breaking free from the dark oppression and superstition of the past, moving ever forward through the power of the natural human reason, aided by technological advance, and leading finally to the perfection of human life in a glorious future of freedom, knowledge, gentleness, harmony, and happiness.

In the final passage of the *Esquisse*, after he described this future paradise, Condorcet wrote the following moving peroration. Drawing on what we have now absorbed from our studies of the several planetary cycles, we can recognize in its rich fusion of imagery, thought, and feeling the simultaneous influences of the Uranus-Pluto archetypal complex (constellated throughout the 1790s and the French Revolution), the Saturn-Pluto complex (of the 1793–94 period during the Terror), and the Uranus-Neptune complex (the conjunction of Condorcet's birth in 1743)—all three fused inextricably into a single impassioned statement.

How this portrait of mankind, free of all these chains, no longer under the rule of chance, or the enemies of progress, and walking with a sure and certain step on the path of truth, of virtue and happiness, presents to the philosopher a sight which consoles him for the errors, the crimes, the injustices which still sully the earth, and of which he is often the victim! In the contemplation of this portrait he receives the reward for his efforts towards the progress of reason and the defence of liberty. He then dares to bind these efforts to the chain of human destiny: there he finds virtue's true reward, the pleasure of having created an enduring good, which fate will no longer destroy with a deadly compensation, by bringing back prejudice and slavery. This contemplation is a refuge for him, where the memory of his persecutions cannot follow; where, living in thought with a humanity re-established in the rights and dignity of its nature, he forgets the one which is corrupted and tormented by greed, fear, or envy; it is there that he exists in reality with those like him, in an Elysium which his reason knows how to create, and which his love for humanity has embellished with the purest enjoyments.

From the Uranus-Pluto archetypal complex of the French Revolutionary decade we see the intense political revolutionary and emancipatory fervor, the overwhelming drive towards radical change, the vivid sense that human progress and freedom are ceaselessly impelled by powerful, unstoppable evolutionary forces that are now breaking forth in a liberating surge. From the Saturn-Pluto complex of the 1793–94 period we recognize not only the immediate background of the Terror with Condorcet as its victim, and the harsh reality of his suffering and impending imprisonment and death, but also the vision of an immense human struggle against vast eras of oppression and corruption, slavery and chains, prejudice and fear, greed and envy, the "deadly compensation" of fate. We can see here too that other side of the Saturn-Pluto gestalt: the noble binding of one's strenuous effort to the chain of human destiny, which creates an enduring good and forges a deep and permanent moral development in human evolution. Finally, suffusing the entirety of the historical vision is the characteristic spirit of the Uranus-Neptune complex: hope and faith in an ideal future that will liberate humankind, the Elysium of the philosopher's imagination that is more real than the corrupt present, the boundless trust in humanity's infinite perfectibility, the creation of a new paradise through the free exercise of human will and reason, and the spiritual transformation of the human condition made possible through the advance of science and technology.[2]

Karl Marx was born in 1818 during the next Uranus-Neptune conjunction following the opposition of Condorcet's birth, with all three of these planetary combinations (Uranus-Pluto, Saturn-Pluto, and Uranus-Neptune all in hard aspect with each other) in a single natal configuration. It is not difficult to discern in the Marxist vision, rhetoric, and historical influence precisely the same motifs that were expressed by Condorcet during the alignments of the French Revolutionary Terror, and again inspired by utopian impulses and expectations intensely independent of religious sources.

As we have seen throughout this book, the archetypal complexes—quite apart from the conscious intentions of the actors involved—appear to express themselves synchronically and diachronically in different forms and inflections that can even be antithetical to each other, as in these diverse secular and religious expressions of the utopian impulse, yet are ultimately rooted in the same underlying archetypal principles. Such a pattern of multivalence and antagonism within an underlying unity was visible, for example, in our discussion of terrorism and governmental retribution in the Saturn-Pluto cycle. It was similarly evident in the mutually demonizing armored conservative reactions on opposing sides during the Cold War. In the present context, whether in the work and vision of Plato or the Apostles, Thomas More or Francis Bacon, Marx or Skinner, the utopian impulse, however variously expressed, bears a consistent correlation with the same planetary cycle, Uranus-Neptune, and displays the distinctive symptoms of the same underlying archetypal complex.

Romanticism, Imaginative Genius, and Cosmic Epiphany

F ew cultural movements more vividly embodied the full range of characteristic archetypal themes of the Uranus-Neptune cycle than Romanticism. In the most recent Uranus-Neptune conjunction before our own, that of 1814–29, Romanticism was at its height. This was the age of Keats, Byron, and the Shelleys, of the poetic and mythic epiphanies of *Ode on a Grecian Urn, Ode to a Nightingale, To Autumn, Hymn to Intellectual Beauty, A Defence of Poetry, Prometheus Unbound*, and the philosophical summation of Romanticism, Coleridge's *Biographia Literaria*. This was the age that brought the inspired final masterpieces of Beethoven, Blake, and Goethe—the Ninth Symphony with its invocation to universal love and the "Ode to Joy," the *Missa solemnis*, the late quartets, *The Everlasting Gospel*, the *Illustrations to the Book of Job*, the completion of *Faust*. It was an age that declared the liberation and awakening of the world-creating imagination, the high spiritual calling of the artist, the emancipating power of love and art. It affirmed the Romantic-Platonic ultimate unity of the Good, the True, and the Beautiful. It brought forth Keats's vision of the world as the "vale of Soul-making." It was an era that especially aspired to realize the transcendent and numinous, the exalted ideal. This was the age of Schubert, Pushkin, Scott, Stendhal, and Lamartine and the formative period for Hugo, Berlioz, Chopin, Schumann, and Liszt.

In philosophy, we see again the characteristic Uranus-Neptune themes: This was the age of Hegel at the peak of his vision and prominence with his immensely influential articulation of absolute Idealism and his conception of history as a vast evolutionary movement that ultimately integrates all opposites—spirit and nature, human and divine—in a higher synthesis. This was also the crucial formative period for American Transcendentalism, when Emerson imbibed the central ideas of Romanticism, Platonism, German Idealism, and Asian mystical traditions to bring forth a new expression of the second Great Awakening then taking place in America. This period brought the cultural emergence of a new and influential appreciation and understanding of the Renaissance, the Middle Ages, and classical Greek antiquity that has endured to our day. This same period also brought a decisive renewal of Platonic and Neoplatonic thought (as in Hegel, Shelley, and Emerson), widespread new interest in Hindu and Buddhist philosophy and religion, a revival of Western esoteric traditions (as in the revival of astrology in England from 1816), the founding of Egyptology and Champollion's breakthrough in the decipherment of Egyptian hieroglyphics using the Rosetta Stone (1822), and the rise of scholarly studies of ancient mythology, folklore, legend, and fairy tale (as in the seminal work of the Grimm brothers in these years).

Often in Romanticism these different Uranus-Neptune motifs would be combined, as with Shelley's invoking of esoteric alchemical imagery to describe the transformative power of the poetic imagination in his *Defence of Poetry*:

> It transmutes all it touches and every form moving within the radiance
> of its presence is changed by wondrous sympathy to an incarnation of
> the spirit which it breathes; its secret alchemy turns to potable gold the
> poisonous waters which flow from death through life.

In the category of new art forms and technical media that subsequently expressed and influenced the cultural imagination, it was during this conjunction that photography was invented, beginning in 1826, by Niepce and Daguerre. (This development was diachronically related to the rapid development of motion pictures during the immediately following Uranus-Neptune opposition at the beginning of the twentieth century.) The overlapping themes of unexpected revelation and technological innovation suddenly bringing new images and new perceptions of reality, new ways of relating to memory, new modes of artistic expression, and the radical change of traditional art forms (as in photography's effect on painting as visual representation) were all evident in the emergence of photography during this conjunction.

John Keats's *On First Looking into Chapman's Homer*, his first great poem and the one that initiated him into his poetic calling, was composed and published in 1816–17 in that especially seminal moment in the Romantic awakening when Jupiter joined Uranus and Neptune to form a rare triple conjunction.[3] With its sublime portrayal of the poet's awakening to the mythic dimension of reality, the poem both describes and embodies in itself several of the most prominent themes of the Uranus-Neptune archetypal complex:

> *Much have I traveled in the realms of gold,*
> *And many goodly states and kingdoms seen;*
> *Round many western islands have I been*
> *Which bards in fealty to Apollo hold.*
> *Oft of one wide expanse had I been told*
> *That deep-browed Homer ruled as his demesne;*
> *Yet did I never breathe its pure serene*
> *Till I heard Chapman speak out loud and bold:*
> *Then felt I like some watcher of the skies*

> When a new planet swims into his ken;
>   Or like stout Cortez when with eagle eyes
>   He stared at the Pacific—and all his men
> Looked at each other with a wild surmise—
>   Silent, upon a peak in Darien.

In this elegant précis of the Uranus-Neptune archetypal complex, we can recognize many of its most characteristic themes: sudden revelation, the unexpected opening to the archetypal realm of being, the evocation of ancient numinosity, the liberation of the creative imagination, the astonishment of discovering new horizons both inner and outer—the sudden sighting of a new cosmic reality, of the Homeric domain of mythos, of an undreamt oceanic expanse—all multivalently comprehended in a unified poetic epiphany.

Keats's comparison of his mythic awakening to an astronomical revelation experienced by "some watcher of the skies / When a new planet swims into his ken" alludes to the momentous discovery of Uranus by William Herschel, who was himself born with a nearly exact Uranus-Neptune opposition in 1738, that of the first Great Awakening. The correlation of the Uranus-Neptune cycle with the births of individuals who experienced and brought into the wider culture epoch-making astronomical discoveries was especially consistent. Copernicus was born during the Uranus-Neptune conjunction in 1473, Galileo and Kepler were both born during the immediately following Uranus-Neptune opposition in 1564 and 1572, respectively, and Isaac Newton was born during the very next Uranus-Neptune conjunction after that, on Christmas Day of 1642.[4]

Each of these individuals experienced an extraordinary cosmological awakening, a sudden revelation that radically shifted their cosmic and metaphysical foundations. Each experienced that awakening as imbued with numinous significance, as a sudden gift from the divine that opened the human mind to the sacred mysteries of the universe. Each mediated that cosmological awakening to the larger culture in a diachronic sequence of progressively ever more encompassing and developed disclosures: Copernicus led to Kepler and Galileo, then all three led to Newton. Remarkably, from the birth of Copernicus to that of Newton there took place one complete 360° unfolding of the Uranus-Neptune cycle, from conjunction to conjunction, and the births of Galileo and Kepler occurred halfway between, at the 180° opposition.

Moreover, there were two especially key transitional moments of cultural awakening to the new cosmos that took place in the course of this 360° cycle between the birth of Copernicus and that of Newton. The first was the spectacular sudden appearance in 1572 of a supernova, an exploding star whose brightness increases exponentially in a very brief time. Brighter than Venus, the new star remained visible to the naked eye for two years before fading. The appearance of the new star directly contradicted the ancient doctrine of the unchangeability of the heavens, dramatically challenging astronomers' long-established assumptions and preparing the way for the Copernican-Newtonian cosmological revolution. The year the supernova appeared, 1572, was the same year as Kepler's birth; both events thus coincided with the Uranus-Neptune opposition that took place halfway in the cycle that unfolded between the conjunctions of Copernicus's birth and Newton's. Tycho Brahe, the preeminent astronomical observer of his age, was taking an evening walk on November 11 of that year when he suddenly saw something he did not think possible. His description of that moment well conveys the quality of revelatory impact characteristic of Uranus-Neptune phenomena:

> Amazed, and as if astonished and stupefied, I stood still, gazing for a certain length of time with my eyes fixed intently upon it and noticing that same star placed close to the stars which antiquity attributed to Cassiopeia. When I had satisfied myself that no star of that kind had ever shone forth before, I was led into such perplexity by the unbelievability of the thing that I began to doubt the faith of my own eyes.

The other pivotal moment in the cosmological revolution that unfolded between the births of Copernicus and Newton took place in 1609–10 with the remarkable convergence, within nine months, of Kepler's publication of *Astronomia Nova,* which contained his brilliant solution to the ancient problem of the planets, and Galileo's telescopic discoveries and his publication of *Sidereus Nuncius.* These events coincided precisely not only with the fourteen-month period of the Jupiter-Uranus conjunction of 1609–10, as discussed earlier, but also with the longer Uranus-Neptune *square* alignment that began in 1607 and lasted for a decade. This Uranus-Neptune alignment, which also coincided with the invention of the telescope itself, took place exactly halfway between the births of Galileo and Kepler and the supernova's appearance, all at the opposition, and the birth of Newton at the following conjunction.

In this sequence of correlations, we see a distinctive synthesis of Uranus-Neptune themes: the sudden awakening to a new cosmological vision that is comprised of, on the one hand, scientific breakthrough, innovative genius, technological invention, and unexpected new astronomical data, all associated with Uranus; and on the other hand, a creative renewal of the Platonic-Pythagorean philosophical vision, the influence and invocation of Hermetic esotericism, a mystical sense of the dissolving of the boundary between the divine mind and the human, and a radically transformative experience of spiritual epiphany and numinous visionary understanding, all associated with Neptune. Thus Kepler's ecstatic declaration: "I yield freely to the sacred frenzy; I dare frankly to confess that I have stolen the golden vessels of the Egyptians to build a tabernacle for my God far from the bounds of Egypt."

Kepler saw astronomers as "priests of the most high God with respect to the book of nature." In the great cosmological revolution of his time, he regarded himself as having been allotted the sacred "honor of guarding, with my discovery, the door of God's temple in which Copernicus serves before the high altar." Similarly, Newton was as fully absorbed in the esoteric, magical, and theological aspects of his research as in what the modern mind would subsequently consider to be science. Between the sudden surge of scientific breakthroughs of his youth (during his Uranus square Uranus transit) and the publication of the *Principia* in his forties (during his Uranus opposite Uranus transit), Newton devoted himself so assiduously day and night to the study of alchemy and biblical prophecy as to far exceed in time and effort the labors in those areas of any other individual of his time or since. As John Maynard Keynes observed in a paper written for the Royal Society celebrations of the Newton Tercentenary, Newton should perhaps be more accurately regarded not as the "first of the age of reason" but as the "last of the magicians, the last of the Babylonians and Sumerians":

> He looked on the whole universe and all that is in it as a riddle, as a secret which could be read by applying pure thought to certain evidence, certain mystic clues which God had laid about the world to allow a sort of philosopher's treasure hunt to the esoteric brotherhood. He believed these clues were to be found partly in the evidence of the heavens and in the constitution of elements . . . but also partly in certain papers and traditions handed down by the brethren in an unbroken chain back to the original cryptic revelation in Babylonia. . . .

> He did read the riddle of the heavens. And he believed that by the same powers of his introspective imagination he would read the riddle of the Godhead, the riddle of past and future events divinely foreordained, the riddle of the elements and their constitution from an original undifferentiated first matter, the riddle of health and immortality. All would be revealed to him if only he could persevere to the end. . . .

As in science, so also in art: The correlation of the Uranus-Neptune cycle with the several distinct but archetypally coherent themes we have seen so often above—cosmological epiphany, the astonishing disclosure often of an esoteric or spiritual nature, the revelation of a mythic dimension of reality, extraordinary poetic inspiration and imaginative genius—can also be observed in the life and work of William Shakespeare. Here again we can recognize a larger synchronic and diachronic patterning at work, at once aesthetic and mathematical, as Galileo and Shakespeare were in fact born within a few weeks of each other in 1564, when Uranus and Neptune were in nearly exact opposition. Whereas Galileo's revelations took place within an astronomical and scientific context, Shakespeare's were expressed in poetic and dramatic form, but with an archetypally similar quality of unexpected awakening to a radically new reality, often with deep metaphysical and spiritual implications. Such epiphanies, sometimes having a stunning, life-changing power, occurred repeatedly in Shakespeare's plays— whether tragic, comic, or romantic—each instance evoking in a different way the basic Shakespearean recognition that more realities exist in heaven and earth than are dreamt of by our current sciences and philosophies.

As the Uranus-Neptune world transit cycle, moving from the opposition of Shakespeare's and Galileo's births, reached the next square alignment in the 1608–12 period, the theme of sudden revelatory surprises and spiritual awakenings became distinctly more pronounced in Shakespeare's plays until such epiphanies reached a climax in *Cymbeline, The Winter's Tale,* and *The Tempest,* the great romance tragicomedies that Shakespeare produced in 1609–11. This was the exact period of Galileo's telescopic discoveries and the dissemination of his *Sidereus Nuncius* ("The Starry Messenger") that brought those discoveries to the attention of the larger culture. (These were also the years in which the luminous King James translation of the Bible was published.) Compared with Shakespeare's earlier tragedies, comedies, and histories, which were written during the Uranus-Pluto and Saturn-Pluto transits discussed earlier, these late plays written during the Uranus-Neptune square explore a more symbolic, fantastic, and experimental mode of drama in which the tragic and problematic dimensions of existence are ultimately embraced within spiritually redemptive narratives that have definite esoteric and mystical overtones. As Ted Hughes wrote in *Shakespeare and the Goddess of Complete Being*:

> Shakespeare's own attitude to his task as dramatist seems to have changed in this final group of plays. From being a prophetic visionary swept along in the dam-burst of historical forces, nakedly exposed to the glories and terrors of creation and human events [visible in his plays during the Uranus-Pluto and Saturn-Pluto alignments discussed earlier] . . . he seems to become more like a kind of Noah among the rising waters, the magus of a Gnostic, Hermetic ritual.

Especially characteristic of the Uranus-Neptune archetypal complex was Shakespeare's intuition of life as a kind of divine play or artistic pageant, much like the Indian view of *maya* and *lila,* and his disclosure of this reality as a dramatic epiphany within his own plays. Appearing in subtle and implicit ways throughout his works, this theme is made most explicit in *The Tempest,* which contains his self-portrait as a magus and was written near the end of Shakespeare's creative trajectory just as the Uranus-Neptune alignment became exact. Here we see the Shakespearean revelation of a mysterious spiritual-imaginative ground (or, in a sense, groundlessness) underlying all reality, dissolving and melting into thin air the literal appearance of all things to reveal the divine dream of life, the spiritual theater of the human condition:

> *Our revels now are ended. These our actors,*
> *As I foretold you, were all spirits, and*
> *Are melted into air, into thin air:*
> *And, like the baseless fabric of this vision,*
> *The cloud-capp'd towers, the gorgeous palaces,*
> *The solemn temples, the great globe itself,*
> *Yea, all which it inherit, shall dissolve,*
> *And, like this insubstantial pageant faded,*
> *Leave not a rack behind. We are such stuff*
> *As dreams are made on; and our little life*
> *Is rounded with a sleep.*
>
> (*The Tempest*, 4.4.148–58)

It is characteristic of Uranus-Neptune eras, and of major cultural figures born during these periods, that a certain *numinosity* often attaches to their legacy in the evolving cultural tradition. This occurs not only with explicitly religious epochs, such as at the birth of Christianity in the time of Jesus and the apostles, but also in philosophical awakenings, like the birth of Platonism in the time of Socrates and Plato, and great epochs of artistic revelation, like the Italian Renaissance of Leonardo, Raphael, and Michelangelo. So too with revered figures of the creative imagination in the history of literature. The status of the Shakespearean canon as virtually a sacred scriptural disclosure for the modern spirit has often been acknowledged, with every ambiguous word and variant meticulously analyzed and debated as if it were an ancient biblical text, and with its complex layers of meaning revealing themselves in new ways to new generations. Melville, just before he began work on *Moby Dick* at the age of twenty-nine, wrote his editor while he was in the midst of his own exultant revelation upon first reading the plays of Shakespeare:

> . . . the divine William. Ah, he's full of sermons-on-the-mount, and gentle, aye, almost as Jesus. I take such men to be inspired. I fancy that this moment Shakspeare in heaven ranks with Gabriel Raphael and Michael. And if another Messiah ever comes twill be in Shakspeare's person. . . .

Dante's *The Divine Comedy*—there were Uranus-Neptune alignments at both the birth of the poet and the writing of the poem—possesses a comparable numinosity and spiritual status in the Western cultural legacy. In a sequence remarkably parallel to that just cited for Shakespeare, Dante was born in 1265 when Uranus and Neptune were in close square alignment, and he composed *The Divine Comedy*, beginning in 1304–06, when the Uranus-Neptune cycle had moved exactly 90° further to reach the conjunction. At the time Dante commenced work on the great poem, the Uranus-Neptune conjunction in the sky was precisely transiting his natal Uranus-Neptune square in an exact T-square configuration, a rare convergence of world and personal transits on a natal aspect in which all six alignments—natal aspect, world transit, and personal transits—involved both Uranus and Neptune.[5] One could say that the very title and essence of *La Divina Commedia* contains in synthesis the two principles associated with Uranus and Neptune: the divinity and sublime visionary quality of Neptune combined with Uranus's trickster awakening, the unexpected opening and resolution beyond the tragic. The same principles are equally relevant to Shakespeare's final divine comedies, the tragicomic romances of *The Tempest* and *The Winter's Tale*.

The special spiritual stature of the works of Shakespeare and Dante in the Western cultural legacy is shared by the great novels of Tolstoy and Dostoevsky: *War and Peace*, *Anna Karenina*, *Crime and Punishment*, *The Brothers Karamazov*. The profundity and revelatory power of their imaginative vision provides a similarly enduring source of spiritual insight and interior deepening. The same could be said of Melville's *Moby Dick*. It is striking that all three of these novelists were born during the Uranus-Neptune conjunction of the 1814–29 period at the peak of the Romantic age. Indeed, this alignment coincided precisely with that remarkable wave of births of imaginative geniuses who made of the nineteenth-century novel a medium of great revelatory power and spiritual vision—not only Dostoevsky, Tolstoy, and Melville but Flaubert, Turgenev, the Brontës, and George Eliot—as well as the equally revelatory poets Whitman and Baudelaire. Dickens was born at the beginning cusp of the alignment, Emily Dickinson at its ending.[6] All these individuals played a crucial role in the transformation of literature in modern culture as it became a form of spiritual disclosure and a vessel for the religious impulses whose traditional expression had been undermined and devalued by the disenchanting implications of modern science. As Charles Taylor has emphasized, this revelatory and transfiguring impulse at work in the literature of this era is true even of anti-Romantic "realists" such as Flaubert and Baudelaire who sought courageously to reveal the disenchanted and meaningless with their art, creatively transfiguring the banal and the deterministic into liberating, epiphanic artistic experience that possessed its own beauty—sometimes even sublime—beyond the conventional standards of earlier artistic canons.[7]

It is important to note here that many of these novelists and poets born during the Uranus-Neptune conjunction of the Romantic era—Dostoevsky, Melville, Flaubert, Baudelaire, George Eliot, Whitman—were born also with the Uranus-Pluto square of the 1816–24 period, as discussed earlier in the Uranus-Pluto section of the book. The combination of these two archetypal complexes, Uranus-Neptune and Uranus-Pluto, seemed to provide an especially dynamic creative drive both for major cultural figures who worked in the period of this three-planet configuration and for the next generation that was born at this time.

Among the former we see this specific archetypal synthesis in Shelley's *Prometheus Unbound* of 1818–19, which depicted a Prometheus who was simultaneously a mythic embodiment of an ideal humanity (Uranus-Neptune) and a titanic force for radical change and emancipation from tyranny (Uranus-Pluto).

At times the combination of these two distinct, even sharply polarized archetypal complexes brought together in a thinker's work divergent views in an unusually idiosyncratic manner. Schopenhauer, for example, in *The World as Will and Idea* published in 1818–19, combined the Uranus-Pluto awakening of nature's chthonic powers, the universal will, and the underworld of human experience in a proto-Darwininan evocation of nature's ceaseless struggle for existence with several interrelated Uranus-Neptune themes: his philosophical view of the world as "idea," something that exists only as our experience, a representation; his appropriation of certain mystical doctrines of Hinduism and Buddhism (the unity of life behind appearances, the world as *maya* or illusion, ascetic-mystical transcendence achieved by negation of the will and worldly attachment); his conception of the Platonic Ideas as universal forms that can be experienced through great works of art; and his exaltation of art and aesthetic experience as providing the possibility of a liberating transcendence from the prison of existence.

In the lives and works of the major cultural figures who were born during this period of the two overlapping cycles (1816–24), the clashing and interpenetration of two such different archetypal complexes seems to have provided an extraordinarily powerful and at times intensely polarized expression of the creative imagination. We have seen something of this profound dialectic and polarization in Marx in his attempted synthesis of titanic struggle and political revolution with utopian and humanitarian idealism. In literature, equally striking is Dostoevsky, who was born in 1821 at the peak moment of the cyclical overlap with an exact Uranus-Neptune conjunction (within ½°) and a very close Uranus-Pluto square (within 3°). In each of his great novels Dostoevsky creatively enacted the themes and conflicts of the corresponding archetypal complexes in a memorably compelling manner.

Particularly in his final masterwork, *The Brothers Karamazov*, we can recognize a striking archetypal pattern in the three Karamazov brothers—Dmitri, Ivan, and Alyosha—each of whom distinctly embodies one of the three archetypal principles associated with the three outer planets. The eldest brother, Dmitri, lustful, volcanic, instinctually driven, is a classic embodiment of the Pluto archetype; Ivan, the brilliant existential rebel, decisively carries the Promethean principle associated with Uranus; the youngest, Alyosha, the religious mystic, is an equally clear incarnation of the Neptune archetype. It appears that Dostoevsky's intimate lifelong experience of these three principles in direct dynamic relation and tense counterpoint, which corresponds to the nearly exact hard-aspect alignment of the three outer planets at his birth, was translated by his creative imagination into their separate personified embodiments in the three strongly defined brothers. In this dramatic context, the archetypal complexes in Dostoevsky's being and in the collective psyche were not only differentiated and articulated, made more conscious, but also brought into direct interaction and urgent dialectical development.

Yet beyond this intricate dialectic *between* the three different archetypal principles, it is also instructive to discriminate a further set of themes and qualities in the works of Dostoevsky in which all three principles—Uranus, Neptune, and Pluto—combine to form a *single* larger archetypal complex. We see this triple combination embodied again and again in the overwhelming potency and unpredictable irruptions of both spiritual and instinctual conditions that so affect and afflict his major characters, almost always with the spiritual and instinctual aspects closely interconnected. We see this larger archetypal gestalt in the highly characteristic Dostoevskian state of extreme mental, emotional, and physical turmoil verging into madness that he called "brain fever." And it is acutely evident in the profundity and often violent intensity of the sudden transformations of consciousness that his characters so often undergo, which are recognizable to every reader of Dostoevsky's highly distinctive works—not only the spiritually revelatory seizures but also more generally the states of overwhelming passion, love or hate, despair or hope, reverent devotion, dark descents, luminous resurrections.

If we precisely discriminate the three separate archetypal principles and the specific nuances of their interactions, we can recognize how all of the above qualities, conditions, and themes, so pervasive in Dostoevsky's novels, perfectly reflect the interplay of the three planetary archetypes in a manner that can be articulated as three different archetypal vectors:

First, we can understand this larger archetypal gestalt as the Pluto archetype of titanic power and chthonic depths tremendously intensifying and compelling the Uranus-Neptune themes of unexpected shifts of consciousness and sudden spiritual awakenings (Pluto→Uranus/Neptune), driving these sudden revelations and shifts of awareness with volcanic elemental potency.

Second, we can recognize the Uranus-Pluto theme of suddenly catalyzed violent intensity being activated by or associated with Neptunian factors such as alcohol, mental and emotional confusion, madness, and mystical apprehension (Neptune→Uranus/Pluto).

Third, we can discern the Promethean principle associated with Uranus as suddenly awakening and catalyzing in unexpected ways, both liberating and disruptive—and also giving brilliant creative expression to—the Neptune-Pluto experience of overwhelmingly intense, even destructive convulsions of consciousness, descents into the underworld, volcanic eruptions from the depths of the archetypal unconscious, hallucinatory visions and projections, and profound, viscerally felt spiritual transformations (Uranus→Neptune/Pluto).

All these themes come together in what is perhaps the central spiritual experience of Dostoevsky's life, one repeated many times, which occurred at the onset of the epileptic seizures to which he was subject for almost his entire adult existence. Dostoevsky described that experience with clinical precision in *The Idiot*, in the interior reflections of Prince Myshkin:

> He was thinking. . . that there was a moment or two in his epileptic condition almost before the fit itself. . . when suddenly amid the sadness, spiritual darkness, and depression, his brain seemed to catch fire at brief moments, and with an extraordinary momentum his vital forces were strained to the utmost all at once. His sensation of being alive and his awareness increased tenfold at those moments which flashed by like lightning. His mind and heart were flooded by a dazzling light. All his agitation, all his doubts and worries, seemed composed in a twinkling, culminating in a great calm, full of serene and harmonious joy and hope, full of understanding and the knowledge of the final cause.
>
> Reflecting about that moment afterwards, when he was well again . . . he arrived at last at the paradoxical conclusion: "What does it matter that it is an abnormal tension, if the result, if the moment of sensation, remembered and analyzed in a state of health, turns out to be harmony and beauty brought to their highest point of perfection, and gives a feeling, undivined and undreamt of till then, of completeness, proportion, reconciliation, and an ecstatic and prayerful fusion in the highest synthesis of life?" . . . That it really was "beauty and prayer," that it really was "the highest synthesis of life," he could not doubt.

As later recounted in memoirs by others who knew him, Dostoevsky described his own epileptically catalyzed revelations in terms that are suggestive of the same overwhelming intensity, noetic power, and spiritual exaltation:

> For several brief moments I feel a happiness unthinkable in a normal state and impossible to imagine by anyone else who has not lived through it. I am then in perfect harmony with myself and the entire universe; the sensation is so powerful and so delightful that for a few seconds of such happiness one would give ten years of one's life, perhaps even one's entire life.
>
> I had the sentiment that heaven had come down to earth and swallowed me up. I really apprehended God and felt him in every fiber of my being.

Before we leave Dostoevsky, it will be instructive to discuss one other remarkable archetypal pattern in his works that can be precisely illuminated by his natal planetary aspects. In all of Dostoevsky's major novels, a crucial element in the narrative drama is the role of the principal female character in relation to the male protagonist for whom she is both romantic partner and spiritual mirror, as for example in *Crime and Punishment*, where each step of Raskolnikov's moral and spiritual transformation was mediated by his relationship to the saintly young woman Sonya. I found it extraordinary that not only was Dostoevsky born when all three outermost planets, Uranus, Neptune, and Pluto, were in a rare nearly exact configuration of dynamic aspects, but on the day of his birth the planet Venus was in exact conjunction with this larger alignment. (Venus was positioned precisely between Uranus and Neptune, which were themselves less than ½° from each other, and all three planets were closely square Pluto.) Because of Venus's archetypal association with romantic love, beauty, and the beloved partner, it seemed to me striking that virtually all of the male protagonists in Dostoevsky's major novels were romantically involved with women who exactly mirrored and mediated the male figures' most essential character traits and existential attitudes, the very traits and attitudes that corresponded so precisely to the three outer-planetary archetypes. Similarly, each of these women played crucial roles in either the extreme turmoil (Uranus-Pluto) or the spiritual awakenings (Uranus-Neptune) that marked the lives of the protagonists—as indeed happened in Dostoevsky's own life, as clearly visible in the sequence of his three most significant relationships with women.

Moreover, such themes as the sudden awakening of romantic love and unexpected perception of beauty, both liberating and disruptive in its effects and often associated with rebellious actions against societal conventions (all Venus-Uranus), the spiritually redemptive power of love and the spiritual beauty of compassionate love (Venus-Neptune), and finally the overwhelming intensity of passionate erotic love with its potential for instinctual and emotional violence (Venus-Pluto) are all prominent in every one of his major novels.

Remarkably, the only other major literary figure who I found was born with this same rare four-planet configuration—Venus closely aligned with Uranus, Neptune, and Pluto all in hard-aspect alignment—is Shakespeare, believed by most Shakespeare scholars to have been born on or within three days of April 23, 1564 (he was baptized on April 26). The exact archetypal themes that we have just seen so explicitly expressed in the life and work of Dostoevsky were evident, with equal intensity and with all their specific nuances and complex interplay, in virtually every one of Shakespeare's plays and poems. The extremity of passion experienced and acted upon, the potential instinctual and emotional violence of romantic and erotic love, the rebellion of lovers against the confining authority of social or familial structures, the sudden awakening of romantic love, the sudden opening to compassionate forgiving love, the enchantments and self-deceptions of romantic enthrallment, the spiritually transformative and redemptive power of love and beauty, the unexpected power of beauty to move the human soul, the crucial role of young girls, women, and lovers in shaping the unfolding drama of human life through beauty and love and bringing the possibility of spiritual

rebirth—all these are expressed in Shakespeare's work with an articulate specificity that could scarcely be more vivid.

Even in an entirely comedic context, as in *A Midsummer Night's Dream*,
Shakespeare precisely conveys this overarching archetypal complex in his telling
juxtaposition of love and madness, both of which he recognizes as akin to the
poet's imaginative capacity to body forth a new reality:

> *Lovers and madmen have such seething brains,*
> *Such shaping fantasies, that apprehend*
> *More than cool reason ever comprehends.*
> *The lunatic, the lover and the poet*
> *Are of imagination all compact:*
> *One sees more devils than vast hell can hold,*
> *That is, the madman: the lover, all as frantic,*
> *Sees Helen's beauty in a brow of Egypt:*
> *The poet's eye, in a fine frenzy rolling,*
> *Doth glance from heaven to earth, from earth to heaven;*
> *And as imagination bodies forth*
> *The forms of things unknown, the poet's pen*
> *Turns them to shapes and gives to airy nothing*
> *A local habitation and a name.*
>
> (*A Midsummer Night's Dream*, 5.1.4–17)

Apart from the presence of the faster-moving Venus in this configuration,
the larger outer-planet configuration of Uranus, Neptune, and Pluto in a T-square
at Shakespeare's birth can be recognized archetypally in the more general quality
of experience that is conveyed in virtually his entire oeuvre: the countless diverse states of overwhelming mental and emotional intensity, of visceral depths
and spiritual heights, so often associated with love but also with ambition,
power, and pride, with envy and jealousy, with hope, despair, revenge, madness,
death, old age, rebirth. The T-square alignment of *any* three planets generally coincides with a challenging archetypal dynamic informed by the relevant planetary principles in tense relation, but a T-square alignment of the three outermost
planets—a configuration that has happened only once in the modern era—
appears to be correlated with an especially profound archetypal interaction
bringing forth an extraordinary range of human experience and deep internal and
external conflicts that often have a transpersonal quality. A certain high tension is wrought by the clashing extremity of the dynamic forces activated—
Promethean, Dionysian, Neptunian—that demands dramatic embodiment and
presses towards an enlargement of human possibility. In many ways one can recognize that, as Harold Bloom and other critics have observed, in the almost
anonymous brilliance of his plays' many-charactered articulations, Shakespeare
himself bodied forth the self-reflective modern character and sensibility in all

their unprecedented complexity—spiritual, instinctual, emancipatory, rebellious, inspired, passionate—at the very moment of its titanic emergence in the sixteenth and seventeenth centuries.

Recalling that Galileo, too, was born in 1564 with this same T-square, except that he had Mercury and the Sun in alignment with the outer three planets rather than Venus as Shakespeare did, we can observe the parallels in these two paradigmatic individuals' roles in mediating the birth of the modern sensibility. In Galileo, the Plutonic factor (he was born with Sun and Mercury in triple conjunction with Pluto, all in a T-square with Uranus and Neptune) seems to have expressed itself as a titanic power struggle of self and intellect (Sun-Mercury-Pluto) in the context of a radical shift of cultural world view (Uranus-Neptune) in which the opposing forces were science and religion. In this opposition of cultural forces, one side was emancipatory and disruptive in its influence (Uranus) while the other affirmed a transcendent sacred dimension of existence (Neptune). This religious impulse, however, was fatefully conflated with the authoritarian structures and dogmatic beliefs of a fearful, armored and punitive Church hierarchy, as described earlier in the sequence of Vatican prohibitions and Inquisitional trials precisely aligned with the Saturn-Pluto cycle. Yet the emerging scientific vision had its own cosmic numinosity (Uranus-Neptune), whose power inspired the Copernican revolutionaries with a certain spiritual conviction as well.

One could say that the epic significance of the Galilean drama in the history of Western civilization lay in its fundamental role in shaping the very nature of reality for the modern world. It also shaped the nature of human knowledge of that reality, and the determination of which cultural authority would have the power to configure that reality for the coming age. The overarching historical and cultural momentousness of this struggle seems to correspond with considerable accuracy, both in its specific meaning and its transpersonal potency, to the dynamic tension constellated by the great principles associated with the three outermost planets of Uranus, Neptune, and Pluto. More specifically, it was Galileo's thinking and writing (Mercury), his essential commitment to the empowered intellect (Mercury-Pluto), the penetrating character of his mind, his intensely polemical words and personality, his extraordinarily dynamic and sometimes destructive sense of sovereign selfhood (Sun-Pluto)—and indeed, his powerful elevation of the Sun to centrality in the universe—that became the historical focal point upon which this vast cultural struggle and titanic transformation centered, as if it were enacting a Shakespearean drama of its own on the stage of world history. But whereas Shakespeare's high altar was consecrated to the goddess of beauty, art, and love, Galileo's high altar was dedicated to the self-empowered mind.

Whether the epiphany took the form of Galileo's telescopic discoveries or Shakespeare's dramatic revelations, Dante's Beatific Vision in *The Divine Comedy* or

Petrarch's epiphany at the summit of Mont Ventoux, Plato's philosophical awakening to the transcendent Ideas in the wake of Socrates's death or the apostles'
Pentecostal awakening of the Spirit in the wake of Jesus's death, the archetypal
theme of epiphanic disclosure revealed itself with luminous consistency in close
coincidence with the alignments of the Uranus-Neptune cycle.

We can recognize a continuing diachronic development of the several interrelated themes of epiphanic disclosure, imaginative genius, and the sacred role
of the creative individual in mediating such disclosures when we follow the
Uranus-Neptune cycle after the era of Keats and the Shelleys, Coleridge and
Emerson, Beethoven and Goethe, Idealism and Romanticism. It was during the
Romantic epoch of this Uranus-Neptune conjunction that the twin concepts of
the creative imagination and the sacred role of the artist in envisioning and
birthing new realities were first fully enunciated and made conscious. These
same ideas and aspirations were then actualized in new ways in the lives and
works of the major creative figures who were born at that time: Wagner and
Dickens at its beginning cusp, then the Brontës, Melville, Whitman, George
Eliot, Dostoevsky, Flaubert, Baudelaire, Tolstoy, Dickinson. This developing impulse then received a decisively new formulation in modernism—at once continuous with and breaking from the Romantic position—during the immediately
following Uranus-Neptune opposition of the 1899–1918 period: beginning with
the work of Cézanne, Mahler, and Henry James, then Rilke and Yeats, Picasso
and Matisse, Joyce and Proust, Pound and Eliot, Stravinsky, Schönberg, Diaghilev, Duncan, Nijinsky, Kandinsky, Mann, Lawrence, Stein, Frost, Stevens.[8]

In the realm of science, no more dramatic cosmic epiphany can be imagined
than that brought forth in this same epoch by Einstein in the special and general
theories of relativity and the sudden opening of a radically new cosmos to the
modern imagination. Essential to this epiphany, and to the simultaneous emergence of quantum physics, was the characteristic theme of a sudden dissolution
of previously established structures and boundaries—between matter and energy, time and space, subject and object, wave and particle, being and nonbeing.

Indeed, the word *epiphany* itself received a new definition and significance
through James Joyce's writings of that time, first appearing about 1907 in his
early unpublished novel *Stephen Hero*, in which the word was invoked to signify
the sudden revelation of the essential nature or meaning of a thing, a person, or
a situation—that moment when "the soul of the commonest object . . . seems to
us radiant." The word epiphany precisely contains the combination and interplay
of the Promethean impulse associated with Uranus—the sudden, unexpected,
illuminating, revelatory, awakening, liberating—with the Neptunian element of
the aesthetic and spiritual imagination, the poetic and numinous, the inner
meaning, the deeper reality, the radiant soul of things.

In turn, many crucial figures who subsequently mediated the spiritual,
philosophical, and imaginative awakenings of the twentieth century were born in
the years of this Uranus-Neptune opposition in the early twentieth century, each

representing a different category of the Uranus-Neptune archetypal complex: seminal poets such as Pablo Neruda and Dylan Thomas; influential mystics and religious innovators such as Thomas Merton, Simone Weil, Karl Rahner, and Bede Griffiths; major scholars of mythology and religion such as Joseph Campbell, Mircea Eliade, Erich Neumann, Henry Corbin, Paul Ricoeur, Jean Gebser, and Marie-Louise von Franz; great innovators in mathematical philosophy such as Kurt Gödel, Alan Turing, and John von Neumann who served at once the Platonic-Pythagorean realm of ideal mathematical forms and the development of set theory, game theory, information theory, and the design of computers; pioneers in the awakening to a more unitive and holistic world view that reflected the intricate interdependence and subtle interconnectedness of nature and reality, such as Gregory Bateson, David Bohm, Rachel Carson, Arne Naess, and Thomas Berry; and leading figures in the emergence of the spiritual counterculture, such as Alan Watts, Albert Hofmann, Abraham Maslow, and J. D. Salinger.

Perhaps one of the most widely appreciated epiphanies in modern American literature is the one with which Salinger graced his readers in *Franny and Zooey*, written and first published in exact coincidence with the most recent Uranus-Neptune square that took place in the 1950s, spanning almost precisely the entire decade. This alignment occurred halfway between the opposition of the early twentieth century and the conjunction of our own time, and coincided with a wave of cultural and spiritual impulses that entered the otherwise conservative postwar collective psyche at that time. This wave was notably visible in the rapid rise of interest in the West in Buddhism, Hinduism, and other forms of Asian mysticism, D. T. Suzuki's influential lectures in New York on Zen to Erich Fromm and others, Joseph Campbell's journey to Asia and his beginning his multivolume encyclopedic work of world mythology *The Masks of God*, Alan Watts's publication of *The Way of Zen*, the seminal teaching of Watts, Haridas Chaudhuri, and Frederic Spiegelberg at the American Academy of Asian Studies in San Francisco, and the emergence of the Beat movement (from "beatific") with Allen Ginsberg, Jack Kerouac, and Neal Cassady—"angelheaded hipsters burning for the ancient heavenly connection" (*Howl*).

Recalling that the discoverer of LSD, Albert Hofmann, was born during the preceding Uranus-Neptune opposition, we can also recognize the characteristic themes of the Uranus-Neptune complex during this period in the introduction of psychedelic experimentation as a path of psychological change and spiritual epiphany, as reflected in Aldous Huxley's *The Doors of Perception* of 1954, Humphrey Osmond's coining the word *psychedelic* ("mind-manifesting") in a letter to Huxley in 1956, Gordon Wasson's meeting the Mexican *curandera* María Sabina and publishing his influential *Life* magazine article on the sacred psilocybin mushroom in 1957, and the beginning of Stanislav Grof's research on LSD in Prague in the same years through which he developed an approach to psychotherapy that integrated psychoanalysis with an openness to transformative mystical experience. Reflecting several themes combining the Promethean and

Neptunian principles, Huxley at this time began writing his utopian novel *Island*, which depicted a society of social compassion and individual freedom whose religious foundation was shaped by the communal ritual ingestion of a psychedelic medicine. Like Huxley and Grof, Alan Watts, Allen Ginsberg, and Ken Kesey all began their psychedelic experiments during this Uranus-Neptune alignment in the 1950s. These pioneering explorations became major influences that contributed to the wider countercultural movement of social rebellion and emancipation during the Uranus-Pluto conjunction of the 1960s.

This Uranus-Neptune alignment of the 1950s also coincided with Martin Luther King's crucial religious opening, the "kitchen experience" in January 1956, in the early months of the civil rights protest movement in Montgomery, Alabama (when Saturn was also square Pluto). Late one night after having received a series of threatening phone calls, when he had reached a dark nadir of fear and discouragement, he suddenly experienced God as no longer merely a "metaphysical category" but rather a powerful divine presence that gave him the moral and spiritual courage to risk his life in leading the new movement and serving "the birth of the ideal of freedom in America" and the "birth of a New Age" (Uranus archetypally associated with birth, freedom, awakening, and the new; Neptune with ideals, spiritual inspiration, and experience of the numinous): "I experienced the presence of the Divine as I had never experienced Him before." Soon after, influenced by Bayard Rustin, King adopted the Gandhian strategy of nonviolent resistance as both a moral principle and an effective force for change. (Gandhi was born during the preceding Uranus-Neptune square; Thoreau and Tolstoy were born during the Uranus-Neptune conjunction just before that.) During this same alignment occurred the widespread Protestant revival and enormous New Evangelical crusades led by the charismatic preacher Billy Graham, epitomized in the summer-long crusade in 1957 at Madison Square Garden in New York—where Graham invited the young King, as a leader of "a great social revolution," to lead the multitude in prayer.

We can further fill in the picture of the Uranus-Neptune quadrature cycle by recalling the wave of other works that emerged during this most recent square alignment of the 1950s and deeply influenced the spiritual development of the second half of the twentieth century: Teilhard de Chardin's *The Human Phenomenon* (1955) and *The Divine Milieu* (1957), with their dissolving of the boundary between science and religion in an integral mystical vision of evolution; Paul Tillich's *The Courage to Be* (1952) and *Dynamics of Faith* (1957), with their passionate Christian engagement with the philosophical and existential tensions of a secular age; Owen Barfield's *Saving the Appearances* (1957), with its influential development of ideas on the evolution of consciousness first advanced by Rudolf Steiner during the preceding opposition; and Hans Jonas's *The Gnostic Religion* (1958), which introduced Gnosticism to modern readers. In philosophy, one can mention here the publication in 1953 of two foundation texts of what would become the postmodern philosophical vision, Wittgenstein's

Philosophical Investigations and Heidegger's *Introduction to Metaphysics*, which was followed by several more works, published in the 1950s, that represented Heidegger's later poetic philosophy focused on the mystery of Being.[9]

This Uranus-Neptune alignment coincided as well with the extraordinary outpouring of Jung's last works in the course of this decade: *Synchronicity, Answer to Job, Aion, Mysterium Coniunctionis, The Undiscovered Self,* and *Memories, Dreams, Reflections.* These works collectively reflect that radical shift in religious psychology, epistemology, and philosophy of history that has become Jung's most provocative and perhaps seminal contribution to the thought and culture of the later twentieth century. Pervaded by the characteristic themes and spirit of the Uranus-Neptune archetypal complex, they can be seen as both an unexpected creative advance in Jung's late thought and the final fruits of the development that was set in motion in Jung's pivotal period of intellectual and psychospiritual transformation during the preceding Uranus-Neptune opposition in the 1913–18 period, exactly 90° earlier in the cycle.

To all these cultural phenomena that suggest the activated Uranus-Neptune complex of this era we should add the sudden wave of spiritually revelatory films of Ingmar Bergman and Federico Fellini—*The Seventh Seal, Wild Strawberries, La Strada, Nights of Cabiria*—that appeared in the 1950s, drew international attention, and started, along with the French New Wave, the British Free Cinema, Akira Kurosawa in Japan, and Satyajit Ray in India, a creative revolution in film that went on to permeate the cultural experience of the 1960s and after.

Simultaneously, the evolution of jazz during the Uranus-Neptune square of the 1950s was influenced in a characteristically mystical way by John Coltrane's famous spiritual epiphany of 1957. Attempting to describe the aura of sacredness and divinity that permeated Coltrane's subsequent concerts, his wife, Alice Coltrane, stated:

> Call it Universal Consciousness, Supreme Being, Nature, God. Call this force by any name you like, but it was there, and its presence was so powerfully felt by most people that it was almost palpable.

Finally, it was Salinger's memorable contribution to this larger spiritual influx of the 1950s to bring forth the revelation that formed the brilliant climax of *Franny and Zooey*, first published in *The New Yorker* as two extended stories in 1955 and 1957 during the heart of the Uranus-Neptune alignment.[10] The celebrated passage narrates a phone call from Zooey Glass to his younger sister, Franny, who is in the next room in the Glass family's apartment in Manhattan. Franny, in the dark throes of a spiritual crisis, refusing to eat and desperately repeating in silence the Jesus prayer of the Russian mystics, is suffering from a state of acute alienation from the spiritless world of shallow egotism that surrounds her in her life as a college student and amateur actress. After several unsuccessful attempts to provide his sister with a way back to her life, Zooey recalls the enigmatic advice their deceased older brother Seymour gave them as children before they went on the air for their weekly radio program, *It's a Wise Child*.

"I remember about the fifth time I ever came on 'Wise Child.' I subbed for Walt a few times when he was in a cast—remember when he was in a cast? Anyway, I started bitching one night before the broadcast. Seymour'd told me to shine my shoes just as I was going out the door with Walker. I was furious. The studio audience were all morons, the announcer was a moron, the sponsors were morons, and I just damn well wasn't going to shine my shoes for them, I told Seymour. I said they couldn't see them anyway, where we sat. He said to shine them anyway. He said to shine them for the Fat Lady. I didn't know what the hell he was talking about, but he had a very Seymour look on his face, and so I did it. He never did tell me who the Fat Lady was, but I shined my shoes for the Fat Lady every time I ever went on the air again—all the years you and I were on the program together, if you remember. I don't think I missed more than just a couple of times. This terribly clear, clear picture of the Fat Lady formed in my mind. I had her sitting on this porch all day, swatting flies, with her radio going full-blast from morning till night. I figured the heat was terrible, and she probably had cancer, and—I don't know. Anyway, it seemed goddam clear why Seymour wanted me to shine my shoes when I went on the air. It made sense."

Franny was standing. She had taken her hand away from her face to hold the phone with two hands. "He told me, too," she said into the phone. "He told me to be funny for the Fat Lady, once." She released one hand from the phone and placed it, very briefly, on the crown of her head, then went back to holding the phone with both hands. "I didn't ever picture her on a porch, but with very—you know—very thick legs, very veiny. I had her in an awful wicker chair. She had cancer, too, though, and she had the radio going full-blast all day! Mine did, too!"

"Yes. Yes. Yes. All right. Let me tell you something now, buddy. . . . Are you listening?"

Franny, looking extremely tense, nodded.

"I don't care where an actor acts. It can be in summer stock, it can be over a radio, it can be over television, it can be in a goddam Broadway theatre, complete with the most fashionable, most well-fed, most sunburned-looking audience you can imagine. But I'll tell you a terrible secret—Are you listening to me? There isn't anyone out there who isn't Seymour's Fat Lady. That includes your Professor Tupper, buddy. And all his goddam cousins by the dozens. There isn't anyone anywhere that isn't Seymour's Fat Lady. Don't you know that? Don't you know that goddam secret yet? And don't you know—listen to me, now—don't you know who that Fat Lady really is? . . . Ah, buddy. Ah, buddy. It's Christ Himself. Christ Himself, buddy."

For joy, apparently, it was all Franny could do to hold the phone, even with both hands.

We can readily recognize here the most characteristic features of the Uranus-Neptune archetypal complex: the sudden resolution to the spiritual crisis in which Franny was entrapped, the unexpected creative synthesis of irreverent wit and the sacred, of the trickster (Uranus) and the mystic (Neptune); the surprising dissolution of boundaries between imaginative literature and religious disclosure; the revelation of the numinous in an entirely unanticipated form and manner; and the sudden shift of both reality and personal identity produced by the epiphany of a universal human divinity. Above all, the passage evokes an unexpected liberation from the seemingly irresolvable human condition of egoic imprisonment, like a window suddenly opening to a new, holy, infinitely spacious world.

As we have seen so often before in the other planetary cycles we have examined, the activation of a particular archetypal complex tends to take the form not only of a new expression of the relevant archetypal themes and qualities, but also of a new interest in and sense of kinship with previous articulations of these themes that coincided with earlier alignments of the same planetary cycle. Each new alignment of a cycle appears to correlate with a highly specific sense of *resonance* with earlier eras, historical phenomena, and cultural figures informed by the same archetypal gestalt. With this resonance emerges a fresh recognition of the significance and contemporary relevance of various events, works of art, and prominent figures from those earlier periods. The religious awakenings of one Uranus-Neptune age draw on those from earlier alignments, as in the cyclical renewals of Christian spirituality and Pentecostal enthusiasm. Buber rediscovers the Hasidism of Ba'al Shem Tov and brings forth his I-Thou philosophy. Keats adapts both the Petrarchan and the Shakespearean sonnet forms to bring forth his own poetic masterpieces of the Romantic era. Petrarch rediscovers the writings of Cicero from the Uranus-Neptune conjunction of the first century BCE and calls for a cultural renaissance based on the glories of classical antiquity. Ficino recovers Plato, Melville discovers Shakespeare, Neruda reads Whitman.

In Salinger's *Franny and Zooey*, repeated references are made throughout to major figures associated with previous Uranus-Neptune historical epochs who reflect the Uranus-Neptune archetypal gestalt—spiritual teachers and mystics such as Socrates, Jesus, and Francis of Assisi, and spiritually illuminated writers such as Pascal, Dickinson, Dostoevsky, and Tolstoy. Quotations from many of these figures were meticulously inscribed on a large white board nailed to the door of the bedroom of the two eldest Glass brothers, Seymour and Buddy, and several were silently read by Zooey as he contemplated his coming conversation with Franny. One of them, from the *Discourses* of the Stoic philosopher and former slave Epictetus—written during the Uranus-Neptune conjunction of 104–117 CE that immediately followed the opposition at the birth of Christianity—can serve as a characteristic example of the archetypal resonance to which I am referring, with its sober step-by-step philosophical analysis that suddenly breaks forth into an unexpected revelation of an intimate and pervasive divine reality.

> Concerning the Gods, there are those who deny the very existence of the Godhead; others say that it exists, but neither bestirs nor concerns itself nor has forethought for anything. A third party attribute to it existence and forethought, but only for great and heavenly matters, not for anything that is on earth. A fourth party admit things on earth as well as in heaven, but only in general, and not with respect to each individual. A fifth, of whom were Ulysses and Socrates, are those that cry:—
>
> *I move not without Thy knowledge!*

Revelations of the Numinous

As we have seen, the period of the most recent Uranus-Neptune opposition in 1899–1918 played an especially catalyzing role in the spiritual history of the twentieth century. As in other such alignment periods, the larger intellectual situation of the age seems to have encouraged new and creative responses to the characteristic Uranus-Neptune archetypal impulses in evidence at that time, responses that were specific to the cultural context. Because of the dominance of modern science in shaping the contemporary sensibility, many spiritually informed thinkers in these years felt compelled to approach the phenomenon of religious experience in a manner that answered the demands of empirical rigor and critical analysis. Many figures discussed earlier engaged in this task—William James, Jung, Steiner, Buber, Bergson, Bucke, and Royce— each bringing different starting points and tools to the effort. To these can be added other important theorists of religion whose work emerged at this time such as Max Weber and Rudolf Otto.

In the context of psychology, it was especially James and Jung who in these years laid the foundation for integrating the religious dimension of the human psyche with the world view of the emerging century. Both transpersonal and archetypal psychology, two of the most vital currents to emerge from the wellspring of depth psychology in the past several decades, originated in the ideas and concerns that these men addressed in the period of this Uranus-Neptune alignment, the most recent opposition before the conjunction of our own time. Both in the study of the numinous and the analysis of mystical reports and psychedelic experiments, this period was extraordinarily seminal for the philosophical and psychological engagement with the spiritual dimension of human experience. As James declared in 1909 at the end of *A Pluralistic Universe*:

> Let empiricism once become associated with religion, as hitherto, through some strange misunderstanding, it has been associated with irreligion, and I believe that a new era of religion as well as of philosophy will be ready to begin.

In the twentieth century, both depth psychologists and scholars of religion came to employ the term "numinous" to signify experiences pervaded by a sense of the holy, the sacred, mystery, divine presence, and religious awe. The concept was developed by Rudolf Otto in a series of works beginning in 1904 and culminating in *The Idea of the Holy* of 1917, all written during the Uranus-Neptune opposition of 1899–1918. Otto's views were influenced by James's *The Varieties of Religious Experience*, with its empirical survey and sensitive analysis of a multitude of reports of religious and spiritual phenomena. The *Varieties* was originally delivered as the Gifford Lectures in 1901–02 at the beginning of the same Uranus-Neptune opposition. In turn, both Otto's ideas and James's studies influenced the work of Jung, who integrated the concept of the numinous as a critical element in his own psychology and philosophy of religious experience, which emerged during this same alignment.

We can discern not only this synchronic but also a distinct diachronic pattern of correlations between the Uranus-Neptune cycle and significant milestones in this area. Otto regarded Friedrich Schleiermacher as his most important precursor and the key figure in the philosophical rediscovery of the sense of the holy in the post-Enlightenment era. The founder of modern Protestant theology, Schleiermacher published his masterwork *The Christian Faith*, the most influential work of nineteenth-century Protestantism, in 1821–22, in exact coincidence with the immediately preceding Uranus-Neptune conjunction that took place at the peak of Romanticism and German Idealism.

In observing the concept of the numinous and the study of numinous phenomena that developed through the work of these scholars—Schleiermacher, Otto, James, Jung—we can recognize what was in essence a *liberation of the idea of the sacred* into modern discourse, an awakening to a previously hidden or suppressed reality in rebellion against the established secularism of the modern mind. This characteristic expression of the Uranus-*Neptune* archetypal complex, the liberation of the sacred, can be seen as both closely analogous to and in contrast with the *liberation of the instinctual,* the awakening to the Dionysian and the id, that occurred for the modern mind in coincidence with the successive Uranus-*Pluto* alignments in the same hundred-year span through the work of Schopenhauer, Darwin, Nietzsche, and Freud.

Moreover, not only its cultural and intellectual effect as a spiritually liberating idea but the very nature of the numinous as it was formulated and discussed by both Otto and Jung precisely embodies the distinctive qualities of the two archetypal principles that constitute the Uranus-Neptune complex. In Otto's perspective, the numinous is defined not only by such terms as sacredness, divinity, inspiration, mystery, and religious awe (all qualities associated with Neptune) but also as something that suddenly confronts human awareness with an unexpected dimension of reality, something that is experienced as "Wholly Other" than the mundane sphere, that utterly transcends and subverts the everyday world of conventional experience, and that disrupts the very ground of one's being as it was previously construed (all these themes reflect qualities associated with Uranus interpenetrated by Neptune). This same archetypal synthesis is evident in Otto's focus on the experience of divine grace's sudden entering of the soul as an unexpected influx of sanctification that catalyzes a radical inner change.

Similarly, Jung repeatedly described the appearance of the numinous as the abrupt intrusion of another reality into the ordinary conscious state, as something that suddenly crosses one's path, that stops one up short, that is imbued with an uncanny, challenging, often destabilizing quality. It overwhelms one with its alterity. It is autonomous, tricksterlike, beyond anticipation or control.

Such an understanding and experience can be seen as underlying Jung's entire psychology with its distinctive emphasis on the unpredictable, autonomous, and ultimately spiritual nature of the unconscious in its interaction with the conscious ego. Through this lens Jung saw the nature and function of dreams, psychological symptoms, slips and errors, synchronicities, suddenly intrusive events whether inner or outer, "fate"—the entire modus operandi of the archetypal dimension as it unpredictably impressed itself upon human experience.[11] The very phenomenon of synchronicity can be recognized as a vivid expression of precisely these two archetypal principles in close interplay: the metaphysical trickster, the unexpected correspondence of inner and outer events that reveals a deeper coherence of meaning in life than had been assumed possible, the inexplicable coincidence that carries a numinous charge, the sudden revelation of a spiritual purpose that works within and subverts the apparent randomness of existence. Here we can recall that Jung's seminal paper on synchronicity—itself something of a cultural awakening to a transcendent dimension, disruptive of established assumptions and conventional logic, and not without its own confusing ambiguities—was published during the Uranus-Neptune square of the 1950s.

Jung's enduring testament to this conception of the numinous that informed his psychology and his life experience, one so consistently expressive of the Uranus-Neptune complex and the tricksterlike unpredictable spontaneity of the divine, was the ancient Latin motto he inscribed above the door of his house on the shore of Lake Zürich, where it can still be read today: *Vocatus atque non vocatus deus aderit* ("Called or not called, [the] God will come").

In *The Varieties of Religious Experience*, William James meticulously examined religious and mystical reports from many sources over the centuries in order to discriminate the specific qualities that seemed most distinctive of this category of human experience. James believed that a mystical stratum existed in human nature, that it was the source of all religions, and that at the core of personal religious experience were mystical states of consciousness. For our present analysis, his survey of these states represents a concise catalogue of characteristic archetypal phenomena and themes associated with the Uranus-Neptune complex. James especially singled out the following qualities as defining the nature of mystical experience, each easily recognizable as embodying a synthesis of these two archetypal principles:

Ineffability: Mystical states are typically experienced as having a character so radically different from ordinary experience and the structures of conventional language that they defy any attempt by the mystic to adequately convey to others their impact or meaning. They are outside the compass of verbal formulation and require direct experience for their meaning to be understood or appreciated.

> No one can make clear to another who has never had a certain feeling, in what the quality or worth of it consists. One must have musical ears to know the value of a symphony; one must have been in love oneself to understand a lover's state of mind. Lacking the heart or ear, we cannot interpret the musician or the lover justly, and are even likely to consider him weak-minded or absurd. The mystic finds that most of us accord to his experiences an equally incompetent treatment.

Noetic quality: Such states are experienced not only as states of feeling but as states of knowledge. Those who experience them have the sense of being the recipient of truths that are so profound as to be inaccessible to the ordinary intellect, and that convey a power of conviction of their veridical reality that can endure a lifetime: "They are illuminations, revelations, full of significance and importance . . . as a rule they carry with them a curious sense of authority for aftertime."

Transiency: Mystical states enter and depart with a spontaneous evanescence, generally lasting for only brief periods before fading into the light of common day. Yet in that sudden opening of a window to another reality, as in the fleeting moments of poetic apprehension received in a state of intoxication, such states give evidence of an intrinsic "mystical faculty of human nature, usually crushed to death by the cold facts and dry criticism of the sober hour."

Passivity: Though often facilitated by preliminary voluntary actions, such as meditation or prayer, fasting, special breathing techniques, or the ingestion of psychoactive plants or compounds, the mystical states themselves are characteristically experienced in a state of passive receptivity, with a surrender of the personal will in favor of a radically receptive embrace of the divine influx: "The mystic feels as if his own will were in abeyance, and indeed sometimes as if he were grasped and held by a superior power."

Other characteristic Uranus-Neptune qualities that James specified as typical of such states include the sudden influx of a dreamlike sense of mystery and timelessness, indescribable awe, a dissolution of the usual sense of self or personal identity, and an often disorienting recognition that ordinary consciousness discloses only a phantasmal unreality. In his survey, James—much like Salinger in his survey in *Franny and Zooey*—recounts reports of mystics and poets who with extraordinary frequency were themselves associated with earlier Uranus-Neptune alignments: Meister Eckhart, Saint John of the Cross, Saint Teresa of Ávila, Jakob Boehme, Whitman. Each is cited to display a different quality or nuance of the mystical spectrum. The paradox and ineffability of mystical experience is illustrated by Eckhart (who led the early fourteenth-century Rhineland mystical awakening during the same conjunction as Dante's *La Divina Commedia*) and Boehme (whose *Aurora*, a foundation work of Christian theosophy, was published in 1612 during the same square as Galileo's *The Starry Messenger*). Saint John of the Cross, whose spiritual awakening occurred during the preceding Uranus-Neptune opposition, is called upon to give witness to that state of high rapture in the "union of love" that escapes the power of verbal description. The soul, John wrote,

> finds no terms, no means, no comparison whereby to render the sublimity of the wisdom and the delicacy of the spiritual feeling with which she is filled. . . . In this abyss of wisdom, the soul grows by what it drinks in from the well-springs of the comprehension of love.

James then calls upon Teresa of Ávila, "the expert of experts in describing such conditions," whose mystical autobiography coincided with the same Uranus-Neptune opposition as that of John of the Cross and the birth of Shakespeare. In the passages James quotes, Teresa's deep intimacy with mystical states is matched only by her transparent spiritual modesty, revealed in each instance in a different manner.

> One day, being in orison, it was granted me to perceive in one instant how all things are seen and contained in God. . . . The view I had of them was of a sovereign clearness, and has remained vividly impressed upon my soul. It is one of the most signal of all the graces which the Lord has granted me. . . . The view was so subtle and delicate that the understanding cannot grasp it.

> God establishes himself in the interior of this soul in such a way, that when she returns to herself, it is wholly impossible for her to doubt that she has been in God, and God in her. This truth remains so strongly impressed on her that, even though many years should pass without the condition returning, she can neither forget the favor she received, nor doubt of its reality. . . . But how, you will repeat, can one have such certainty in respect to what one does not see? This question,

I am powerless to answer. These are secrets of God's omnipotence which it does not appertain to me to penetrate. All that I know is that I tell the truth; and I shall never believe that any soul who does not possess this certainty has ever been really united to God.

What empire is comparable to that of a soul who, from this sublime summit to which God has raised her, sees all the things of earth beneath her feet, and is captivated by no one of them? How ashamed she is of her former attachments! How amazed at her blindness! What lively pity she feels for those whom she recognizes still shrouded in the darkness! . . . She groans at having ever been sensitive to points of honor, at the illusion that made her ever see as honor what the world calls by that name. . . . She laughs at herself that there should ever have been a time in her life when she made any case of money, when she ever desired it . . . . Oh! if human beings might only agree together to regard it as so much useless mud, what harmony would reign in the world! With what friendship we would all treat each other if our interest in spurious honor and in money could but disappear from earth! For my own part, I feel as if it would be a remedy for all our ills.

As an example of the "sporadic" type of mystical experience, James cites Whitman's well-known lines from *Leaves of Grass* in which he described an embracing spiritual epiphany that suddenly suffused the poet's sensibility:

> *I believe in you, my Soul . . .*
> *I mind how once we lay, such a transparent summer morning.*
> *Swiftly arose and spread around me the peace and knowledge that*
>   *pass all the argument of the earth,*
> *And I know that the hand of God is the promise of my own,*
> *And I know that the spirit of God is the brother of my own,*
> *And that all the men ever born are also my brothers,*
>   *and the women my sisters and lovers,*
> *And that a kelson of the creation is love.*

Whitman, born in 1819 during the Uranus-Neptune conjunction of the Romantic epoch, is also called upon for his description of what James believes was "a chronic mystical perception" in the poet's life:

There is, apart from mere intellect, in the make-up of every superior human identity, a wondrous something that realizes without argument, frequently without what is called education (though I think it the goal and apex of all education deserving the name), an intuition of the absolute balance, in time and space, of the whole of this multifariousness, this revel of fools, and incredible make-believe and general unsettledness, we call *the world*; a soul-sight of that divine clue and unseen thread which holds the whole congeries of things, all history and time, and all events, however trivial, however momentous. . . . [Of] such soul-sight and root-center for the mind mere optimism explains only the surface.

For a similar epiphany awakened by nature, James uses a passage from the *Memoirs of an Idealist* of Malwida von Meysenbug, born in 1816 during the same Uranus-Neptune conjunction as Whitman. Social reformer and feminist, a friend of both Wagner and Nietzsche, and a warm-hearted supporter of a generation of young German artists and thinkers, von Meysenbug for many years had found it impossible to pray because of her materialistic philosophical beliefs. In the following account, it is the sea that both symbolizes and catalyzes her mystical opening, and her metaphors are explicitly suggestive of the fluidity, infinity, and reconciling unity of Neptune conjoined with the sudden unexpected liberating impulse of Uranus:

> I was alone upon the seashore as all these thoughts flowed over me, liberating and reconciling; and now again, as once before in distant days in the Alps of Dauphiné, I was impelled to kneel down, this time before the illimitable ocean, symbol of the Infinite. I felt that I prayed as I had never prayed before, and knew now what prayer really is: to return from the solitude of individuation into the consciousness of unity with all that is, to kneel down as one that passes away, and to rise up as one imperishable. Earth, heaven, and sea resounded as in one vast world-encircling harmony. It was as if the chorus of all the great who had ever lived were about me. I felt myself one with them, and it appears as if I heard their greeting: "Thou too belongest to the company of those who overcome."

Even the anonymous reports James cites bear precise testimony to the specific character of this archetypal complex, as in this example of a "sudden realization of the immediate presence of God" that occurred in an unlikely environment far from the mystic's monastic cell or inspiring sea.

> I know an officer on our police force who has told me that many times when off duty, and on his way home in the evening, there comes to him such a vivid and vital realization of his oneness with this Infinite Power, and this Spirit of Infinite Peace so takes hold of and so fills him, that it seems as if his feet could barely keep to the pavement, so buoyant and so exhilarated does he become by reason of this inflowing tide.

Finally, it is James's recounting of his own now-famous illumination, which occurred during his experiment with the psychoactive drug nitrous oxide, that brings forth his paradigmatic statement concerning the mystery of nonordinary states of consciousness:

> One conclusion was forced upon my mind at that time, and my impression of its truth has ever since remained unshaken. It is that our normal waking consciousness, rational consciousness as we call it, is but one special type of consciousness, whilst all about it, parted from it by the filmiest of screens, there lie potential forms of consciousness entirely different. . . . No account of the universe in its totality can be final which leaves these other forms of consciousness quite disregarded. How to regard them is the question—for they are so discontinuous with ordinary consciousness. Yet they may determine attitudes though they cannot furnish formulas, and open a region though they fail to give a map. At any rate, they forbid a premature closing of our accounts with reality.

This classic Jamesian affirmation of an open universe, inner and outer, and an intellectual and spiritual posture of radical openness to its mystery became ever more articulate in James's writings during the Uranus-Neptune opposition that coincided with the last decade of his life. Beyond that pragmatic affirmation of openness, James sounded one other note in this account of his own experiences in the *Varieties*. It is a note heard again and again in the mystical philosophies, poetic illuminations, and religious awakenings associated with Uranus-Neptune epochs and individuals—the experience of sudden *reconciliation,* the unexpected resolution of what had seemed to be irrevocably opposite principles or forces into a larger complex unity: the *mysterium coniunctionis.* "Looking back on my own experiences," James concluded,

> they all converge towards a kind of insight to which I cannot help ascribing some metaphysical significance. The keynote of it is invariably a reconciliation. It is as if the opposites of the world, whose contradictoriness and conflict make all our difficulties and troubles, were melted into unity. Not only do they, as contrasted species, belong to one and the same genus, but *one of the species,* the nobler and better one, *is itself the genus, and so soaks up and absorbs its opposite into itself.* This is a dark saying, I know, when thus expressed in terms of common logic, but I cannot wholly escape from its authority. I feel as if it must mean something. . . . Those who have ears to hear, let them hear.

The Great Awakening of the Axial Age

It is now time to examine the only period in recorded history when all three of the outermost planets, Uranus, Neptune, and Pluto, were in a virtually exact triple conjunction. This world transit was part of the larger Uranus-Neptune cycle we have been surveying, but it was the only time in the past several thousand years that a conjunction of Uranus and Neptune was exactly conjoined by Pluto as well. On the basis of the many correlations so far, we would expect this historical period to be of special interest, even serving as a test case for the entire perspective.

As it happens, the long Uranus-Neptune-Pluto triple conjunction occurred in the extraordinary era, historically unprecedented and still unparalleled, that extended from the 590s to the 550s BCE. These decades constituted the very heart of the great Axial Age that brought forth the birth of many of the world's principal religious and spiritual traditions. While exact dates for the events and figures of this distant epoch are often difficult to ascertain—generally, only the decade is known rather than the year—the historical evidence for the unique significance of this period is overwhelming. This was the age of Buddha, bringing the birth of Buddhism in India; of Mahavira and the birth of Jainism in India; of Lao-Tzu and the birth of Taoism in China, which was followed a decade later by the birth of Confucius, Lao-Tzu's younger contemporary. This same epoch coincided with that sudden wave of major prophets in ancient Israel—Jeremiah, Ezekiel, and the Second Isaiah—through whom a deep transformation in the Judaic image of the divine and understanding of human history was forged, one that is still evolving. In this same era the Hebrew Scriptures were first compiled and redacted. The traditional dating for the immensely influential Zoroaster and the birth of Zoroastrianism in Persia, though still elusive to historians, has long centered on the sixth century.

In Greece, the period of the triple conjunction exactly coincided with the birth of Greek philosophy itself, as the first Greek philosophers, Thales and Anaximander, flourished during these decades of the 580s through the 560s, and Pythagoras, towering figure in the history of both Western philosophy and science, was born. In Greek religion, Orphism was emerging and the oracle of Delphi was at the height of its influence. During the same period flourished the first great lyric poet of Western culture, Sappho, whose creativity and mastery of the art were so highly revered that classical authors called her the tenth Muse. Born in this same period was Thespis, the father of Greek tragedy whose crucial artistic innnovation, giving individual actors lines of dramatic dialogue previously spoken only by the traditional chorus, is considered to have marked the invention of drama itself.

On yet another front, these same decades brought the statesman-poet Solon's revolutionary legal and economic reforms in Athens that paved the way for the development of democracy, so characteristic of the Uranus-*Pluto* cycle's correlation with periods of radical change, liberal political reform, and an intensified impulse for social and cultural progress. (The Age of Pericles in Athens coincided with the immediately following Uranus-Pluto conjunction a century and a half later in 443–430.) During this period Solon established rules for the public recital of the Homeric epics, which became the enduring basis of Greek education and the classical imagination, reflecting a consistent theme in later Uranus-*Neptune* alignment periods such as those in Roman antiquity (Cicero, Virgil), the Renaissance, and the Romantic era.

The great figures and events, ideas, movements, awakenings, and transformations of the collective consciousness that were brought forth during this prodigious epoch have pervaded the subsequent evolution of humankind. I found it most impressive that the era universally acknowledged as the single most significant in the entire religious and spiritual history of the world coincided with the only exact triple conjunction of Uranus, Neptune, and Pluto, the very planets whose cyclical alignments were associated with archetypal meanings so precisely relevant to such an extraordinary global epoch of spiritual awakening and cultural transformation. Indeed, having spent a lifetime studying these cyclical planetary cycles, I found that the astonishing coincidence of this specific epoch with the triple conjunction of the three outermost planets possessed a certain numinosity of its own.

Astronomically, this was the only era in recorded history in which the Uranus-Neptune cycle, the Uranus-Pluto cycle, and the Neptune-Pluto cycle coincided in such a close triple conjunction. All three planets were within 2° of exact alignment near the middle of this period, in 577–576 BCE. Viewed, as it were, through a wide-angle telescopic lens, the coinciding historical and cultural phenomena seem to have formed an enormous archetypal wave in the half century from 600 to 550, which almost exactly encompassed the period in which Neptune and Pluto were within 30° of conjunction (602–552). As I noted earlier when discussing other triple conjunctions of the outer planets, such as the remarkable Jupiter-Uranus-Pluto conjunction of 1968–69, the presence of three planets in such a configuration seemed to coincide with a significant broadening of the orb in which the archetypally relevant events occurred. In the Uranus-Neptune-Pluto conjunction of the first half of the sixth century BCE, the three planetary cycles formed a series of precisely concentric alignments within this longer

period, tightly overlapping in such a way that the spans of their conjunctions became increasingly narrow in the 590s and 580s, reached their closest alignment
in the years 578–575, then gradually separated through the 560s and 550s.[12]

Virtually all the characteristic themes of the Uranus-Neptune cycle that we
surveyed in the preceding chapters are visible here, but, appropriate to the triple
conjunction with Pluto, they seem to have been expressed in a spectacularly
seminal manner—massive and profound, deeply evolutionary, transformative on
a vast scale both temporally and globally. The basic theme of *spiritual awakenings and the birth of new religions* during this era and its aftermath is of course
the most conspicuous of these Uranus-Neptune motifs: the great religious revolutions of Buddhism, Taoism, Confucianism, Jainism, and the rest. From the
perspective of Western religious history, we see exemplified in the prophetic disclosures of Judaism during this era the quintessential Uranus-Neptune theme of
a radical transformation of the God-image and a revolutionary new understanding of the divine will acting in history—the latter especially appropriate to the
presence of Pluto in the configuration with its archetypal association with both
evolution and a universal will.

With respect to the characteristic Uranus-Neptune theme of the *birth of
new philosophies,* we discover here the very birth of Western philosophy itself,
visible in Thales, Anaximander, and Pythagoras, who all sought through a newly
emergent capacity for critical reason to discover the fundamental *archai,* the orig-
inating unitive causes that underlie the flux and diversity of the world. Another
Uranus-Neptune theme, the emergence of *philosophies of a specifically idealist
metaphysical character,* is evident in Pythagoras's understanding of the transcendent mathematical forms and universal intelligence that govern the cosmos. Remarkably, it was the very next Uranus-Neptune conjunction, exactly one cycle
later, that coincided with the birth of Platonism, which was deeply influenced by
Pythagoras.

The *astronomical* motif of the Uranus-Neptune cycle that we saw in the
cyclical sequence of Copernicus, Kepler, Galileo, and Newton is evident here in
the birth of Western astronomy itself through the work of Thales, Anaximander,
and Pythagoras. This epochal beginning was marked by Thales's earliest astronomical speculations (including his reputed prediction of an eclipse in 585);
Anaximander's positing of the first scientific cosmology, which had the Earth
suspended freely in the center of a spherical universe; and Pythagoras's positing of a spherical Earth enclosed in the rotating sphere of the fixed stars, with
the planets rotating in the opposite direction. (Again, the diachronic pattern is
visible here as well: Eudoxus, the first Greek astronomer to propose a detailed
cosmology that explained the diverse planetary motions, was born during the
immediately following Uranus-Neptune conjunction at the turn of the fourth
century.)

Among the many intellectual breakthroughs and new beginnings of the
triple-conjunction Axial era, Anaximander produced the first map of the Earth,

and postulated the first known theory of evolution, which proposed that life first arose from the sea and that the first humans resembled fish. This is an especially interesting correlation in view of Pluto's association with biological evolution and the subsequent coincidence of Uranus-Pluto cyclical alignments with the emergence of evolutionary theories (e.g., those of Darwin and Wallace during the 1840s–50s conjunction, those of Erasmus Darwin, Geoffroy Saint-Hilaire, Goethe, and Lamarck during the preceding opposition of the 1790s, and those of the "second Darwinian revolution" during the most recent conjunction of the 1960s). That this particular Uranus-Pluto conjunction included Neptune in the alignment is aptly suggestive of the dominant oceanic motif of Anaximander's evolutionary theory, and of the extraordinary imaginative and intuitive leap required for such a speculation at that time.

The Uranus-Neptune theme of *cosmic epiphany,* especially one revealing a spiritual dimension of the universe, is superbly expressed in the Pythagorean revelation of the transcendent harmony of the spheres that unites astronomy and music in a divinely ordered whole. It is expressed as well in Pythagoras's use of the word *kosmos* to describe a living universe that is pervaded by spiritual intelligence, beauty, and structural perfection. In Pythagoras we also see that *unity of science and religion,* the complete absence of categorical boundaries, which represents another frequent Uranus-Neptune motif. As regards the *creative emergence of esoteric traditions,* which we have so often observed in coincidence with later Uranus-Neptune alignments, we see in the founding of the Pythagorean brotherhood and philosophy a wellspring of those several Western esoteric traditions for which Pythagoras was the ancient origin and revered charismatic authority.

Another characteristic Uranus-Neptune motif in evidence during this epoch was the *birth of new forms of artistic expression,* visible in the beginning of tragic drama and the actor's role believed to have been initiated by Thespis (from whose name the word "thespian" is derived). Again, we see the diachronic cyclical pattern here: the first great tragedian, Aeschylus, emerged during the immediately following Uranus-Neptune opposition; in 485 BCE he won the first of his many first prizes in the annual Athenian festival, and he went on to write ninety plays altogether in the course of his long life. Shakespeare, his Renaissance heir, was born during the Uranus-Neptune opposition two millennia later.

The emergence of new artistic forms and creative genius was also beautifully embodied during the period of the triple conjunction in the luminous figure of Sappho, who beginning in the 580s flourished precisely during this period. Not unlike Pythagoras, a spiritual charisma has come to be attached to Sappho as the high priestess of the isle of Lesbos who presided over a feminine cult of love, beauty, and poetry. Even in the few extant fragments, it is evident to us many centuries later that her work represented not only a creative breakthrough of the poetic imagination but also a profound psychological shift in the posture of the artist. Sappho brought forth a newly personal, emotionally intimate form of poetic disclosure. She creatively transformed lyric poetry in both technique and style as she moved from the tradition of poetry written from the perspective of gods and muses to one expressing the personal vantage point of the individual. Writing in the first person, depicting love and loss as these affected her personally, she seems to have mediated through her art a distinct advance in the impulse towards individuation that was then emerging in the Greek psyche.

We can also recognize in Sappho two significant Uranus-*Pluto* themes that we saw consistently in correlation with that cycle in later centuries, such as during the 1960s, 1896–1907, 1845–56, and the 1790s: first, the *social empowerment of women*; and, second, *Dionysian awakening and erotic liberation*. The distinct presence of the full archetypal complex associated with the three planets in combination can be sensed in the pronounced depth of feeling and intensity of lyrical expression that marks Sappho's work, a revelation of eros overpowering in its visceral and instinctual potency (Uranus-Pluto) that is inextricably intertwined with the poetic, romantic, and imaginative dimensions of her art (Uranus-Neptune).

> That man seems to me on a par with the gods
> who sits in your company and listens to you so close to him
> speaking sweetly and laughing sexily,
> such a thing makes my heart flutter in my breast,
> for when I see you even for a moment,
> then power to speak another word fails me,
> instead my tongue freezes into silence,
> and at once a gentle fire has caught throughout my flesh,
> and I see nothing with my eyes, and there's a drumming in my ears,
> and sweat pours down me, and trembling seizes all of me,
> and I become paler than grass,
> and I seem to fail almost to the point of death in my very self.

Something of the Shakespearean eruption of romantic-erotic intensity is present here, a lyrical inflection of the Dostoevskian brain fever, and a suggestion of Whitman's full-bodied poetic eros as well. The same three planets were in dynamic alignment in every instance, but this time as a triple conjunction.

The compression of these dazzling wonders of the ancient world—cultural, religious, scientific, philosophical, artistic—into a brief period in exact coincidence with the Uranus-Neptune-Pluto conjunction was paralleled in the contemporary architectural magnificence of Nebuchadnezzar's imperial capital of Babylon. The reign of Nebuchadnezzar as King of Babylon from 605 to 562 BCE coincided almost precisely with the entire epoch. During that period he restored virtually every temple in the empire over which he presided. Babylon was a great city of palatial grandeur, with monumental public buildings faced with brightly colored enameled tiles, canals, broad avenues, winding streets, and the Hanging

Gardens filled with exotic flora and irrigated by waters carried from the Euphrates.

It was this Babylon that was the setting and crucible for the great metamorphosis of Judaism that took place during this epoch. The capture and destruction of Jerusalem in 586 by Nebuchadnezzar and the deportation of most of the Jewish population to Babylonian captivity took place in exact coincidence with the world transit of *Saturn* in close square alignment to Pluto and Neptune (just before Uranus reached close conjunction with the other two outermost planets). In the ensuing decades, the profound response of the Jewish prophets to those cataclysmic political and spiritual events essentially wrought the transformation of Judaism into a world-historic religion characterized by a monotheistic universalism and an ethical individualism. The writings of Jeremiah and Ezekiel during this era expressed a radically new emphasis on the individual's relationship to God. Those of the Second Isaiah, born during the triple conjunction, brought forth an especially powerful declaration of a loving God sovereign over all history and all humanity, inspiring generations to come with a vision of hope for the ultimate arrival of the kingdom of God that would liberate his people from the sufferings and injustices of the present age.[13] The metamorphosis of the prophetic imagination at this time became the source of inspiration for countless religious figures and movements in later centuries, including many utopian and millennialist visions that emerged again and again during later cyclical alignments of the Uranus-Neptune cycle, from the New Testament period to the twentieth-century civil rights movement:

> Thus saith God the Lord, he that created the heavens, and stretched them out; he that spread forth the earth, and that which cometh out of it; he that giveth breath unto the people upon it, and spirit to them that walk therein: I the Lord have called thee into righteousness, and will hold thine hand, and will keep thee, and give thee for a covenant of the people, for a light of the Gentiles; to open the blind eyes, to bring out the prisoners from the prison, and them that sit in darkness out of the prison house.

> The voice of him that crieth in the wilderness, Prepare ye the way of the Lord, make straight in the desert a highway for our God. Every valley shall be exalted, and every mountain and hill shall be made low: and the crooked shall be made straight, and the rough places plain: And the glory of the Lord shall be revealed, and all flesh shall see it together.
>
> (Isaiah 42:5–7; 40:3–5)

We have seen the three-planet combination of Uranus, Neptune, and Pluto before, in the quadrature configurations of the sixteenth and nineteenth centuries when we discussed the epochal struggles and complex clashing of powerful forces visible in the lives and works of Shakespeare, Galileo, and Dostoevsky. With these paradigmatic figures in mind, we can perhaps to some small degree grasp how overwhelming a transformation of consciousness the Axial Awakening of the sixth century BCE wrought in innumerable human beings across the civilizations of the ancient world, from China and India to Persia, Babylon, Israel, and Greece: the destruction of the old and the birth of the new, the unprecedented shifts in the perception of reality, the epoch-making power of the revelations, the awakening of radically new religious, philosophical, and scientific perspectives—indeed the very birth of philosophy and science as our civilization came to understand them, and the birth of religious traditions that are to this day foundational for the human community. Moreover, in regard to the social aspect of religious evolution, the Axial Age opened up for humanity the possibility of direct engagement with the divine much more widely to individuals, to mystics, prophets, philosophers, and sages whose religious experience and spiritual authority represented an emancipation from the archaic social hierarchy of divine kingship that had previously mediated such experience.

As we consider the advancing Uranus-Neptune cycle and the diachronic patterns of archetypally connected cultural phenomena that unfolded during subsequent alignments, like the births of Platonism and Christianity, we can recognize that many of the great religious and philosophical epiphanies of the Axial Awakening were centered on a profound and enduring *transformation in the experience of the numinous.* This transformation took radically divergent forms in the various civilizations and traditions—Buddhist, Taoist, Confucian, Jainist, Zoroastrian, Judaic, Greek—each differing in basic ways from each other and developing divergent orientations within their own traditions. The commonality in these various transformations was the disclosure of both a new possibility of relationship and a newly potent distinction, which often became a radically polarized dichotomy, between a reality of ultimate and radically superior spiritual value and a reality perceived as intrinsically or provisionally inferior. The two realities were discerned and defined on many levels, which often overlapped: the divine world of eternity and the empirical human world of flux and finitude, the ontologically primary and the derivative, the transcendent and the immanent, spirit and matter, good and evil, light and dark, above and below, the perfect and the imperfect, the one and the many, reality and illusion, Brahman and maya, nirvana and samsara, the Tao and the conventional world, the kingdom of God and the secular world, the redeemed future and the fallen present, salvation/ enlightenment and the dark imprisonment of the ordinary human condition, the philosopher-prophet-mystic-sage and the unilluminated.

Each religious tradition developed these differentiations and strove to overcome them in diverse ways, those in Asia doing so with far different spiritual and philosophical outcomes from those of the West. Upon these polarities was established the spiritual and intellectual foundation for a great deal of the historical evolution of human consciousness that has transpired since that age, especially in the West, where these dichotomies were especially pronounced and consequential. In a Hegelian and Jungian spirit, one could say that this epochal revelation of dynamically related metaphysical opposites in human experience began a great evolutionary process of dialectical tensions and syntheses, a process in which our own era is now fully engaged.

The great Axial Awakening of the triple conjunction period was an extremely complex phenomenon, a *fons et origo* with multiple streams. From the moment of their emergence, each of the many religions and philosophies that were born or transformed during this epoch contained an internal complexity that was creatively developed and differentiated in the ensuing centuries. Each stream underwent multiple ramifications, internal divisions, and new divergences seemingly in every possible manner. The new autonomy of the individual, the new capacity for a reflexive awareness that is aware of itself, the new will to question the received and the given, the challenges to long-established religious beliefs and assumptions, the prophetic and philosophical defiance of secular powers and conventional values, the new role of mystics and sages, the new modes of artistic expression that supported greater individuality and critical reflection on the human condition, the general emerging impulse away from the local and towards the universal and away from the traditional and towards the novel, and, not least, the awakening to a transcendent reality that ultimately sought a new kind of incarnation in the world of human history and aspiration: all these crucial characteristics of the Axial epoch set in motion processes that unfolded and dialectically developed in the succeeding centuries and millennia.

From one perspective, then, we can recognize the archetypal dynamics of the triple conjunction as an expression of the titanic evolutionary power, depth, and intensity of the Plutonic principle impelling and empowering the archetypal phenomena of the Uranus-Neptune cycle the alignments of which coincided so consistently with the births of new religions, mystical awakenings, cultural renaissances, artistic revelations, new philosophies, utopian visions, and cosmic epiphanies (Pluto→Uranus-Neptune). In this view, the basic phenomena of the Axial Age during the triple conjunction are clearly those we have seen as characteristic of the Uranus-Neptune cycle, but here they are given an epochal intensity and enduring transformative potency by the presence of Pluto.

From another perspective, we can recognize the archetypal vector during the period of the triple conjunction as one in which the Neptune principle spiritualizes and gives religious, metaphysical, and imaginative form to the characteristic Uranus-Pluto cycle phenomena of sudden radical change and revolutionary upheaval, widespread empowerment of creativity, and an intensified collective impulse towards progressive innovation and the striving for new horizons (Neptune→Uranus-Pluto).

Finally, we can approach the triple-planet archetypal complex during this period of the Axial Awakening as an expression of the Promethean principle of Uranus as it suddenly and unexpectedly liberates, awakens, and catalyzes the characteristic phenomena associated with the Neptune-Pluto cycle (Uranus→ Neptune-Pluto).

The Neptune-Pluto cycle, involving the two outermost planets, is the longest of all planetary cycles, and its synchronistic historical and cultural phenomena are in certain respects the most profound and consequential. It is approximately five hundred years in length, and the intervening oppositions occur some two hundred and fifty years after each conjunction. The period of each such alignment of Neptune and Pluto on its own, with the 15° orb, lasts approximately twenty-five to thirty years, and with the broader 20° orb, more than a third of a century.

Limiting ourselves here to Western cultural history, we can briefly follow the sequence of Neptune-Pluto cyclical alignments and their extraordinarily consistent coincidence with the beginnings and endings of immense historical epochs of great cultural magnitude. As we have just seen, the triple conjunction of the sixth century BCE coincided not only with the heart of the global Axial Age but also with the rise of Greece and its rapid emergence as a world-historic civilization. The following opposition of Neptune and Pluto of 345–315 BCE coincided precisely with the climax of the classical Greek period and the beginning of the Hellenistic era in coincidence with Alexander the Great's enormous transformation of the Mediterranean world and western Asia.

The following Neptune-Pluto conjunction coincided with the full ascendancy of Rome in the age of Julius Caesar and Augustus (first century BCE), the next conjunction coincided with the fall of the western Roman Empire and the beginning of the Middle Ages (fifth century CE), the next with the beginning of the High Middle Ages (tenth century), and the conjunction after that with the end of the Middle Ages and the beginning of the Renaissance (turn of the fifteenth century). At the midpoint of the five-hundred-year modern period, the opposition alignment of Neptune and Pluto took place at the climax of the Scientific Revolution in the middle of the seventeenth century. Finally, the most recent Neptune-Pluto conjunction coincided with the great fin de siècle epoch of the last decades of the nineteenth century and the turn of the twentieth (1880–1905), which commenced the five-hundred-year cycle in which we now find ourselves.

The Neptune-Pluto cycle with its corresponding archetypal complex demands a detailed survey and analysis of its own, which I will provide elsewhere. What can be mentioned briefly here is that, besides the great epochs marking the rise and fall of civilizations suggested above, the major Neptune-Pluto cyclical alignments appear to have coincided with especially profound transformations of cultural vision and the collective experience of reality, which often took place deep below the surface of the collective consciousness. We can recognize some of its characteristic themes in the great crucible of metaphysical destruction and regeneration that Western culture passed through during the last Neptune-Pluto conjunction at the end of the nineteenth century—that end of an age and

THE NEPTUNE-PLUTO CYCLE

Axial alignments since 600 BCE

15° orb		Exact alignment <1°
590–565 BCE (BC)	*conjunction**	579–577
345–315	*opposition*	333–327
96–71	*conjunction*	85–82
150–180 CE (AD)	*opposition*	162–68
399–424	*conjunction*	410–13
645–674	*opposition*	656–662
893–918	*conjunction*	904–06
1137–1167	*opposition*	1150–55
1386–1411	*conjunction*	1397–1400
1631–1660	*opposition*	1643–48
1880–1905	*conjunction*	1891–93

20° orb adds three to five years before and after dates given for 15°.

*For the Uranus-Neptune-Pluto triple conjunction of the sixth century BCE, 20° orb:

Neptune-Pluto conjunction	594–560
Uranus-Neptune conjunction	586–566
Uranus-Pluto conjunction	583–570

transformative threshold which was symbolized in the Nietzschean transvaluation of all values, the dying of the gods that had ruled the Western spirit for two millennia and more, the subterranean dissolution of conventional Christian belief and Enlightenment assumptions, the powerful upsurge of "the unconscious" in many senses (including its first being conceptualized at this time), the global interpenetration of the world's religious and cultural traditions, and the emergence in Western culture of a range of long-suppressed and long-developing cultural phenomena and archetypal impulses that led to the intensely dynamic world of the twentieth century.

Such underlying transformations of the Neptune-Pluto eras tend to be brought to the surface of cultural life in more explicit form during the immediately following Uranus-Pluto and Uranus-Neptune alignments, often as creative breakthroughs and sudden awakenings. We saw just such a wave of events and figures in the revolutionary changes and cultural epiphanies that occurred during the overlapping Uranus-Pluto and Uranus-Neptune oppositions at the beginning of the twentieth century. These immense, evolving transformative impulses in the deep collective psyche brought forth a further cyclical eruption of intensified cultural creativity and change during the next Uranus-Pluto conjunction of the 1960s. This brings us to the Uranus-Neptune conjunction of our own time.

The Late Twentieth Century and
the Turn of the Millennium

Our final example of the Uranus-Neptune cycle is the most recent conjunction, which was within 15° of exact alignment from 1985 to 2001. Seen more broadly in its 20° span, this alignment extended through 2004, and the correlations in the later stages suggested the usual "sunset" phenomenon at the close of an extended and cumulative archetypal development.

Looking back over this extraordinary period of the late twentieth century and the turn of the millennium, we can recognize that virtually every one of the major categories evident in past Uranus-Neptune eras played a dominant role in the life of the world community during this most recent alignment: the widespread spiritual renewal of the age, the astonishing multiplicity of spiritual paths and traditions from many cultures and eras disseminating and merging throughout the world, the burgeoning of religious movements in Latin America, Africa, Russia, and East Asia, the Islamic revival in the Middle East and elsewhere, the rapid spread of Pentecostalism and other Christian missionary initiatives on many continents. We can discern the familiar signs of the Uranus-Neptune archetypal complex during this conjunction in the pervasiveness and intensity of contemporary Western interest in Buddhism, Sufism, Hinduism, and Taoism, in meditation and mysticism, in esoteric traditions and mythology, in Jungian and archetypal psychology, in transpersonal theory and consciousness research, in shamanism and indigenous traditions, in nature mysticism, in the convergence of science and spirituality, and in the emergence of holistic and participatory paradigms in virtually every field.

Yet this era was an unusually fluid and complexly ambiguous one, both intellectually and spiritually, and this fluidity and complex ambiguity were similarly reflective of the same archetypal gestalt. Another equally characteristic motif of the Uranus-Neptune cycle that was evident during the period of this alignment was the decisive emergence of "postmodernity," which developed and in many ways climaxed intellectual and cultural impulses that were set in motion in the late nineteenth and early twentieth centuries during the convergence of outer-planet alignments discussed at the end of the last chapter. Increasingly central to the life and vision of both academic culture and the larger society during the later 1980s and 1990s, the postmodern sensibility mediated a rapid dissolution and deconstruction of long-established structures and boundaries, roles and hierarchies, and many once-firm certainties, beliefs, and assumptions, all in the service of emancipation.

Reality Isn't What It Used to Be declared the title of a characteristic book of the 1990s summing up these postmodern intellectual and cultural developments. The recognition of both objective reality and personal identity as "constructed," as having no independent ground, as being a kind of social myth, with all the liberating and disorienting ramifications of this recognition, was a dominant theme of this era. The postmodern epistemological critique of modern science and its claims to possessing a unique or intrinsically superior access to objective truth played a similarly pervasive role in the cultural life of this period. This critique and dissolution of established structures of belief extended to the presumption of intellectual, spiritual, and cultural hegemony on the part of Western civilization more generally, and it simultaneously undermined and liberated the Western mind, from both within and without.

Essential to this era and precisely reflective of the Uranus-Neptune archetypal gestalt was the widespread sense that the collective Western consciousness had entered into a liminal state that was situated fundamentally between paradigms—unprecedentedly free-floating, uncertain, epistemologically and metaphysically untethered and confused, yet in its radically pluralistic flexibility open to possibilities and realities not permitted in the arena of conventional collective discourse in earlier generations.

A deeply consequential expression of this archetypal complex took place in the international political arena with the rise of perestroika and glasnost during the Gorbachev era in the Soviet Union in exact coincidence with the beginning of the Uranus-Neptune conjunction in the mid-1980s. From this time, a gradual movement towards increased political openness and flexible innovation emerged in what had until then been perhaps the most tightly closed and armored society on the planet. Another sign of the same archetypal complex that emerged during these same years was the extraordinarily widespread and spirited awakening to an impulse for global unity and peace that was felt by both sides of the Cold War schism as well as by the larger international community. In Europe, the entire period of the Uranus-Neptune alignment was dominated by the political and economic movement towards the establishment of the European Community, which dissolved long-established national boundaries and societal structures in favor of a continent-wide community of freely circulating people, ideas, and goods. In all these contexts, the impulse towards unification and peace was closely associated with—and catalyzed by—the increasing dissolution of global barriers (Neptune) by the rapid spread of communication technologies (Uranus).

The new impulses and developments in the Soviet Union and Eastern Europe during the second half of the 1980s that were characteristic of the Uranus-

Neptune complex—emancipatory, unitive, innovative—did not arise smoothly but rather precipitated considerable resistance and strife. Throughout just these years, from 1985 to 1991, Saturn was in a rare triple conjunction with Uranus and Neptune, the only one of the twentieth century. The tensions between the old order and the new, the various collapsing structures and destabilizations, and the increasing loss of faith in the communist dream—a collective shift of consciousness widely catalyzed by television broadcasts that crossed borders and revealed the reality of life beyond the Iron Curtain—all reflected themes typical of these planetary complexes in intricate tense interplay.

It was precisely when Jupiter moved into close opposition alignment to this triple Saturn-Uranus-Neptune conjunction from the summer of 1989 to the summer of 1990 that the revolutions that swept Eastern Europe took place, as did the release of Nelson Mandela and the beginning of the end of apartheid in South Africa. The atmosphere of collective euphoria in the witnessing of seemingly miraculous sudden radical change, almost entirely nonviolent, accompanied by a definite spiritual dimension (as articulated by Václav Havel, for example), was eloquently reflective of the characteristic archetypal themes associated with the combination of Jupiter, Uranus, and Neptune. The fall of the previously impenetrable Berlin Wall and the dismantling of the long dividing barrier between East and West Germany took place with such astonishing speed that reporters and photographers were forced to run frantically simply to record it. As the Associated Press reported: "And wherever the dike collapsed, rivers of cheering, weeping Germans burst through." Here we see the characteristic Neptunian metaphors—rivers of people weeping—combined with the Saturn-Uranus motif of suddenly collapsing structures, amid the Jupiter-Uranus themes of euphoria, dazzling speed, and freedom's sudden victory.

The liberation not only of millions of people from the oppression of Soviet communism but of the collective consciousness of the international community from the imprisonment of the Cold War and its constant threat of nuclear apocalypse precisely coincided with the period of this multi-planet alignment. Also appropriate to the Uranus-Neptune complex in particular was the decisive spread throughout the world of the democratic ideal in the years of the conjunction. The synthesis of the emancipatory Promethean impulse with a mythically embodied idealism was vividly illustrated in the spring of 1989 by the appearance in Tiananmen Square of the Goddess of Liberty statue constructed by Chinese student rebels.[14]

The spectacular transformation of both individual and collective experience produced by the rapid development and dissemination of high technology, above all the personal computer and the Internet, is of course basic to an understanding of this entire era and is equally reflective of the characteristic motifs of the Uranus-

Neptune archetypal complex. Here we can briefly note a few major themes that clearly reflect the combination of Uranus and Neptune: the synthesis of techno-logical innovation with radical changes in consciousness, the unprecedented speeding up of the flow of information and the internal experience of life, the ceaseless stream and instantaneity of communication produced by email, the sense of unlimited interconnectivity, the accelerated dissolving of boundaries (re-lational, global, economic, epistemological). The experiential dimension of these changes clearly reflects the Uranus-Neptune complex in the sudden, liberating and, to many, bewildering opening up of unlimited networks of connections and access to new sources of data. So also the addictive, druglike, trance-inducing aspect of Internet use.

Equally suggestive of this archetypal gestalt are such characteristic terms and metaphors as "cyberspace," the "World Wide Web," "surfing the datastream," "hypertext," and the dynamic and nonlinear amorphous "sea" of virtually infinite sources of information, complexly interconnected through hypertext links, all mediated by genie-like search engines that have revolutionized the search for and transmission of knowledge. The many allusions to the Internet as facilitating the emergence of a "global mind," "Gaia mind," the "Teilhardian noosphere," and "Indra's net," with Internet connections, high-speed fiber-optic cable (much of it undersea), and wireless technology that can potentially link every individual node of consciousness to every other on the planet, clearly reflect the Uranus-Neptune archetypal complex. We can also recognize the distinctive signs of this planetary combination in the widespread utopian, even mystical aspirations that emerged during these years in direct connection with the new technologies.

Many characteristic Uranus-Neptune themes were evident in the sciences during these same years. The rise of theories of hyperspace, alternative realities, virtual particles, invisible dark matter and dark energy, and multidimensional string theory (with the universe composed of strings "so small that a direct ob-servation would be tantamount to reading the text on this page from a distance of 100 light-years") all suggest this archetypal gestalt. Similarly reflective of the Uranus-Neptune complex is the increasingly popular "multiverse" theory, with our universe seen as but one of countless other universes existing in other di-mensions, with new self-reproducing inflationary universes being endlessly pro-duced out of black holes and big bangs like bubbles out of an infinite sea of bubbles. Here we see the spontaneous rise in the scientific mind of Neptunian metaphors and qualities (sea, bubbles, infinity, invisible dimensions of reality, un-fettered speculative imagination) combined with Uranian themes (astronomical science, surprising new realities, ceaseless cosmic creativity and new beginnings).

More generally, the rapid rise of cosmology itself and the catalyzing of crea-tive cosmological speculation during this alignment is a correlation we have observed repeatedly in association with the Uranus-Neptune cycle. Such specu-lations and theoretical advances were greatly accelerated throughout these years by new data made possible by improved telescope technology, computer-based image processing, satellites, and probes (much as Galileo's telescope provided a similar stimulus for new understandings of the solar system and the cosmos centuries earlier during another such alignment). Remarkably, at the beginning of the Uranus-Neptune conjunction, the first images of the planets Uranus and Neptune themselves were sent back to Earth by Voyager II, in 1986 and 1989, respectively. Evidence for the existence of planets outside our own solar system was demonstrated in a series of discoveries beginning in 1989, with more than one hundred extrasolar planets discovered by the end of the alignment period. The Cosmic Background Explorer (COBE) satellite's discovery, announced in 1992, of primordial ripples in the cosmos that date from three hundred thousand years after the big bang provided unprecedentedly precise information for such crucial cosmological parameters as the deep structure, geometry, and expansion rate of the universe. Yet the most spectacular stream of revelations was provided by the Hubble Space Telescope, "the single most important instrument ever made in astronomy."

Launched during the Jupiter-Uranus-Neptune alignment of 1989–90 that also coincided with the fall of the Berlin Wall and the Velvet Revolution, the Hubble Telescope transmitted images year after year during this conjunction that made possible an extraordinary series of astronomical advances. Its four hundred thousand parts making it perhaps the most complex instrument ever constructed, the space telescope enabled astronomers to calculate the age and expansion rate of the universe and opened human vision and the human imagination to cosmic realities across vast distances in both space and time. Countless discoveries were announced during the alignment. As the end of the Uranus-Neptune conjunction approached in 2004 (and in coincidence with the Jupiter-Uranus opposition that occurred one full cycle and fourteen years after that of its launch), the Hubble made possible the deepest telescopic view into the universe ever obtained by humankind. Among the ten thousand new galaxies it revealed were what appeared to be infant galaxies that emerged during the first half-billion years after the big bang, in the "dark ages" before the formation of stars was possible.[15] The era of the Uranus-Neptune conjunction was repeatedly celebrated by both scientists and journalists as having produced a "golden age" and a "renaissance" in astronomy.

The character of much scientific discourse and theory during this period suggested yet other expressions of the same archetypal complex, such as the growing ascendancy of systems theory, complexity theory, and chaos theory with their focus on ever-shifting networks of relationship, nonlinear dynamics, and the complex interdependence of living systems. Here too could be mentioned the widespread popularity of holistic and participatory scientific perspectives such as those of David Bohm (wholeness and the implicate order in physics), Ilya Prigogine (the theory of dissipative or non-equilibrium structures in chemistry), Rupert Sheldrake (morphic field theory in biology), Barbara McClintock ("a feeling for the organism" in biological and genetic research), Edgar Morin (transdisciplinary complex holism in both social and physical sciences), Stuart Kauffman and the Santa Fe Institute (self-organization and complexity in evolution), Humberto Maturana and Francisco Varela (the theory of autopoeisis and enactive co-creation of reality in cognitive neuroscience), and Ervin Laszlo (the postulation of a "psi field" that acts as an underlying cosmic plenum or superfluid energy sea that conserves all information and conveys interconnected patterns of coherence), among many others.

Several overlapping Uranus-Neptune motifs were often visible in a single theory, as in Mark and Dianna McMenamin's "Hypersea" hypothesis in geology and evolutionary biology, in which the subject matter examined, the metaphors used, and the principles posited all reflect this specific archetypal field (sea and ocean, fluid interconnectedness, symbiosis, all terrestrial life forms in their extraordinary diversity seen as a single intricately nested inclusive life form joined by its inner sea of nutrient-carrying body fluids). Suggestive of yet other motifs of this archetypal complex are Terrence Deacon's work on the evolutionary consequences of symbolic cognition (*The Symbolic Species*) and George Lakoff's and Mark Johnson's exploration of the pervasively metaphorical character of human perception and understanding (*Metaphors We Live By*). The sharp rise in interest in a multidisciplinary "science of consciousness" during the 1990s expressed in many conferences, journals, and academic programs is another characteristic expression of the Uranus-Neptune complex.

An expecially vivid reflection of this archetypal field was the rapprochement between science on the one hand and religion, theology, and spirituality on the other that was visible in the countless books and symposia devoted to such themes during the decade of the 1990s. The widely followed dialogues held between Western scientists and the Dalai Lama, as well as the decade-long research project that studied the biology and neuoroscience of meditation pursued in cooperation with the Dalai Lama and Buddhist monks that was begun in 1992, were typical expressions of the Uranus-Neptune complex that was constellated in the collective psyche at this time. The "neurology of religious experience" became a notable subject of scientific research and public discussion. Equally characteristic of this archetypal impulse was the widespread aspiration to reconcile religious perspectives with evolutionary theories, whether by synthesizing ancient Asian mystical ideas with contemporary Western science, generating theories of intelligent design shaped by biblical principles, or developing sophisticated philosophical and cosmological conceptions influenced by such thinkers as Teilhard de Chardin and Alfred North Whitehead.

A radically heightened fluidity and openness entered into the major religious traditions of the world during this era: Christian, Jewish, Buddhist, Hindu, Islamic, Taoist, the various indigenous and shamanic streams in South and North America,

Africa, and Australia. The complex interminglings, dialogues, and creative fusions of these traditions took place, both within cultures and within individuals, with unprecedented speed and depth during the years of this Uranus-Neptune conjunction. Within the specific traditions themselves, major reformations and even revolutionary developments took place, with creative changes in ritual, doctrine, hierarchical structures, and practices. Many of these changes reflected the influence of the emancipatory streams that had developed during previous Uranus alignments, moving the mainstream religious traditions to become more democratized and antihierarchical, more socially emancipatory across genders and sexual orientations, and more socially and politically engaged.

More specifically, this period brought a many-sided impulse in the various religious traditions to open themselves to the embrace of values clearly associated with the Uranus-Neptune archetypal complex of meanings—to become less rigidly structured and separate, more relational, more open to the whole, more ecological and cosmological, more integrally embodied, more directly experiential, more open to the mystical dimension of religion, more pluralistic and dialogical, more oriented to the larger world community, and, in many senses of the word, more participatory. All these developments are suggestive of a catalyzed Promethean impulse that expressed itself through and within the domain of Neptune—religion and spirituality, the dissolving of boundaries, the movement towards unity and interconnectedness.

Apart from these more liberalizing trends, the period of this conjunction coincided with that general heightening of religiosity throughout the world that has been a characteristic theme of Uranus-Neptune epochs. Many Christian movements—Pentecostal, evangelical, charismatic, revivalist, holiness—during these years underwent dramatic growth that began in local communities and moved out into the world through both traditional missionary efforts and the disseminating powers of electronic communications media. Driving the growth was an upsurge of charismatic phenomena, intensely emotional religious rituals, faith healings, rebirth experiences, numinous visitations, and other forms of personal spiritual transformation. The era's heightening of religiosity took a wide diversity of forms in many religions—dramatically in Islam but scarcely less so in the resurgence of Russian Orthodoxy and Slavic Catholicism, the spread of Mormonism, the rise of Korean megachurches, of grassroots Chinese movements, of South American syncretistic churches—that were all clearly suggestive of a strongly constellated Uranus-Neptune complex in the collective psyche.

As the major religious traditions underwent these various developments and transformations, with consequences that remain unforeseeable, much of the characteristic spiritual dynamism of the age took place outside the traditions. The influx of esoteric and mystical impulses into the collective psyche during the period of this conjunction was especially pronounced, as in the spread of Buddhist Vipassana meditation, Christian esotericism, and new forms of gnosticism.

The remarkably widespread wave of intensified interest in the world's mythological traditions in the aftermath of the posthumous broadcast of the Joseph Campbell interviews in the spring of 1988 is indicative of this larger movement in the culture. In the later 1980s and throughout the 1990s during this conjunction, the national best-seller lists in the United States often included an unusually high proportion of works written by Jungian and archetypally oriented authors such as Campbell, Robert Bly, Thomas Moore, Clarissa Estes, Marion Woodman, and James Hillman, and the word "soul" was in the titles of countless popular works.

Such journals as *Gnosis*, *Alexandria*, *Parabola*, *Common Boundary*, *The Quest*, *Culture and Cosmos* (England), *Esoterica* (United States), *Esotera* (Germany), and *Universalia* (Prague) became widely popular and were accompanied by a renewal of interest in mysticism, Hermeticism, Gnosticism, Pythagoreanism, the Kabbalah, theosophy, and anthroposophy. Scholarly conferences and books were devoted to topics such as divinatory practices in classical antiquity, the history of Hellenistic astrology, the use of psychoactive entheogens in the Eleusinian mysteries, shamanic rituals in the Amazon rainforests, esoteric currents in Renaissance art and thought, the origins of the Mithraic mystery religion, Byzantine magical practices, feminist perspectives on Tantric Buddhism, sacred geometry in Western architecture, the Rosicrucian Enlightenment, alchemy and the Hermetic tradition in seventeenth-century Prague, and the like. The combination of the astronomical and the esoteric-mystical was reflected in heightened popular interest in archaeoastronomy, Stonehenge and the Pyramids, Native American star prophecies, the Mayan calendar, and Harmonic Convergences.

Fictional works that explored metaphysical and esoteric subjects, such as *The Celestine Prophecy* and *The Da Vinci Code*, were read by millions. The highest-selling books throughout the world during this alignment were J. K. Rowling's series of Harry Potter novels about magic and the occult arts (beginning with *The Sorcerer's Stone* or *The Philosopher's Stone*, the original explicitly alchemical British title—in 1997 during the triple conjunction with Jupiter). Other characteristic Uranus-Neptune themes and topics—mystical near-death experiences, life after death, past lives, angels, auras, channeling, divination, developing the intuition and creative imagination, dream interpretation, the tarot, the I Ching, yoga, t'ai chi, holistic healing methods, mind-body healing, spiritual healing, prayer circles, bringing spirituality and social idealism into business practice, the spiritual dimension of ecology, spirituality and gender healing, dance as a spiritual path, art as a spiritual path, spiritual pilgrimages to sacred places around the world, mystical poetry—flooded the collective consciousness during the period of this conjunction. The best-selling poet in North America during the 1990s was the thirteenth-century Sufi mystical poet Rumi, in numerous translations.

More generally, the Uranus-Neptune complex was evident in what appeared to be the collective awakening of a spiritual and existential desire to merge with a greater unity—to reconnect with the Earth and all forms of life on it, with the global community, with the cosmos, with the spiritual ground of life, with the community of being. This archetypal impulse was visible as well in the new awareness of and invocation of the *anima mundi,* the soul of the world, the archetypal dimension of life, and in the widespread call for a reenchantment of the world—the reenchantment of nature, of science, of art, of everyday life. The archetypal gestalt associated with Uranus-Neptune especially could be discerned during this era in the nearly ubiquitous urge to overcome old separations and dualisms—between the human being and nature, spirit and matter, mind and body, subject and object, masculine and feminine, intellect and soul, cosmos and psyche—and to discover a deeper integral reality and unitive consciousness.[16] All these tendencies can be understood as expressions of the archetypal impulse associated with the *coniunctio oppositorum,* the conjunction of opposites, and the *hieros gamos,* the sacred marriage. This impulse, reflecting Hermetic, Kabbalistic, and Christian mystical themes that, as we have seen, correlated with past Uranus-Neptune alignments, was articulated most recently by Jung, in the context of depth psychology, in coincidence with the preceding opposition and square alignments of this same cycle, as discussed above.

With all these impulses and developments at work, a certain quality of spiritual expectation concerning a shift in the ages seemed to be overtaking the collective psyche. Prophecies from many traditions abounded and were read against the backdrop of heightened historical urgency produced by accelerating geopolitical, nuclear, and ecological developments in the world. The heavens themselves produced unusual and spectacular phenomena during this conjunction, as with the extraordinarily vivid appearance of the Hale-Bopp comet, the widely viewed dramatic crashing of the Shoemaker-Levy 9 comet into Jupiter, and the preternaturally bright Mars as it orbited nearer to the Earth than at any time in recorded history. Other phenomena such as the continuing mysterious appearance of highly complex crop circles throughout the world provided a terrestrial counterpart to this celestial spectacle, as did increasingly unpredictable and strange weather patterns, the melting of the polar ice caps, and scientific predictions of global climate change. The combination of these diverse phenomena compelled some to call to mind the ancient biblical prophecy: "And I will show wonders in heaven above, and signs in the earth beneath."

The collective psyche's highly activated thirst for spiritual transcendence and holistic unities during this period also displayed the problematic side of this archetypal complex, which was visible in a wide range of less exalted impulses and behaviors. The intensified religious consciousness of the age gave rise to many New Age infatuations and eccentric cult movements while simultaneously inspiring and bolstering fundamentalist fanaticisms in many religions throughout the world. Cults as diverse in their beliefs as Heaven's Gate, the Solar Temple, Aum Shinrikyo, and the Branch Davidians all reflected the heightened religiosity and metaphysical suggestibility of the era. Self-encapsulating religious communities and belief systems encouraged varying forms of world-rejection that ranged from the isolationist to the suicidal.

Especially consequential were certain characteristics of the widespread evangelical Christian revival in the United States, which often took the political form of an unreflective reactionary conservatism. In its active mode, this revival aggressively asserted "biblical values" against those of a pluralistic secular society and sometimes combined this assertion with a messianic nationalism (especially catalyzed during the Saturn-Pluto alignments discussed earlier, as in 2000–04). In other instances, the evangelical impulse, much like certain streams in the New Age movement, was combined with an inward-turning withdrawal from active engagement with the complex challenges of modern life and a willful ignorance of the ecological and economic realities of the international community. Especially suggestive of the Uranus-Neptune complex was the widespread belief in an imminent mass "rapture" that would result in the instant physical disappearance of Christian believers as they would be suddenly swept up into the celestial realm with Jesus, leaving behind a world that would descend into apocalyptic tribulation. Over forty million copies of the "Left Behind" series of novels disseminating this belief were sold between 1995 and 2004, second only to the Bible among Christian religious texts in the extent of its readership. The climax of the series came in 2004—appropriately in coincidence with the Jupiter-Uranus opposition as well—with the publication of the twelfth volume, *Glorious Appearing*, which described the triumphant return of Jesus to the world.

More generally, an intensified psychological tendency towards escapism and denial, passivity and narcissism, credulity and delusion was widely in evidence, aided by a radically increased collective immersion in the artificial reality created by the mass media. These tendencies and pathologies reflect the shadow side of the Uranus-Neptune complex, as does the saturation of the collective consciousness by technologically produced hyperstimulating images signifying nothing. Particularly reflective of this complex was the widespread hypnotic fascination with and addiction to image ("image is everything") and a collective tendency towards acute epistemological confusion—the conflation of the real with the virtual and illusory, part-fiction biographies and histories, dramatized news, government video releases disguised as television news reports, political spin, docudramas, infomercials, "reality shows," Internet rumors, fabricated news stories and fraudulent journalism, plagiarized scholarship and term papers, the electronically accelerated dissemination of the unsubstantiated and the spurious— a continuous display of postmodern relativism in vulgar form subtly infecting and shaping popular culture. All these suggest the shadow side of Neptune (illusion, disorienting dissolution of boundaries, confusion and conflation, deception and self-deception, fantasy, image, mesmerized passivity) as catalyzed by Uranus (high-speed electronic technology, innovation, the thirst for excitement and stimulation, the new, the ever-changing).

Such themes were epitomized in the dominant MTV video aesthetic, which became increasingly pervasive during the period of this alignment from the mid-1980s through the 1990s. Rapidly shifting disjunctive juxtapositions of images driven by repetitive musical rhythms produced a form of mass-hypnotic entertainment that thrived on dissolving the structures of narrative rationality and personal identity. These cultural tendencies were in turn combined with a widespread susceptibility to and obsession with addictions of all kinds—drugs, alcohol, consumerism, television, mindless channel surfing, celebrity media coverage, video games, pornography, the Internet—all suggestive of the problematic side of the Neptune archetypal principle: addictive, escapist, narcissistic, illusory, mesmerizing. These and many other forms of intensified *maya* in the global culture compromised the positive potential of such other characteristic Uranus-Neptune phenomena as interactive electronic multimedia, artificial intelligence, the development of spectacularly creative cinematic special effects, and virtual reality.

As we have repeatedly seen, such a combination of positive and problematic manifestations of the same archetypal complex during a particular planetary alignment is altogether characteristic of the historical evidence we have explored in this book. Yet it is in periods of alignments involving Neptune that a quality of irresolvable ambiguity, fluidity, and epistemological confusion seems to be especially prominent. Where does one draw the line between the positive and problematic in many of the above phenomena? Who is to draw such a line? The archetypal perspective suggests something like a metaperspective on this issue, for the radically interpretive, perspectival, situated, and relative nature of all judgments reflects a philosophical position—one might call it postmodern reflexivity—that is itself precisely expressive of the Uranus-Neptune archetypal complex. This viewpoint and mode of consciousness became pervasive during the years of the Uranus-Neptune conjunction, with multiple consequences that have been simultaneously freeing and disorienting. In the end, as in past alignments of this planetary cycle, the outcome was the emergence of a radically heightened creative fluidity and metaphysical flexibility in the collective consciousness of our time.

Many of the most controversial and challenging developments of this era can be seen as reflecting a characteristic vector of the Uranus-Neptune complex—the dissolving of boundaries into unities through technology and change—in its negative form: the loss of distinct cultural traditions, languages, religions, and communities through the mass media, globalization, immigration and assimilation, diffusion and appropriation, thereby provoking many tensions and defensive reactions. A similar dynamic can be recognized in the arts and intellectual property that has resulted from the digitization of all information and the potentially universal instantaneous free access to download music, films, images, and texts—"content"—from the Web. All these were susceptible to technological revisions and intersplicings with results that ranged from the creative and amusing to the distortive and falsifying. Even the characteristic mode of sociopathic adolescent rebellion during this period—the dissemination of strategically deceptive computer viruses through the World Wide Web—reflected another aspect of the Uranus-Neptune complex.

The extraordinary rise of the cell phone with its many complex sociological and psychological ramifications in the 1990s is an especially vivid symptom of the Uranus-Neptune gestalt. Its nearly ubiquitous use by the end of the Uranus-Neptune conjunction period had not only dissolved boundaries between individuals and locations in ways never before experienced, it also made permeable the boundaries between those on the cell phone and those in their physical vicinity—in restaurants, subways, airports, sidewalks—who could not avoid hearing the conversation and absorbing the other's private reality into their own. The widespread use of cell phones also produced with unprecedented frequency the phenomenon of experiencing multiple realities simultaneously: individuals conversed on the phone while meeting or partying with others, doing homework, driving in traffic, or walking down the street, remaining continuously engaged, often intensely so, in another world—"multitasking." Such situations, repeated countless times daily across the world, also contributed to the increasing emergence of "virtual communities" of relationship and dialogue, often combined with a virtual disappearance from the immediate physical context. Several people might be physically present in the same location yet for all practical purposes were invisible to each other as they engaged in conversations with others not present.

The mobility of the phones provided not only an unprecedented degree of accessibility but also frequent confusion and disorientation (and sometimes deliberate deception) about where the person on the cell phone was located at that moment, which might be just outside the door or in a country on the other side of the globe. Interaction across multiple time zones became a daily experience. This condition of "nonlocality" was paralleled in the world of cyberspace and the Internet, there combined with the widespread phenomenon of users adopting multiple virtual identities in chat rooms and other Internet forums. An especially characteristic form of nonlocality that widely emerged at this time was the experience of many well-informed individuals, embedded in the electronically mediated lifeworlds of cyberspace and global television, who found themselves more intimately aware of the state of the world and distant regions of the planet than of their own neighborhood. All these newly emergent qualities of experience in the collective psyche—the dissolving of boundaries, unlimited interconnectivity and accessibility, nonlocality, multiple realities, virtual realities, multiple virtual identities, disorientation, confusion, illusion, global interconnectedness and unity, all mediated by the new technologies—eloquently reflect various distinct expressions of the Uranus-Neptune archetypal complex.

Just as the era of the 1960s with its Uranus-*Pluto* conjunction displayed both a powerful emancipatory creative dynamism and a destructive unleashing of instinctual energies in almost every area of human activity, so also the period of this most recent Uranus-*Neptune* conjunction displayed a distinctly bivalent expression of the relevant archetypal impulses, almost equally divided between the admirable and the problematic. Yet whether they took positive or negative forms, the relevant phenomena during both conjunctions showed the distinctive qualities corresponding to the specific archetypal principles associated with the two outer planets in conjunction at that time. In this very indeterminacy lay both the potential creative freedom and the moral responsibility of the individual and the human community to engage and enact these archetypal forces in the most life-enhancing manner.

Comparing the Sixties and the Nineties

The 1960–72 period was the first era whose correlations we examined in this book's survey of outer-planet cycles. Here at the end of this survey we may now find it valuable to compare and contrast the two periods—roughly the Sixties and the Nineties—that coincided with the only conjunctions of the outermost planets in the past hundred years. The next such conjunction, between Uranus and Pluto, will not occur for another century. For *two* such conjunctions of the outermost planets to occur in a single generation is a rare phenomenon, affording us a special opportunity for historical comparison. Both periods are recent enough that for many readers the comparison can rest as much on direct knowledge and experience as on the historical record. This particular comparison also has the advantage of dealing with two conjunctions that had one planet in common, Uranus, so that we can observe both the distinct archetypal similarities, related to the presence in both cases of the highly activated Prometheus principle, and the archetypal differences, related to the presence of Pluto in one alignment and Neptune in the other.

Let us briefly compare the two periods in several categories of cultural phenomena, using as shorthand "the Sixties" to encompass the full period of the Uranus-Pluto conjunction that began about 1960, was exact in 1965–66, and extended into the early 1970s; and "the Nineties" to encompass the full period of the somewhat longer Uranus-Neptune conjunction that began in the mid-1980s, was exact in 1993, and extended through the 1990s into the beginning of the new millennium.

The set of archetypal qualities shared in common by the two eras can be discerned easily enough, and indeed, the similarity between the Sixties and the Nineties has been repeatedly remarked upon. Both were periods of extraordinarily rapid change, and each era was notable in its own way for the widespread destabilization of previously established structures, accelerated creativity, and a radically heightened impulse towards emancipation and experiment. All of these themes of course reflect the Prometheus archetype associated with Uranus, the planet common to the two alignments. Within that archetypal commonality, the differences between the two eras can to a remarkable degree be recognized as reflecting the dominant archetypal presence of Pluto in the 1960s and of Neptune in the 1990s.

Politically, the Sixties were characterized by a volcanic eruption of revolutionary and emancipatory activity that affected virtually every area of human experience. Even the antiwar demonstrations that called for peace and love were infused with an often uncontrollable elemental heat, an overwhelming visceral intensity that repeatedly spilled over into violence and fierce confrontation. Virtually every major university campus in the United States was the site of extremely charged confrontational rebellion, and most of the major cities incurred massive fiery destruction in the urban riots of the decade. By comparison, one thinks of the Velvet Revolution and indeed almost the entire revolutionary collapse of the Iron Curtain in the 1989–90 period, which were accomplished with virtually no bloodshed, a phenomenon that was almost inconceivable until it happened. It was as if a subtle but pervasive liberating shift of the collective consciousness had suddenly emerged in nation after nation, so that long-established structures rapidly dissolved before one's eyes. This "revolution by dissolution," as it has been called, is precisely reflective of the two forces at work in the Uranus-Neptune complex, and is as applicable to the World Wide Web and the computer-driven revolution of global commerce and corporate structures as to the radical changes that occurred in the political domain during the same period.

An equally reflective illustration of this contrast between the two eras can be found in China. Beginning in the mid-1960s, during the Cultural Revolution initiated by Mao Zedong, tens of thousands of young Red Guards brought forth an eruption of raging instinct, astonishingly violent on a vast scale for years, that affected millions and caused immense destruction throughout the country, all in the name of revolution and freedom. This tableau of political frenzy during the Uranus-Pluto conjunction can be seen in sharp contrast to the actions of the gentle student rebels in Tianenmen Square in China in 1989 during the Uranus-Neptune conjunction, with their Goddess of Liberty idealism and the enduring image of pacifist defiance and pathos that was embodied by the lone student standing unprotected yet quietly resistant in front of the advancing tanks of the Chinese military.

Similarly, the African-American civil rights movement of the 1960s, despite the nonviolent policy of King and many others (which began during the Uranus-Neptune square of the 1950s), moved steadily through the Uranus-Pluto decade towards the heightened militancy of the Black Power movement, the rise of the Black Panthers, armed takeovers of university buildings, and the "Burn, baby, burn" desperate violence of the countless urban conflagrations of the decade; again, over 120 cities were torn by riots just in the one summer of 1967. By contrast, the Million Man March in 1995 during the Uranus-Neptune conjunction was marked by mass prayer and collective expressions of religiosity, an explicit spiritual impulse and call to unity characterized more by evangelical than revolutionary fervor. Even in the aftermath of the 1992 Los Angeles riots (during the

Saturn-Pluto square), what was heard most poignantly and enduringly was the brief final utterance by the central figure in the drama, Rodney King, in his cri de coeur for a humane community of peaceful tolerance and mutual sympathy, "Can't we all get along?"

Of course the historical shift from the one era to the other is not one of simple contrast. In the examples cited for the period of the Uranus-Neptune conjunction, we can see both the definite continuation of emancipatory impulses and the highly charged drive towards radical change that decisively arose during the Uranus-Pluto conjunction in the 1960s. As discussed in earlier chapters, the underlying archetypal forces that emerge during a specific alignment do not suddenly cease after the alignment is over but continue to unfold in a multitude of ways. These subsequent manifestations are significantly shaped by the new contexts of the later epochs, and informing these new contexts, I believe, are the new archetypal dynamics of the later eras, which correspond to the new planetary alignments then taking place in the various unfolding cycles. It is not, therefore, a matter of simplistically comparing two eras as if they were entirely distinct and separate Newtonian objects. Rather, to use a homely (albeit Olympian) metaphor, the process more resembles the passing of a baton, which is carried into the new context. The later era seems to *contain the earlier within it* in a causally efficacious manner, and continues to embody and evolve the dominant archetypal impulses that explicitly emerged during the earlier planetary alignment. But it does so in a way that distinctly reflects the changing archetypal dynamics of the new era, corresponding to its own specific convergence of planetary alignments.

The feminist revolution during the Uranus-Pluto conjunction of the 1960s, for example, was centered above all on achieving the empowerment and personal autonomy of women—political, economic, sexual—as the means for and measure of their liberation. This powerful impulse continued throughout the following decades, evolving and critically redefining itself year by year. During the Uranus-Neptune conjunction of the later 1980s and 1990s, the feminist impulse expressed itself in a new diversity of forms, many of which favored the cultivation of what were experienced and identified as "feminine values": greater holistic awareness in various forms, with an emphasis on intuition and empathy, relational sensitivity, ecological embeddedness, a more fully embodied consciousness, creative pluralism, the preference for peaceful dialogue over competitive aggression, nurture and care, the dignity of the maternal, the sacredness of childbirth, with all these values and qualities often associated with explicitly spiritual themes. A new recognition and cultivation of "women's ways of knowing" emerged, reflecting epistemological orientations different from those of the mainstream modern mind.

During the later 1980s and 1990s, the spiritual and religious dimension of feminism became far more pronounced than it had been in the 1960s. The affirmation of women's spiritual authority in religion became a central concern, with widespread pressure to permit the ordination of women as ministers and priests, often in defiance of conservative authorities, and with similar developments in Jewish, Buddhist, and other religions. The increased recognition of the feminine dimension of the divine, the rapid rise of a movement that sought to recover a "Goddess tradition" of religious imagery and ritual, the growth of the Wiccan movement and the invocation of an "Earth wisdom," the emergence of ecofeminist spirituality, the increasing popularity of Sophianic Christianity, the upsurge of interest in and reported visions of Mary in Roman Catholic popular piety, and the founding of academic programs in women's spirituality during this period all suggest the constellation of the Uranus-Neptune archetypal complex. Historical perspectives were similarly configured through this lens, as the pioneering archaeological work of Marija Gimbutas was embraced by many as demonstrating the existence in ancient Europe of a peaceful egalitarian and matristic society that reflected the primacy of spiritual and aesthetic values. Such perspectives encouraged fresh renewals of a utopian idealism not unlike other forms of utopian visions we have seen associated with Uranus-Neptune alignments in the past, but now centered on the restoration of women and the feminine dimension of existence to the center of cultural and spiritual life.

A parallel shift can be observed in the history of gay and lesbian emancipation in these two eras. Again, the dominant impulse that emerged in the 1960s and early 1970s was the assertion of personal freedom, political empowerment, and sexual liberation. While these aspirations continued to be significant in the following decades, they were joined by new concerns and values that reflected themes characteristic of the Uranus-Neptune conjunction that began in the mid-1980s. Partly under the impact of the AIDS epidemic (which started during the Saturn-Pluto conjunction in the period just before the beginning of the Uranus-Neptune conjunction), a new spirit of compassionate service focused on healing, altruistic sacrifice of often heroic proportions, and the recognition of the spiritual dimension of life emerged. As this period progressed, through the 1990s and the turn of the millennium, the collective impulse in the gay and lesbian community increasingly reflected an affirmation of relational and spiritual values, expressed through an insistence on the right to enter into marriage sanctioned by both religion and civil society, and to serve as priests, ministers, and bishops in positions of religious authority in the free and open exercise of their spiritual beliefs.

Science and Technology

Scientific theories during the Uranus-Neptune conjunction were influenced by this archetypal gestalt in highly visible ways as well. First among these was the postmodern deconstructive recognition that all such theories were radically affected and permeated, usually unconsciously, by nonempirical factors—gender, class, race, ethnicity, language, myth, personal ambition, the human impulse towards self-aggrandizement, the urge to control or conquer nature, and so forth.

While the basic revolutionary insight into the nature of paradigms first decisively emerged during the 1960s in the aftermath of Thomas Kuhn's *The Structure of Scientific Revolutions* of 1962, it was during the later 1980s and 1990s that this insight became pervasive in both the academic world and popular culture. Nor was it simply a matter that Kuhn's theory became more widespread. Rather, it was further developed and revised in specific archetypally appropriate ways, having been articulated, for example, in new, more psychologically nuanced forms, such as the feminist turn given Kuhn's theory by Evelyn Fox Keller and Carolyn Merchant, the ecological turn given by the work of Theodore Roszak and Ralph Metzner, and the transpersonal and archetypal inflections given by the work of Stanislav Grof and James Hillman.

Specific disciplines within the sciences appear to have been significantly affected by these shifting archetypal dynamics from the one era to the other. For example, cosmological theory in the 1960s was dominated by the discovery of the cosmic background radiation that gave powerful evidence for the big bang theory of cosmogenesis. The sudden liberation of unimaginably potent elemental forces at the birth of the cosmos, driving cosmic evolution in a massive centrifugal explosion of energy and stellar matter from an extremely hot, dense primordial condition, is superbly reflective of the Uranus-Pluto archetypal complex, simultaneously Promethean and Dionysian in mutual activation. While this theory continued to be developed during the succeeding decades, a shift occurred in the 1990s, partly because of new information mediated by the Hubble Space Telescope, as new and more complex multidimensional cosmological theories emerged that incorporated processes and phenomena scarcely conceivable by the ordinary human imagination—not unlike the situation that resulted from the Einsteinian relativity revolution during the last Uranus-Neptune opposition at the beginning of the twentieth century.

Another facet of the same complex that was visible in the field of cosmology during the Uranus-Neptune conjunction was the extraordinary rise of theories of cosmological evolution that specifically integrated a spiritual dimension. This impulse was evident in a range of forms, including John Barrow and Frank Tipler's widely discussed proposal of an anthropic cosmological principle in which certain universal constants in cosmic evolution are seen as precisely calibrated to permit the existence of human life, and various spiritually suggestive statements by prominent scientists such as the astronomer Allan Sandage's declaration that the big bang could only be regarded as a "miracle." The same impulse was expressed more comprehensively during this alignment in the development of a "sacred cosmology" and spiritually informed vision of cosmic evolution, Teilhardian and Whiteheadian in inspiration, by such thinkers as Thomas Berry, Brian Swimme, and David Ray Griffin. Each age reconfigures its cosmology, its historical perspectives, and its evolutionary metanarratives in accord with its own zeitgeist, one of whose most exact indications is, I believe, the specific state of archetypal dynamics associated with the planetary configurations of the time.

The metamorphosis of the Gaia hypothesis from the 1960s to the 1990s displays the same archetypal progression. In its original formulation by Lovelock in the late 1960s, the Gaia hypothesis was principally a theory concerning the dynamic interrelationship of the Earth's physical, biological, and chemical processes, which suggested that the Earth was a systemically integrated web of life with emergent properties of self-regulation. In the course of the 1980s and 1990s, the Gaia hypothesis came to be seen by the wider culture as the basis for a more spiritual and mythopoetic orientation towards ecological issues, whereby the Earth was regarded not only as an intricately self-sustaining and self-organizing life system but as Gaia herself, the Earth goddess, a cosmic being of sacred status and value in the universal scheme of things. Despite attempts by the scientific community and Lovelock himself to restrict the hypothesis to entirely scientific and naturalistic parameters, the term "Gaia" in the discourse of the wider culture was increasingly associated with an attitude of reverence towards all forms of life on the planet, with sacred rituals and invocations, and with an ecological activism ultimately informed by spiritual values and an underlying sense of mystical unity with nature.

Theories of biological evolution during the two eras also suggest a shift of the dominant archetypal influences corresponding to the two different planetary conjunctions. Characteristic theories of human and primate evolution in the Sixties were embodied in widely disseminated works by Konrad Lorenz, Robert Ardrey, and others that emphasized the struggle for survival and the innately aggressive, territorial, sexually rapacious naked ape—generally imaged as a male hunter—all strongly suggestive of the Uranus-Pluto archetypal complex. By contrast, research and theories in the Nineties, as reflected in the work of scientists such as Jane Goodall and Frans de Waal, emphasized innate tendencies towards cooperative behavior in primates, the relational imperatives of the community, the greater role of maternal factors, ecological embeddedness, creative play, and distinctive signs of an emergent consciousness and even an emergent morality in nonhuman animals. Comparable shifts in scientific theory and research in these years occurred in related fields such as interspecies communication and cultural anthropology.

The scientific exploration of space in the two eras presents an analogous pattern of development. We have repeatedly observed the close association of Uranus and the Prometheus archetype with the scientific-technological impulse to break free of gravitational constraints, explore new horizons, ascend into the air and into outer space, and open up the possibility of a fundamentally new relationship to the cosmos. The difference between the Uranus-Pluto conjunction period of the 1960s and the Uranus-Neptune conjunction of the 1990s is instructive. The Sixties saw the titanic achievement of the first manned space flights and climaxed in the Moon landings, which required the deployment of unprecedentedly powerful technologies of propulsion to break through the gravitational pull of the Earth and to reach intended destinations in outer space. The entire trajectory, from the first flights by Gagarin and Shepard in 1961 to the last Moon landing in 1972, took place precisely during the only Uranus-Pluto conjunction of the twentieth century. By contrast, the most exciting advances in the exploration of space during the 1990s were largely centered on and made possible by the technological breakthrough of the Hubble Space Telescope and the flood of unprecedented images and new vistas of the cosmos that it afforded, with immediate consequences for cosmological theory and the astronomical imagination.

The Hubble Telescope of the 1990s captured public attention more than any scientific venture since the space program and Moon landing of the 1960s. The Promethean principle of technological breakthrough and liberating advance associated with Uranus was vividly present in the major space activities of both decades, but the activities of the 1960s had a distinctly Plutonic quality and potency while those of the 1990s were distinctly Neptunian, when nearly all such efforts were concerned with electronically transmitting new images, which radically shifted the cultural vision and stimulated the cosmological imagination, revealed the previously invisible, opened up the possibility of new and multidimensional realities, and aroused feelings of cosmic wonder and spiritual awe. Even the space station, one of the few space projects of this era that involved astronauts rather than instrumental probes and telescopes, was of a different character from that of the 1960s' feverishly competitive "space race." Instead, the space station constituted a multinational collaborative effort, one dedicated to forming globally cooperative and collective living arrangements in space, themes that distinctly echo the idealistic, boundary-dissolving, utopian impulses of the Uranus-Neptune complex.

Interestingly, efforts during the 1990s to repeat or extend the manned space explorations of the 1960s consistently collapsed while the more archetypally apt observational activities flourished. Conversely, just as the Uranus-Neptune conjunction approached the 20° point in 2004, the Hubble Telescope, in the absence of regular maintenance, began to lose its functionality. The National Aeronautics and Space Administration provisionally decided to cut funding for the future maintenance of the Hubble Telescope in favor of future manned space expeditions to the Moon and Mars, which it has scheduled, coincidentally, for the period when Uranus next moves into alignment with Pluto in the 2010s.[17]

The dominant technologies of the two decades also closely reflect the two different archetypal complexes, Uranus-Pluto and Uranus-Neptune. The characteristic technologies of the 1960s were not only the rocket-powered propulsion of the space flights but also other technologies of a similarly Promethean-Plutonic nature such as nuclear power and jet propulsion, as deployed in the rapid proliferation of nuclear power plants and global jet aviation during that decade (including, for example, the development of the supersonic Concorde, whose first flights took place in 1969). By contrast, the dominant technologies of the 1990s involved the nearly invisible silicon chip, subtle rather than titanic in its workings, which brought a radical expansion and acceleration of the computer revolution and the rapid development of a plethora of digital, multimedia, and communication technologies. Here too could be mentioned the emerging vision of molecular nanotechnology as the foundation for a future manufacturing revolution. Above all, the new technological capabilities of this decade were expressed not in rocket propulsion and nuclear power but in the rapid pervasive shift of the collective consciousness produced by the high-tech dissolution of global, commercial, relational, and epistemological structures and barriers—all characteristic Uranus-Neptune motifs. These technologies were in turn often associated with utopian, esoteric, and mystical ideas and impulses.[18]

A family of sciences and technologies that appears to be especially correlated with the Uranus-Neptune cycle is that of chemistry and biochemistry, microbiology, genetics, and pharmacology. In this category, the Promethean impulse—scientific, experimental, liberating, defying limits, bringing sudden breakthroughs, opening new possibilities of human autonomy with respect to nature—is combined with such Neptunian themes as the chemical and liquid, the microscopic and invisible, processes involving fusions and mergings, and a concern with healing, drugs, and chemically influenced changes in both the body and the psyche. The diachronic correlations in this category can be recognized historically as going back to the ambiguous borderline of alchemy and chemistry, as in the work of Robert Boyle, a student of alchemy and a pioneer of chemistry, whose experiments began in 1654 during the Uranus-Neptune conjunction of the 1650s. Lavoisier, the founder of modern chemistry, was born in 1743 during the immediately following Uranus-Neptune opposition. Gregor Mendel, the founder of genetics and the discoverer of the laws of heredity, was born in 1822 during the immediately following conjunction, and his major discoveries were first published during the years 1865–69, in exact coincidence with the following Uranus-Neptune square. This sequence of quadrature alignments continued: Mendel's advance remained unrecognized until, as discussed earlier, it was simultaneously rediscovered by three different scientists and the science of genetics was first named by William Bateson, all in 1900, just as the following Uranus-Neptune opposition was beginning.

The quadrature sequence continued yet again: It was during the immediately following Uranus-Neptune square alignment in 1953 that Francis Crick and James Watson discovered the double-helix structure of the DNA molecule at the Cavendish Laboratory, and thereby revealed the means by which inherited characteristics are transmitted from one generation to the next. Finally, completing the quadrature cycle, it was during the Uranus-Neptune conjunction of the late 1980s and the 1990s that these developments came to a climax in the Human Genome Project, the rapid acceleration of biotechnological science and industry, recombinant DNA research, and widespread experimental genetic manipulation of cell tissue, plants, and animals. The first successful genetic cloning, of the sheep Dolly, took place in Scotland in 1997 (coinciding as well with the most recent Jupiter-Uranus conjunction), and the first successful cloning of a human embryo took place in 2004 in South Korea at the end of the Uranus-Neptune alignment period (during the most recent Jupiter-Uranus opposition in a diachronic sequence with Dolly's cloning).

Related to these developments are the many rapid advances made in pharmacology, virology, microbiology, and immunology. A plethora of new drug treatments for physical and mental illnesses, from immune-system diseases such as AIDS to mood disorders such as depression, emerged during the period of this alignment. Especially notable have been the social ramifications of pharmacological experimentation and its many products such as Prozac, Zoloft, Viagra, and Botox that have been widely embraced in contemporary society. We see reflected in these technological innovations a characteristic family of Uranus-Neptune qualities that are variously consciousness-altering, psychologically liberating, and concerned with affecting either external image or what is subjectively apparent ("cosmetic psychopharmacology"), and that dissolve the boundary between reality and illusion. The enormous number of individuals, children and adolescents as well as adults, who during the 1990s were prescribed psychoactive drugs for such psychological conditions as hyperactivity or depression and whose experience of reality was significantly defined by chemical technologies is strongly suggestive of the Uranus-Neptune archetypal complex. So also is the explosive use of steroids, human growth hormone, beta-blockers, and other performance-enhancing drugs in athletic and other activities in those years. In a diachronic pattern, a similar wave of pharmaceutical breakthroughs and social consequences took place in the 1950s during the immediately preceding Uranus-Neptune square with the development of the polio vaccine and antibiotics, and also of tranquillizers and antipsychotic drugs, such as Thorazine, which have played a large role in medicine and psychiatry ever since.

We can also recognize the familiar motifs of the Uranus-Neptune complex in this same area at the theoretical level, where neurochemistry and brain research have essentially dissolved the boundary and distinction between the brain's ever-changing "natural" biochemical condition and "drugs," many varieties of which the brain itself produces. A similar theoretical state is evident in the field of genetic research, where the subtle interplay between genetic and environmental factors in shaping human behavior, health, and disease is now recognized to be so complex in its recursive interaction as to defy any reductive causal understanding. The manner in which any specific gene will express itself in a given individual will be affected by the action of other genes, chemicals in the cell, various biographical circumstances, and the prenatal environment. Not only has the nature vs. nurture dichotomy been dissolved in this complex interplay but the role of human volition and activity is recognized as a further crucial factor that can unpredictably affect the outcome of the already fluid genetic-environmental interaction. The Uranus-Neptune archetypal motifs are thus visible across the range of themes cited: the technical breakthroughs in fields such as neurochemistry and genetics, the intellectual awakenings that dissolve previously assumed boundaries and distinctions, the new recognition of the mutual interpenetration of contributing causal factors, the fundamental indeterminacy of such fluidly interactive complexity, and the unpredictable role of autonomous human intervention in shaping the ultimate outcome of this fluid multicausal interaction.

The Arts

We see an equally striking contrast and archetypal shift between the two eras in the arts. Again, as we explored in the Uranus-Pluto chapters, the popular music of the 1960s was driven by an unprecedented elemental force. On the one hand, it was Promethean in its insistent impulse towards liberation, creative freedom, improvisation, protest, and rebellion, as well as in its technological empowerment through electricity. On the other hand, the music was emphatically Dionysian in its erotic and rhythmic power, with themes of sexual freedom, political revolution, and sympathy for the demonic, instinctual, and shadow elements of the human psyche. While such themes and impulses have continued since that decade, from indie rock to hip-hop, the Uranus-Neptune conjunction of the later 1980s and 1990s distinctively coincided with such archetypally appropriate musical developments as the emergence of world music, bringing a fusion of and creative interplay between multiple musical genres from different continents and cultural traditions, and the rise of electronica, electronic trance, and New Age music. Especially characteristic of the Uranus-Neptune complex has been the emergence of a pervasive postmodern "sampler" culture in which DJs employ digital mixing technologies to produce an improvisatory collage of musical genres such as hip-hop, techno, ambient, minimalism, chants, and world music, interspliced with samples from various past recordings and genres. Practitioners speak of developing a multimedia art form involving the creative mixing of any sound, image, or text from the entire collective memory of humankind.

Also reflective of this archetypal field has been the widespread occurrence during this conjunction of various "technospiritual" ritual musical events (Uranus as the technological, Neptune as the spiritual). This was notably exemplified by the extraordinary phenomenon of raves, in which every weekend in large cities, wilderness areas, and beaches throughout the world, beginning in 1988 and extending through the 1990s and beyond, millions of youths participated in mass dance events using Ecstasy and music to enter ecstatic unitive states that dissolved interpersonal boundaries and elicited experiences of self-transcendence and spiritual euphoria.[19] Regarded by many as a crucible of youth spirituality during the 1990s, raves were seen as having "transmuted the role that organised religion once had to lift us onto the sacramental and supramental plane."

During those same years occurred the equally extraordinary phenomenon of the Grateful Dead's concert tours. Though they originated in the 1960s, it was in coincidence with the Uranus-Neptune conjunction from the mid-1980s until Jerry Garcia's death in 1995 that they essentially became mass rituals of transformation attended faithfully by hundreds of thousands in large venues throughout the world. The widespread popularity of the band Phish, so similar to the Dead in the spirit of its countercultural idealism, cult following, and improvisatory concert rituals, exactly spanned the entire Uranus-Neptune conjunction period. The annual Burning Man Festival that arose during this same period displayed the same combination of archetypal motifs relevant to the Uranus-Neptune gestalt: collective ritual transformation, unconstrained experiment and creativity, the technological and the spiritual combined with rebellion and eccentricity, ubiquitous use of psychoactive drugs and sacred visionary plants, a cultivation of the nonordinary in both consciousness and free self-expression, and the formation of a temporary utopian community that encouraged both extreme creative individualism and unitive states of collective merging.

Similarly reflective of the same impulse, though with a very different inflection, was the rapid spread of electronically amplified "praise and worship" music and Christian rock in large ritual services and evangelical music tours in which thousands of young Christians participated. These technologically enhanced events characteristically ended with the appearance of the words "Sacred Revolution" on giant video screens, another suggestion of the Uranus-Neptune complex. Here too can be mentioned the spread during this time of cyberchurches, interactive virtual religious ministries and communities; and rave masses, free-spirited liturgies accompanied by rock and trance music introduced by Anglicans in England in the early 1990s and brought to the United States soon after by the dissident Catholic priest Matthew Fox.

Equally suggestive of the Uranus-Neptune archetypal complex was the sudden rise of popular interest in the sacred music of other cultures and eras, such as Indian kirtans and Gregorian chant, and their creative assimilation into modern musical idioms. We can recognize here a distinct diachronic pattern of major creative periods in the history of sacred music in coincidence with Uranus-Neptune cyclical alignments: the wave of religious masterworks by the great polyphonic composers Palestrina and Tallis during the Uranus-Neptune opposition of 1556–74, coincident with the era of Teresa of Ávila and John of the Cross; by Bach and Handel during the following Uranus-Neptune opposition of 1728–46 coincident with the era of the Great Awakening (Mass in B Minor, *Saint Matthew Passion*, *Messiah*); and by Beethoven and Schubert during the following conjunction of 1814–29 coincident with the age of Romanticism (*Missa solemnis*, the spiritually idealistic Ninth Symphony, *Ave Maria*, the six masses), to name a few iconic examples.

A continuation of this diachronic pattern can be discerned in major works of sacred and spiritually profound music in the twentieth century, where again specific qualities reflective of the Uranus-Neptune archetypal complex—numinosity, a mystical spirit, the evocation of religious wonder—were vividly embodied in compositions during each of the quadrature alignment periods. The relevant works of Alexander Scriabin (the mystical trilogy of 1905–11, *The Divine Poem*, *The Poem of Ecstasy*, and *Prometheus*), of Charles Ives (the Fourth Symphony of 1909–16), and of Ralph Vaughan Williams (the *Fantasia on a Theme of Thomas Tallis* of 1910), were all composed during the most recent Uranus-Neptune opposition. The spiritually resonant slow movements of Mahler's Fourth and Fifth Symphonies composed during these years could also be cited. The most recent square alignment of the 1950s coincided with Alan Hovhaness's *Mysterious Mountain*, and the conjunction period of the later 1980s and 1990s brought a wave of sacred works by John Tavener (*Resurrection*, *Hymns of Paradise*) and Arvo Pärt (*Te Deum*, *The Beatitudes*), and works with explicitly spiritual themes such as Philip Glass's compositions for the films *Anima Mundi* and *Kundun*.

We can recognize this archetypal pattern as well in the cinema. Films in the 1960s were notable for an unprecedented freedom in portraying sexuality and violence, and their content focused on such Uranus-Pluto motifs as political and social revolution (*The Battle of Algiers*, *Z*, *Medium Cool*, *Adalen 31*, Godard's many films), countercultural rebellion (*Easy Rider*, *Alice's Restaurant*, *Woodstock*), space exploration (*2001: A Space Odyssey*), the criminal underworld (*Bonnie and Clyde*, *The Godfather*, *The French Connection*), eroticism (*La Dolce Vita*, *Blowup*, *Last Tango in Paris*), and the unleashed id (*Fellini Satyricon*, *If*, *A Clockwork Orange*).

By contrast, the creative breakthroughs in films of the 1990s were especially evident in the immensely expanded capacity to create special effects, computer animation, and other technologies producing *maya*-like virtual realities and multidimensional fantasias in a wide range of genres. As in form, so in content. The most widely viewed and characteristic films of the Uranus-Neptune period, while continuing the subject matter opened up in the 1960s, increasingly treated a plethora of distinctly more Neptunian subjects: myth, legend, and fantasy (*The Lord of the Rings* trilogy, the Harry Potter series), virtual realities (*The Matrix* trilogy, *The Truman Show*, *Pleasantville*), dreams, visions, magical realism (*Field of Dreams*, *The Secret of Roan Inish*, *Amélie*, *Chocolat*, *Talk to Her*, *Forrest Gump*, *Big Fish*, *American Beauty*, *Crouching Tiger Hidden Dragon*), religious and biblical subjects (*The Mission*, *The Last Temptation of Christ*, *The Passion of the Christ*), the Shakespeare renaissance (*Much Ado About Nothing*, *Romeo and Juliet*, *A Midsummer Night's Dream*, *Hamlet*, *Othello*, *Henry V*, *Prospero's Book*, *Shakespeare in Love*), the animation renaissance (*Who Framed Roger Rabbit?*, *The Little Mermaid*, *Beauty and the Beast*, *Aladdin*, *The Lion King*, *Kiki's Delivery Service*, *Princess Mononoke*, *Spirited Away*, *Toy Story*, *Chicken Run*, *Shrek*, *Finding Nemo*, *The Incredibles*), ocean and sea narratives (*Titanic*, *Whale Rider*, *The Perfect Storm*, *Master and Commander*), diverse spiritual themes (*Seven Years in*

Tibet, Kundun, Baraka, Babette's Feast, Life Is Beautiful, Dead Man Walking, The Shawshank Redemption), life after death (*What Dreams May Come, Ghost, The Sixth Sense, The Others*), unexpected shifts of reality and consciousness (*Memento, Mulholland Drive, Being John Malkovich, Adaptation, Eternal Sunshine of the Spotless Mind, A Beautiful Mind, Vanilla Sky, Artificial Intelligence: A.I., Minority Report, Contact, Big, Groundhog Day, Alice in Wonderland*).[20]

To these could be added the innumerable films of this period that engaged other characteristically Neptunian subjects such as God and divine beings of various kinds, spirits, angels, aliens, hallucinations, time travel, past lives, multiple identities and multiple realities, and the exploration of other dimensions of existence. One of the most frequent motifs in this era's films, which represented both a new technological capacity and a new metaphysical fluidity, was the "morphing" of various entities, characters, and entire environments from one form to another in an unexpected and often highly creative manner.

A comparable pattern of archetypal contrast between the two decades is discernible in the theater during the two eras. The 1960s brought many plays clearly reflective of the Uranus-Pluto archetypal field, such as *Who's Afraid of Virginia Woolf?, Marat/Sade, Hair*, and *O Calcutta!*, the Off Broadway revolution associated with Edward Albee and Sam Shepard, and the radically experimental Living Theatre of Julian Beck and Judith Malina. These developments can be contrasted with, for example, the paradigmatic drama of the 1990s, Tony Kushner's *Angels in America*, with its many visions and angelic intercessions, posthumous visitations, religious overtones, and spiritual epiphanies, and with its fantasia of imaginal ambiguities and unexpected sudden shifts among multiple fluidly intersecting realities. Yet here again we can recognize how the latter work entirely depended on and developed out of the revolutionary experiments of the 1960s. *Angels in America* brought the new Uranus-Neptune motifs into a threatrical tradition that had already been liberated from the constraints of established conventional structures and themes during the preceding Uranus-Pluto era.

We can observe a similar pattern in a specific genre such as dramas about the criminal underworld and the Mafia. The *Godfather* films of the 1960s' Uranus-Pluto conjunction represented a creative eruption of the Plutonic underworld, and also a diachronic development from the Uranus-Pluto square of the 1930s and the earlier wave of classic gangster films such as *Public Enemy* and *Scarface*. This emergence of the underworld into the collective psyche was both sustained and transformed with the dominant television drama at the turn of the millennium, *The Sopranos*. In this widely viewed and influential series, the various Uranus-Pluto motifs continued unabated from *The Godfather* epoch—the artistic revelation of the criminal underworld, shocking violence, illicit sexuality, the unleashed instincts, dark motivations, the distinctive mobster ethos and language, the incessant power struggles and ever-lurking danger of death. But in the new archetypal context of the Uranus-Neptune period, the underworld boss was undergoing unpredictable shifts of consciousness, confusing dreams with waking realities, reflecting inwardly on his motivations, and seeing a psychiatrist—taking antidepressant drugs, experiencing drug-side-effect visions and hallucinations, interpreting dreams and projections, recovering childhood memories. All these were explored with a postmodern complexity of narrative technique, multiple viewpoints, and rapidly shifting images, camera-angles, and juxtapositions. The characters themselves frequently watch and allude to films of the earlier Uranus-Pluto epochs like *The Godfather* and *Public Enemy*, which produces a characteristically Uranus-Neptune field of cinematic cross-references, mirrorings, and postmodern "intertextuality." Much like the persona of the *Sopranos'* protagonist, the boundaries of the gangster genre itself have been dissolved: the series' gangster persona constantly merges in unpredictable ways with other genres and identities—psychological drama, comedy, family drama, narrative of spiritual discovery—which subverts expectations and opens up a new multidimensional fluidity of artistic experience.

Technological innovation (Uranus) in the service of image and illusion (Neptune) is especially reflective of the Uranus-Neptune archetypal complex, and the major advances in this domain are closely associated with the unfolding alignments of this planetary cycle. Photography emerged during the Uranus-Neptune conjunction of the 1820s with the work of Niepce and Daguerre. Motion pictures rapidly emerged as a major cultural phenomenon and art form during the following opposition of the 1899–1918 period. The immediately following square alignment of the 1950s coincided with the rapid dissemination and public embrace of television, which brought with it all of its characteristic Uranus-Neptune elements, both positive and problematic. The generation of children born with this square (1950–60) was the first to grow up with television as a principal shaping influence on its consciousness and mode of experiencing the world. It was also during this alignment that Marshall McLuhan—who was born in 1911 during the preceding Uranus-Neptune opposition, in close alignment with his Sun—first developed his influential theories on technology as an extension of the human nervous system, the transformative impact of the television medium on the cultural consciousness, and the emergence of a "global village" unified and shaped by electronic information technologies (hence McLuhan's prophetic role as "father of cyberspace").

Finally, at the completion of this Uranus-Neptune cycle that began with the 1820s conjunction and the birth of photography, the conjunction of the later 1980s and 1990s coincided with the explosion of television and multimedia technologies: hundreds of cable stations accessible worldwide through satellite and high-speed fiber-optic connections (instantly selected or dismissed with a remote control device), videos and DVDs of potentially every film ever made, high-definition television, TiVos, camcorders, cell phone cameras, the digitalization of images and other forms of cultural expression, and numerous other technological advances whose rapid dissemination took place during the period of this conjunction. Also relevant to this archetypal complex are the many cultural, social, and psychological consequences of this revolution. The globalization of culture, the democratizing effect on the creation and dissemination of information, and the often catalyzing influence that television and computers have had on revolutionary social and political developments (the Eastern European revolutions of 1989, China throughout the 1990s) are all related to these technological advances. Equally reflective of the Uranus-Neptune field has been the decisive dominance of the television media in shaping the collective imagination during this era, the supplanting of the print media by the televised image, and the development of a hyperkinetic mode of visual and aural communication through rapidly shifting juxtapositions of image and sound. An especially problematic consequence of these advances has been the widespread emergence of a form of consciousness that is predominantly concerned with entertainment and consumption, and is at once passive and ceaselessly restless—hyperstimulated, fragmented, decontextualized, and ahistorical—with concrete consequences as diverse as attention deficit disorder and U.S. foreign policy.

Psychology

As a final example of the archetypal shift from the 1960s to the 1990s, we may cite the transformation of psychology, which underwent two distinct developments during the latter period, both of which reflect characteristic themes of the Uranus-Neptune complex. The dominant psychiatric approach at the end of the twentieth century, impelled by advances in pharmacology and neuroscience, and also by pressures from the insurance industry, has been to regard and treat psychological illnesses as essentially biochemical conditions that can be rectified, or their symptoms suppressed, by the use of drugs. The subjective qualities of human experience are regarded as entirely a function of biochemical conditions of the brain. This biochemical orientation can be contrasted with the dominant emphasis in psychiatry in the 1960s on the liberation of the individual from traumatic childhood experiences and repressive familial and cultural influences.

Beyond the neurosciences, conventional psychiatry, and the medical-pharmaceutical-insurance complex, however, a collective shift in the culture's psychological understanding and sensibility took place during the 1990s that reflected those deeper archetypal themes and impulses that we have observed throughout this exploration of the Uranus-Neptune cycle. Here, too, the contrast with the 1960s is readily apparent. The major innovative psychological theories and therapies that emerged during the Uranus-Pluto conjunction of the 1960s were especially concerned with the cathartic release of repressed instinctual and emotional material: The breakdown of somatic armoring, the discharge of aggression, and the achievement of orgasmic potency and erotic freedom were regarded as crucial for the attainment of psychological health. The spirit of the time, in psychology as in other areas of culture, was dominated by a synthesis of the Promethean and Dionysian impulses in mutual activation. The empowered autonomy of the individual was the overriding goal. In many writings and theories, psychological and somatic liberation was closely associated with social emancipation and political revolution. The ideas and philosophical orientation of Freud were central to these developments during the 1960s (as they had also been during the Uranus-Pluto square alignment of the 1930s), and the ideas of Nietzsche, Darwin, and Marx loomed in the background. The psychological milieu of the Sixties was pervaded by the concepts and practices of such figures as Wilhelm Reich, Fritz Perls, R. D. Laing, Norman O. Brown, Herbert Marcuse, Albert Ellis, Ida Rolf, Will Schutz, and Arthur Janov. The characteristic innovative modalities of the era were bioenergetic release, emotionally intensive encounter groups and gestalt therapy, physically intensive Rolfing and other forms of somatic intervention, the primal scream, nude marathons—all distinctly reflective of the Promethean-Dionysian archetypal complex.

In contrast to the more agonistic spirit of the 1960s, the psychological theories and therapies that emerged prominently during the later 1980s and 1990s were of a distinctly different tenor, having such key themes as the care of the soul, the awakening to the significance of the spiritual dimension of life, the integration of psychotherapy with meditation and spiritual practice, and the acknowledgment of the healing potential of numinous and religious experiences. New attention was given to the mythic and archetypal dimension of dreams, art, and religious experience. Jungian analysis, archetypal psychology, and transpersonal psychology became especially widespread and influential orientations. National newsmagazines of the 1990s noted the shift towards Jung and away from Freud as many individuals pursued psychological quests that had an emphatically spiritual character. Psychology and psychotherapy were increasingly regarded as paths of spiritual discovery and transformation that supported the task of "soul-making" (reviving John Keats's phrase and perspective that was articulated in 1819 during the preceding Uranus-Neptune conjunction). Depth psychology was now seen as an authentic *via regia* to the sacred for the post-Enlightenment age. Its character and aspirations seemed especially relevant to an era that was simultaneously secular and spiritual, restlessly experimental, globally interrelated, and pervaded by a new religious pluralism. It also provided crucial support for an era that was discovering religious symbols that for many were not adequately expressed or honored in the inherited religious traditions.

Rather than the struggle for and achievement of a sharply differentiated autonomous self, as favored in the 1960s, the attainment of psychological health was increasingly seen as better served by the cultivation of a relational self with more permeable boundaries, one capable of intimacy and reciprocity as well as self-sovereignty. New value was given to the capacity for compassionate openness to the other and the cultivation of an increased sensitivity to one's embeddedness in larger communities of being—local, ancestral, ecological, spiritual, planetary. New significance was given to the task of liberating the individual psyche from the narrow concerns and limitations of its illusory separateness, and opening awareness to the larger realities and claims of the collective psyche, the transpersonal domain, the ecological unconscious, the global community, the cosmos.

Connected to these orientations was a new recognition of the psychological importance of healing the split between inner and outer, reconnecting psyche and world, recovering the *anima mundi,* mediating "the return of the soul to the world." This recognition was in turn closely allied with the impulse to recover and revalue the archetypal feminine, in both women and men, and in both the individual psyche and the collective—restoring it to its rightful place in the psychic cosmos, and moving ultimately towards a healing integration of feminine and masculine. To a remarkable degree, each of these many interrelated impulses specifically reflected the characteristic motifs and concerns of the Uranus-Neptune archetypal complex.

Similarly, instead of the models of the psyche that dominated the 1960s, which emphasized instinctual and emotional release and orgasmic liberation, a new appreciation of the complexly multidimensional character of the psyche emerged as dominant in the 1990s. This multidimensionality took many forms—archetypal, transpersonal, integral, multicultural, multiperspectival—all of which were characterized by a new awareness of the mysterious and limitless nature of the interior universe. The healing potential of nonordinary states of consciousness, the use of entheogens and sacred medicines from shamanic traditions, special breathing methods such as holotropic breathwork, wilderness vision quests, meditative disciplines and techniques, and the study of esoteric traditions such as alchemy and Hermeticism, the Kabbalah, and Gnosticism were characteristic themes of the emerging psychological theories and therapies.[21] Many embraced the relevance of other cultures' symbol systems and religious traditions for their individual journeys of psychological transformation. The nature of symbolism itself shifted, as the Freudian approach to symbols, interpreted reductively as straightforward substitute signs of instinctual desires or fears, increasingly gave way to the Jungian approach to symbols as multivalent living principles that mediate access to deeper realities and have spiritually transformative power.

The psychological goals and models favored by the 1960s did not, of course, simply disappear. Rather, they were transformed in the new archetypal context. Sexuality, for example, remained liberated, but increasing emphasis was placed on the cultivation of a capacity for reciprocal relationship and erotic merging rather than simply the achievement of powerful orgasmic release, personal empowerment, and individual autonomy. Religious traditions of sacred sexuality, Tantric and Taoist sexual practices, and Native American approaches to the spiritual dimension of sexual experience were widely studied, and there was greater focus on transcendence of the individual self, melted ecstasy, and sacralized interpersonal fusion. Similarly, the call for a psychological emancipation that empowers political engagement, social activism, and environmental awareness continued from the 1960s but became increasingly informed by spiritual themes and associated with movements such as socially engaged Buddhism, the interfaith commitment to social justice and freedom articulated by the Jewish Tikkun community, various politically focused prayer and meditation circles, and an ecological activism that explicitly drew upon spiritual resources and the experience of underlying oneness with the Earth community. A similar pattern can be seen in the development of feminism within depth psychology from the 1960s to the 1990s, which increasingly shifted towards integrating a range of feminine archetypes, acknowledging numinous experiences of female deities from various religious and mythological traditions, and deepening the understanding of the collective unconscious to encompass the *anima mundi*.

One final example of this dynamic continuity and transformation from one era to the next is the "participatory turn" in contemporary spirituality and psychology. Here the focus on freedom, empowerment, and erotic embodiment from the 1960s joined with the postmodern pluralism and mystical-spiritual impulses of the 1990s to bring forth a call for not only an *awakening* to the spiritual and archetypal dimensions of being but an awakening to a new *relationship* to those dimensions of being—radically participatory, co-creative, pluralistic, and dialogical. Such a perspective affirmed the validity of a multiplicity of spiritual liberations in which various spiritual traditions and practices cultivate and enact, through co-creative participation in a dynamic and indeterminate spiritual power, a plurality of authentic spiritual ultimates. The ideal invoked was at once unitive and pluralistic, emancipatory and relational, socially engaged and spiritually informed, embodied and ensouled.[22]

More generally, these diverse developments during the Uranus-Neptune conjunction of the late twentieth century and the turn of the millennium can be seen as representing the cyclical activation and creative renewal of cultural impulses that we have observed as having coincided again and again with the alignments of the Uranus-Neptune cycle over the centuries. The diachronic pattern of correlations involving the evolution of the archetypal perspective from Plato to Jung is especially vivid. The widespread interest in and development of Jungian ideas and the mythic perspective in the late twentieth century, particularly in the writings of Joseph Campbell and James Hillman, Robert Bly, Stanislav Grof, Edward Edinger, Marion Woodman, Clarissa Estes, and Thomas Moore, can of course be traced back to the period of the immediately preceding Uranus-Neptune opposition of the early twentieth century, when Jung's psychology was forged. This was also when James Joyce and Thomas Mann—Campbell's other heroes whom he so often invoked along with Jung—began to create their mythically informed work. So also Rilke, who played a similar role for Robert Bly.

The tradition of imagination that Hillman invoked as the cultural stream from which archetypal psychology emerged shows a similarly remarkable correlation with the Uranus-Neptune cycle: Again, first back to Jung and the others of the early twentieth century during the last opposition; then to Romanticism, Keats, and Coleridge during the immediately previous Uranus-Neptune conjunction of the early nineteenth century; then further back to the Renaissance, Ficino, and the Florentine Academy during the conjunction of the later fifteenth century; then to Petrarch, from the preceding conjunction of the early fourteenth century; and finally back to the Greeks and the Platonic tradition that emerged from the Uranus-Neptune conjunction at the turn of the fourth century BCE. The long diachronic sequence constitutes a kind of procession of ancestors and sources of inspiration for the evolution of the archetypal perspective, which has emerged during this most recent conjunction to bring forth another creative efflorescence in new historical circumstances and with new horizons opening before it.

As we have seen, many such cultural lineages that extend back through the centuries have unfolded with remarkable consistency and precision in correlation with the Uranus-Neptune cycle. To cite one final motif: the many instances of individuals who strive for and experience a sudden recognition of an underlying pattern of meaning, what might be called the archetypal "Rosetta Stone" experience. Here could be mentioned the original Rosetta Stone breakthrough itself by Champollion in deciphering Egyptian hieroglyphics; Kepler's ecstatic discovery of the elegant mathematical laws that solved Plato's ancient problem of the planets; the discovery of the double-helix structure of DNA by Watson and Crick; the Elizabethan magus-scientist John Dee and his Kabbalistic and Hermetic quest to unveil the sacred language and mysteries hidden in nature; Pythagoras's discovery of the transcendent mathematical forms that structure the cosmos, from musical tones to the planetary motions; Newton's scientific and alchemical passion to unriddle the mystic clues that hold the key to understanding the world and history; Einstein's relativity breakthroughs—all emerging in individuals and eras correlated with alignments of the Uranus-Neptune cycle.

Here too could be cited Gregory Bateson's lifelong focus on the "patterns which connect": patterns that reveal an immanent mind pervading all of nature, and that disclose "a world in which personal identity merges into all the processes of relationship in some vast ecology or aesthetics of cosmic interaction." (Bateson defined the aesthetic faculty as "responsiveness to patterns which connect.") Especially suggestive of this motif is Jung's concept of synchronicity itself with its focus on spontaneous coincidental patterns of events that suddenly reveal unexpected meanings and an underlying unity of the inner and outer worlds. And most recently, Stanislav Grof in many lectures during the 1990s referred to archetypal astrology as a Rosetta Stone for the understanding of the human psyche. In all these, a common archetypal theme is evident: the revelation of a long-hidden pattern of intelligibility, an intangible but encompassing principle of order—often with numinous and aesthetic overtones, even in the most scientific contexts—that unifies what previously had been separate and unintelligible, and evokes a sense of sudden liberation, awakening, and unexpected illumination.

In retrospect, these two great eras of radical cultural change and creativity which coincided with the two great conjunctions of the second half of the twentieth century, Uranus-Pluto and Uranus-Neptune, can perhaps best be understood in relation to the enormous epochal transformation that was set in motion during the most recent five-hundred-year-cycle Neptune-Pluto conjunction. As discussed in the preceding chapter, this alignment extended through the last decades of the nineteenth century into the beginning of the twentieth. Historically, the axial alignments of Uranus—first with Pluto, then with Neptune—that immediately follow the conjunctions of Neptune-Pluto have coincided with periods that bring to the surface, in the form of sudden creative breakthroughs and emancipatory surges, processes that were seeded during the Neptune-Pluto conjunction. More generally, the Uranus-Pluto and Uranus-Neptune cycles which have been the focus of so much of this book appear to be associated with historical phenomena in which the Promethean principle of creativity, emancipation, and unpredictable change has dynamically impelled the long unfolding dialectic between the archetypal principles associated with Pluto and Neptune—using the traditional terminology, the dialectic between "Nature and Spirit."

The most recent Neptune-Pluto conjunction, which ended a century ago, coincided with a profound reconfiguration of the perceived relationship between nature and spirit in the Western sensibility that was visible in the ideas, movements, and figures that emerged or were born at that time—from Nietzsche to Teilhard, theosophy to depth psychology, the encounter with the unconscious to the world parliament of religions. In light of the great triple conjunction of Uranus, Neptune, and Pluto during the Axial Awakening period of the sixth century BCE, it is striking that many of the impulses established at that time more than 2500 years ago have been moving toward a climactic moment of transformation in the course of the past hundred years. Reflecting this epochal historical development, prophetic voices in the 1990s, such as the theologian Ewert Cousins, began to suggest the possible coming in our time of a second Axial awakening comparable to the first:

> If we shift our gaze from the first millennium BCE to the eve of the twenty-first century, we can discern another transformation of consciousness. It is so profound and far-reaching that I call it the Second Axial Period.
>
> In an era that has brought a global awareness to humanity for the first time, when the planet Earth with all its inhabitants can be seen in its entirety in cos-

mic space as the single celestial body that it is, and when the universe has been revealed as a creative vastness expanding through millions of galaxies and billions of years of cosmic evolution from the big bang to the present, the collective consciousness now emerging recognizes as was never before possible that all participate in a single enormous history. At the same time, that history, for humanity and the Earth community, has reached a stage of rapidly deepening crisis and peril.

As countless thoughtful observers have asserted, the future depends on how humankind meets this unprecedented moment of challenge and choice: how it negotiates the tensions between unity and multiplicity in the world's nations and religions, and how it resolves the polarity between spirit and nature in the evolving consciousness of a technologically empowered human species. The first Axial Age brought a decisive stage of differentiation and individuation to human spirituality—of the newly emergent individual self out of the collective, of the newly emergent historic religious traditions that developed their distinct orientations out of the primordial shamanic and archaic religions, and of the newly emergent reflexive human consciousness out of the primordial matrix of nature, the Earth, and the cosmos. Our time appears to represent a critical moment in which the evolutionary developments that were set in motion at that time, two and a half millennia ago, are moving to a climax, and perhaps to a new stage of cultural evolution that is more complexly dialogical and participatory in every one of these respects.

VIII

Towards a New Heaven and a New Earth

A mood of universal destruction and renewal . . . has set its mark on our age. This mood makes itself felt everywhere, politically, socially, and philosophically. We are living in what the Greeks called the kairos—*the right moment—for a "metamorphosis of the gods," of the fundamental principles and symbols. This peculiarity of our time, which is certainly not of our conscious choosing, is the expression of the unconscious human within us who is changing. Coming generations will have to take account of this momentous transformation if humanity is not to destroy itself through the might of its own technology and science. . . . So much is at stake and so much depends on the psychological constitution of the modern human.*

—C. G. Jung
The Undiscovered Self

Planetary democracy does not yet exist, but our global civilization is already preparing a place for it: It is the very Earth we inhabit, linked with Heaven above us. Only in this setting can the mutuality and the commonality of the human race be newly created, with reverence and gratitude for that which transcends each of us singly, and all of us together. The authority of a world democratic order simply cannot be built on anything else but the revitalized authority of the universe.

—Václav Havel
The Spiritual Roots of Democracy

Understanding the Past,
Creating the Future

To approach the issue of future planetary alignments in the light of the evidence we have examined so far, we must first clearly grasp the limitations of the present study. For the sake of simplicity and clarity in this initial survey of archetypal correlations with planetary movements, I have restricted the focus of this book almost entirely to a few major cycles of the outer planets. The larger astrological picture, however, is far more rich and complex, with many more interpenetrating variables. Of the three principal forms of correspondence described in this book—natal charts, personal transits, and world transits—I have focused mainly on the latter. In that category I limited the above survey to only four planetary combinations, and in those cycles to only the quadrature alignments: the conjunctions, oppositions, and squares. Cyclical alignments having a different character, such as the trine and sextile, were not included. I mentioned only briefly such significant planetary cycles as the Neptune-Pluto and Saturn-Uranus cycles, while still others, such as Saturn-Neptune, I have not yet discussed at all.

These limitations have resulted in my focusing on certain dominant themes and qualities of the periods examined while ignoring or bracketing other significant motifs that in another context I would have highlighted. Similarly, these constraints have resulted in my considering at length certain historical periods while scarcely mentioning others. The later part of the 1970s, for example, was not explored, nor were the mid-1920s, though many important cultural phenomena are associated with those periods, and the relevant planetary alignments are as noteworthy and illuminating as those we have examined. Every era has its own significance, its own nobility, its own complex drama, each with its unique pattern of unfolding planetary alignments and corresponding archetypal dynamics.

To give just one illustration of a category of correlations that we have so far not considered: An especially notable planetary alignment in Western cultural history, one that involved the trine aspect, was the rare "grand trine" configuration of Uranus, Neptune, and Pluto that took place approximately between 1765 and 1777, when the three outermost planets moved into an equilateral triangle, each being positioned in an angular relationship of 120° with the other two. Grand trines between any three planets characteristically coincide with a particularly pronounced harmonious mutual activation and interpenetration of the three archetypal principles involved. Such a grand trine of the three outermost planets occurred only once in the modern era. The period of that alignment coincided with the very height of the Enlightenment, when there took place many of that era's most distinctive milestones, such as the completion of the *Encyclopédie*, the eighteenth century's great intellectual bible of intellectual emancipation, by Diderot and the other leading philosophes. The grand trine coincided also with the beginning of the American Revolution led by Jefferson, Adams, Washington, Franklin, and others as a self-conscious expression of Enlightenment ideals and principles. Here too we can recognize the archetypal background of the distinctive numinosity, the sense of providential blessing and divinely ordained destiny, that has historically been attached to those founding events and figures. This numinosity and spiritual idealism (Neptune) was in turn radically interwoven with the impulse towards liberty and revolution (Uranus-Pluto), a complex of themes powerfully articulated later by Lincoln and, often more problematically and exploitatively, by others.

This same period of the grand trine of the later 1760s and 1770s also coincided with the great birth of Romanticism in Germany that introduced that seminal and profound cultural impulse into the European mind. From the work of Herder and Goethe in these years emerged a new conception of nature, spirit, and history—and of language and art, intellect and feeling, interiority and imagination, sensuality and spirituality, humanity and divinity—that would dramatically bear fruit, as we have seen, during the immediately following Uranus-Pluto and Uranus-Neptune axial alignments from the 1790s through the 1820s (and indeed beyond those periods to the most recent such alignments of the 1960s and 1990s). In addition, virtually the entire central generation of Romantics was born during the decade of this grand trine: Wordsworth, Coleridge, Schelling, de Staël, the Schlegel brothers, Schleiermacher, Hölderlin, Novalis.

The powerful confluence of brilliant creativity and the urge for freedom and change (Uranus), of imagination, spiritual aspiration, and charismatic idealism (Neptune), and of nature, evolution, instinct, and eros (Pluto) that began to enter into the world at this time and was then given artistic and philosophical form by the generation born during this period corresponds exactly to the character of a grand trine involving these planets and archetypal principles. Remarkably, during the period when the three planets were in especially close alignment, in 1769–70, three world-historic individuals were born whose lives and influence especially embodied this archetypal confluence: Napoleon, who was born with *Mars* on the grand trine; Beethoven, who was born with *Venus* on the grand trine; and Hegel, who was born with *Mercury* on the grand trine.

To a far greater extent than can be explored within the limits of this book, an enormous range of comparable evidence has now emerged concerning the natal charts and personal transits of historically significant individuals. The comprehensive set of data comprising all three forms of correspondence expands the evidence of synchronistic patterning to include all the archetypal combinations associated with the planets and luminaries in all their possible pairings: Sun-Pluto, Moon-Pluto, Mercury-Pluto, Venus-Pluto, Mars-Pluto, Jupiter-Pluto, etc.; Sun-Neptune, Moon-Neptune, Mercury-Neptune, Venus-Neptune, and so forth. The correlations presented in the preceding chapters involving just four cycles of world transits are thus only a highly restricted sample and illustration of this much larger body of evidence. They provide us with a limited, though still potentially valuable, foundation for looking at future planetary alignments.

Before turning our attention to the future, it will be helpful to consider briefly the way I went about assessing the evidence surveyed in the preceding chapters, and how this journey of inquiry led to a gradual transformation in my research assumptions and, more generally, my approach to knowledge.

In any sustained rigorous inquiry, many apparent anomalies will arise in the course of systematic research. Something as infinitely complicated and mysterious as human history, or even a single human life, can never be neatly comprehended by any theoretical structure, no matter how complex, supple, and encompassing that structure may be. Over the years, I would often examine biographical and historical phenomena for which I could not immediately recognize any planetary correlations that made sense in terms of the coherent patterns consistently visible in most other cases. Yet in the course of time, with more data, or with a deeper grasp of the astrological principles at work, a new horizon of understanding would often open up. I would then realize that I had been attempting to compress the data too rigidly into an inadequate theoretical structure or, conversely, attempting to apply a viable structure to inadequate or insufficiently understood data. These are problems familiar to researchers in every discipline as they work within a particular paradigm. As Kuhn and other historians of science have observed, confronting anomalies constitutes an essential aspect of the growth of knowledge and the process of paradigm change.[1]

To respond to such challenges, the researcher must engage in a constant negotiation between theory and data, reconsidering each in the light of the other in a continuous process of recursive feedback—tentatively modifying the theoretical structure, probing the evidence more deeply, patiently observing. In my case, the evidence was of two kinds, astronomical and historical-biographical, both of which had to be carefully examined and precisely compared to determine whether significant correspondences were present. The task therefore required a disciplined alertness to subtle clues of genuine patterning yet also to the hazards of distorting projection and insufficient knowledge. Like Scylla and Charybdis for Odysseus, the dangers lay in both directions: on the one side, being skeptically armored to the point of impenetrability against the possible reality of correlations that would challenge the conventional modern world view, and on the other, being uncritically overcommitted to a mass of inherited astrological theories that could promiscuously find patterns everywhere.

In the end, making proper assessments of correlations seemed to involve the continuous interplay of "multiple intelligences," to use Howard Gardner's helpful term. To maintain the double-edged alertness to both potential patterns and potential projections, the exercise of critical reason of the usual sort was crucial. But so also was something more like psychological self-awareness, with a cultivated willingness to challenge one's own structurings of reality and limiting assumptions of all kinds. The task seemed to require not only an intellectual but an emotional capacity to tolerate a state of unknowing, to withhold oneself from premature conclusions—either skeptical or affirmative—that merely bolstered one's sense of existential security at the expense of encountering the unknown.

Equally crucial was the role of aesthetic and imaginative discernment, without which the archetypal forms and patternings at the heart of the phenomenon would have been entirely invisible—or inaudible, as if the archetypal forms were a language the cosmos spoke, for those who had ears to hear. No less important was a capacity for empathic insight into the underlying character of different historical eras and diverse cultural figures. This in turn needed to be combined with a sound historical sense for what events and individuals were significant in a particular field, in what ways, and with what interconnections and lines of influence. Always, what had to be honored was the evidence—life itself, in all its complexity, particularity, and sovereign autonomy. What I sought to explore and understand seemed to demand the engagement of my whole being for it to open up its deeper patterns and meanings, its intelligibility. The long journey of research was in itself not unlike a spiritual path.

Looking back over the past three decades, I can now recognize that after a certain critical threshold was reached in both the quantity and the quality of correlations, my starting posture underwent an essential transformation of perspective similar to the one described in the Two Suitors chapter: Instead of assuming a general cosmic randomness, as one usually would, then checking skeptically for highly unlikely inexplicable coincidences that might contradict the conventional view, I now began to assume, flexibly but with some degree of confidence, an underlying order. When I encountered an event or cultural phenomenon for which convincing planetary correlations were not immediately apparent, I continued to pursue the inquiry, staying open to the possibility that a significant correlative pattern might well emerge over time as I learned more. Far more often than not, this is just what occurred. In retrospect, attending closely to anomalies resistant to understanding proved to be an important part of the research. Such an approach in the end often produced valuable conceptual breakthroughs, sometimes many years after I first encountered the challenging problem.

Yet without the starting posture of methodological openness, neither impenetrably armored nor naïvely overcommitted, the deeper and more compelling patterns would most likely not have become visible, because the starting structure of my assumptions would have impatiently precluded their eventual appearance. I found that the conventional modern assumption that the cosmos and its processes are intrinsically random and meaningless constituted an extraordinarily effective barrier to further knowledge. So also did the uncritical acceptance of many conventional astrological doctrines. Finding the middle path between these two obstacles turned out to be essential to opening a path of discovery that would not otherwise have presented itself.

As I continued the research in this manner and in this spirit, year after year, the intelligibility of the historical record began to unfold. In the preceding chapters, the reader will perhaps have observed a similar process. For both researcher and reader, the success of such an unfolding seems to require a flexible combination of critical questioning, freedom from a predisposition of closed skepticism, and patience.

Any discussion of future alignments, whether for world transits or personal transits, presents extraordinary challenges and responsibilities to the astrological researcher. Because we have seen how similar planetary configurations in the past have coincided with specific archetypal phenomena with considerable consistency, and because we can mathematically determine the upcoming alignments with great precision, one might say that, in a sense, we know something about the future. But in another sense, we do not know. I believe that the extent to which we have embraced this epistemological humility is a decisive measure of the potential value or harmfulness of our analysis. The difference between concrete prediction and archetypal prediction is something like the difference between fate and free will. Stated more precisely: It is the difference between an inevitably constraining and likely misconceived assertion of a pregiven future and the potential empowerment of a co-creative self consciously participating in an archetypally structured unfolding of life in an open universe. It could well be said that the entire modern and postmodern development of human autonomy and critical self-awareness has prepared us to be better able to walk the tightrope presented to us by the contemporary archetypal astrological perspective and evidence—in particular, by the knowledge of the outer planets' existence and their corresponding archetypal principles, by the retrospective knowledge of the historical correlations, and by the foreknowledge of future planetary alignments.

I began my systematic astrological research in the mid-1970s. In the course of the next several years the basic framework of understanding that underlies the present book emerged fairly rapidly. At that time, therefore, a number of the more recent planetary alignments I have discussed in the preceding chapters were still in the future. When I saw, for example, that a Saturn-Pluto conjunction was going to occur in the 1981–84 period, or that a much longer Uranus-Neptune conjunction would take place from the mid-1980s through the rest of the century, I tentatively anticipated that humanity's collective experience during those eras would bear something like the distinctive archetypal character I had observed in so many earlier instances of the same configurations. On occasion, I would have a specific intuition—essentially an educated guess, based on the evidence available to me—as to what kinds of concrete events might take place during a particular alignment. From the perspective of the late 1970s one could easily surmise that the upcoming Saturn-Pluto conjunction of 1981–84 might very well coincide with a period of widespread conservative empowerment, an acute increase in Cold War tensions, and a crisis in the Middle East, given the occurrence of just such phenomena during every previous quadrature alignment of the Saturn-Pluto cycle since the preceding conjunction in 1946–48 when the Cold War began and the state of Israel was born. Similarly, during the Uranus-Neptune conjunction of the later 1980s and 1990s into the new millennium, the likelihood of a sustained era of widespread spiritual awakening, heightened religious belief, and new interest in esoteric, mystical, and holistic perspectives seemed to me a fairly straightforward prospect, given the historical record.

While these anticipations of the future proved well-founded, there occurred many specific events and trends in those periods that I did not anticipate. Before it happened I did not foresee that anything like the Internet revolution and the globalizing impact of the World Wide Web would happen during the Uranus-Neptune conjunction of the 1990s, and the same is true of countless other cultural phenomena of that era discussed in the preceding chapter that I now can easily recognize as reflecting the Uranus-Neptune archetypal complex. Conversely, other possibilities that I feared might occur during these periods did not in fact take place. In the Saturn-Pluto conjunction of the 1981–84 period, when so many geopolitical circumstances clearly resembled those of the 1914–16 Saturn-Pluto conjunction two cycles earlier that had coincided with the sudden catalyzing of a global war among all the European powers and alliances, I was not entirely certain during the first Reagan administration that the world would manage to get through that conjunction without a direct and perhaps catastrophic conflict between the mutually demonizing and nuclear-overarmed Cold War superpowers—something many foreign policy experts feared at the time as well, often making explicit references to the European situation of 1914. Such an outcome seemed especially plausible given the extent to which the world situation in 1981–84 appeared to be moving towards a climax of the Cold War whose beginning had coincided with the 1946–48 conjunction exactly one Saturn-Pluto cycle earlier. A cyclical pattern seemed clear; the principal question was how it would turn out. Instead of a catastrophic conflict, however, what happened was an intensification of these global tensions and dangers, as well as many local wars, to a point that catalyzed both widespread public criticism and severe economic stresses, and eventually produced a very different outcome: the mutual effort in the second half of the 1980s by both superpowers during the Uranus-Neptune conjunction for nuclear arms control and increased diplomatic understanding, which finally led to the end of the Cold War itself in 1989–90, when Jupiter reached this alignment.

Most recently, in the case of the Saturn-Pluto opposition of the 2000–04 period, on the basis of past correlations I felt I could justifiably anticipate another period of conservative or reactionary empowerment, historical crisis and contraction, and a widespread increase of divisiveness, hostility, and mass violence in the world. The possibility certainly loomed as well of another wave of terrorist activity, just as had taken place during the preceding Saturn-Pluto quadrature alignments in the present cycle in 1981–84 and 1992–94. As I discussed earlier, astrologers knew that the Saturn-Pluto opposition would first reach exactitude in August 2001 and move into an especially challenging grand cross configuration with the Sun and Moon in September. But when the events of September 11 took place, my response was probably similar to the vast majority of astrological researchers throughout the world: We immediately knew what planetary alignment was relevant, and what archetypal complex had just been tragically and devastatingly constellated. But astrological comprehension of the *specifics* of the event, though virtually immediate, was archetypal and retrospective, not concretely predictive.[2]

In the vast majority of cases in which I have considered the likely coinciding events for future alignments, whether in my personal life, the lives of other individuals, or the life of the human community, I have been surprised—both by the many ways in which the relevant archetypal complexes *actually* manifested themselves beyond what I imagined, and by the ways in which they did *not* manifest themselves as I might have thought or feared. Instead, in countless instances, I received a new lesson in the infinite creativity of the cosmos as it unpredictably unfolded its processes and events in extraordinarily consistent archetypally patterned correlation with the ongoing planetary movements.

I am therefore far more interested in using the archetypal astrological lens for better understanding the present and the past than for predicting the future. It is indeed a powerful lens, with a range that now encompasses the trans-Saturnian planets, and a depth that now more fully registers the complex multidimensional character of the archetypal principles involved. We have, in a sense, been given a powerful archetypal telescope for a vast archetypal cosmos at the same moment that we have developed extraordinarily powerful space telescopes for apprehending the vast physical cosmos. Both kinds of instruments are immensely expanding our universe, each in its own way. But though such instruments permit an unprecedented understanding of the present and the past, their value for understanding the future is considerably more limited and subtle. The very nature of this form of archetypal understanding in relation to the concrete particulars of life requires a knowledge of *both* the concrete particulars *and* the relevant planetary alignments for the two categories to be mutually explicated. The particular is illuminated by the archetypal at the same moment that the archetypal is embodied in the particular. Before that moment, the archetypal is a structural potentiality, a wave form of probabilities, a vessel of possibility awaiting realization.

Not only does knowing the archetypal illuminate the particular (archetypal→particular), but conversely, knowing the particular can shine new light on the archetypal (particular→archetypal), as when our examination of specific historical and cultural events and figures gives us a deeper understanding of the archetypal principles they embody and exemplify. We gain new understanding of Prometheus and Dionysus by recognizing the precise nature of their presence and interaction in the 1960s. We comprehend the Saturn-Pluto complex better when we have studied the particularities of its expression in the lives and work of Kafka, Melville, Marx, Calvin, and Augustine, or in Frida Kahlo's paintings, or Maya Lin's Vietnam Memorial, or Shakespeare's tragedies, or the Inquisition, or the events of September 11, or their aftermath. Each concrete particular gives new insight into how a given archetypal complex can manifest. Each event or figure or work of art deepens our grasp of the ways of those gods in the planetary pantheon. By contrast, knowing the planetary alignment but not the particular embodiment provides only a general kind of information at a very high level of abstraction—the archetypal wave form before it has been concretely embodied, particularized, inflected, and creatively enacted. In general, therefore, the insights that archetypal astrology makes possible retrospectively into the dynamic patterns of human experience can be precise, nuanced, and consistently far more revealing than the always problematic and often inept attempts at concrete prediction of a literalistic future-oriented astrology.

The same contrast is true with respect to statistical tests of predictive astrology. While such research is no doubt valuable in the short term for stimulating scientific dialogue about astrology, even the most statistically significant positive results, such as the Mars effect and other correlations of the Gauquelin experiments, have yielded few useful insights for better understanding the complexities of human experience. They have provided a source of endless controversy for skeptics and scientists discomfited by the existence of anomalous data so starkly incompatible with their cosmological beliefs. Yet compared with the archetypal approach to astrological analysis, the methodology of statistical research appears to be fundamentally inadequate for examining the actual scope and intricacy of astrological correlations, hampered as it is by simplistic epistemological assumptions inherent to that mode of investigation. Such tests are both incapable of registering archetypal multivalence and blind to the necessity of full participatory engagement in the act of cognition. What is true of synchronicities in general is true as well of astrological correlations: The evaluation of such coincidences depends deeply on the sensitive perception of context, nuance, and multiple lev-

els of meaning. The suggestive patterning and subtle precision of detail characteristic of such phenomena notoriously escapes the net of quantitative experiments
and objectivistic assessments. The task is better suited to a Sherlock Holmes
than a Scotland Yard.

The conviction that statistical research should constitute the final arbiter of
all positive knowledge of the world rests on the no longer tenable assumption
that the world can ultimately be known only as a detached object to be mechanistically tested and measured, rather than as a multidimensional, complexly unfolding relational field to be participated in with all our human faculties. It was
just this presumption that the world could finally be mastered by calculation
that Weber defined as the essence of disenchantment. Statistics can clearly be
invaluable in some areas of research, as in testing the efficacy of a specific drug
for a particular medical purpose. But astrology represents a far more complex
reality; it presents an epistemological challenge that transcends the competence
of quantitative testing. Several decades of statistical experiments of astrology,
though perhaps performing a helpful service by disturbing the status quo of
scientific assumptions, have in the end provided little in the way of profound
historical, cultural, or psychological insight. Given the mismatch between the
mode of investigation and the phenomena investigated, that situation is unlikely
to change.

Yet all this still leaves open the question of archetypal astrological analysis of
future planetary alignments. We live in an exceptionally precarious era in the history of the world, when the problems of the Earth community are both deepening and accelerating. In such circumstances, we are naturally inclined to consult
every source of information and insight that could possibly increase our self-
understanding and the effectiveness of our present strategies. In this context
and with this motivation, knowledge of the major future alignments of the outer
planets and their corresponding archetypal principles and complexes could indeed prove helpful, like knowing the weather reports before setting out to surf in
large waves with winds coming from multiple directions. Our challenge, therefore, is to maintain a constant vigilance to avoid the many traps endemic to this
kind of analysis—above all, the projection of fears or wishes, the drawing of definite conclusions on the basis of limited data, and the urge to control life rather
than participate in it.

One other point about the value and limitation of this kind of survey is perhaps appropriate here. Every individual has his or her own birth chart with its
particular set of planetary configurations and ongoing personal transits, with a
unique unfolding drama that is specific to that person alone. Generalizations
about historical epochs and the larger cycles of the planets must always be balanced against the infinitely varied particularities of individual lives. Nevertheless, we can also recognize that the drama of the individual life always takes
place within the larger drama of the human community, just as our personal psyche and personal unconscious are always embedded within the collective psyche

and collective unconscious. With these qualifications and caveats, then, the major world transit alignments of the outer-planet cycles are, I believe, the principal data we now possess for understanding the archetypal dynamics of the coming years. The extent to which we are aware of those dynamics, and participate consciously and courageously in their unfolding, could play a pivotal role in the future we are about to create.

Observations on Future
Planetary Alignments

As I was completing work on this book, the most recent axial alignments of three of the four planetary cycles we have surveyed in this book simultaneously came to an end: the twenty-three-month Jupiter-Uranus opposition, the nearly four-year Saturn-Pluto opposition, and the twenty-year Uranus-Neptune conjunction. All three cycles reached the final 20° point in the course of the year 2004. This fortuitous circumstance has allowed us in the preceding chapters to look back upon and survey the cultural phenomena and archetypal correlations for most of the duration of all three alignment periods just ending.

Yet as I have emphasized, alignments are not off-and-on light switches. The historical trends and cultural impulses that were set in motion and flourished during these several alignments will no doubt continue to unfold in the coming months and years, often bringing to public consciousness significant archetypally relevant developments that are currently unknown or seemingly peripheral. The observed archetypal patterns consistently display an essential wavelike indeterminacy—both in their specific timing and in the unpredictable diversity of their concrete expression—that bears close resemblance to the observations of quantum physics.

Moreover, the events of the last stages of any axial alignment of the outer planets during the penumbral period between the 15° and 20° point of separation can often be recognized as representing the cumulative result of that alignment's archetypal developments. The Promethean and Dionysian spirit of the Uranus-Pluto conjunction of the 1960s, for example, was in general far more evident at its end in the 1972–74 period than at its beginning in 1958–60. This sunset phenomenon seems to be especially pronounced when a long alignment of two outer planets is joined in its final phases by a third planet, as in the present case of Jupiter's joining the currently ending Uranus-Neptune conjunction to form a broad, shorter-lasting three-planet configuration (Jupiter opposite Neptune and Uranus in closely overlapping succession), extending from the summer of 2002 through the summer of 2004.[3]

The many cultural phenomena and experiential themes reflective of the long Uranus-Neptune conjunction now coming to an end have so saturated our collective experience during the past two decades that it is difficult to perceive this era from outside its archetypal domain. It is like a vast all-permeating sea in which we have been deeply immersed for many years: the pervasive postmodern milieu of interpenetrating pluralism and ceaseless change, free-floating consciousness and epistemological uncertainty, the accelerated cultural and technological innovation, the heightened mystical-esoteric-mythic impulses, the utopian tendencies, the elevated idealism and religiosity, the dissolving of many kinds of boundaries, the multiple globalizing influences, the ubiquity of communication technologies such as cell phones and the Internet, the constant universal interconnectivity, the mass entrancement by the corporate media and political image-makers, the technologically mediated *maya*-like experience of the collective consciousness, the widespread concern with multiple paradigms, virtual realities, nonordinary states of consciousness, new cosmic vistas, the fluid shifts and manipulations of reality and experience produced by computers, pharmaceuticals, and biotechnology. Yet because we have been living in it, rather than looking back on it as a cultural epoch that we can examine only through the historical record, perhaps we can in this instance also recognize more directly and clearly the extent to which the relevant archetypal impulses and qualities of the zeitgeist still continue to unfold at the end of the conjunction, and we can observe more precisely the nature of their continuing presence in the future well after the alignment is over.

It is worth noting that in its later stages, as the Uranus-Neptune conjunction reached the 15° point of separation in 2001, many of the characteristic Uranus-Neptune themes and tendencies were radically challenged by the events that coincided with the Saturn-Pluto opposition's reaching exact alignment—the September 11 attacks, the response and subsequent actions of the Bush administration, the Iraq war, the sharp increase in terrorist activity and counterterrorist repression. In particular, the enormity of the trauma caused by the events of September 11, the tremendous impact of the mass death and suffering, seemed to many to signify "the end of postmodern relativism," the forced emergence of a new moral decisiveness and epistemological realism, and the sobering close of an era of narcissistic escapism and naïveté—all characteristic Saturn-Pluto motifs. Compared with the long period of the 1990s that preceded these events, an emphatically different mood now pervaded the collective consciousness, with a new sense of the dangers of global interconnectedness, porous boundaries, and relaxed pluralism, as well as of heightened religiosity—all themes suggestive of the shadow side of the Uranus-Neptune complex as seen through a Saturn-Pluto lens. In turn, these realizations and the new collective mood brought forth an aggressive divisiveness and rigidity into the spirit of the time: the rapid establishment of armored boundaries, highly restrictive legislation and government policies, a moral certitude tending towards absolutism, a simplistic polarization between good and evil, and a new realpolitik ruthlessness in political and military activity—again, all characteristic themes of the Saturn-Pluto archetypal complex.

As time passed, however, during the last phases of the Uranus-Neptune conjunction from 2001 to 2004 as it moved beyond 15° towards the final 20° point, it became apparent that the characteristic themes of the Uranus-Neptune archetypal complex in effect *merged* with those of the concurrently activated Saturn-Pluto complex, each assimilating the other in mutual interpenetration. The resulting fusion was visible in the widespread emergence of a more grounded idealism, a joining of spiritual aspiration with political realism expressed through well-organized nonviolent efforts to oppose oppressive and belligerent government policies. A new moral gravitas was combined with emancipatory hope in an often courageous encounter with destructive historical forces and entrenched political power. Problematically, the fusion of these same two archetypal complexes was evident during the 2001–04 period in the heightened state of religious and ideological enthrallment in the service of reactionary violence and oppressive impulses on both sides of various world conflicts, the Orwellian manipulation of deceptive rhetoric, symbols, and images to sway public opinion, and a state of collective mesmerization facilitated by the media that for some time effectively neutralized efforts to bring greater critical awareness to the global situation.

As we now examine the major planetary alignments of the immediate future, restricting ourselves first to the specific cycles and alignments we have surveyed in this book, we can begin with the *Uranus-Pluto* cycle, the first cycle we examined. Following the most recent conjunction of 1960–72, the next Uranus-Pluto alignment, a square, will be within 10° orb from 2007 to 2020. It is just now entering this alignment, moving inside the penumbral 15° range from 2004 to 2006.

The next *Saturn-Pluto* alignment, a square, will occur mainly during the years 2009–11. It first reaches the penumbral 15° range in September 2008 and 10° in November.

The next *Jupiter-Uranus* conjunction will be within 15° orb from March 2010 to April 2011. (Add one month at each end for penumbral 20° orb.)

Much further into the future, the next *Uranus-Neptune* square alignment will occur in the years 2035–45, first reaching 15° penumbral orb beginning in 2032.

To these alignments from the four familiar outer-planet cycles should be added upcoming alignments for outer-planet cycles we have not yet examined:

Saturn opposite Neptune, 15° orb, takes place from November 2004 to August 2008 (first moving into 20° orb in August 2004).

Saturn opposite Uranus, 15° orb, will occur from September 2007 to July 2012 (first moving into 20° orb in October 2006).

Jupiter conjunct Pluto, 15° orb, will occur from January 2007 to October 2008. (For 20° orb in Jupiter alignments, add one month at each end.)

Jupiter conjunct Neptune, 15° orb, will occur from February 2009 to March 2010.

Jupiter opposite Saturn, 15° orb, will occur from March 2010 to March 2012.

From the survey of planetary cycles we have already studied we can tentatively extrapolate from previous correlations as well as from current trends to assess what kinds of cultural and historical phenomena might coincide with these next alignments. The immediately preceding alignments of any cycle tend to be especially relevant. For example, the already approaching Uranus-Pluto square alignment that will extend through 2020 points to the possibility of a significant cyclical development of the cultural impulses and archetypal dynamics that emerged during the 1960s. Characteristic themes we have observed for this cycle in past centuries include heightened impulses for radical social change and cultural creativity, accelerated technological and scientific advance, the empowerment of progressive and reformist political movements, intensified feminist, civil rights, and countercultural activity, increased drive for freedom and autonomy at both the individual and collective level, pressure towards radicalization in many spheres of action and ideas, intensified ecological activism, an awakening of the instincts and nature in many senses, changes in the global balance of power, large demographic shifts, and the activation of mass energies and mass movements of various kinds. Generally speaking, Uranus-Pluto eras have tended to bring forth the catalyzing of powerful forces in many forms, the awakening of a will to power that can be both creative and destructive, and a tangible intensification and acceleration of human experience.

All of these specific themes have been strongly in evidence during past Uranus-Pluto alignments with considerable consistency. Yet as to which of them will be visible during these next fifteen years, we of course cannot know. If we consider feminism, for example—from Mary Wollstonecraft and the women of the French Revolution through the Seneca Falls women's rights convention in 1848 and the suffragettes of the early 1900s to the women's liberation awakening of the 1960s—the Uranus-Pluto cycle has been highly consistent in its correlations. The developing diachronic pattern suggests that with this next dynamic alignment of Uranus-Pluto another period of both the spontaneous empowerment of women and an intensified striving for equality and self-sovereignty is on the immediate horizon. Because the alignment is a square, the potential for stress and struggle in that process is high, but considering the clear sequence of past correlations, it seems to me altogether likely that another feminist propulsion will infuse itself into the culture and that women will emerge from the next decade and a half with considerably more political and economic power than now. Yet one can never be certain how these archetypal forces will become concretely embodied, only that they will tend to do so in a way that is consistent with their character and grounded in the developing cultural context.

The several upcoming alignments involving Jupiter or Saturn are shorter in duration and have their own characteristic archetypal vectors—the Jupiter alignment periods tending towards the expansive and elevating, the Saturn towards the problematic and restrictive. Yet more subtly, the converse is also true: Jupiter always has its complicating shadow, Saturn its hard-earned gifts.

The natural human tendency is to want to know that the general outlook for the foreseeable future is uniformly positive and will only get better, with blue skies as far as the eye can see. Yet there are advantages to knowing of a potentially challenging reality in advance, facing it squarely, preparing for it, and recognizing its signs and characteristic motifs, its dangers, and its positive potential when it is consciously assimilated and enacted. Perhaps equally important, it can be psychologically centering and spiritually fortifying to recognize that such periods may represent the unfolding of larger cycles of archetypal development and human evolution in a context that is in some sense cosmic, subtly ordered and intelligible, rather than arbitrary, random, and meaningless.

Of all the cycles listed, the Saturn-Neptune opposition will be of special relevance for understanding the immediate period, from later 2004 to 2008. The archetypal combination of Saturn and Neptune is an exceptionally complex and profound one. The two archetypal principles are radically different from each other in character, even in ontology—they rule two entirely different universes of meaning. The many ways in which those meanings can interact, oppose each other, interpenetrate, and be synthesized deserve as extensive an exploration as we have given to each of the four combinations already surveyed. Without an extensive survey of historical and biographical correlations, one cannot convey the rich diversity of possible inflections inherent in this archetypal complex, nor can we glimpse the diachronic and synchronic patternings that preceded—and form a context for understanding—the current alignment. Before such an analysis, however, a few headlines may be helpful, as long as we keep in mind the considerable simplification that such a brief overview necessitates.

For our present purpose, the earlier chapters' survey of Saturn and Neptune in the context of other planetary cycles can suggest some of the characteristic themes that tend to be constellated in the collective psyche when these two archetypes are combined. The Saturn-Neptune complex can be seen as in many ways comparable to the Saturn-*Pluto* complex because of the dominance in both of Saturnian themes and an unmistakable Saturnian atmosphere. The enormous difference between the two complexes is that this general Saturnian cast is now pervaded with a Neptunian quality rather than a Plutonic one.

Saturn-Neptune can also be compared to the *Uranus*-Neptune complex, but instead of the Promethean impulse interacting with Neptune, we have Saturn.

The dominant tendency is thus not that of awakening and liberating the Neptunian dimension but rather setting up dichotomies and tensions with it, bringing out its problematic qualities, opposing and negating them, judging them; or disciplining, structuring, grounding, forging, and maturing them, thus giving the Neptunian dimension concrete embodiment.

A characteristic motif of Saturn-Neptune eras is a heightened tension and dialectic between ideals, hopes, and beliefs on the one hand and the hard realities of life on the other. The same complex can express itself in the form of heightened conflicts between religion and secularism—"belief and facts," "faith-based and reality-based" (and in the United States, "red states" and "blue states")—each side perceiving the other to be living in a state of delusional self-deception. Intensified secular skepticism towards religious beliefs of any kind tends to be constellated at the same time as intensified commitment to conservative religiosity, which often takes the form of antiscientific biblical literalism ("God vs. science"). The conflict between creationism and evolution is a characteristic expression of this archetypal polarity, as in the case of the Scopes trial during the Saturn-Neptune square of 1925, and of Darwin himself, born during the Saturn-Neptune conjunction of 1809. Sensitivity to the oppressive and constraining aspects of religious belief tends to be heightened, bringing forth sharp criticism of religion as "mere myth"—superstitious nonsense, naïve fantasy, the "opium of the people" in the words of Marx, born during the Saturn-Neptune square that followed Darwin's conjunction; a psychologically motivated illusion, in the view of Freud, born during the Saturn-Neptune square exactly one cycle later. Issues surrounding skepticism generally—the discernment of truth and illusion, and the confronting of deception and delusion—frequently emerge.

There is also a tendency during Saturn-Neptune eras to experience a subtle but pervasive darkening of the collective consciousness, sometimes as a diffuse and difficult-to-diagnose social malaise, at other times as a direct response to deeply discouraging or tragic events. Reflecting the complex in its most intense form, such eras are frequently marked by collective experiences of tragic loss, the defeat of ideals and aspirations, the death of a dream, which are accompanied by a sense of profound sorrow. The current Saturn-Neptune opposition first reached the 15° range in November 2004. The bitter disappointment and vast sadness that overcame half the U.S. population and much of the rest of the world as a result of Bush's reelection just as the alignment reached the 15° threshold is highly characteristic of the Saturn-Neptune complex. The pervading sense that an ideal had been lost took many forms—the loss of the ideal image of what the United States had once represented both to its citizens and to the world, the defeat of widespread hopes for a change in the world's leadership at a critical time in history, the sense of futility felt after so much work on behalf of that cause, the loss of faith in the democratic process, lingering doubts about the truthfulness of the vote count and the legitimacy of the election. Highly characteristic of the Saturn-Neptune complex was the pervasive experience of discouragement and depression, resignation, pessimism, despair, and dazed disorientation that descended on many in the following weeks and months like an immense dark cloud.

The same complex was visible even more acutely one month later in the wake of the tsunami in Asia, with its tidal wave of grief, inconsolable loss and anguish, and mass rituals of mourning. Here too were other characteristic Saturn-Neptune themes: death caused by water, the ocean as source of suffering and loss, contamination of water, water-borne and infectious diseases, numberless haunting images of death and sorrow transmitted throughout the world and permeating the collective consciousness.

As the Saturn-Neptune alignment moved closer in orb in the late summer of 2005, virtually all of these themes dramatically repeated themselves in the catastrophic flooding that overwhelmed New Orleans after the Gulf Coast hurricane Katrina. Many characteristic motifs of the Saturn-Neptune complex pervaded the event and its aftermath: death and disaster through water; the floodwaters breaching the protective levees; the stream of globally televised images of suffering and death; the drowning of a city and legacy that represented the soul of much of American culture; floating corpses, the contaminated and diseased water, the widespread dehydration, the lack of critical drugs, the countless medical crises, the powerless hospitals and nursing homes; the strange paralysis of the government; the collective sense of hopelessness and despair; the steady focus on the suffering of the poor, the abandoned, the sick and the frail, the very old and very young, the dying, the homeless, the grieving.

A comparison of the central crises of the two consecutive Saturn oppositions—first with Pluto, then Neptune—that have marked this first decade of the twenty-first century is instructive. The fiery hell and ashes of Ground Zero in New York on September 11 followed by the "shock and awe" destruction of the Iraq invasion during the Saturn-*Pluto* alignment stand in sharp contrast with the tragic water nightmares of the Asian tsunami and the New Orleans flood during the Saturn-*Neptune* alignment. The difference in the collective emotional responses of the two crises is striking as well—the intensified power struggle, conservative empowerment, grave determination, armored security, and mutually demonizing hostility during the Saturn-Pluto alignment, compared with the widespread sense of diffuse helplessness, disillusionment and despair, bitter disappointment with the government's massive failure and negligence, and private outpouring of compassion, prayer, sacrifice, and aid during the Saturn-Neptune alignment.

Similarly, whereas in the aftermath of the 2001 crisis during the Saturn-Pluto period the focus of collective judgment and division (Saturn) was on power, violence, terrorism, and war (Pluto), both in the United States and abroad, the focus of collective judgment and division in the aftermath of the 2005 crisis during the Saturn-Neptune period was on empathy and the failure of empathy, on systemic negligence, the acute as well as chronic lack of care for the poor and disadvantaged, the narcissistic bubble enclosing the current U.S. leadership and its policies, and the immense human cost of that blindness and insensitivity. With a kind of precision of symmetry and aesthetic coherence, the reactionary structures that were empowered by fiery events and ruthless violence in the earlier period were now weakened or dissolved by watery events and compassionate concern. As often occurs during Saturn-Neptune alignments, the hidden shadow of past actions and policies became visible, haunting the present.

While only an extensive historical overview of the Saturn-Neptune cycle could give the reader an adequate basis for discerning the full range of correlations that will be relevant for understanding the current alignment, it is worth mentioning here that one of the most frequent themes historically has been a widespread sense of *discontent* and *loss of faith* pervading the social and political atmosphere, as in the sustained "crisis of confidence" of 1978–79 during the Saturn-Neptune square that occurred in the later years of the Carter administration. In wartime, Saturn-Neptune alignments often coincide with the later stages of a war when a collective sense of physical and spiritual exhaustion, disillusionment, and low morale—often on both sides—is dominant, as happened at the end of World War I (conjunction of 1916–19), World War II (square of 1943–45), Vietnam (opposition of 1970–73), and the Cold War (conjunction of 1987–91). Virtually the entire American Civil War was fought during the Saturn-Neptune opposition of 1861–65. The sense of being caught in a futile and endless "quagmire" is often felt and voiced, as in the current case of the Iraq War in 2004–05.

To the above list could be added the Korean War, most of which was fought during the Saturn-Neptune conjunction in 1951–53. One of the most characteristic responses to periods informed by this archetypal complex is the acute sense of irony, wry or bitter humor, a deep awareness of the absurd and insane in life. The dark humor reflects a response to suffering and hopelessness that in some sense is an attempt to preserve one from going insane or succumbing to despair. To mention one example to stand for many, the film *M*A*S*H* was based on the experiences in 1951–52 of a surgeon who served in a military medical unit attempting to cope with the endless casualties and horror of war during the Saturn-Neptune conjunction of the Korean War. The film was released in 1970 (followed by the television series in 1972) in coincidence with the immediately following Saturn-Neptune opposition of 1970–73, when it precisely captured the mood of the nation and its soldiers trapped in the demoralizing war in Vietnam. The film was directed by Robert Altman, who was born with the Saturn-Neptune square, and whose many films have been consistently notable for their deeply ironic spirit.

Frequently seen on the spiritual level during Saturn-Neptune eras are dark nights of the soul and severe challenges to religious faith, such as Nietzsche's announcement of the "death of God" during the Saturn-Neptune conjunction of

1881–82, or John Lennon's song "God" in late 1970 ("God is a concept by which we measure our pain"), as well as his bitter postmortem for the 1960s during that same 1970–73 alignment: "The dream is over." Often individuals during these periods question the existence of an all-loving God who would permit tragic events and vast human suffering, as many voiced after the tsunami in Asia in the winter of 2004–05, or as countless people experienced in 1943–45 during the period of greatest horror and anguish in the concentration camps. A more particularized form of this sense of collective tragedy took place during the Saturn-Neptune square in 1963 with the worldwide grief and the mass ritual of mourning after the assassination of John Kennedy. Yet an equally strong expression of the Saturn-Neptune archetypes in combination is the impulse to sustain faith and hope in the darkness, as in Martin Luther King Jr.'s courageous, inspired and inspiring "I have a dream" speech before the Lincoln Memorial in 1963 during the same Saturn-Neptune alignment, or Lennon's influential song "Imagine" during the following one in 1971.

Paradoxically, as we have often seen with other cycles, such periods tend to coincide with collective expressions of opposite sides of the same complex: loss of faith and disillusionment but also a forging of a deeper faith in the face of harsh or tragic realities. The latter response can take many forms: a search to discover a foundation of hope in a greater though not-yet-visible reality, an inward-turning withdrawal from the world to contact inner spiritual resources and ideals, a strengthened commitment to religious tradition, a turning to spiritual discipline and practice, ritual, prayer, and meditation. The same archetypal complex can also constellate an individual or collective impulse to engage the world in a manner that is both spiritual *and* pragmatic, to devote oneself to overcoming the disparity between the ideal and the actual through service and spiritually informed action. Here the synthesis of Saturn and Neptune is expressed through the strenuous effort to embody spiritual values and compassionate ideals by enacting them within the concrete realities and challenges of the human community. A call for service and sacrifice is strongly felt. The Dalai Lama, who was born with Saturn opposite Neptune, is a paradigmatic example of this potential expression of the complex. Frequently, the experience or witness of suffering serves to dissolve rigid boundaries and past enmities, and to call forth unitive and compassionate healing impulses (as was visible, for example, in many instances in the wake of the tsunami, such as in Sri Lanka).

Nevertheless, as with the many Saturn-Pluto hard aspects we have examined, Saturn-Neptune periods generally present a significant challenge to the collective spirit of an age. Social anomie and spiritual malaise are frequent, sometimes intensified to a state of profound alienation. (Salman Rushdie in 2005: "The cold war is over, but a stranger war has begun. Alienation has perhaps never been so widespread.") In their milder expression, these tendencies can take the form of an underlying mood of confusion, doubt, uncertainty, and ambivalence. A range of psychological symptoms tends to be more in evidence:

free-floating anxiety, narcissism, apathetic inertia, escapism and denial, psychic numbing, dissociation, autistic introversion, tendencies towards addiction and dependency of various kinds, insomnia and dream disturbances, physical and spiritual fatigue, world-weariness, listlessness and weakening of the will, concern with chronic and debilitating illnesses, with influenza and malaria and other infectious diseases, viruses and vaccines, posttraumatic stress disorders, "phantom diseases," and difficult-to-diagnose mental and physical conditions (as in chronic fatigue syndrome and Gulf War syndrome, both of which emerged during the last Saturn-Neptune conjunction of 1987–91).

Here too could be mentioned problematic reactions, side effects, and abuses of drugs of all kinds, prescription and otherwise, and increased public awareness of these problems, often as a result of new data that disclose a dark reality hidden behind a carefully manipulated image, as in the corporate abuse of testing protocols and the suppression of negative data. This motif was evident in the first year of the Saturn-Neptune opposition in 2004–05 in such phenomena as the methamphetamine epidemic (in a diachronic pattern with the crack cocaine epidemic of the preceding conjunction and heroin epidemics during this and earlier alignments); the wave of drug scandals among professional athletes involving the use of steroids and other performance-enhancing drugs; and the concurrent wave of pharmaceutical companies that were forced to withdraw from the market or issue warnings for once-celebrated drugs (e.g., Vioxx, Plavix, Bextra, Celebrex) because of newly revealed negative side effects and dangers linked to their use.

The Saturn-Neptune theme of poisoning, pollution, toxic chemical effects, and subtle poisoning of the public mind or political environment can take a remarkable variety of forms—the literal, as in the dioxin poisoning of the Ukrainian presidential candidate Viktor Yushchenko, and the less literal but equally toxic, as in cynical and deliberately deceptive Machiavellian political advertising like that of the "Swift Boat Veterans for Truth" on behalf of the Bush presidential campaign, both themes clearly in evidence precisely in coincidence with the first months of the Saturn-Neptune opposition in 2004. (Machiavelli himself was born with Saturn and Neptune in close opposition.) The original "Willie Horton" advertisement that provided a model for this form of political deception was produced in coincidence with the last Saturn-Neptune conjunction in 1988, on behalf of the presidential campaign of the elder Bush. In both 1988 and 2004 (Saturn-Neptune conjunction and opposition, respectively), the widely disseminated deceptive advertisements with their dark, fear-inducing images played a critical role in the defeat of the opposing presidential candidate.

Not only deception but also self-deception is a characteristic expression of this complex when negatively constellated. A state of delusion about one's actual condition in the world is carefully maintained by filtering out and denying all information that might cast question on the validity of one's rigidly protected belief system, thereby creating a closed feedback loop. Such tendencies can range from an individual state of mental illness requiring professional treatment to a more pervasive collective delusion in which, for example, a nation's leadership encapsulates itself in an impenetrable bubble of denial and self-reinforcing belief, often tinged with religious themes and self-idealizing fantasies, that is starkly at odds with its concrete consequences and the reality perceived by the rest of the world. Avoidance of critical self-reflection conspires with support from naïve or opportunistic followers to prevent, at least for a time, the intrusion of realities that would disturb the elaborately defended illusion.

Yet the same archetypal complex also tends to constellate a strong impulse to unmask deception, to reveal the illusion, to cut through the denial, to confront the dark reality behind the surface image. "Credibility gaps" arise. A sharper eye for shadow tends to develop in the collective cultural vision, resulting in a more acute sense of irony (sometimes bitter irony, as with Jonathan Swift and Mark Twain, both born with Saturn and Neptune in hard aspect), with increased tendencies towards ironic distancing and intensified skepticism about political rhetoric, conventional wisdom, naïveté, hypocrisy, and deceit. The sharply increased public recognition in 2004–05 of the Bush administration's systematic deception in beginning the Iraq War, its false claims concerning Iraq's "weapons of mass destruction" and terrorist links to September 11, which paralleled concurrent revelations and skepticism about athletes and drugs, the pharmaceutical industry, journalists' hoaxes in major news media, and the Bush administration's deceptive editing of scientific reports about global warming and other environmental matters, is highly characteristic of the Saturn-Neptune pattern of truth and illusion, deception and unmasking deception.

Underlying and uniting many of the above tendencies is the central theme of *disenchantment* and *disillusionment*—in both the negative and positive senses and encompassing the entire range of their meanings. These include not only loss of faith, discouragement, social alienation, and sense of existential meaninglessness but also the empowerment that can emerge from confronting an illusion, shedding a faith that is no longer viable, waking as if from a dream, lucidly recognizing the consensus madness, demystifying the received version of reality—as in the collective disillusionment with communism that rapidly spread through the peoples of Eastern Europe and the Soviet Union during the Saturn-Neptune conjunction of 1987–91, in the triple conjunction with Uranus. A subtle dissolving of oppressive structures can take place on many levels, affecting structures of belief as well as of institutions.

Yet another important form this motif can take is the dichotomy between materialistic reductionism (Saturn) and imaginative vision (Neptune), between matter and spirit, and between cosmic disenchantment and an ensouled universe. Here the characteristic Saturn-Neptune issue of judging what is truth and what is illusion becomes especially relevant, as each side views the other as captured by an illusion. The possibility that modern disenchantment, in Weber's sense, is itself at a deeper level a form of delusional enchantment, a self-enclosed state of alienated consciousness that has systematically filtered out the spiritual dimensions of existence, offers yet a further amplification of these characteristic Saturn-Neptune themes. Weber himself, the great theorist of disenchantment, was born during the Saturn-Neptune opposition of 1864, and he articulated the concept of disenchantment in his lecture "Science as a Vocation" during the Saturn-Neptune conjunction in 1919.

To briefly summarize, the dichotomy between the Neptunian imaginative-spiritual-religious axis and the Saturnian literalist-skeptical-scientific axis that is characteristic of eras and individuals informed by this complex can be seen as taking three distinct forms. First, one finds a strong tendency towards metaphysical skepticism: an impulse to doubt the existence of transcendent or spiritual realities, and to regard the imagination as primarily a source of subjective distortion. Metaphysical, spiritual, mystical, and imaginative dimensions of existence are firmly negated in favor of a sober critical rationalism in engagement with the concrete empirical world. This negation often takes the form of a strong impulse to demystify religious belief as a principal cause of both oppression and illusion in human life. Here we see such figures born with Saturn-Neptune aspects as David Hume, the paradigmatic skeptic in the history of philosophy and acute critic of religion (*On Miracles*, *Dialogues Concerning Natural Religion*); Bertrand Russell, who played the same role in twentieth-century philosophy (*Why I Am Not a Christian*); and Freud, who understood all religion as the psychological residue of childhood needs and projections of parental omnipotence (*The Future of an Illusion*).

The second form this dichotomy can take reflects an exactly contrary tendency, in which a firm commitment to the superiority of the poetic and spiritual imagination directly opposes the distorting constraints of conventional perception and scientific materialism. Here William Blake, born with Saturn and Neptune in close opposition, can stand as a paradigmatic figure:

If the doors of perception were cleansed, everything would appear to man as it is, infinite. For man has closed himself up, till he sees all things thro' narrow chinks of his cavern.

May God us keep
From single vision and Newton's sleep!

In every cry of every Man,
In every infant's cry of fear,
In every voice, in every ban,
The mind-forg'd manacles I hear.

Poetry fetter'd Fetters the Human Race.
Nations are Destroy'd or Flourish in proportion as
Their Poetry Painting and Music are Destroy'd or Flourish.

Art Degraded Imagination Denied
War Governed the Nations.

An equally frequent expression of the Saturn-Neptune polarity takes the form of a kind of Romantic existentialism in which spiritual and imaginative aspirations are confronted with the reality of a tragic or disenchanted world, with a resulting sense of melancholic loss, longing, and disillusionment. Here the aesthetic preference is characteristically for elegies, adagios, nocturnes, requiems, pietas, laments, or the blues, reflecting the poignant encounter of the poetic and spiritually sensitive temperament with the tragic, oppressive, and sorrowful aspects of existence (as expressed, for example, in Samuel Barber's quintessential *Adagio for Strings*, both the composer and the composition born during Saturn-Neptune alignments; or *Both Sides Now* or *Blue* by Joni Mitchell, likewise born with Saturn-Neptune; or Dylan's *Sad-Eyed Lady of the Lowlands*, composed during a Saturn-Neptune personal transit). The pervading atmosphere is one of poignancy and pathos, world-weariness and spiritual resignation, unquenchable yearning of the soul; or a state of profound unknowing, melancholic ambiguity, an impasse between two incommensurable universes—inner and outer, subjective and objective, poetic sensibility and tough-minded logic, the aspiring soul and the hard facts of life.

Saturn-Neptune periods tend to be among the most psychologically and spiritually demanding of times as well as the most likely to call forth genuine nobility of spirit and profundity of vision. They can engender a darker cast to the imagination yet also a more realistic spirituality. In perhaps its most admirable form, the Saturn-Neptune complex appears to be associated with the courage to face a hard and often tragic reality without illusion and still remain true to the ideals and dreams of a better world. Instead of provoking despair or passivity, the painful gap between the ideal and the real inspires one to undertake whatever sustained labor is necessary to transform the resistant structures of the world (political, economic, religious, philosophical) in service of one's highest spiritual intuitions.

Robert Kennedy, born with the Saturn-Neptune square directly on his natal Sun, came to reflect just this expression of the archetypal complex. Grief-stricken in the wake of his brother's assassination in 1963 (when Saturn and Neptune were again in square alignment), Kennedy suffered a virtually paralyzing spiritual and emotional crisis in the following months and years as he struggled to assimilate the tragedy, and to confront the shattered image of the good God inherited from his childhood Catholic faith. Transformed by this crucible of suffering, and helped by long meditations on the works of poets such as the elegist Alfred Tennyson (born with the Saturn-Neptune conjunction), Kennedy gradually returned to public life with those distinctive ideals and attitudes with which he is now most identified, and which reflected an inner resolution of the archetypal dialectic associated with the Saturn-Neptune complex: a deeper spiritual faith mediated by the encounter with death and suffering, hope that transcends tragedy, compassionate action on behalf of the poor and the oppressed, a commitment to a life of service and sacrifice on behalf of the larger human community, and faith in the possibility of a better world—as in his frequent quoting of Tennyson's "Come my friends, 'tis not too late to seek a newer world."

Finally, a paradigmatic figure in this regard was Abraham Lincoln, born in 1809 with the Saturn-Neptune conjunction. His lifelong sufferings from intense depression and grief, the many tragic deaths and losses that marked his life, his spiritual struggle with the finality of death, his skepticism about orthodox religious beliefs, his deep sense of resignation, and his pronounced capacity for irony all vividly reflect this archetypal combination. So also does his commitment to the compassionate care of the oppressed, the wounded, the widowed and orphaned, his consecration of the dead, his forgiveness of the enemy, his spiritual tentativeness and humility. Lincoln was, essentially and poignantly, a "man of sorrow and reconciliation" (sorrow as an expression of Saturn, reconciliation as an expression of Neptune). Above all, we can recognize this archetypal synthesis in Lincoln's capacity to perceive in the suffering and death of so many—including himself—all sacrificed on the altar of a higher ideal, the mysterious workings of a spiritual purpose acting in and through the mortal struggles of human history.

This is close to the heart of the Saturn-Neptune complex and its potential *coniunctio oppositorum:* the recognition of spirit in matter, of the universal in the particular, of the archetypal in the concrete, the redemptive shining through of the eternal soul within the mortal body of the empirical world. As iconically reflected in Michelangelo's *Pietà* (1499), Saturn-Neptune transits tend to coincide with periods of profound spiritual loss and contraction, in the many senses suggested above, but also periods of profound spiritual forging, soul-making, the redemptive embodiment of spirit, reflecting the struggle and higher synthesis of incarnation.

No alignment, such as the Saturn-Neptune opposition just discussed, takes place in a vacuum as the only relevant factor in understanding the archetypal dynamics of a specific period of time. As we have seen throughout this survey, at any given moment multiple planetary alignments are in orb, overlapping each other, with a corresponding interaction of multiple archetypal forces simultaneously in play. Often these different archetypal combinations are sharply divergent in character, influencing the cultural atmosphere in highly distinct ways, and sometimes interpenetrating with extraordinary unexpected consequences. For example, the qualities associated with the Uranus-Pluto alignment that has recently begun its approach could scarcely be more different in character from the Saturn-Neptune opposition. Only a "complexity theory" adequate to such intricately complicated archetypal interactions and multiple influences would be of use in assessing the unfolding continuum of history. Needless to say, a fundamental recognition of indeterminacy and unpredictability is the bedrock of the entire perspective articulated here.

With that caveat in mind, let us look a little further forward at the upcoming alignments. If we can judge by past experience, the most significant and potentially dramatic configuration on the horizon is the convergence of three planetary cycles that will produce a close *T-square* alignment of *Saturn, Uranus,* and *Pluto* during the period 2008–11. The last time that these three planets were simultaneously in hard aspect was from 1964 to early 1968, when Saturn opposed the longer Uranus-Pluto conjunction of the 1960s and when both revolutionary and reactionary impulses were intensely constellated and complexly interpenetrating in the collective psyche. This was the period of greatest polarized tensions and convulsions during that tumultuous decade, when there was a rapid acceleration of cultural change and stressful development. The preceding hard-aspect configuration in the twentieth century involving these three planets was the T-square that occurred between 1929 and 1933, at the beginning of the long Uranus-Pluto square that extended through the 1930s. We examined several other such periods in earlier centuries.

Historically, as we have seen, the archetypal dynamics during eras in which these three planets were in such a configuration have been especially powerful, challenging, and transformative. The forces involved seem to demand, as well as bring forth the possibility of, a deepened capacity for the creative resolution of intensely opposing forces—the old and the new, the past and the future, order and change, tradition and innovation, stability and freedom. A general atmosphere of power struggle is typical. Underlying tensions between established social authority and newly empowered countercultural impulses tend to be exacerbated. So also the generational tensions between old and young and the political tensions between conservative and progressive. A quality of accelerated maturation is usually notable in the collective psyche. Entrenched assumptions and expectations confront the unpredictable and the disruptive. Whether the result is a destructive encounter between forces of revolutionary change and forces of rigid reaction or a pragmatic synthesis of creative innovation and resolute discipline in recognition of irrevocable new realities depends on factors beyond what can be seen astrologically. Such periods have generally been marked by critical events and cultural phenomena that both climax and catalyze longer-term processes. International tensions and geopolitical divisions can intensify, so that radically new approaches are required to resolve long-standing antagonisms and conflicting values. Issues surrounding the unforeseen consequences of technological development tend to rise to public consciousness. In the current global situation, it appears likely that large-scale ecological as well as political and social structures will be affected during this period, with an increased urgency to resolve problems involving the allocation and preservation of the world's natural resources.

Yet much will depend on what steps are taken during these next years, and what kind of awareness—both collective and individual—is brought to bear on the challenges now facing the human community. As I have emphasized throughout this book, an extremely wide range of archetypally relevant "scenarios," as the futurists say, is possible for any such alignment, reflecting different potential inflections of whatever archetypal forces are at play. These different scenarios and inflections in turn reflect that irreducible multivalent indeterminacy that resides in the very nature of archetypes. Some may view the observed consistency of correlation between patterns of human experience and planetary movements as evidence that history has, in some essential way, already been determined in its basic outlines, if not in every detail. Such a conclusion, I believe, reflects simplistic assumptions about causality and determinism lingering from the modern (and premodern) mind-set. It may also reflect deep psychological tendencies, collective as well as personal, rooted in unconscious feelings of helplessness and victimization. Rather than reinforcing a sense that one is bound by a definite fate, however, knowledge of upcoming world transits, like the knowledge of one's personal transits and natal chart, can open the possibility of a more informed and creative response to the archetypal forces at work at any given time. Numerous unpredictable factors are at work in co-constituting the events to come: the long-developing and still shifting and pliable historical trends, the spontaneous social and political responses to newly emerging conditions, the state of the collective moral conscience, the extent to which the constellated energies are unconsciously and blindly acted out or consciously engaged and assimilated—and no doubt many other trans-empirical factors beyond our ken, such as perhaps karma and grace.

Even in astrological terms, indeterminacy and creative unpredictability are part of the archetypal pantheon, as essential manifestations of the Uranus-Promethean principle. All periods involving major Uranus alignments tend to constellate these themes in concrete events, each cycle doing so with different inflections according to the second planet involved. The Jupiter-Uranus conjunction of 2010 and the early 2011 will take place during the peak of the T-square, and is likely to coincide with unexpected new beginnings, expansive impulses, and creative breakthroughs of many kinds that will shape the larger whole—some immediately visible to public awareness, some of a more hidden nature that fully emerge later.

A crucial role will be played during the years of the T-square and beyond by the coming to power of the generation born during the Uranus-Pluto conjunction of the 1960s and its aftermath. So will the coming of age of the generation of children born during the Uranus-Neptune conjunction just ending. Moreover, for many years to come, the sustained infusion into the collective psyche of the idealistic cultural impulses, creative visions, and spiritual awakenings that emerged during that long Uranus-Neptune era will continue to unfold its consequences for many years into the future, often in new ways that cannot now be predicted. Finally, the very knowledge of the powerful archetypal dynamics involved—the foreknowledge of the planetary alignments, their timing, and their potential significance—could provide us with an important further level of insight and self-awareness by which we might better navigate this critical transition in our world's history.

Nothing is certain, or at least nothing can be said to be certain. When it comes to the future, we are all seeing through a glass darkly. Yet some glasses are perhaps less opaque than others. Given the consistent pattern of correlations involving these planets in the past, it does seem reasonable to prepare for the possibility that the years of the upcoming Saturn-Uranus-Pluto T-square configuration will present the human community with a convergence of major challenges on many fronts. The Uranus-Pluto square that will continue through 2020 could well represent something like a combination of the 1930s and the 1960s in a twenty-first-century context: a sustained period of enormous historical change requiring humanity to radically expand the scope of its vision and draw upon new resources and capacities in ways that could ultimately be deeply liberating. Whatever form this coming era will take, I believe that the great global transformations and emancipatory movements that have coincided with the long sequence of axial alignments of Uranus, Neptune, and Pluto surveyed in this book, as well as the deep human suffering and moral evolution that took place during the Saturn-Pluto, Saturn-Neptune, and other such challenging alignments, have prepared the world to enter this critical threshold with a collective awareness that could make a significant difference in its outcome.

One last planetary alignment should be mentioned. We have discussed the various upcoming dynamic or hard-aspect alignments of the outer-planet cycles. There still remain the trines and sextiles of these cycles. Of these, by far the most significant is the century-long *Neptune-Pluto* sextile, which began in the mid-twentieth century and will continue until near the middle of the twenty-first. This long sextile takes place once each five-hundred-year Neptune-Pluto cycle, beginning about a half-century after the conjunction. Its unusual duration results from Pluto's eccentric 248-year orbit, which twice each Neptune-Pluto cycle brings it close to and, briefly, even inside Neptune's orbit—the first time as a sextile, the second as a trine.

Historically, such sustained sextile or trine alignments of Neptune and Pluto have coincided with long epochs in which a certain profound evolution of consciousness appears to be propelled and sustained in a gradual, harmoniously unfolding manner, moving beneath and through the fluctuations and crises that might occur at a more immediate empirical level. The grand trine of Uranus, Neptune, and Pluto in the 1760s and 1770s cited in the previous chapter, which coincided with the peak of the Enlightenment, the birth of Romanticism, and the beginning of the American Revolution, occurred as part of the most recent much longer Neptune-Pluto trine of the eighteenth century. These century-long epochs generally seem to impel the collective experience of a more confluent relationship between nature and spirit, between evolutionary and instinctual forces (Pluto) and the spiritual resources and idealistic aspirations of the pervading cultural vision (Neptune). The archetypal dynamics involved characteristically provide, at an almost subterranean level in the collective psyche, a sustained stabilizing impulse.[4]

This particular category of alignment has special significance: first, because it involves Neptune and Pluto, the two outermost planets; and second, because it lasts longer than any other planetary alignment. The current sextile is also historically noteworthy because of its role in the larger cyclical movements of all three outermost planets, since it coincided with the first Uranus-Pluto and Uranus-Neptune conjunctions to occur after the Neptune-Pluto conjunction of the 1880–1905 period. From a long-term historical perspective, therefore, we are living today at the moment when all three of these cycles, the largest planetary cycles known to us, have just completed their conjunctions in succession, marking the full initiation of the corresponding archetypal dynamics for the next several centuries.

If we consider, then, the unfolding cycles of the three outermost planets—taking into account the current alignment between Neptune and Pluto, the number of years since the most recent Neptune-Pluto conjunction a century ago, and the completion of the subsequent Uranus-Pluto and Uranus-Neptune conjunctions of the 1960s and 1990s, respectively—our present moment in history is most comparable, astronomically, to the period exactly five hundred years ago with which we began the book: the era that brought forth the birth of the modern self during the decades surrounding the year 1500. This too was an epoch of extraordinary turbulence and uncertainty, and also of great cultural creativity and dynamism. It was the moment of the High Renaissance of Leonardo and Michelangelo, Erasmus and Thomas More, in the immediate aftermath of Pico della Mirandola's new vision of human possibility in the *Oratio* and Ficino's Platonic Academy in Florence—a period shaped by the rapid spread of a powerful new medium of universal communication, the printed book; the first expeditions to a vast new world that, at enormous human and ecological cost, led to the opening of the global community to itself; and the immense spiritual and cosmological transformations, still unfolding, represented by Luther's start of the Reformation and Copernicus's conceiving of the heliocentric hypothesis.

Our postmodern age of ceaseless flux and irresolvable complexity, for all its metaphysical disorientation, and despite the collective entrancement produced by the mass media and corporate marketing, has nevertheless brought forth new conditions and possibilities that could prove invaluable for our future. As a result of the many extraordinary changes—cultural, psychological, spiritual—that have unfolded in the past half-century, the collective psyche has undergone a pervasive and in certain respects deeply benign transformation that cannot easily be measured and yet, for all its subtlety, is no less pregnant with historical significance. The rapid dissemination during this era of a fundamental new openness to the perspectives and realities of different cultures, eras, religions, races, classes, genders, sexual orientations, age groups, even different species and forms of life has been an essential characteristic of our time. It is perhaps not too much to say that, in this first decade of the new millennium, humanity has entered into a condition that is in some sense more globally united and interconnected, more sensitized to the experiences and suffering of others, in certain respects more spiritually awakened, more conscious of alternative future possibilities and ideals, more capable of collective healing and compassion, and, aided by technological advances in communications media, more able to think, feel, and respond together in a spiritually evolved manner to the world's swiftly changing realities than has ever before been possible.

Opening to the Cosmos

With increasing accord and insistence, many disciplines and perspectives in our time have been pointing towards a more participatory and spiritually informed vision of the cosmos, as if a greater underlying impulse were at work through these diverse intellectual and cultural streams. Yet outside the private intuitions of a few and the private yearnings of many, the encompassing power of modernity's disenchanted cosmology has continued unabated. The world picture that emerged and established itself during the Enlightenment in the wake of the Scientific Revolution still effectively informs the activities and values that most influence the world today, and the various challenges to its hegemony have until now been largely peripheral and tentative. The modern self still lives in a vast and, in a fundamental sense, alien universe that is the random consequence of exclusively material evolutionary processes—a universe devoid of any meaning or purpose, indifferent to humanity's spiritual and moral aspirations, and relentlessly silent.

In the course of our civilization's history, this determinedly "neutral" world picture has in certain respects been deeply emancipatory. It has freed the modern self from long-established structures of cosmic meanings and purposes that, while perhaps sustaining and numinous, were often problematically interpreted, shaped, and enforced by cultural authorities—whether political or religious—whose vision was not always profound, their motives not always beyond question. We have come to realize, however, not only the great liberation but the great loss that the triumph of the mechanistic world picture brought in its wake. The liberation and the loss at the heart of modernity have been inextricably connected.

It was in response to this realization that I proposed the thought experiment of the two suitors. If our intellectual self-awareness now requires a further evolution, perhaps the first step is to recognize that our engagement with the universe would be more deeply fruitful if it more resembled a genuine dialogue. When the cosmos is assumed to be fundamentally incapable of purposeful communication, of depth and complexity of meaning, then no communication at that level can possibly take place. Such communication is excluded at the very outset of the inquiry. Yet in any authentic relationship—that is, in a relationship of true reciprocity—the potential communication of meaning and purpose must be able to move in both directions, in this instance between self and world. For this to occur, a patiently developed sense of intellectual and imaginative empathy—of receptive, respectful, trusting observation and analysis, inward and outward—is essential. Awareness of this need has moved our age to turn with new respect to those eras, traditions, and cultures in which such epistemologies have long been cultivated: ancient, indigenous, shamanic, mystical, esoteric.

Compared with the modern stance of systematic self-distancing and objectification, it appears that our present task is to cultivate a capacity for opening ourselves more fully to "the other" in all its forms—to listen with more keenly discerning ears to other voices and perspectives, other ways of being and knowing, other cultures and other ages, other forms of life, other modes of the universe's self-disclosure. As in any genuine dialogue, we must be willing to enter into that which we seek to know, not keep it distanced as a silent object imprisoned by the framework of our limiting assumptions. We need to allow that which we seek to know to enter into our own being.

Our best philosophy of science, like our most acute self-reflections, has taught us the radical extent to which our assumptions configure and create our world. Not only reason and empiricism but depth of self-honesty, inward receptivity, richness of imagination, openness to beauty, steadfastness of passion, faith, hope, spiritual aspiration all play a major role in constellating the reality we seek to know—as do fear, prejudice, mistrust, stubbornness, egocentricity, greed, impatience, lack of imagination, absence of empathy. And this is perhaps the underlying message of our modern Enlightenment's unexpected darkening of the world: At the hidden heart of cognition is a moral dimension. As the Greeks knew, the quest for the true cannot be separated from the quest for the good.

Nor, perhaps, can the search for the true and the good be ultimately separated from our search for beauty. The modern world view recognizes cosmic beauty as only an accident, an arbitrary coincidence of subjective human perception and superficial local appearance. Yet that beauty secretly inspires all cosmologists, even in their attempts to explain the entire cosmos with an abstract "theory of everything" that falls so conspicuously short of the world's rich complexity, mystery, and interior depths. A fundamental yet virtually unexamined issue in cosmology today is the question of whether all beauty in the universe is merely a random product of blind evolution and subjective circumstance or whether that beauty is in some sense significant and intentional, an expression of something more ensouled, more profound, intelligently relational, mysterious.

"Perhaps it seems surprising that physicists seek beauty," Jeanette Winterson has written, "but in fact they have no choice. As yet there has not been an exception to the rule that the demonstrable solution to any problem will turn out to be an aesthetic solution." Whatever their conscious motivations, scientists have always been compelled by a theory's aesthetic superiority. Yet perhaps our understanding of what is aesthetically superior in a cosmological theory must be fundamentally expanded, beyond that of mathematical elegance alone as in contemporary science, to encompass what might be infinitely deeper dimensions of the universe's aesthetic reality. Perhaps what we regard as a rigorously "scientific" engagement with the cosmos must be radically enlarged and developed so that the intellectual, aesthetic, and moral imaginations of scientist-philosophers of the future are fully integrated, deepening and enriching each other in their mutual interplay. It is possible that the deeper truths not only of our spiritual life but of the very cosmos require, and reward, an essentially aesthetic and moral engagement with its being and intelligence, and will forever elude a merely reductive, skeptical, objectifying judgment issued by a single proud but limited faculty, "reason," narrowly defined and rigidly isolated from our full being.

Yet this larger engagement with the cosmos will require of us a profound shift in what we regard as legitimate knowledge. It will demand an initial act of trust in the possible reality of an ensouled cosmos of transformative beauty and purposeful intelligence. In the inner politics of the modern mind, a "hermeneutics of suspicion" has completely overpowered and eclipsed a "hermeneutics of trust." That suspicion has been directed towards nature, towards the universe, towards other cultures and other world views, towards the spiritual dimension of life, even towards the human being in her embodied and ensouled wholeness. From Bacon and Descartes on, the modern mind directed its suspicion at everything except its own stance of skeptical objectification. The modern blindness to its own posture was precisely what many postmodern thinkers sought to correct, yet in doing so the postmodern strategy tended to produce an even more absolute negation: all reality perceived as nothing more than a social-linguistic construct, a local projection serving power and enforced by power. Because the postmodern intellectual milieu uncritically continued the modern assumption of cosmic disenchantment, the major modes of postmodern deconstruction essentially made their valid critical insights the final limit of any metaphysical understanding. Every attempt at a larger coherence, every discernment of an underlying spiritual meaning or purpose, was fundamentally suspect as nothing more than another totalizing move, another surreptitious attempt to expand the power of one part over the whole. Every imagination of an intelligible whole imbued with a larger significance drew deconstructive forces towards it like heat-seeking missiles.

In the course of the modern and postmodern periods, the necessary balance between the two basic intellectual postures of suspicion and trust, that essential creative tension of opposites, was lost. The consequences of this loss and imbalance have been immense. The fundamental skepticism of the modern and postmodern mind, its state of chastity that once served a larger purpose, has become a permanently confining end in itself, an armored state of intellectual constraint and spiritual unfulfillment. The strategy of skeptical self-distancing from the world has impelled and shaped the modern self—differentiating it, empowering it, but eventually so isolating it that it has come to dwell inside a solipsistic prison of its own assumptions. Worse, in its inflation and increasingly manic desperation, the civilization possessed by that objectifying stance has now become a centrifugal force of destruction and self-destruction in a world too intimately interconnected to accommodate such a titanic juggernaut so out of balance with the whole.

Humanity's "progress of knowledge" and the "evolution of consciousness" have too often been characterized as if our task were simply to ascend a very tall cognitive ladder with graded hierarchical steps that represent successive developmental stages in which we solve increasingly challenging mental riddles, like advanced problems in a graduate exam in biochemistry or logic. But to understand life and the cosmos better, perhaps we are required to transform not only our minds but our hearts. For our whole being, body and soul, mind and spirit, is implicated. Perhaps we must go not only high and far but down and deep. Our world view and cosmology, which defines the context for everything else, is profoundly affected by the degree to which *all* our faculties—intellectual, imaginative, aesthetic, moral, emotional, somatic, spiritual, relational—enter the process of our knowing. How we approach "the other," and how we approach each other, will shape everything, including our own evolving self and the cosmos in which we participate. Not only our personal lives but the very nature of the universe may demand of us now a new capacity for self-transcendence, both intellectual and moral, so that we may experience a new dimension of beauty and intelligence in the world—not a *projection* of our desire for beauty and intellectual mastery, but an *encounter* with the actual unpredictably unfolding beauty and intelligence of the whole. I believe that our intellectual quest for truth can never be separated from the cultivation of our moral and aesthetic imagination.

As Goethe recognized, it is often the case that the very faculties we require for our knowledge can be developed only through our receptive engagement with what we wish to comprehend, which transforms us in the very process of our inquiry. Thus the study of archetypal forms opens the archetypal eye. And thus the open encounter with the potential reality of an *anima mundi* makes possible its actual discernment. In this view, only by opening ourselves to being changed and expanded by that which we seek to understand will we be able to understand at all. Such a shift involves gradually opening our awareness to a dimension of reality that, though potentially of deep significance, may at first seem scarcely perceptible, the subtle "patterns which connect"—patterns of meaning within and without, the delicate and elusive, the repressed and denied, that which is obscured by our certainties, that which suggests and intimates rather than commands and proves. Such a transformation in our approach to life requires, as Jung saw, a new openness to our *own* "other," our interior other: our unconscious, in all its plenitude of forms. For here, perhaps, we begin to encounter the interior mystery of the cosmos itself.

Sources of the World Order

I n every field of inquiry, an adequate paradigm reveals patterns of coherent relations in what are otherwise inexplicable random coincidences. A good theory makes observed patterns intelligible. As the physicist and philosopher of science P. W. Bridgman famously observed, "coincidences" are what are left over after one has applied a bad theory. In the course of the three decades during which I have examined correlations between planetary movements and the patterns of human affairs, I found there were simply too many such "coincidences" evident in the data, which were too consistently coherent with the corresponding archetypal principles, and too strongly suggestive of the workings of some form of complex creative intelligence, to assume that they were all meaningless chance anomalies. Plato's words from his final dialogue, the *Laws*, when he criticized the disenchanted mechanistic cosmology of the physicists and Sophist philosophers of the preceding century, now seemed to me uncannily prophetic.

> The truth is just the opposite of the opinion which once prevailed among men, that the sun and stars are without soul. . . . For in that short-sighted view, the entire moving contents of the heavens seemed to them only stones, earth, and other soulless bodies, though these furnish the sources of the world order.

Yet the data that has now emerged suggests that what Plato called the "world order" is of a special kind. The evidence points to a cosmic ordering principle whose combination of participatory co-creativity, multivalent complexity, and dynamic indeterminacy was not entirely comprehensible to the ancient vision, even a vision as intricate and penetrating as Plato's. The relationship between the unfolding realities of human life and a dynamic archetypal order reflected in the planetary movements appears to be more fluid and complex, more creatively unpredictable, and more responsive to human intention and quality of consciousness or unconsciousness than was articulated in the classical tradition. One important task before us, therefore, is to understand the long development that separates Plato's vision of an archetypal participatory cosmos from our own. Another is to grasp how the nearly pervasive astrological cosmology of classical antiquity, after deeply influencing the medieval and Renaissance imagination, gradually receded in cultural significance and intellectual legitimacy until it came to appear utterly untenable to the modern mind. Yet another task is to seek insight into why it has reemerged in our own time, radically transfigured. Running through all these questions, I believe, is the great mystery of the unfolding Copernican revolution, which seems to have played the role of cosmological vessel and mediator of a vast initiatory process in the evolution of the modern self.

Beyond these, the survey we have now completed in the present book has brought up a multitude of other issues and questions that require careful attention and response—historical, philosophical, psychological, methodological. Significant cultural figures and events not yet discussed, complicating factors in those that have been discussed, and larger metaphysical and cosmological issues that now loom before us all call for discussion. Moreover, other significant categories of evidence, some of which will shine a new light on what we have seen in the preceding chapters, still remain to be presented. But I believe that we have examined a sufficient range and quantity of data at this point to consider, at least provisionally, their larger implications. Taking into account both the evidence set forth here and the larger body of research that I have so far completed, plus the findings of many fellow researchers in this field, I would briefly summarize my own tentative conclusions in the following way.

The current body of accumulated data makes it difficult to sustain the modern assumption that the universe as a whole is best understood as a blind, mechanistic phenomenon of ultimately random processes with which human consciousness is fundamentally incoherent, and in which the Earth and human beings are ultimately peripheral and insignificant. The evidence suggests rather that the cosmos is intrinsically meaningful to and coherent with human consciousness; that the Earth is a significant focal point of this meaning, a moving center of cosmic meaning in an evolving universe, as is each individual human being; that time is not only quantitative but qualitative in character, and that different periods of time are informed by tangibly different archetypal dynamics; and, finally, that the cosmos as a living whole appears to be informed by some kind of pervasive creative intelligence—an intelligence, judging by the data, of scarcely conceivable power, complexity, and aesthetic subtlety, yet one with which human intelligence is intimately connected, and in which it can consciously participate. I believe that a widespread understanding of the potent but usually unconscious archetypal dynamics that coincide with planetary cycles and alignments, both in individual lives and in the historical process, can play a crucial role in the positive unfolding of our collective future.

As I can attest from my own initial encounter with this evidence, there are many reasons why a person with a twentieth-century education and the usual background of modern cosmological assumptions would find it difficult to accept even the remotest possibility of meaningful correspondences between the movements of the planets and the patterns of human experience. I believe that historically some of those reasons have indeed been justified, and I have sought to address these. Yet I also believe that the evidence now available, when examined and explored with an open mind and an open heart, speaks for itself better than any defense I could attempt to provide. I have found the archetypal astrological perspective, properly understood, to be uniquely capable of illuminating the inner dynamics of both cultural history and personal biography. It provides extraordinary insight into the deeper shifting patterns of the human psyche, both individual and collective, and into the complexly participatory nature of human reality. It places the modern mind and the modern self in an altogether new light, radically recontextualizing the modern project. Perhaps most important, it promises to contribute to the emergence of a new, genuinely integral world view, one that, while sustaining the irreplaceable insights and achievements of the modern and postmodern development, can reunite the human and the cosmic, and restore transcendent meaning to both.

Epilogue

It is returning, at last it is coming home to me—my own Self and those parts of it that have long been abroad and scattered among all things and accidents.

—Nietzsche
Thus Spoke Zarathustra

The modern mind has long assumed that there are few things more categorically distant from each other than "cosmos" and "psyche." What could be more *outer* than cosmos? What more *inner* than psyche? But today we are obliged to recognize that, of all categories, psyche and cosmos are perhaps the most consequentially intertwined, the most deeply mutually implicated. Our understanding of the universe affects every aspect of our interior life from our highest spiritual convictions to the most minuscule details of our daily experience. Conversely, the deep dispositions and character of our interior life fully permeate and configure our understanding of the entire cosmos. The relation of psyche and cosmos is a mysterious marriage, one that is still unfolding— at once a mutual interpenetration and a fertile tension of opposites.

It seems we have a choice. There are many possible worlds, many possible meanings, living within us *in potentia,* moving through us, awaiting enactment. We are not just solitary separate subjects in a meaningless universe of objects upon which we can and must impose our egocentric will. Nor are we blank slates, empty vessels, condemned to playing out passively the implacable processes of the universe—or of God—or of our environment, our genes, our race, our class, our gender, our social-linguistic community, our unconscious, our stage in evolution. Rather, we are miraculously self-reflective and autonomous yet embedded participants in a larger cosmic drama, each of us a creative nexus of action and imagination. Each is a self-responsible microcosm of the creative macrocosm, enacting a richly, complexly co-evolutionary unfolding of reality. To a crucial extent, the nature of the universe depends on us.

Yet it is no less certain that our *own* marvelously complex nature depends upon and is embedded in the universe. Must we not regard the interpenetration of human and cosmic nature as fundamental, radical, "all the way down"? It seems to me highly improbable that everything we identify within ourselves as specifically human—the human imagination, human spirituality, the full range of human emotions, moral aspiration, aesthetic intelligence, the discernment and creation of narrative significance and meaningful coherence, the quest for beauty, truth, and the good—suddenly appeared ex nihilo in the human being as an accidental and more or less absurd ontological singularity in the cosmos. Is not this assumption, which in one form or another still implicitly pervades most modern and postmodern thought, nothing other than the unexamined residue of the Cartesian monotheistic ego? Is it not much more plausible that human nature, in all its creative multidimensional depths and heights, emerges from the very essence of the cosmos, and that the human spirit is *the spirit of the cosmos itself* as inflected through us and enacted by us? Is it not more likely that the human intelligence in all its creative brilliance is ultimately the cosmos's intelligence expressing *its* creative brilliance? And that the human imagination is ultimately grounded in the cosmic imagination? And, finally, that this larger spirit, intelligence, and imagination all live within and act through the self-reflective human being who serves as a unique vessel and embodiment of the cosmos—creative, unpredictable, fallible, self-transcending, unfolding the whole, integral to the whole, perhaps even essential to the whole?

If so, perhaps the approach of the second suitor to the mystery of the universe will ultimately be a more fruitful and appropriate strategy than one that presumes the universe's fundamentally meaningless and purposeless nature as the very starting point of legitimate knowledge. Let us recall those remarkable words of Sir James Frazer a century ago at the end of his twelve-volume magnum opus, *The Golden Bough*:

> In the last analysis magic, religion, and science are nothing but theories of thought; and as science has supplanted its predecessors, so it may hereafter be itself superseded by some more perfect hypothesis. . . . Brighter stars will rise on some voyager of the future—some great Ulysses of the realms of thought—than shine on us. The dreams of magic may one day be the waking realities of science.

Yet perhaps those stars will have been there all along, hidden by the bright dawn of our modernity. And our Ulysses will be but awakening to a very ancient cosmos whose vast intelligence, beauty, and mystery we have been slowly preparing ourselves to know.

> *We shall not cease from exploration*
> *And the end of all our exploring*
> *Will be to arrive where we started*
> *And know the place for the first time.*

Notes

Part I: *The Transformation of the Cosmos*

1. I explore many of these complexities in *The Passion of the Western Mind: Understanding the Ideas That Shaped Our World View* (New York: Harmony, 1991; Ballantine, 1993). Charles Taylor in *Sources of the Self: The Making of the Modern Identity* (Cambridge, Mass.: Harvard University Press, 1989) presents an especially comprehensive and nuanced account of the complex historical roots and development of the modern self. Robert Bellah's 1964 paper "Religious Evolution," in *Beyond Belief: Essays on Religion in a Post-Traditional World* (Berkeley: University of California, 1991), provides an invaluable historical analysis of the evolving relationship between religious world view, human self-image, and social-political developments in which various forms of world rejection (from the Axial Period) and disenchantment (from the Reformation and modernity) play a pivotal role. This compact and still essential essay will be considerably expanded and developed in Bellah's forthcoming *Religious Evolution*.

Part II: *In Search of a Deeper Order*

1. The primary texts by Jung are the 1951 Eranos conference lecture "On Synchronicity" and the longer 1952 monograph *Synchronicity: An Acausal Connecting Principle*, both in *Collected Works of Carl Gustav Jung*, trans. R. F. C. Hull, ed. H. Read, M. Fordham, G. Adler, W. McGuire, Bollingen Series XX (Princeton, N. J.: Princeton University Press, 1953–79), vol. 8. While invaluable and seminal, these works by Jung are marked by many conceptual incoherencies and confusions, perhaps inevitable in the first presentation of a new principle of understanding that so radically challenged existing assumptions. Moreover, as discussed in note 5 below, Jung's lecture and monograph focused on categories of phenomena, such as paranormal events and experimental data from physics, that obscured the human, psychologically transformative dimension of synchronistic phenomena, though the latter was in fact far more central in Jung's own life experience and clinical observations.

   Other relevant texts by Jung can be found in *Jung on Synchronicity and the Paranormal*, edited and with an introduction by Roderick Main (Princeton, N. J.: Princeton University Press, 1997). For synchronicity's implications for the psychology of religion, see Robert Aziz, C. G. *Jung's Psychology of Religion and Synchronicity* (Albany: State University of New York Press, 1990): "The synchronicity concept is, arguably, the single theory with the most far-reaching implications for Jung's psychology as a whole, particularly for his psychology of religion" (p. 1). Jung's acute alertness to synchronistic phenomena in his life and their possible implications is emphasized through Aziz's analysis (see especially pp. 84–90, 159–166). For synchronicity's relevance to physics and the scientific world view, see Victor Mansfield, *Synchronicity, Science, and Soul-Making* (Chicago: Open Court, 1995). Other significant writings on synchronicity include books or essays by Arthur Koestler, Antony Flew, Michael Fordham, Ira Progoff, Marie-Louise von Franz, Aniela Jaffé, Allan Combs, Mark Holland, Michael Conforti, Jean Shinoda Bolen, David Peat, Sean Kelly, and Ray Grasse.

2. Hillman's discussion of Petrarch's ascent of Mont Ventoux in *Re-Visioning Psychology* is important to our concerns on two further counts beyond its exemplification of a synchronicity that was both personally and culturally consequential: first, Hillman's understanding of soul—psyche, the locus of meaning and purpose—as something existing not only within but beyond "man"; and second, his

analysis of the Renaissance as marking the emergence of a new kind of inner vision, tied to a new sense of self and a new vision of the world. Thus Hillman continues:

> If one looks again at the passage Petrarch was reading which so stunned him, one finds that Augustine was discussing *memoria*. Book X, 8 of the *Confessions* is important to the art of memory. It is about the soul's imaginative faculty. "Great is this force of memory [imagination] excessive great, O my God; a large and boundless chamber! who ever sounded the bottom thereof? yet is this a power of mine, and belongs unto my nature, nor do I myself comprehend all that I am. Therefore is the mind too strait to contain itself."
>
> These sentences immediately precede the passage Petrarch opened on the mountain. In them Augustine is wrestling with the classical problems, beginning with Heraclitus, concerning the measureless depth of the soul, the place, size, ownership, and origin of the images of *memoria* (the archetypal unconscious, if you prefer). It was the wonder of this train of thought that struck Petrarch, the wonder of the interior personality, which is both inside man and yet far greater than man. . . . The revelation on Mont Ventoux opened Petrarch's eyes to the complexity and mystery of the man-psyche relationship and moved him to write of the marvel of the soul. . . . Renaissance psychology begins with a revelation of the independent reality of soul. . . . It is not the return from nature to man that starts the Renaissance going but the return to soul. (Hillman, *Re-Visioning Psychology*, pp. 196–97 [bracketed and parenthetical interpolations in Hillman]; Augustine, *Confessions*, X, 8, 15, trans. E. B. Pusey [New York: Dutton Everyman, 1966], pp. 212–13)

Hillman is seeking here to correct the "humanistic fallacy" of Renaissance scholarship, in which Petrarch's "commentators and translators interpret the 'soul' and the 'self' in his writing as 'man': to them the event on Mont Ventoux signifies the return from God's world or nature to man. . . . It cannot hold the Augustinian paradox that keeps psyche and human as two factors 'in' each other by virtue of imagination. Therefore the humanistic fallacy fails to acknowledge what Petrarch actually wrote: Soul is the marvel" (pp. 196–97).

I would add that the ambiguous conflation of "soul" and "self" with "man" does not begin with Renaissance scholarship but is in an important sense central to the birth of the modern self in the Renaissance, visible in Pico and Ficino and in the larger ethos of the age. This underlying ambiguity in Renaissance Humanism permitted an empowerment of the human self that was in turn greatly heightened by the further unconscious conflation of human reason with the image of divine reason, the transcendent Solar Logos, that emerged in the course of the Copernican revolution, Scientific Revolution, and Enlightenment. Both of these "humanistic" developments—the human appropriation of both *psyche* and *logos*—had roots and precedents in ancient Greek thought, as well as in the biblical tradition. In the modern secular context, however, freed of the transcendental constraints of the classical religious sensibility, these developments took dramatically new forms with new consequences.

3. Whereas Augustine interpreted his synchronistic reading of St. Paul's words as a foundation for overcoming an intense inner conflict and permanently redirecting his life in accordance with his revelation, Petrarch's reading of Augustine's words seems to have produced a more complex result, one appropriate to the modern self of which he was a major precursor. Over the past two centuries, Petrarch's ascent of Mont Ventoux in 1336 has been interpreted by many prominent scholars as an extraordinarily epochal event that heralded the new spirit of the Renaissance and modernity, yet they have interpreted that event in remarkably diverse and at times entirely opposite ways. The nineteenth-century historian Jacob Burckhardt saw Petrarch's ascent as a great milestone in the modern discovery of the beauty of nature and landscape (*The Civilization of the Renaissance in Italy*, Part Four, "The Discovery of the World and of Man"). Jean Gebser declared that the ascent signified "the first dawning of an awareness of space that resulted in a fundamental alteration of European man's attitude in and toward the world . . . an unprecedented extension of man's image of the world," and that it prophetically "inaugurates a new realistic, individualistic, and rational [perspectivally objective] understanding of nature" (*The Ever-Present Origin*, trans. N. Barstad and A. Mickunas, rev. ed. [Athens: Ohio University Press, 1991], pp. 12–15). Petrarch's biographer Morris Bishop called him the first modern mountain climber, whose novel motivation was to scale the peak for its own sake (*Petrarch and his World*, Bloomington: Indiana University Press, 1963, pp. 103–04).

Representing the mainstream of twentieth-century scholarship, Paul O. Kristeller stated that

Petrarch's response to reading Augustine on the mountain, and his life work generally, "expresses for the first time that emphasis on man which was to receive eloquent developments in the treatises of later humanists and to be given a metaphysical and cosmological foundation in the works of Ficino and Pico. This is the reason that the humanists were to adopt the name 'humanities' (*studia humanitatis*) for their studies" (*The Encyclopedia of Philosophy*, s.v. "Petrarch," vol. 6, ed. P. Edwards [New York: Macmillan and Free Press, 1967, 1972], p. 127; see also "Augustine and the Early Renaissance," *Studies in Renaissance Thought* [Rome: Storia e Letteratura, 1969], pp. 361–62).

In contrast to the latter position, James Hillman evoked not a new "emphasis on man" but rather a "return to soul" as genuinely emblematic of the Renaissance. In Hillman's rendering, Petrarch's attention to the boundless mystery of interiority, his care for the intellectual imagination, his devotion to the classical authors, his passion for writing and excellence of style, and his enduring attachment to the image of Laura all represented a cultivation of soul, not only as opposed to a "return to man" but also, ultimately, as a movement away from the spiritual path represented by Augustine. "Petrarch's experience is called the Ascent of Mont Ventoux. But the crucial event is the *descent,* the return down to the valley of soul" (*Re-Visioning Psychology*, p. 197).

Petrarch himself, however, in his famous letter carefully describing the experience to his friend and confessor, portrays the event above all as a powerful metaphor for the arduous spiritual ascent to God, and he depicts his reading of Augustine's words as dramatically, even chastisingly, calling him back to that most important commitment. Though this perspective on the event is surprisingly absent, even suppressed, in the major commentaries and interpretations just cited, it is clearly the most compelling dimension of the experience for Petrarch himself. After mentioning the synchronicity involved in Augustine's conversion experience, Petrarch recalled yet another example of such a coincidence and its transformative consequences, and then began his larger meditation on the spiritual challenge of life:

> The same thing happened earlier to Saint Anthony, when he was listening to the Gospel where it is written, "If thou wilt be perfect, go and sell what thou hast, and give to the poor, and thou shalt have treasure in heaven: and come and follow me." Believing this scripture to have been read for his especial benefit, as his biographer Athanasius says, he guided himself by its aid to the Kingdom of Heaven. And as Anthony on hearing these words waited for nothing more, and as Augustine upon reading the Apostle's admonition sought no farther, so I concluded my reading in the few words which I have given. I thought in silence of the lack of good counsel in us mortals, who neglect what is noblest in ourselves, scatter our energies in all directions, and waste ourselves in a vain show, because we look about us for what is to be found only within. I wondered at the natural nobility of our soul, save when it debases itself of its own free will, and deserts its original estate, turning what God has given it for its honour into dishonour. How many times, think you, did I turn back that day, to glance at the summit of the mountain which seemed scarcely a cubit high compared with the range of human contemplation—when it is not immersed in the foul mire of earth? With every downward step I asked myself this: If we are ready to endure so much sweat and labour in order that we may bring our bodies a little nearer heaven, how can a soul struggling toward God, up the steeps of human pride and human destiny, fear any cross or prison or sting of fortune? How few, I thought, but are diverted from their path by the fear of difficulties or the love of ease! . . . How earnestly should we strive, not to stand on mountaintops, but to trample beneath us those appetites which spring from earthly impulses. With no consciousness of the difficulties of the way, amidst these preoccupations which I have so frankly revealed, we came, long after dark, but with the full moon lending us its friendly light, to the little inn which we had left that morning before dawn. ("The Ascent of Mount Ventoux: To Dionisio da Borgo San Sepolcro," in *Petrarch: The First Modern Scholar and Man of Letters*, ed. and trans. J.H. Robinson [New York: Putnam, 1898], pp. 318–19)

It is certainly true that the impulse and will to make the ascent at all and the sharply polarized nature of the inner dialogue he conducts with himself as he climbs the mountain and later reflects on the event suggest that Petrarch is indeed, in spite of himself, beginning to break from the powerful hold of the Augustinian medieval spirit while simultaneously assimilating it. But his own account makes clear just how immense was the struggle to do so. We should also note that the Latin word Petrarch uses that Hillman and others translate as "soul" is not *anima* but *animus*. This can also be translated as "spirit," or as the "soul" in the Christian spiritual sense rather than as the more psychological and imaginative "soul" developed by Hillman and archetypal psychology.

Finally, in yet a further dimension of the ascent that is implicitly recognized and enlisted by all these interpretations—those of Burckhardt, Gebser, Bishop, Kristeller, Hillman, and Petrarch himself—it is especially the inspiration and recovery of the great authors of classical antiquity, from Virgil and Ovid to Augustine himself, that permeates the event and pervades Petrarch's account from beginning to end, as their eloquence and wisdom are brought to bear on every aspect of his experience as it unfolds that day. Even the idea of making the ascent was catalyzed by Petrarch's reading of another ancient author on the day before: "The idea took hold upon me with especial force when, in rereading Livy's *History of Rome*, yesterday, I happened upon the place where Philip of Macedon, the same who waged war against the Romans, ascended Mount Haemus in Thessaly, from whose summit he was able, it is said, to see two seas, the Adriatic and the Euxine" (Robinson, ed., *Petrarch*, p. 308). Here as well, then, can be seen the birth of both Renaissance classicism and the modern man of letters.

We can perhaps understand the now-famous ascent on that long clear day in April 1336 in its more encompassing significance by recognizing that it is this newly articulate complexity and conflict of values, motivations, and experiences to which Petrarch gave voice in his account that we must see as central—spiritual and moral, literary and humanistic, naturalist and perspectival, aesthetic and romantic, scholarly and classicist. The event was a great *complexio oppositorum*, a complex interplay and synthesis of opposites: at once reflective and questing, looking both to the past and to the future, both outward and inward, both ascending and descending. It is precisely this divergent multiplicity of values, this tension of many conflicting impulses, by which Petrarch heralds the new sensibility of the Renaissance and the emergence of the modern self with its unprecedentedly multiform character. The Ascent of Mont Ventoux, and the descent afterwards, is a superbly ambiguous event, and in just this complex multivalence lies its essential character and magnitude.

4. Robert Aziz comments: "For Jung, the call to individuate arises from the deepest sources of life and is supported inwardly and outwardly by the compensatory activities of nature. It is a call, therefore, that is not to be taken lightly. Both inwardly and outwardly nature strives unceasingly to bring about the realization, in the life of the individual, of a unique pattern of meaning. . . . [A]s evidenced by his own writings on synchronicity and, perhaps more importantly, by the way he lived his own life, the individuation process extends beyond the psychological realm and assumes the character of a drama that takes the whole of nature for its stage. What we normally regard as the discontinuous inner and outer worlds become enclosed within the same circle of wholeness. Inwardly and outwardly nature works, through the compensatory patterning of events, to further the movement of the individual toward wholeness. . . . Now one is challenged to achieve a full understanding of the meaning that conjoins one, not only to the unconscious, but to nature in its entirety. This is the new spiritual challenge of individuation. It is the task of experiencing within the sacred circle of nature as a whole the meaning of an individual existence" (*C. G. Jung's Psychology of Religion and Synchronicity*, pp. 165–66).

Jung's attitude closely resembles the characteristic primal and shamanic alertness to nature's symbolically significant patterning, as well as ancient Chinese Taoist philosophy, in which the dominant principles are pattern, order, symbolic correlations, the unity of human and cosmos, and the interdependence of all things. Cf. Richard Wilhelm, *The Secret of the Golden Flower*: "[Chinese philosophy] is built on the premise that the cosmos and man, in the last analysis, obey the same law; that man is a microcosm and is not separated from the macrocosm by any fixed barriers. The very same laws rule for the one as for the other, and from the one a way leads into the other. The psyche and the cosmos are to each other like the inner world and the outer world. Therefore man participates by nature in all cosmic events, and is inwardly as well as outwardly interwoven with them" (trans. C. F. Baynes [New York: Harcourt, Brace & World, 1931, 1962], p.11, quoted in Aziz, p. 135). Cf. also Joseph Needham, *Science and Civilisation in China*: "The keyword in Chinese thought is *Order* and above all *Pattern*. . . . The symbolic correlations or correspondences all formed part of one colossal pattern. Things behaved in particular ways not necessarily because of prior actions or impulsions of other things, but because their position in the ever-moving cyclical universe was such that they were endowed with intrinsic natures which made that behaviour inevitable for them. . . . They were thus parts in existential dependence upon the whole world-organism. And they reacted upon one another not so much by mechanical impulsion or causation as by a kind of mysterious resonance" ([Cambridge: Cambridge University Press, 1956, 1991], vol. 2, p. 281).

5. This formulation of synchronicity in terms of *qualitative time,* from 1930, reflects Jung's early astrological research, beginning in 1911, and his experiments throughout the 1920s with the I Ching: "Jung's first theorizing about synchronicity was done with reference to astrology and the *I Ching* and focused on the fact that things arising in a particular moment of time all share the characteristics of that moment. It appears to have been this understanding of the role of time, an understanding in which simultaneity does indeed play an essential part, which led Jung to coin the term 'synchronicity,' with its emphasis on the element of time (Gk. *syn* = together, *chronos* = time)" (R. Main, *Jung on Synchronicity and the Paranormal*, p. 23).

In later years, Jung increasingly focused on synchronicity's parallels with twentieth-century physics. He was influenced first by his conversations about relativity with Einstein (a dinner guest on several occasions in the 1909–12 period) and several decades later through his discussions about quantum mechanics with his patient and friend Wolfgang Pauli. Reflecting the parallels with both physics and the parapsychological experiments of J. B. Rhine at Duke University that started in the 1930s, Jung began to broaden the concept of synchronicity to include many phenomena—various paranormal phenomena such as precognition and telepathy, the discontinuities of modern physics, the properties of natural numbers—for which simultaneity, qualitative time, and meaning were not always relevant factors. Instead, he began to stress "the psychic relativization of time and space" and "general acausal orderedness." However, as many commentators have noted (Koestler, Aziz, Mansfield, Main), some of these additions stretched the parameters of the concept to include phenomena for which the original term "synchronicity" was now problematic and less obviously appropriate.

In his efforts to include the various phenomena from parapsychology and physics, Jung essentially combined into one overarching concept several separate classes of events which in many cases seemed to confuse and overlook their fundamental differences. For example, an especially important difference was concealed by Jung's conflation of two basic categories, the meaningful coincidence of simultaneous events and the experience of clairvoyant cognition. The first category can be said to represent the classic form of synchronicity, illustrated by the paradigm case of the golden scarab, in which the outer world unexpectedly brought forth a concrete external event that closely paralleled in meaning a simultaneous psychological state. The second category was centered on cases in which an individual experienced internally—by intuition, dream, or vision—some external event in a future time or at a distant location.

But it is only in the first category—the one on which Jung placed far greater emphasis—that the crucial possibility of a meaning-embedded world presents itself, one that has all the metaphysical implications associated with the concept of synchronicity. By contrast, in cases of paranormal experiences like clairvoyance, telepathy, and precognition, the individual in question can be seen as simply exercising some not yet understood perceptual or cognitive faculty that has no implications for the outer world's capacity to embody meaning in a manner that transcends the human psyche. Such cases would thus provide evidence pointing only to the need for a revised understanding of human abilities and the parameters of human consciousness. Other cases, such as those in the parapsychological experiments and in quantum physics, present comparable differences, as well as additional ones that eliminate the presence of meaning as a central factor altogether.

It seems likely that the scientific status of physics and the statistical-experimental nature of the parapsychological research played a significant role in moving Jung in the above direction, encouraging him to modify the terms of his original concept and add further categories to it in his hope to elevate the viability of his challenging hypothesis in the science-dominated intellectual ethos of the mid-twentieth century (see, for example, Ira Progoff, *Jung, Synchronicity, and Human Destiny* [New York: Dell, 1973], p. 143; Aziz, p. 2; Mansfield, pp. 33–34; and Main, pp. 15–17, 23–27). This also perhaps explains Jung's 1954 letter to André Barbault in which he contrasted synchronicity with the qualitative time hypothesis he had earlier proposed, suggesting now that the idea of synchronicity replaced rather than manifested the principle of qualitative time (C. G. Jung, *Letters 2: 1951–1961,* ed. G. Adler, A. Jaffé, trans. R. F. C. Hull [London: Routledge & Kegan Paul, 1976], p. 176). Jung here described the latter concept as tautological because "time in itself consists of nothing" and is only "qualified" or defined by events.

This apparent change in Jung's position probably reflected not only his larger shift in emphasis towards a more broadly inclusive and science-oriented formulation of the synchronicity principle, but also his desire to locate the essence of synchronistic phenomena in the parallel patterning of the phenomena themselves rather than in some a priori characteristics of time apart from the phenomena. Thus, contrary to some commentaries on this topic, Jung's later objection was not to the idea of time having a de facto qualitative dimension but rather to the idea that time *itself* was the a priori determining factor of the observed qualities. Instead, Jung clearly viewed the determining factor, in the sense of what "arranged" the qualitative patterning in the flux of events, to be not time per se but rather the constellated archetype. In Aristotelian terms, the archetype is the formal cause of the synchronicity. Time is thus regarded as possessing a qualitative dimension, but the quality that will be manifest at any given time is indeterminate and potential until a specific archetype is constellated.

In retrospect, by the time Jung wrote his principal analysis on synchronicity in the early 1950s, his increasing focus on parapsychology and physics had in a sense partly colonized the original concept and thus obscured the reality of how he had integrated his experience of meaningful coincidences into his life and clinical practice. Jung's original and most familiar examples of synchronicities emerged in psychological, therapeutic, religious, divinatory, and esoteric contexts (as compared with experimentally tested extrasensory perception, psychokinesis, out-of-body and near-death experiences and other paranormal phenomena, and the discontinuities of physics, for all of which alternative explanations have been given that are arguably more apt than synchronicity). For the more characteristic original categories of meaningful coincidences, such as the golden scarab and stopped watch examples cited in the text, the idea of qualitative time (i.e., time as possessing a qualitative dimension), along with the elements of simultaneity and meaning, clearly remains relevant as part of a larger theoretical conception in which the archetypal meaning that informs and connects the synchronistic events serves as a fundamental explanatory principle.

Many aspects of relativity and quantum mechanics are indeed relevant to synchronistic phenomena: a relativized space-time continuum, the collapse of strict linear causality and of a fully independent objective world, complementarity, probabilistic indeterminacy, nonlocality, and the interconnected and interdependent nature of reality. Other essential elements of synchronicities, however, have no parallels in physics—above all, the fundamental presence of meaning as the structuring factor, and the apparent teleological or purposive aspect of such events.

In traditional philosophical terms, these two basic elements of synchronicities—meaning and purpose—represent straightforward expressions of what Aristotle called formal and final causes, respectively. Compared with the simpler (or simplistic) modern view of causality, which is entirely linear-mechanistic in nature, Aristotle's more nuanced and capacious formulation defined "cause" as that which is a necessary, though not in itself sufficient, condition for the existence of something. Such conditions included formal and final (teleological) factors, in addition to the material and efficient factors stressed by mainstream modern science. When Jung originally employed the term "acausality" and emphasized that synchronicities were fundamentally acausal in nature, he provided a helpful and probably necessary counterpoint to the narrow conventional scientific understanding of linear-mechanistic causality that was then (the first half of the twentieth century) nearly ubiquitous. But the clear applicability of Aristotle's richer classical formulation of causality for understanding synchronicities within a Jungian archetypal and teleological perspective places in question the continued usefulness or appropriateness of the term "acausality" in this context.

6. Marie-Louise von Franz: "The most essential and certainly the most impressive thing about synchronistic occurrences, the thing which really constitutes their numinosity, is the fact that in them the duality of soul and matter seems to be eliminated. They are therefore an *empirical* indication of the ultimate unity of all existence, which Jung, using the terminology of medieval natural philosophy, called the *unus mundus*. In medieval philosophy this concept designates the potential preexistent model of creation in the mind of God in accordance with which God later produced the creation. It is, according to John Scotus Erigena, 'God's vital or seminal power which changes from a Nothing, which is beyond all existence and non-existence, into countless forms' " (M.-L. von Franz, *C. G. Jung: His Myth in Our Time* [Toronto: Inner City Books, 1998], p. 247).

7. *Senex,* from the Latin: old man, elder, age, as in senescence, senator, senility. Reflecting the complex and ambiguous constellation of qualities, positive and problematic, characteristic of old age—from narrowness, rigidity, and pessimism, and the concern with order, control, and death, to gravitas, experience, and wisdom—the *senex* is closely associated with the Saturn archetype. The *senex* is the polar complement to the *puer* or *puer eternus* (eternal child), with which it is mutually implicated. For a richly perceptive exploration of the *senex,* see two early papers by James Hillman, "On Senex Consciousness," *Spring: An Annual of Archetypal Psychology and Jungian Thought* (1970), pp. 146–65; and his 1967 Eranos paper, "Senex and Puer: An Aspect of the Historical and Psychological Present," in J. Hillman, ed., *Puer Papers* (Dallas: Spring Publications, 1991), pp. 3–53.

8. This understanding of Jung's evolution is at the center of Aziz's analysis: "In 1937 when Jung exhorted his Yale audience to move beyond the confines of established religion and accept the challenge of 'immediate religious experience,' what Jung had in mind was for them to enter consciously into a direct encounter with the unconscious. For those for whom the rituals of conventional religion had lost their efficacy, what Jung offered as an alternative was an intrapsychic ritual which, properly followed, would lead to the emergence of a highly personalized spiritual wholeness. What Jung had in mind in 1937, then, was a ritual to be enacted within the sacred circle of the psyche. . . . [H]owever, this earlier Jungian notion of religious ritual has been dramatically transformed by the synchronicity concept, indeed, so much so that we can now say that Jung's notion of 'immediate religious experience' may be taken to refer not simply to an intrapsychic encounter, but to a direct encounter with nature in its entirety. The Jungian ritual, to put it simply, is now a ritual which is to be enacted within the sacred circle of nature as a whole. . . . [F]or Jung the 'holy' is encountered as much outwardly, in the synchronistic patterning of events, as it is inwardly. Accordingly, the individual in search of 'immediate religious experience' is now required to attend to the compensatory images with which nature presents one outwardly with the same religious seriousness with which one attends to the 'images of wholeness offered by the unconscious.' . . . The religious need, as Jung puts it, longs for wholeness, and here the wholeness to which one must open oneself is a wholeness that is not only transmitted intrapsychically, but transmitted to the individual through the synchronistic patterning of events in one's environment (Aziz, pp. 167–68).

9. Cf. R. Main, "Religion, Science, and Synchronicity," *Harvest: Journal for Jungian Studies* 46, no. 2 (2000), pp. 89–107. "In a 1955 letter to R. F. C. Hull, Jung reported: 'The latest comment about "Synchronicity" is that it cannot be accepted because it shakes the security of our scientific foundations, as if this were not exactly the goal I am aiming at. . . .' On the same day he wrote to Michael Fordham of 'the impact of synchronicity upon the fanatical one-sidedness of scientific philosophy.' Specifically, Jung thought that his work on synchronicity demonstrated the need to expand the current conception of science in order to include, in addition to the classical concepts of time, space, and causality, a principle of acausal connection through meaning. This, he concluded, would introduce the psychic factor of meaning into our scientific picture of the world, help get rid of 'the incommensurability between the observed and the observer', and make possible a 'whole judgement'—that is, a judgement that takes into consideration psychological as well as physical factors. Because for Jung the psychological mediates between the physical and the spiritual, to link the physical and psychological in this way entails setting up a potential bridge between the physical and the spiritual, hence between science and religion. These bold conclusions and implications from Jung's work on synchronicity resonate with many subsequent attempts to develop more holistic models of science—some directly exploring Jung's suggestions, for instance those of David Peat and Victor Mansfield, others working independently but aware of Jung's contribution and possibly influenced or inspired by it, for instance those of David Bohm and Rupert Sheldrake."

10. See, for example, the lecture given by Jung's daughter, Gret Baumann-Jung, "Some Reflections on the Horoscope of C. G. Jung," trans. F. J. Hopman, in *Spring: An Annual of Archetypal Psychology and Jungian Thought* (1975), pp. 35–55. See also Jung's letter to B. V. Raman, September 6, 1947: "In cases of difficult psychological diagnosis I usually get a horoscope in order to have a further point of view from an entirely different angle. I must say that I very often found that the astrological data elucidated certain points which I otherwise would have been unable to understand" (Jung, *Letters 1*, p. 475).

11. To this list could be added Galileo and Francis Bacon. Galileo's long practice of astrology, not only for patrons, such as the Medici, the grand dukes of Tuscany, but also for his own family, is documented by N. Kollerstrom et al. in an issue of *Culture and Cosmos* devoted entirely to this subject (*Galileo's Astrology*, vol. 7, no. 1, 2003), and by H. Darrel Rutkin in "Galileo Astrologer: Astrology and Mathematical Practice in the Late-Sixteenth and Early-Seventeenth Centuries," *Galilaeana* 2 (2005), pp. 107–43. Bacon set out a detailed argument for a reform of astrology on empirical principles in his *De dignitate et augmentis scientiarum*, the expanded Latinized 1623 reworking of his *The Advancement of Learning* (1605). See Rutkin, "Astrology, Natural Philosophy and the History of Science, c. 1250–1700: Studies toward an Interpretation of Giovanni Pico della Mirandola's *Disputationes Adversus Astrologiam Divinatricem*," Ph.D. thesis, Indiana University, 2002.

Concerning the Greek origins of Western astrology, modern historians generally either disregarded them or considered astrology an inexplicable aberration of the Greek mind, an uncharacteristic succumbing to irrational non-Greek influences. But as S. J. Tester remarked in his survey *A History of Western Astrology* (Suffolk, England: Boydell, 1987):

> Those who have admired the Greeks for their clear rationalism (and who have always ignored anything they saw as contrary to it as un-Hellenic, no matter whether the author was a Greek and the language Greek and the time Classical) have so pre-conditioned their own thinking as to misunderstand both astrology and its appeal to the Greek mind. . . . It was not the uneducated and superstitious who accepted and developed it. It was the philosophers, like Plato, who prepared the ground, and the Stoics—who were among the greatest logicians and physicists of their times—who most fully worked it into their system. It was the doctors and the scientists like [Aristotle's student and successor] Theophrastus who accepted it and developed its associations with medicine. . . . The point, and it is a very important point indeed, is that astrology appealed to the educated Greeks precisely because they were rational. . . . It is not an accident that the two greatest of the Greek astronomers, Hipparchus and Ptolemy, were both also astrologers, the latter the author of the most influential ancient textbook of astrology. Nor were the Greeks necessarily wrong about this; but right or wrong, they accepted astrology, and its acceptance as a learned and scientific study was the common, if not the normal, attitude to it down to the eighteenth century, and it is impossible to understand men like Kepler and Newton unless astrology is seen for what the Greeks made it, a rational attempt to map the state of the heavens and to interpret that map in the context of that "cosmic sympathy" which makes man an integral part of the universe. (pp. 17–18)

See also George Sarton, *A History of Science: Hellenistic Science and Culture in the Last Three Centuries B.C.* (Cambridge, Mass.: Harvard University Press, 1959), p. 165; and Otto Neugebauer's comment that, "compared with the background of religion, magic, and mysticism, the fundamental doctrines of astrology are pure science" (*The Exact Sciences in Antiquity*, 2nd ed. [Providence, R.I.: Brown University Press, 1957], p. 171). In her study of the Christian cardinal, philosopher, and astrologer Pierre d'Ailly, whose astrological writings played a significant role in inspiring Columbus to make his transatlantic voyage, Laura Ackerman Smoller cites the works of prominent scholars working in this area such as Thorndike, Neugebauer, Pingree, and North, and adds, "No one can read these works without an appreciation of what a sophisticated and demanding science was practiced by the medieval astrologers" (*History, Prophecy, and the Stars: The Christian Astrology of Pierre d'Ailly, 1350–1420* [Princeton, N.J.: Princeton University Press, 1994], p. 5).

12. *Ptolemy's Tetrabiblos*, trans. J. M. Ashmand (Symbols and Signs, 1976); Johannes Kepler, "On the More Certain Fundamentals of Astrology," foreword and notes by J. B. Brackenridge, trans. M. A. Rossi, *Proceedings of the American Philosophical Society* 123, 2 (1979): pp. 85–116; *Kepler's Astrology: Excerpts*, trans. and ed. K. Negus (Princeton, N.J.: Eucopia, 1987); Alan Leo, *Art of Synthesis* (London: Fowler, 1968); *How to Judge a Nativity* (London: Fowler, 1969); Dane Rudhyar, *Astrology of Personality* (1936; Garden City, N.Y.: Doubleday, 1970); Charles E. O. Carter, *Principles of Astrology* (London: Fowler, 1970); *Astrological Aspects* (London: Fowler, 1971); Reinhold Ebertin, *Combinations of Stellar Influence* (Aalen, Germany: Ebertin-Verlag, 1972); John Addey, *Astrology Reborn* (London: Faculty of Astrologers, 1972); *Harmonics in Astrology* (1976); Robert Hand, *Planets in Transit* (Gloucester, Mass.: Para Research, 1976); *Horoscope Symbols* (Rockport, Mass.: Para Research, 1981); Liz Greene, *Saturn: A New Look at an Old Devil* (York Beach, Maine: Weiser, 1976); Stephen Arroyo, *Astrology, Karma, and Transformation* (Davis, Calif.: CRCS Publications, 1978); Charles Harvey, Michael Baigent, Nicholas Campion, *Mundane Astrology* (London: HarperCollins, 1984). Among many other works, I also consulted the widely used texts by Frances Sakoian and Louis Acker, *The Astrologer's Handbook* (New York: Harper & Row, 1973), and *Predictive Astrology* (New York: Harper & Row, 1977), and also, from 1976, the bimonthly issues of the British *Journal of the Astrological Association*, and the biannual *Correlation Journal of Research into Astrology*.

13. An important exception to this general statement is the continued practice of traditional horary astrology, essentially a form of divination that employs elaborate rules of astrological interpretation in combination with an active intuitive role by the practitioner to arrive at highly specific predictions

about particular issues of concern to the inquirer. An insightful epistemological analysis of this prac-tice is developed by Geoffrey Cornelius in *The Moment of Astrology: Origins in Divination* (New York: Penguin, 1994). Historically, most traditional astrological practice before the twentieth century shared much in common with the divinatory methodology of horary, and indeed the earliest forms of astrology that emerged from Mesopotamia seem to have been largely divinatory. This has become considerably less true in the major texts and practices of leading figures in contemporary Western as-trology, whose principles and purposes I believe are better described in terms of archetypal under-standing rather than literal prediction. The unexamined (and often problematic) conflation of these two very different methodological goals—archetypal insight and concrete prediction—is no doubt the result of the absence throughout the history of astrology until fairly recently of a sustained tradi-tion of epistemological analysis and critical reflection.

Part III: *Through the Archetypal Telescope*

1. Cf. Aby Warburg's description of astrology as uniquely "the meeting and confrontation point be-tween the demands of a rational order, as in Greek science, and the myths . . . inherited from the East: between logic and magic, between mathematics and mythology, between Athens and Alexan-dria" (Eugenio Garin, *Astrology in the Renaissance*, trans. C. Jackson and J. Allen, rev. C. Robertson [London: Arkana, 1983], p. xi). Similarly, Gustav-Adolf Schoener, following the classical philologist Franz Boll's statement that astrology at its essence seeks to be "religion and science at the same time," defines astrology as "a tightrope walk between religion and scientific astronomy" (G.-A. Scho-ener, "Astrology: Between Religion and the Empirical," trans. S. Denson, *Esoterica: The Journal*, IV [2002]: 30).

2. Weber used the term "rationalization" to signify the systematic deployment of reason in any social activity, whether in law, science, or religion, to effect greater calculability, efficiency, predictability, and control. The tendency towards an increasingly rigid mechanistic determinism that accompanied this development in the history of astrology can be seen as another form of Weber's "iron cage," a state of oppressive depersonalization and alienation, here with ancient and medieval rather than modern sources.

3. See, for example, Michel Gauquelin, *Cosmic Influences on Human Behavior* (New York: Aurora Press, 1973). For a thorough discussion of the Mars effect, see Suitbert Ertel and Kenneth Irving, *The Tenacious Mars Effect* (London: The Urania Trust, 1996), and Hans J. Eysenck and David Nias, *Astrology: Science or Superstition?* (London: Penguin, 1982). For an insider's account of the scandal of the attempts by the Committee for the Scientific Investigation of the Claims of the Paranormal (CSICOP) to discredit the Gauquelin results (the account of the scandal was written by one of the committee's own founding members and chief researchers), see Dennis Rawlins, "sTARBABY," *Fate*, No. 32, October 1981 (http://cura.free.fr/xv/14starbb.html). See also John Anthony West, *The Case for Astrology* (New York: Viking Arkana, 1991), and G. Cornelius, *The Moment of Astrology*.

4. This brief overview of astrology's historical development in the West is highly schematic and in-tended only to suggest its larger evolutionary vector. At each stage in this development, many factors—societal and cultural, philosophical, religious, scientific, commercial, biographical—played a role in shaping the astrological perspective and practice of any particular era or individual. In any given instance, elements from these different stages and periods continued to live on and intermin-gled in complicated fusion and compromise formations. This multilayered complexity can be seen to have existed like a palimpsest in all of the cultural epochs in which astrology flourished—from Hel-lenistic Alexandria and the Roman Empire through Persian and Arabic culture under Islam and the High Middle Ages and Renaissance in Europe to its worldwide revival in the twentieth century. This complexity is especially characteristic of the contemporary astrological milieu, in which many schools and practices, traditional and novel, concurrently flourish. Despite these complications, however, an evolutionary pattern of development does seem discernible.

5. Part of the confusion generated by the clash of paradigms—modern scientific and ancient astrological—lay in the shifting meaning of ancient terms and concepts as used in later eras. For ex-ample, even in the more causal-mechanistic perspectives of later Hellenistic astrology, the planetary emanations that radiated their influences from the celestial spheres to the Earth were not merely

physical forces as the modern mind thinks of them. They were as much spiritual and symbolic as they were physical and literal in nature; they permeated the world with their analogical currents and thus contained the possibility of multiple significations: i.e., they were archetypal.

6. I have examined these several stages in the evolution of the archetypal perspective in the history of Western thought at greater length in *The Passion of the Western Mind*. For the Platonic doctrine of archetypal Forms and its complex relationship to Greek myth, see pp. 4–32. For Aristotle's contrasting view of universals, see pp. 55–72. For later classical developments, see pp. 81–87. For Christian, medieval, and Renaissance developments, see pp. 106–11, 165–70, 179–91, and 200–21.

7. An additional difference between Platonic and Jungian archetypes was emphasized by classical Jungians (e.g., Edward Edinger, Marie-Louise von Franz), who regard Platonic principles as inert patterns as compared with Jungian archetypes, which are seen as dynamic agencies in the psyche, independent and autonomous. The problem with this simple distinction is that Plato's archetypal principles are of widely varying kinds, which shift in nature from dialogue to dialogue. While some are indeed inert patterns (e.g., the mathematical forms), others possess a spiritual dynamism whose epiphanic power transforms the philosopher's being and whose ontological power moves the cosmos (the Good, the Beautiful). Similarly, Plato's discussion of Eros in *The Symposium* suggests a psychological dynamism not unlike what one would find in a Jungian context (and, here, Freudian as well). There is more continuity between Plato's Forms and the ancient gods than the inert-pattern characterization seems to indicate.

The dynamism of universal forms becomes fully explicit in Aristotle, but at the expense of their numinosity and transcendence. In effect, Jung draws on different aspects of the Platonic and Aristotelian conceptions, integrating them with Freudian-Darwinian instincts and Kantian categories. Jung does not, however, always keep these differing and overlapping aspects of archetypes in view or sufficiently distinguished, which has produced confusion and controversy in many discussions of Jungian archetypes in recent decades (see the following note).

8. When Jung made such statements as ". . . in the symbol the *world itself* is speaking" or "Synchronicity postulates a meaning which is a priori in relation to human consciousness and apparently exists outside man," it is clear that he had transcended the Kantian epistemological framework with its decisive division between subjectively structured phenomena and unknowable noumena (things-in-themselves beyond the reach of human subjectivity). Archetypes whose meaning could be said to "exist outside man" and that inform both the human psyche and the "world itself" were clearly not bound by the Kantian structure of knowledge and reality.

Yet in his own mind, as reflected in many statements both public and private, Jung loyally upheld the Kantian framework throughout his life, and never ceased to insist on its essential relevance and validity for his findings. The paradoxes, contradictions, and confusions of the Jung-Kant relationship deeply affected important dialogues in which Jung participated in the course of his life, and they have riddled Jung scholarship for decades. (See, for example, Stephanie de Voogd, "C. G. Jung: Psychologist of the Future, 'Philosopher' of the Past," *Spring: An Annual of Archetypal Psychology and Jungian Thought* [1977], pp. 175–82; Barbara Eckman, "Jung, Hegel, and the Subjective Universe," *Spring: An Annual of Archetypal Psychology and Jungian Thought* [1986], pp. 88–99; and many contributions from Wolfgang Giegerich.)

Certainly Jung's continuing loyalty to Kant was biographically understandable, given not only the enduring effect of his reading Kant and Schopenhauer (his entrée to Kant) in his youth but also the cultural and intellectual context in which he worked throughout his life. From the beginning of Jung's career, Kant's thought provided him with crucial philosophical protection vis-à-vis conventional scientific critiques of his findings. Jung could always defend his controversial discussions of spiritual phenomena and religious experience by saying that these were empirical data that revealed the structure of the human mind and had no necessary metaphysical implications. But as many commentators have noted, not only did Jung often make statements with vivid metaphysical implications and assumptions; in addition, the Kantian framework became less and less capable of assimilating the discoveries and theoretical advances of his later work, particularly in the area of synchronicity and what he now called the "psychoid" (psyche-like) archetype that he saw as informing both psyche and matter, challenging the absoluteness of the modern subject-object dichotomy. As a result, his statements on these epistemological and metaphysical issues became increasingly ambiguous and self-contradictory. (See, for example, Sean Kelly's insightful discussion from the Hegelian perspective in *Individuation and the Absolute* [New York: Paulist Press, 1993], pp. 15–37.)

I believe there was a further reason that the later Jung invoked the Kantian framework so often when he discussed archetypes. If I can try to sum up a complex situation briefly, it appears that Jung unwittingly conflated the issue of archetypal multivalence with the issue of whether archetypes can be directly knowable. On the one hand, Jung recognized and often stressed that archetypes are always observed and experienced in a diverse multiplicity of possible concrete embodiments, so that the full essence and meaning of the archetype must be regarded as fundamentally transcending its many particular manifestations. On the other hand, he often conflated this crucial insight with the quite separate epistemological issue of whether archetypes can be directly experienced and known as principles that transcend the human psyche, or only indirectly inferred by observing the configurations of psychological phenomena which are structured by archetypes that are ultimately "unknowable" in themselves (noumena). In his understandable attempt to preserve the multivalent indeterminacy of archetypes that transcend every particular embodiment, Jung called upon a Kantian framework of phenomenon and noumenon that entailed the unknowability of the archetypes in themselves, their humanly unreachable essence beyond every diverse manifestation.

Jung seems not to have fully grasped the epistemological and ontological possibility of a genuine direct participation (in both the Platonic sense and the contemporary sense of co-creative enaction) in a dynamically multivalent archetype that in some sense remains indeterminate until concretely enacted. This theoretical limitation also informed and, I believe, helped produce Jung's many contradictory and confusing statements about the unconscious and the psyche, and about various metaphysical and spiritual issues such as God and the God-image, that fueled his famous controversies with Martin Buber and Fr. Victor White.

Jung's occasional lack of clarity about the nature of archetypes seems also to have been increased by his unconscious conflation of two different Kantian ideas in his discussions of archetypes. Jung saw archetypes on the one hand as a priori forms and categories, and on the other hand as unknowable transcendent noumena that exist behind and beyond all phenomena (a point made by de Voogd). Thus for Jung, archetypes essentially fulfilled both functions in the Kantian framework—categories of experience and noumenal things-in-themselves—but he did not seem aware that he moved back and forth between these two separate functions in his various statements and formulations.

Doubtless part of the confusion underlying Jung's many discussions of archetypes reflects the extremely complex and enigmatic problem of *projection*—namely, how constellated archetypes can configure our lived reality and give meaning to our experience not only by shaping and constituting our perceptions but also, at times, by deeply distorting them. This issue is connected with another, equally complex and enigmatic. For in the background of Jung's conflicting philosophical loyalties and statements loomed his lifelong struggle with the disenchanted modern cosmos, which he both took seriously and saw through, and which had similarly shaped and confused Kant's philosophical struggles and formulations. Against the overwhelming contemporary scientific consensus on the disenchanted nature of the cosmos and the workings of nature, Jung could never be quite sure how much trust he should place in his spiritually revelatory observations and intuitions about a world embedded with purpose and meaning, even though the data repeatedly seemed to break out of a subjectivist or psychologistic confinement. So he hedged his bets by frequent allusions to Kant's philosophical strictures (while reminding scientists that in their materialistic presuppositions they were in no different a position). Jung's many ambiguous and contradictory statements about astrology reflect this same inner struggle with the disenchanted modern cosmos.

Since Jung's death, the extraordinary expansion of astrological research and evidence compared with the more limited astrological data Jung worked with, combined with a deeper philosophical and psychological understanding of the complex ontology and epistemology of archetypes, has helped to clarify the challenging issues with which he was increasingly confronted with each passing decade of his life and work. These issues have important philosophical implications beyond the fields of psychology and astrology. I believe that many of the major points of conflict and ambiguity in the postmodern mind about the social construction of knowledge, projection, subjectivism, relativism, pluralism, and participation will be helpfully illuminated by these developments in the archetypal astrological field.

9. The ancient Greek root for the word "planet"—*planetes*—meant "wanderer" and signified not only Mercury, Venus, Mars, Jupiter, and Saturn but also the Sun and Moon, i.e., all the visible celestial

bodies that, unlike the fixed stars, moved through the sky in ways that differed from the simple single motion and eternal regularity of the diurnal westward movement of the entire heavens. Though a distinction is often made between planets and luminaries, the astrological tradition has generally retained the original more encompassing meaning, referring to the Sun and Moon as planets. One finds this usage in the European literary tradition as well, as in Shakespeare's *Troilus and Cressida*: "Therefore is the glorious planet Sol / In noble eminence enthroned and sphered." The ambiguous definition of "planet" continues in a different form in astronomy today, with the recent discovery of Pluto-like objects in the Kuiper Belt placing in question the exact status of both Pluto and the new objects.

10. See A. E. Taylor's translation of *Plato's Philebus and Epinomis*, with an introduction by R. Klibansky (London: Thomas Nelson, 1956).

11. I first discussed the issue of Uranus's archetypal meaning in a monograph entitled "Prometheus the Awakener," written in 1978–79 and privately circulated among colleagues. A preliminary analysis intended mainly for the Jungian, archetypal psychology, and astrological communities, it was later published in the *National Council of Geocosmic Research Monographs* (1981) and, in slightly expanded form under the title "Uranus and Prometheus," in *Spring: An Annual of Archetypal Psychology and Jungian Thought* (1983), edited by James Hillman. One version or the other was published in several other astrological journals in Europe and the United States during the following decade. The monograph was later published as a small book in an updated version as *Prometheus the Awakener*, first in England (Oxford: Auriel Press, 1993), subsequently in the United States (Woodstock, Conn.: Spring Publications, 1995). Other discussions of the parallels between the astrological Uranus and the mythological Prometheus can be found in Stephen Arroyo, *Astrology, Karma, and Transformation* (1978), p. 40, the earliest mention of the correspondence of which I am aware, and in Liz Greene, *The Art of Stealing Fire* (London: CPA Press, 1996), a more recent, longer treatment that draws in part on my monograph.

12. Galle and his assistant Heinrich d'Arrest discovered the new planet within 1° of the position predicted by LeVerrier, on September 23, 1846, during the first hour of their search at the Berlin Observatory after receiving his letter containing the prediction. A year earlier, the English mathematician John Couch Adams had hypothesized the existence and position of the new planet because of the observed Uranus perturbations, but his efforts to persuade English astronomers to conduct a search at that time were unsuccessful, and his estimate of the new planet's position was somewhat less accurate than LeVerrier's. For a discussion of recently uncovered evidence concerning Adams's ambiguous role in the discovery, see Nick Kollerstrom, "Neptune's Discovery: The British Case for Co-Prediction," *Science and Technology Studies*, University College London, http://www.ucl.ac.uk/sts/nk/neptune/index.htm; and W. Sheehan, N. Kollerstrom, and C. Waff, "The Case of the Pilfered Planet," *Scientific American*, December 2004.

Neptune was actually first observed by Galileo in 1612, when he recorded it as a star of the 8th magnitude rather than a new planet. A similar history occurred in the case of Uranus, which was sighted but not identified as a planet several times prior to its discovery by Herschel; the earliest recorded instance was by John Flamsteed in 1690.

13. William James: "In cases of conversion, in providential leadings, sudden mental healings, etc., it seems to the subjects themselves of the experience as if a power from without, quite different from the ordinary action of the senses or of the sense-led mind, came into their life, as if the latter suddenly opened into that greater life in which it has its source. The word 'influx,' used in Swedenborgian circles, well describes this impression of new insight, or new willingness, sweeping over us like a tide. . . . We need only suppose the continuity of our consciousness with a mother sea, to allow for exceptional waves occasionally pouring over the dam" ("Human Immortality: Two Supposed Objections to the Doctrine" [1898], in *Essays in Religion and Morality* [Cambridge: Harvard University Press, 1982], pp. 93–94).

14. I found that the most significant factors in natal and transit correlations, other than the planets and their major aspects, were first, planetary alignments with the Ascendant-Descendant (horizontal) axis and the Midheaven-IC (vertical) axis; second, planetary "midpoints," configurations in which one planet is positioned precisely halfway between two other planets, or in

close aspect to that point; and third, certain other planetary alignments, sometimes called "minor aspects," such as the 45° and 135° aspects (semisquare and sesquisquare), and the 150° aspect (quincunx).

Besides the signs and houses, other significant interpretive factors in both traditional and contemporary astrological practice include the elements (air, water, fire, earth), qualities (cardinal, fixed, mutable), rulerships, progressions and directions, returns and ingressions, other celestial bodies such as fixed stars and minor planets, locality charts, relationship charts, and harmonics. For the sake of simplicity and clarity in the present book, I have not incorporated these additional factors in the presentation of evidence; instead, I have limited the analysis to correlations involving major planetary aspects in world transits, personal transits, and natal charts. Because such a research program does not use the zodiacal signs as interpretive factors, it is unaffected by the complex issue of the two zodiacs, sidereal and tropical, the difference between which is produced by the precession of the equinoxes.

15. The astronomical data used for calculations in the present book are based on the Swiss Ephemeris, which in turn is based on the most recent planetary and lunar ephemeris developed by NASA's Jet Propulsion Laboratory, DE405/406. All calculations were checked using the Solar Fire 5.0 program, which employs the Swiss Ephemeris and JPL computations.

16. Generally speaking, archetypal correlations were evident for personal transits when the transiting planet was within 3°–5° before and after exact major aspect with the natal planet. The smaller figure represents the range of greater intensity and frequency of observed correlations, while the larger figure represents a penumbral range within which correlations were still observed but with lessening intensity. In personal transits, correlations tend to occur with greater frequency and intensity during a larger range of degrees before exact alignment and typically diminish within a smaller range after exact alignment. The concurrence or partial overlapping of other transits appeared to affect the range of this operative orb, with the archetypal character of the coinciding events showing corresponding complexities and inflections according to which planets were involved in the other transits.

Because of variations caused by the planets' apparent retrograde motion (which in the case of Uranus is produced by the slower-moving Uranus's being viewed from the faster-moving Earth as both planets orbit the Sun), a transiting planet can move in and out of this range more than once in the course of a single transit. Though tending to occur in a wavelike continuum in coincidence with the transit's degree of exactitude, archetypal correlations were generally in evidence from the first time the planets moved into the 3°–5° range to the last time they moved beyond it.

The orb for personal transits was also affected by which transiting planet and which aspect were involved. For example, correlations with Mars transits consistently tended to begin somewhat earlier than with other planets, while correlations with Saturn transits consistently tended to continue longer after exact alignment had been reached. For all planets, the hard-aspect quadrature alignments tended to have larger orbs than the soft aspects; conjunctions and then oppositions had the largest (4°–5°), sextiles the smallest (2°–3°). A special case is that of the transiting conjunctions of an outer planet as it returns to its own natal position at the end of its full 360° cycle; here the operative orb appears to be especially large. As we will see in the next chapter, this was particularly evident in the case of the Saturn return at the end of its 29½ year cycle.

17. In the case of Einstein, Uranus reached the 180° opposition point of its cycle during the years 1918–21. In November 1919, the Royal Society in London announced that its scientific expedition to Príncipe Island, which was formed for the purpose of photographing a solar eclipse earlier that year, had completed calculations that demonstrated a deflection of light at the rim of the Sun, thereby giving dramatic support to Einstein's general theory of relativity. Einstein was immediately heralded as a genius without precedent, and the theory of relativity was for the first time widely acclaimed by both the scientific community and the larger public. However, the initial major scientific breakthrough in Einstein's life took place in the summer and fall of 1905, when he published the four papers in the scientific journal *Annalen der Physik* that transformed modern physics; these contained the special theory of relativity, the equivalence of mass and energy, the theory of Brownian motion, and the photon theory of light. Uranus was exactly at the 120° trine point of its cycle during the years 1904–06, the trine being the major aspect of the Uranus transit cycle that precedes the

opposition by approximately fourteen years. On the day that *Annalen der Physik* received Einstein's epoch-making paper on special relativity—June 30, 1905—Uranus was within 1° of exact alignment to its position at Einstein's birth. This exactitude of alignment takes place for a period of less than six months altogether.

The same correlation occurred with Darwin. Uranus had reached the 180° opposition point of its cycle in Darwin's life during the years 1852–54. It was at this time that the Royal Society first recognized Darwin's work as a biologist, by awarding him its Royal Medal in 1853 for his research on coral reefs and on barnacles. This work proved to be crucial both for his deepening grasp of the transmutation of species and for his credibility with scientists when he would later publicize his theory. However, it was earlier in Darwin's life, when Uranus had reached the 120° trine point of its cycle, from February 1837 through December 1839, that he achieved his most important conceptual breakthrough: the first formulation of the theory of evolution in his private notebooks. In 1837, soon after his return from the *Beagle* expedition to South America and the Galápagos Islands, Darwin recognized that many of his observations could only be understood if species changed over time and evolved in different directions from a common ancestor. The theory lacked a mechanism by which evolution took place until, on September 28, 1838, Darwin read Malthus's *Essay on the Principle of Population* with its theory of the necessary relationship of human population growth to food supply. Extrapolating from Malthus's idea, Darwin realized that nature enforced its selection of species by eliminating those variations that could not fit into available ecological niches and favoring those that could. On that day, Darwin entered into his "Notebook on the Transmutation of Species" the note that demonstrated that he had solved the problem of natural selection. On that day, transiting Uranus was within 1° of exact trine alignment to its position at Darwin's birth, again a transit that lasts altogether less than six months within that range of exactitude.

18. I found that both of these forms of Uranus transits (with Uranus either as the transiting planet or as the natal planet being transited) were equally likely to coincide with Promethean phenomena such as significant creative breakthroughs. For example, in their joint discovery of the structure of DNA in 1953, announced in the April 25 edition of the journal *Nature*, James D. Watson was undergoing the one type, transiting Uranus to natal Sun, while Francis Crick was undergoing the other, transiting Pluto to natal Uranus.

19. A more recent example of this same pattern is Joseph Campbell, who, like his mentors Freud and Jung, lived into his eighties. Campbell's pivotal work, the one with which he will always be most closely identified, was *The Hero with a Thousand Faces*, in which he explored the mythology of the liberating hero who confronts an unexpected radical change, inner and outer, to enter a new world of meaning and purpose that he or she then mediates for others. This book was completed in 1948 and published in 1949, in exact coincidence with Campbell's Uranus-opposite-Uranus transit, with the planet at the 180° opposition point of its cycle from mid-1947 to mid-1950. Campbell lived to be eighty-three, dying in October 1987 in the middle of his Uranus return just as the planet was reaching the 360° conjunction point of its cycle. Before he died, he recorded the famous series of interviews with Bill Moyers, the television broadcasts of which during the remaining months of his Uranus return transit after his death brought unprecedented public attention to his ideas and life work.

The occurrence of such posthumous correlations was in fact noted by Jung. In a lecture on Jung's birth chart delivered in 1974 in Zurich, his daughter Gret Baumann-Jung mentioned the following anecdote: "Shortly before his death, as we talked about horoscopes, my father remarked: 'The funny thing is that the darned stuff even works after death' " (G. Baumann-Jung, "Some Reflections on the Horoscope of C. G. Jung," trans. F. J. Hopman, *Spring: An Annual of Archetypal Psychology and Jungian Thought* [1975], 55).

20. In personal transits involving the return of an outer planet such as Saturn or Uranus to its natal position (the Saturn return or the Uranus return), archetypally relevant events consistently began as early as 20° or more before exact alignment and often continued as many degrees afterwards. In the case of the first Saturn return, relevant events and psychological changes typically began to emerge at age twenty-eight (sometimes as early as twenty-seven) and were strongly in evidence through age thirty. The second Saturn return coincided with a similarly extended wave of such events one cycle later, in the late fifties through age sixty.

21. The intensified activation of the Saturn archetype during the first Saturn return period between the ages of 28 and 30 reflects what in Jungian archetypal psychology is referred to as the constellating and potential integration of the *senex* principle, linked with a rapid transformation, and sometimes suppression, of the *puer* principle, or child archetype, with which the senex is in dialectical tension. (See note 7 for Part II above, p. 499.)

22. In addition to taking into account the cultural and biographical context, I found that any particular planetary alignment in a natal chart could be understood only within the larger context of the other intersecting planetary alignments that occurred at an individual's birth. The archetypal tendencies that characteristically coincided with a Sun-Uranus conjunction or any other natal planetary alignment took different forms in accordance with which other planets were in close aspect with that alignment at the person's birth, thereby forming a larger multi-planet configuration. Shelley again provides an instructive example. Shelley was born not only with a Sun-Uranus conjunction but with both the Sun and Uranus in a close triple conjunction with Venus. This astronomical reality seemed to be elegantly mirrored in the specific character and quest of Shelley's unbound Prometheus, whose liberation of humankind specifically brought to the world a new reign not only of freedom but of *love and beauty.*

Viewed by itself, Shelley's Sun-Uranus conjunction can be seen as his powerful self-identification (Sun) with the Promethean impulse of freedom and rebellion (Uranus), to the point that he depicted Prometheus himself as the heroic center of his most prominent literary achievement. In turn, the triple conjunction with Venus can be recognized in the particular inflection Shelley gave to the Promethean myth, in which love and beauty—the qualities of the archetypal Venus—became essentially tied to freedom, rebellion, and the heroic manifestation of the self. Similarly characteristic of the Venus-Uranus planetary combination were Shelley's lifelong tendencies towards romantic freedom and unpredictability, sudden awakenings of new love and erotic attraction, impulsive acts of rebellion in the service of love and beauty, and repeated situations of love that defied conventional limitations and structures, as in premarital and extramarital liaisons and other relationships condemned by social opinion or parental authority.

One other example of this same archetypal correspondence involving a Sun-Venus-Uranus configuration will be helpful to cite here. Richard Wagner, like Shelley, was born with both Sun and Venus in close alignment with Uranus (an opposition). In Wagner's life and personality, and in the major narratives and heroic characters of his operas, one can readily recognize virtually identical archetypal themes and impulses as those just cited for Shelley: the close association of artistic creativity with romantic freedom, rebellion, and unpredictability; sudden awakenings of new love and erotic attraction; repeated situations in which the impulsive pursuit of such relationships broke free from previous commitments, upset societal conventions, and disrupted established life structures.

Equally instructive is the timing of Wagner's transits involving this same natal configuration. Transiting Uranus opposed Wagner's natal Uranus (the same transit as those cited in the last chapter for Galileo, Descartes, Freud, Jung, Friedan, et al.) and conjoined his natal Sun-Venus conjunction in 1857–59. These were the three years during which Wagner composed *Tristan und Isolde,* his most revolutionary musical work, which marked a critical creative threshold in his artistic evolution. Both in its radically innovative musical character and in its narrative of suddenly awakened romantic and erotic love that defies established social structures *Tristan und Isolde* precisely reflects the archetypal complex constituted by the Prometheus and Venus principles in dynamic synthesis. Moreover, it was during just these years that the married Wagner suddenly fell in love with Mathilde Wesendonck, the young wife of a patron, and explosively disrupted both marriages. Wagner's personal romantic drama and his composition of *Tristan und Isolde,* both precisely reflective of the Venus-Uranus archetypal complex, were so interconnected and mutually inspiring that biographers and musicologists continue to debate the question of which was cause and which effect.

Often two individuals are born with two very different alignments involving the Sun, as in Shelley's Sun-Uranus conjunction and Schopenhauer's Sun-Saturn conjunction, with correspondingly contrasting personality traits and biographical tendencies, yet have another planetary combination in common and clearly share the corresponding archetypal themes in their lives. For example, Schopenhauer and Shelley were both born with Venus and Uranus in major aspect (a trine, for Schopenhauer). We can recognize in Schopenhauer's philosophical thought a suggestive parallel to this alignment, for in the larger context of his pessimistic, profoundly Saturnian philosophy, Schopenhauer also taught as one of his central doctrines that of all areas of human experience, art and aesthetic contemplation (Venus) especially allowed the human being to be suddenly lifted up and temporarily liberated (Uranus) from the bondage of ordinary existence.

In turn, it was specifically this element of Schopenhauer's thought that influenced Wagner—not the general pessimism but the doctrine of emancipation through art and the special role of artistic genius in mediating that transfiguration—and it was the Venus-Uranus planetary combination that the two men had in common. In other respects, Wagner's personality more resembled Shelley's unconstrained heroic Promethean self—indeed, his Promethean self was more extreme than Shelley's—than it did Schopenhauer's much more Saturnian self and existential posture. Again, this underlying resemblance in personality and self-expression between Wagner and Shelley is paralleled by their sharing of natal Sun-Uranus alignments, in contrast with Schopenhauer's Sun-Saturn.

23. In epistemological terms, the active, interpretive, participatory role in archetypal cognition is comparable to and anticipated by Aristotle's concept of the active intellect, *nous poietikos*. The active intellect is the faculty of the mind that permits the recognition of universals in phenomena in much the same way that light permits the potentially existing colors in things to become actual. (See W. D. Ross, *Aristotle: A Complete Exposition of His Works and Thought*, 5th ed. [New York: Meridian, 1959], pp. 146–49.) The original text for the concept is Aristotle's *De Anima*, and the perspective has been further developed by Aquinas, Goethe, Rudolf Steiner, and Owen Barfield.

Part IV: *Epochs of Revolution*

1. By way of visual analogy, a 15° orb on each side of exactitude is approximately the range within which the Full Moon is visible as such, when the Sun is aligned in opposition to the Moon; and conversely, the same orb is the range within which the New Moon is invisible, when the Sun is in conjunction with the Moon. Because of variations caused by the planets' apparent retrograde and direct motion (produced by their heliocentric orbits as seen from the perspective of the Earth moving in its orbit), the outer planets can move in and out of this 15° range more than once in the course of a single alignment or aspect, though correlations are generally in evidence from the first time the planets move into this range to the last time they move beyond it. Also, the concurrence or overlapping of other major planetary alignments affects the range of this operative orb, and the archetypal character of the coinciding events shows corresponding complexities and inflections.

2. Among countless possible examples from either period, this decree by the French Revolutionary Convention in the 1790s is a characteristic reflection of the era's historical self-awareness and the epochal transformation a revolutionary generation believes it is responsible for realizing:

> The French nation, oppressed, degraded during many centuries by the most insolent despotism, has finally awakened to a consciousness of its rights and of the power to which its destinies summon it. . . . It wishes its regeneration to be complete, in order that its years of liberty and glory may betoken still more by their duration in the history of peoples than its years of slavery and humiliation in the history of kings. (Cited in J. Barzun, "The French Revolution," in *Columbia History of the World*, ed. J. A. Garraty and P. Gay [New York: Harper & Row, 1972], p. 771)

3. See I. Bernard Cohen, *Revolution in Science* (Cambridge, Mass.: Harvard University Press, 1985), pp. 209, 212. The 1790s brought the definitive replacement, outside astronomy, of the earlier meaning of "revolution" as a cyclical return to an earlier condition on the model of planetary revolutions, as in Copernicus's *De Revolutionibus Orbium Coelestium* ("On the Revolutions of the Celestial Spheres," 1543). Cohen's work provides a valuable survey of the complex historical relationship between these two meanings and of the long evolution of usage during the sixteenth to eighteenth centuries when the two meanings were ambiguously juxtaposed and combined.

4. The juxtaposition of the historical past and the breaking present, and the fluid movement back and forth between literal and archetypal, individual and collective, was characteristic of the Rolling Stones' music at that time, as it was of the era's self-consciousness generally:

> *Everywhere I hear the sound of marching charging feet. . . .*
> *'Cause summer's here and the time is right for fighting in the street. . . .*

> *Think the time is right for a palace revolution. . . .*
> *But what can a poor boy do, except to sing for a rock 'n' roll band.*

Cf. *Sympathy for the Devil*, *Jumping Jack Flash* (both 1968), *Gimme Shelter*, *Midnight Rambler* (both 1969).

5. As we will see in Part V, this historical sequence was characteristic of the larger interweaving of planetary cycles in which, for example, major sustained developments initiated during the long period of a Uranus-Pluto alignment subsequently came to a crisis and breakdown of some kind when Saturn moved into hard-aspect alignment with Uranus. Here, the wave of heightened abolitionist activity and other political and social developments during the 1845–56 period led to the Civil War, which began when Saturn moved into square alignment with Uranus in 1861. A similar pattern was visible in the sustained surge of radical impulses and activities in Russian political life during the 1896–1907 Uranus-Pluto opposition (including the founding of the Bolshevik party by Lenin and Trotsky and the Revolution of 1905–06), which led to the Bolshevik Revolution when Saturn moved into opposition to Uranus in 1917.

6. "A number of historians—among them Roger B. Merriman (1938), H. R. Trevor-Roper (1959), E. Hobsbawm (1954), and J. M. Goulemot (1975)—have called attention to the almost simultaneous occurrence of revolts, uprisings, or revolutions in different parts of Europe in the middle of the seventeenth century—in England, France, the Netherlands, Catalonia, Portugal, Naples, and elsewhere. This was obviously a time of crisis and instability, and it would almost seem that there was a general revolution, of which the geographically separate events were but individual manifestations" (Cohen, *Revolution in Science*, p. 77).

7. After noting that revolutionary developments in science were taking place in the same general era as the widespread revolutionary political events of the mid-seventeenth century, Cohen adds: "But so far as I know, no one has linked the Scientific Revolution to the other revolutions that occurred in that same century, or speculated that the revolutionary spirit which moved in the realm of politics might have been the same as that which caused upheavals in the sciences" (*Revolution in Science*, p. 78). Readers of Cohen's meticulous work will immediately note the extraordinarily consistent correlation of the major revolutionary epochs and events he recognizes as paradigmatic, in both the intellectual and political realms, with the cyclical sequence of Uranus-Pluto conjunctions and oppositions discussed here: the English Revolution, the French Revolution, the 1848 revolutions, the 1960s; Copernicus and Vesalius; Kepler, Galileo, and Gilbert; Descartes and Boyle; Lavoisier and Hutton; Faraday and Maxwell; Marx and Engels; Darwin and Wallace; Planck, Einstein, and Freud; plate tectonics and Kuhn; and so forth. Further significant correlations of a more precisely timed character with Newton, Darwin, Einstein, and others are discussed in the section on the Jupiter-Uranus cycle.

8. The diachronic sequence of correlations of the Uranus-Pluto cycle with significant historical developments in the power of the press, the struggle to establish freedom of the press, and the emergence of mass communication can be quickly sketched: The conjunction of 1960–72 coincided with an unprecedented flourishing of the underground press with hundreds of alternative weekly newspapers suddenly arising in cities throughout North America and Europe, the influential publishing of the Pentagon Papers by *The New York Times* and *The Washington Post* in conflict with the U.S. government, the new dissemination and power of the mass media generally, and more specifically the unprecedented influence of the media in reflecting and influencing mass opinion against the Vietnam War. The preceding Uranus-Pluto opposition of 1896–1907 coincided with the new power of progressive-reformist, muckraking, and yellow journalism, especially under Joseph Pulitzer and William Randolph Hearst, that affected both domestic and international policies and decisions in that era and afterwards. The conjunction of 1845–56 coincided not only with the proliferation of revolutionary and socialist publications in association with the revolutions of the 1848–49 period and Marx and Engels's *The Communist Manifesto*, but also with the role of the new telegraph in accelerating mass communication throughout the world, the invention of the rotary press that permitted mass printing, the founding of both the Associated Press and Reuters News Service, the *London Daily News*'s beginning publication as the first cheap British newspaper (edited by Charles Dickens), and the start of publication of the *Daily Telegraph* in London, *Le Figaro* in Paris, *The New York Times*,

and *The Chicago Tribune*, the first prominent women's rights newspaper (*Lily*, edited by Amelia Bloomer), and the rapid proliferation and expanded influence of daily newspapers in the United States generally during those years.

The preceding opposition of the 1787–98 French Revolutionary epoch coincided with the establishment of freedom of the press in the United States by the ratification of the Bill of Rights in 1789, as well as with numerous developments in this area associated with the revolution in France such as Babeuf's publishing of the first socialist journal, *Le Tribun du Peuple*. The conjunction of 1705–16 coincided with the rapid development of the press and political and cultural journalism in England. Publications included Daniel Defoe's *Review*, Jonathan Swift's *The Examiner*, and Addison and Steele's *The Tatler* and *The Spectator*. The preceding opposition of the English revolutionary period of 1643–54 coincided with a similar flourishing of the dissident press in England, and with John Milton's seminal manifesto for freedom of the press in 1644, the *Areopagitica*. The preceding opposition during the radical Reformation coincided with Luther's influential publishing of his German Bible in 1534, the same year as Henry VIII's rejection of papal control in England. Finally, the first conjunction of the early modern period, 1450–61, coincided with Gutenberg's development of the printing press itself, which made possible the entire sequence of subsequent cyclical developments just cited.

9. Thus Wordsworth's famous lines from *The French Revolution As It Appeared to Enthusiasts at Its Commencement*:

> *Bliss was it in that dawn to be alive,*
> *But to be young was very heaven!*

And from *The Prelude* (Book VI, 340–42):

> *Europe at that time was thrilled with joy,*
> *France, standing on the top of golden hours,*
> *And human nature seeming born again . . .*

So also Wordsworth's contemporary, the young Romantic poet Robert Southey:

> Few persons but those who have lived in it can conceive or comprehend what the memory of the French Revolution was, nor what a visionary world seemed to open upon those who were just entering it. Old things seemed passing away, and nothing was dreamt of but the regeneration of the human race. (*The Correspondence of Robert Southey with Caroline Bowles*, ed. E. Dowden [Dublin, 1881], p. 52)

10. *The Persecution and Assassination of Jean-Paul Marat as Performed by the Inmates of the Asylum of Charenton Under the Direction of the Marquis de Sade*, stage play by Peter Weiss (1964), film directed by Peter Brook (1967).

11. The Uranus-Pluto conjunction of 1705–16 that coincided with the beginning of the Industrial Revolution and the births of Rousseau and Diderot also coincided with the massive social upheavals, revolutionary transformation, and intensive modernization of Russia propelled by Peter the Great during these same years, and with the great shift in the balance of imperial power in Europe, from Spain and France to England, produced by the War of the Spanish Succession from 1702 to 1714.

12. Freud was born in May 1856 when Uranus was 16° from exact conjunction with Pluto (with the Sun 4° from Uranus, 12° from Pluto). I regularly found such configurations, when the Sun was positioned between two other planets, to be correlated with heightened expressions of the relevant archetypal principles in complex interaction.

13. There were three quadrature alignments of the Uranus-Pluto cycle in the life of Schopenhauer: the opposition of the French Revolutionary epoch, when he was born; the following square, when he wrote and published *The World as Will and Idea*, in 1818–19; and finally the conjunction at the end of the cycle, during the 1845–56 period when his philosophy was first widely read and began to exert

its cultural influence, which occurred after the publication in 1851 of his volume of essays and aphorisms entitled *Parerga und Paralipomena*.

14. Nietzsche was born in October 1844, when Uranus had moved to 19° from exact conjunction with Pluto. As we will examine later, at this time Jupiter was in close conjunction with Uranus (7°) at the beginning of a broad triple conjunction with Pluto. Nietzsche was also born with Sun and Pluto in exact opposition, comparable to Freud's Sun-Pluto conjunction though considerably more exact, which is often associated with a strong personal identification with the Dionysian principle.

15. The steep rise in the numbers of nuclear power plants ordered each year beginning in the 1960s is well represented by a graph from the Nuclear Energy Institute showing the "rise and fall of nuclear power," available at http://www.pbs.org/wgbh/pages/frontline/shows/reaction/maps/chart2.html. The rise begins at the time of the exact Uranus-Pluto conjunction in 1965–66 and extends through 1974, when the conjunction reaches the 20° point of separation, after which there is a steep decline. The arc of the timeline in close correlation with the Uranus-Pluto alignment closely resembles the trajectories of other archetypally relevant phenomena during those same years, such as the number of manned space expeditions in the Moon program or the annual number of student rebellions, antiwar demonstrations, civil rights marches, black power demonstrations, and urban riots. Measures of other relevant phenomena show a rapid rise beginning with this period but not declining afterwards, as in statistics measuring sociological shifts in sexual mores, divorce, births to unmarried women, number of pornographic institutions (from 9 in New York City in 1965 to 245 in 1977), and the like. Similarly, in the category of industrial technology during the preceding Uranus-Pluto opposition of 1896–1907, the number of cars produced during that decade increased from 25 per year at its start to 25,000 at its end, and continued to increase thereafter.

16. In his youth Nietzsche first employed the word *Übermensch* to refer to Byron; the term took on a radically transformed meaning in his mature work. Elvis Presley, who embodied and anticipated the disruptive awakening and eruption of the Dionysian that fully emerged on the collective level during the 1960s, was born during the Uranus-Pluto square of the 1930s (in close alignment with Venus and the Sun).

17. The intimate relationship between Shelley's life and work on the one hand and the French Revolutionary period on the other, both born during the Uranus-Pluto opposition, was played out in a multiplicity of ways. Shelley wrote both insightful analyses and impassioned poetry on the significance of the French Revolution. The direction of his political convictions was deeply influenced by William Godwin's *An Enquiry concerning Political Justice*, which Godwin was writing in the year Shelley was born (published 1793). Finally, Shelley eloped with and later married Mary Godwin, the daughter of William Godwin and Mary Wollstonecraft, the two proponents of English radical thought of the 1790s whose work was so emblematic of that era and influential in subsequent Uranus-Pluto periods; both were born during the preceding Uranus-Pluto square.

18. The close association of the Uranus-Pluto cycle with technological advances, the drive for progress, and the impulse for invention and experiment is suggested not only by the many milestones in the history of technology cited in the chapter but also by this cycle's frequent correlation with the birth of individuals whose lives and work reflected these themes in especially significant ways. Benjamin Franklin's pioneering discoveries of the nature of electricity and lightning and the multitude of his practical inventions (Franklin stove, lightning rod, bifocal glasses) are representative of this tendency. The archetypal association of both the astrological Uranus and the mythic Prometheus with electricity (the fire stolen from the heavens) is evident here as well.

Franklin was born during the Uranus-Pluto conjunction of the early eighteenth century, in 1706, and during the immediately following opposition, in 1791, was born Michael Faraday, the great experimental scientist who discovered electromagnetism and invented the electric motor, generator, and transformer, which ultimately moved the Industrial Revolution from steam power to electricity. The immediately following Uranus-Pluto conjunction of the mid-nineteenth century coincided with the births of both Edison (1847) and Tesla (1856). Many individuals in the generation born in the 1960s during the most recent conjunction, being notably comfortable with high technology, have played central roles in advancing and disseminating the computer revolution that began during the era of their birth.

19. Many other characteristic themes of the Uranus-Pluto cycle are in evidence for the conjunction period of 1592–1602 in addition to the milestones of the Scientific Revolution, the intensified creativity of the Elizabethan period, and the titanic struggle and unleashed instincts of Shakespeare's plays cited in the text. The heightened impulse to explore new horizons and assert power again clearly expressed itself through the rapid advance of European global exploration and commerce at this time: Both the Dutch East India Company and the British East India Company were founded during this alignment and sent out voyages and began colonization; both England and France penetrated into North America (John Smith on a whaling expedition explored and named New England, the French built settlements on the St. Lawrence); the Spanish-Basque navigator Vizcaíno sailed north along the California coast, and reached and named Monterey Bay. The sustained Irish rebellion led by Hugh O'Neill, Earl of Tyrone, took place throughout the period and repeatedly defeated the British armies sent by Elizabeth to quell it. A major milestone in the history of religious freedom was marked by the Edict of Nantes (1598), which granted the Huguenots (Protestants) religious freedom in France. An interesting form of the theme of unleashing the forces of nature's power can be recognized with the start during this decade of the *encierro* (running of the bulls) in Pamplona, Spain.

20. As on several other occasions in these chapters, I am here considering from a different vantage point many of the same phenomena that I examined earlier. Though the earlier themes—scientific and technological revolution, for example, or erotic liberation—often overlapped with the present category, my specific focus here is on cultural *creativity* per se. The phenomenon of creativity seems to be associated with all three of the outermost planetary archetypes, each with a different inflection. We will examine correlations with Neptune and its distinctive qualities and motifs in a later section. In the Uranus-Pluto cycle here discussed, the Promethean principle associated with Uranus comprises those aspects of creativity that involve inventiveness, sudden unexpected awakenings and quantum leaps, the exciting impulse to bring forth the new, sudden shifts in the unfolding of reality, brilliant and dazzling breakthroughs, and the urge to free the human being from constraints and burdens. By contrast, the Plutonic-Dionysian principle concerns more the *elemental* aspect of creativity—from the depths, from the evolutionary wellspring of nature and from the depths of the unconscious, chthonic and libidinal—i.e., creativity as the polar complement and counterbalance of the destructive aspect of the same encompassing and fundamentally ambiguous Pluto archetype.

Thus the dynamic synthesis of these two archetypal principles, Promethean and Dionysian, that tends to occur during alignments of the Uranus-Pluto cycle is especially synergistic in constellating creativity. Shakti, the supreme Indian goddess and the principle of divine creative power, is in many respects a synthesis of these two principles (combined with Neptune as well). Uranus-Pluto periods can be seen as eras marked by the especially vivid awakening and empowerment of Shakti in the collective psyche, as expressed in sustained and widespread surges of cultural creativity and eros.

21. A similar comparison could be made to Whitehead's process philosophy, in which the concepts of causal efficacy and concrescence suggest the continual inheritance and composition of the entire past into every present actuality.

22. On this fragment from Xenophanes, W. K. C. Guthrie comments: "The emphasis on personal search, and on the need for time, marks this as the first statement in extant Greek literature of the idea of progress in the arts and sciences, a progress dependent on human effort and not—or at least not primarily—on divine revelation" (*A History of Greek Philosophy*, vol. 1, *The Earlier Presocratics and the Pythagoreans* [Cambridge: Cambridge University Press, 1962], 399–400).

Part V: *Cycles of Crisis and Contraction*

1. See, for example, Robert Hand, "A Crisis of Power: Saturn and Pluto Face Off," *The Mountain Astrologer*, July-August 2001 (also available at http://www.mountainastrologer.com/planettracks/hand/hand.html), and Robert Zoller's analysis, discussed in Luke Andrews, "Prediction and 11th September 2001," http://new-library.com/zoller/features/.

2. The Saturn-Pluto conjunction of 1946–48 that coincided with the start of the Cold War and the nuclear arms race first reached the penumbral 20° point in August 1945. The dropping of the atomic bombs on Hiroshima and Nagasaki on August 6 and 9, 1945, took place when Saturn and Pluto were 21° from exact alignment. At that time, the Sun was in close conjunction with Pluto, 4° from exact alignment. (Cf. the *Bhagavad Gita*'s invocation of the Pluto archetype as recalled by J. Robert Oppenheimer when he witnessed the first atomic explosion: *"Now I am become Death, the destroyer of worlds."*)

3. The widespread awakening of terrorist activity in the second half of the twentieth century occurred most notably during the Uranus-Pluto conjunction of the 1960s; assassinations, terrorism, and violent dissidence pervaded the entire decade. As discussed in that section, the periods of earlier Uranus-Pluto alignments, such as the French Revolution, the 1848 period, and the turn of the twentieth century, all coincided with similar waves of assassinations, terrorism, and the emergence of philosophies of anarchy and violent revolution. I believe this can be understood as the disruptive awakening or liberation (Uranus) of violent instincts and social turmoil (Pluto) in association with revolutionary or emancipatory impulses and agendas (Uranus). Subsequent or overlapping *Saturn*-Pluto quadrature alignments seem to coincide consistently with major crises of terror and repression; both sides of the conflict often express both sides of the archetypal gestalt in complex synthesis.

4. After the major aspects, one of the categories with the most consistent archetypal correlations in historical and biographical research was that of planetary midpoints. When one planet was positioned in very close (within 2° to 3°) aspect, especially in conjunction, to the exact midpoint of two other planets, all three corresponding planetary archetypes appeared to be brought into complex mutual interaction. In October 1929, just before the longer T-square alignment they were about to enter, Saturn, Uranus, and Pluto formed an exact midpoint configuration. Uranus reached the exact midpoint of Saturn and Pluto as the latter two planets approached their opposition alignment for the first time. On October 29, 1929, Uranus was exactly—less than 0°10'—at the Saturn/Pluto midpoint. The three planets then moved into an increasingly close T-square that lasted from 1930 to 1933. After Saturn moved out of this alignment, Uranus and Pluto continued to be in a 90° square within 10° orb until 1937 and within 15° orb until 1939. Just as the longer Uranus-Pluto alignment was finished, Saturn moved into square to Pluto in 1939 in coincidence with the beginning of World War II.

5. In addition to the major scandals associated with the Catholic Church hierarchy and many corporations such as Enron, the Saturn-Pluto opposition of 2000–04 also coincided with accusations against the Bush administration of complicity in the events of September 11, most notably by the philosopher and theologian David Ray Griffin in *The New Pearl Harbor* (Interlink, 2004). Many others made references to Watergate during this time, including John Dean, a central figure in the revelations that brought about the resignation of Nixon during the Saturn-Pluto square of 1973–75 (John W. Dean, *Worse Than Watergate: The Secret Presidency of George W. Bush* [Boston: Little, Brown, 2004]).

Numerous other historic scandals similar to Watergate and the Dreyfus Affair that coincided with the Saturn-Pluto cycle could be cited, such as the series of scandals surrounding the Environmental Protection Agency during the first Reagan administration in 1981–84 or the Teapot Dome scandal during the Harding administration beginning in 1921 during the Saturn-Pluto square. In France, the famous Affair of the Diamond Necklace and the resulting trial before the Parlement that involved Cardinal de Rohan, Marie-Antoinette, and the court of Louis XVI took place during the Saturn-Pluto conjunction of 1785–87, just before the French Revolution. Innumerable less historic but in their own circles significant scandals coincided with alignments of this cycle, such as the one that occurred at the San Francisco Zen Center during the last Saturn-Pluto conjunction in 1983.

The same pattern is evident in personal transits to individual natal charts: Both Clarence Thomas and Bill Clinton were born during the Saturn-Pluto conjunction of 1946–48 and underwent major personal transits of Saturn or Pluto across their natal Saturn-Pluto conjunction at the time of the scandals involving accusations of sexual misbehavior in 1991 and 1998, respectively. In both cases we see such characteristic themes of the Saturn-Pluto complex as trial and judgment about sexual activities, deep public humiliation, and, with Thomas, the vivid metaphor with which he attacked his judges, "This is a high-tech lynching."

6. Kennan's preference for the containment strategy was for skillful and steadfast political, diplomatic, and cultural efforts rather than military interventions, with his greatest emphasis placed on the importance of strengthening the spiritual and moral vitality of American society. The following sentence adds further nuances that reflect the Saturn-Pluto complex's distinctive qualities: "It is important to note, however, that such a policy has nothing to do with outward histrionics: with threats or blustering or superfluous gestures of outward 'toughness.'" His concluding paragraphs underscore these qualities:

> Thus the decision will really fall in large measure in this country itself. The issue of Soviet-American relations is in essence a test of the overall worth of the United States as a nation among nations. To avoid destruction the United States need only measure up to its own best traditions and prove itself worthy of preservation as a great nation.
>
> Surely, there was never a fairer test of national quality than this. In the light of these circumstances, the thoughtful observer of Russian-American relations will find no cause for complaint in the Kremlin's challenge to American society. He will rather experience a certain gratitude to a Providence which, by providing the American people with this implacable challenge, has made their entire security as a nation dependent on their pulling themselves together and accepting the responsibilities of moral and political leadership that history plainly intended them to bear. ("The Sources of Soviet Conduct," *Foreign Affairs*, July 1947)

7. William McNeill's *The Rise of the West*, which was written in part as a response and counterpoint to Spengler's *The Decline of the West*, was published during the *Uranus*-Pluto conjunction in 1963, and reflected that era's zeitgeist of propulsive evolutionary advance on many levels—political, social, technological, intellectual—as compared with the *Saturn*-Pluto complex that is more evident in Spengler's historical vision.

8. Reflecting a related Saturn-Pluto motif, Cheney's characteristic modus operandi after September 11, 2001—working in a secret underground bunker from which he exerted control over foreign policy and domestic security activities—bore a striking resemblance to the strategies and psychology of the underground mole depicted in Kafka's *The Burrow*.

9. The biographical parallels to the sequence of Saturn-Pluto conjunctions during the life of Schopenhauer is instructive. There were three Saturn-Pluto conjunctions in his life. The first coincided with his birth in 1788. The second coincided with the publication of *The World as Will and Imagination* in 1818, at which time the book was almost entirely ignored. This did not change until many years later, when Schopenhauer published his more accessible collection of essays and aphorisms entitled *Parerga und Paralipomena*. This occurred in 1851 during the very next Saturn-Pluto conjunction, the one that coincided with the publication of Melville's *Moby Dick*. This was also the period of the Uranus-Pluto conjunction of the revolutionary 1845–56 epoch, an era marked by many events and movements in the collective psyche that suggest the liberation of the id, nature's struggle for survival, and an opening to the deep instinctual ground of life. It was only from the time of the Uranus-Pluto conjunction—in rare triple conjunction with Saturn at the time of the publication—that Schopenhauer's ideas begin to exercise their deep influence on European thought and culture, from Wagner and Nietzsche to Freud and Jung.

10. Many of these same themes again arose with renewed force and in new forms during the Saturn-Pluto opposition of 2000–04. A characteristic reflection of this archetypal complex's again being constellated during this period is the summary of world events and geopolitical tendencies contained in a widely discussed essay by Walter Russell Mead, a senior fellow at the Council on Foreign Relations, entitled "It's the Dawning Age of the Apocalypse. . ." (*The Washington Post*, February 2, 2003). The various motifs, current realities, and rising fears cited in the brief essay, written when the alignment was close to exactitude, represent a dense litany of Saturn-Pluto themes and historical references: mass terrorism; September 11; weapons of mass destruction brandished by nations of the Axis of Evil; widespread fear of terrorist nuclear attack by rogue nuclear weapons; threats by North Korea that "the United States is in danger of falling into the grave that it has dug" and if it does, it "will never again survive"; nuclear threats by Pakistan against India and vice versa; references to

World War I, World War II, the Holocaust, and Hiroshima; the doomsday clock on the cover of the *Bulletin of the Atomic Scientists* that shows how close the world is to annihilation; the federal government's implementation of Big Brother security measures; the drastic and sustained fall of the stock market and widespread economic depression; fear of technology in the hands of enemies as turning like a Frankenstein monster against its creators; the global epidemic advance of AIDS and malaria; the belief of a majority of Americans polled by Time/CBS that the biblical apocalypse will come true, 17 percent believing that the end of the world will happen in their lifetimes; the belief of fundamentalist Christians that Israel's victory in the Six Days' War of 1967 and its annexation of the West Wall signified the hand of God in history; the Islamic fundamentalist response to Western influence in the Middle East; escalating zealot actions and reactions to Israel-Palestine conflicts and fundamentalist Christian support of Israel that potentially can lead self-fulfillingly to Armageddon—all of which has created a "witches' Sabbath of madness and turmoil." Mead concludes by stating: "Apocalypse anxiety has moved into the mainstream of American politics and culture. . . . [A] line has been crossed. . . . The Age of Progress is in the past and this is the era of Shiva, destroyer of worlds."

11. Cf. journalist Bill Moyers's observation about the Republican right and the 2001–04 Bush administration, in a *New York Review of Books* essay entitled "Welcome to Doomsday": "Many of the constituencies who make up this alliance don't see eye to eye on many things, but for President Bush's master plan for rolling back environmental protections they are united. A powerful current connects the administration's multinational corporate cronies who regard the environment as ripe for the picking and a hard-core constituency of fundamentalists who regard the environment as fuel for the fire that is coming" (March 24, 2005, p. 10).

12. The radical deepening of gravitas that tends to emerge in the collective psyche during Saturn-Pluto alignments is well conveyed in an essay by Charlene Spretnak written within a month of the events of September 11, 2001:

> The initial shock and grieving after the terrorist attacks instilled in the American psyche a gravitas, a deep sense of grounding that seemed to slow time in our mad-dash world and draw us into silent reflection rather than quick talk. Thinking felt as if it were weighted in our entire body. It refused to click into easy patterns as we sought to grasp the unimaginable new reality. In that palpable grounding the first week, we were all bonded with the dead and with each other, causing us to reach out to family and friends around the country in shock and loving support. It felt as if our suddenly having to bear the unbearable had delivered us to another way of being, one shaped by the trauma of immense tragedy and the movement into regeneration. Even mainstream commentators noted that the trivial concerns of our consumer culture seemed extremely irrelevant. We had entered a new time and a new psychological space. (*The San Francisco Chronicle*, October 5, 2001)

13. John Hersey, whose *Hiroshima* galvanized the American public's moral response to the dropping of the bombs and helped set the terms for the nuclear debate during the following decades of the Cold War, was born during the preceding Saturn-Pluto conjunction in 1914. As with many other authors and artists born with this aspect, the themes of his most significant work were consistently reflective of this archetypal complex. Hersey's most famous novel, *The Wall*, depicted both the extreme inhumanity and the extreme courage displayed during the Nazi destruction of the Warsaw ghetto during World War II.

14. An especially enduring and consequential embodiment of the many conflicting and interpenetrating qualities, both positive and negative, intrinsic to the Saturn-Pluto complex can be recognized in the distinctive character and legacy of the the U.S. Constitution, which came into being during the Saturn-Pluto conjunction of 1785–88. Created at the Constitutional Convention in Philadelphia of 1787, analyzed and defended in *The Federalist Papers*, and ratified in succession by the individual states in 1787–88, the Constitution was both forged and legally established entirely during that conjunction. (Reflecting other characteristic themes of the Saturn-Pluto complex, this was the same conjunction that coincided with the period of severe economic depression and widespread famine,

affecting many parts of the world, that in France established the critical social conditions and imme-diate provocation for the French Revolution, which began the next year as Jupiter and Uranus moved into conjunction.)

In the U.S. Constitution, several motifs that suggest the positive synthesis of the two principles associated with Saturn and Pluto can be discerned: the enduring and firmly established powerful authoritative structure, legally binding and hallowed by tradition, history, and longevity, that provided for a stable organization (Saturn) of power (Pluto) in a complex system of checks and balances that would carefully hold the tension and interplay of conflicting political forces and impulses. All these qualities precisely represent the characteristic dynamics of the Saturn-Pluto archetypal complex.

Reflecting a diachronic cyclical pattern, James Madison, the principal architect of the Consti-tution, was himself born in 1751 during the immediately preceding Saturn-Pluto conjunction, ex-actly one full cycle and thirty-six years before the birth of the Constitution he designed. The sustained effectiveness of the Constitution's structural control of immense power, its stable contain-ment of the tension of opposing forces, and its enduring character and continued potent authority all owe much to Madison's mind and character. Madison was himself inspired by the writings on the separation and balance of powers by John Locke, who was born under an exact Saturn opposite Pluto a century earlier (in 1632, the same alignment that coincided with the trial of Galileo).

We can recognize the characteristic spirit and ambiance of this complex as well in the grave and weighty intonations that accompany almost all public pronouncements about the Constitution, such as "the great wisdom of our American Constitution" or "What our Founding Fathers established over two centuries ago." Similarly, the grave accusation, "That is unconstitutional!" or the dire warn-ing, "Our nation is in a constitutional crisis," as at the time of Watergate and also after the 2000 presidential election. Both crises were exactly coincident with Saturn-Pluto alignments. We also see the relevant themes in the Constitution's virtually unassailable authority, which is in certain respects suggestive of a structure of religious law that has been invested with the legitimacy of omniscient wisdom and unquestionable divine authority.

Here we can begin to observe the shadow side of the same archetypal complex, the very strengths and virtues of the Constitution being linked with its profound flaws. Thus, for example, its extreme resistance to modification even when such change is crucial to save its democratic princi-ples and even when a majority of citizens wish to modify it. Especially reflective of the shadow di-mensions of the Saturn-Pluto complex, despite the better intentions of its principal architects, was the Constitution's authoritative sanctioning of slavery that was carefully built into its original struc-ture because it was required by the slave-holding southern states as the price of ratification.

This enduring legacy of what has been called the nation's "original sin" permitted and sustained the immeasurable suffering of countless enslaved men, women, and children—as well as the im-measurable corruption and hardening of the slavemasters' souls—and led to the catastrophic cleans-ing of the Civil War. Its legacy continued with the many laws, such as Jim Crow and poll taxes, to disenfranchise and segregate blacks that were enacted and extended with almost systematic regu-larity in coincidence with subsequent Saturn-Pluto alignments. That legacy continued as well in the stubbornly enduring effects of racism that pervade and wound American society, which become es-pecially evident during Saturn-Pluto alignments such as the 1964–67 opposition, or again during the most recent square of 1992–94, when urban riots touched off by racial injustice shook the nation.

Moreover, as the nation discovered in the 2000 election at the start of the most recent Saturn-Pluto opposition, the distortions that the Constitution and the Electoral College wrought in the structure of presidential elections continued as well, resulting, in 2000, in the election of a candidate with half a million fewer votes than his opponent. The further significant role played during this election by the thousands of confirmed cases of systematic disenfranchisement of African-American voters and, finally, the determinative role played by the Supreme Court also represent characteristic expressions of the archetypal complex associated with Saturn-Pluto alignments. The victim's side of the Saturn-Pluto complex was vividly reflected in the widespread conviction that an historic defeat of democratic values had occurred in the 2000 election, accompanied by a sense of electoral disen-franchisement and judicially enforced impotence that was experienced by many in the wake of the Supreme Court decision.

The Supreme Court itself, which was established by the Constitution during the same Saturn-Pluto conjunction of 1787–88, has long carried with it much the same mantle of solemn authority: the dark gravitas of its black robes, its hallowed chambers, the granite and marble solidity of its tem-ple, the patriarchal authority of its considered pronouncements, its reverence towards the Founding

Fathers, its overwhelmingly male-dominated bench of aging justices, its long, slow deliberations and penetrating consideration of deep judicial problems and conflicts, its solemn and binding judgments. We also see the Saturn-Pluto complex in the Court's persistent concern with "the original intent" of the Founding Fathers, and the tremendous power of precedent and past judgments in its debates and the determining of decisions. It is visible as well in the highly conservative tendencies of the Court (with significant exceptions, such as the liberal activism of the Warren Court during the Uranus-Pluto conjunction of the 1960s). Finally, in its status as the last court of appeal and its authoritative determinations and final judgments, particularly with respect to death sentences and executions, another archetypal theme of the Saturn-Pluto complex can be discerned, that of the Last Judgment. The installation of a 5,280-pound granite monument bearing the Ten Commandments in the Alabama State Supreme Court lobby by the state's chief justice from 2001 to 2003 during the most recent Saturn-Pluto alignment suggests the close archetypal association in the American unconscious between the U.S. Constitution and biblical authority.

15. In *Memories, Dreams, Reflections*, Jung spoke of Schopenhauer as "the great find":

> He was the first to speak of the suffering of the world . . . and of confusion, passion, evil. . . . Here at last was a philosopher who had the courage to see that all was not for the best in the fundaments of the universe. He spoke neither of the all-good and all-wise providence of a Creator, nor of the harmony of the cosmos, but stated bluntly that a fundamental flaw underlay the sorrowful course of human history and the cruelty of nature: the blindness of the world-creating Will. (p. 69)

16. Both the Ku Klux Klan and the Knights of the White Camelia, the two principal organizations in the South founded by former Confederates to oppose Reconstruction and terrorize African-Americans, were founded during the Saturn-Pluto opposition of 1866–67. The Plutonic character of the Klan pervaded the mythos of its organization: each state or Realm was governed by a Grand Dragon, aided by eight Hydras as staff; clusters of counties were ruled by a Great Titan and six Furies; each county was overseen by a Grand Giant aided by four Night Hawks; and each Den was governed by a Grand Cyclops with two Night Hawks. Members were known as Ghouls.

Moreover, the second Ku Klux Klan was founded in 1915 during the Saturn-Pluto conjunction that coincided with World War I. This incarnation of the Klan spread throughout the United States, north and south, with a fundamentalist religious orientation and a virulently nativist political program, and with hundreds of thousands of members as it broadened its agenda of white supremacy and the violent suppression of African-Americans to include anti-Semitism and anti-Catholicism.

17. Holst was familiar with astrology, and he composed each movement of *The Planets* to reflect the distinct archetypal character of each planet: Mars, Venus, Mercury, Jupiter, Saturn, Uranus, and Neptune. (In 1914 the planet Pluto had not yet been discovered.) The opening movement, "Mars," accurately reflects the aggressive, military qualities associated with the Mars archetype, but at a deeper level the music is clearly pervaded by the archetypal complex that we have seen associated with the Saturn-Pluto cycle: the overwhelming elemental power, the highly ordered relentlessness of its titanic driving force, the destructive violence on a mass scale, the chthonic depths of darkness and horror, the suggestion of mechanized warfare and totalitarian terror with thousands of armored tanks, planes, and jackbooted regiments that destroy everything in their path—all evoked in music composed before the events they portray took place.

18. Joyce's *A Portrait of the Artist as a Young Man* was published in installments as Joyce completed them in Ezra Pound's *The Egoist* in 1914–15, then as a book in the United States in 1916, all during the Saturn-Pluto conjunction. Joyce himself was born in 1882 at the cusp of the immediately preceding Saturn-Pluto conjunction one cycle earlier, near the beginning of the rare (occurring once in five hundred years) Saturn-Neptune-Pluto triple conjunction of 1881–84 that also coincided with the births of Kafka, Stravinsky, and Virginia Woolf, and Nietzsche's declaration of the death of God.

Joyce's portrait of hell makes clear the extent to which the concept and image of hell can be approached archetypally not only as Saturn's judgment and punishment of the Plutonic id (sexuality, the bestial instincts, the demonic, the underworld) but also as the Pluto archetype's overwhelming intensification of the Saturn principle of *time* (and other Saturnian themes, such as confinement, punishment, guilt, suffering, and death) to its absolute extreme. From this perspective, Joyce's rendering of the nature of *eternal* damnation at the climax of the preacher's sermon (employing as well the paradigmatic Saturnian metaphor of the clock) is especially memorable:

> Last and crowning torture of all the tortures of that awful place is the eternity of hell. Eternity! O, dread and dire word. Eternity! What mind of man can understand it? And remember, it is an eternity of pain. Even though the pains of hell were not so terrible as they are, yet they would become infinite, as they are destined to last for ever. But while they are everlasting they are at the same time, as you know, intolerably intense, unbearably extensive. To bear even the sting of an insect for all eternity would be a dreadful torment. What must it be, then, to bear the manifold tortures of hell for ever? For ever! For all eternity! Not for a year or for an age but for ever. Try to imagine the awful meaning of this. You have often seen the sand on the seashore. How fine are its tiny grains! And how many of those tiny little grains go to make up the small handful which a child grasps in its play. Now imagine a mountain of that sand, a million miles high, reaching from the earth to the farthest heavens, and a million miles broad, extending to remotest space, and a million miles in thickness; and imagine such an enormous mass of countless particles of sand multiplied as often as there are leaves in the forest, drops of water in the mighty ocean, feathers on birds, scales on fish, hairs on animals, atoms in the vast expanse of the air: and imagine that at the end of every million years a little bird came to that mountain and carried away in its beak a tiny grain of that sand. How many millions upon millions of centuries would pass before that bird had carried away even a square foot of that mountain, how many eons upon eons of ages before it had carried away all? Yet at the end of that immense stretch of time not even one instant of eternity could be said to have ended. At the end of all those billions and trillions of years eternity would have scarcely begun. And if that mountain rose again after it had been all carried away, and if the bird came again and carried it all away again grain by grain, and if it so rose and sank as many times as there are stars in the sky, atoms in the air, drops of water in the sea, leaves on the trees, feathers upon birds, scales upon fish, hairs upon animals, at the end of all those innumerable risings and sinkings of that immeasurably vast mountain not one single instant of eternity could be said to have ended; even then, at the end of such a period, after that eon of time the mere thought of which makes our very brain reel dizzily, eternity would scarcely have begun.
>
> —A holy saint (one of our own fathers I believe it was) was once vouchsafed a vision of hell. It seemed to him that he stood in the midst of a great hall, dark and silent save for the ticking of a great clock. The ticking went on unceasingly; and it seemed to this saint that the sound of the ticking was the ceaseless repetition of the words—ever, never; ever, never. Ever to be in hell, never to be in heaven; ever to be shut off from the presence of God, never to enjoy the beatific vision; ever to be eaten with flames, gnawed by vermin, goaded with burning spikes, never to be free from those pains; ever to have the conscience upbraid one, the memory enrage, the mind filled with darkness and despair, never to escape; ever to curse and revile the foul demons who gloat fiendishly over the misery of their dupes, never to behold the shining raiment of the blessed spirits; ever to cry out of the abyss of fire to God for an instant, a single instant, of respite from such awful agony, never to receive, even for an instant, God's pardon; ever to suffer, never to enjoy; ever to be damned, never to be saved; ever, never; ever, never. O, what a dreadful punishment! An eternity of endless agony, of endless bodily and spiritual torment, without one ray of hope, without one moment of cessation, of agony limitless in intensity, of torment infinitely varied, of torture that sustains eternally that which it eternally devours, of anguish that everlastingly preys upon the spirit while it racks the flesh, an eternity, every instant of which is itself an eternity of woe. Such is the terrible punishment decreed for those who die in mortal sin by an almighty and a just God. (New York: Modern Library, 1996, pp. 177–80)

19. Mel Gibson was born during the Saturn-Pluto square in 1956, within 1° of exact alignment (with Mars in the configuration as well). This was the same year and Saturn-Pluto alignment during which Cecil B. DeMille directed and produced *The Ten Commandments*, another culturally influential film with a biblical subject and similar motifs—the stern religious authoritativeness of Moses,

the thundering power of Yahweh as he issued the divine commandments, the ruthless punishment of evil, and so forth. The film starred Charlton Heston, who was born during the Saturn-Pluto square of 1923 and who became another leading conservative Hollywood figure. DeMille was himself born during the Saturn-Pluto conjunction of 1881. He made two versions of *The Ten Commandments*, the first during the Saturn-Pluto square of 1923 (when Heston was born), the second during the Saturn-Pluto square of 1956 (when Gibson was born). Many of DeMille's other films embodied characteristic themes of the Saturn-Pluto complex: *The Sign of the Cross, The Crusades, Samson and Delilah, Forbidden Fruit, Madame Satan, The Godless Girl, Temptation*.

20. Such correlations were evident even in a genre as unlikely to be reflective of Saturn-Pluto archetypal themes as musical comedy. The film musical *Chicago*, produced and widely viewed during the most recent Saturn-Pluto opposition in 2002–03, was saturated with Saturn-Pluto motifs: murder and revenge, ruthless ambition, corruption, the criminal and sexual underworld, prison and death row, trials, judgments, guilt, executions, a view of human motivation as dominated by relentless selfishness, and a pervasive aesthetic of blackness and shadows, dungeons and guns. The original Broadway play was conceived and produced during the Saturn-Pluto square of 1973–75.

21. In many of Kafka's stories, the protagonist is an entrapped animal, often a rodent or insect, the prey of life, as in *The Burrow, The Metamorphosis*, and *Josephina the Mouse Singer, or The Mouse Folk*. The same motif was brilliantly exploited by the comic artist Art Spiegelman in his two-part graphic novel published as *Maus: A Survivor's Tale* and *Maus II: From Mauschwitz to the Catskills*. Based on his parents' experiences as survivors of the concentration camps, *Maus* depicted the Jews as mice and the Nazi Germans as predatory cats ("Katzies"). Spiegelman was born during the postwar Saturn-Pluto conjunction of 1946–48. The subjects of his principal works have consistently reflected the Saturn-Pluto complex; *Maus*'s focus on the Holocaust was followed by his 2004 work, *In the Shadow of No Towers*, which addressed the destruction of the Twin Towers on September 11, 2001, and its devastating psychological aftereffects. Spiegelman's all-black *New Yorker* magazine cover immediately after September 11 subtly rendered the towers in silhouette in an even darker shade of black.

22. Auden's *September 1, 1939* explores many Saturn-Pluto themes relevant to the events of September 11, 2001: the dark end of an era, evil done by those to whom evil is done, blind steel and concrete skyscrapers and the cold thrusting power of imperialism, a psychopathic god served by an enemy gone mad. Perhaps especially relevant is its insight concerning humiliation and violence: "The poem, as Joseph Brodsky once pointed out, is really about shame—about how cultures are infected by overwhelming feelings of shame, their 'habit-forming pain,' and seek to escape those feelings through violence. What drives men mad—drives them to psychopathic gods—is the unbearable feeling of having been humiliated" (Adam Gopnik, *The New Yorker*, October 1, 2001).

23. One of the more striking patterns I found in my research was a consistent correlation between alignments of the outer-planet cycles (Saturn-Pluto, Jupiter-Uranus, Saturn-Neptune, and so forth) with the simultaneous writing and publication of large numbers of books about historical events and dominant themes from earlier alignment periods involving the same planets. A comprehensive body of such evidence can readily be assessed by a systematic examination of all reviews of just-published books, both fiction and nonfiction, in any extensive weekly book review, such as the *New York Times Book Review* or comparable publications such as the *New York Review of Books*, the *London Review of Books*, or the *Times Literary Supplement*.

The collective psyche appears to be shaped by and spontaneously attracted toward particular motifs and phenomena that closely reflect the archetypal qualities of the current planetary alignments, qualities that were in turn dominant in the events and spirit of earlier eras with the same alignments. The relevant archetypal qualities are thus regularly visible in the writing and publication not only of books that focus on contemporary expressions of those themes but also of works that explore earlier historical manifestations. This results in an increased public awareness during such periods of both the relevant archetypal motifs and their most vivid historical embodiments—for example, during Saturn-Pluto alignments, the publication of works, both fiction and nonfiction, about the Holocaust and concentration camps, the gulag, the world wars and the cold war, terrorism and fundamentalism from other ages, imperialist domination, scandals and sins in the history of the Church, witch hunts, the Watergate scandal, the history of slavery, and so forth.

24. Edmund Morel, the British investigative journalist and the founder of the Congo Reform Association, viewed the title of Conrad's work as synonymous with the horrific reality of European cruelty and African suffering in the Congo, and considered Leopold II to be "a great genius for evil." Leopold himself was born with his Sun closely conjoined with a Saturn-Pluto opposition (and all three in close T-square alignment with Mars). On a separate but related note, in 1939, when Einstein wrote the letter to Roosevelt to recommend the development of the atomic bomb, the greatest known supply of the uranium necessary for producing the nuclear reaction lay in the Belgian Congo, where it was mined as ore by a Belgian mining company.

25. After finishing *Answer to Job*, Jung wrote to a friend, "I have landed the great whale." Born with Saturn square Pluto, Jung wrote *Answer to Job* during an illness in a white-heat state of archetypal possession in 1951–52, the one time in his life that transiting Pluto crossed his natal Saturn-Pluto configuration (Pluto opposite Saturn, square Pluto).

26. Stowe's *Uncle Tom's Cabin*, the letter from her friend, and the public outcry against the Fugitive Slave Act all also reflect the widespread awakening of antislavery feeling and heightened emancipatory impulses that occurred during the long Uranus-Pluto conjunction of the 1845–56 period discussed in the preceding chapter, when the abolitionist activities of Frederick Douglass, Harriet Tubman, John Brown, and many others reached a height of intensity before the Civil War. The shorter Saturn-Pluto conjunction of 1850–53 took place near the middle of that period at the time of closest conjunction of Uranus and Pluto, when the three planets were in a rare tight triple conjunction. The remarkable phenomenon of *Uncle Tom's Cabin*—Stowe's writing of the novel, the catalyzing circumstances, and the immense popular response to its publication—can be understood as the Saturn-Pluto and the Uranus-Pluto complexes being simultaneously constellated with unusual potency.

27. *Night and Fog* (*Nuit et Brouillard*, 1955, Saturn-Pluto square), *The Pawnbroker* (1965, opposition), *Sophie's Choice* (1982, conjunction), *Shoah* (documentary interviews, 1981–85, conjunction), and *Schindler's List* (1993, square). A similar pattern can be recognized in Philip Roth's novel *The Plot Against America*, written during one Saturn-Pluto period (2001–04) while it re-imagined another Saturn-Pluto period, focused on the year 1940. The novel is suffused with characteristic Saturn-Pluto themes and events, such as repressive conservative empowerment, anti-Semitic prejudice and hostility, an atmosphere of pervasive menace and fear, the Holocaust, global war, and helplessness in the face of dark and overpowering historical forces.

28. Because Wilde was born with a close natal Mercury-Uranus opposition, transiting Uranus was also exactly conjoining his natal Mercury at this time, a natal aspect and transit I frequently found correlated with heightened linguistic facility, brilliant and often irreverent wit, an inclination towards bons mots, wisecracks, unexpected twists of meaning, word play, and verbal irreverence (as in Wilde's "I can resist everything except temptation" or his famous statement to the customs official upon entering the United States, "I have nothing to declare except my genius").

29. It is important to keep in mind that personal transit correlations, such as those cited for Shakespeare, always take place within a larger, more complex context of world transits and the ongoing cycles of the outer planets. For example, the world transit of the Saturn-Pluto opposition of 1598–1601 (the one that coincided with the Inquisition's trial and execution of Giordano Bruno) took place in exact coincidence with the beginning of Shakespeare's tragic period (*Julius Caesar* in 1599–1600, *Hamlet* in 1601), as if the collective zeitgeist were initiating what became Shakespeare's more sustained personal encounter with the same energies and themes during his long personal transit of Pluto to his own natal Saturn. I found this to be typical of the "overdetermining" coincidence of simultaneous personal and world transits in such correlations.

  Any discussion of Shakespeare's possible transits necessarily entails the question of the authorship of the Shakespearean canon. It is possible that the character of the natal chart and the evidence of precisely timed archetypal correlations with personal transits could contribute a new source of insight on this issue.

30. Cited in Robert Hollander, *Dante: A Life in Works* (New Haven: Yale University Press, 2001), p. 91. Based on his own words in *La Divina Commedia*, Dante was born between May 18 and

June 17, 1265. We therefore can be certain of his natal Saturn position with a margin of error of less than 2°.

Part VI: *Cycles of Creativity and Expansion*

1. Because of retrograde and direct apparent motion, the oppositions of Jupiter and Uranus (and, very rarely, the conjunctions) often move in and out of the 15° range over a longer period of up to about twenty-three months. In these cases the archetypal correlations, and in particular the cyclical diachronic patterns, were no less apparent, but the synchronic patterns were somewhat more diffuse and less sharply punctuated than in the concentrated fourteen-month alignments. The 1782–83 opposition was such an example, Jupiter and Uranus having been within 15° of exact alignment for approximately sixteen months spread out over the twenty-three month period from January 1782 to November 1783. With few exceptions, the conjunctions occurred in concentrated periods of fourteen consecutive months (as in 1775–76 and 1788–89), while the opposition periods were more often extended and discontinuous. As we will see, Jupiter-Uranus oppositions not infrequently coincided with cultural milestones and creative breakthroughs that had an especially significant and climactic nature.

2. The subsequent history of the *Bounty* mutineers and the Polynesian women and men who joined them, first on Tahiti and then as they lived in complete isolation on Pitcairn Island from 1789 through the 1790s, seemed virtually a precise microcosm of what happened on a larger scale halfway around the world in France in the same period: the initial successful rebellion during the Jupiter-Uranus conjunction followed by a sustained eruption of bloody violence, murder, and power struggle during the longer Uranus-Pluto opposition—the plotting, revenge, and madness, the boiling over of irrational impulses in an otherwise paradisiacal setting, the self-destruction of an entire society. The Dionysian nature of this eruption was also evident in the new sexual freedom experienced by the British sailors in the Polynesian environment, and in the frequently sexual nature of the sources of conflict that resulted in the repeated outbursts of murderous aggression in the Pitcairn community.

3. When Jupiter-Uranus alignments coincided with the Uranus-Pluto cycle (i.e., took place at the same time that Uranus and Pluto were within 15° alignment), as in 1968–69, with the triple conjunction of Jupiter with Uranus and Pluto, the range of degrees within which archetypally relevant correlations were in evidence for the Jupiter-Uranus alignment consistently appeared to be extended beyond the 15°–20° range. For example, by the beginning of 1968, when Uranus and Pluto were within 7° of each other, Jupiter had moved to within 17° of Pluto and 23° of Uranus. Cultural phenomena characteristic of the Jupiter-Uranus cycle were clearly in evidence at this point and throughout the 1968–69 period, though events suggestive of the triple archetypal complex notably increased in frequency as the three planets moved into closer range in the course of 1968. The climax of the triple conjunction was the summer of 1969 (the Apollo Moon landing, the Woodstock music festival, and many other relevant phenomena) when all three planets were within 7°–8° of each other.

I believe such observations underscore the importance of recognizing the fluidity and interpenetration of archetypal principles and forces rather than assuming a more atomistic ontology and causality (i.e., expecting archetypally relevant phenomena to stop and start in mechanistic correlation with the alignments rather than to unfold in a more complex continuum of multiple overlapping wave forms).

4. The original technical meaning of "quantum leap," as distinct from the popular use of the phrase, signifies a shift from one energy level to another by a subatomic particle, such as when an electron changes from one energy level to another in a distinct leap without passing through any of the intermediate values of energy. The archetypal theme of "quantum leap" that I observed in coincidence with Jupiter-Uranus alignments seems to embrace simultaneously the technical meaning (the sudden jump from one energy level to another without intermediate steps), the popular meaning (a sudden and unexpected major shift or radical expansion of any kind), and the link between the two (the fact that the original quantum hypothesis proposed by Planck reflected not only a sudden energy leap but also an extraordinary anomaly, a scientifically unexpected phenomenon in itself, that in turn precipitated a major leap in the growth of scientific understanding). This striking metaphoric

flexibility and creative multivalence was consistently observable in archetypal correlations related to each of the planetary cycles and combinations.

5. The 1961–62 Jupiter-Uranus opposition had an unusual span: It was centered on the year 1962 but had an early approach in the spring of 1961 and finished in early 1963. (See end of this note for exact months and orbs.) The representative Promethean phenomena of this period closely paralleled this extended pattern. The first space flights by Gagarin and Shepard took place in a three-week period in April and May of 1961 when Jupiter and Uranus were within 17° and 15° of alignment, respectively. During the main span of the alignment, in 1962, occurred John Glenn's space flight, the launch of the Telstar satellite, and the launch of the first orbiting solar observatory.

A similar timing is visible in the history of the civil rights movement of the 1960s: the Uranus-Pluto conjunction spanned the decade, while the Jupiter-Uranus opposition in the spring of 1961 and 1962 coincided with significant milestones in that longer trajectory. The movement was first decisively galvanized on a national scale in May 1961 when the Freedom Riders, organized by the Congress of Racial Equality and comprising more than 70,000 students of both races, began their demonstrations throughout the South to break down segregation barriers in interstate transportation. In September 1962, James Meredith attempted to enter the segregated University of Mississippi. The ensuing riots, deployment of federal troops, and national attention further galvanized the growing movement for racial equality. Note 15 below examines other events of this Jupiter-Uranus alignment that served as catalysts for the longer-term cultural movements and processes of the Uranus-Pluto conjunction of the 1960s.

Jupiter and Uranus first moved within 20° orb in late March 1961 and were within 15° for most of May. Because of retrograde motion, Jupiter moved back outside the 15° range at the end of May and outside the 20° orb in early July; it did not return until January 1962 (within 20° then 15° in that month). The two planets remained within 15° orb for the entire year of 1962; they finally moved beyond the 15° point in February 1963, and beyond the 20° point in March.

6. Kennedy (who was born with a Jupiter-Uranus square) made a second widely quoted speech that summoned the nation to reach the Moon, on Sept. 12, 1962, when the Jupiter-Uranus opposition was closer to exact:

> We choose to go to the Moon in this decade and do the other things, not because they are easy, but because they are hard, because that goal will serve to organize and measure the best of our energies and skills, because that challenge is one that we are willing to accept, one we are unwilling to postpone, and one which we intend to win.

A diachronic echo of these first manned space flights took place in coincidence with the most recent Jupiter-Uranus opposition in October 2003, when China successfully launched its first astronaut into space, thereby becoming the third country, after the United States and the USSR, to accomplish this feat.

Jupiter-Uranus alignments seem to coincide with not only the achievement of such feats in the field of space travel and aviation but also the impulse to do so, irrespective of the outcome. During the Jupiter-Uranus opposition of 2003–04, a distant echo of Kennedy's commitment to land a man on the Moon was George W. Bush's call for another such landing by 2020 to facilitate a subsequent manned expedition to Mars. During the immediately preceding Jupiter-Uranus opposition in July 1989, Bush's father when president had proposed a similar program of a return to the Moon as a stepping stone to Mars. The project was dropped after NASA's cost estimate of $400 billion was viewed as beyond the capacity of the U.S. budget. (Saturn was in conjunction with Uranus at that time, and both planets were opposite Jupiter.)

7. Such a feat did take place, however, in earlier eras in the human imagination, and it is striking how consistently the theme of space flight and aviation in the realm of literary fiction and the cinema was correlated with the Jupiter-Uranus cycle. Jules Verne's *From the Earth to the Moon*, which made many assumptions about space flight that later proved to be accurate, was published during the Jupiter-Uranus opposition of 1865. H. G. Wells wrote *The First Men in the Moon* during the conjunction of 1900. In film, Kubrick's *2001: A Space Odyssey*, the first epic space flight film, coincided with the triple conjunction of 1968–69. George Lucas's *Star Wars* was produced during the succeeding opposition of 1976–77 (released in May 1977, two months after the opposition ended). The following

conjunction of 1983 coincided with *The Right Stuff*, which was based on the first astronauts' space flights (which had occurred during the Jupiter-Uranus opposition of 1961–62).

In a related category, Ronald Reagan's "Star Wars" speech of March 1983, in which he set forth his technological fantasy of a nuclear space defense system, took place during the same Jupiter-Uranus conjunction of 1983 (and coincided as well with the Saturn-Pluto conjunction of 1981–84 and the greatly intensified Cold War tensions and fears of a nuclear Armageddon that dominated that period). Edgar Allan Poe's famous "Balloon Hoax," in which he published a widely believed newspaper report about a supposed transatlantic balloon flight that landed on the coast of South Carolina, took place during the Jupiter-Uranus conjunction of 1844–45 (cf. the Wright brothers' first flights on the coast of North Carolina during the conjunction of 1900 and Lindbergh's actual transatlantic flight during the conjunction of 1927).

8. The extraordinary conjunction of the Sun, Jupiter, Uranus, and Pluto at Descartes's birth on March 31, 1596, was also aligned in conjunction with Mercury—aptly paralleled by Descartes's fundamental assertion of the *cogito* and rationality as both the foundation for the identity of the autonomous self and the method for establishing its existence: "I *think,* therefore I *am.*"

9. The specific milestones were Jeremy Bentham's *Introduction to the Principles of Morals and Legislation* (1789), the classic exposition of Utilitarianism; David Ricardo's *On The Principles of Political Economy and Taxation* (1817), the most important work in economic theory between Adam Smith and Marx; Alexis de Tocqueville's famous nine-month visit to the United States (1831), which resulted in his classic political analysis, *Democracy in America.* During the period of the next conjunction (1844–45), Marx and Engels began their historic association: They met in Paris in August 1844, collaborated on *Die heilige Familie*, the first statement of the theory of Marxist communism, and published it in February 1845. During this same fertile period, Engels wrote *The Condition of the Working Class in England*, while Marx wrote what are now known as the *Economic and Philosophical Manuscripts of 1844* and the *Theses on Feuerbach*, which set forth the philosophical foundations of Marx's thought. Fourteen years later, during the next conjunction (1858–59), John Stuart Mill—heir to Hume, Bentham, Ricardo, and Tocqueville—published his most renowned and most conspicuously Promethean work, *On Liberty*.

10. The conjunction centered on the year 1858 was astronomically unusual in that, because of their apparent retrograde movements relative to each other, Jupiter and Uranus were within 15° of exact conjunction in three separate periods between July 1857 and March 1859 (July to October 1857, February to August 1858, and December 1858 to March 1859), approximately fourteen months spread out over a twenty-month period. Wagner began the composition of *Tristan* in August 1857 near the beginning of the conjunction and completed it twenty-four months later. The Darwin-Wallace announcement of the theory of evolution occurred during the central segment of the conjunction in July 1858, while John Stuart Mill's *On Liberty* was published during the last segment in March 1859.

The Jupiter-Uranus conjunction centered on the year 1803 that coincided with the *Eroica* was another case of this kind. The alignment first moved within 15° in October 1802 and finally left it in July 1804. This extended period of the conjunction closely coincided with the full span of Beethoven's composition of the *Eroica*: The first sketches for the symphony were done in October 1802, the principal period of composition took place in the summer and fall of 1803 when the conjunction was exact, and he completed the final fair copy by April of 1804.

Generally speaking, I found that such discontinuous alignments tended to coincide with archetypally relevant phenomena from the time the planets first moved within the orb to the time they moved beyond it for the last time. This was also true of personal transits of the outer planets, in which similar retrograde and direct movements across the natal chart positions occur.

11. As in 1968–69, when a Jupiter-Uranus alignment took place near the end of or soon after a longer Uranus-Pluto alignment, events that were clearly climactic expressions of the Promethean-Dionysian archetypal impulses that had been developing during the longer alignment regularly coincided with the approximately two-year period when all three planets—Jupiter, Uranus, and Pluto—were in broad conjunction. The wave of epoch-making events in modern thought and culture that took place in the 1857–59 period closely coincided with Jupiter's moving into alignment with the Uranus-Pluto conjunction, which began as the latter had entered the final penumbral 15°

to 20° range: Wagner's composition of *Tristan und Isolde* (1857–59), the publication of both Flaubert's *Madame Bovary* (April 1857) and Baudelaire's *Les Fleurs du mal* (June 1857), Darwin's and Wallace's announcement of the theory of natural selection and Darwin's beginning *The Origin of Species* (July 1858), and the publication of John Stuart Mill's *On Liberty* (February 1859). All five of these cultural milestones can best be understood in the context of the long Uranus-Pluto conjunction of the 1845–56 period that led up to their concrete emergence during the later penumbral period of the triple conjunction. The ideas and impulses expressed in these works were not only being developed during that longer period; they also all clearly reflect the characteristic themes of the Uranus-Pluto archetypal complex.

In Darwin's and Wallace's evolutionary theory, these themes are evident not only in its revolutionary impact on society and cultural beliefs but also in its focus on and intellectual-cultural awakening to such Plutonic themes as the struggle for existence, nature "red in tooth and claw," biological instinct, ceaseless transformation and evolution—with these in turn combined with Promethean themes of evolution's unpredictable variation and ceaseless creative innovation. In Mill's *Liberty*, they are evident in that essay's specific focus on Promethean themes of political freedom and emancipation, and its direct association with the political and intellectual developments of the two immediately preceding revolutionary Uranus-Pluto eras of 1845–56 and the French Revolution.

With Baudelaire's *Les Fleurs du mal*, we see the presence of the Uranus-Pluto complex in its Promethean liberation or awakening of Plutonic themes previously not explored so directly and powerfully in poetic literature—the violent and erotic, the perverse and morbid, the sordid and taboo, the instinctual and urban underworlds. Flaubert's *Madame Bovary*, which like *Les Fleurs du mal* was prosecuted for immorality, was as transformative for the modern novel as Baudelaire's work was for modern poetry. Wagner's *Tristan* similarly represented a Promethean revolution in the history of nineteenth-century music while also embodying the Dionysian energies so characteristic of Uranus-Pluto periods. Moreover, its character was associated with the revolutionary political developments and upheavals in European society and culture during the preceding Uranus-Pluto decade, such as the revolutions of 1848–49 which Wagner directly participated in and publicly supported.

This same period of the broad triple conjunction of Jupiter, Uranus, and Pluto in 1857–59 also coincided with significant revolutionary political phenomena in several areas of the world, such as the Sepoy Mutiny (which began in May 1857), which was the direct outgrowth of developments in India that had taken place during the 1845–1856 period of the Uranus-Pluto conjunction and bore the characteristic features of the latter archetypal complex. Similarly, the Lincoln-Douglas debates of 1858 during the Jupiter-Uranus conjunction, which both articulated and galvanized the national antislavery debate just before the Civil War, grew directly out of the radical changes in social attitudes and intensified abolitionist sentiment in the United States that had developed during the 1845–56 period of the Uranus-Pluto conjunction.

12. A remarkable wave of significant works of short fiction was produced during the fourteen-month period of that conjunction, from September 1885 to November 1886. In addition to Arthur Conan Doyle's writing of the first Sherlock Holmes story, Robert Louis Stevenson wrote *The Strange Case of Dr. Jekyll and Mr. Hyde*, Tolstoy wrote his greatest short work, *The Death of Ivan Illich*, Joseph Conrad wrote his first story (the prototype of *The Black Mate*), and the stories of Anton Chekhov first received public and critical acclaim.

13. Salinger began writing stories during the Jupiter-Uranus opposition of 1934. He wrote his first Holden Caulfield story seven years later during the conjunction of 1940–41. Seven years after that during the opposition of 1948 he published in *The New Yorker* his first mature work, *A Perfect Day for Bananafish*, which was also the first Glass family story. And seven years after that during the conjunction of 1954–55 he published *Franny*, the first work of his final phase of longer stories. Salinger's most famous work, *The Catcher in the Rye*, was published in 1951 when Uranus was transiting in exact conjunction to his natal Jupiter, a once-in-a-lifetime personal transit that lasts three years.

14. For simplicity and clarity, I have focused this survey of the relatively brief Jupiter-Uranus cycle on the conjunctions and oppositions only. However, as with the other cycles we have examined, the square alignments halfway between the conjunctions and oppositions consistently coincided with archetypally relevant events that formed intricate synchronic and diachronic patterns with the axial alignments we have been examining. For example, the Jupiter-Uranus square alignment of 1951 coincided with the song that after years of debate was recognized by the Rock and Roll Hall of Fame as

the first rock and roll song: *Rocket 88* by Ike Turner, produced by Sam Phillips in Memphis. Phillips later discovered and recorded Elvis Presley when the 1954–55 Jupiter-Uranus conjunction occurred, at the start of the larger wave of songs (by Chuck Berry, Bo Diddley, Bill Haley and the Comets, and Buddy Holly) that marked the birth of rock and roll.

The 1951 square alignment also coincided with the publication in July of that year of Salinger's *Catcher in the Rye*, which has been called the beginning of the specific youth counterculture whose end was marked by the death of John Lennon twenty-nine and a half years later in December 1980 (exactly one Saturn cycle later). It was also in 1951 during this square that Jack Kerouac wrote most of *On the Road* in a legendary three-week creative burst of nonstop single-spaced typing on a 120-foot "scroll" of paper he had taped together (April 2–22).

15. In addition to the emergence of Dylan, the Beatles, and the Rolling Stones, as well as the major milestones in space flight and the civil rights movement (see note 5 above), the Jupiter-Uranus opposition centered on the year 1962 coincided with the dawn of the ecology movement with Rachel Carson's *Silent Spring*, the start of the women's movement with the completion of Betty Friedan's *Feminine Mystique* (July 1962) and the publication of Doris Lessing's early feminist classic *Golden Notebook*, and the revolution in philosophy of science marked by the 1962 publication of Thomas Kuhn's *The Structure of Scientific Revolutions*. It was also in this year that Harry Hess postulated the theory of sea-floor spreading that started the plate-tectonics revolution in the Earth sciences, and Benoit Mandelbrot invented fractal images.

The Esalen Institute opened in 1962, inspired by Aldous Huxley and other prophets of a coming transformation of humanity, and began the human potential movement as the first of countless similar growth centers that flourished in the following years. Maslow's *Toward a Psychology of Being* marked the beginning of humanistic psychology. Timothy Leary and Richard Alpert first took LSD at Harvard, the Good Friday experiment using psilocybin was conducted at the Harvard Divinity School, and Ken Kesey, the future leader of the Merry Pranksters, published *One Flew over the Cuckoo's Nest*. Marshall McLuhan published *The Gutenberg Galaxy*. Pop art emerged with Andy Warhol's paintings of Campbell's Soup cans and Roy Lichtenstein's first one-man show in New York. In the same year Tom Hayden and the Students for a Democratic Society (SDS) drafted the influential Port Huron Statement, their founding declaration that advocated student activism in the pursuit of radical social reform. Cesar Chavez founded the National Farm Workers Association in the same year. Michael Harrington wrote *The Other America*, which helped catalyze social reform and the War on Poverty. Algeria won its revolutionary war of independence from France (having started it in late 1954 during the immediately preceding Jupiter-Uranus conjunction; this parallels the same sequence of the American revolutionary war of independence from England, which began in 1775 during the Jupiter-Uranus conjunction and was won during the following opposition of 1782–83).

Finally, it was in 1962 that Pope John XXIII convened the Second Vatican Council, which commenced the radical transformation of the Roman Catholic Church during the Sixties. And in the Soviet Union, the landmark publication in 1962 of Aleksandr Solzhenitsyn's *One Day in the Life of Ivan Denisovich* signaled a new period of cultural liberalization under Khrushchev. Both of these institutions' liberalizing phases were sharply slowed and to some extent ended when Saturn opposed the Uranus-Pluto conjunction in the mid-1960s after Pope John XXIII was succeeded by the more conservative Paul VI and Khrushchev was replaced by Brezhnev.

16. The 1968–69 triple conjunction also marked the turning point for Miles Davis's virtuoso sidemen of this time—John McLaughlin, Herbie Hancock, Tony Williams, Wayne Shorter, Josef Zawinul, Keith Jarrett, and Chick Corea—all of whom went on to form their own groups, which in turn became the dominant influences in the evolution of jazz-rock fusion in the 1970s.

17. In the poem Keats famously confused Balboa with the Spanish conquistador Hernando Cortés (Cortez), who invaded Mexico six years later: "Or like stout Cortez when with eagle eyes / He stared at the Pacific . . ."

18. During the intervening Jupiter-Uranus conjunction between these two oppositions, in 1872, Nietzsche published his first book, *The Birth of Tragedy*. During the following conjunction, in 1886, he wrote his philosophical summation, *Beyond Good and Evil*.

19. The Statue of Liberty was conceived of and proposed during the Jupiter-Uranus opposition of 1865 by the Frenchman Édouard Laboulaye, chairman of the French antislavery society, who was inspired by Lincoln's death and the emancipation of the slaves at the end of the Civil War. Frédéric-Auguste Bartholdi, the sculptor of the statue, was present at the dinner in which Laboulaye made the proposal.

20. There were two times in which Jupiter, Uranus, and Pluto came into broad triple conjunction in the nineteenth century, though neither was as close as the 1968–69 conjunction. These alignments occurred at the very beginning and end of the Uranus-Pluto conjunction of the mid-nineteenth century. The first time was in 1844–45, when the three planets moved within 20° of exact alignment, at times reaching as close as 15°. The second time, discussed in notes 10 and 11 above, took place in 1857–58 at the very end of the same Uranus-Pluto conjunction when Jupiter returned and the three planets moved to within 21° of exact alignment.

The coincidence of the first of these periods, 1844–45, with the start of Marx and Engels' collaboration, Darwin's first exposition of his evolutionary theory, Thoreau's Walden Pond period, Wagner's *Tannhäuser*, and the birth of Nietzsche are all suggestive of this larger triple-planet archetypal complex. The later 1857–58 period, which extended to the spring of 1859 when Jupiter and Uranus were still within 15°, coincided with the various milestones discussed in note 11 above: Wagner's *Tristan und Isolde*, Baudelaire's *Les Fleurs du mal*, Flaubert's *Madame Bovary*, Darwin's and Wallace's joint public announcement of the theory of evolution and the beginning of Darwin's writing *The Origin of Species*, and Mill's *On Liberty*, as well as such political phenomena as the sustained upheaval in India initiated by the Sepoy Mutiny, and the Lincoln-Douglas debates in the United States.

Halfway between the above two periods, in 1850–52, was the closest axial alignment of Jupiter, Uranus, and Pluto during the nineteenth century, when Jupiter moved into opposition to the nearly exact Uranus-Pluto conjunction,. This long opposition (moving in and out of 15° range between November 1850 and October 1852) coincided with the Saturn-Pluto conjunction of 1850–53, discussed at length in earlier chapters, which coincided with its own archetypally distinctive cultural phenomena that were often antithetical in character to the Jupiter-Uranus-Pluto complex. Yet the latter was conspicuously in evidence, even if always combined with the Saturn-Pluto complex. The power of Melville's *Moby Dick* of 1851, Sojourner Truth's "Ain't I a Woman?" speech to the women's rights convention in Akron in 1851, the emancipatory and transformative impact of Stowe's *Uncle Tom's Cabin* of 1852, the widespread cultural reaction against religious orthodoxy influenced by Schopenhauer's philosophy after the publication of his essays in 1851, and the enormous display of technological and scientific progress in London's Great Exhibition and Crystal Palace of 1851 are all suggestive, each in its distinctive way, of this larger combination of multiple archetypal influences (*Jupiter*-Uranus-Pluto as well as *Saturn*-Uranus-Pluto).

The triple Saturn-Uranus-Pluto conjunction, lasting from 1850 to 1853, was also reflected in the harsh conservative backlash of the European powers in the aftermath of the events of 1848 and the many measures taken during that period to suppress radical and revolutionary political movements. It was of course 1848 that brought the greatest eruption of social and political turmoil during the Uranus-Pluto conjunction of the nineteenth century—indeed, at any time in the nineteenth century—and this wave of revolutionary upheaval coincided precisely with the brief period in which Jupiter was in close square alignment with both Uranus and Pluto and when Saturn was not in the configuration.

21. In astronomy and space exploration during the Jupiter-Uranus opposition of 2002–04, there occurred the first manned Chinese space flight; the first successful private space flight (SpaceShipOne); the launching of the Spitzer Space Telescope and its first major discoveries of early star formation and the youngest planet ever observed (in a diachronic pattern with the launching of the Hubble Space Telescope during the immediately preceding Jupiter-Uranus opposition of 1989–90); the successful Mars probe which beamed images back to the Earth from the robotic rovers Spirit and Opportunity; the Cassini's reaching Saturn; and the launching of the Stanford space probe to test Einstein's general theory of relativity (in a diachronic pattern with the announcement of the Príncipe Island expedition's results during the opposition of 1919–20). Also at this time occurred the first successful quantum teleportation (achieved independently and simultaneously in Austria and the United States).

In the area of Promethean social and political phenomena, besides the global demonstrations against the war in Iraq, characteristic Jupiter-Uranus events included the wave of same-sex marriages celebrated in New England and on the West Coast in the wake of the landmark Massachusetts court ruling (in a diachronic pattern with the Stonewall uprising during the conjunction of 1968–69), and the unprecedented success and popular embrace of anti-establishment documentaries such as Michael Moore's *Bowling for Columbine* and *Farenheit 9/11*, as well as *The Fog of War*, *The Corporation*, *Outfoxed*, *Uncovered: The Whole Truth About the Iraq War*, and *The Yes Men*.

Characteristic of the Jupiter-Uranus complex as well was the revolution in the music-recording industry produced by the rapid spread of iTunes during the same period (much as CDs produced a comparable revolution during the Jupiter-Uranus conjunction of 1983). Other cultural phenomena of a Promethean character include the Internet's rapid transformation during the 2002–04 period into a conduit and amplifier of political dissidence and intellectual independence (against the backdrop of the conservative empowerment during the Saturn-Pluto opposition of these same years), evident in the widespread influence of progressive activist organizations, such as MoveOn.org, and the surge in popularity of blogs and other websites that carry news and opinion outside the mainstream media.

Part VII: *Awakenings of Spirit and Soul*

1. Swedenborg's doctrine of correspondences, which was later taken up by Baudelaire (born during the following Uranus-Neptune conjunction) and which linked the natural and human world with the spiritual and divine through linguistic analogy as in the tradition of the Jewish Kabbalah, was set forth in his essay "A Hieroglyphic Key" in 1741 during this Uranus-Neptune alignment.

2. Contemplating the poignancy of this passage, which was written while Condorcet was hiding from the Revolution's punitive terror, his death in prison only a few months away, Charles Taylor remarks, "There were, indeed, 'errors, crimes, injustices' for which he needed consolation. And it adds to our awe before his unshaken revolutionary faith when we reflect that these crimes were no longer those of an ancien régime, but of the forces who themselves claimed to be building the radiant future" (*Sources of the Self*, p. 354).

3. During the fourteen months of this Jupiter-Uranus conjunction within the larger Uranus-Neptune conjunction that continued for another decade, a wave of major creative activity occurred in English Romanticism. In the first month of the Jupiter-Uranus conjunction (December 1816), the works of Percy Bysshe Shelley and of John Keats received their first major public attention when Leigh Hunt published his influential article on the "Young Poets." Keats then published his first volume of poems, which included *On First Looking into Chapman's Homer*, and met Shelley and Wordsworth for the first time. Shelley published his *Hymn to Intellectual Beauty* and wrote *The Revolt of Islam*, his visionary defense of the revolutionary impulse. Mary Shelley wrote most of *Frankenstein: A Modern Prometheus* at this time. Byron completed his major autobiographical poem *Childe Harold's Pilgrimage* and wrote *Manfred*, his first poetic drama, while Coleridge published his seminal work of Romantic philosophy, *Biographia Literaria*. Many other milestones of Romanticism took place in 1817 as well, such as Beethoven's beginning the composition of the Ninth Symphony and Hegel's publishing his *Encyclopedia*. This was the same rare configuration (Jupiter, Uranus, and Neptune in triple conjunction) that occurred at the time that Dante began to compose *La Divina Commedia* (1306) and that Pico composed the *Oratio de Dignitate Hominis* (1486).

4. In the Julian Calendar then in use in England, Newton's birth occurred on December 25, 1642 (Old Style), which with the introduction of the Gregorian Calendar became January 4, 1643 (New Style). Scholars have speculated that Newton's birth on Christmas Day, combined with the absence of a worldly father (who died when Newton was in utero) in echo of the birth of another world redeemer, influenced Newton's self-image, mystical leanings, and biblical obsessions.

5. During the crucial years at the start of the *Divine Comedy*'s composition, 1304–07, Dante had personal transits of Uranus opposite natal Uranus, Neptune opposite Uranus, Uranus square Neptune, and Neptune square Neptune. This combination of transits is essentially identical to what Jung had in the 1913–18 period when he underwent his own midlife period of psychospiritual transformation and creative awakening (see note 11 below).

6. Charles Dickens, born in 1812 just as the Uranus-Neptune conjunction of the Romantic epoch reached the 20° range, is a good example of how certain individuals born at these cuspal or penumbral moments just at the start or end of an outer-planet axial alignment seem to serve as important outliers of the larger archetypal impulses that emerged at that time. In Dickens (whose Sun and Moon were in close major aspect to Uranus and Neptune, respectively), the distinct presence of the Uranus-Neptune gestalt is evident in the sustained act of imaginative revelation he brought to the nineteenth-century novel as a genius of the creative imagination not unlike Shakespeare or his contemporaries Dostoevsky and Tolstoy. It is also visible in his repeated rendering of highly characteristic Uranus-Neptune themes, such as the sudden spiritual epiphany that climaxes *A Christmas Carol*: supernatural apparitions and revelatory visions, the unexpected influx of divine grace, radical shifts of consciousness, the experience of resurrection and rebirth, and the awakening of universal compassion. Also relevant was Dickens's enduring role in awakening the collective consciousness of the Victorian age to a new empathy for the poor and helpless of humanity.

7. See Taylor, *Sources of the Self*, pp. 430–32.

8. The complex relationship between Romanticism and modernism, the latter being at once a development and an antithesis of the former, is explored by Taylor in *Sources of the Self*, "Epiphanies of Modernism," pp. 456–93.

9. To these could be added two immensely influential works of philosophy from two radically different perspectives that have shaped postmodern thought, W. V. O. Quine's *Two Dogmas of Empiricism* (1951) at the beginning of the alignment and Hans-Georg Gadamer's *Truth and Method* (1960) at the end.

10. In addition to the close Uranus-Neptune square alignment world transit in 1955–57, during these years Salinger was simultaneously undergoing a personal transit of Neptune trine natal Uranus and transiting Uranus conjunct natal Neptune, a remarkable convergence of Uranus-Neptune personal and world transits.

11. As discussed in the chapter "Personal Transit Cycles," the crucial period for the formation of Jung's psychology was 1913–18. This period began with Jung's break from Freud, the series of intense prophetic dreams just before World War I, and his sudden confrontation with the archetypal unconscious, and continued through the years of sustained psychological and intellectual ferment from which emerged Jung's basic understanding of the psyche and the process of individuation. The entirety of this period coincided with the world transit of the Uranus-Neptune opposition. It also coincided with an extraordinary convergence of once-in-a-lifetime personal transits for Jung of both Uranus and Neptune in the sky transiting in hard aspect to both his natal Uranus and Neptune configurations. These natal aspects were especially significant in Jung's birth chart, since he was born with Neptune in exact square alignment to the Sun (less than 1°) and with Uranus in exact square alignment to the Moon (less than 1°).

Such a convergence of world and personal transits of Uranus and Neptune both in the sky and in the natal chart is rare and suggests a potentially extraordinary activation of the archetypal gestalt associated with the Uranus-Neptune combination: as a world transit, constituting a general condition in the collective psyche, and as a series of personal transits. Every one of these alignments, both transiting and natal, was a dynamic quadrature aspect (conjunction, opposition, or square). As discussed in note 5 above, a similar convergence of Uranus-Neptune world and personal transits occurred to Dante as he wrote *La Divina Commedia* (except that we do not know the position of the Sun or Moon at Dante's birth, only the slower-moving outer planets such as Uranus and Neptune).

12. In the series of overlapping alignments, the longest of the three, the Neptune-Pluto conjunction, was within 20° orb between 594 and 560 BCE, the Uranus-Neptune conjunction was within 20° orb between 586 and 566, and the Uranus-Pluto conjunction was within 20° orb between 583 and 570.

13. The First Isaiah, whose themes closely anticipated those of the second, began his prophecies between 750 and 740 BCE, in coincidence with the immediately preceding Uranus-Neptune conjunction. This earlier conjunction, which was within 20° orb from 758 to 737, also coincides with the approximate period scholars estimate for the composition of Hesiod's *Theogony* and *Works and Days*.

(The dating for the Homeric epics continues to be too ambiguous and elusive to permit any reliable correlations.)

14. The Tianenmen Square protests, crackdown, and massacre took place in June 1989, when Saturn was in close conjunction with Uranus (8°) and Neptune (1°) and when the Jupiter-Uranus opposition was just beginning (17°). One can see the familiar Jupiter-Uranus motif in the Tianenmen protests both in the heightened impulse for freedom and rebellion and in the eloquent allusion to the Statue of Liberty, which was erected during the Jupiter-Uranus conjunction of 1885–86 (and conceived during the Jupiter-Uranus opposition of 1865). The archetypal complex associated with the Saturn-Uranus (and Neptune) conjunction was in evidence in the crackdown and defeat of the idealistic demonstrators for freedom. The Jupiter-Uranus alignment moved into close opposition during the summer of 1989 and was in close orb throughout the period of the rapid consecutive Eastern European revolutions in the fall of 1989. I will explore elsewhere the important archetypal correlations involving the longer Saturn-Uranus-Neptune triple conjunction of 1986–91.

15. In its capacity to reveal unimaginably remote cosmic epochs, the Hubble Space Telescope essentially functioned in the role of a time machine, transporting astronomers through time itself. This capacity suggested another characteristic theme of the Uranus-Neptune archetypal complex: the technologically mediated dissolving of and liberation from seemingly absolute structures of time and space. H. G. Wells, the author of the original *Time Machine*, was born during the Uranus-Neptune square in 1866.

16. In this light, the archetypal complex associated with the Uranus-Neptune conjunction can now perhaps be seen as subtly pervading the entire vision and tenor of the present work (which took form throughout the long period of this conjunction), invisibly shaping its themes and orientation in the same way that Flaubert (born in 1821 with an exact Uranus-Neptune conjunction) said an author should be in his novel: like God in the world, present everywhere and visible nowhere.

17. Major space and aviation accidents, such as the Apollo I disaster in 1967 and the crash of the Challenger space shuttle in 1986, showed a tendency to coincide with Saturn-Uranus hard aspects. These contrast with the correlation of successful breakthrough flights in coincidence with Jupiter-Uranus alignments: e.g., the first manned space flights by Gagarin, Shepard, and Glenn in 1961–62; the first Moon landing in 1969; the successful Apollo-Soyuz linkup in space and the first successful Mars probe by Viking I in 1975–76; the Galileo space probe to Jupiter, the Cosmic Background Explorer (COBE), and the Hubble Space Telescope all launched in 1989–90; and the first successful Chinese manned space flight in 2003.

We see for example the successful landing of the Mars Pathfinder's Sojourner Rover during the *Jupiter*-Uranus conjunction in 1997 followed by the failure of the Mars Polar Lander during the *Saturn*-Uranus square in 1999. This was followed most recently by the two successful Mars landings of the Spirit and Opportunity rovers during the next *Jupiter*-Uranus opposition in 2004. (An exception to this pattern was the crash of the space shuttle *Columbia* over Texas in February 2003 during the Saturn-Pluto opposition, 3° from exact, one month before the U.S. invasion of Iraq; Jupiter and Uranus were then near the beginning of their opposition, 15° from exact.)

In some cases, both Jupiter *and* Saturn were in alignment with Uranus, as during the Hubble launch in 1990, which initially failed to provide clear images due to a microscopic flaw in the telescope's primary mirror. At this time Saturn was in a rare triple conjunction with Uranus and Neptune, appropriate to the technical error that produced a failure of astronomical vision with the hopelessly blurred images, and a crushing disappointment for astronomers. The imperfection was repaired in December 1993 by astronauts during five dramatic spacewalks just as the Uranus-Neptune conjunction reached exactitude. After this, the flood of spectacular images commenced and continued through the rest of the Uranus-Neptune conjunction period.

18. An insightful survey of many relevant phenomena in this category during the 1990s is Erik Davis, *TechGnosis: Myth, Magic, and Mysticism in the Age of Information* (New York: Three Rivers, 1998), "a secret history of the mystical impulses that continue to spark and sustain the Western world's obsession with technology, and especially with its technologies of communication" (p. 2). In his introduction, Davis describes the current milieu with lively metaphors, all of which are saturated with the archetypal motifs of Neptune and Uranus in combination:

Even as many of us spend our days, in that now universal Californiaism, surfing the data-stream, we can hardly ignore the deeper, more powerful and more ominous undertows that tug beneath the froth of our lives and labors. You know the scene. Social structures the world over are melting down and mutating, making way for a global McVillage, a Gaian brain, and a whole heap of chaos. The emperor of technoscience has achieved dominion, though his clothes are growing more threadbare by the moment, the once noble costume of Progress barely concealing far more wayward ambitions. Across the globe, ferocious postperestroika capitalism yanks the rug out from under the nation-state, while the planet spits up signs and symptoms of terminal distress. Boundaries dissolve, and we drift into the no-man's zones between synthetic and organic life, between actual and virtual environments, between local communities and global flows of goods, information, labor, and capital. With pills modifying personality, machines modifying bodies, and synthetic pleasures and networked minds engineering a more fluid and invented sense of self, the boundaries of our identities are mutating as well. The horizon melts into a limitless question mark, and like the cartographers of old, we glimpse yawning monstrosities and mind-forged utopias beyond the edges of our paltry and provisional maps.

From this summary of the dissolving, disorienting consequences of the new techologies, Davis immediately turns to the religious, mythic, mystical, and esoteric impulses that are no less conspicuous and widespread themes of the age:

Regardless of how secular this ultramodern condition appears, the velocity and mutability of the times invokes a certain supernatural quality that must be seen, at least in part, through the lenses of religious thought and the fantastic storehouse of the archetypal imagination. Inside the United States, within whose high-tech bosom I quite self-consciously write, the spirit has definitely made a comeback—if it could be said to have ever left this giddy, gold rush land, where most people believe in the Lord and his coming kingdom, and more than you'd guess believe in UFOs. Today God has become one of Time's favorite cover boys, and a Black Muslim numerologist can lead the most imaginative march on the nation's capital since the Yippies tried to levitate the Pentagon. Self-help maestros and corporate consultants promulgate New Age therapies, as strains of Buddhism both scientific and technicolor seep through the intelligentsia, and half the guests on Oprah pop up wearing angel pins. The surge of interest in alternative medicine injects non-Western and ad hoc spiritual practices into the mainstream, while deep ecologists turn up the boil on the nature mysticism long simmering in the American soul. This rich confusion is even more evident in our brash popular culture, where science-fiction films, digital environments, and urban tribes are reconfiguring old archetypes and imaginings within a vivid comic-book frame. From The X-Files to occult computer games, from Xena: Warrior Princess to Magic: The Gathering playing cards, the pagan and the paranormal have colonized the twilight zones of pop media.
   These signs are not just evidence of a media culture exploiting the crude power of the irrational. They reflect the fact that people inhabiting all frequencies of the socioeconomic spectrum are intentionally reaching for some of the oldest navigational tools known to humankind: sacred ritual and metaphysical speculation, spiritual regimen and natural spell. For some superficial spiritual consumers, this means prepackaged answers to the thorny questions of life; but for many others, the quest for meaning and connection has led individuals and communities to construct meaningful frameworks for their lives, worldviews that actually deepen their willingness and ability to face the strangeness of our days. (pp. 1–2)

19. Ecstasy, which during these years of the Uranus-Neptune conjunction became the most widely used psychoactive drug after marijuana in the United States, was first synthesized during the Uranus-Neptune opposition in 1912. Though, like LSD and marijuana, it has been proven in numerous studies to have therapeutic value, its prohibition by the U.S. government has confined its use to underground countercultural recreational and ritual purposes, often on a mass scale.
   It was during the immediately preceding Uranus-Neptune conjunction in 1821 that Thomas De Quincey invented the discourse of recreational drug use with the publication of Confessions of an English Opium Eater. Baudelaire, the next major Western writer to describe the effects of recreational

drug use, was born in 1821 (the same year as De Quincey's *Confessions*) during the same Uranus-Neptune conjunction exactly one cycle ago.

Here too should be mentioned the close association of unitive and mystical experiences with biochemical changes in the body variously produced, whether by visionary plants, synthesized psychoactive substances, or specific somatic methods such as special breathing or dietary practices. The enormous popularity of the use of MDMA or Ecstasy during the conjunction period of the later 1980s and 1990s, the dissemination throughout the world of indigenous shamanic rituals using visionary plants such as ayahuasca and mushrooms, the unprecedented ubiquity of psychoactive drug use among the young, the spread of transformative breathing practices such as holotropic breathwork, the wave of scholarly conferences devoted to psychedelic therapy and shamanic practices, and the popularity of works explicating such experiences by authors such as Terence McKenna and Huston Smith are all characteristic of this theme of the Uranus-Neptune complex.

As regards the diachronic sequence in this area, it was during the preceding Uranus-Neptune opposition in 1901 that William James first articulated the philosophical and religious implications of such practices in *The Varieties of Religious Experience*, and it was during the intervening square of the 1950s that extensive psychedelic research and therapy began, and that Aldous Huxley explored the significance of chemically mediated mystical experiences in *The Doors of Perception*. Underlining the special connection between the chemical and the spiritual—two seemingly distinct categories within the Neptunian archetypal complex—Huxley addressed the critique made by conservative religious authorities against the spiritual validity of experiences mediated by such substances as psilocybin, mescaline, and LSD:

> God, they will insist, is a spirit and is to be worshiped in spirit. Therefore an experience which is chemically conditioned cannot be an experience of the divine. But, in one way or another, all our experiences are chemically conditioned, and if we imagine that some of them are purely "spiritual," purely "intellectual," purely "aesthetic," it is merely because we have never troubled to investigate the internal chemical environment at the moment of their occurrence. Furthermore, it is a matter of historical record that most contemplatives worked systematically to modify their body chemistry, with a view to creating the internal conditions favorable to spiritual insight. (*The Doors of Perception* [New York: Harper Perennial, 1990], p. 155)

20. *Alice in Wonderland*, whose many themes and general character represent a paradigmatic expression of the Uranus-Neptune archetypal complex—sudden unexpected shifts of reality, fantastic transgressions of conventional logic, the synthesis of the trickster and the imagination, the ingestion of psychoactive substances—was published by Lewis Carroll in 1865 during the Uranus-Neptune square alignment of 1863–74, as was *Through the Looking-Glass*, in 1872. Lewis Carroll (Charles Dodgson) was born near the end of the immediately preceding Uranus-Neptune conjunction with his Sun halfway between Uranus and Neptune in broad triple conjunction. The widely viewed and highly creative cinematic adaptation of 1999 cited in the text was made for television during the most recent Uranus-Neptune conjunction, exactly one cycle after Lewis Carroll's birth. The most widely viewed previous version was the 1951 Disney animation feature which was produced in coincidence with the preceding Uranus-Neptune square.

21. A similar continuity and archetypal shift between the two eras can be seen with respect to shamanism itself. While, for example, the writings of Carlos Castañeda that began to be published in the late 1960s (*The Teachings of Don Juan, Journey to Ixtlan, Tales of Power*) emphasized the achievement of extraordinary personal power such as that of a traditional sorcerer, and portrayed his teacher don Juan as a shamanic *Übermensch*, the characteristic spirit of the 1990s was that of sacramental participation in shamanic rituals using sacred medicines such as ayahuasca or mushrooms, shared in groups that formed sacred circles, with the purpose of opening to states of religious ecstasy and psychospiritual transformation. Increasing numbers of American and European seekers traveled to South America and other indigenous tribal areas to experience such rituals and undergo shamanic initiations. Brazilian churches such as the Santo Daíme and the Uniao do Vegetal, with thousands of members combined shamanic and Christian practices and symbols, centering these on the ritual ingestion of ayahuasca as the sacrament of communion. Rapidly spreading in the later 1980s from the rain forests of Brazil to large cities such as Rio de Janeiro, ayahuasca ceremonies in the 1990s began to be held in many European cities—Madrid, Barcelona, Amsterdam, Munich, Frankfurt,

Berlin—and in several areas of the United States in an underground manner, becoming one of the faster growing religious practices in the world despite attempts by the U.S. government to suppress it.

22. A key work in articulating the participatory turn in the philosophy and psychology of religion is Jorge Ferrer's *Revisioning Transpersonal Theory: A Participatory Vision of Human Spirituality* (Albany: State University of New York Press, 2002).

Part VIII: *Towards a New Heaven and a New Earth*

1. In addition to Thomas Kuhn, *The Structure of Scientific Revolutions*, 2nd ed. (Chicago: University of Chicago Press, 1970), see especially Imre Lakatos and Alan Musgrave, eds., *Criticism and the Growth of Knowledge* (Cambridge: Cambridge University Press, 1974). In the present context, typical research problems included attempting to "fit" a given event into a particular planetary cycle with too simplistic and Cartesian an understanding of the multiple cycles' complex interaction; prematurely assessing the event in question, misjudging its deeper character and significance; measuring the planetary alignments with consistently too narrow an orb; and insufficient understanding of the relevant archetypal complex.

2. As with any future event, it is possible that a combination of astrological insight, empirical observation of the context, and the employment of some other intuitive faculty—divinatory, clairvoyant, precognitive—could have produced a specific prediction of terrorist activity on that day. But I believe that the contemporary Western astrological paradigm, apart from any contribution from an intuitive divinatory faculty, is best understood as archetypally rather than concretely predictive.

3. I observed this on a personal level in the course of writing the present book, whose final composition took place at a rapid pace during this twenty-four month period of the Jupiter-Uranus-Neptune alignment in 2002–04, after a much longer gestation period of research and reflection that extended throughout the twenty-year period of the Uranus-Neptune conjunction.

4. In the course of each five-hundred-year Neptune-Pluto cycle, the two planets move into one sextile (60°) alignment and one trine (120°) alignment that are unusually long, each lasting approximately one hundred years. The most recent example of such a trine began at the end of the seventeenth and lasted for almost the entire eighteenth century, the pivotal century of the Enlightenment, Romanticism, and the emergence of the democratic revolutions. In the last chapter I discussed the much shorter grand trine of Uranus, Neptune, and Pluto that took place in the later 1760s and the 1770s (about three-quarters of the way through the longer Neptune-Pluto trine). The century-long Neptune-Pluto trine on its own terms coincided with an age that bore the marks of a confluent activation of this archetypal combination. Relevant here, in the Western context, are the diverse intellectual and cultural impulses and the powerful evolution of the human spirit associated with those many remarkable individuals who flourished, were born, or both during this alignment: in music, for example, this alignment encompassed the period from Bach and Handel to Mozart and Beethoven; in the emergence of the modern novel, from Defoe and Richardson to Fielding, Sterne, and Austen; in the development of modern philosophy, from Leibniz, Locke, and Berkeley to Hume, Kant, and Hegel. We can also recall the many other lastingly influential thinkers of the Enlightenment, from Voltaire, Vico, Swift, Montesquieu, and Diderot to Condorcet, Gibbon, Smith, Godwin, and Wollstonecraft; the founding fathers and mothers of the American nation, from Franklin and Jefferson to the Adamses and Madisons; the major Romantics, from Rousseau, Herder, Goethe, and Schiller to Blake, Wordsworth, Coleridge, de Staël, Novalis, and Hölderlin.

The preceding instance of such a sustained Neptune-Pluto trine during the previous five-hundred-year cycle occurred at the peak of the High Middle Ages and lasted most of the thirteenth century, the century of Chartres Cathedral, of *Parzival* and *Tristan and Isolde*, of Francis of Assisi and Dominic, of Albertus Magnus and Thomas Aquinas, and of the births of Dante and Meister Eckhart. The profound evolutionary shift in the relationship between spirit and nature associated with the Neptune-Pluto archetypal complex is highly visible, for example, in the personality and religious sensibility of Francis of Assisi, as it is also in the philosophy of Thomas Aquinas.

For the current Neptune-Pluto sextile, a comprehensive comparison of the Uranus-Pluto conjunction of the 1960s and the Uranus-Neptune conjunction of the 1990s should take into account that Neptune and Pluto were in sextile alignment with each other during both periods. The Uranus-Pluto conjunction of the 1960s was therefore always in confluent aspect to Neptune and had a distinct corresponding archetypal confluence between the Neptune archetype and the dominant Promethean-Dionysian impulse of the era. Suggestive evidence for this confluence can be found in the pervasive idealism as well as the important spiritual, esoteric, and unitive dimension (Neptune) of the 1960s' counterculture. The major role of psychedelic experience in shaping and inspiring the emancipatory sensibility of that era strongly suggests such a complexified archetypal gestalt.

Conversely, the Uranus-Neptune conjunction of the later 1980s and 1990s formed a sextile aspect to Pluto throughout the period of that alignment. A corresponding Plutonic inflection of the dominant Uranus-Neptune complex can be observed: for example, the distinct presence of such Plutonic themes as the role of sexuality, political power, and evolutionary and ecological issues in shaping the various manifestations of the Uranus-Neptune gestalt discussed in the text.

Looking forward to significant multi-planet configurations in the distant future: The next *Jupiter-Uranus-Pluto* triple conjunction, such as last occurred in 1968–69, will take place one hundred years from now, in 2106–07. The next *Uranus-Neptune-Pluto* triple conjunction, as occurred at the time of the great Axial Awakening of the sixth century BCE, will take place during the thirty-year period of 3357–87, in the next millennium. In the year 3370, all three of the outermost planets will be within 2° of exact alignment, for the first time since the Axial Age.

Sources

Part I: *The Transformation of the Cosmos*

3: *"all was Light"*: Alexander Pope, *Epitaph: Intended for Sir Isaac Newton* (1730).

4: *"whatever shape thou shalt prefer"*: Pico della Mirandola, "On the Dignity of Man" (1486), in E. Cassirer, P. O. Kristeller, and J. H. Randall Jr., eds., *The Renaissance Philosophy of Man* (Chicago: University of Chicago Press, 1948), pp. 224–25.

6: *"six thousand years for a witness"*: Johannes Kepler, *The Harmonies of the World*, V (1619), trans. Owen Gingerich, in *Dictionary of Scientific Biography* (New York: Charles Scribner's Sons, 1970), vol. 7, s.v. "Kepler, Johannes."

7: *"noble and arduously won discoveries"*: Nicolaus Copernicus, *De Revolutionibus Orbium Caelestium* (1543), trans. D. F. Dobson and S. Brodetsky, *Occasional Notes of the Royal Astronomical Society*, vol. 2, no. 10 (London: Royal Astronomical Society, 1947). Quoted in Thomas S. Kuhn, *The Copernican Revolution: Planetary Astronomy in the Development of Western Thought* (Cambridge, Mass.: Harvard University Press, 1957), p.137.

7: *"not the Earth"*: Martin Luther, *Table Talks* (1539), quoted in Kuhn, p. 192.

7: *"above that of the Holy Spirit"*: John Calvin, *Commentary on Genesis* (1554), quoted in Kuhn, p. 192.

7: *"towns and mountains thrown down"*: Jean Bodin, *Universae Naturae Theatrum* (1597), quoted in Kuhn, p. 190.

9: *"mistress of their belief"*: Galileo Galilei, *Dialogue Concerning the Two Chief World Systems—Ptolemaic and Copernican* (1632), trans. S. Drake, 2nd rev. ed. (Berkeley: University of California Press, 1967), p. 328.

13: *"wrong in what they denied"*: John Stuart Mill, "Coleridge" (1840), in *Essays in Politics and Culture*, ed. Gertrude Himmelfarb (New York: Doubleday, 1962), p. 136.

14: *"whose contradictory is also true"*: Oscar Wilde, "The Truth of Masks" (1889), in *The Artist as Critic: Critical Writings of Oscar Wilde*, ed. Richard Ellmann (Chicago: University of Chicago Press, 1998), p. 432.

20: *"disenchanted"*: ("the knowledge or belief that . . . there are no mysterious incalculable forces that come into play, but rather that one can, in principle, master all things by calculation"): Max Weber, "Science as a Vocation" (1919), *From Max Weber: Essays on Sociology*, trans. and ed. H. H. Gerth and C. Wright Mills (New York: Oxford University Press, 1946), p. 139.

21: *"definitive and irreversible"*: Charles Taylor, *Hegel* (Cambridge: Cambridge University Press, 1975), pp. 8–9; see also pp. 3–11.

27: *"one conception of reality with reality itself"*: Robert Bellah, "Between Religion and Social Science" (1969), in *Beyond Belief: Essays on Religion in a Post-Traditional World* (New York: Harper & Row, 1970; Berkeley: University of California, 1991), p. 246.

28: *"curious accident"*: Bertrand Russell, *Religion and Science* (1935), (Oxford: Oxford University Press, 1961), pp. 23, 222.

28: *"seems pointless"*: Steven Weinberg, *The First Three Minutes: A Modern View of the Origin of the Universe* (1977), 2nd ed. (New York: Basic Books, 1993), p. 154.

29: *"only by chance"*: Jacques Monod, *Chance and Necessity: An Essay on the Natural Philosophy of Modern Biology* (1970), (New York: Knopf, 1971), p. 180.

30: *"we are strange in the universe"*: Primo Levi, *Other People's Trades*, "The New Sky" (1985), trans. R. Rosenthal (New York: Summit Books, 1989), p. 22.

33: *"level of civilization never before achieved"*: Max Weber, *The Protestant Ethic and the Spirit of Capitalism* (1905), trans. Talcott Parsons (New York: Charles Scribner's Sons, 1958), p. 182.

34: *"night continually closing in on us"*: Friedrich Nietzsche, *The Gay Science* (1882), trans. Walter Kaufmann (New York: Random House, 1974), p. 181.

35: *"heaps of atoms in empty space"*: Paul Feyerabend (1978), *Science in a Free Society* (London: Verso, 1982), p. 70.

Part II: *In Search of a Deeper Order*

43: *"where the difficulties really reside"*: Joseph Campbell, *The Hero with a Thousand Faces* (Princeton: Princeton University Press, 1949), p. 17.

44: *"fills me with dread"*: Blaise Pascal, *Pensées* (written 1659–62, published posthumously, 1670), trans. A. J. Krailsheimer, rev. ed. (Harmondsworth, UK: Penguin, 1995), p. 66. *"Le silence éternel de ces espaces infinis m'effraie."*

44: *"the moral law within me"*: Immanuel Kant, *Critique of Practical Reason* (1788), trans. and ed. Mary Gregor (Cambridge, UK: Cambridge University Press, 1997), p. 133.

44: *"the psychological century"*: Peter Homans, "History of a Movement: From Jung to the Present" (Paper presented at the History of Analytical Psychology Symposium, Tiburon, California, April 2002). See also Homans's *Jung in Context: Modernity and the Making of a Psychology*, 2nd ed. (Chicago: University of Chicago Press, 1995), and *The Ability to Mourn: Disillusionment and the Social Origins of Psychoanalysis* (Chicago: University of Chicago Press, 1989).

47: *"to preserve our civilization"*: C. G. Jung, letter of September 23, 1949, to Dorothy Thompson, in *C. G. Jung, Letters 1: 1906–1950*, ed. G. Adler, A. Jaffé, trans. R. F. C. Hull (London: Routledge & Kegan Paul, 1973), p. 537.

52: *"continued with satisfactory results"*: Jung, "On Synchronicity," (1951), *Collected Works of Carl Gustav Jung*, trans. R. F. C. Hull, ed. H. Read, M. Fordham, G. Adler, W. McGuire, Bollingen Series XX (Princeton, N.J.: Princeton University Press, 1953–79), vol. 8, par. 982, pp. 525–26.

52: *"at last begin to move"*: Jung, *Synchronicity: An Acausal Connecting Principle* (1952), *Collected Works*, vol. 8, pars. 843, 845, pp. 438–39.

52: *"performed the act"*: Esther Harding, in *C. G. Jung Speaking: Interviews and Encounters*, ed. W. McGuire and R. F. C. Hull, Bollingen Series XCVII (Princeton, N.J.: Princeton University Press, 1977), pp. 182–83.

53: *"animum esse mirabile"*: James Hillman, *Re-Visioning Psychology* (New York: Harper and Row, 1975), p. 195–96.

53: *"the same thing in his own case"*: Petrarch, "The Ascent of Mount Ventoux: To Dionisio da Borgo San Sepolcro" (1336), in *Petrarch: The First Modern Scholar and Man of Letters*, ed. and trans. J. H. Robinson (New York: Putnam, 1898), p. 317.

54: *"book should be published"*: Henry Fierz, in *C. G. Jung, Emma Jung and Toni Wolff: A Collection of Remembrances*, ed. F. Jensen (San Francisco: The Analytical Psychology Club of San Francisco, 1982), p. 21. This case is also explored in Robert Aziz, *C. G. Jung's Psychology of Religion and Synchronicity*, pp. 86–90.

57: *"the quality of this moment of time"*: Jung, "Richard Wilhelm: In Memoriam" (1930), *Collected Works*, vol. 15, pars. 81–82, p. 56.

57: *"apparently exists outside man"*: Jung, *Synchronicity*, par. 942, pp. 501–02.

59: *"transconscious, metapsychic factors"*: Jung, letter of July 10, 1946, in *C. G. Jung, Letters 1: 1906–1950*, p. 433; quoted in Aziz, pp. 176–77.

59: *"the culture of scientific materialism"*: Victor Mansfield, *Synchronicity, Science, and Soul-Making* (Chicago: Open Court, 1995), p. 1.

59: *"I don't know where they are"*: Marie-Louise von Franz, "Passions of the Soul," Ikon Television (Netherlands), 1990, quoted in Mansfield, p. 22.

62: *"remarkable things have turned up"*: Jung, letter to Freud, June 12, 1911, in *C. G. Jung, Letters 1: 1906–1950*, p. 24.

62: *"all the psychological knowledge of antiquity"*: Jung, "Richard Wilhelm: In Memoriam" (1930), *Collected Works*, vol. 15, par. 81, p. 56.

Part III: *Through the Archetypal Telescope*

76: *"in process of being born"*: Hans J. Eysenck and David Nias, *Astrology: Science or Superstition?* (London: Penguin, 1982), pp. 208–09.

77: *"Everything breathes together"*: Plotinus, *Enneads*, II, 3, 7, "Are the Stars Causes?" (c. 268), quoted in Eugenio Garin, *Astrology in the Renaissance*, trans. C. Jackson and J. Allen, rev. C. Robertson (London: Arkana, 1983), p. 117.

81: *"question of meaning altogether"*: W. K. C. Guthrie, *The Greek Philosophers: From Thales to Aristotle* (1950), (New York: Harper Torchbook, 1960), pp. 10–11.

82: *"powerful mythology"*: Ludwig Wittgenstein, *Lectures and Conversations on Aesthetics, Psychology and Religious Belief*, ed. C. Barrett (Oxford: Blackwell, 1970), p. 51; quoted by Hillman in *Re-Visioning Psychology* (pp. 155, 249), where he provides a depth psychological alternative to Wittgenstein's implied simple Enlightenment contrast of "mythology" with "scientific explanation." Not only does every fantasy have its archetypal reason, Hillman argues, but every reason has its archetypal fantasy.

83: *"imaginative vision and emotion of the soul"*: Hillman, *Re-Visioning Psychology*, pp. xiii–xiv (xix–xx in 1992 edition).

83: *"I cannot but be in them"*: Hillman, *Re-Visioning Psychology*, pp. 169–70.

83: *"to one God or another"*: Hillman, *Re-Visioning Psychology*, pp. 168–69.

85: *"resolved into algebraic equations"*: Jung, "The Syzygy: Anima and Animus" (1948), in *Aion: Researches into the Phenomenology of the Self, Collected Works*, vol. 9, part ii, par. 25, p. 13.

86: *"pour into human cultural manifestation"*: Joseph Campbell, *The Hero with a Thousand Faces* (Princeton N.J.: Princeton University Press, 1949), p. 3.

86: *"the world itself is speaking"*: Jung, "The Psychology of the Child Archetype" (1940), in *The Archetypes and the Collective Unconscious, Collected Works*, vol. 9, part i, par. 291, p. 173 (emphasis in original). Jung's reference is to Karl Kerényi's companion essay, "The Primordial Child in Primordial Times."

87: *"makes any unilateral formulation impossible"*: Jung,"Archetypes of the Collective Unconscious" (1934), *Collected Works*, vol. 9, part i, par. 80, p. 38.

89: *"they change their shape continually"*: Jung, "The Psychology of the Child Archetype," par. 301, p. 179.

97: *"being one with the external world as a whole"*: Sigmund Freud, *Civilization and Its Discontents* (1929), trans. W. Strachey (New York: Norton, 1989), pp. 11–12. The term was originally employed and the phenomenon described in a letter to Freud from his friend Romain Rolland who after reading Freud's *The Future of an Illusion* wondered whether the "oceanic feeling" of an underlying connection with the universe that he observed in himself and others was perhaps the true source of humanity's religious urges.

105: *"who themselves have not tried them"*: Kepler, Letter to Herwart and Feselius, *Kepler's Astrology: Excerpts*, trans. and ed. Kenneth G. Negus (Princeton, N.J.: Eucopia, 1987), p. 13.

106: *"harmony of the celestial aspects"*: Kepler, *On the More Certain Fundamentals of Astrology*, (1602), in *Kepler's Astrology: Excerpts*, p. 13.

108: *"ultimately of all existence"*: David Bohm and David Peat, *Science, Order, and Creativity* (New York: Bantam, 1987), p. 134.

108: *"current ways of thinking"*: Bohm and Peat, pp. 133, 136.

112: *"but once in a lifetime"*: Freud, *The Interpretation of Dreams*, preface to third English edition, in *The Basic Writings of Sigmund Freud*, trans. A. A. Brill (New York: Modern Library, 1938), p. 181.

112: *"the secret of dreams was revealed"*: Ernest Jones, *The Life and Work of Sigmund Freud*, 3 vols. (New York: Basic Books, 1953–57), vol. 1, pp. 323, 354.

112: *"as a hen at a hawk"*: Jones, *Freud*, p. 242.

113: *"both intellectually and emotionally"*: Jones, *Freud*, p. 255.

113: *"at the beginning of 1896"*: Jones, *Freud*, p. 351.

113: *"the prima materia for a lifetime's work"*: Jung, *Memories, Dreams, Reflections*, recorded and edited by Aniela Jaffé, trans. R. and C. Winston, rev. ed. (New York: Vintage, 1965), p. 199.

114: *"to make her own heaven or hell"*: Betty Friedan, *The Feminine Mystique* (preface, July 1962; 1st edition published 1963), (New York: Norton, 2001), p. 12.

117: *"the threshold of intellectual maturity"*: D. T. Whiteside, quoted in *Dictionary of Scientific Biography*, vol. 10, p. 48.

117: *"more than at any time since"*: Isaac Newton, quoted in *Dictionary of Scientific Biography*, vol. 10, p. 50.

120: *"willingly devote continued labor"*: Gertrude Stein, *Fernhurst* (1904–05), in *Fernhurst, Q. E. D. and Other Early Writings* (New York: Norton, 1971), pp. 29–30; quoted in Stephen Arroyo, *Astrology, Karma, and Transformation* (Davis, Calif.: CRCS Publications, 1978), p. 84.

121: *"irresponsible days of my youth are over"*: Tennessee Williams, "Amore Perdida," *Michigan Quarterly Review* 42 (Summer 2003), p. 545. "The old life seemed to be over. The new one had not begun yet. This was a time in between."

123: *"only more inveterate habits"*: W. J. Earle, summarizing James's mature philosophy as having emerged directly out of his earlier psychological insights, in "William James," *Encyclopedia of Philosophy* (New York: Macmillan, 1967), vol. 4, p. 248.

127: *"hardly before the age of twenty-eight"*: Arthur Schopenhauer, "Of Women," *Parerga and Paralipomena* (1851), trans. T. B. Saunders (New York: A. L. Burt, n.d.), p. 436.

127: *"slowly does it come to maturity"*: Schopenhauer, *Parerga and Paralipomena: Short Philosophical Essays* (1851), vol. 2, trans. E. F. J. Payne (Oxford: Oxford University Press, 1974), p. 615.

128: *"I change but I cannot die"*: Percy Bysshe Shelley, "The Cloud" (1819), *The Norton Anthology of Poetry*, ed. A. Allison et al. (New York: Norton, 1975), p. 672.

134: *"differentiation without difference"*: J. N. Findlay, "The Logical Peculiarities of Neoplatonism," in *The Structure of Being: A Neoplatonic Approach*, ed. R. Baine Harris (Albany, N.Y.: State University of New York, 1982), p. 1.

136: *"of the arts, of ideas and culture"*: James Hillman, "Why 'Archetypal' Psychology?" in *Loose Ends* (Zurich: Spring Publications, 1975), p. 139.

Part IV: *Epochs of Revolution*

145: *"I'll rail at all his servants"*: Mick Jagger and Keith Richards, "Street Fighting Man," from the album *Beggar's Banquet* (1968).

146: *"the dominant reality of the human community"*: William H. McNeill, *The Rise of the West: A History of the Human Community* (Chicago: University of Chicago Press, 1963), pp. 726–27.

150: *"but over themselves"*: Mary Wollstonecraft, *A Vindication of the Rights of Woman* (1792), 2nd ed., ed. Carol H. Poston (New York: Norton, 1988), p. 62

150: *"it is as great to be a woman as to be a man"*: Walt Whitman, "Song of Myself," *Leaves of Grass* (New York: Oxford University Press, 1990), p. 45.

154: *"we are free at last"*: Martin Luther King, Jr., Speech at the March on Washington, August 28, 1963. Available online at U.S. Department of State International Information website, http://us info.state.gov/usa/infousa/facts/democrac/38.htm. Accepted as part of the Douglass Archives of American Public Address (http://douglass.speech.nwu.edu) on May 26, 1999. Prepared by D. Oetting (http://nonce.com/oetting).

157: *"turned upside down"*: Christopher Hill, *The World Turned Upside Down: Radical Ideas during the English Revolution* (New York: Viking, 1972).

157: *"how men thought before it was made"*: Christopher Hill, *The Century of Revolution*, 2nd ed. (London: Sphere Books, 1972), pp.165 ff.

158: *"rebellion was everywhere in the air"*: Orest Ranum, "The Age of Revolutions," in *Columbia History of the World*, ed. J. A. Garraty and P. Gay (New York: Harper & Row, 1972), p. 730.

160: *"controlled and sustained flight"*: John Noble Wilford, "How the Wright Brothers Did What No One Else Could," *New York Times*, December 9, 2003.

162: *"on the origin of species in the years 1794–95"*: Charles Darwin, *The Origin of Species, 1st edition with An Historical Sketch* (1859), (New York: Avenel, 1979), p. 55.

164: *"a second Darwinian revolution"*: I. Bernard Cohen, *Revolution in Science* (Cambridge: Harvard University Press, 1985), p. 297.

170: *"Exuberance is beauty"*: William Blake, *The Marriage of Heaven and Hell* (1793), in *The Poetry and Prose of William Blake*, 4th printing with revisions, ed. D. V. Erdman, commentary by H. Bloom (New York: Doubleday, 1970), pp. 34–37.

173: *"social principles are or should be"*: Jacques Barzun, "Society and Politics," in *Columbia History of the World*, p. 699.

174: *"in the history of life"*: Max Eastman, quoted in Robert Gottlieb, review of *Isadora: A Sensational Life* by Peter Kurth, *New York Times Book Review*, December 30, 2001.

177: *"the drench of my passions"*: Whitman, *Leaves of Grass* (1855), pp. 78, 9, 30, 86, 88, 94.

179: *"I feel as if I had not created this myself"*: Letter from Mahler to his friend and colleague, the soprano Anna Bahr-Mildenburg, July 18, 1896. Quoted in Edward Downes, *Guide to Symphonic Music* (New York: Walker, 1976), pp. 535–36.

180: *"in the geological sciences in this century"*: William Glen, *The Road to Jaramillo: Critical Years of the Revolution in Earth Science* (Stanford: Stanford University Press, 1982), p. 271. Quoted in Cohen, *Revolution in Science*, p. 463.

181: *"the preservation of the world"*: Henry David Thoreau, from his essay "Walking," which began as a lecture called "The Wild," delivered at the Concord Lyceum on April 23, 1851. Thoreau gave this lecture many times during the 1850s, eventually turning it into an essay published posthumously in 1862 in the *Atlantic Monthly*.

185: *"distinct from his soul is to be expunged"*: Blake, *The Marriage of Heaven and Hell* (1793), in *The Poetry and Prose of William Blake*, pp. 34–38.

192: *"we still believe it is fine weather"*: Jung, "Wotan" (1936), in *Civilization in Transition, Collected Works*, vol. 10, par. 375, p. 182; par 389, p. 186.

193: *"and other purposes through nuclear 'transmutation' "*: Leo Szilard, 1934, quoted in Nuclear Age Timeline, Nuclearfiles.org: A Project of the Nuclear Age Peace Foundation, http://www.nuclearfiles.org/hitimeline/1930s.html.

193: *"make this old world vanish in smoke"*: Ernest Rutherford, quoted in R. W. Clark, *Einstein: The Life and Times* (New York: Avon, 1971), p. 661.

195: *"the sceptre from tyrants"*: Anne-Robert-Jacques Turgot, quoted in *Encyclopaedia Britannica*, 15th ed., s.v., "Franklin, Benjamin."

195: *"begun with the Discourse on Method"*: Jules Michelet, quoted in Paul Schrecker, "Revolution as a Problem in the Philosophy of History," *Nomos*, 1967, 8:34–53.

Part V: *Cycles of Crisis and Contraction*

228: *"values of discipline and restraint were denigrated"*: Margaret Thatcher, quoted in Arthur Marwick, "How We Taught the World to Swing," *The Sunday Times Magazine* (London), 30 May 2004.

235: *"war of opposing fundamentalisms"*: John Mack, "Considering the Current Crisis," Conference of the International Transpersonal Association, Palm Springs, California, June 2004.

238: *"burst his hot heart's shell upon it"*: Herman Melville, *Moby Dick or The Whale* (1851), (Franklin Center, Penn.: Franklin Library, 1979; based on the revised and corrected 1947 Oxford University Press edition), p. 181.

238: *"I act under orders"*: Melville, *Moby Dick*, p. 515.

239: *"fury and vengeance"*: Owen Chase, *The Wreck of the Whaleship Essex*, ed. I. Haverstick and B. Shepard (New York: Harcourt Brace, 1999), p. 12.

240: *"very latitude of the shipwreck"*: Herman Melville, quoted in afterword of Chase, *The Wreck of the Whaleship Essex*, p. 100.

240: *"choose a mighty theme"*: Melville, *Moby Dick*, pp. 423–24.

241: *"significance lurks in all things"*: Melville, *Moby Dick*, p. 401.

243: *"long-term and vigilant containment"*: George F. Kennan ("X"), "The Sources of Soviet Conduct," *Foreign Affairs*, July 1947.

244: *"not be mistaken for missionary work"*: Henry Kissinger, testimony before U.S. congressional committee, 1975, quoted in *The Observer*, August 12, 2001.

245: *"martyr in the calendar of philosophy"*: Karl Marx, doctoral dissertation (1841), quoted in *Encyclopaedia Britannica*, 15th ed., s.v. "Marx, Karl."

254: *"animals the souls they torment"*: Arthur Schopenhauer, "The Christian System" (1851), in *Religion: A Dialogue and Other Essays* (New York: Macmillan, 1891), pp. 105–17.

256: *"fully exploit space until we can control it"*: United States Air Force Space Command, *Strategic Master Plan FY04 and Beyond* (Peterson AFB, Colorado: November 5, 2002), pp. 4–5.

256: *"not'ing more dan de shark well goberned"*: Melville, *Moby Dick*, p. 286.

259: *"knowledge which they cannot lose"*: J. Robert Oppenheimer, "Physics in the Contemporary World," *Bulletin of the Atomic Scientists* IV, 3 (March 1948), p. 66.

261: *"to gratify its desires"*: Saint Paul, Letter to the Romans, 13:13–14, Revised Standard Version.

261: *"all the shadows of my doubts were swept away"*: Augustine, *Confessions*, VIII, in *Augustine of Hippo: Selected Writings*, trans. and intro. Mary T. Clark (Mahwah, N.J.: Paulist Press, 1984), p. 98.

263: *"no widening of the spiritual horizon"*: Jung, "After the Catastrophe" (1945), in *Civilization in Transition, Collected Works*, vol. 10, par. 240, pp. 215–16.

263: *"on whom a world depends"*: Jung, "The Undiscovered Self" (1957), *Collected Works*, vol. 10, par. 587–88.

266: *"With kindest regards, C. G. Jung"*: Letter of August 20, 1945, Bollingen, in C. G. Jung *Letters Vol. I: 1906–1950*, ed. G. Adler, A. Jaffé (Princeton: Princeton University Press, 1973), p. 375.

267: *"is where God learns"*: Rainer Maria Rilke, "Just as the Winged Energy of Delight" (*Da dich das geflügelte Entzücken*, 1924), trans. Robert Bly, *Selected Poems of Rainer Maria Rilke* (New York: Harper & Row, 1981), p. 175.

272: *"the anger of the Godhead"*: James Joyce, *A Portrait of the Artist as a Young Man* (New York: Modern Library, 1996), pp. 160–64.

274: *"summary court in perpetual session"*: Franz Kafka, quoted from his notebooks in introduction to *Selected Stories of Franz Kafka*, trans. Willa and Edwin Muir, intro. Philip Rahv (New York: Random House, 1952), p. x.

275: *"more than Art imitates Life"*: Oscar Wilde, "The Decay of Lying" (1885), in *The Artist as Critic: Critical Writings of Oscar Wilde*, ed. Richard Ellmann (Chicago: University of Chicago Press, 1998), p. 307.

276: *"Our world in stupor lies"*: W. H. Auden, "September 1, 1939," in *Chief Modern Poets of England and America*, 4th ed., ed. G. D. Sanders et al. (New York: Macmillan, 1957), vol. 1, p. 360.

277: *"ever written on the subject"*: Edmund Dene Morel, founder of the Congo Reform Association. Quoted in *Reforming the Heart of Darkness: The Congo Reform Movement in England and the United States*, ed. J. Zwick, http://www.boondocksnet.com/congo/congo_heart.

278: *"our beloved though guilty country"*: From *Letters of a Nation*, ed. A. Carroll (New York: Kodansha International, 1997), pp. 103–04.

283: *"only one thing for me now, absolute humility"*: Oscar Wilde, *De Profundis* (written 1897, first published posthumously 1905), (New York: Penguin, 1976), pp.143–44.

285: *"stand me now and ever in good stead"*: Joyce, *A Portrait of the Artist as a Young Man*, p. 273.

286: *"fulfill our assigned role"*: Thomas Berry, *The Great Work: Our Way into the Future* (New York: Bell Tower, 1999) pp. 1, 3, 7.

287: *"colliding in the North Atlantic"*: William Rivers Pitt, "Of Gods and Mortals and Empire," *Truthout*, Perspective, February 21, 2003, http://truthout.org/docs_02/022203A.htm. ("It sounded like two behemoth icebergs colliding in the North Atlantic, but you needed the right kind of ears to hear it. . . .")

297: *"cooperation of a whole generation of physicists"*: Niels Bohr, "Discussions with Einstein on Epistemological Problems in Atomic Physics" (1949), available at http://www.meta-religion.com/Physics/Quantum_physics/discussions_with_einstein.htm.

Part VI: *Cycles of Creativity and Expansion*

305: *"most remarkable computer-technology demonstration of all time"*: John Markoff, *What the Dormouse Said: How the 60s Counterculture Shaped the Personal Computer Industry* (New York: Viking, 2005), p. 149.

305: *"the most influential environmental photograph ever taken"*: Galen Rowell, photographer *US Nature*, http://www.abc.net.au/science/moon/earthrise.htm.

308: *"since Newton enunciated his principles"*: Clark, *Einstein: The Life and Times*, pp. 289–90.

310: *"may furnish means of new knowledge"*: Benjamin Franklin to Sir Joseph Banks, letter of July 27, 1783, *Oxford Book of Letters*, ed. F. Kermode and A. Kermode (Oxford: Oxford University Press, 1995), p. 156.

311: *"expensive to accomplish"*: John F. Kennedy, May 25, 1961, "Special Message to the Congress on Urgent National Needs," John F. Kennedy Library and Museum, http://www.cs.umb.edu/jfk-library/j052561.htm.

318: *"Titan, wrestling with the Gods"*: Richard Wagner, quoted in Milton Cross and David Ewen, *Encyclopedia of the Great Composers and Their Music*, rev. ed. (Garden City, N.Y.: Doubleday, 1962), vol. 1, p. 45.

319: *"The coincidence of date is amazing"*: The New Grove Dictionary of Music and Musicians, ed. Stanley Sadie (London: Macmillan, 1980), vol. 20, p. 123.

331: *"upon a peak in Darien"*: John Keats, "On First Looking into Chapman's Homer," *The Norton Anthology of Poetry*, p. 699.

332: *"one experiences only oneself"*: Nietzsche, *Thus Spoke Zarathustra*, trans. R. J. Hollingdale (Harmondsworth, UK: Penguin, 1961, 1969), p. 173.

339: *"away from all dusty rooms"*: Nietzsche, *Thus Spoke Zarathustra*, p. 147.

340: *"Or, my brothers. Or?"*: Nietzsche, *Daybreak: Thoughts on the Prejudices of Morality*, trans. R. J. Hollingdale (Cambridge: Cambridge University Press, 1997), 228–29.

340: *"an officer storming the barricades"*: Nietzsche, quoted in introduction to Lou Salomé, *Nietzsche*, trans. and ed. Siegfried Mandel (Urbana, Ill.: University of Illinois Press, 2001), p. xxxiv.

340: *"many brave pioneers are needed now"*: Nietzsche, *The Gay Science*, trans. Hollingdale, quoted in introduction to *Thus Spoke Zarathustra*, p. 18.

341: *"all instincts are holy"*: Nietzsche, *Thus Spoke Zarathustra*, p. 102.

341: *"it is called my Will"*: Nietzsche, *Thus Spoke Zarathustra*, p. 135.

341: *"overcome itself again and again"*: Nietzsche, *Thus Spoke Zarathustra*, p. 138.

341: *"to give birth to a dancing star"*: Nietzsche, *Thus Spoke Zarathustra*, p. 46.

342: *"with your equals and yourselves"*: Nietzsche, *The Gay Science*, 283, trans. Hollingdale, quoted in introduction to *Thus Spoke Zarathustra*, p. 18.

342: *"only where there are graves are there resurrections"*: Nietzsche, *Thus Spoke Zarathustra*, p. 136.

342: *"Become what you are!"*: Nietzsche, *Thus Spoke Zarathustra*, p. 252.

344: *"I know both, I am both"*: Nietzsche, *Ecce Homo*, trans. Hollingdale (Harmondsworth, UK: Penguin, 1979), p. 38.

344: *"cannot obey himself will be commanded"*: Nietzsche, *Thus Spoke Zarathustra*, p. 137.

344: *"into the icy breath of solitude"*: Nietzsche, *Thus Spoke Zarathustra*, p. 89.

345: *"closing in on us"*: Nietzsche, *The Gay Science*, trans. Kaufmann (New York: Random House, 1974), p. 181.

345: *"absolutely fresh and cheerful January days"*: Nietzsche, quoted in Hollingdale, introduction to *Thus Spoke Zarathustra*, p. 22.

346: *"it is mine also"*: Nietzsche, *Ecce Homo*, pp. 102–03.

346: *"the discipline of great suffering"*: Nietzsche, *Beyond Good and Evil*, 225, trans. and quoted in Hollingdale, *Nietzsche: The Man and His Philosophy*, rev. ed. (Cambridge: Cambridge University Press, 1999), p. 191.

347: *"had not first become ashes"*: Nietzsche, *Thus Spoke Zarathustra*, p. 90.

347: *"kill the Spirit of Gravity"*: Nietzsche, *Thus Spoke Zarathustra*, p. 68

347: *"a sacred Yes"*: Nietzsche, *Thus Spoke Zarathustra*, p. 55.

347: *"a god dances within me"*: Nietzsche, *Thus Spoke Zarathustra*, pp. 68–69.

347: *"played with the goad of freedom"*: Nietzsche, *Thus Spoke Zarathustra*, p. 215.

347: *"Spare me for one great victory"*: Nietzsche, *Thus Spoke Zarathustra*, pp. 231–32.

348: *"Keep holy your highest hope!"*: Nietzsche, *Thus Spoke Zarathustra*, p. 71.

349: *"department of science on which they bear"*: Thomas Bell (May 24, 1859), quoted in M. White and J. Gribbin, *Darwin: A Life in Science* (New York, Dutton: 1995), p. 210.

Part VII: *Awakenings of Spirit and Soul*

362: *"the spiritual in the human being to the spiritual in the universe"*: Rudolf Steiner, letter to Anthroposophical Society (February 17, 1924), trans. George and Mary Adams, in *The Essential Steiner: Basic Writings of Rudolf Steiner*, ed. and intro. by Robert A. McDermott (San Francisco: Harper and Row, 1984), p. 415.

363: *"touch with our physical hands"*: Rudolf Steiner, *Knowledge of the Higher Worlds and Its Attainment* (1904), trans. George Metaxa, with revisions by H. B. and L. D. Monges (New York: Anthroposophic Press, 1947), p. 1.

363: *"is mere merchandise"*: Isadora Duncan, quoted in Gottlieb, *New York Times Book Review*, December 30, 2001.

366: *"expositions of the books"*: Hildegard von Bingen, quoted in Sabina Flanagan, *Hildegard of Bingen, 1098–1179: A Visionary Life* (London: Routledge, 1989), p. 4.

367: *"Authority is the weakest source of proof"*: Thomas Aquinas, *Summa Theologica*, trans. Fathers of the English Dominican Province (Notre Dame, Indiana: Christian Classics, 1981), vol. 1, qu. 1, art. 8, obj. 2.

368: *"and one in loving"*: Meister Eckhart: A Modern Translation, trans. R. B. Blakney (New York: Harper & Row, 1941), p. 206.

368: *"as being, as activity, as power"*: Meister Eckhart, ed. F. Pfeiffer, trans. C. Evans (London: Watkins, 1947), vol. 1, "Sermons and Collations," no. 2, pp. 9–10.

369: *"were and are endowed"*: Dante Alighieri, The Divine Comedy, Paradiso, trans. J. D. Sinclair (Oxford: Oxford University Press, 1971), canto V, p. 75.

369: *"not only in my eyes is Paradise"*: Dante, The Divine Comedy, Paradiso, canto XVIII, p. 257.

369: *"is all gathered in it"*: Dante, The Divine Comedy, Paradiso, canto XXXIII, p. 483.

370: *"the Love that moves the sun and the other stars"*: Dante, The Divine Comedy, Paradiso, canto XXXIII, p. 485.

371: *"since the dayis of the Apostillis"* ("The most perfect school of Christ that ever was on the Earth since the days of the Apostles"): John Knox (1556), quoted in "The Reformation: Doctrine," The Columbia History of the World, p. 529.

374: *"profound and solemn festival of knowledge"*: Rudolf Steiner, An Autobiography, trans. Rita Stebbing, ed. P. M. Allen (Blauvelt, N.Y.: Rudolf Steiner Publications, 1977), p. 319.

377: *"philosophical testament of the eighteenth century"*: K. M. Baker, "Marquis de Condorcet," in The Encyclopedia of Philosophy, ed. P. Edwards (New York: Macmillan, 1967), vol. 2, p. 184.

378: *"embellished with the purest enjoyments"*: Marquis de Condorcet, Esquisse (1793), trans. and quoted in Taylor, Sources of the Self, p. 354.

381: *"waters which flow from death through life"*: Percy Bysshe Shelley, Defence of Poetry, quoted in Taylor, Sources of the Self, p. 581.

382: *"Silent, upon a peak in Darien"*: John Keats, "On First Looking into Chapman's Homer." The Norton Anthology of Poetry, p. 699.

383: *"doubt the faith of my own eyes"*: Tycho Brahe, Progymnasata, quoted in Timothy Ferris, Coming of Age in the Milky Way (New York: Anchor Books, 1989), p. 71.

383: *"priests of the most high God with respect to the book of nature"*: Kepler, letter to Johann Herwart, March 16, 1598, The Portable Renaissance Reader, rev. ed., ed. J. B. Ross and M. M. McLaughlin (New York: Penguin, 1977), p. 603.

384: *"before the high altar"*: Kepler, Letter to Johann Herwart, The Portable Renaissance Reader, p. 604.

384: *"persevere to the end"*: J. M. Keynes, "Newton the Man," The Royal Society Newton Tercentenary Celebrations 15–19 July 1946 (London: Royal Society, 1947; New York: Basic Books, 1966), p. 96.

385: *"the magus of a Gnostic, Hermetic ritual"*: Ted Hughes, Shakespeare and the Goddess of Complete Becoming (London: Faber and Faber, 1992), p. 331.

386: *"twill be in Shakspeare's person"*: Melville, letter to Evert Duyckinck, February 24, 1849, in J. Leyda, ed., The Melville Log: A Documentary Life of Herman Melville, 1819–1891 (New York: Gordian, 1969), pp. 288–89.

390: *"he could not doubt"*: Fyodor Dostoyevsky, The Idiot (1868), trans. D. Magarshack (Harmondsworth, UK: Penguin, 1960), p. 258.

390: *"felt him in every fiber of my being"*: Dostoevsky, as recounted by Nikolay Strakhov, Biografiya; and Sofya Kovalevskaya, Memoirs; quoted in Joseph Frank, Dostoevsky: The Years of Ordeal, 1850–1859 (Princeton, N.J.: Princeton University Press, 1990), pp. 196–97. For a slightly different translation of these accounts, see http://www.charge.org.uk/htmlsite/dost.shtml.

394: *"seems to us radiant"*: James Joyce, Stephen Hero, quoted in William Rose Benét, The Reader's Encyclopedia, 2nd ed. (New York: Crowell, 1965), s.v. "epiphany," p. 318.

396: *"as I had never experienced Him before"*: Martin Luther King, Jr., this and the preceding quoted phrases from King cited in the introduction to The Papers of Martin Luther King, Jr., Volume III: Birth of a New Age (Dec. 1955–Dec. 1956), ed. Clayborne Carson et al. (Berkeley: University of California Press, 1997).

397: *"it was almost palpable"*: Alice Coltrane, quoted in J. C. Thomas, Chasin' the Trane: The Music and Mystique of John Coltrane (New York: Doubleday, 1975), p. 126.

399: *"even with both hands"*: J. D. Salinger, Franny and Zooey (New York: Little, Brown, 1961), pp. 200–02.

400: *"I move not without Thy knowledge"*: Epictetus, Discourses (c.104–107), Book 1, ch. 12, trans. H. Crossley, in Harvard Classics (New York: P. F. Collier & Son, 1909–14), vol. 2, part 2; quoted in Salinger, Franny and Zooey, p. 176.

401: *"new era of religion as well as of philosophy will be ready to begin"*: William James, A Pluralistic

Universe, in *The Works of William James* (Cambridge, Mass.: Harvard University Press, 1977), p. 142.

404: *"an equally incompetent treatment"*: William James, *The Varieties of Religious Experience* (1902), (New York: Simon & Schuster, 1997), p. 300.

404: *"a curious sense of authority for aftertime"*: James, *Varieties*, p. 300.

404: *"cold facts and dry criticism of the sober hour"*: James, *Varieties*, p. 304.

404: *"grasped and held by a superior power"*: James, *Varieties*, p. 300.

405: *"the well-springs of the comprehension of love"*: St. John of the Cross, *The Dark Night of the Soul*, book 2, ch. 17, quoted in James, *Varieties*, p. 320.

405: *"the expert of experts in describing such conditions"*: James, *Varieties*, p. 321.

405: *"the understanding cannot grasp it"*: Teresa of Ávila, *Autobiography*, quoted in James, *Varieties*, p. 323.

406: *"really united to God"*: Teresa of Ávila, *The Interior Castle, Fifth Abode*, quoted in James, *Varieties*, pp. 321–22.

406: *"a remedy for all our ills"*: Teresa of Ávila, *Autobiography*, quoted in James, *Varieties*, pp. 325–26.

406: *"the creation is love"*: Whitman, *Leaves of Grass*, quoted in James, *Varieties*, p. 311. A kelson is a long timber that runs lengthwise internally along the bottom structure of a ship and holds everything together.

407: *"optimism explains only the surface"*: Whitman, *Specimen Days and Collect* (1882), quoted in James, *Varieties*, p. 311.

407: *"the company of those who overcome"*: Malwida von Meysenbug, *Memoiren einer Idealistin* (first published 1868 during the Uranus-Neptune square), quoted in James, *Varieties*, p. 311. It was at Meysenbug's house in Rome that Nietzsche first met Lou Salomé.

407: *"the immediate presence of God"*: James, *Varieties*, p. 309.

407: *"by reason of this inflowing tide"*: R. W. Trine, *In Tune with the Infinite* (1899), p. 137, quoted in James, *Varieties*, p. 309.

408: *"a premature closing of our accounts with reality"*: James, *Varieties*, p. 305.

408: *"who have ears to hear, let them hear"*: James, *Varieties*, pp. 305–06.

413: *"to the point of death in my very self"*: Sappho, Greek text in *Lyrica Graeca Selecta*, ed. D. L. Page (Oxford: Oxford University Press, 1968), no. 199; English translation in *The Oxford Dictionary of Quotations*, 4th ed., ed. Angela Partington (Oxford: Oxford University Press, 1991), p. 556.

420: *"Reality Isn't What It Used to Be"*: Walter Truett Anderson, *Reality Isn't What It Used to Be: Theatrical Politics, Ready-to-Wear Religion, Global Myths, Primitive Chic, and Other Wonders of the Postmodern World* (New York: Harpercollins, 1990).

421: *"rivers of cheering, weeping Germans burst through"*: Marcus Eliason, Associated Press, "Ten Years Later, Iron Curtain Is Vanished, Unmourned But Not Forgotten," *Turkish Daily News*, October 23, 1999.

422: *"from a distance of 100 light-years"*: Brian Greene, *The Fabric of the Cosmos: Space, Time, and the Texture of Reality* (London: Penguin, 2004), p. 352.

423: *"the single most important instrument ever made in astronomy"*: Sandra Faber, University of California at Santa Cruz, quoted in *New York Times*, July 27, 2003.

423: *"feeling for the organism"*: Evelyn Fox Keller, *A Feeling for the Organism: The Life and Work of Barbara McClintock*, 10th Anniversary Edition (New York: Times Books, 1984), p. 101.

440: *"onto the sacramental and supramental plane"*: interview with Ray Castle, "trancetheologian," quoted in *Rave Ascension: Youth, Techno Culture and Religion*, ed. Graham St. John (forthcoming).

449: *"vast ecology or aesthetics of cosmic interaction"*: Gregory Bateson, *Steps to an Ecology of Mind* (New York: Ballantine, 1972), p. 306.

449: *"responsiveness to the patterns which connect"*: Gregory Bateson, *Mind and Nature: A Necessary Unity* (New York: Dutton, 1979), p. 8.

450: *"the Second Axial Period"*: Ewert H. Cousins, *Christ of the 21st Century* (Rockport, Mass., Element Press, 1992), p. 7.

Part VIII: *Towards a New Heaven and a New Earth*

458: *"multiple intelligences"*: Howard Gardner, *Frames of Mind: The Theory of Multiple Intelligences*, 2nd ed. (New York: Basic Books, 1993).

473: *"perhaps never been so widespread"*: Salman Rushdie, *New York Times Book Review*, April 17, 2005.

476: *"thro' narrow chinks of his cavern"*: Blake, *The Marriage of Heaven and Hell* (1793), in *The Poetry and Prose of William Blake*, p. 39.

476: *"single vision and Newton's sleep!"*: Blake, Letter to Thomas Butts, November 22, 1802, in *The Poetry and Prose of William Blake*, p. 693.

477: *"mind-forg'd manacles I hear"*: Blake, "London," *Songs of Experience* (1794), in *The Poetry and Prose of William Blake*, p. 27.

477: *"and Music are Destroy'd or Flourish"*: Blake, *Jerusalem* (1804), in *The Poetry and Prose of William Blake*, p. 144.

477: *"War Governed the Nations"*: Blake, *The Laocoön* (1820), in *The Poetry and Prose of William Blake*, p. 271.

485: *"will turn out to be an aesthetic solution"*: Jeanette Winterson, *Gut Symmetries* (New York: Alfred Knopf, 1997), pp. 99–100.

488: *"sources of the world order"*: Plato, *The Laws* XII, 967c, trans. A. E. Taylor, in *The Collected Dialogues,* ed. Edith Hamilton and Huntington Cairns (Princeton, N.J.: Princeton University Press, 1965), p. 1512.

Epilogue

492: *"the waking realities of science"*: Sir James George Frazer, *The Golden Bough* (1911–15), (New York: Touchstone, 1996), pp. 825–26.

492: *"know the place for the first time"*: T. S. Eliot, "Little Gidding," *Four Quartets* (1943), (New York: Harcourt, 1968), p. 47.

Acknowledgments

During the many years that I was writing and thinking about this book I often remembered the poem by Issa that was posted on Seymour and Buddy Glass's bedroom door in *Franny and Zooey*:

O snail
Climb Mount Fuji,
But slowly, slowly!

In this case, the snail's progress has had to be witnessed and tolerated by many others—my children, Christopher and Rebecca, whose entire lives have been lived with the book's looming presence in their family life; my wife Heather, who has deeply believed in the value of this work and supported it in ways beyond counting; my parents, who hoped I was up to something worthwhile; my brothers and sisters, who trusted my long journey; and many friends, from different stages of my life over the past three decades, who made countless allowances for my commitment to this project as only true friends can do. I warmly thank them all. Yet I know that no words can do justice to what has been given.

Far more than is usual for a book with a single author, this book has been a collaborative work, especially in the final three years when I was helped by more than thirty trusted colleagues. Their close reading of the manuscript as I completed each stage and their detailed responses to each chapter were essential in shaping and refining the final text. I gratefully acknowledge the following who read the manuscript in its entirety, in many instances more than once, and who provided me with invaluable critical comments, recommendations, and support: Christopher Bache, Anne Baring, Jorge Ferrer, James Fournier, Gerry Goddard, Ray Grasse, Stanislav Grof, Suzi Harvey, Kris Hulsebus, Will Keepin, Sean Kelly, Keiron Le Grice, Norma Lewis, Robert McDermott, Rod O'Neal, Jordi Pigem, Sheri Ritchlin, Jacob Sherman, Jonathan Stedall, David Steindl-Rast, Matthew Stelzner, and Van Wishard. For expert readings of specific chapters I am indebted to Bruno Barnhart, Robert Bellah, Stuart Brown, Lionel Corbett, Owen Gingerich, Christopher Hunt, Deane Juhan, Thomas Kirsch, Joseph

Prabhu, and Brian Swimme. The manuscript also benefited in its final stage from the perceptive readings and comments of Callie Cardamon, Roberta De-Doming, Jennifer Freed, Christina Hardy, Chad Harris, June Katzen, Kevin Kohley, Philip Levine, Frank Poletti, Bill Streett, and Barbara Winkler. For her heartfelt support and many shared insights, I am deeply grateful to Terra Wise.

It was an immeasurable benefit to have so many gifted men and women devote themselves with such generosity and care to bringing the book to birth. In some sense they all made this project their own, transforming my personal task into a collective effort that enriched the book in small ways and large. Yet their contribution went far beyond scholarly and editorial counsel. No author can take on a task like this and sustain it without another kind of support, of the heart and the spirit, and I will always be grateful to those who provided it over such a long period.

In particular, I owe more than I can say to Stanislav Grof, with whom I have researched, discussed, and taught the material contained in this book for thirty years, beginning with our work together in the 1970s at Esalen Institute in Big Sur, California. His friendship and intellectual fellowship have been a continuing, deeply appreciated gift in my life. James Hillman has been a crucial contributor to this book from the beginning, not only as the encouraging and guiding editor and publisher of its early incarnations as *Prometheus the Awakener*, but also through the influence of his many brilliant lectures and writings. I wish to gratefully acknowledge Charles Harvey, who as president of the British Astrological Association was both the earliest and, for over twenty years until his death in 2000, the most patient and steadfast supporter of my work within the international astrological community. For guidance in the initial stages of my research, I am indebted to Hans Hofmann, Craig Enright, Georgia Kelly, Arne Trettevik, Giles Healey, and Robert Hand. I also want to thank the many remarkable students who participated in the graduate courses and seminars I have taught over the past twelve years at the California Institute of Integral Studies in San Francisco and Pacifica Graduate Institute in Santa Barbara. As was once wisely said, the teacher is the person in the classroom who is learning the most.

This book would not have found its way into print had it not been for the faith in its value, sustained for many more years than could reasonably be expected, shown by my literary agent, Frederick Hill, and my publisher, Clare Ferraro. I am deeply grateful to both. I am also indebted to Bokara Legendre, Robert Wyatt, and Peter Guzzardi for their important early roles in initiating the publication of this book. I wish to thank Carole DeSanti and Beena Kamlani for their very helpful editorial suggestions and many hours of heroic work on a large and complicated manuscript. My thanks go also to Tara Sanders for her skill and patience in translating my various instructions into elegant diagrams and helping with the cover illustration.

For financial support that sustained my work at key stages over the years I am deeply grateful to Norma and David Lewis, Robert Tarnas and Barbara

Raskin, Joan Reddish, Deborah Wittwer-Kopp, Alexandra Marston, Michael Marcus, George Zimmer, and Arthur Young. I also gratefully acknowledge the generosity and vision of the late Laurance S. Rockefeller, whose decade-long support of my teaching at the California Institute of Integral Studies, and of the Philosophy, Cosmology, and Consciousness graduate program that I cofounded there, played an important role in the formation of this book. In this regard I owe a special debt to Robert McDermott, who as president of that school invited me to join the faculty and create a program while continuing research and writing, and who has been unflaggingly generous in his support and friendship.

Finally, I wish to express my gratitude to the extraordinary land and sea here in coastal California where I have lived, learned, and received inspiration throughout the years of my journey with this book—a journey that began at Esalen in Big Sur with the luminous night sky of stars and planets that I watched in wonder, night after night, season after season, from the high cliffs overlooking the Pacific.

Index